May you enjoy the fascinating
Journey of the Wagner Experience,
With best wishes from
Paul Dawson-Bowling

THE
WAGNER
EXPERIENCE

First published in Great Britain in 2013 by Old Street Publishing Ltd
Trebinshun House, Brecon LD3 7PX
www.oldstreetpublishing.co.uk

ISBN 978-1-908699-43-5

10 9 8 7 6 5 4 3 2 1

A CIP catalogue record for this title is available from the British Library.

Typeset by James Nunn

Printed and bound in Great Britain by CPI Group (UK) Ltd, Croydon, CR0 4YY

To My Wonderful Wife
Elizabeth

Was je ich ersehnt, ersah ich in dir

THE
WAGNER
EXPERIENCE

AND ITS MEANING TO US

VOLUME I

Paul Dawson-Bowling

LIST OF CONTENTS

Vol. I

Preface by Sir Donald McIntyre ix
A Note on the Illustrations xi
Introduction xiii
Thanks and Acknowledgments xxvi

1. A Brief Biography of Richard Wagner 3
2. Towards a Definition of Wagner's Fascination 20
3. Towards an Understanding of Wagner's Fascination 44
4. The Child is Father of the Man   I. *Riddles from the Dark* 73
5. The Child is Father of the Man   II. *Sources of a Genius* 101
6. The Child is Father of the Man   III. *Faces of a Genius* 133
7. Femme Inspiratrice, Femme Fatale:
   Minna Wagner and her Successors 157
8. The Miracle of the Music 196
9. Puzzles, Obstructions and Objections 242

Vol. II

10. *Der Fliegende Holländer* 4
11. *Tannhäuser* 41
12. *Lohengrin* 117
13. *Der Ring des Nibelungen* 147
14. *Das Rheingold* 180
15. *Die Walküre* 221
16. *Siegfried* 268
17. *Götterdämmerung* 304
18. *Tristan und Isolde* 360
19. *Die Meistersinger von Nürnberg* 418
20. *Parsifal* 479
List of Illustrations 533
Bibliography 537

PREFACE

by Sir Donald McIntyre

There are many conflicting views on Richard Wagner's life but I have certainly been spellbound by his crazy, bipolar and controversial mind that enabled him to produce all his profound works of genius with utter integrity. 'The thin line between madness and genius'! Thankfully, none of his characters display the one-sided goodies-versus-baddies mentality equivalent to 'Cowboys and Indians'. All his characters are in need of balance to resolve their ingrained conflicts. Conflict is inside each of Wagner's characters. The resulting tension is the essence of the drama in all of Wagner's works. The alternative is boring. Conflicts are inherent inside all of us. Balancing them is the best possibility in resolving them.

Typical of Wagner is how very many questions he asks. These need to be considered by his audiences or, in this case, by the readers of this book. I am nearly 80 but I am forever looking for adequate answers to Wagner's questions. I've had many telephone calls with Paul and he is undoubtedly the man to examine the many questions that Wagner posed. These questions are now waiting to be explored by you, the reader.

Read Paul's book! He has lots of convincing answers to many of these questions Wagner asks. And after reading this book, each of you will be better qualified to come up with your own personal ideas. Paul has challenged us all with his own findings: he has certainly challenged me. He has also provided us with many facts about Wagner as man and artist. 'Ask and you will find.'

Paul has already inspired me to write my own personal biography, which I have now started, about my life as a singer, particularly of the works of Wagner. In so doing, I am in a constant state of excitement while exploring deeper. Therefore, what I am most intrigued by is Paul's assessment of Wagner as a man. I confess I didn't know enough about Wagner's life and had read unreliable assessments. However, what I've long been sure of is what I have studied in his works and tried to portray throughout my career: sheer genius!

A Note on the Illustrations

The nature of the illustrations in this book is largely determined by the archetypes inherent in Wagner's great dramas, a dimension which the book reveals as fundamental to their meaning. Few Wagner illustrators over the last hundred years have related to these archetypes at all, and it was therefore inevitable that Arthur Rackham should feature extensively, especially as modern techniques applied here have minimised the sallow tinge of the fading paper in his original books. I also include some remarkable production photographs, and have made whimsical use of several sets of cards, similar to cigarette cards, which marketed a sort of German Oxo, 'Leibig's Fleisch-Extrakt'. They are true enough to the archetypes, and they are remarkable for their detail, as well as demonstrating how Wagner was popularly presented 100 years ago.

However I am most excited at being able to offer the best of twelve illustrations by Ferdinand Leeke, presented in refined versions which are evidently unavailable in any other modern form. They come from an exceedingly rare publication of the first decade of the twentieth century, entitled simply Richard Wagner: 12 Illustrationen von Ferd. Leeke, *that presents them in far finer detail than in Ernest Newman and Landon Ronald's* Stories of the Great Operas, *or McSpadden's* The Stories of Wagner's Operas, *themselves both rare enough. Unfortunately the originals of many Leeke paintings disappeared at the end of the Second World War, either looted or destroyed. This confers on the examples in this book a special value and interest. They have a nineteenth-century flavour that is both quaint and authentic; they are true to the archetypes in the Wagnerian depths; and they go straight to the heart of the matter.*

P D-B

INTRODUCTION

This is a book of enthusiasm. It is addressed to everyone with an interest or a potential interest in Richard Wagner. People who take to the Wagner Experience encounter something wonderful, like gazing into a silver mirror which dissolves into a miraculous, self-contained world, glinting with life-changing possibilities. There are others who sense its appeal but find it difficult, and the first aim of this study is to provide an Open Sesame for anyone wanting it. My intention is to make things easier for newcomers by presenting Wagner's works as they stand before us.[1] The book also offers good things to old-timers, scholars and longstanding enthusiasts in virtue of the distinctive disciplines and viewpoints which it reveals; but for all those drawn to the Wagner Experience, the key factor is the direct encounter with his ten great music dramas as they are. This accounts for the first main purpose of this study, to describe them in all their immediacy.

This is not to belittle the background, or deny its importance. The man Wagner, his background and his output are so interwoven that an awareness of his circumstances, his influences, his sources,

---

[1] The question how best to refer to Wagner's works is an interesting one. In form they evolved, with some backsliding, from 'opera' to 'drama' and 'music drama', but the categories are not watertight, and sometimes one term suits better, sometimes another. I tried greater descriptive accuracy in earlier drafts but the result was only a lot of qualifications and exclusions, which added nothing but length and verbiage. It seemed best to use whatever term suited the context.

his explanatory prose works, the psychological considerations, the performance history and the reception history – all these things can deepen the Wagner Experience. Adding the right background can be like adding the right lenses during an eye test. As more lenses are added, what was blurred takes on new focus and depth, and we see more clearly and better. Even so, trouble arises when anyone turns the background into the foreground in a way that inflates features from the margins and distorts Wagner's explicit intentions. He created mysterious worlds of knights in shining armour, grottos of enticing eroticism, magic fire and quests for the Holy Grail. Does it add meaning if people are led to think of *Das Rheingold* as not really about beautiful Rhinemaidens swimming in luminous depths and not about the Rhinegold shining through the waters? How does it help if even in telling the story it is reconstituted in line with some unusual element from the background, if the gold is recast as faeces and Alberich the dwarf is made into a Freudian symbol of a deprived infant, wanting to play with his own excrement?[2] What if the Ring which Alberich forges from the gold becomes a bizarre combination of an anal and vaginal sphincter? This kind of thing may produce interesting glosses, according to taste, but it is not Wagner, and when someone promotes it as the real Wagner, I believe that error is at work, and a reworking of his intentions which is unwarranted. This is a particularly glaring example to make the point, but it is real; and a particular drawback of these reworkings is that they can put off newcomers who are trying out the Wagner Experience. The same can happen if *Die Meistersinger von Nürnberg* is set up as a Luddite manifesto attacking industrialisation, because Wagner later had a violent argument with a factory owner about factory conditions and because *Die Meistersinger*'s main characters are manual craftsmen. The reason for making this point so emphatically is that these things happen so commonly with Wagner, and they are not like better lenses but distorting mirrors. My own guiding principle about background is straightforward: anything which heightens

2   Artin, Tom, *The Wagner Complex: Genesis and Meaning in* The Ring, [Sparkill, N.Y.,] 2012, p. 83 et seq.

the Wagner Experience is worthwhile, but if something from the background results in confusion or disappointment or otherwise gets in the way, then bringing it in is a mistake.

This is a main reason why this book approaches Wagner largely from the centre, from his masterpieces themselves. They are above all vital, existential dramas. They succeed because of their music, their plots and their narratives, their tensions and their dénouements, and because Wagner populated them with warmly alive individuals who involve us in their destinies. However his aims went beyond drama. He wanted his creations to be instruments of change. His is a didactic art. Its very nature is to instruct, challenge and encourage. Not that this in itself makes it 'better'. It is rare for anything artistic to be better because of the ideas in it. The opposite is more likely, with the ideas weighing it down; but Wagner had the genius to avoid this, and in practice his ideas do enhance his dramas through a distinctive richness and depth of their own. There are ideas philosophical and practical, ideas about personal ideals, relationships, the erotic phenomenon, politics, religion, and many other things that are important to human beings, and they centre on becoming who we want to be, living life better, and creating a better world. Wagner presented his ideas as bold possibilities, compelling schemes and challenging directives.

This brings me to the second main purpose of this study, which is to explain the ideas and the lessons built into his dramas and to draw them out. He frequently set out his guidance and suggestions in the personal reflections and debates of his stage characters, but equally he enshrined them in the stories themselves. His dramas are like parables or the fables of Aesop, where the meaning and the moral are acted out, and in Wagner the meanings run deep, as relevant today as they have ever been. The one quality that they do not and could not possess is simplicity, and this is my reason for a sizeable book which elaborates the experience, even after emphasising the importance of a direct approach. The importance of a direct approach remains true, but it is equally true that the better we understand Wagner's dramas, the more rewarding they will be. Even viewed directly, Wagner's dramas could never be simple; there is always too much going on in them for that. First, they fill our attention as fascinating stage plays. Then there is the music, mesmerising but dense. Then again, there are the rational propositions and the directives which Wagner moulded into them.

They also operate at another level which is quite different, the realm of myth and the psyche, and the pull of the spirit towards the unknown. For some people their myth-invoking quality registers immediately, without thought or effort, but in general it reveals its secrets more readily to a mind seasoned with insights into myth and psychology of the kind presented by Carl Jung.[3] Along with Sigmund Freud,[4] Jung was one of two commanding figures in the new science of psychology which was acquiring form and prestige in the five decades after Wagner's death. Their ideas, particularly Jung's about myth and archetypes, are interesting in their own right, but their importance for Wagner is that they deepen the meaning of dramas. Fashions change, and recently there have been reactions against both, partly because they barely used the experimental and statistical methods which are the backbone of psychology now. The period of their main activity came before these methods were developed, but unfashionable does not mean untrue, and it does not lessen the truth of their discoveries that they did not corroborate them by the methods of today. Many of the theories of Freud and Jung are indeed corroborated, but by other means than experiment. They hang together, they sit coherently with our general experience, and they work. Just as successful journeys validate the maps used to make them, so too the successful outcomes achieved by applying Jung's ideas validate those ideas. Jung's unwitting contribution to the Wagner Experience is particularly enlightening because the revelations in Wagner's dramas come as much through myth and its effect on the unconscious as through rational exposition. Jung's 'unconscious' was not the 'unconscious' of Freud, a dark,

---

3   Carl Jung (1875-1961), Swiss co-founder with Freud of modern psychology.

4   Sigmund Freud (1856-1939), Viennese father of modern psychology. Both Freud and Jung will feature in this book.

disordered repository of repressed desires and inadmissible memories, but a world that is just as vital and real as the world of the intellect, but wider and richer. It is partly *to* the unconscious and *through* the unconscious that Wagner's operas address their revelations. Operas do not generally spell out dictionary definitions or argue their points step by logical step, and they would be pretty stony going if they did.

The Wagner Experience can work on us without being aware of it, but if we understand how it works we can enter into it more fully and make better use of it. The Wagner Experience has the power to touch most aspects of life, not the fine detail but the principles. It will not tell anyone whether the 10.45 train from Paddington is the right one, but it will help with the wider existential questions, what kind of journey is the right one and where it should lead.

One incomparable feature of Wagner's stage works is the music, and it is largely because of the music that many people find the Wagner Experience overwhelming. It is also the music, his extraordinary music, which summons his imaginary worlds into being. His dramas are not simply *set to* music but *expressed in* music. It is through the music that Wagner stages his dramas on the threshold of the mind. Wagner's worlds and his dramas have been stigmatised from his day to ours as artificial, a matter of smoke and mirrors, but although the means may be artificial and consist of play-acting, stage props, and people playing their instruments, the revelations and experiences themselves are real. It is above all because of the music that the dramas work their incomparable effect, their joint appeal to reason and the imagination. It is the music which confers on the dramas their power to rearrange and transform us, working on us almost like action manuals of applied psychology.

At the same time there is something about the dramas and the music, a mix of power and seduction, which stirs up antagonism. We shall see that this antagonism has some deep causes, first of all certain emotions and modes of awareness aroused by Wagner which are unfamiliar and disturbing. Wagner can also make people feel that they are being confronted by an ancient mariner who takes them by the scruff of the neck and overwhelms them, provoking resentment and even outrage. His very personality is a chequered spectacle, and in a sense he was a pathological personality, but only in the sense that Isaac Newton, Winston Churchill, St Paul, Gandhi and John Milton were pathological. Like these men and many others possessed of towering greatness, he had his share of inconsistencies and unappealing characteristics. There were certainly times 'when he gratified the pettier feelings that great men have in common with small ones,' as George Bernard Shaw put it.[5] To understand his personality, we shall need to go into his early years and examine his upbringing against the principles of developmental psychology, or at least its basic elements. This will make it clear how emotionally deprived his upbringing was, and how Wagner's erratic, frightening childhood was not one to give rise to a well-balanced adult, a confident, rounded human being. He was a man of serious disunities and these gave rise to his distinctive 'shadow' and his potent 'shadow side'. An awareness of these facts sets up a better perspective (better lenses) through which to view Wagner, and this in turn allows a better view of his dramas and all that they can tell us.

What is unusual and strange about Wagner's negative features is the reaction they provoke, and the strength of it. He was certainly not a profoundly good man, as his English translator, William Ashton Ellis, and his son-in-law, Houston Chamberlain, have claimed, but nor was he an ogre rampaging up and down Europe, as his American biographer Robert Gutman suggests. The truth is that he was a strange mix of these extremes and of everything in between. This is part of the enigma and fascination of Wagner, and it is not surprising that he stirs mixed feelings. What is surprising is the degree of *ill* feeling evident in many of today's writings on the subject. Perhaps this is partly a matter of his attitude to the Jews and his weird, improbable, posthumous association with Hitler. The claim which I heard in Leipzig (of all places) in 2012, that Wagner was well known regularly

5   Shaw, George Bernard, *The Perfect Wagnerite*, Leipzig, 1913, p. 189.

to have had breakfast with Hitler, was bizarre, but the essential point is that politically Hitler was far to the right, whereas Wagner was at the extreme left, almost a Marxist, and all the evidence shows that he never changed. It is a mistake to believe that he turned into a right-wing nationalist. This was a role foisted onto him posthumously.

The American Robert Gutman or the German Joachim Köhler have made great attempts to identify an over-arching unity which entirely embraced the man and his entire output, in virtue of which both have written groundbreaking accounts of his life and work. The difficulty is that both Wagner's life and his work changed and mutated. To be sure, each of his dramas possesses a distinctive quality, an unremitting Wagnerian intensity, and this can produce the illusion of a constancy running through them all, but they were like the man, in that the individual dramas consist of warring elements which hold together only under great tension, and the whole series is just as variegated. Wagner's life was like his dramas; it embraced so much that was dissonant, was so titanic in its range, and evolved so drastically, that there could be no ordinary unity about it. Wagner's progress through the world was somewhat like that most iconic of rivers, the Rhine, which alters drastically over its long course from Lake Constance to the North Sea. The Rhine Falls and their thunder are as different from the river's silent, elemental surge past the Lorelei rock as the composer of *Der Fliegende Holländer* is different from the composer of *Tristan und Isolde*. In one sense the river is the same, but it has transformed, and Wagner resembled it. He went against the general tendency to keep to the same courses as life progresses and simply broaden then out, because his moral outlook, his cast of mind, his fundamental values, his way of composing, everything about him took flight in new and unimaginable directions. Without intending it consciously, he reconfigured himself repeatedly and radically. Wagner was always Wagner and nobody else could have produced what he did, but his transformations were extraordinary.

The question of translations from the German is an interesting one. Wagner's prose is difficult, but his is not the only example of a nineteenth-century style, German or English, which seems difficult today. The prose of the past, even that of a great stylist like Thomas Carlyle, can seem inaccessible now because it follows unfamiliar conventions; and even at the time Wagner's idiosyncratic style created particular challenges. As Francis Hueffer, Wagner's early American advocate, put it,

> As soon as he comes upon a topic that really interests him, be it music or Buddhism, metaphysics or the iniquities of the Jews, his brain gets on fire, and his pen courses over the paper with the swiftness and recklessness of a racehorse, regardless of the obstacles of style and construction, and sometimes of grammar. His meaning is always deep, but to arrive at that meeting sometimes seems to set human ingenuity at defiance. It would of course have been possible, by disentangling dovetailed sentences, and by giving the approximate meaning where the literal was impossible to turn all this into fairly smooth English. But in such a process, the strength and individual character of the original would inevitably have been lost. [6]

Hueffer chose to 'to indicate the diction which a man of Wagner's peculiar turn of mind would have used if he had written in English instead of in German.' His translation was 'intended to be an exact facsimile of the German original.' William Ashton Ellis, author of the classic eight-volume translation of Wagner's prose works which was published between 1892 and 1899, did not spell out his method so definitely, but in practice he did much the same. It is fashionable nowadays to criticise these translations, and with some justice. Sometimes they stray far from accuracy, and sometimes they go the other way and are all too accurate, but the result is not always English. Trying now a hundred years later to do any better than Ashton Ellis

6   *Correspondence of Wagner and Liszt*, tr. Francis Hueffer, New York, 1889, Preface.

creates recognition of another difficulty, that the idea and thoughts themselves are often the kind that many people do not think nowadays. Doom, Romantic Love, Redemption, Profane, Evil: it is the ideas themselves which have a quaint museum tinge for many people. Any attempt to translate them into modern English distorts the ideas, but fidelity to the originals can raise an indulgent or ironic smile. For these many reasons, nobody has yet done the job of translating the prose works better than Ellis, and he certainly caught the peculiar flavour of Wagner's style. I have ended up gratefully taking over his versions but making amendments where he seems misleading or obscure, marking the fact in footnotes. Translations of the verse are even more challenging because the problems of translating the prose are all heightened in verse, but Andrew Porter did wonders, translating several of Wagner's opera texts in a style that was Wagnerian and genuinely singable and yet not old-fashioned. The various verse translations in this book are all provided with attributions, except where they are my own.

Despite the ramified quality of Wagner's prose, his thinking and ideas were often compelling and original. In this he was like Hegel, that very German philosopher who showed that it was possible to write in a congested, tortuous style, but yet alter outlooks, reshape human thought, and change the history of the world. Francis Hueffer grasped that something like this was equally true of Wagner, that beneath his reckless style, his thought did run deep, something which latter-day experts sometimes deny. 'Wagner was no philosopher' said Ernest Newman,[7] and because of Newman's massive authority, these words are often quoted by modern specialists as a self-sufficient reason for not considering the evidence and not bothering with Wagner as a thinker. 'Newman is right to reject Wagner as a philosopher,' said Laurence Dreyfus in his recent book[8] and went on to accuse Wagner of woolly thinking and vagueness on the subject of 'Love'. Is it not

---

7   Newman, Ernest, *Wagner as Man and Artist*, London, 1924, rev. 1924, p. 275.

8   Dreyfus, Laurence, *Wagner and the Erotic Impulse*, Cambridge, Mass., 2010, p. 44.

rather that the idea of 'Love' itself that is woolly and indeterminate, evading definition? Critics of Wagner as a philosopher should examine Wagner's credentials and also assess Ernest Newman's own credentials with more rigour. The fact is that Ernest Newman was not only 'no philosopher', but not really competent to judge philosophers because at the time he had little interest or understanding of the subject. He gave the game away when he asked,[9] 'Who is to decide between rival philosophies or sociologies?' and answered, 'Personally, I believe that one philosophy is about as good as another, and worse.' It is baffling that such a tremendous intellect could not see the simple fact that 'a choice of a philosophy' has real consequences, because philosophy is not about the number of angels that can dance on a pinpoint, but about the values by which we live. Immanuel Kant's philosophy was strong on values and the reasons why no human individual should simply serve the ends of another. The philosophy of the Nazis was strong on the reasons why the sole purpose and function of the individual was to serve the state. The Nazi view had very real consequences, and the man who could not see that different philosophies were certainly not 'about as good, one as another' was not the best man to judge Wagner as a philosopher. This is not to disparage Newman's *Wagner Nights*, an incomparable exposition of Wagner's ten main works, with which this book is not in competition, nor his superlative account of Wagner's life, one of the great biographies of the English language.

When it comes to the illustrations for this book, my choices may look old-fashioned, but there is a reason. Any Wagner illustrations must both reflect Wagner's own vision and sit happily with the *archetypes* inherent in his dramas. Archetypes, a discovery of Jung, have considerable value towards understanding the mind and genius of Wagner; and to recognise their significance in his creations is a help towards understanding what they signify for us. Archetypes consist largely of collective memories and inborn dispositions. Archetypes generate counterparts in consciousness of the instinctive patterns

9   Newman, *op. cit.*, p. 319.

laid down in the brain, but the archetypes themselves are inaccessible to consciousness. They occupy unconscious regions, and are only knowable through their effects. As Jung expressed it, 'the stirring of archetypes is generally associated with emotions and feelings of great power,' and the archetypes that pervade Wagner's works give them part of their power to influence the imagination. Pictures, illustrations, stage sets, and productions of Wagner which are at odds with the archetypes negate their effect, and this in turn damages their power over the imagination and detracts from all that the Wagner Experience can tell us.

There are certain Wagner topics which have been regularly misconstrued over the years, and four in particular deserve a fresh look, the first being Wagner's childhood, which is routinely described as happy. It was nothing of the kind. The second topic is Minna Wagner, the composer's first wife, often regarded as slight and unmeritable, but Chapter 7 establishes her immense significance for Wagner. The third is Paris and his first stay there, without which he might never have created *Der Ring des Nibelungen*. The fourth is *Parsifal*, reappraised as being a very distinctive instrument for change since it promoted superior models of society and better patterns of spiritual wholeness.

Chapter 8 is about how and why the music casts its spell, but my aim is to keep things simple, and not attempt a specialised account of the music. There are others who do it better, and there simply is not room to describe the music even in the moderate detail of Ernest Newman in *Wagner Nights*. Rudolf Sabor has done this well for *The Ring*, but only Roger North in his compendious book on *Tristan und Isolde*[10] has achieved a full account of a music drama by Wagner, albeit in a book which is twice the size of the *Tristan* score. The plan here is to explain the main musical tendencies, the salient motives and the more important features of the music, but it would need several more books to expound the full complexities of Wagner's symphonic combinations. For all that, I still discuss certain aspects of the music

10   North, Roger, *Wagner's Most Subtle Art*, London, 1996.

which deserve more recognition than they have been granted hitherto, and any semi-technical terms employed should be well-known to anyone who has sung in a choir at school or the local church, or played the piano to a modest level. There are some rare occasions when it is necessary to see the orchestral score in full, but the musical examples will generally take the form of single staves or piano reductions.

My own experience plays a role in this study. I concentrate on Wagner's works as they are, but nobody can present Wagner's creations without presenting reflections in a mirror and revealing something of himself. I have tried to avoid reading anything into Wagner which is not there, but my life's work as a family doctor (General Medical Practice) brings to the book a distinctive angle based on what I have learnt. It is rather as Jean Shinoda Bolen said in her book on *The Ring*,[11] 'As a psychiatrist and a Jungian analyst, I try to recognise what rings true psychologically.' I can relate to what she says, because psychiatry was an important part of General Medical Practice until recent years. During my time, between 1978 and 2007, General Practice, then truer to its name, called for a general involvement with patients, and it was all the more rewarding and because it frequently went beyond health matters into their lives. Often patients became friends, but friends who might confide anything. It is no small thing to be trusted with the secrets of many hearts, and my professional life provided telling illustrations for some points in this study, until I had to realise that it would breach 'patient confidentiality' to use them. It was obviously right to discard them, and I was happy to do so, but I lost some useful illustrations about the benefits of the Wagner Experience.

My own life-experience has demonstrated the encouraging fact that nobody needs to devote themselves unduly to Wagner to gain worthwhile things from the experience. Most of us lead complex and busy lives, and any leisure activities come with an opportunity cost, in that time spent on one thing cannot be spent on another. In my case there were all of twenty years when my involvement with Wagner did

---

11   Bolen, Jean Shinoda, *Ring of Power: The Abandoned Child, the Authoritarian Father, and the Disempowered Feminine*, New York, 1992.

not and could not amount to more than occasionally enjoying an LP (vinyl disc); nonetheless the Wagner Experience was an old captivity which surreptitiously increased its hold during this Wagner exile.

My experience has resulted in a book which is different from most others on Wagner, because its aims and its emphasis are different. Everyone reading it should gain a fair idea of the plots and music, but the aim is to provide access to the whole Wagner Experience and to all that it can offer. It is a catalyst towards appreciating what the experience *is*, what it can teach us, and how above all it enables us to have life more abundantly.

THANKS AND ACKNOWLEDGMENTS

I owe my thanks and acknowledgments to a great many people. First to my daughter Leonora who cajoled me into getting down and writing the book, has provided thoughtful suggestions and technical skills, and done much generally to make the enterprise possible. Dr Michael Tanner, Prof. Robert O'Neill, Prof. Gaines Post and Christopher Fyffe provided useful early advice about approaches and methodology. Christopher Argent and Charles Ellis both read and advised on substantial sections of the text. Canon Christopher Irvine, Canon Librarian of Canterbury Cathedral, read and commented perceptively on the *Parsifal* chapter. Christopher Johns and his brother Patrick have ably converted many of my rough musical excerpts into Sibelius-perfect examples, latterly helped equally ably by Andrew Brinsford. Lionel Friend, conductor of one of the greatest recordings I know of *Götterdämmerung*, read a number of chapters, criticising and improving their substance and ironing out ambiguities. Robert S. Fisher (of the Wagner Society of Northern California) and Malcolm Rivers (of The Mastersingers, the incomparable training organisation for British Wagner singers) have been constant in their encouragement, as has Roger Lee, editor of *Wagner News*. I owe much thanks to all the following; Eric Adler, The Robin and Mary Gill Trust, Daniel and Hilary Chapchal, Prof. John Derry, Dr Martin and Nicola Francis, Francesca Fremantle, Graham Ives, Anne and Stephen Johns (my sister and her husband), the Revd John Wates, Dr Richard Philips, Prof. Tegid Wyn Jones, Bryan and Sikka Sanderson, Thomas and Marney Swan, Rudi Saunders, Gerald Brinsdon, Keith Hodgson and Roger Lee without whose financial support, often very generous, publication would have been impossible. I am grateful to my other adult children, Sebastian and Melissa, for their support in many ways, not least when events brought a slight dipping of the spirits. I value greatly the assistance of my meticulous editor, Henry Howard. His faith in the book gave it a publisher. He then had to edit an author who had no idea how to be edited, and did so with humour and diplomacy. I also appreciate the commitment of Ben Yarde-Buller of Old Street Publishing. I owe to Raymond Browne, Gary Kahn, Dr Jim Prichard, Jeremy Rowe, Malcolm Rivers, and Malcolm Spence, all of the Wagner Society, many opportunities to present educational events for the Society, particularly my 'Annual Paul Dawson-Bowling Presentations'. Over a decade, these provided the testing ground for many ideas that now appear. None of these good people are responsible for any faults that may also appear.

My thanks are due to Tina Rykker, then of Seattle Opera, whose request, long ago, for an article on the meaning of *Der Fliegende Holländer* was the beginning of all that now takes form, and to Sir Donald McIntyre who has set his seal on the end-product by writing the preface. Finally I thank my wife Elizabeth, for her help, her self-sacrifice, and her loving kindness at every stage from beginning to end.

PART I

PART I

ONE

A BRIEF BIOGRAPHY OF RICHARD WAGNER

Wagner's life was a roller coaster affair, but a roller coaster that took a peculiar zigzagging path. Trying to keep track of it can be like trying to chart the trail of a jumping jack. Apart from revealing its intrinsic interest, a brief sketch of it now will help keep in focus Wagner's main staging posts, year by year. It is not necessary to absorb the detail, but some idea of its shape and direction contributes towards a feel for the Wagner Experience and its meaning to us.

1813   On 22 May Wagner is born at Leipzig, ninth child of Carl Friedrich Wagner and his wife Johanna Rosine (née Paetz).

1813   On 23 November Wagner's father dies of typhus.

1814   On 28 August Wagner's mother marries Ludwig Geyer, actor and painter; the family soon move to Dresden, and Wagner is brought up with the surname Geyer.

1820   Aged 6, Wagner is enrolled as a border at Pastor Wetzel's school at Possendorf, near Dresden; his instruction apparently includes piano.

1821   On 30 September Geyer dies. Wagner is transferred to Eisleben to the care of his uncle Karl. There he is befriended by his grandmother, the aged Frau Geyer but she also soon dies. He attends the school of Pastor Alt but often truants.

1822   His uncle Karl marries, leaving no room for Wagner; he briefly stays with uncle Adolf Wagner at Leipzig, but Adolf does not want him and he returns to his mother and family at Dresden. He enters the Kreuzschule there as Richard Geyer. He makes excellent academic progress in any subjects which interest him.

1826   The rest of Wagner's family moves to Prague, but for the sake of his education Wagner stays in Dresden as lodger with a Dr Böhme.

1827   Wagner visits Prague, and falls for the Pachta sisters. At the end of the year he returns to his family in Leipzig.

1828   He enrols at the Nicolaischule, Leipzig as Richard Wagner. He is angry and resentful at being demoted a class, and does no work. He begins the tragedy *Leubald*. He begins to study harmony and music theory with Christian Gottlieb Müller.

1829   Wagner creates his first compositions, including two piano sonatas (none extant).

1830   He is expelled from the Nicolaischule, and enters the Thomasschule. He studies violin briefly. He makes a piano transcription of Beethoven's Ninth Symphony, and composes four overtures (no longer extant). His 'Drumbeat' Overture is performed at a Christmas Day concert conducted by Heinrich Dorn.

1831   He enrols at University of Leipzig. He has private composition lessons with Christian Theodor Weinlig, Cantor of St Thomas

Church, Leipzig. His Overture in D minor is performed on 25 December at the Leipzig Hoftheater.

1832   He begins a friendship with Heinrich Laube, novelist and social thinker and a leading figure in the Young Germany movement. He visits Vienna and Prague. His Symphony in C is first performed at Prague Conservatory in November. He first sees the dramatic soprano Wilhelmine Schröder-Devrient on stage – probably as Agathe (23 December), and Leonore (27 December) – a transforming experience.

1833   On 17 January he begins appointment as chorus master at Würzburg; he is intensely active. He composes an opera *Die Feen*, based on play by Gozzi.

1834   On 15 January he returns to Leipzig via Nuremberg. He plans *Das Liebesverbot*, an opera based on Shakespeare's *Measure for Measure*. He begins his first engagement as a conductor at Bad Lauchstädt, performing *Don Giovanni* with a scratch orchestra and without a rehearsal. His does this to secure an appointment as Music Director with Heinrich Bethmann's company based at Magdeburg, after becoming besotted with Minne Planer, the leading straight actress of the company.

1835   He maintains a hectic pace as Music Director and a hectic relationship with Minna. In November she leaves for an engagement in Berlin but returns after a storm of imploring letters from Wagner.

1836   On 29 March *Das Liebesverbot* receives its first disastrous performance in Magdeburg, disastrous because of violent disputes onstage among the cast which bring the performance to a premature conclusion. The Bethmann company was already going bankrupt, and now does so. Wagner, unfunded and jobless, has no success with proposals to stage *Das Leibesverbot* in Berlin. Minna takes up an engagement at Königsberg in East Prussia, forever famous as the city of Kant, and Wagner follows, hoping for a job as Music Director, but for months nothing materialises. On 24 November Wagner marries Minna.

1837   On 1 April he finally begins as Music Director at Königsberg. On 31 May Minna leaves him for a Jewish merchant, Dietrich. Wagner reads Lord Lytton's historical novel *Rienzi* in translation, and starts to sketch an opera on the subject. He is appointed Music Director at Riga, starting 1 September. There he continues his immense activity directing operas.

1838   He completes the text for a comic opera, *Männerlist grösser als Frauenlist*, composes two numbers, and stops. Instead he creates the libretto for an immense grand opera *Rienzi* and begins the music. He also conducts concerts. It is largely from his experience at Magdeburg, Königsberg and Riga that he forms himself artistically.

1839   He is replaced as Riga Music Director by Heinrich Dorn, who had once promoted his Overture at Leipzig. To escape creditors and make his name at the Paris Opera, as he hopes, he and Minna make perilous journeys by land and sea to London and Boulogne. There he unexpectedly meets the wealthy and successful opera composer Giacomo Meyerbeer. Meyerbeer treats him kindly and gives him recommendations for Paris, where he arrives on 17 September. He begins the first movement of his *Faust Symphony*, but fails to make headway in Paris.

1840   Wagner is challenged by major financial difficulties. He achieves a solitary performance of his *Columbus* Overture at Conservatoire. He forms ideas for *Der fliegende Holländer*. Financial stringency leads him to embark on musical journalism.

He writes for the *Revue et Gazette musicale*, proprietor Maurice Schlesinger, and makes popular arrangements from fashionable French operas. He continues work on *Rienzi*, completing this immense score, his biggest, on 19 November.

1841   There is a second performance of the *Columbus* Overture under Maurice Schlesinger on 4 February. Wagner moves out to the suburb Meudon to continue *Der fliegende Holländer*, returning to Paris on 30 October. Meanwhile *Rienzi* is accepted at the Dresden Court Opera, thanks in no small part to Meyerbeer's kind recommendation. Wagner completes the orchestral score of *Der fliegende Holländer* in mid November.

1842   On 7 April the Wagners leave Paris by road for Dresden, arriving 12 April. He has ideas for *Tannhäuser* while on summer holiday in Teplitz. 20 October sees *Rienzi's* premiere, with clarion-voiced Josef Tichatschek in the title role, Wilhelmine Schröder-Devrient as Adriano, and Carl Gottlieb Reissiger conducting. The enthusiasm of cast, orchestra and audience is tumultuous, and this is probably the greatest single triumph of Wagner's entire life.

1843   2 January: *Der fliegende Holländer* is premiered at Dresden with Wagner conducting, but the work creates a sense of anticlimax after *Rienzi*. Nonetheless Wagner is appointed Royal Kapellmeister on 1 February. He creates the religious cantata *Das Liebesmahl der Apostel* which is performed under his direction with vast forces in the Frauenkirche, Dresden on 6 July. He eagerly accepts the formal offer of friendship from the rising physician Anton Pusinelli. He has an enormous workload but continues work on *Tannhäuser*.

1844   On 7 January he conducts Berlin premiere of *Der fliegende Holländer* and 21 March Hamburg premiere of *Rienzi*, both with mixed receptions and no nationwide breakthrough, for which he had hoped.

1845   On 13 April he finishes the orchestral score of *Tannhäuser*. He passes a life-changing summer vacation at Marienbad, where he conceives plans for most of his life's remaining work, and creates prose drafts for *Die Meistersinger* and *Lohengrin*. On 19 October he directs the premiere of *Tannhäuser*, with Tichatschek in the title role, Wilhelmine Schröder-Devrient as Venus, and Wagner's niece by adoption, Johanna, as Elisabeth. Initial audience disappointment is followed by growing enthusiasm at every performance.

1846   On 5 April in the face of widespread opposition, Wagner conducts Beethoven's 'unperformable' Ninth Symphony at the Palm Sunday orchestral benefit concert, and scores a major artistic and box office triumph. From May to July he is allowed generous convalescence-leave of absence to compose *Lohengrin*, but is again increasingly beset with financial problems.

1847   He repeats the triumph with Beethoven's Ninth Symphony, but has to move to cheaper rooms. On 24 October he conducts the Berlin premiere of *Rienzi* but he jokingly and unwisely described it 'as a sin of my youth'. The press publicised this and *Rienzi* was duly vilified.

1848   On 9 January Wagner's mother dies. Encouraged by events in this year of revolutions, he becomes politically very active, writing articles and delivering speeches. He nonetheless completes orchestral score of *Lohengrin* on 28 April. On 20 October he produces the prose draft of *Siegfrieds Tod*; and on 28 November the verse version.

1849   Wagner engages in much revolutionary activity, including the draft for a five-act revolutionary drama *Jesus of Nazareth*. On 16 February Franz Liszt performs *Tannhäuser* in Weimar. In March Wagner meets Michael Bakunin, the Russian anarchist. On 30 April King Friedrich August II of Saxony abolishes the Constitution. 4 May: the Dresden uprising begins with Wagner playing a heroic and reckless role. As the uprising is put down with brutality and atrocities by Prussian troops, Wagner escapes. With Liszt's help he passes through Weimar to Lindau and thence by boat to Switzerland, arriving in Zurich on 28 May. He completes *Art and Revolution* (July) and *The Artwork of the Future* (November). Minna joins him in Zurich early in September.

1850   Wagner is offered an annual allowance by two admirers, Julie Ritter and Jessie Laussot, an Englishwoman married to a French wine merchant. In March he visits the Laussot family at Bordeaux, and becomes infatuated with Jessie. He embarks on plans of utter folly, to elope with her, but these are foiled by her mother and husband, who threatens to shoot Wagner. On 3 July Wagner returns to Zurich and to Minna. On 28 August Liszt directs the premiere of *Lohengrin* at Weimar, provoking much hostile criticism but also an enormous stir. Wagner's anti-Semitic treatise, *Jewry in Music*, is published in September. Through his energy as an organiser and his quality as a conductor, he transforms Zurich's main orchestra and its concert life.

1851   He completes *Opera and Drama* in January, and the poem of *Der Junge Siegfried* in June, and sets about making sketches for *Das Rheingold* and *Die Walküre* in October and November, in spite of spending two months at the Albisbrunn hydropathic centre undergoing a water cure.

1852   Wagner is seriously depressed by the *coup d'état* of Louis-

Napoleon in France the previous 2 December. Throughout the year he conducts concerts and operas, and it is through these that he meets Otto Wesendonck, a wealthy entrepreneur trading silks to America, and his wife Mathilde. He finishes the poem of *Die Walküre* on 1 July and *Das Rheingold* on 3 November, and revises *Der Junge Siegfried* and *Siegfrieds Tod* ready for publication of the complete *Ring* poem early the following year. He is further outraged when Louis-Napoleon declares himself French Emperor Napoleon III, also on 2 December, just a year after his coup.

1853   Wagner publishes 50 copies of his *Ring* poem book in February, and in May he conducts three concerts of music from his own works. In July Liszt visits Wagner and introduces him to his symphonic poems. In August Wagner is funded for a holiday in Italy by Otto Wesendonck, and then may have experienced the so-called 'vision of Spezia' triggering the composition of *Das Rheingold*. Between 1 November and the 25 January the following year, Wagner composes the music of *Das Rheingold*.

1854   He continues to work on the orchestral score of *Das Rheingold* as he begins the composition of *Die Walküre* on 28 June. He is often ill. He is assailed by more and worsening problems of finance, of Minna's inexorably deteriorating health, and by a sense of political hopelessness, as reactionary forces increasingly re-establish themselves through Europe. He is ripe for his autumn encounter with Schopenhauer's cardinal work, *The World as Will and Representation*. Ideas for *Tristan und Isolde* also begin to throng his mind.

1855   He conducts the *Faust Overture*, recently revised. Between March and June, he is in London to conduct eight concerts for the Old Philharmonic Society of London as it was known, being wrongly led to believe that these will prove very profitable; in fact he barely covers his costs. Berlioz was simultaneously in London conducting the New Philharmonic.

1856   He completes the orchestral score of *Die Walküre* on 23 March. In September he makes his first compositional drafts for *Siegfried*. In October Liszt comes to stay for six weeks and plays some additional symphonic poems which have a profound influence on Wagner.

1857   On 28 April the Wagners move into The Asyl, a pleasant house of modest pretensions, near the almost finished villa of the Wesendoncks. He becomes a domineering visitor there, organising concerts and playing his musical drafts on the piano. On 9 August, Wagner finally breaks off from the composition of *Siegfried*, at the end of Act II. He completes the poem of *Tristan und Isolde* by 18 September, in spite of many visits and other distractions, and on 1 October he begins to compose the music.

1858   Jealousies at the Wesendonck ménage worsen, and on 7 April, Minna intercepts Wagner's 'Morning Greeting', a letter actually trying to make peace with Mathilde after a furious row with her over the character of Faust in Goethe. (Mathilde saw Faust as an ideal; Wagner as a tragic failure.) In a literal sense Minna misinterprets Wagner's letter to Mathilde, but is correct in recognising Wagner's emotionally adulterous relationship with Mathilde. Wagner and Minna leave The Asyl to go their separate ways, Minna to Dresden, Wagner to Venice. He stays at the Palazzo Giustiniani with only one companion, Karl Ritter, son of his benefactress.

1859   He continues to compose *Tristan und Isolde* Act II, completing the orchestral score on 18 March, but he is virtually expelled from Venice on 24 March, because Venice was at that time an

Austrian territory, and Austria belatedly followed the Dresden line that Wagner was a dangerous outlaw. Wagner moves to Lucerne, and completes the orchestral score of *Tristan* Act III on 6 August. In spite of the extreme instability of his circumstances and emotional and mental upheavals, Wagner has in less than six years composed more than three and a half of his greatest works. It takes him from 1859 to 1882 to create and compose the remaining three and a half. In September he moves to Paris and presses Minna to join him, which she does in mid November.

1860   In Paris Wagner conducts three concerts of excerpts from his works, which are financially disastrous, but enthral an audience largely composed of Paris's leading artists and intellects; many of them come to all three concerts. On 15 July, an amnesty allows Wagner to return to Germany, except for Saxony. Under pressure from Princess Metternich, wife of the Austrian ambassador, Napoleon III, Wagner's especial bête noire, gives commands that *Tannhäuser* be staged at the Paris Opera. In September rehearsals begin, but Wagner succumbs to a series of illnesses including the often lethal typhoid, and his debility delays progress. He still manages to complete the revised version of the 'Venusberg scenes' of Act I.

1861   *Tannhäuser* is staged at Paris Opera, on 13, 18 and 24 March, but it is whistled off the stage by the Jockey Club. An unsettled period follows, nomadic to a degree unusual even for Wagner, but he hears *Lohengrin* for the first time while visiting Vienna. It is such a good performance that it raises his hopes that he might perform *Tristan und Isolde* there. On realising that nothing will come of it he decides to create *Die Meistersinger* as a money-spinner, an intention confirmed when he meets the Wesendoncks in Venice. He returns to Paris late in December and works on the *Meistersinger* poem and formulates elements of the music.

1862   He completes this poem, and early in February travels to Mainz to read it at the house of Schott, the music publisher who has made him financial advances on the work. He takes lodgings at nearby Biebrich, and Minna comes to join him unexpectedly. A brief period of happiness is ruined by the belated arrival of a Christmas present from Mathilde Wesendonck which has apparently been following him round Europe. After 'ten days of hell', Wagner and Minna separate finally. On 1 November, the *Meistersinger* Overture is first performed in Leipzig. He moves to Vienna to give three concerts of excerpts from his works, and Brahms is among the copyists.

1863   He tours Germany and Eastern Europe as far as Moscow, giving many financially successful concerts of his own works; but in May moves into a villa at Penzing, a Viennese suburb, furnishing it in a lavishly sybaritic style and living a life of reckless extravagance. On 28 November 1863, while he is stopping off at Berlin for 24 hours almost by chance, he and Cosima von Bülow become lovers.

1864   On 23 March, Wagner escapes from Vienna in disguise to avoid his creditors. On 29 April he arrives in Stuttgart, and is planning to disappear he knows not where on May 3, but the evening before he is run to earth by Herr von Pfistermeister, secretary to the newly-acceded King Ludwig II of Bavaria. Ludwig wants to support him, and instead of disappearing next day he travels to Munich and on 4 May he meets the King. Ludwig offers to pay off his debts and support him with his money and his love, installing him at once on the Starnberger See at the Villa Pellet. Cosima joins him on 29 June, and they resume their sexual relationship. On 15 October, he moves to Munich at 21 Briennerstrasse. Hans von Bülow is given a royal appointment and moves with his family to Munich five weeks later. Wagner continues his affair with Cosima, amidst varying degrees of lies, connivance and deception until 1869, when Bülow agrees to a divorce.

1865   Preparations go ahead for the Munich premiere of *Tristan and Isolde*, and Wagner works on *Die Meistersinger*. On 10 April, Cosima bears Wagner a daughter, Isolde. On 10 June, Hans von Bülow conducts the model first performance of *Tristan and Isolde*. On 17 July, Wagner begins his autobiography at the request of the king. On 21 July 20 Ludwig Schnorr von Carolsfeld, his ideal tenor and original Tristan, dies. There is increasing hostility to Wagner at the Munich court and among the Munich public, which reaches a crisis on 10 December when Wagner is asked by a heartbroken Ludwig to leave Munich for a while.

1866   On 25 January Minna dies in Dresden while Wagner is vainly searching for somewhere to live in France. He returns to Geneva four days later, and does not attend the funeral. On 23 March, he finishes the orchestral score of *Die Meistersinger* Act I. On 15 April he moves to Tribschen on Lake Lucerne. Cosima and her children arrive for a visit on 12 May, and are horrified when Ludwig makes a surprise incognito appearance to Tribschen for Wagner's birthday. Worse, he tells them he plans to abdicate so as to be with Wagner forever. Wagner does everything to dissuade him, and Ludwig remains king. Wagner continues work on *Die Meistersinger*, entertaining streams of visitors and fending off more, while Cosima vacillates, torn between her passion for Wagner and the resistance of her husband and her father.

1867   On 17 February Cosima bears Wagner a second daughter, Eva. On 11 June, *Lohengrin*'s 'model performance' enrages King Ludwig because the aging Tichatschek neither looks nor sounds as he hoped, and he blames Wagner for the other singers' imperfections as well. On 22 June Wagner completes the orchestral score of *Die Meistersinger* Act II, and on 24 October of Act III, in spite of stresses over Cosima, not least the stress of her father, Liszt, visiting Tribschen to give unwelcome advice.

1868   On 21 June, Hans von Bülow conducts first performance of *Die Meistersinger*, to immense acclaim, but Wagner scandalises the old Munich diehards by standing up and bowing from the royal box, Wagner, a mere genius. On 14 September, Wagner visits Italy for three weeks with Cosima, and she decides to seek a divorce from von Bülow, while Wagner undertakes to let King Ludwig know. On 16 November, Cosima arrives at Tribschen with Wagner's daughters, and tells him that she means never to leave him again.

1869   Cosima begins her diary. Wagner completes the orchestral score of *Siegfried* Act II on 23 February, and republishes his anti-Semitic *Jewry in Music*. On 15 May, Nietzsche visits Wagner at Tribschen, the first of 23 visits. He is staying there on 6 June when Cosima bears Wagner a son Siegfried, with significant post-partum haemorrhage. Less than a fortnight later, Hans von Bülow at last agrees to divorce. On 22 September, *Das Rheingold* is successfully premiered in Munich for King Ludwig, against Wagner's wishes.

1870   Wagner works on *Siegfried* and *Götterdämmerung*. On 5 March *Die Walküre* is first performed for King Ludwig, and although this too is against Wagner's wishes it is a tremendous success. On 19 July France declares war against Prussia, and is eventually defeated and humiliated. Wagner and Brahms both eventually produce tasteless celebrations, Wagner with his comic opera pastiche libretto *A Capitulation*, which he seriously thought his acolyte conductor Hans Richter should set to music. On 25 August, Wagner marries Cosima at the Protestant Church in Lucerne. She finally becomes a Lutheran in October the following year. On 25 December, Wagner directs the *Siegfried Idyll* on the stairwell at Tribschen, with Hans Richter playing the brief trumpet part.

1871   On 5 February, Wagner completes the orchestral score of *Siegfried* Act III. On 16 April Wagner and Cosima visit the Margrave's Opera House at Bayreuth, and although they realise that it is unsuitable for *The Ring*, they decide on Bayreuth anyway as the place to build a new opera house dedicated to *The Ring*. They wishfully imagine that the first performances can take place in 1873.

1872   On 8 January, Wagner chooses his site for the theatre, where it stands today. In February, he acquires the site for his own house, and establishes a committee to organise the enterprise at Bayreuth. In April, he moves to Bayreuth. On 22 May, he lays the foundation stone for his new theatre, and conducts Beethoven's Ninth Symphony at the Margrave's Opera House. He works on *Götterdämmerung* from temporary accommodation at 7 Dammallee, where he is living with wife and children which he numbered at five, always treating Bülow's children with the same enthusiastic affection as his own.

1873   Wagner continues work on *Götterdämmerung*, but spends much time and effort travelling and attempting to raise funds for the Bayreuth enterprise. Ludwig, heartbroken and angry at not having *The Ring* for Munich, refuses to help. Wagner is also on the search for suitable singers.

1874   On 26 February, King Ludwig relents a little, and agrees to a loan of 100,000 thalers, which would be liquidated from the receipts of the festival. Although this destroys Wagner's ideals and intentions that entry should be free, he feels compelled to accept. On 28 April, Wagner moves into his new villa,

Wahnfried. He spends the summer selecting and rehearsing singers, and on 21 November, he finally completes the orchestral score of *Götterdämmerung*.

1875   The year is dominated by the need for fundraising, including many concerts conducted by Wagner. He coaches singers in summer, and in the autumn he visits Vienna to coach at rehearsals for *Tannhäuser* and *Lohengrin*.

1876   The year is likewise dominated by preparations for the three original cycles of *Der Ring des Nibelungen* and the aftermath. It is attended by royalty and leading lights throughout the civilised world. The Emperor of Germany who had not helped financially but did attend, commented 'I never thought you would bring it off.' Wagner's friendship with Judith Gautier ripens into a passionate attachment, but no more. To Wagner's despair, the loss from the festival amounts to 148,000 marks, annihilating his hopes of repeating the festival and putting right the faults next year. He spends three months touring Italy with his entourage, attempting to salvage his own seriously declining health.

1877   Wagner begins to set about *Parsifal* in earnest, completing the poem on 19 April. He conducts eight concerts at the Royal Albert Hall, London along with Hans Richter in the attempt to reduce the festival deficit, and is so depressed and disillusioned that he thinks seriously of emigrating to America. At the same time (15 September), he makes plans with the patrons of Bayreuth to found a music school there and perform all his works from *Der fliegende Holländer* in series at the Bayreuth Theatre. Late in September he begins to compose *Parsifal*.

1878   King Ludwig does a deal on 31 March: the King can perform all Wagner's works at Munich, in exchange for a 10% royalty from the performances which will be used to pay off the existing loan from the King. The King will also loan free of charge the orchestral and choral forces of the court opera, along with their conductor, for the Bayreuth *Parsifal*, upon which Wagner now continues to work more confidently.

1879   Wagner continues with *Parsifal*. He enjoys family life as an enthusiastic, kindly and romping parent, often slightly at odds with Cosima's more authoritarian approach; Cosima for instance always expected her children to kiss her hand when they came into the room.

1880   Wagner spends almost the whole year in Italy, leaving Bayreuth on New Year's Eve 1879, and arriving back on 17 November. He is still trying to protect his health in the milder Mediterranean climes. On the way back, he once more meets King Ludwig, but is thereafter never to see him again.

1881   Wagner makes more progress with *Parsifal*, and is reasonably satisfied with two cycles of *The Ring* in Berlin during May. In November he again escapes from the now dangerous winter climate of southern Germany, and makes for Palermo.

1882   There in Palermo at the Hotel des Palmes, Wagner completes the orchestral score of *Parsifal* on January 13 1882. He stays in Palermo until 20 March, arriving in Bayreuth on 1 May. There are 16 performances of *Parsifal*, between 26 July and 29 August, with changing casts. At the final performance, Wagner takes the baton from Hermann Levi for the last part of Act III. On 14 September, Wagner leaves Bayreuth for the last time, travelling to Venice where he has rooms in the Palazzo Vendramin. On 25 December, he conducts a private performance of his youthful C major Symphony at the Teatro la Fenice.

1883   On 13 February in Venice, Wagner has a fatal heart attack, and dies. Cosima, rushing the scene but probably just too late, cradles him in her arms and cannot bear to release him. (The story that the English flower maiden, Carrie Pringle, played any part in Wagner's demise has long been exposed as a 'canard' by Stewart Spencer.) Wagner's body is brought back to Bayreuth in state, for an impressive funeral, and he is mourned throughout the civilised world, even by those who had been his enemies in life.

TWO

Towards a Definition of Wagner's Fascination

Wagner. Weaver of Spells. Pied Piper of Bayreuth. What is the secret of his hold over the imagination? How does it work, and what is its significance? Can it offer something worthwhile to the world and to each of us personally? These are questions for longstanding Wagnerians, for newcomers, for puzzled outsiders and even for anti-Wagnerians. They are questions which have fascinated me since first being drawn into my father's enthusiasm more than half a century ago. They are fundamental to the Wagner Experience, and the hope of discovering some answers was a spur to this book.

Wagner's impact often gains from the sheer surprise, the mix of joy and disbelief that go with first discovery. This was the case with my father, and his introduction to Wagner is so telling that it is worth describing. As a boy during the early 1920s my father watched a silent film which had nothing to do with Wagner but whose background music, even as a primitive piano duet, gripped his imagination. The film was soon lost to memory, but the music stayed with him forever; and it turned out to be the 'Ride of the Valkyries'. A decade later in the 1930s, Hitler had a scheme for foreign students to come and help build his Autobahns and witness his economic miracle, and my father was one of them. For two weeks' tough manual labour, students were given some money and a third week's pass to travel anywhere on the German State Railways. My father took the opportunity to go Nuremberg for a Nazi rally, and then on to Munich and *The Ring*. He was profoundly disturbed by Nuremberg, but this did not spoil his experience of *The*

Ring. It was love at first sight, and like the music at the silent film, it stayed with him forever.

Wagner had exactly this same impact on C.S. Lewis and Anton Bruckner, to name but two. Lewis, whose Narnia books are still children's best-sellers in many languages after half a century, described in his autobiography how 'in the dark crowded shop of T. Edens Osborne, I first heard a record of the *Ride of the Valkyries.* The experience came like a thunderbolt. It was not a new pleasure but a new kind of pleasure, if indeed pleasure is the right word, rather than trouble, ecstasy, astonishment, "a conflict of sensations without name".'[12] Wagner was just as much 'trouble, ecstasy and astonishment' for Anton Bruckner, the great Austrian symphonist. Bruckner's first encounter with Wagner's music was *Tannhäuser* at Linz in 1863.[13] Previously Bruckner had composed church music of high quality but provincial aspirations, and he had become a formidable theoretician, but it was *Tannhäuser* that unlocked the wellsprings of his creative imagination, not so much as a musical experience as something like falling in love or a religious conversion. *Tannhäuser* sparked off the symphonies which send Bruckner's name resounding round the world and which, significantly, are quite unlike the work which triggered them off.

This instant, life-changing impact was what Wagner always hoped for, and this is exactly the experience of many who fall under his spell, but it is not how everybody comes to Wagner. It can be a 'slow burn' as Sir Simon Rattle has described it; and access to the Wagner Experience can be difficult, even for people whose interest has been aroused. Robert S. Fisher, one of America's leading West Coast Wagnerians and editor of the Californian *Leitmotive*, has observed, 'How often have I encountered someone who is a newcomer to Wagner, and is tremendously excited by hearing the enthusiasm that Wagnerians uncontrollably express; he thereupon decides to attend the next Wagnerian performance, only to be gravely disappointed

---

12   Lewis, C.S., *Surprised by Joy, an Autobiography*, London, 1955, p.76.
13   Göllerich, August, and Max Auer, *Anton Bruckner: Ein Lebens- und Schaffens-Bild*, Regensburg, 1932, iii, part 1, pp. 142-3.

and mystified. Whatever the elusive element that the initiated comprehend, our newcomer finds only long, tedious and boring. I am not sure exactly how one does enter the inner circle, but we owe it to the uninitiated to warn them of something like an apprenticeship before one experiences the transcendental euphoria.'[14] Some people understand Wagner's language easily and intuitively. Others need help with it, and this book helps with finding the wavelength.

Wagner hoped to make his special, decisive impact on his audience from the very outset of his career, as he made clear after the Berlin premiere of *Der Fliegende Holländer*. He wrote happily to his first wife, Minna, 'I had achieved my aim: I had woven a spell round the audience, such that the first act had transported them into that strange mood which forced them to follow me wherever I chose to take them.'[15]

This study often quotes Wagner directly (in translation), because his own words are often best at making the points. His vast correspondence vividly summons up his views and ideas and the cast of his personality, both letters written by him and other peoples' letters to him or about him. These letters come by the thousand, and they are excellent primary sources. Another rich primary source but more chequered is his autobiography, *Mein Leben*, and equally important are Cosima's *Diaries*, the nearly-shorthand account of their life together by his permanently infatuated and worshipful second wife. (She was also rigid, ruthless and authoritarian, and she often told him how he ought to behave.) Her diaries are a mix of banalities ('My father and R. agreed that they would both write to the wine merchant'), vignettes of the Wagner household, and shafts of blinding illumination into his life and work, with frequent verbatim accounts of what he said.

---

14   *Leitmotive*, vol. XXI no. 2. (Summer 2007), p. 17 (Wagner Society of Northern California. P.O. Box 8832 Emeryville, California 946662 USA). 'Transcendental euphoria' was a description coined by the late Professor William O. Cord, an authority figure on the American Wagner scene.

15   *Richard to Minna Wagner: Letters to his First Wife*, tr. *William Ashton Ellis*, London, 1909.

Perhaps the peculiar hues of Wagner's character and its fascinating variety emerge most immediately from the letters he wrote himself. Over twelve thousand survive; and his son-in-law, Houston Stewart Chamberlain, said of them, 'These show us the *man*; he seems to step out of them bodily before our eyes.'[16] This is true but not the whole truth; the reality was more complicated, and with Wagner the reality was always more complicated. He had a passion for unburdening himself on the page, and yet there were always aspects of himself that he kept back from particular correspondents, so that his letters rarely give more than a partial picture. His personal correspondence reveals how he was driven to preach under pressure of ideas, above all by his conviction in the transforming power of art, his art. Even writing to his young niece, Franziska, he entreated her to recognize his aspirations and understand 'the significance of an artwork, where a human soul is telling them its joys and sorrows ... my only holdfast is the individual in whom I can see that I have preached to his conscience, and stung him up to free himself from the lies and hypocrisy, making him a fellow fighter against the empty reign of worldly wisdom.'[17] (What *did* the young girl make of that?)

Another source for Wagner, both facts and ideas were his published prose works, the huge essays which acted as vehicles for his development. Written as the occasion demanded, they set out his theories on art and a vast welter of topics; and they were part of his method for formulating his ideas and principles. *Opera and Drama* (*Oper und Drama*, Leipzig, 1852) was the testing ground where he worked out the ground-rules for the new musico-dramatic forms that he was then fashioning, above all for *Der Ring des Nibelungen*. These rules were like the grammar of a language which he was both creating and teaching himself. A knowledge of the grammar, the syntax and the vocabulary of a language is the foundation from which people go on to speak it

---

16   *Richard Wagner's Letters to August Röckel*, tr. Eleanor C. Sellar, Bristol, [1897], Preface, p. 7 (Chamberlain's italics).

17   *The Family Letters of Richard Wagner*, tr. William Ashton Ellis, London, 1911, p. 181 (amended).

freely. After a person has absorbed its elements he is barely conscious of them when actually speaking. Wagner was in an especially demanding position in that he needed first to formulate the grammar, syntax and vocabulary of the new musico-dramatic language he was forging, and then learn and absorb it so fully that it became second nature. Without doing this, he could never have gone on to express himself so freely. He explained his method of training and teaching himself to his loyal Dresden supporter, Theodor Uhlig,[18] the court violinist, telling him that *Opera and Drama* was his textbook, so that 'through *Opera and Drama*, I am always coming to a better understanding of myself'. He expanded this explanation for the composer Franz Liszt,[19] telling him that his purpose in *Opera and Drama* was 'to draw into the light the things dawning inside me, in order once again to cast myself back into the lovely unconsciousness of artistic creation'.

He had instinctively grasped the principle that language does not simply describe and define our experience; it actually shapes it and makes it real. It was the Frenchman, Jacques Lacan,[20] who is credited with recognising this. Lacan advanced our understanding of how language gives to our experiences a new solidity and strengthens their meaning, and has unwittingly made it even clearer why Wagner needed new languages, verbal and musical, to encompass his new masterpieces and make them real. It is difficult to imagine how he could have created *The Ring* without new languages to represent it. Later there would be times when he would bend his new languages and even swerve from them, but as Richard Strauss would one day say, in order to break the rules you have to know the rules. Wagner had

---

18   *Richard Wagner's Letters to his Dresden Friends*, tr. J.S. Shedlock, London [1890], letter to Theodor Uhlig, 12 December 1850.

19   *Correspondence of Wagner and Liszt*, tr. Francis Hueffer, London, 1897, letter of 25 November 1850 (amended).

20   Jacques Marie Émile Lacan (1901-81) was Freud's most rebarbative disciple. His prose style is the acme of obscurity, but his polemical emphasis has done much to establish how far our ideas and our identities are formed by language.

seen to it that he had created theoretical foundations so strong and knew them so well, that he was able to extend his new-found powers and go beyond their original limits.

His prose works are not a unified system of thought, because he wrote them as the occasion demanded; and because the demands continued to evolve, his prose works expressed a process, and a mental state that was continuously evolving, and never a final, definitive standpoint. Wagner continued publishing his views on an ever wider miscellany of subjects, and opinions have long been divided between those who see Wagner's stage works as expounding the same ideas as those in his prose works and those who see a gulf between them. Some of Wagner's essays now seem bizarre, like the one late in life where he suggested that the entire population of Europe should decamp to the tropics to facilitate a vegetarian diet and a healthier life, on the unfounded assumption that it was only the miserable and unhealthy climate of Europe that made it necessary to eat meat.[21] However this suggestion of a mass migration from Europe was not Wagner's idea, but a popular one at this period; and Cosima's *Diaries* show that Wagner had taken it from his friend, Count Gobineau.

---

21   *Religion and Art: Prose Works*, tr. William Ashton Ellis, vol. vi, London, 1897. It is as well to grasp that many of the ideas in Wagner's writings that appear to us bizarre are not personal but common to the period. He has faced stinging criticism and open derision for his thoughts on Beethoven's skull, his reflections about how far its thickness was responsible for Beethoven's character and his music, but they may seem less of a Wagnerian aberration if we remember that the 'phrenology' which they reflect was a sphere of medicine that was considered very advanced in the nineteenth century. Many medical specialists of the day seriously believed that the characteristics of a skull determined a person's qualities and could reveal them; and the belief was widely accepted. For example, the captain of the *Beagle* was a tough, nautical man, and yet his appraisal of Charles Darwin's character, before he would accept him on board for his momentous voyage, included a detailed assessment of his skull and its characteristics. Wagner's ideas may seem mad now but they were a madness of his times and not his own.

Wagner was neither the first nor the last to demonstrate that in a great mind brilliant ideas and profound truths could sit side by side with nonsense; and his methods fell short of the unvarying severity of another great prophet of the nineteenth century, Karl Marx, whose career and methods, and even his convictions, often ran parallel with Wagner's, as we shall see in *Der Ring des Nibelungen*. Wagner did not always gather and sift his facts with the same rigour as Marx before taking them as the basis for a theory, but his prose works still contain many important ideas and Wagner *did* often support them with a sound basis of evidence. They may represent flights of imagination, but his proposals for action also came with practical suggestions for their implementation in the most intricate, meticulous detail.[22] His

---

22   His ideas often have a contemporary relevance that can be unsettling because they seem almost Cassandra-like, true but unheeded, because they go against the popular ideas of the day. In *Religion and Politics*, for instance, written for the young King Ludwig, he offered penetrating advice about public opinion, the power of the press, and the way human motivation works in society. He fulminated against the power and the unbridled freedom of the press. He describes how an admirable intention, liberal in origin, to create freedom for the press from censorship and governmental control had been exploited, and become a façade. The absence of any censorship or regulation had enabled the press to exercise a tyranny over public opinion more absolute than any dictator. A few pages later he was writing about '*Wahn*', the force or forces that drive all living things, including mankind, and included some of the points made by Richard Dawkins in *The Selfish Gene*: altruism and self-sacrifice is often not free-willed idealism but a quasi-Darwinian survival mechanism inbred over millennia to promote the species; self-sacrifice may result in the destruction of the individual but save the group. Wagner goes on to indicate that altruistic qualities are often exploited by despots for their own personal advantage. Already too it emerges from his writings from Zurich in the 1850s that he had regarded capitalism as wasteful. He saw gross inefficiencies in the working of the price mechanism in that many businesses making the same products and vying for the market were competing to the point of destruction; and the inevitable consequence of the destruction of the less competitive

writings are at their best and most popular when discussing music and drama, and they contain some of the finest thinking ever documented on these topics. There were many areas of his ideas where his prose works demonstrate a powerful and original mind at work. They never set out a single system of thought but nor for that matter did Freud and Jung, Marx, Keynes or Nietzsche; and their ideas were not the less valid and influential on that account. Hans Richter, Wagner's Hungarian protégé who conducted the original cycles of *The Ring* at Bayreuth, probably spoke for most people when he was asked what he thought of the master's prose works, and answered that he would gladly give them all in exchange for one more score. But anyone who comes to terms with Wagner's overloaded style and actually reads his prose works usually appreciates why it was that at the end of the nineteenth century, when they were at the height of their influence, his devotees saw them as the fount of all wisdom. That was the grand era of Wagnerism, and although it has faded, Wagner was a figure of real significance both as a literary thinker and essayist. Many of his ideas and theories have a timeless relevance; but it was not as a thinker and essayist that he earned his place high among the immortals.

Incomparably greater was his achievement as a creative artist. His ten dramas expressed in music are as vital as ever. The spell that they cast maintains its hold more powerfully; and the importance of what they tell us seems, if anything, to grow. The Introduction described how they are concerned with the great issues, and also express compelling arguments why these concerns are vital, the advantages of taking them seriously, for the individual, for society, and for the world. They also offer warnings if we neglect these concerns, the *dis*advantages for the individual, for society, and for the world. Many of Wagner's ideas

---

businesses and the bankruptcies and job losses would waste resources. Communism and mutualism, mutual ownership and central planning, would avoid all this. Would anyone today call this thinking senseless? Many of his prose works are worth taking far more seriously than commonly happens now, but these instances given are enough to indicate that Wagner's position was at least well-reasoned.

about drama and its importance come from Aeschylus, the tragedian of ancient Athens who appeared to him incomparable (and with good reason). He told Cosima that the *Oresteia*, the one surviving trilogy of Aeschylus (the only extant series of three consecutive dramas) was 'the most perfect thing in every way, poetic, philosophical, and religious,' and at the celebration banquet after the first Bayreuth Festival, Franz Liszt, who was by then his father-in-law, gratified Wagner by suggesting that the mantle of Aeschylus (and indeed of Shakespeare as well) had fallen on Wagner. Wagner conceived of Athenian drama, and above all the *Oresteia*, as an ideal fusion of the arts, bringing catharsis to those who experienced it. Catharsis was an idea formulated by Aristotle, the great philosophical polymath of the ancient world, and it can be summarised, if only superficially, as the ordering and balancing of the emotions through vicarious experience, principally that of drama. Wagner idolised the drama of the Athenians, envisaging it as High Culture with a spiritual dimension, which could yet somehow, amazingly, enthral the entire population of 'ordinary' Athenians. It was as if the members of the great British public who now throng the stadiums for football matches were to go there instead for a performance of *Hamlet* or Beethoven's *Missa Solemnis* or some extraordinary mixture of both. Thanks to its cathartic effect, what the Athenians experienced in the theatre would refashion their engagement with the gods, the world, and other people. It worked, as Wagner understood it, because the Athenian drama originated from the spirit of the whole people, the Athenian '*Volk*', even though it was the creation of an individual playwright. It was a drama which both validated human existence and paid homage to the gods, and it embodied a life-enhancing ideal of high culture that Wagner took as his own. He exhorted his violinist friend Theodor Uhlig, 'Let us not forget that culture alone can enable us to enjoy what man in his highest fullness can enjoy,'[23] and again and again in *Opera and Drama* and *Art and Revolution* (1849) he made it clear that the specific culture he had

23   *Richard Wagner's Letters to his Dresden Friends*: letter to Theodor Uhlig, Zurich, 22 October 1850.

in mind was its highest form, which for him meant drama. His drama would be one which would fulfil and regenerate those experiencing it as he believed Greek drama had done. He would not try to resurrect Aeschylus or copy him literally because 'the resurrection of Greekism' (Ashton Ellis) struck him as both impossible and not even desirable in a world so utterly changed. Moreover he saw the Athenian model as fatally flawed because it was built on slavery, and slavery had led to its downfall. Even so, Greek tragedy provided his model and shaped his aspirations. Like the Athenian dramatists, Wagner would reanimate myth, whose truths were relevant to humanity 'for all time; however the epochs may change'. He would make his own the idea that drama should be a fusion of all the arts and should transform consciousness. He above all absorbed the *Oresteia*, and it specifically influenced *The Ring*, its shape, its myth, and even some of its action and characters. In the early prose drafts of *The Ring*, for instance, there is a turning point in the action when the three Norns, three very Northern creatures, warn Wotan, the supreme god, that he must give up the Ring to avoid the curse placed upon it by Alberich.[24] Eventually Wagner reassigned this warning to a new character, Erda. Erda is the spirit of the earth and source of all wisdom in *The Ring*, but before Wagner Erda was unknown to Northern mythology. She is a direct import of the Greek earth-goddess Gaia. This is just one example how Greece and the *Oresteia* hover in the background of *The Ring* and mould its action, glinting through its fabric like a mysterious presence. Part of the transforming potential of his Greek originals which Wagner took over was that he too would hold up a mirror for people, a miraculous mirror showing them in a better, more ideal form, revealing them as they should be. He believed that this picture would spur them on to better and fulfil themselves. As well as his debt to Aeschylus, Wagner acknowledged another to Shakespeare, his other favourite dramatist. He saw Shakespeare as absolute in his veracity, in his 'holding up a

---

24   'The Nibelungen Myth considered as a Sketch for a Drama' (1848), *Prose Works*, vii, p. 302.

mirror to nature and his intimate grasp of humanity'.[25] 'Shakespeare sees people and sets them before us … Shakespeare's histories contain the whole history of man … Nobody understood humanity as well as Shakespeare.' These quotes come from Cosima's *Diaries*, and they are just a few from the hundreds documenting Wagner's unstinting admiration for Shakespeare.

In all this Wagner adopted an aesthetic approach recognised by Maurice Kufferath in his book, *Parsifal*, published in Paris in 1890, an ideal of drama 'which finds in artistic sensibility the expression of man's highest aspirations, of the eternal Desire for the Best, and makes art the complement of ethics and morality'. This was Wagner's approach, and Kufferath contrasted it with an attitude 'which reduces art more or less to the level of agreeable entertainment,' although Wagner was realistic enough to grasp that if artistic creations did not provide people with a positive feeling and some kind of pleasure, however exalted, they would never promote the things which were important.

Wagner actually went deeper than Greek drama in his ability to 'sting up' his audience because, as the Introduction hinted, he possessed an intuitive grasp of depth psychology long before its founding fathers had formulated it. His dramas are steeped in psychology and myth, and they look forward, as constructive prescriptions for the future. This purposive view is distinctly un-Freudian. Freud's views on art, myth and dreams were more often what is known as 'reductive'. Freud saw art largely as a coping mechanism for dealing with the traumas of life and coming to terms with them, and particularly for resolving damage from the deep past. For Freud artistic experience provided escapes and sublimations, particularly escapes into wish-fantasy. If art could perform this Freudian function and heal past damage, this was no mean achievement, but Wagner was in line with Jung in believing

---

25   In his autobiography he tells us that his first drama, written when he was fifteen years old, 'had drawn largely upon Shakespeare's *Hamlet*, *King Lear* and *Macbeth* and Goethe's *Götz von Berlichingen*.' *My Life*, *authorized translation from the German*, London, 1911, p. 29.

that art could do far more. Wagner saw myth as revealing meaning in things, and the myths which he enveloped in his 'equinoctial music' (the words of Laurens van der Post) offer suggestions by which to live. The most obvious illustration of a purposive myth is in *Siegfried*, the third part of *Der Ring des Nibelungen*. For now, the point is that *Siegfried* is a hero myth representing the universal patterns and challenges facing young men (and nowadays young women). As a person absorbs a myth, it moulds and guides his outlook and actions.

Wagner believed that in creating his prescriptive, didactic dramas he was creating something universal for the world which was yet very German, just as Greek tragedy is universal but very Greek. He had taken over from Herder an idea of German-ness as embodied in the German *Volk*. The *Volk* possessed a common heritage of German myth and wisdom, and this German, '*völkisch*' quality was both provincial and universal. This was part of a paradoxical outlook which he shared with various contemporaries, the belief that the values of the *Volk*, the community, were local and homely, and yet supra-national. The *Volk* and its values signified a nourishing sense of community for Wagner and many of his contemporaries, which they considered to be at risk when people aggregated in great, soulless cities. Wagner particularly disapproved of cities such as Paris or London, because they cut people off from their roots, and they were not places fit for human beings. When Wagner extols the *Volk*, it is the character of provincial Nuremberg and Weimar that he evidently has in mind. After Goethe and Schiller had lived there, Weimar regarded itself and was regarded widely by others as the ideal of a German state. Weimar was even compared with Bethlehem, the birthplace of Jesus Christ, as another town which was great in its very smallness. The *Volk* in such places could keep better in touch with its sources of natural wisdom, and as a result it could siphon them up and broadcast them out to the world to its universal enrichment, which was why these sources of wisdom were both local and universal. Wagner explained, 'Whereas the Greek work of art expressed the spirit of a splendid nation, the Artwork of the Future [his own art] is intended to express the spirit of the people regardless of all national boundaries.' He also said, 'The National Element in it must be no more than an ornament, an added individual charm, not a limiting restriction.' This is not exactly the strident German nationalism often attributed to Wagner. He intended his art and its *völkisch* wells of wisdom to enrich humanity, not to subjugate it. All this points to something further which the *Volk* signified for Wagner, something that came close to the 'collective unconscious', the innate source of knowledge, ideas and dispositions postulated by Jung as common to all. For Wagner the *Volk* personified Jung's 'wisdom of the unconscious', and this was part of Wagner's inveterate tendency to personify, a tendency which stood him in good stead as a dramatist.

These are some of the background factors that make the Wagner Experience so eternally relevant, 'however the epochs may change'. Much of Wagner's own background thinking, the intellectual soil from which his works blossomed, was richly positive because it was so humanitarian and high-minded. As we shall see from what he tells us in *The Ring*, Wagner was fundamentally a liberal intellectual, and he always remained so at heart, however far he was driven to compromise. Many writers on Wagner seem not to realise that he always struggled against being a political suspect. He spent years striving to overturn his banishment and exile, and in the new industrialised Germany of the Bayreuth years he was at a very real risk of being in trouble again, and so he did compromise his ideals.

There were other aspects of his intellectual firmament which were genuinely objectionable and which I discuss in due course, but these seldom materialise in his dramas. His dramas were like roses growing in a fertile loam where some rank compost had once been dug in. The compost is metabolised to be part of the richness, but the roses themselves are not like the compost. The rankest element of that compost was his racist theorising, but it was only one element and, as Chapter 9, on obstacles to the Wagner Experience, will explain, racial prejudice was not a specifically Wagnerian property, but commonplace.

Access to the Wagner Experience does not come through following a set of rules and formulas, as happens with access to maths or physics, or in learning a foreign language. I emphasise again that its essential requirement is to spend time on the dramas themselves. For the Wagner Experience to work, we need to make it our experience. This was one reason why Wagner was eager that his works should speak in ways which communicate directly. Equally he wanted us to participate in the experiences of the principal characters of his drama. Although he inherited his drama from Aeschylus and Shakespeare, he determined to recast it in a language that was as easy as possible to understand, so that 'nothing should be left to the synthesising intellect'.

Drama was always Wagner's ideal, but it is important to grasp what he meant by 'drama'. For Wagner, the drama is emphatically not the music. It is not the text. It is not the staging or the acting. It is expressed and articulated by these things, but they are simply the means to an end. The drama is something different, an abstraction shimmering away beyond the means, and Wagner described it as 'the poetic intent'. It may be the music, the text, the staging and the acting which convert that underlying intent into a form that we can apprehend, but this is all rather different from the widespread belief that Wagner regarded his texts as fundamental, the real thing, and the music as some kind of handmaid, a minor subordinate. This belief may have arisen from his startling metaphor, that music is 'the womanly element, the bearing element that needs the poetic aim as a begetting seed'. He held that music needs a text; 'after music has received the fertilising seed from the poet, it forms and ripens the fruit by its own individual powers.'[26] This gave rise to the notion that he saw the music as colouring and the text as the essential, but the truth of the matter was established early by Wagner himself, as far back as *Lohengrin*. *Lohengrin* is the ultimate romantic opera and was completed before Wagner defined his ideas of music drama, and yet he wrote to Liszt at Weimar about *Lohengrin*, to spell out 'the only purpose that guided me, I mean the simple and bare intention of the *drama*!'[27] (The emphasis is Wagner's own.) Drama was already the essential, so much so that soon afterwards he was

26 *Opera and Drama: Prose Works*, ii, p. 297.
27 *Correspondence of Wagner and Liszt*, pp. 91-92.

writing another letter to make the same point to Baron Ziegesar, then *Theaterintendant* at Weimar, and urging him that every element in the *Lohengrin* performance at Weimar should support the *drama*.

The reason for Wagner's apparent emphasis on text in *Opera and Drama* was that in traditional opera, he saw music looming too large and 'behaving like a tyrant'. *Opera and Drama* described the music as 'a mightily waxing monster', whose 'shameless insolence ... made poetry lay down her whole being at her feet.' In the category of opera Wagner saw music as subverting the plot, stamping its shape on the text, and deforming the metres of verse and accents of speech. Such concerns were not new. In 1691, while writing a new version of *King Arthur* as a vehicle for music by Henry Purcell, the poet Dryden wrote that 'the Numbers of Poetry and Vocal Musick are sometimes so contrary that in many places I have been obliged to cramp my verses and make them rugged to the hearer'.[28] Dryden nevertheless took his secondary position under Purcell in good part; 'Because these sorts of Entertainments are principally designed for the Ear and Eye, my Art, on this occasion, ought to be subservient to his.'[29]

Wagner the poet would have none of it. He never allowed music to impose false accents on the words, and he even later built his ordinance into the plot of *Die Meistersinger*, where Hans Sachs, the cobbler poet, pillories Beckmesser's song in Act II because its melody does indeed 'cramp his verses' and impose false accents on the metre. From *The Ring* onwards, Wagner himself succeeded in creating verses and melodies where the speech accents match the musical accents. He had also been just as unhappy about operas where the music was allowed to twist the drama out of shape, spinning out minor episodes to give opportunities for arias, ensembles, and choruses, but throwing away the action's pivot points in some perfunctory recitative 'because they do not lend themselves to operatic numbers'. 'Every

---

28   Quoted by Robert King, *Henry Purcell*, London, 1994, p. 184.

29   The issues about reconciling text and music were still not resolved 250 years later when Richard Strauss took them as the basis for his final opera, *Capriccio* (1942).

bar of dramatic music is justified only by the fact that it explains something in the action, or in the character of the actor,' as he wrote in his letter to Liszt, and he demanded that 'Music should do no more than contribute towards its full share of making the drama clearly and quickly comprehensible. People should not *think* of the music at all, but only *feel* it in an unconscious manner, while their fullest sympathy should be wholly occupied by the action represented.'[30] His aim was not to take music's previous dominance and transfer it to the text, but to secure an equal balance among all the ingredients. This synthesis would give the drama its character and make it so compelling that we lose ourselves in it, as Wagner once described happening to himself during a performance of *Tristan und Isolde*. He lost all awareness of the music as such, and became transported into the drama owing to the prodigious achievement of Ludwig Schnorr von Carolsfeld,[31] the dramatic tenor who sang the title role. Wagner described how 'in his overwhelming portrayal of the Act III Tristan, the orchestra completely disappeared beside him, or more accurately, appeared to be subsumed into his delivery'.

In some of his works, most obviously *Das Rheingold, Die Walküre, Tristan* and *Parsifal*, he devised the drama simultaneously in words and music. He told the same story in parallel texts of words and sound, and there are such rigorous connections between them that it becomes impossible to separate the story from the twin registers of its expression. We know more about Wagner's composition process in *Parsifal* than any other work, because he had then established his base at Bayreuth, and in *Parsifal* the musical composition largely went hand in hand with writing the text, each building on the other in a kind of mutual leapfrog. Wagner actually remodelled the words of Christ which are intoned by a mystical choir during the 'Communion Scene' in Act I, in order to make them fit the music he was inspired to write for them. The bond between his words and his music was not always so close, and the links between creating the text and composing

30   *Correspondence of Wagner and Liszt*, p. 101.
31   'Ludwig Schnorr of Carolsfeld' (1864-5), in *Prose Works*, iv, p. 236.

the music varied greatly in directness and intimacy. *Götterdämmerung* stood at the other extreme from *Parsifal*, because he eventually set about composing the music fifteen years after completing the text. Although it was still a poem (Wagner's term) designed for music, any memory of his original intentions had become shadowy, and as a composer he had advanced so far that it was almost like creating music for another man's text. The case of *Die Meistersinger* was different again, because he had the overture complete in his head before even thinking his way through the drama, and this Overture eventually provided leitmotives for words and ideas that did not exist when it was conceived. With Wagner there was no standard practice.

All of this brings us up against a paradox. The Wagner Experience centres on the drama, but it is expressed in music; and the music is at the heart of the Wagner Experience. It is ecstatic in its own right. It is mesmerising. If the drama is a mirror through which to view new realms, it is the music which dissolves the mirror in a silver mist and draws us through it. It is the music which summons into being Wagner's undiscovered countries; and it is the music which spirits us away to them. The music acts as a magical intermediary, relating the drama to the audience. It makes the connection between the world of Wagner's imagination and the audience's own real world. 'What was impossible for Shakespeare, that is, to act every one of his roles, is something that the composer achieves with the greatest ease, speaking directly through his performing musicians.'[32]

The music conjures up the very experience of his characters for the imagination. The French writer Édouard Schuré, who had been at the original Munich performances of *Tristan und Isolde*, recalled this effect of the music, that 'the interior of the characters became transparent … All the currents and undercurrents of thought insinuated themselves into me in such an all-encompassing manner and with such overwhelming force, that everything that occurred within Isolde occurred within me.'

32   'The Destiny of Opera', public lecture, 1871, *Prose Works*, v, p. 150.

The music also enables its hearers to live the drama as a whole, partaking in the entire drama as a parallel reality. Wagner stated as much, putting his words into the mouths of the chorus towards the end of *Die Meistersinger*. The Knight Walther von Stolzing has related his dream, his visionary experience of Eva, and recreated it in music, in his prize song. He stands for Wagner and for what Wagner's music could do; and the chorus comments:

> *So hold und traut,*
> *wie fern es schwebt,*
> *doch ist es grad',*
> *als ob man selber alles miterlebt.*

> However far it soars,
> It is so fair and familiar;
> *It is as if one experienced it all with him.*

Thanks to the music, people do find that they 'experience it all with him'. Wagner's music also persuades us of worlds, actions, events, that would otherwise not seem real, and his recommendations about staging his works were all directed towards increasing the suspension of disbelief induced by the music. It may be the drama that presents his political, philosophical, psychological, and spiritual directives to his audience, but it is the music which endows them with a uniquely persuasive force.

Wagner's music gains its power of persuasion by connecting with the imagination at many levels. The chapter on Wagner's music explains the form and structure that people sense in Wagner's music, even though it is only distantly related to normal rules of musical forms, and its peculiar capacity to connect with the unconscious.

In this capacity as a composer, Wagner saw himself as the successor to Beethoven, rather as he regarded himself as the descendent of Aeschylus and Shakespeare in drama. It was Beethoven 'in whom there thrived the power of shaping the unfathomable, the never-seen, the ne'er experienced, which yet becomes the most immediate experience, of most transparent comprehensibility'.[33] It was Beethoven who had 'opened up the faculty of instrumental music for expressing elemental storm and stress,'[34] and Beethoven's *Eroica* Symphony exemplified for Wagner the his mentor's 'seer-like ability' to create a work where 'all the truly human feelings are present, feelings of love, of grief, of force, nothing human is a stranger, the most feeling softness married to the most energetic force.'[35] In Beethoven 'music became the syllables, the words and phrases of a speech where a message yet unheard could express itself, where the inexpressible could proclaim itself.'[36] As the context makes clearer, Wagner meant musical speech, the musical language which Beethoven had forged in his symphonies and which Wagner aimed to take further. Wagner also believed that in Beethoven musical meaning, which had hitherto been oceanic but vague and indeterminate, came nearest to the precision of words; that in Beethoven the feeling and the meaning of the music almost crystallised in spoken language. Wagner saw the Ninth Symphony as the landmark ('*Grenzstein*') where Beethoven's expression had finally erupted out beyond music into words, and he hailed it as the 'redemption of music from her own peculiar element into the realm of *universal art*. After this, only the perfect artwork of the future can follow, the universal drama to which Beethoven had forged the key.'[37]

Wagner believed, with some justice, that he was the one to turn that key and unlock the door. He created for his dramas a music which was as transcendental as Beethoven's. Music of such expressive force added to the problems and challenges of making sure that his dramas were not hijacked by 'music's overweening dominance', but Wagner succeeded. In Wagner the music, however compelling, invariably

---

33 'Beethoven' (1870), *Prose Works*, v, p. 92.
34 *The Artwork of the Future* (1849), *Prose Works*, i, p. 121.
35 'Beethoven's "Heroic Symphony"' (1851), *Prose Works*, iii, p. 222.
36 *The Artwork of the Future*, p. 121 (amended).
37 Ibid., p. 126.

serves the drama, enhancing it with intimations that neither the words nor the actions of the performers could express.

Partly because of its relationship to unconscious mental processes, Wagner's is a music of unusual power and intensity, a music where even the silences are hypnotic. It has not only a unique expressive force but a uniquely seductive persuasion. Wagner himself recognised this when he modified his belief that music and the other arts should make equal contributions, as he did after encountering Schopenhauer's most influential work, *The World as Will and Representation* (as it is usually translated). Thereafter Wagner became increasingly convinced that music stood apart. He came to regard music as unique, sinking a deep shaft into an ultimate reality which was otherwise unattainable. In music 'the world displays its essence directly, whereas in the other arts, this essence has to pass through the medium of understanding before it can be displayed.'[38] Many years previously Wagner, only twenty, had written to Rosalie, his adored sister, that his music 'so poured from my innermost soul' that 'it must pass to the souls of others'.[39] Wagner had not then developed to the point of being able to make this happen, but in time he succeeded in creating a music which does pass to the souls of others. In his late essay on the term 'Music Drama' he said 'I should have been happy to describe my dramas as deeds of music become visible.'[40]

What was actually visible at Bayreuth in Wagner's time often raises a condescending smile today. James Treadwell in his book *Interpreting Wagner*[41] exemplifies the belief that staging has immeasurably progressed. He describes his incredulity that anything so primitive, ineffective and outmoded as the original stage models in the museum in Bayreuth should ever have appeared convincing. It is even suggested that Wagner had no visual sense, and that his own stagings were

38 'Beethoven', p. 72.

39 *The Family Letters of Richard Wagner*, p. 6, letter to Rosalie, 11 December 1833.

40 'On the name "Musikdrama"' (1872), *Prose Works*, v, p. 303.

41 Treadwell, James, *Interpreting Wagner*, New Haven and London, 2003.

obstacles to his works. Obstacles, however, was not precisely what they seemed originally. Henri Fantin-Latour was a painter possessed with an undeniable visual sense, and here is what he wrote after seeing the opening scene of *Das Rheingold*:

Oh, it is unique. Nothing else is like it. It represents a feeling as yet only partially understood … there is nothing more beautiful, more realised among my '*féerique*' memories. The movements of the Maidens who swim while singing are perfect, Alberich who desires the gold, the lighting, the beam of light which the gold throws down into the water, is ravishing. It is feeling, it is not music, nor theatre décor, nor subject, but the enthralment of the spectator – yet spectator is not the right word, nor is auditor correct. All is contained.[42]

Obstacles and hostilities to Wagner do genuinely exist, but as we can see in Chapter 9 many of them are grounded not in fact but in illusions, often the result of false information about Wagner. Some authorities on Wagner, such as Hartmut Zelinsky or Robert Gutman evidently detest the subject of their preoccupations, whereas I mainly feel an enormous admiration for this strange and troubled man, but the question whether one loves or loathes him does not affect the value of what he offers us. Nietzsche denied any such value after his estrangement from Wagner, and he virtually objected that the Wagner Experience was nothing but an opium, a flight from reality that was intrinsically pernicious.

No-one would reasonably deny the greatness of Nietzsche, but as a doctor I can only disagree. In the same way that Freud failed later to see that art was more than a compensation for traumas, Nietzsche after breaking with Wagner lost his previous awareness that the Wagner Experience could be more than an escape from life. Nietzsche was right that harm can come from taking anything, whether it is Wagner,

42   Quoted in Wilton, Andrew and Robert Upstone, *The Age of Rossetti, Burne-Jones and Watts: Symbolism in Britain 1860-1910*, London, 1997, p. 214.

religion, charitable works, sex, or mind-altering chemicals, and using it as an escape, as a means of avoiding the facts and challenges which we need to accept. People who depend on fantasy agents to make them more comfortable and bury their heads in the sand soon find that they are in the grip of disturbing addictions, but except for mind-altering chemicals, these same agents can be deployed rightly, and then they can centre us, replenish us, and empower us. The difficulty is that the dividing line between what is escapist and what enables us to handle life better is often a hazy one with a fair amount of overlap. There is no clear distinction. Even a complete flight from reality can be refreshing and positive if it is just an occasional resource. The challenge is about getting the balance right and avoiding dependencies, including the dependency on Wagner. Anyone can misuse Wagner as a route to illusion and wishful thinking, as Nietzsche warned, and we shall look at more of Nietzsche's objections in Chapter 9.

However the more important point about the Wagner Experience is that it is not so much an escape from life, as forward looking towards making a better job of life. This entire study is in a sense about why Nietzsche was mistaken in believing Wagner was 'bad for your health'. The Wagner Experience could almost be described as psychotherapeutic, and like the best kind of psychotherapy, the 'cognitive' kind, it requires that the person fully understands and participates to the point of embracing the process. The picture of the psychiatrist or therapist as a remote, inaccessible figure imposing godlike interpretations on submissive patients is far removed from an active participation such as the best therapists encourage, and in the same way, any quasi-psychotherapeutic effect from Wagner works better if we understand the process and embrace it. However, the term 'psychotherapy' is not quite right, because it implies something amiss, a pathology calling for a remedy, whereas Wagner's benefits extend far beyond people with disorders. Even in good mental health, the human condition calls for constant stressful adjustments, such as those between our animal aspects and our higher selves. There is always some disunity among the different aspects, and this means that there is only a wavering, shifting line between damaging mental illness calling for psychiatric intervention, and the 'normal' disunity which is the common heritage of humanity. Even normal people can still benefit from better balance and integration. In both mental illness and this existential disunity, the Wagner Experience can help. In both cases the experience can open up and present new and positive possibilities.

I have mentioned one of the most appealing things about the Wagner Experience, its summoning of undiscovered realms from which we can and do return, replenished and enriched. Wagner's dramas are reliable companions, friends in fair weather and foul, and they are like the promise of the mediaeval mystery play: 'Everyman, I will go with thee, and be thy guide in thy most need to go by thy side,' constantly touching our actions and re-framing our engagement with life.

They do this partly by acting as templates that align with our life events, recasting them and conferring on them a new value. They can disclose the gold in what seemed base metal or even dross. The positive they can enhance, and the negative and the ordinary they can transform. This is all part of that 'redemption' which Wagner was concerned to present. By the end of his life he clearly and openly intended his dramas to provide something close to religious redemption or salvation. In his late essay, *Religion and Art*, he described 'art' (his art) 'as destined to reach its zenith in its affinity with religion,' and he went on to explain how his art offered a redemption that was not far different from religion. The experience of his art can actually have an effect almost like the liturgies and observances of religion in their transforming effect. And like the liturgy and the services of organised religion Wagner's works can signify different things on different occasions and at different stages of life. This is not for one moment to suggest that the Wagner Experience is itself a religion or a religious substitute, and as we shall see, Wagner vehemently rejected any such notion. Although five of his 'big ten' are set in a Christian context that looms larger in Wagner than in any other operatic composer, the Wagner Experience demands no metaphysical beliefs, nor any faith in a transcendent power (with the probable exception of *Parsifal*; and we shall come to that). It imposes no Ten Commandments or Sharia law. On the other hand, for these very reasons, it is not incompatible with religious beliefs, and it can be life-enhancing in much the same way as religion. Like religion at its best, it can centre us, creating fulfilment and integration, and it can also create an expansion of consciousness and a widening of sympathies. It too can transfigure life. That is why the Wagner Experience is so important, why it is perhaps that 'Everyone needs Wagner'.

THREE

Towards an Understanding of Wagner's Fascination

… While with an eye made quiet by the power
Of harmony, and the deep power of joy,
We see into the life of things.

William Wordsworth
('Lines Written a Few Miles above Tintern Abbey')

Wagner's fascination permeates this book. Several aspects of that fascination have now been mentioned, the euphoric sense of perceptions widened, of boundaries enlarged, of increased potentials, and of greater meaning. The sense of empowerment which goes with it is not imaginary or artificial, as many examples have demonstrated: Bruckner's new-found power to compose his symphonies, the summoning forth of poetry from T.S. Eliot or Baudelaire, and the drive towards the personal growth of D.H. Lawrence and C.S. Lewis. Just as important is Wagner's empowerment of ordinary people, enabling them to live lives which are more inwardly fulfilling and more outwardly effective. This chapter discusses how and why the fascination works, but it is important to emphasise that aesthetic theories cannot be proved logically. Aesthetic theories belong to a domain where formal proof is intrinsically impossible; they belong to the same sphere as theories of history, science and economics, theories about the French Revolution and its causes, theories of light, theories explaining the rise of money: empirical categories where there can be no final, logical proofs, no mathematical QED. The important point is that the theories should appeal to reason: does an idea make sense; does it explain the facts? Is it the simplest explanation on offer? Does it sit happily with our general experience, and does it hold its own when faced with new information? These are the criteria for the theories of Wagner's fascination presented here.

The first point to make is that the fascination of the Wagner Experience is an exceptional example of something quite common, the general appeal of artificial experiences. Given the chance, most people prefer to spend significant amounts of their time engaged with happenings and encounters which are not real. Paul Bloom, Professor of Psychology at Yale, has gone into the matter in detail,[43] and draws on Time Management studies in the USA demonstrating how far Americans retreat into imaginary experiences whenever they are free to do what they want. They prefer to spend their leisure in 'fictions', a category which Paul Bloom takes to include any artificial worlds that are of someone else's making, such as novels, films, video games, and television (in the USA over four hours a day on average), but also in the worlds which people create for themselves, worlds of daydream or fantasy. The appeal of fictions and artificial experiences is partly to do with the extent to which they take on the mantle of reality. Imaginary experiences can speak to people and affect them as much as if they were real. Paul Bloom gives as an example how people had nightmares for weeks after watching Alfred Hitchcock's film *Psycho*, just as if they had actually witnessed its events. Again, J.K. Rowling, of Harry Potter fame, has described how she received letters, and not only from children, begging her to keep alive and safe such characters as Hagrid, Hermione, or Ron, because they meant so much to her readers. They had lived through many vital events with her characters, and had become as fond of her creations as if they were real-life friends. There are countless examples to illustrate this point, that people are eager to identify with fictions and keen to live out the non-existent experiences

---

43   Bloom, Paul, *How Pleasure Works*, London, 2011, p. 156. Paul Bloom informs us by contrast that on average Americans spend four minutes a day on sex, the same time as on tax returns.

of non-existent characters. People who have discovered Wagner find that his creations score highly simply as imaginary experiences which they can live out rewardingly.

In a way, non-real experiences and characters can have a certain advantage over reality, because reality and our own real lives have some unexciting stretches, whereas fiction can be, as Clive James put it, 'life with the dull bits left out'. Fictions also possess the advantage of being wider in range. Novels, plays, histories, biographies and television all spirit us away to interesting worlds and interesting people, not necessarily pleasant, who would otherwise remain outside our experience. This absorption into worlds beyond our own is common to the appeal of Homer, Macaulay, Dante, Dostoevsky, Shakespeare, television soap operas and now computer games, as well as Wagner. Paul Bloom provides evidence that vicarious experiences exercise this fascination in every culture where there is any evidence on the matter.

This is a first explanation for the appeal of fiction, and there is a second which is closely related. Bloom argues convincingly that human beings are innately designed to respond to fictions because they bring an evolutionary, perhaps even a survival value. There are good reasons (which space forbids elaborating further) for accepting that an important function of pleasure is to motivate behaviour which is 'good for the genes'. The pleasure which comes from fictions, fables, novels, dramas, films and staged representations can often inspire beneficial behaviour. Stories instil suggestions for safe practice and achieving good things, as *Siegfried* well illustrates, and stories can give rise to essential change even among the unthinking and reluctant. Cautionary tales particularly provide warnings about avoiding unpleasant things and dangerous situations, or at least about preparing for them. There is thus an evolutionary advantage in these fictions, so that the human race has become conditioned over the ages to respond to them positively. Aristotle over two millennia ago said something like this of tragedy, a specialist branch of cautionary fiction. In a sense, all tragedy is didactic and cautionary, because it presents behaviour that is *de*structive and implicitly warns against it (as happens in *Lohengrin*). Tragedy often additionally provides pointers to ways that are *con*structive. No artificial experiences offer these benefits more generously than those presented by Wagner.

There is a third, related, reason for the appeal of fiction, that stories can be a 'prime mechanism for how societies get nicer', even if the opposite is also possible, how 'moral insights such as the evils of slavery can be packaged in a form that persuades others and eventually becomes accepted as the status quo'.[44] Multimillion-pound advertising industries are built on the fact that people emulate behaviours and standards which they witness on television, because 'life follows art' (applying the term 'art' in a broad, inclusive sense). Likewise Wagner's dramas do not just model particular practices and values; they demand that we should adopt them, and this is only possible because the dramas and their characters draw us in.

Hence when Neville Cardus, the unforgettable music critic of the *Manchester Guardian*, asked himself the reasons for Wagner's fascination, his first answers were 'the exciting story represented in the drama' and that 'the public are attracted by his dramatic genius and the range of it'. The public were also attracted by its ideals; 'The interest is the same in such old fashioned matters as idealism matched against corruption, in the revolt of youth against custom, in love as a solvent. And ordinary human nature will still respond to an imaginative representation of crude villainy and of selfless heroism soon to suffer disillusionment ... Even in this age, the superstition still clings to many that a god can be symbolised by a genius, even if it is a god in chains.' The range of ideas, examples and recommendations which Cardus compressed into this short passage is extraordinary.

The fascination of Wagner's dramas is heightened by the music, and some people would go further, asserting that Wagner's fascination *is* the music, a point of view which Neville Cardus half endorsed: 'The appeal of *The Ring* to the audiences that flock to it is the vivid illustrative orchestral sound with its hammer rhythms for Nibelheim,

---

44   Ibid., p. 173.

its lilt and surge for the Rhine scenes, the tumult of the Valkyries' ride, the gigantic stamping of the giants, the forging of Siegfried's sword, the low-crawling heavings of Fafner the dragon, the evocation of fire and the sleep of Brünnhilde.' In that he could translate these things into music, 'Wagner was among the greatest and completest of musicians.' The idea that it is the music that really *is* Wagner's fascination can often appear to be borne out at concert performances where members of the audience are visibly 'blissed out' by the music.

In a distinctive assessment of *The Ring*, Prof. William O. Cord took the matter of Wagner's fascination beyond the action and the music. What he said of *The Ring* is set out here abbreviated, and his assessment applies to Wagner's fascination generally.

There is a Universality about Wagner's creative works, a Universality in theme, in topic, in content, of context, in nature, in character, in intellect, in interpretation, in expression, and in metaphor. This Universality is most obvious in *The Ring*. *The Ring* has a kind of cosmic authority which cannot be grasped in a physical or even a rational manner ... As the words and the sound of *The Ring* continue to strike the senses, the drama's continuous present allows the emotional essence of the mind to unfold, to extend itself, without bounds, and then to spread throughout the total being of the viewer ... This stirs some element of emotional experience, some factor of individual understanding, some philosophic or psychologic insight ... such that Reason drifts into an outer circle separated from the core of emotion that now presides. This, then, is the 'Transcendental Euphoria' of *The Ring*.[45]

45 Cord, William O., 'Assessment of the Secrets of the Power Wagner's Work Holds over Us', *Leitmotive*, vol. XXI no. 2 (Summer 2007), p. 17. In full the passage reads: 'There is a Universality about Wagner's creative works, a Universality in theme, in topic, in content, of context, in nature, in character, in intellect, in interpretation, in expression, and in metaphor. This Universality is most obvious in *The Ring*. *The Ring* has a kind of cosmic authority which cannot be grasped in a physical or even a rational manner, but can only be perceived sensorially, and only then

William Cord does not exactly explain *why* 'philosophic or psychologic insight' should create euphoria, and in any case some might baulk at the idea of euphoria as a source of Wagner's fascination because the action in his dramas is often not euphoric. *Lohengrin* ends in irreparable loss. Elsa, the heroine, dies 'of a broken heart' after asking Lohengrin the forbidden question who he is. Lohengrin has lost her, his great

---

by one who approaches the drama with some seriousness. This strength, this force, is an essence depicted as an instantaneous and continuous present. This present stands alone, and is infinite; it exists without beginning or end, without limits or boundaries. Without past, without future, it is ever-current and continuous, and it is instantaneous, bursting into being the instant the first dark notes of *Das Rheingold* resound in the darkened theatre. These notes now begin a journey through the emotional psyche, and the experience of the timeless present sets in immediately. As *The Ring* unfolds, the state of mind grows and expands; as the drama progresses, the limitless present envelopes all that the mind controls, to prevent the rational or logical exerting its influence. As the words and the sound of *The Ring* continue to strike the senses, the drama's continuous present allows the emotional essence of the mind to unfold, to extend itself, without bounds, and then to spread throughout the total being of the viewer. At this point the senses dominate. They define a comprehension of the drama that only feeling can acknowledge and that is personal to the individual who listens to the sounds intently.

Now there is a pleasant insight that roams unfettered by cultural modes or social mores. The rational understanding that *The Ring* projects has become one with the most intimate emotions of the audience. It is because of their timeless present that Wagner's mature works and especially *The Ring* allow each epoch, each culture, each age, each individual, to find itself. A flood of feeling then flows freely about the internal condition of the human spirit. This state regularly stirs some element of emotional experience, some factor of individual understanding, some philosophic or psychologic insight. Such personal reactions diffuse osmotic-like within the psyche, to such an extent that all other affairs become shadows. Reason has now drifted into an outer circle separated from the core of emotion that now presides. This, then, is the 'Transcendental Euphoria' of *The Ring*.'

and only love. The troops are distraught as he departs down the river Scheldt back to Montsalvat. What makes it worse is that Lohengrin has of necessity struck down their previous war-leader, Telramund. The visiting German King-Emperor Henry is equally upset. Even Ortrud, Telramund's terrifying wife, has lost out completely. There are no winners, and it is easy to understand the chorus's final '*Weh*: Woe! Alas! Misery!'

Even so Professor Cord's suggestion holds up convincingly. However poignant its action may be, the total experience of *Lohengrin* actually *is* euphoric, indeed rapturous. Cord might have protested that he was actually writing about *The Ring* and that I have misapplied his transcendental euphoria to the sad story of *Lohengrin*, but *The Ring* is just as 'sad'. In 1854, Wagner wrote to Princess Caroline zu Sayn-Wittgenstein, that there was no suffering in the world that did not find its most excruciating expression in *Die Walküre*, and yet *Die Walküre* supports William Cord's contention. Even if Wagner's description of such suffering in *Die Walküre* had not been an exaggeration, it would not detract from the fact that the *Die Walküre* as a whole creates a positive, exalted effect. As it happens, not every drama of Wagner is tragic; *Siegfried*, *Meistersinger* and *Parsifal* all end 'happily'; but even Wagner's tragic works were of a highly unusual kind, because each one, taken as a whole, offers us not only Aristotelian catharsis but a full measure of euphoria.

Part of the euphoria is that Wagner's dramas rearrange and transform the thinking and feeling of those who relate to them in a way that resolves the intrinsic disunities of the human condition. These disunities stem from the fact that man is on the one hand an instinctive animal, a creature driven by biology and the need to survive, stay well and replicate itself. On the other hand he is an intelligent machine, a cerebral computer, given to rational thinking. The human computer evolved out of the human animal to serve its purposes, but the end result is a being that yokes together forces which frequently pull in different directions, a rational mind straining against instinctive drives. There are additional disunities between the older, more primitive animal brain and the large, complex brain unique to man. However, the disunities and the conflict are creative too, and out of them has arisen one of the strangest and most amazing phenomena of the universe, human consciousness, the mind, the psyche, the spirit, the soul.[46] With this comes an awareness of values, beauty and ugliness, good and evil, loyalty and perfidy, affections and disaffections, and of humanity's spiritual and aesthetic dimensions. However, the disunities remain serious, a potential source of emotional disturbance, conflict and mental illness. Religions, philosophies, psychologies, as well as great poets and artists have all attempted various ways of resolving the disunities, of reconfiguring and overcoming them, but Wagner stands out as very special indeed, because he addressed them in ways that go far to resolving them.[47]

Indeed a distinctive appeal of the Wagner Experience is that by providing a resolution of the disunities, it offers a kind of secular redemption; and there are certain ideas from the writings of Hans Keller and Bryan Magee which are relevant and helpful about this. Hans Keller was a pivotal figure at the BBC between the 1960s and the 1980s and his book, *Criticism*, indicates briefly a conception of

---

46   Gilbert Ryle in *The Concept of Mind* (London, 1951) denied the existence of this conscious awareness, poking fun at the idea of a 'ghost in the machine', but most of us would assert from first-hand experience that there is a ghost in the machine, because we are that ghost; we know it more nearly than we know anything: '*Cogito, ergo sum.*'

47   Young, Wayland, *Eros Denied*, Brattleboro, Vt., 1964, p. 186 on Christianity: 'It dismantled man wherever it went and reassembled him afresh. Every feeling, every belief, every image of himself and of his fellows, every duty, every right, every impulse, reaction and reflection, every sentiment of community and of distinction, was changed through and through.' Wagner had a great deal of sympathy for views like this. The dismantling, reassembling process might be partly positive as a mechanism for resolving man's divisions, but it was a flawed because it required too much suppression of his animal aspect. This created conflicts of its own, as Wagner expounded in *Tannhäuser*.

Wagner's fascination which he seems to have taken for granted.[48] 'Wagner's music, like none other before or indeed after him, let what Freud called the dynamic unconsciousness, normally inaccessible, erupt with a clarity and seductiveness that will always be likely to arouse as much resistance (to the listener's own unconsciousness) as its sheer power creates enthusiasm.' Hans Keller's laconic formulation had a precedent in Bryan Magee's remarkable little book, *Aspects of Wagner*.[49] Magee wrote:

> We have a music that gets at people – not everyone, of course, but a remarkable number – in a unique way; gets under their skins, stirs passions that no other music touches, and draws reactions that, favourable or unfavourable, are certainly immoderate ... Wagner gives expression to things that in the rest of us and in the rest of art are unconscious because they are repressed. Modern psychology has familiarised us with the idea – and convinced most of us of its truth – that in the process of growing up and developing independent personalities, and learning to live in society, we have to subordinate some of our most powerful instinctual desires, especially erotic and aggressive ones, for instance passionate erotic feelings towards parents and siblings, or the urge to attack and destroy those on whom we are emotionally dependent so that these are driven underground, below the level of consciousness, and kept there at the cost of some strain, as a result of which they remain charged with a high level of emotional voltage. Most of the really important taboos in our society, such as the incest taboo, relate to them. This repression, this inner conflict, is inseparable from living, and is part of the personality of each one of us. I believe it is from, and to, this level of personality that Wagner's music speaks.

Bryan Magee's exposition was initially intended to explain the fascination of the music, but it went beyond his intention 'to embrace

48   Keller, Hans, *Criticism*, London, 1987, p. 95.
49   Magee, Bryan, *Aspects of Wagner*, London, 1968.

the plots', which are 'to a remarkable degree the subject matter of depth psychology. Even today, audiences would be shocked if the first act of a new drama were to consist in a prolonged, passionate love-scene between brother and sister that culminated in sexual intercourse as soon as the curtain went down. Yet this is the first act of *Die Walküre*.' Magee continues,

> While archetypal psycho-sexual situations are being acted out on-stage at exhaustive length, the orchestra is pouring out a flood of inexpressible feelings associated with them. And this is the heart of the matter: it is in the orchestra, as Wagner and everyone since has been aware, that the innermost aspects of the drama are being realised. The most important things in life, namely its psycho-emotional fundamentals as inwardly experienced, are articulated here, as they can never be in words, or on the stage, or in any other outward terms. The Wagnerian orchestra is, to quote Thomas Mann, 'the Kingdom of subliminal knowledge, unknown to the word Up There'.

Magee effectively re-frames Wagner's analysis of the relation between sung text and orchestra in quasi-Freudian terms, and Bryan Magee's analysis has helped a good many people with access to the Wagner Experience. Although his discussion is largely about the plots and not about why the music works, this does not detract from the quality of his insights.

A minor failing of his book is its unquestioning acceptance of Freud's view of the unconscious, at best a shallow place containing experiences too insignificant to register, but more like a cesspool of unacceptable impulses and suppressed infantile urges, topped up with more recent experiences that were too unpleasant to remember, too traumatic and criminal, or simply too filthy and degrading to countenance. For Freud the unconscious was a disordered world committed to a war on the humanity of its owner and only to be exorcised by psychoanalysis. Another idea follows close, that the satisfactions of the Wagner Experience come from a process whereby people come to terms with the dark and detestable phantoms of their unconscious, and gain some degree of relief.

I have already hinted how Jung regarded this kind of thinking as misguided (as I do), and perhaps it is closer to the truth to see the Wagner Experience as positive, as helping to resolve the disunities of being human. Freud was at his best in his analysis of these disunities and in the theories he formulated concerning their origins, about thirty years after Wagner's death. Freud's thinking led him to believe that the disunities result from the tensions among our basic impulses, because they exist in a state of conflict. As he argued, the human mind functions as an uneasy balance between three groups of impulses which exist in a mix of cooperation and antagonism. The first of these groups consists of blind drives and instincts, which he termed the 'id'. We feel the id in its imperative demands for such things as food, warmth, safety, a supportive environment, and procreation. Incidentally, this is not merely a matter of conjecture or unfounded theoretical fantasy, because there is an anatomical and physiological counterpart to the id in the hypothalamus, that part of the brain which directs, activates and coordinates the other areas devoted to fulfilling instinctive needs and fundamental drives. The demands of the id create an inner unrest which can only be allayed by satisfying them. Satisfying them leads, in Freud's terminology, to 'pleasure', and Freud called the process of satisfying them the 'pleasure principle'.

The second group of impulses which Freud identified are the rational ones, operating to devise ways and means for satisfying the id. Driven by its demands, the rational aspect of the mind works out how to get food, how to earn money, how to find and keep a job, a house to live in, and a mate. At a physiological level the hypothalamus supports these objectives through its direct connections with all those parts of the brain which are responsible for perceiving, thinking, forming intentions, and carrying them out: the higher functions of the mind. The rational element which takes on these higher functions is known in Freud-speak as the 'ego'.

The third group of impulses identified by Freud are those from the regulating conscience, the 'super-ego'. Freud believed that the super-ego is formed in infancy from bruising encounters with others in a child's surroundings. From earliest life there are conflicts because the id drives a child to pursue its own ends in selfish disregard of everyone else, impelling the child to do things that often do not suit other people at all. This leads to conflicts with the powerful figures in the child's surroundings, with other children and above all with parents, who curb its impulses. They also coerce it to do things that are contrary to its id instincts, and it learns to cooperate in order to avoid the pain of having these powerful figures react unpleasantly if it simply follows its impulses. A child soon realises that it is less disagreeable to create its own internal checks. It comes to anticipate external restraints, and to defuse them by assimilating them, making them its own, and pre-empting them. In other words, the child internalises the conflict between the id and external pressures, and the restraints on the id become half-instinctive. This process in Freud's view, though not Jung's, forms the real basis of conscience. Of these three mental dimensions, only the ego is rational. The id and the super-ego are subliminal drives.

There may be large numbers of instincts and drives, but it is important for an appreciation of Wagner that Freud came to believe that libido, life force or sexuality, was all-important; while Jung, although he found evidence for a good many others, recognised two as specially significant: 'Eros' and the 'will to power'. These twin drives were those which Wagner had already identified and which found their way into his dramas, above all into *The Ring*. Interestingly the 'will to power' was an idea and an expression which Jung took from another pioneer psychologist, Alfred Adler. Adler himself had taken it from Nietzsche and Nietzsche originally took it – from Wagner! Wagner's own name for the musical theme which we know as 'the Ring' was the 'Will to Power'. Jung regarded 'Eros' and the will to power as the two impulses principally responsible for our intellectual energy and drive. For Jung as in Wagner, 'The Will to Power is surely as mighty a demon as Eros, and just as old and original'[50] and just as impossible to confine. If 'love is an elastic concept that stretches from heaven to hell and combines in itself good and evil, high and low,' so is the will to power, and the opposition of love or Eros and the will to power lies at the heart of *The Ring*. As in Jung so too in Wagner, it is this tension and conflict of two basic drives which gives rise to human energy, the impulse to act and achieve. It also adds to our inner unrest. As Jung put it, 'The growth of culture consists in the progressive subjugation of the animal in man. It is a process of domestication which cannot be accomplished without rebellion of the animal nature.'[51] This conflict is at the heart of *The Ring*, and provides its mainspring.

The Wagner Experience helps to resolve the disunities as does almost no other art. The Wagner Experience can make possible an acceptance of 'the dog beneath the skin', but both for Wagner and for Jung, the point of accepting instincts 'was not, as many would have it, with a view to giving them boundless freedom, but rather to *incorporating them in a purposeful whole*'.[52] Here was Jung's crucial recognition, replicated in Wagner's precepts to us, above all in *The Ring* and *Parsifal*, that unless a person is in full possession of his/her personality, including his *shadow side* (his more reprehensible aspect), it will crop up elsewhere in an ugly and dangerous form. 'It is a frightening thought that man has a shadow side consisting of a positively demonic dynamism.'[53] 'We cannot be whole without this negative side; we have a body and if we deny the body we cease to be three dimensional.'[54] And 'if men can be educated to see the shadow side of their nature clearly,' (and assimilate it), 'it is to be hoped that they will be educated to understand and love their fellow-men better.'

50   Jung, C.G., *Über die Psychologie des Unbewussten*, revised edition, Zurich, 1945, tr. R.F.C. Hull as 'On the Psychology of the Unconscious', in *Two Essays on Analytical Psychology*, New York, 1956, p. 43.
51   Ibid., p. 28.
52   Ibid., p. 36 (my italics).
53   Ibid., p. 39.
54   Ibid., p. 40.

Wagner's works from *Der fliegende Holländer* onwards actualise and model this very quest towards integration. The integration of the shadow side consists of a reconfiguring process which can be helped forward and even instilled in us by Wagner's works. The relief from inner dissonance which Wagner's works confer is a source of their fascination and appeal, and is one reason why we experience Wagner's dramas not only as *recon*figuring but as *trans*figuring.

It is highly relevant to the Wagner Experience and its meaning to us that Jung was also led by his clinical experience to recognise the need for myths and religion as innate and universal. Jung argued that we need them in order to live by them,[55] and this is where the Wagner Experience can play an especially fulfilling role. The Wagner Experience does include myths by which to live, and it helps us to deal with the universal issues confronting humanity, which are much the same as they have ever been. Man has barely altered in physiology or psychology since he first evolved; nor has his psychological journey through life much changed. In all places, in all cultures, there are the same basic needs, and this certainly includes the need for ideas by which to live, something vividly illustrated and explained in Jung's early example of the Pueblo Indians of North Mexico with their singular myths and beliefs. Jung explained how these people believed that the sun was their father, and they believed that they assisted the sun to make his daily journey across the sky by practising their religion and performing certain rituals. 'In this they did something which

---

55   The relationship between myth and religion is hazy. The Shorter Oxford English Dictionary defines myth as *fictitious* narrative, whereas religion is 'the recognition by man of a higher unseen power as having control of his destiny and entitled to obedience, reverence and worship, together with the general mental and moral attitudes resulting from this belief, both as they affect the individual and the community.' The fundamental difference is that myth is taken as fictional whereas religious beliefs are accepted as true, and for those who hold them an ultimate truth. At certain phases of his life, Jung seemed to deny any distinction. He saw no reason not to accord the same truth value to religion and to myth, indeed the same as to science and history.

they saw as being of great value to the world, and this gave their lives significance, because it was they who maintained the sun in all his glory.' Without their efforts, 'the sun would wither and perish, and the earth go dark and die.' Jung commented, 'I then realised on what the "dignity", the tranquil composure of the individual Indian, was founded.' This illustrated his point that when a myth confers meaning and purpose on life, as here and in Wagner's dramas, then it fulfils an essential function. However untenable the myth may be as science, it is life-enhancing for the people who live by it and it has therefore a crucial psychological validity. The trouble is that today no educated person could live by this myth about the sun, however attractive it may be to feel so significant, because it is so obviously false to the facts.

Something of the kind applies to the religious beliefs of today in that they can only work for the well-being of people who believe in them, and Jung was deeply concerned at the compelling evidence that men and women without religion or myths do lose their sense of value. This is where Wagner offers something that is both fascinating and extraordinary. His dramas express myths which we know to be untrue; they are not historical or scientific realities (*Parsifal* may be the exception; and the 'myths' of *Parsifal* and their status warrant a special discussion) but the important, amazing thing is that it does not matter. It is still possible to live by them, possible for them to make sense of our lives *without our having to believe that they are true*. This does not mean that the Wagner Experience is simply a conscious escape into make-believe or wishful thinking, most importantly because the life-enhancing effect which it produces is a material fact. Even if the myths of the Wagner Experience are fictions and everyone knows they are fictions, the benefits which originate in them are real. What happened to C.S. Lewis, Bruckner, Baudelaire, Nietzsche, and countless others, was real. That is the first point, and the second is that Wagner's life-enhancing effect is more than repairing the past and healing existing disunities, though this is no small benefit in itself. Wagner's dramas go further; they look forward to the future and offer directions about living life better.

This is part of the secular salvation which Wagner offers, and in addition to relief from the disunities common to humanity, it offers liberation from particular shortcomings and personal errors. As most people will recognise from their own experience, actions undertaken freely can loom up later like alien powers. Some degree of redemption from their stranglehold is one of the central benefits of Wagner, and it offers the means to escape the prison of the past and go forward. This redemption is not unique to Wagner, and in fact I believe it is easier to explain initially by drawing on a parallel redemption, the experience offered by J.S. Bach in the *St Matthew Passion*. Even though the redemption which this offers is not secular, it works on the imagination in ways which illuminate the way that Wagner's secular version can also work. A point of contrast between Bach and Wagner is that the redemption in the *St Matthew Passion* is bound to mean more to people who believe in Christianity, because redemption is for them a factual, material reality, a possibility which does not arise with the secular version provided in *The Ring*. There is a passage in the *St Matthew Passion* which gives a special reality to redemption, the passage which tells the story of 'Peter's Denial'. The account in St Matthew's Gospel as it stands is one of the most poignant and involving things in the whole of western literature. It begins with Jesus Christ's warning to his followers that after his arrest they will simply fly to save their own skins. Christ warns them that anyone accused of being associated with him will simply deny all knowledge and claim never to have met him. Peter was one of the followers, and Peter was a bluff, energetic character who felt affronted by what he saw as a put-down. He retorted that everyone in the world might deny knowing Jesus, but he never would. Jesus' response was that before cock-crow next morning, Peter would have denied him three times, which is exactly what happened. Jesus was arrested, and Peter followed him through the darkness in a state of fearful vagueness, wondering 'what next?' He was in the courtyard outside the judgment hall where Jesus was in trial, and he was shivering in the cold and huddled by the fire when he was recognised. A maid came up and accused him of being one of Jesus' men; Peter answered evasively that he was not. Then another maid came up with the same claim and Peter denied it with more heat. It all then happened a third time, with several people saying they were sure of their facts and that his Galilean accent gave him away. Peter began to curse and to swear 'I do not know the man!' and immediately the cock crew. Then Peter remembered the word of Jesus, how he had said that before the cock crowed, Peter would deny him thrice. And Peter went out, and wept, bitterly.

Here is a devastating situation with universal resonances, and Christianity contains a great deal that is of universal resonance. Here is an agonising example of human disunities creating conflict and turmoil. The animal in the man wanted to escape. Self-preservation is a basic drive. However it conflicted with imperatives from the higher functions of the mind and spirit, and perhaps with some archetypal ordinances as well. The pain of the conflict is unendurable, the pressure and the guilt appalling. This situation furthermore represented a paradigm of irrevocable failure; of Peter having 'talked the talk and not walked the walk', of his having let somebody down who was very dear. There is something universal about the experience of being weighed in the balance and found wanting, of Peter recognising that Christ had seen through him and knew him exactly as he was. Peter sees himself as contemptible in his own eyes as in Christ's; *and there is absolutely nothing that he can do about it*. This is a situation where many people have experienced parallels, perhaps most people beyond the age of about five (unless they are irredeemably narcissistic or in denial, and here I assert gently again that as a family doctor I knew the secrets of many hearts).

It is the general achievement of true, original Christianity to forgive and absolve such guilt, failure and wrong, if it is admitted and confessed. It is Bach's particular achievement to take this episode and others like it, and make the forgiveness a reality. Bach in effect takes such failures and transfigures them. His music pours a shower of beauty on Peter's anguish, and continues to do so in the aria that follows, '*Erbarme dich, mein Gott*, Forgive me, my God!' Bach refracts a tormenting, self-lacerating experience through his music in a way that re-frames its terms of reference. The power of the music draws people into the experience, so that they participate in it, and live in it. They also live through it, and emerge redeemed. Bach's genius, musical, dramatic, psychological and religious, irradiates the episode and rearranges the psyche in such a way as to make real the experience of being made whole again. They are then free to move on and go forward and make progress. Unless they are as thick as a brass ox, even the most irreligious must recognise the *St Matthew Passion* as a frightful story about the betrayal, persecution and hideous, torturing death of a profoundly good man[56] and Bach illuminated it and transformed our involvement through music which touches the mind and psyche at every level. In this the *St Matthew Passion* offers something similar to Wagnerian redemption or *Erlösung*. At the very least the *St Matthew Passion* offers a kind of secular salvation for people who go deeply through the experience of it, a salvation wrought by mind-altering art at its most sublime. People who believe the Christian creed expressed in the *St Matthew Passion* regard the redemption it expresses as something more, something beyond Bach's masterpiece which comes through heavenly grace and Christ's atonement. From either viewpoint, secular or sacred, it is the music that mediates the redemption, making it available and palpable both as a psychological and a metaphysical experience. The *St Matthew Passion* works a fair amount of its redemptive effect even for people who do not believe in the creed it represents, because the music can envelope any sensitive person in the experience. It suffuses the imagination, and people are then free to move forward with a new freedom, with mistakes un-made and potentials rejuvenated.

Wagner achieves the same effect, again a kind of secular salvation created through mind-altering art, as becomes fully obvious a little later, from the individual operas, but for an immediate illustration there is 'Wotan's Farewell' in *Die Walküre*. At this point in the action,

56   It is interesting that Götz Friedrich, the committed Marxist, staged it in Berlin with a profound respect for its ideals and for the person of Jesus.

Wotan has arrived at a situation where his mistakes have ruined and wrecked the universal order which he had created, and where his attempts to put matters right have simply made them worse. Not only that, but he has lost the affections of his wife, the life of his dear son, and worse, the daughter who is his beloved alter ego. It is his fault and his mistakes that have created the catastrophe. Wotan sees himself as having totally failed, and (again) *there is absolutely nothing that he can do about it*. This too is a situation where many people have could testify to parallel experiences of their own. As happens with Bach, Wagner's music and drama also pour down a shower of beauty, refracting the experience in a way that transforms its terms of reference. Here again the effect is to draw people into the experience, so that they participate in it, live in it and live through it, and this time it is Wagner's genius, musical, dramatic, psychological, that irradiates it and reorders the psyche in ways as that make real the experience of being whole again. It too creates a new freedom to make progress and move forward with enlarged potentials. In fact Wagner's dramas transform many poignant and forbidding aspects of life, achieving this by means of music and drama that connect with us at a conscious and an unconscious level; and it is no mere whimsy to wonder whether it was a shared affinity for something more than music which led Wagner increasingly towards Bach in his final decade. Like Bach, Wagner's music envelopes us in myth-invoking experiences and saturates our minds in them. Bach and Wagner both infuse life events with something that transforms the possibilities, but Wagner requires no religious belief for the Wagner effect to work. The separate chapters on each of Wagner's ten great dramas go specifically into what they can each offer towards this.

The next reason for Wagner's uncanny fascination has come up already, though not in full focus. Quite apart from the specific transformations wrought by many specific experiences through which we are drawn in Wagner's dramas, their very language has the capacity to reconfigure the mind. For this they deploy language in two different registers, the language of words and the language of music. Wagner believed that music could actually speak, and that music was a language as specific and compelling as any words. In Wagner, both text and music speak the drama.

Both can also condition and recondition the mind, altering its way of experiencing things, sometimes in small ways, sometimes with immense effect, and in order to understand how this is possible, it is important to look again at the discoveries of Jacques Lacan and others after him about the modelling effect of language. Lacan convincingly argued that language does not simply express ideas; it forms and shapes them, and in the process it forms and shapes us, our minds and our identity. This happens because we are all born into a world of language. Language surrounds an infant from the beginning. As the infant grows and develops its receptive capacity for language, both for understanding it and speaking it, so too the language of its encounters moulds its ways of thinking. There is a constant developmental interaction between language and the child's mind, as language takes the child's amorphous mental glimmerings and crystallises them. Language makes it possible to experience things with more focus and definition. Language is doing more here than putting ideas and experience into words; it is determining them, and the process continues into adulthood and beyond. The economy, religion, romantic passion, meaning and reason are all concepts created in and through language. In creating them, language defines both the style of a person's thoughts and the person who thinks them. Hence it is that in a world where language is dominated by computers and computer-speak, children are more likely to incline towards computers in the way that they think, logically and in steps. In environments dominated by economic-speak and statistic-speak, children would be more likely to imagine human beings as consumers and think of them generally in terms of numbers and populations. In a world dominated by psychiatry-speak, people's outlook is permeated by psychological viewpoints, viewing human beings as controlled by non-rational impulses rooted in neurology or experience. There is no time or age limit to this process. It is possible to come to law or music late in life, and however late it is, people's ideas and their minds are remodelled by the new linguistic terms they encounter.

In a mental world where Wagner looms large, people's outlooks are likewise conditioned by the language, verbal and musical, of his ten great dramas. Wagner's twin languages embody his ideas, and a mind that absorbs them is affected and altered by them. People actually form and modify their identities in terms of the language they encounter in Wagner's works, just as much as they do from any other language in their surroundings. What they gain from Wagner's language is of special importance for reasons put forward by another Frenchman, Jean-Luc Marion. He contends that language today has become more limited and has closed down the scope of our experience. Jean-Luc Marion, a Roman Catholic theologian of some distinction, has suggested convincingly that contemporary language is unable to offer any adequate expression for many of the experiences that matter most to people, such as love. Jean-Luc Marion's book, *The Erotic Phenomenon*[57] (a surprising book from a devout Roman Catholic theologian) begins, 'We no longer have the words to speak it, the concepts to think about it, nor the strength to celebrate it.' In consequence, many people only sense such experiences vaguely, without understanding them or determining them properly. He argues that this is part of a larger problem, the shrivelling away of many facets of language which should colour and enhance our thinking and enlarge our experience. It is language which generally enables us to determine our ideals, but Marion claims convincingly that the cast of contemporary language results in a disdain for ideals and even an implicit denigration of any words that express and formulate them. He takes as an illustration the word 'charity' and all that it represents;[58] if used now the word generally causes 'a

---

57   Marion, Jean-Luc, *The Erotic Phenomenon*, Chicago, 2007.

58   Marion believes that religion has itself degraded ideals of grace, the sacred and the soul. These abound and resonate throughout the translation of the Bible authorised by King James, famously described as the only work of genius ever put together by a committee. The second half of the Bible, The New Testament, tells how Jesus Christ, the central figure of the Bible, was and is the Saviour of the world. The Authorised

strange linguistic embarrassment'. 'Even charity's magnificent name is snatched away, and it is covered by rags deemed more acceptable, such as "fellowship", "solidarity", "humanitarian aid".'

This brings us to the particular aspect of Wagner's appeal and fascination that I mentioned, that the experience of his twin languages offers the possibility of recovering ideals and restoring them. The verbal language of Wagner's great dramas is rich enough to express ideals and concepts with which to clothe them and think about them. Combined with the musical language of those dramas it makes experiences possible for which we previously lacked the capacity. The Wagner Experience opens up the imagination to possibilities to which contemporary language and thought gives short shrift. People evidently do need these possibilities because they crave after them, and 'try and recreate them, albeit in pared down, pallid versions'. As Jean-Luc Marion points out, people seem impelled to fabricate replicas, poor substitutes, 'the desperate sentimentalism of popular prose, the frustrated pornography of the idol industry, or the shapeless ideology of that boastful asphyxiation known as "self-actualisation".'[59] In doing so, people are reaching out beyond the identities assigned to them socially, their identities as commodities and consumers, to a world of the imagination and the spirit, or romance and ideals. Ideals are spiritual affairs, and people naturally reach out towards ideals in a manner that supports Jung's axiom that human beings are naturally predetermined to spirituality, religion and wholeness. The language of myth and religion is one which gives form and shape to these possibilities, and the language of Wagner does the same.

Wagner's fascination is, in addition, related to the capacity of his

Version describes in beautiful English how he was baptised in the river Jordan; whereupon the heavens opened and a voice from above said, 'Thou are my beloved son, in whom I am well pleased.' It was a surprise when the Archbishop of Canterbury commended a new version which reads 'That's my boy; you're doing fine!' which has few resonances, or at least resonates very differently.

59   Ibid., p. 2.

dramas to reach into the mind, stirring the archetypes and producing mental realignments which people mostly experience as pleasurable, sometimes even ecstatic. This is the right point to look in more detail at archetypes and the way they work. They are central to Jung's psychology and just as central to our understanding of Wagner. Unfortunately he never gave a definition of 'archetype' but from his use of the term it is evident that archetypes are something like the programmes which enable a computer to accept and process information. Archetypes fulfil this function in the mind, but they are innate. Hence a person without an archetypal predisposition towards rhythm, melody and harmony will never grow to appreciate music; it can only seem a noise. Some of the most universal archetypes and most relevant to Wagner are to do with parents. Through its archetypes every newborn child is preconditioned to relate to parents and to assume that it is their nature to be a sovereign, kindly authority, a conviction which often endures in the face of glaring evidence to the contrary. Archetypes have their being in the deeps of the mind, and incidentally this sense of 'depth in the mind' is a common experience. It is a common experience to feel sleep as a sinking down into unconsciousness, and awakening as an emerging up out of it. It is also a common experience to feel that we draw memories and old thoughts and ideas up from the depths. The sense of mind as an actual place with levels and dimensions is virtually inescapable, and it is not unreasonable to envisage its depths, as Jung did, as a territory occupied by archetypes and myths. Jung regarded archetypes as inborn and as having evolved through human prehistory. He saw them as unknowable in themselves, and described them as 'representatives of unconscious states and processes whose nature can be only imperfectly inferred and realised from the contents that appear in consciousness.'[60] They send up counterparts, flashes or whole pictures that flicker across the television screen of consciousness, and it is then that they may take the form of thoughts, mental images and emotions. It is then that 'mythological images are

60 Jung, Carl, *On the Nature of the Psyche*, tr. R.F.C. Hull, Abingdon, 1969, p. 100.

awakened … An interior spiritual world opens out. Its images are intense … When an archetype appears in a dream, in a fantasy or in life, it always brings with it a certain power, by virtue of which it exercises a numinous or a fascinating effect, or impels to action.'[61] Activity among the archetypes is sensed as a stirring of great force and significance. A good illustration comes again from C.S. Lewis and his description of discovering Wagner:

> The sky turned round. It was as if the Arctic itself, all the deep layers of secular ice, should change not in a week or an hour, but instantly, into a landscape of grass and primroses and orchards in bloom, deafened with bird songs and astir with running water … How did I know at once and beyond question, that this was no Celtic or sylvan, or terrestrial twilight? But so it was. Pure Northernness engulfed me: a vision of huge clear spaces hanging above the Atlantic in the endless twilight of Northern Summer, remoteness, severity … and almost at the same moment I knew that I had met this before, long, long ago. And with that plunge back into my own past there arose at once almost like heartbreak, the memory of Joy itself, the knowledge that I had once had what I now lacked for years, that I was returning at last from exile and deserts to my own country; and the distance of the Twilight of the Gods and the distance of my own past Joy, both unattainable, flowed together into a single, unendurable sense of desire and loss … And at once I knew that to have it again was the supreme and only object of desire … You will misunderstand everything in this autobiography unless you realise that Asgard and the Valkyries seemed to me incomparably more important than anything else in my experience.[62]

It is difficult to imagine a more poetic and penetrating description of this layer of the Wagner Experience, of archetypes stirred to action, and the joy and fulfilment that goes with it. The Wagner Experience

---

61   Id,, *Two Essays on Analytical Psychology*, tr. R.F.C. Hull, New York, 1956, p. 80.
62   Lewis, C.S., *Surprised by Joy*, London, 1955, p. 74.

was radiant illumination for Lewis, and it gave his life a value and worthwhileness which religion had not supplied, or at least not yet. Christianity was real for him, but it meant nothing yet compared to Wagner. He even castigated himself because the religion in which he wanly believed gave him so much less and meant so much less than the myths of Wagner in which he did not believe; and this reinforces the important point that what he experienced in Wagner did not have to be materially true for it to transform his life. The Wagner Experience still imparted the sense of integration (C.S. Lewis called it a renaissance) which Jung regarded as the central objective of religion, although neither Lewis nor anyone else mistook the Wagner Experience for a religion. For the experience to work for Lewis, it was enough that his mind should be filled with it and that the archetypes in it should become active. They worked for him as Jung believed that they always worked, with a purposeful objective 'which I [Jung] have called individuation. This transcendent function … which is capable of uniting the opposites … is a purely natural process which may pursue its course without the knowledge or assistance of the individual and can some times forcibly accomplish itself in the face of opposition. The meaning and purpose of the process is the realisation of the personality, the production and unfolding of its original, potential wholeness.'[63]

This then is another fascination that Wagner confers, another source of his appeal, that the Wagner Experience also acts and helps towards personal integration. Most people will understand this more easily if they compare it with falling in love. There it is an acquaintance with a particular person that creates resonances which are experienced as a joy, but it can also produce a particular equilibrium and a heightened awareness. Wagner's dramas likewise create mental resonances which a person experiences as a joy; and it too can produce a particular equilibrium and heightened awareness. People may find it helpful towards understanding this mental reconfiguring which comes from

---

63   Jung, *Two Essays on Analytical Psychology*, p. 121.

Rosine Wagner, painted by her second husband Ludwig Geyer

Ludwig Geyer, self-portrait of 1803

Adolf Wagner, Richard's uncle

Heinrich Laube, writer and leader of the Young Germany movement, in 1836

Minna Planer in 1836, painted by an admirer, Alexander von Otterstedt

Minna Wagner in 1853 with her dog Peps, painted by Clementine Stockar-Escher

Arthur Schopenhauer, painted in 1859 by Jules Lunteschutz

Franz Liszt in 1865

Mathilde Wesendonck in 1850, by Karl Ferdinand Sohn

King Ludwig II of Bavaria as a young man

Cosima Wagner in 1879, by Franz von Lenbach

Richard and Cosima Wagner in Vienna in 1872, photographed by Fritz Luckhardt

Bühnenfestspielhaus
in Bayreuth.

Aufführungen am 13.—17., 20.—24. u. 27.—30. August

von

Richard Wagner's Tetralogie
Der Ring des Nibelungen.

Erster Abend: Rheingold.
Personen:

Wotan,		Herr Beh von Berlin.
Donner,	Götter	„ Elmblad „
Froh,		„ Unger v. Bayreuth.
Loge,		„ Vogl v. München.
Fasolt,		„ Eilers v. Coburg.
Fasner,	Riesen	„ Reichenberg v. Coln.
Alberich,	Nibelungen	„ Hill v. Schwerin.
Mime,		„ Schlosser v. München.
Fricka,		Fr. Grün von Coburg.
Freia,	Göttinnen	Frl. Haupt von Cassel.
Erda,		Frl. Jaide v. Darmstadt.
Woglinde,		Frl. Lehmann I v. Berlin.
Wellgunde,	Rheintöchter	„ Lehmann II v. Cöln.
Floßhilde,		„ Lammert v. Berlin.
Nibelungen.		

Ort der Handlung: 1. In die Tiefe des Rheines.
2. Freie Gegend auf Bergeshöhen a. Rhein.
3. Die unterirdischen Klüfte Nibelheims.

Zweiter Abend: Walküre.
Personen:

Siegmund	Herr Niemann von Berlin.
Hunding	„ Niering von Darmstadt.
Wotan	„ Beh von Berlin.
Sieglinde	Frl. Scheffsky von Würzburg.
Brünnhilde	Fr. Materna von Wien.
Fricka	Fr. Grün von Coburg.
Acht Walküren.	

Ort der Handlung: 1. Das Innere der Wohnung Hundings.
2. Wildes Felsengebirge.
3. Auf dem Brunhildenstein.

Dritter Abend: Siegfried.
Personen:

Siegfried	Herr Unger v. Bayreuth.
Mime	„ Schlosser v. München.
Der Wanderer	
Alberich	„ Hill v. Schwerin.
Fafner	„ Reichenberg v. Cöln.
Erda	Fr. Jaide v. Darmstadt.
Brünnhilde	Materna von Wien.

Ort der Handlung: 1. Eine Felsenhöhle im Walde.
2. Tiefer Wald.
3. Wilde Gegend am Felsenberg.

Vierter Abend: Götterdämmerung.
Personen:

Siegfried	Herr Unger v. Bayreuth.
Gunther	„ Gura von Leipzig.
Hagen	„ Kögl v. Hamburg.
Alberich	„ Hill v. Schwerin.
Brünnhilde	Fr. Materna von Wien.
Gutrune	Frl. Weckerlin von München.
Waltraute	Fr. Jaide v. Darmstadt.
Die Nornen.	
Die Rheintöchter.	
Mannen. Frauen.	

Ort der Handlung: 1. Auf dem Felsen der Walküren.
2. Gunther's Hofhalle am Rhein.
Der Walkürenfelsen.
3. Vor Gunther's Halle.
4. Waldige Gegend am Rhein.
Gunther's Halle.

Eintritts-Karten (½ Patronatschein) zu beziehen durch den

Kölner Richard Wagner-Verein.

Druck und Verlag der Langen'schen Buchdruckerei (Albert Ahn), Köln.

W. 502.

Poster announcing the first Ring cycle as a *Tetralogie*, 1876

Franz Betz, the original Wotan, in 1876

Amalie Materna, the original Brünnhilde, in 1876

Friedrich Schorr, the leading Wotan of the 1920s and 30s

The following pages contain six scenes from Wagner's life: a set of six late nineteenth-century collectible cards advertising Liebig's Fleisch-Extrakt

archetypes being activated, if I use a slightly bizarre analogy about iron filings strewn on a card (this analogy should not be pressed too far). If someone brings a magnet underneath the card, the filings are energised and leap into new formations of strange beauty. Wagner is the magician who applies the magnet to the randomly strewn disunities of the mind and who reorders them. This adds another aspect to Cord's transcendental euphoria. In the light of the better equilibrium, the altered and the heightened awareness which it creates, we are disposed to live life more fully and even to make better decisions.

The passage quoted from C.S. Lewis provides exactly a description of archetypes projecting their scintillating imagery up into consciousness, of positive emotions materialising as the archetypes 'exercised their numinous or fascinating effect'. Archetypal indeed is the description of the Arctic, of all the deep layers of ice, 'changing not in a week or an hour but instantly into a landscape of grass and primroses and orchards in bloom'. These are symbols reflecting archetypes, as were the deafening bird songs and the stir of running water; and archetypal too was the awareness that this was no Celtic or sylvan, nor any terrestrial twilight. So was the pure Northernness, that vision of huge clear spaces hanging above the Atlantic in the endless twilight of Northern summer, the remoteness, the severity. And he even tells us that it was almost at the same moment that he knew that he had met this before, long, long ago. He describes the experience as a plunge back into his own past, but it was almost certainly a plunge backwards into a deeper and more ancient past than his own. It was not from his personal past but from the collective subconscious that he derived 'almost like heartbreak, the memory of Joy itself, the knowledge that I had once had'. He said he had lacked this knowledge for years, but the earlier stretches of his autobiography indicate that he had never previously possessed it at all; it had previously existed only as an inchoate potential. His return 'at last from exile and deserts to my own country' was in fact a new journey, resulting from his encounter with Wagner. In his case that journey would ultimately lead to Christianity, but to reaffirm his essential point, 'The distance of the Twilight of the Gods and the distance of my own past Joy, both unattainable, flowed together into a single, unendurable sense of desire and loss ... And at once I knew that to have it again was the supreme and only object of desire.' What a description of the Wagner Experience and its fascination! The strange thing is that at the exact point in life where C.S. Lewis located this renaissance, he had not, as he maintained, encountered any of Wagner's music or anything but the title, *The Twilight of the Gods*. However, his account goes on to describe how the music so completely filled out his every expectation that it creates the likelihood that he was reading back into the first encounter revelations which dated later from his first hearing of the music.

What matters is that the achievement of integration and wholeness or at least a move towards them is at the heart of Wagner's endless fascination. Some degree of integration is always accessible in the Wagner Experience, a recurrent replenishment more easily repeated now than in Wagner's day because sound recordings and video make it easier to enjoy much of the experience at will.

My own first encounter with the Experience was through *Das Rheingold*, an old black label Columbia '78' of 'The Entry of the Gods into Valhalla'. I did not really find that it meant much at first; there was no instant impact, and yet there was something about it that kept me going back, and in the end it exerted a mesmerising fascination: a slow burn. The passage comes at the end of *Das Rheingold*, and it calls on many symbols that have an archetypal dimension. It is about mists that clear to reveal the sunset, and about Wotan, lord of all the gods, hailing Valhalla, his glorious new fortress. It is about a river in the valley below, where beautiful Rhinemaidens lament the loss of their stolen gold. It is about Loge, god of fire and guile who facetiously advises them to bask in the gods' newborn splendour. It is about a rainbow, shimmering and evanescent, over which the gods proceed magisterially to their new home. Mists, sunsets, rainbows, gods in glory, gold, mighty fortresses in the sky, a river in the depths of a gorge, beautiful maidens singing a lament, these pour forth in coruscating abundance, and their compelling representation in music largely accounts for the impact and fascination of the passage, an effect which is literally indescribable.

At the end of *Das Rheingold*, Wagner fused together an astonishing abundance of symbols and actualised them in music that is equally astonishing. The fusion is more fascinating than the sum of the parts could ever be. Even individually, archetypes have an aura that is numinous, but when configured in harmonious arrangements and encompassed in music as here, the combined effect is immense, truly a source of the Wagner fascination. What was interesting is that the music on its own could summon up so much of the Wagner Experience.

There is sometimes an objection raised against Wagner, that such heightened experiences make ordinary life look monochrome and unacceptable. The return to the world can even seem like Plato's picture of smoky images and spooky shadows, such as are thrown by cardboard cut-outs in the flickering firelight onto the wall of the cave. Previously we had mistaken these shadows for reality, but as Plato saw it there can be no return to accepting the shadows after once seeing reality in the noonday sun. However, things are different in the case of Wagner. When we come back to real life, the spell may fade, albeit slowly, but something of the transforming, integrating effect persists. Inevitably the integration is buffeted by life events and may even become unsettled, but it never fades entirely, and it can be invoked and worked again. A drama by Wagner is the portal to a fascination that is real and constructive, and no one whose life is enhanced by the experience should worry about being seen as a lotus-eater bent on an escape from the world, essentially Nietzsche's accusation, because they are more likely to return to it, but replenished and empowered.

My first experience of *The Ring* in a theatre was not merely replenishing, but cried out for admiration, almost worship, both for some of its characters but also for the experience itself; and anyone who has ever felt Wagner's fascination is likely to understand this. The transcendental euphoria of the Wagner Experience is even comparable with what William Wordsworth described in 'Lines Written above Tintern Abbey', lines repeated from the beginning of the chapter:

> ... *While with an eye made quiet by the power*
> *Of harmony and the deep power of joy,*
> *We see into the life of things.*

The Wagner Experience creates the same mix of heightened sensibility and harmony, the same wholeness and integration. This is a central part of Wagner's fascination, which permeates the book and becomes ever more prominent as we consider what each of Wagner's 'big ten' can bring to our lives. However any attempt to determine Wagner's fascination should – as Neville Cardus suggested – place the music at its centre, and so before the chapters on the individual dramas there is one devoted to the music and to the reasons for the music's particular fascination.[64]

---

64   Before we move on and consider what went into the making of Wagner, there is a further point about the fascination of his dramas, that may not be a single and uniform entity, but multiple. It may be like 'the Hapsburg look', a concept popular among Oxford philosophers in the 1960s (perhaps it still is). The essential feature of the Hapsburg look, the facial appearance of the Hapsburg dynasty, is that there is no single set of facial characteristics or features that define it. There are a number of features that are important, and anyone with the look must have some of them. But nobody with the look needs all of them, and several people can still have the Hapsburg look without having any features in common. The same could be true of the Wagner Experience. It may offer separate fulfilments to different people, and perhaps there are no single aspect of it that affects everybody. Readers must decide for themselves.

FOUR

THE CHILD IS FATHER OF THE MAN

I. Riddles from the Dark

Wer nie sein Brod mit Tränen aß,
Wer nie die kummervollen Nächte
Auf seinem Bette weinend saß,
Der kennt euch nicht, ihr himmlischen Mächte.

> Johann Wolfgang von Goethe,
> *Wilhelm Meisters Lehrjahre*, Book Two, Chapter 13

Who never ate with tears his bread,
Who never through night's heavy hours
Sat weeping on his lonely bed,–
He knows you not, ye heavenly powers!

> tr. Edward Alfred Bowring
> (*The Poems of Goethe*, London, 1853)

Wagner's dramas and their ideas were shaped by the same factors as shaped the man, and they mean and convey more if we understand them through the man. Both his nature and his nurture were extraordinary. Any heavenly powers gathered together at his conception endowed him with a nature that was biologically and mentally exceptional – even odd – and they then tempered his nature with an upbringing that was fractured, tempestuous, and often frightening. To yoke together in one man such a bizarre assortment of ingredients as went into Richard Wagner might well have resulted in mental chaos or even madness, but Wagner possessed a cord of steel and a titanic strength of will that held the warring elements in balance.

The first way in which he was odd was genetic. Some of the oddness was a blessing, some was neutral, and some was a blight. He was blessed with a volatile neurology, a phenomenal energy and a massive intellect. He was gifted with a torrential imagination and a mind that sparkled with original ideas. He was endowed with a compulsive drive and an obdurate conviction. More neutrally he manifested a grand-scale libido from adolescence onwards, along with a mightier still enthralment to Eros and an equally potent will to power. He was a man whom ideas could dominate as much as emotions; both could deprive him of any peace of mind.

The major *problem* arising from his abnormal genetics was the common one, that a person who is oddly made in one way is often oddly made in others. One consequence of his unorthodox constitution was that his exceptional mind was located in a strange body. He was an unusual shape. He was short, 5' 5½", and with his massive intellect came an enormous head. His proportions looked wrong, and he always felt mis-shapen and that his appearance could be off-putting. This was why he told Cosima late in life that he sympathised with his character Alberich from *Der Ring des Nibelungen*, 'the longing of ugliness for beauty'.

His exceptional mind also rested on a fitful, unstable biological infrastructure which easily fell into a sad state of disrepair and hampered him in all that he was driven to do. He was prone to allergies and skin infections, a hazard in themselves and evidence of an even deeper problem, an erratic and disordered immunity. During his first Swiss exile, he was constantly afflicted with erysipelas as he told Liszt in his letter of July 12th 1856, explaining that he had just gone down with his twelfth attack since the previous winter had begun. Erysipelas is a fulminating dermatitis which would now lead straight to hospital and intravenous antibiotics. It was also in Switzerland that he apparently contracted shingles at an age which was early for a condition generally associated with the elderly.[65] His skin was always a hazard for him, and in Venice, when trying to compose Act II of *Tristan und Isolde*, he was disabled for weeks by a huge and painful abscess in his leg. His skin became ever more difficult and sensitive; and people who look down their noses at Wagner's love of silks and satins might be less judgmental if they could experience five minutes of truly intractable itch. Itch: it sounds so trivial! A real itch is not trivial, but an obsession as frantic and all-consuming as any pain, driving the sufferer to hysterics and even suicide; and nobody who has any insight into *pruritus* could regard Wagner's affliction and his attempts to assuage it as a matter for mirth or contempt.

It may be helpful explain in parenthesis that patients with appalling skin conditions often do develop an unusual preoccupation with smooth emollients, rich scents and silky textures, as Wagner did, and it is not unusual for this to border on obsession or even evolve into a full-scale compulsive-obsessive disorder. There is no evidence that matters went so far in Wagner's case, but such a tendency, related to his skin disorders, assuredly played as much of a role in his addiction to silks and satins as any fetishism, any sexually displaced satisfaction related to his pretty sisters and his contact with their silk underwear. It is significant that the crates of silks discovered in the basement at Wahnfried, his last home, remained unopened, because this suggests a compulsion to acquire rather than a fetishist compulsion to feel them. Not suggestions but assertions of Wagner's fetishism exploded throughout the British media seven years ago when *The Wagner*

---

65 Shingles is a viral illness which gives rise to a strip of excruciating skin rash, and is notorious for the unpleasant effects which come with it, often months or even years of recurrent pain in the area affected, lethargy, and moderate to severe depression. This illness has changed its course, and during the last fifteen years, it has become more common in middle age or even younger. It can only occur in those who have previously had chickenpox.

Journal was launched, because of an unfounded article proclaiming the fetishism as a fact. It is true that he recorded in his autobiography, *Mein Leben*, how the company of his sisters after his return to Leipzig made him feel he was in heaven, but it was the intimacy and security of being back in a family which he loved. Further evidence of his compulsive tendency was his obsession with water-cures, described in Chapter 5, an obsession which rapidly resolved, and his obsession with the Jews which was lifelong. These examples bear out the picture of Wagner as a thoroughly addictive personality. Fortunately his compulsive, addictive drive helped to fire up his colossal enthusiasms, his ambitions and his successes as well. This picture also fits well with the context of emotional deprivation when young, and we shall see shortly that Wagner had hard experience of this.

His health was not only undermined by his flawed genetic inheritance but by his early childhood hardships; these, and other later ones when he was attempting to make his name in Paris, help to explain the premature decline of his health and that of his first wife, Minna. Heart disease would ultimately kill them both; and a chronic Irritable Bowel Syndrome would periodically pole-axe Wagner with agonising abdominal pain.[66] He suffered from headaches and pains 'in the nerves

---

66   For example it was again when writing to Mathilde Wesendonck from Paris (23 October 1859), that Wagner commented, 'Trivial as it may sound, Schopenhauer is perfectly right in naming among the chief physiological requirements for Genius a good digestion. Through my extra-ordinary moderation, I have mostly kept that requisite in service-able order; still I foresaw in Berlioz's sufferings those probably pre-destined for myself ... Next day a small error of diet (one glass of red wine with my bouillon at lunch) and soon afterwards a regular catastrophe, which laid me by the heels in a trice.' It laid him 'full length in utter prostration, seized at the body's very citadel.' Ferdinand Praeger too was later to confirm in his reminiscences of Wagner (published in 1892), how 'Wagner ate very quickly, and I soon had occasion to notice the fatal consequences of such unwise procedure, for although a moderate eater, he did not fail to suffer severely from such a pernicious practice.' A little later he commented that Wagner's smoking 'increased the ma-

of his head' and this together with his irritable bowel this lends force to the possibility that he was subject to abdominal migraines. He suffered from ongoing respiratory problems, and ended up with both cardiac and bronchial asthma. By the age of thirty-five he had bilateral hernias, which means that his insides were ballooning out through weaknesses in the muscle wall on both sides of his abdomen. The worst thing was the heart disease mentioned already. By the time of the first Bayreuth Festival in 1876, he was a prey to angina, a cramping chest pain which he wryly called his crab. As well as giving pain to its victims, angina generally creates a terrifying sense of imminent dissolution. This added to the array of his disorders which grew ever more severe and extensive, particularly throughout the composition of *Parsifal*: how on earth did he manage to write anything at all, let alone one of the supreme masterpieces of western civilisation? A final heart attack destroyed him less than a year after it was first performed.

This then was the fitful and wayward physique that supported Wagner's wonderful mind, the unstable synthesis that was to be buffeted by the circumstances of his early life. This chapter and the next two will trace the main factors that went into the making of the man. The inputs from his physiology and his environment were inextricable and there is nothing to be said for trying to tease them out separately. What matters is how they worked together, and how they resulted in the mental matrix upon which circumstances engraved their richest and strangest impressions. Not that he was merely a composite of his inputs. He was what he made of them. He transformed them to create his own distinctive identity. He also transformed them into an art of towering greatness. The capacity for converting life into art is the essence of expressionist art. Though expressionism, as a formal artistic movement, did not reach its zenith until the 1910s and 20s, there is a very real sense in which Wagner's art can be called expressionist. In expressionist art, life-experience is grist to the mills of the imagination,

---

lignity of his terrible dyspepsia.' His digestive irritability was always a nuisance, featuring even more frequently among his adversities at Bayreuth.

and it was the character of Wagner's genius and his strength of will, not only to recreate his experience in his chosen media, but to transform it with heightened intensity.

His crucial experiences were mostly of two kinds: on the one hand his direct life experiences, and on the other his intellectual influences drawn from history, philosophy, myth, economics, religion, social and political theory. These made twin currents which often converged and swirled together to bring his dramas their special depth. Intellectual influences always played a major role in everything that he produced, especially from *The Ring* onwards. We shall come back to them, both in context and specifically in Chapter 5, but our immediate concern now is with his personal experiences, his emotional, psychological and spiritual imprints, and effect of these on the man and his dramas.

The experiences of his early years were particularly vital. His upbringing was rich, varied and unsettled, and from the first he had to deal with adversities in battalions. There are parts of *Mein Leben*, his autobiography, which were designed specifically to re-create his life as a myth-fantasy. *Mein Leben* is an enthralling document as explained already but in it Wagner often reinvented his life as he wishfully imagined it, and he did it for the sake of King Ludwig, for posterity and above all for himself. As always, deception of others is closely associated with deception of self, and a lot of the deception is not so much deliberate fraud as the unconscious reinvention of a reality which was too painful to face. However it is not difficult to read between the lines, and it is in the account of his childhood that the gap between what he tells us and what he thought he was telling us is especially wide. On the positive side it was a childhood that provided a staggering variety of experience, weird though it was; but his narrative assumes that we, his readers, would go along with him and swallow his account of a happy childhood which he took for granted. What he actually reveals is a childhood that was wayward, erratic and often terrifying. Of his many biographers, it is Joachim Köhler[67] who seems

67 Köhler, Joachim, *Richard Wagner: The Last of the Titans*, tr. Stewart Spencer, New Haven and London, 2004.

to have pierced through his inventions about his childhood and grasped something of what a dreadful experience it often was. It is impossible to appreciate his childhood without a grasp of its background, and my aim is to build up an edifice of the background with enough detail to ensure that the story really is appreciated.

It is a story of damage and deprivation. Circumstances deprived him. His early life was a sequence of insecurities and upheavals, and to borrow a cogent, biblical expression common to Victorian writing, his lines were not laid in pleasant places. There was not even consistency in the unpleasant places where his lines were laid, because he was constantly uprooted and moved. The brief biography has demonstrated eight transfers to new and unknown locations by the time he was fourteen: new faces, new places, new situations, where he was always the outsider. After a while the circumstances of each new situation would change, and he was turned out and sent off again. No wonder that as an adult he was drawn to the lonely figure of Ahasuerus, the Wandering Jew, and yet detested him as a symbol of a past which was too painful to acknowledge.

Richard Wagner was born at Leipzig on 22 May 1813. By the end of October, when he was six months old, his father, Friedrich Wagner, was dead from typhus (or typhoid; the sources are not entirely clear). The spectre of destitution loomed, as it did time and again for the Wagner family, but they were rescued by his mother's second marriage to the actor and painter Ludwig Geyer. Geyer was at one stage the subject of personal doubts for Wagner, as to whether he might have been Wagner's real father, but he almost certainly was not. Whatever the case, moral scruples and a 'desire to atone' (for adultery?) seem to have promoted Geyer's marriage to Friedrich Wagner's widow. If so, Geyer did well by her, taking on her large family and half-adopting them. Wagner himself took the name 'Geyer' and became Richard Geyer until he was fourteen. This did not save him from being dispatched from one corner of Saxony to another, to strangers, even if they did their best for him by their own strange lights. Geyer, his stepfather, had taken on a major commitment with the numerous

Wagners, and it relieved the financial pressures when he secured 'an unexpected improvement in his position, a permanent engagement as a character actor at the Court Theatre in Dresden' as Wagner tells us in *Mein Leben*.[68] Geyer's new job meant that he removed his new family to Dresden before Wagner was two.

Only four years later, when he was just six, Wagner's stepfather, 'in his concern to give me a good education', sent him off to a country boarding school at Possendorf, three hours' journey on foot from Dresden. The school was run by a Lutheran clergyman, Pastor Christian Wetzel, whom Wagner seems to have liked, but we will shortly need to consider what kind of education and upbringing were likely to have come from such a source. In any case it was less than a year before the next destabilisation; Wagner was dragged off on an exhausting journey – on foot – to see his stepfather in the final throes of tuberculosis, just before he died. This was a harrowing event in itself, but he had no chance to work through any horror or stupefaction, as he was taken back to Possendorf by Pastor Wetzel that same afternoon. Additionally, Geyer's death straitened the household and cut off the money for Wagner's education. He was taken away from Pastor Wetzel's school only a week later, by Geyer's younger brother Karl. Karl Geyer took him to live at Eisleben where he was a goldsmith. He had already taken on Wagner's elder brother Julius as an apprentice, and Wagner lodged with them in the house of a soap-boiler. Wagner makes no mention of the toxic and disgusting stench which goes hand-in-hand with soap-boiling, but this may perhaps account for a damaged sense of smell later, even if his later addiction to snuff can only have made it worse, in virtue of which he would always crave smothering fragrances, simply because softer scents were inaccessible.

More positively it was at Eisleben that he found someone who treated him well and with whom, briefly, he was able to establish a relationship, his step-grandmother, the ancient Frau Geyer, who

<hr>

68   The direct quotations in this chapter are all from *Mein Leben*, Wagner's autobiography, unless described otherwise (*My Life, authorized translation ...*, New York, 1911).

was a fellow-lodger. He delighted her with pet robins he had caught for her, and she in return befriended him and 'kept me tidy and clean'. It was also at Eisleben that he first awoke to the full horror and outrage of cruelty and suffering. The event that particularly affected him was 'the drowning of some puppies in a shallow pool behind my uncle's house. Even to this day', he wrote almost forty years later, 'I cannot think of the slow death of these poor little creatures without horror.' Wagner had to witness the routine and unpreventable cruelty of adults without anyone to share his reactions, let alone put a stop to what was going on. It was his memories that led him to record at this point of *Mein Leben*: 'The sorrows of others, in particular those of animals, have always affected me deeply.' It was true; and in spite of some disturbing blind spots, Wagner became radically compassionate in theory and in practice.

He soon had to cope with another bereavement, this time his step-grandmother. For almost year afterwards, he still 'made himself at home with the soap boiler's family,' but then his step-uncle married and his wife moved in, leaving Wagner no space or haven there any more. He was taken for a short stay with his uncle Adolf Wagner in Leipzig, a brief but memorable respite from isolation, which is evaluated again later, and he was then returned to his immediate family in Dresden, where they had been 'obliged to settle down as well as they could'. He was not the only one adversely affected; 'My eldest brother Albert, who originally intended to study medicine, had started a theatrical career in Breslau.' At least the family and his mother 'still occupied the same comfortable home which my (step)father had made for them. Thanks to her great energy and to help received from various sources, my mother managed so well that even my education did not suffer.' Actually it did, and the next disruption was on its way. When he was thirteen, 'my sister Rosalie, who had become the chief support of our household, obtained an advantageous engagement at the theatre in Prague where my mother and her children moved in 1826, giving up the Dresden home altogether.' They did not take Wagner with them but left him in Dresden for the sake of his schooling at the famous

Kreuzschule. He had 'to board and lodge with a family called Böhme', a 'rough, poor and not particularly well conducted family', and within a year he had left and set up on his own, 'in a small garret, where I was waited on by the widow of a court plate-washer who served up thin Saxon coffee as almost my only nourishment.' It was at this period that Wagner, under no parental regulation and yet only fourteen, took it into his head to walk to Prague with a son of the Böhme household. He hitched lifts and foraged where he could, sleeping rough or in a barn on a journey which was haphazard and potentially dangerous.

Things finally changed for the better when another sister, Luise, was engaged at the theatre in Leipzig. Leipzig again became the family's central focus, and over Christmas 1827 Wagner returned there, to the town of his birth and to his mother, to his sisters Luise and Ottilie, his half-sister Cäcilie, and his adored Rosalie. It was harbour at last after years of living like a refugee, eight times displaced. He had been an outsider, a nomad like so many of his future characters, the Dutchman, Tannhäuser, Lohengrin, Siegmund, Kundry or Parsifal, but he now came in from the cold. The move back to Leipzig also marked a radical shift in his identity because he again took the surname Wagner. The whole experience of the home in Leipzig had positive associations; and he discovered in his alluring sisters all the femininity and warmth he represented later in Senta, Elisabeth, Elsa, and Sieglinde. As he later recalled, 'I fancied myself in heaven.'

This account makes it clear how the first major challenge to Wagner from his early years was that they were so unstable. His lines were laid in quicksands and minefields which blew up in his face time and again. To understand the other challenges to Wagner during his formative years calls, as mentioned, for a structure of ideas, an edifice of information that is built up now block by block.

Its foundation was the biography of his young life just presented, and the next stage in the edifice is a solid awareness of child development and of how parental influences and circumstances affect a child's upbringing. With this awareness it becomes clearer how few of the right conditions applied to Wagner. John Bowlby's attachment theory, though elegant, is too elaborate for the space available, but an appreciation of the experiments by Harry Harlow should effectively set the scene. In his classic if unethical experiments, Harlow took baby monkeys, the closest he could get to human infants, and inflicted 'wells of despair' on them, consisting of parental deprivation and – although he fed and watered them – a general sensory deficit. The deprived monkeys became blank and barren, pining and wasting away and developing exactly the behaviours of depressive and psychotic human beings. Wagner's uprootings through his eight new households meant that he was likewise deprived of attachments, and he too had lifelong battles with his own 'wells of despair'. Harlow performed another experiment, exposing the monkeys to two crude mother substitutes, one a bare metal frame that supplied milk and the other a frame covered with terrycloth which supplied nothing; and it was the terry cloth version, however crude and inadequate as a mother substitute, which the deprived monkeys desperately preferred. Wagner described his mother as lacking maternal warmth and never fondling him, and he also described her with a desperate affection. The unfulfilled needs of his childhood always haunted him.

Another pillar in the structure of ideas about Wagner's development concerns the inborn tendency of children to follow and mimic examples. There was another experiment, by the psychologist Albert Bandura, which involved making a series of films; they showed children watching adults who were beating some Bobo dolls viciously. The films then showed these children doing the same. Bandura also filmed other children treating these dolls in a friendly fashion after seeing adults behaving well towards them. These findings created a revolutionary shift away from the previous dominant belief, rooted in the far distant ideas of Aristotle about catharsis, that the sight of violence led to revulsion and steered people towards empathy. Bandura also went on to show, less disquietingly, that children become capable of modifying and changing their behaviour once they are old enough to reflect rationally. Another innate predisposition also then comes into play, an opposite tendency towards compassion for a person under threat. However, an important point emerged, that compassion and empathy need fostering to develop. Otherwise the sight of other peoples' injuries and tragedies is less likely to lead to compassion than to sharing in the aggression against them. Once a capacity for compassion develops, most people possess two available responses to brutality which are in direct conflict, to imitate it or to mitigate it. Wagner always swung equivocally between the two, and the reasons for this weather-cocking will be more obvious once we recognise the style of upbringing to which children, including Wagner, were generally then subjected.

The next element in the edifice of information about Wagner's young life concerns the style of pedagogy which was then in vogue. It was often dire, and there are compelling reasons for believing that Wagner was subjected to it, which meant that he had not only to cope with the traumas of his particular circumstances but also the ordeals and damage which were then common practice in bringing up children and educating them. It was a common practice which persistently brutalised children 'for their own good'. We cannot know exactly what Wagner's childhood was like, but a disturbing picture emerges which is internally consistent, which explains the facts, and which matches the circumstantial evidence. It is significant that before he was six Wagner routinely underwent 'chastisement' at the hands of his stepfather. *Mein Leben* tells that he was so badly frightened by nightmares that he craved the relief of any human contact, even his 'chastisement' which was the inevitable consequence of his making a fuss. He saw the chastisements themselves as too commonplace to be worth recording, and only mentioned them because he was describing his nightmares. Then again, *Die Meistersinger* provides circumstantial evidence of 'chastisement' as acceptable practice. It is clear that even the 'wise, kindly Hans Sachs' is always hitting David, his apprentice, because David ruefully tells Walther von Stolzing about it in Act I, and in Act III David is terrified to find Sachs alone, because his past experience tells him that Sachs is going to start beating him.

Most important of all is Wagner's highly revealing letter to his

friend Theodore Uhlig from December 1851. Wagner was agreeing
to stand godfather to Uhlig's son Siegfried, but told Uhlig, 'I should
like to hear your programme respecting this boy's education. Will you
inoculate him with the poison of our bringing up, and so leave it to
chance whether he shall spit out the poison or whether it shall bring
him to ruin? I do not ask this jokingly. We have the future in our
hands. Shall we be such abject cowards as to expose our children to
the same fatal course which (let us be frank) has made us incapable,
half and half, and bad?'

This lends force to the conviction that Wagner's upbringing followed
the poisonous patterns laid bare by Katharina Rutschky in her historical
analysis, *Schwarze Pädagogik*[69] (*Black Pedagogy* or *Poisonous Upbringing*)
and by Alice Miller in her two books *Am Anfang war Erziehung*[70] (*For
Your Own Good*), and *Das Drama des begabten Kindes*[71] (*The Drama of
Being a Child*). Alice Miller, the Polish-Swiss authority, became the better known in England, and her books describe the child-rearing orthodoxies of Central Europe over three centuries. A few examples must
suffice to indicate the standards and styles rife in Wagner's day.

Miller instances a certain Dr. Moritz Schreber, author of a series
of books on child-rearing so extravagantly popular in Germany that
several of them ran to forty printings and were translated into foreign
languages. In 1858 he gave this advice:

The little ones' displays of temper as indicated by screaming or crying
without cause should be regarded as the first test of your spiritual and
pedagogical principles ... Once you have established that nothing is
really wrong ... you should proceed in a somewhat more positive way
by appropriately mild corporal admonitions repeated persistently at the

---

69   Rutschky, Katharina, *Schwarze Pädagogik*, Berlin, 1977.
70   Miller, Alice, *Am Anfang war Erziehung*, Frankfurt am Main, 1983, tr.
     Hildegarde and Hunter Hannum (as *For Your Own Good*), London,
     1987.
71   Ead., *Das Drama des begabten Kindes*, Frankfurt am Main, 1979, tr.
     Ruth Ward (as *The Drama of Being a Child*), London, 1987.

intervals until the child quiets down or falls asleep … this procedure will be necessary only once or at most twice, and then you will be master of the child forever.

Perhaps it is not surprising that Schreber's own son ended up needing psychiatric help from Sigmund Freud, no less. Wagner's date of birth in 1813 fell midway between Schreber's advice from 1858 and the similar recommendations of Johann Gottlob Krüger a hundred years earlier, in 1752:[72] 'You are justified in answering force with force in order to ensure his respect, without which you will be unable to train him. The blows you administer should not be merely playful ones but should convince him that you are his master.' And with an early but truly poisonous insight into child psychology, Johann Georg Sulzer, writing in 1748, had recommended,[73] 'One of the advantages of these early years is that force and compulsion can be used. Over the years children forget everything that happened to them in early childhood. If their wills can be broken at this time, they will never remember afterwards that they had a will, and for this very reason the severity that is required will not have any serious consequences.'

It is disturbing that sections of the Church often lent their support. Miller quotes an example from 1796 where a certain Mr Kiefer related how he had punished and beaten his son Konrad and then gone to his pastor about it, because 'my heart was sore'. The Pastor comforted him; 'You did the right thing, dear Mr. Kiefer … if you have used the rod sparingly not only would it have done no good on this occasion but you would always have to whip him in the future … Now while the lashes are still fresh in your Konrad's mind I advise you to take advantage of it … when you come home, see that you order him about a good deal. Have him fetch you your boots, your shoes, your pipe, and take them away again; have him carry the stones in the

---

72   Krüger, Johann Gottlob, *Gedanken von der Erziehung der Kinder* (*Thoughts on the Education of Children*), Halle, 1752.

73   Sulzer, Johann, *Versuch von der Erziehung und Unterweisung der Kinder* (*An Essay on the Education and Instruction of Children*), 1748.

yard from one place to another. He will do it all and will become accustomed to obeying.'

It is plain that this virulent attitude towards children was common over several centuries. Adolf Matthias[74] wrote in much the same vein in 1902, asking,

> Is it not 'doting' when the baby is coddled and pampered in every way from infancy? Instead of accustoming the baby from the first day of his life on earth to discipline and regularity in his intake of nourishment and thereby laying the groundwork for moderation, patience, and human happiness, 'doting' lets itself be guided by the infant's crying ... It is the opposite of true love which does not shrink from punishment. The Bible says, 'He who loves his son chastises him often with the rod, that he may be his joy when he grows up.'

This whole approach is rooted in the belief that human nature is fatally flawed; that children will become evil adults unless purged sadistically of their innately vicious tendencies. In England there was the proverbial 'Spare the rod and spoil the child,' and this approach was common throughout the Western world in Wagner's time.

What is also relevant to Wagner is that if the brutality itself is damaging, it is more damaging if the children are banned from any normal response to it. A child by the name of Christoph Meckel provides an example that is particularly pertinent to Wagner.[75] For ten days Christoph Meckel's father took him down to the cellar and systematically beat him every morning and then expected his tormented son to adopt a spirit of manly camaraderie and appreciate his father's strongminded concern to bring him up well. What the son remembered was, 'For ten days, an unconscionable length of time, my father blessed the palms of his child's outstretched four-year-old

---

74 Matthias, Adolf, *Wie erziehen wir unseren Sohn Benjamin?* (*How shall we bring up our son Benjamin?*), 1902.

75 Meckel, Christoph, *Suchbild: über meinem Vater* (*Wanted: My father's Portrait*), Düsseldorf, 1979.

hands with a sharp switch. Seven strokes today on each; that makes 140 strokes and then some. This put to an end to the child's innocence … It was my father drove me out of paradise.'[76] This was the climate when Wagner was young, and the harsh pedagogy applied to him is a working hypothesis that matches all the circumstantial evidence and fits Wagner's character as we understand it.

The twin traumas of rootlessness and of vicious nurturing tempered the genius that Wagner became, but they also helped give rise to it. The confusion, the punitive severity, and the insecurities slot into place within the mosaic of his character and help to explain it. They were the source of turbulence which led to an inner agitation and unrest but which also stirred his personality to action and drove him on to achievement. Along with his inborn gifts and the variety of his youthful experiences, they powered his creativity. This is not to imply that a turbulent, damaged childhood automatically leads to great things, like the writing of great music dramas. The numbers of those who can transform inner damage into something positive as Wagner did is not large, and a traumatic childhood is not a sufficient or necessary condition for genius.

For all that, there are causal associations. They may be obscure and poorly understood, but there are many examples which serve as evidence; and in Wagner's case we can certainly distinguish some reasons why he made something positive of his youthful experiences, even his traumas. There has been mention already of his intellect and the innate strength of will, the ego which enabled him to reforge his experiences and recast them into something new, both in the person that he was and in the art that he created. In each of his works he drew this flux of experiences into a new synthesis.

Given his fitful background it would be a surprise if there were an overarching consistency to Wagner. On the one hand he evolved organically, and he could progress through his life and work with a singleness of mind that verged on grandeur, but he was equally prone

---

76   Miller, Alice, *For Your Own Good*, p.3.

to vary and switch on the spur of the moment. In this one corner of his personality he was fundamentally unstable. He was even schizoid, capable of an unusual ambiguity and double-think, and of what psychologists describe as cognitive dissonance. As a good example, there is his letter to Mathilde Wesendonck[77] which begins by describing his horror at the slaughter of a chicken. Wagner took this event as the basis for some illuminating insights generally, and for a specific self-awareness. In particular, he said that he recognised compassion 'as the strongest feature in my moral being' and the wellspring of his art. This contained a real truth, but came strangely from a man who was in the thick of an affair with the very lady to whom his letter was addressed. The affair, though non-carnal, blasted her marriage and inflicted pain and catastrophe on her husband as damaging as any physical adultery, and yet Wagner apparently saw no inconsistency in proclaiming a gospel of compassion while doing things which were the very opposite, the very image of callousness and self-obsession. When this cognitive dissonance was at work, he failed to see truths which were staring him in the face. In Wagner's mind and thinking, the partitions were constantly shifting ground and altering their permeability. At times there was utter clarity and transparency in his thoughts and attitudes, and the inferences which he drew and the connections which he achieved among distant ideas were penetrating and remarkable. At other times the clearest associations, the most obvious conclusions and the plainest consequences would elude him. This schizoid dissonance would also enable him simultaneously to make different plans that were wholly incompatible. Five years before the letter to Mathilde Wesendonck just quoted, he was doing everything in his power to bring his wife to Zurich in Switzerland to be with him. At the same time he was making cloud-cuckoo-land plans to elope with Jessie Laussot, the English wife of a Bordeaux wine-merchant, and go ... to Greece! These incompatible plans were the mark of a man seriously out of touch with reality, and out of joint with himself.

77   *Richard Wagner to Mathilde Wesendonck*, tr. William Ashton Ellis, London, 1905, pp. 44 et seq.

Instability and inconsistency were part of Wagner; and they were also principal causes of his creativity, contributing to the strange vibrancy of the man and his output. He was a man never at peace with himself, and he was galvanised by the forces and the energy which his inner dissonances generated. Let people who doubt the reality of psychic (or intellectual) energy simply ask themselves how constantly they are stirred to action by enthusiasm, anxiety or some other energising sentiment. It is this energy from feelings which drives people to do things and perform actions. When the action is complete, this psychic or intellectual energy is usually discharged, restoring equilibrium (something on the lines of Freud's pleasure principle). However the feelings and the energies generated by the traumas of Wagner's youth were more complicated. In many a situation in his early years there was no action by which Wagner could discharge the energies which the situation generated, so that they became chronic and uncontrollable, like the steam in a boiler with no safety valve. They were a restless force which was unlimited and lifelong. It supercharged his ability to get things done, and it gave him the strength to manage the harsh, abrasive world and the hostility to himself which he helped to arouse. On 14 October 1849, he wrote to Liszt with considerable self-awareness,

Dear Friend, look on me with a serious but kindly glance. All the ills which have happened to me were the natural and necessary consequences of the discord of my own being. The power that is mine is quite unyielding and indivisible. By its nature it takes violent revenge when I try to turn or divide it by external force. To be wholly what I can be, and therefore, no doubt, what I should be, is only possible for me if I renounce all those external things which I could gain by dint of the aforesaid external force. That force would always make me fritter away my genuine power, would always conjure up for me the same evils. In all that I do and think, I am only an artist. If I am to throw myself into our modern publicity, then I cannot conquer it as an artist, and God preserve me from dealing with it as a politician. Poor

and without means for a bare life, without goods and heritage as I am,
I should then be compelled to think only of acquisition; but I have
learnt nothing but my art.

This was the height of egoism. It was also remarkable self-knowledge
and the plain truth. Without husbanding 'the power that was his', he
could never have succeeded in bringing his masterpieces into being,
and nor could he have established their place in the world.

For all his divisions Wagner had a mind with an exceptional ability
to regulate itself, thanks in part to the mighty ego that was in control.
The tendency of the mind to self-regulate operates even in childhood,
especially in childhood, and it enables someone like Wagner to survive
even in the most extreme adverse circumstances. If children experience
brutal 'chastisement' or rejection as Wagner did, this can poison them
in the way that Wagner warned Uhlig to avoid with his own children.
The poisoning can be difficult in itself, but it makes a stress beyond
all bearing if the children are threatened not only if they respond with
anything but meek, kind thoughts, but also threatened that they must
always be truthful and never tell a lie. Here was an incompatible,
impossible combination of demands. How can such children cope?

Here Alice Miller can provide something more towards the growing
edifice of ideas relevant to the child Wagner's psychology. She was able
to describe from her own casework how the pressure to fulfil such
impossible demands can create 'such an intensity of pain that the
people concerned could never have survived except by suppressing their
authentic responses'.[78] A good way to 'suppress authentic responses'
is by denial and repression, the process by which people, particularly
children, instinctively try to annihilate unbearable experiences. They
consign these experiences to oblivion – or they try. But the mind cannot
wipe out the experiences so easily; they refuse to disappear. Instead
the mind consigns them to the unconscious and commonly draws a
veil over them by rewriting reality. Children are driven to batten them

---

78   Miller, *op. cit.*, p. 26.

down in this limbo and to substitute an imaginary picture, a fiction: which is just what Wagner did, as is clear from the contrast between his rosy picture of his childhood in *Mein Leben* and the reality that he lived. The repressed memories are not erased, but persist in a subterranean realm of the mind whence they may rise up unbidden, resulting in bad dreams by night and schizoid divisions by day.

Children damaged by their upbringing commonly create fictions that bear out their innate preconceptions of how their lives should have been. Happily, as just mentioned, Wagner's resort to fiction provided him with something else that was entirely positive: the ingredients for his creative talent and the vital intellectual energy that ignited it. The alternative realities which his situation led him to invent could only have come from the bizarre miscellany of his particular experiences. It is instructive to consider how something similar happened to Anthony Trollope, because Trollope's situation shares many features with Wagner's and supports the developing picture of Wagner's creative powers. Trollope also had an appalling childhood, and he explained in his autobiography how it resulted in desperate escapes into a fantasy world; he would literally invent make-believes and try and live himself into them.[79] Where Anthony Trollope and Wagner differed from each other was that Wagner's imagination had an individual and special access to the world of dreams, primordial images and the collective unconscious, along with the mythical material that mirrored the archetypes in their submerged world. Whereas Trollope's fictions were populated with people drawn from the society he knew well, Wagner's were related additionally to the dark continents of the unconscious which he likewise knew well, and were populated with mythical figures and archetypal images.

A telling contemporary illustration of how a damaged, fragmented childhood like Wagner's can lead to inventiveness appeared in *The Times* newspaper on 5 September 2012; it was provided by a young

---

79   Trollope, Anthony, *An Autobiography*, Edinburgh and London, 1883.

woman with the pseudonym of Rosie who was neglected and homeless from her childhood onwards.

> I lived on the streets for a lot of my childhood. I slept in tumble dryers in laundrettes, under benches, in playgrounds, car parks, doorways, skips. The list goes on. I was also trying to go to school. I was always in trouble for the days I didn't make it in, or the days I got there late; when I did get there I would often fall asleep at the desk or have a panic attack when someone spoke to me and run for the door. I tried to keep myself out of the sludge at the bottom by reading, learning, and drawing on whatever I could find. *I learnt that if I used different words in different ways people responded to me better, and I could split myself into as many personalities as I needed just by learning to understand what other people were like.* I was quite proud when I managed to achieve my GCSE's by studying on the night buses. At the time I saw myself as an intrepid explorer taking each day as it came with ninja-like agility and X-ray vision. *These fantasies kept me going, as the reality was that I was a totally forgotten child who was robbed of childhood. I had no stable home, no one to watch my back and make me feel I was not too crinkled to be allowed in this world.'* (My italics.)

Compare and contrast Richard Wagner living on coffee in Dresden or sleeping in barns and ditches on his way to Prague! In this connection, there are some further facts about children to explain how and why they create fictions which contrast with the truth. It is a poignant fact that children often want to stay with parents or substitutes who did not and do not want them. Such children maintain a compulsive belief that their elders loved them and were somehow acting for the best. The more loveless they are, the more frantically they try to construct a contrasting reality, and so come to build ever more fictions around their lives. Even after growing up they often idolise their childhood and cling to the illusion that they were happy and loved. Wagner did something like this, building the fictions of his happy childhood into his memory and enshrining them in *Mein Leben*.

It may seem bizarre to identify any additional *positive* features from his random billetings and uprootings for Wagner, but they brought him a peculiar advantage; it saved him from ever having a single adult who might have dominated, engulfed and overwhelmed his childhood. A person in Wagner's shifting situation can escape being taken over and brainwashed into denial of his emotions and experiences. His intermittent freedoms allowed Wagner windows of opportunity to recognise or half-recognise the realities of his situation and his past. People who have experienced these escapes are better able later on to recognise and come to terms with their past, and they end up less damaged than those who had no let-up. I have already mentioned the brutalised Christoph Meckel. His vicious domination by his father was likewise incomplete because his father was a military man, often away from home. This gave his son breathing space so that he never absorbed his father's values inwardly. He never metabolised into himself his father's ordinance that he deny the frightfulness of his experiences, and so he could later recognise how badly he had been treated and look back with anger. 'Those who were permitted to react appropriately throughout their childhood – i.e. with anger – to the pains, wrongs, and denial inflicted upon them either consciously or unconsciously will retain this ability to react appropriately in later life too. When someone wounds them as adults they will also then be able to recognise and express this verbally.'[80] And this is just what Wagner did.

Perhaps it would be truer to say that it was just what Wagner *half*-did. Wagner's situation was distinctive because he *half*-repressed and *half*-admitted unpalatable facts. This division occurred because his circumstances were too unstable for any consistency. Of course we can never be sure what his young days were really like for him, and how far he was allowed his own authentic reactions. What actually happened at Eisleben when he saw the puppies drowned? Did he scream and shout? Were there gigantic adults around who shouted back angrily

---

80   Miller, *op. cit.*, p. 65.

and grabbed him and hit him for being a nasty, troublesome little tyke? Was he forced to look on? Did Wagner's elders threaten to drown him along with the puppies, to teach him a lesson? We can never know. The details and the flavour of his childhood are shrouded in a darkness that is unlikely to lift, unless a hoard of new information somehow becomes available.

There are still other important facts to add to the growing structure of information about the young Wagner. They concern the psychic and intellectual energies already described, which were in part powered by anger, the anger generated by conflicted thoughts and feelings such as the young mind represses. Alice Miller asked rhetorically 'What becomes of this forbidden and therefore unexpressed anger?' and Wagner partly followed the pattern suggested in her answer by transforming his suppressed and negative feelings into the energy that went into creating great art. He did not canalise it all in this way. He also followed the more common pattern, where it is 'transformed with time into a more or less conscious hatred directed either against the self or substitute persons, a hatred that will seek to discharge itself in various ways permissible and suitable for an adult.'[81] The redirection of this energy and hatred 'to substitute persons' (as Alice Miller described it) helps to explains why repressed anger seeks out scapegoats, why Wagner created scapegoats, and why he felt such hatred towards them. Wagner's wracked, unstable psyche was an area of conflict where his strength of will only just contained the chaos and imposed order. The energies in the blast furnace might erupt like streams of molten metal at those who least deserved to be hurt. Particularly at risk were those before whom he had abased himself to win their support. The figures of Giacomo Meyerbeer and Franz Liszt glimmer poignantly before us.

When they become adults, people in Wagner's situation are often inconsistent in coping with stresses, pressures and injuries. They can veer from one extreme to another, from chill dissociation to extreme emotion, and this was exactly what happened with Wagner. He could

---

81 *Ibid.*, p. 61.

oscillate from cold detachment to the fullest and the most vehement empathy and expression, as well as anything between. At Bayreuth late in life Wagner was delighted to give a whole thaler, very real money, to a child running in the rain without shoes; but when the Ringtheater am Schottenring, the principal opera theatre in Vienna, caught fire on 8 December 1881 and many of the audience burnt to death, he was unaffected, and although he rationalised his chilling absence of feeling with plausible-sounding explanations, the roots lay deeper. (It is important to remember too that he was by then a very sick man, with less than eighteen months to live.)

It seems almost certain that the shifting locations and inconsistencies of his upbringing did *half*-allow Wagner to acknowledge his adverse experiences, and as a result they never become a repressed force that was disastrous. Wagner's account in *Mein Leben* makes it plain that he had one outlet in the old lady whom he supplied with pet robins, and another, more dramatic, with his strange and remarkable uncle at Leipzig. There were others but these both offered him particular kindness and understanding. Without such let-ups he might have ended up a psychopath instead of a genius, and, chillingly, Alice Miller's *For Your Own Good* contains three brief biographies of devastating relevance to the psychopathic side of Wagner. Here she presented three human disasters when there were no let-outs, no safety valves: three life stories providing a 'compare and contrast' with Wagner, in that Wagner possessed the makings of a personality that was just as pathological. The difference was that he redeemed it through his art and by his strength of will.

The first of Alice Miller's comparative examples was Christiane F, a Berlin drug addict whose tragedy became the subject of an international best-seller and a film that became famous, or infamous, throughout Germany thirty years ago. Second was Adolf Hitler, no less. Last was Jürgen Bartsch, a sadistic child-killer in the mould of Ian Brady, the English 'moors murderer'. In all three Alice Miller dissects a traumatic, disturbed childhood resembling Wagner's but affording no windows of opportunity for acknowledging it, integrating it and defusing it. She comments that if Hitler, when young, had been able to express himself constructively in an art-form, he might have made something positive of his repressions instead of the paranoias, the hatreds and the energy which drove him to become a monster. It is significant that in *The Ring*, Wagner objectified brutal psychosis in the character of Alberich, a kind of prototype for Hitler. We shall see that in both Alberich and Klingsor (in *Parsifal*) Wagner reveals an intuitive understanding of how deprivation and humiliation could generate a fearsome retributive energy and a malignant narcissism. Alberich shakes his fist at the Rhinemaidens who will not gratify him, but because he is powerless in their direction, he displaces his fury and energy. Instead he directs his retribution against the dwarves whom he enslaves and torments. Wagner demonstrates both how the product of emotional trauma could be a person who created tyranny, slavery and suffering, and how such a person could then remain completely aloof, or take a vicious satisfaction in it. To grasp this and understand how such things might be, Wagner had only to look within.

Fortunately he *was* blessed with this crucial escapes, literal escapes when a child, and mental escapes into artistic creation later. His creations were more than safety valves; they transformed his dissonant energies into something wholly positive. He personalised his conflicts in dramas of genius, something of immortal value. His initial efforts were firstly an abreaction, a purging process which consists of reliving disturbing experiences and violently expressing emotions which were forbidden at the time. Those efforts were also an integration of his disunities, and this was a pattern which continued throughout his life's work. It was no chance that his drama *Leubald*, which he later misremembered as *Leubald und Adelaide*, contained so many deaths and murders that he had to bring back half its cast of forty as ghosts to finish the plot. Abreaction and integration are not incompatible, but were complementary ways by which Wagner came to terms with the past. What is striking is how well he came to understand his functioning and his own mind. As he would one day tell Mathilde

Wesendonck,[82] 'Everything with me is so linked together: that has its disadvantages as it allows common and remediable grievances to exert a frequently excessive influence on me: yet it also has this advantage, that I derive from this same interconnection the means of reassurance, for just as everything streams towards my ultimate life task, my art, so from it flows back the fount that dews the arid paths of my life.'

The different elements in Wagner were 'linked together' but were never integrated smoothly. They always strained against one another, and he was a man never at peace with himself. At times the driving energies were barely enough to hold him together and he did almost disintegrate. He might have killed himself. On 15 January 1854, after some particularly vicious attacks on *Lohengrin* at its first presentation in Leipzig had set the seal on his growing despair, he confided to Liszt,[83] 'Dearest Franz, not one of the latter years has passed without bringing me at least once to the verge of a resolution to end my life.' There was an element here of manipulation, but the whole tone of Wagner's letters was one that clearly indicates a risk of imminent collapse into a major depressive illness. If, as a practising doctor, I had heard something like this from Wagner as a patient, I would have treated it as a psychiatric crisis which was life-threatening.

Wagner's creations were thus a method of grappling with the black abysses and the mystical powers which he encountered in dark nights of the soul, and of integrating them. In this same letter to Liszt, he went on to write that art was a stopgap for him in the literal sense, a plug in the dyke against the despair which would otherwise overwhelm him. Art fulfilled his need 'to dive into the waves of artistic fancy, to find contentment in a world of imagination,' even if the process was utterly exhausting. His acts of creation invariably consumed him. As he also told Liszt, 'The Rhinegold is done but I am done for!', and it was only partly manipulation when he wrote to Liszt; 'My fancy should at least be borne up, my imagination supported. I cannot live like a dog. I

---

82   *Richard Wagner to Mathilde Wesendonck*, p. 188, 29 October 1859.
83   *Correspondence of Wagner and Liszt*, tr. Francis Hueffer, New York, 1889,
     ii, pp. 2-8.

cannot sleep on straw and drink bad whisky. I must be coaxed in one way or another if my mind is to accomplish the terribly difficult task of creating a non-existent world.' Certainly this was arrogance, but it was also the simple truth. He did need all the resources, the energies and the comforts that he could command for his achievements, for harnessing to good purposes the turbulent '*Wahn*' energy he described in *Die Meistersinger* in the character of Sachs, about which more later. Only thus could he create something 'noble', the music dramas which he bequeathed to the world. Sometimes he did understand himself with the uttermost penetration, as when he revealed, also to Mathilde, how he, the artist, 'had very cunningly contrived to weather the eternal conflict. Yes, to be in perpetual conflict, never to arrive at full inner repose, ever to be haunted, lured, hurled aside, – indeed that is the life of seething, whence inspiration blooms like a flower of despair.'[84] His disunities were like wild horses pulling in different directions, but he harnessed the energies unleashed to element and determine his particular 'flowers of despair': his masterpieces. Wagner's dramas were a means of enhancing and promoting his grasp on reality, an ecstatic release and an integration of his disunities; and for this reason he could also write of the joy of creation, the very opposite of his despair. Logically his joy and his despair were incompatible, but the wellsprings of artistic creation are not logical. All the available evidence confirms that his art gave shape, meaning, joy and order to his life; and just as important, it can do the same for us.

All these elements of psychological information are an essential part of the edifice of ideas without which there can be no full understanding of Wagner. It is only these ideas and this understanding which can put an end to the idea, entrenched far and wide but entirely erroneous, that he had a happy childhood. It is only through the awareness of his childhood as it really was that we can really begin to comprehend his strange and marvellous mind, his unspeakable challenges and his stupendous achievement. His happy childhood was a fiction even

---

84 *Richard Wagner to Mathilde Wesendonck*, p. 225, 10 April 1860.

more fanciful than Joachim Köhler divined, and to get inside Wagner's formative years, to understand the reasons for his fictionalising them, to grasp the extent to which those years influenced all that he became, and is to open up better access to 'the Wagner Experience and its meaning to us'.

FIVE

The Child is Father of the Man

II. Sources of a Genius

Nimmer kann ich ruhig treiben,
Was Die Seele stark befaßt,
Nimmer still behaglich bleiben,
Und ich stürme ohne Rast.

Karl Marx, *Juvenilia*

Never can I work in peace at
That which holds my soul in thrall;
Never rest but storm forever
Onwards without peace at all.

The last chapter was concerned with Wagner's psychological imprints. This one is about his cultural inputs. Of Wagner's parents and quasi-parents it was his mother, Rosine Wagner, whose cultural influence ran deepest in all that he became. *Mein Leben* describes no influences at all from his father who after all was dead when he was six months old. On the other hand, it warms over his recollections of his step-father, Ludwig Geyer; 'This excellent man … also took my education in hand with the greatest care and affection.' When Wagner was seriously ill, he felt supported by 'the noble part played by my excellent step-father'.

In fact the role of Geyer was ambiguous. We cannot know what strains Geyer brought with him from his own early struggles, what were the stresses of trying to support his adopted family, or when he first sickened with the illness that resulted in his early death. It is never easy to be such wise, all-caring parents as developmental psychologists expect because parents have other worries as well as their children; nevertheless, reading between the lines, it is clear that Geyer could be very caring to Wagner, dubbing him affectionately 'My little Cossack'.

At the same time the last chapter explained how Geyer was the source of the chastisement which Wagner could expect whenever his nightmares awoke the family. We know that he thrashed Wagner for buying a whip with stolen money, while his sisters cried outside the door. Brought up in the 'school of hard knocks', Geyer was in certain ways a martinet, the slave-driving theatrical trainer of Wagner's sisters. He was apparently driven by his anxiety to make them self-sufficient and save them from the near-destitution which he had experienced himself when young. Destitute people starved in those days, as they are beginning to again now. It is easy to condemn overweening father figures of the past (Leopold Mozart was another) when they were doing their best to ensure that their children would be able to fend for themselves in social circumstances which very different from most of ours today. In addition, Geyer was soon to die of tuberculosis, which provides its victims with awful premonitions of an unpleasant end. We do not have his details, but people dying of pulmonary tuberculosis usually grow more and more breathless and cough up blood and disgusting rubbery material, which is actually their own rotting lungs. Because of what was happening, it would have been strange if Geyer had not been depressed and fearful for himself and anxious about his adoptive family. The young and impressionable Wagner had also seen him in menacing roles onstage, one of his specialities, and in some ways he was a prominent factor towards Wagner's frightening, unsettled childhood.

On the purely cultural side Geyer contributed two crucial elements: painting and theatre. Geyer had originally made a name as a painter, largely self-taught after his 'extreme poverty made him break off his studies at University'. His two paintings included in this book, of Geyer himself and of Wagner's mother Rosine, show that at least as a portrait painter he possessed an ability which most of us would be glad to own, and under the encouragement of Wagner's father Friedrich, who befriended him, he had additionally developed a flair for acting, starting out as amateur and then turning professional. Geyer provided Wagner with his first experience onstage, using him as an extra to play an angel in *Der Weinberg an der Elbe*. The music for this was by Wagner's future hero, Weber, and these experiences began to light up the realms of imagination which Wagner's dramas later expressed so compellingly. Although Wagner was only eight when Geyer died, it was evidently Geyer who gave Wagner some early sense of self-worth; it was Geyer who saw to his education and had found him roles in plays; and it was the dying Geyer whom Wagner serenaded with a piano solo, and who then commented, 'Is it possible he has musical talent?'[85]

---

85 Even so, the character of Geyer's influence on Wagner remains questionable and this illustrates how difficult it can be to establish an objective truth. Compare the views of two Wagner scholars of ability and integrity, Joachim Köhler and Jean-Jacques Nattiez. Köhler displayed his view of the Wagner–Geyer relationship in his statement, 'The truth of the matter is that the boy was afraid of him,' depicting Geyer as a cold-hearted, sadistic tyrant who thrashed Wagner with a whip during his life, and haunted Wagner after he was dead. 'In his imagination and his nightmares, Geyer was a constant threat.' Jean-Jacques Nattiez's interpretation goes to the opposite extreme. For Nattiez, Wagner's relationship with Geyer was 'close and affectionate', so much so as to give rise to a strong strain of homoeroticism; 'his libido was directed at his stepfather,' born of 'the feeling of gratitude towards his protective stepfather.' The two views are not totally incompatible but they do not exactly point in the same direction. Köhler, Joachim, *Richard Wagner: The Last of the Titans*, tr. Stewart Spencer, New Haven and London, 2004; Nattiez, Jean-Jacques, *Wagner Androgyne*, tr. Stewart Spencer, Princeton, 1993.

His mother's influence was even stronger. Wagner adored her,[86] and there is a letter in which where he poured out his love and admiration to her more fulsomely than to any other woman in his life except his first wife Minna; 'I am overcome with feelings of gratitude for the glorious love of which you gave such heart-felt proofs, so much so that I might be tempted to write in the tender tones of a lover addressing his beloved ... I only want to thank you and thank you again.'[87] His description in *Mein Leben* of her erratic parenting is seasoned with sympathy and understanding of her predicament; 'Her trying position at the head of a numerous family (of which I was the seventh surviving member), the difficulty of obtaining the wherewithal to rear them, and of keeping up appearances on very limited resources, did not conduce to evolve that tender sweetness and solicitude which are usually associated with motherhood.' This explained why he 'had no recollection of her as a young and pretty mother or of her ever having fondled me'. Earlier, 'her chief characteristics seem to have been a keen sense of humour and an amiable temper,' and the portrait painted by Geyer 'provided a favourable impression of what she might have been'.

Wagner also praised 'her great energy', but having registered admiration he then went on to disparage her; she was distant and undemonstrative; and when he was ill she showed him little warmth; 'At one time during my early boyhood I became so weak from some childish ailment that my mother told me later she used almost to wish me dead, for it seemed as though I should never get well,' information that could not have encouraged a cheery sense of self-worth. It was an exceptional experience for him to see his mother 'looking at him proudly and fondly when being put to bed and speaking of me to a visitor with a certain amount of tenderness.' His childhood needs for security and maternal nurturing generally went unmet, and later he told Minna, 'On the whole I had a pretty miserable time of it.' To be

---

86   *The Family Letters of Richard Wagner*, tr. William Ashton Ellis, London, 1911, letter to his mother, 20 September 1835.

87   *Selected Letters of Richard Wagner*, ed. and tr. Stewart Spencer and Barry Millington, London, 1987, no. 7: letter to his mother, 25 July 1835.

sure, he made his most critical comments after his mother was dead and his memories had been blighted by later experiences of her in old age. In particular, Wagner had been confused and angry when she grew senile, criticising her 'perversion of the truth, distortion and gossip-mongering',[88] and 'her constant chatter which is almost completely brainless' (as it probably was, poor woman, if she was dementing), her meanness with money, her inconsistencies and her dirtiness. Much of this seemed to Wagner like manipulation but as we can see all too well from today's vantage point, these were simply features of senility, most likely a vascular dementia, and the confused emotions touched by anger which Wagner experienced are common to adult children when confronted with elderly parents beginning to crumble, above all when they start to burble and smell bad. Like others in this situation, Wagner was evidently disturbed by his ambiguous feelings and resented the fact that his mother was causing them, letting him down and sabotaging his earlier, happier impressions; but also angry with himself for his aversion to his own mother.

Earlier, because she meant so much, she had been a major cultural influence. Three features of that influence stand out. First, Wagner was affected by 'the strange enthusiasm and almost pathetic manner with which she spoke of the great and the beautiful in Art.' Second and surprisingly, 'She never let me suppose that she included dramatic arts under this heading, but only poetry, music and painting. Consequently she even often threatened me with a curse if I should express the desire to go on the stage.' Third, she was very religious. 'With intense fervour, she would often give us long sermons about God and the divine quality in man. She used to assemble us around her bed and one of us would read out a hymn or part of the church service from the prayer book before she took her coffee.' Thus his mother impressed on Wagner her exalted views on art, her positive responses to poetry, music and painting, and her religious devotion.

---

88   *The Family Letters of Richard Wagner*, letter to his sister Cäcilie and her husband Eduard Avenarius dated 11 September 1842.

The question of Wagner's religious convictions have become a wordy tug-of-war between those who want Wagner to have been religious and those who want him not to, but a religious dimension stalks Wagner's life and work like a ceaseless ostinato. However far his particular convictions may have flickered and changed, Christianity forms the background to almost half his thirteen completed stage works, and in his youth Christianity was taken for granted in everyday life, like the air that he breathed. Much later, when Cosima was writing her *Diaries*, page after page describes some passionate avowal by Wagner about Jesus Christ or some polemical reference to anyone who dared challenge his divinity, however much Wagner may have disliked organised religion and its institutions as he perceived them. *Mein Leben* does not tell much about his religious observances when young, his churchgoing or otherwise, but his bashful revelation of stealing the money intended for his confirmation classes and spending it on sweets at least tells us that he must have been going to confirmation classes for this to have happened. These classes would have been part of the general Lutheran upbringing and influence which Wagner experienced. The reason why religious observances do not feature greatly in *Mein Leben* is that they were too routine and commonplace to warrant a mention, and the only reason why he mentioned the confirmation classes was because of something which struck him as *not* commonplace, the peculiar shiver, the pang of conscience at his first communion from his recollection of the pastor's fees embezzled for sweets; this *Schauer* was emphatically not a religious sensation, as some writers on Wagner choose to believe. It was just as inevitable that he should have had a full exposure to Lutheranism when boarding at Pastor Wetzel's school in Possendorf, even though he does not mention that either.

Along with her positive impact, Wagner's mother's behaviour reinforced a lifelong failing engendered by the shifting circumstances and the emotional rootlessness of the last chapter, his unsatisfiable hunger for the womanly affection which she had always been too busy or distant to provide. A deprivation of maternal 'fondling' contributed to his insatiable need for feminine 'fondling' later. Even his mother's negative attitude to the stage (if true) may well have affected him, if only as a counter-suggestion. She may have provoked in Wagner a fascination with the theatre as a kind of counter-response, causing him unconsciously to dig his heels in, but this is conjecture. What is fact is that he was deeply affected by the world-famous musical and theatrical figures visiting his mother's home. Weber called often and Spohr actually stayed there, and even if his mother expressed opposition to the theatre verbally, she actually presided over the successful stage launch of Wagner's sisters and elder brother.

As a child Wagner was naturally impressionable, and his erratic, frequent upheavals at least exposed him to substitute families and a variety of influences which bristled not only with adversities but with intriguing stimuli. On the one hand he was always a new boy in every social group. As a lad of seven at Eisleben, the location of the drowned puppies, he had 'frequent tussles with the town boys who were constantly mocking at me for my square cap'. He may have been small, but it was never in Wagner's character to be intimidated. He had long been pugnacious, and this was partly the reason why Geyer had nicknamed him his 'little Cossack'. On the other hand Eisleben was also the home of Kolter, the outstanding tight-rope specialist of the day, and Wagner witnessed 'performances by a troupe of acrobats, in which a man walked a rope stretched from tower to tower across the square, an achievement which long inspired me with a passion for such feats of daring. Indeed I got so far as to walk a rope fairly easily myself with the help of a balancing pole.' Even in 1865, when dictating *Mein Leben*, Wagner tells us, 'Even now I feel the urge to gratify my acrobatic instincts.'[89] He was then in his fifties and still climbing the walls up to the first floor windows at Tribschen, to the horror of those present, who feared that he would fall. Even later, in his sixties, he would climb trees at Bayreuth; and at the rehearsals of *Die Walküre*, Act II it would likewise appal the cast to see him balancing precariously on a high narrow platform at the back as he showed everyone how to do it.

89   *My Life, authorized translation* ... , New York, 1911, p. 7.

Throughout his young days he was thus exposed to many fantastical impressions; and there are good reasons for accepting the suggestion that the mind subjected to these cultural stimuli was by nature out of the ordinary. It was not only the impressions but Wagner's physiological computer which was absorbing them that was unusual, but unusual in a manner that was not substandard but exceptional. Another feature that bears out the suggestion of an exceptional neurology was his exceptional dream pattern, the frequency and vividness of his dreams. Cosima's *Diaries* give accounts of more than four hundred of them, quite different from the small number and vague recollections of most people. For the period of the *Diaries* the picture was increasingly complicated by the drugs Wagner was taking. These were prescribed for his very real, and desperate, health problems, but they upset his sleep and affected his dreams. However, this need late in life for medication was obviously not the reason why he dreamed so much and so strangely when young. 'Even during the latest years of my boyhood, not a night passed without my waking out of some ghostly dream and uttering the most frightful shrieks ... They put me to sleep as far away as possible from the others, without thinking that my cries for help would only be louder and longer.'[90] The most convincing explanation why Wagner's night terrors took such heightened form is that he possessed an unusual neuro-physiology. It is relevant that 'from my earliest childhood certain mysterious and uncanny things exercised an enormous influence over me. If I were left alone in a room for long, I remember that, when gazing at the lifeless objects such as pieces of furniture, and concentrating my attention upon them, I would suddenly shriek out with fright because they seemed to me alive.' The account of things dancing and vibrating has points of distant association with epilepsy but in Wagner's case it was more to do with a mind humming with abnormal and excessive activity than some neurological deficit.

Further evidence in support of his exceptional intelligence and

---

90   Ibid., p. 14.

unusual brain was that as a boy he was outstandingly bright and quick in the uptake. The early age at which he translated Homer, his precocious discussions of Shakespeare, Dante and Goethe, and the speed with which he would master music theory are just some of the features that point to an outstanding intelligence. It is similarly significant that throughout life Wagner would describe himself as beset by 'pains in the nerves of his brain' when over-excited, a description that is difficult to decipher now medically but is important when trying to fathom his mentality. There is even the fascinating possibility that Wagner had synaesthesia, a mental cross-talk between the different senses and another mark of an unusual neurology; the idea of his synaesthesia is best considered later in connection with the music.

Wagner tells us that he returned briefly to Leipzig after leaving Eisleben in September 1822, and his time there had its quota of wonders and terrors. He was now aged nine, and stayed at the Thomä House with his uncle Adolf and his aunt Friederike, a stay that held a significance out of all proportion to its brief duration, although the vividness of his memories probably dates from his return later, in 1827. Wagner was given a bed in one of the state rooms normally reserved for the Saxon royal family when they visited Leipzig. Wagner loved these

large strange rooms, luxurious with heavy silk and rich rococo furniture ... and looking out on the bustling market square and the students in their old-fashioned 'club' attire. There was only one portion of the decorations of the rooms that I thoroughly disliked. This consisted of the various portraits, but particularly those of highborn dames in hooped petticoats, with youthful faces and powdered hair. These appeared to me exactly like ghosts; when I was alone in the room, they seemed to come back to life, and filled me with the most abject fear. To sleep alone in this distant chamber, in that old-fashioned bed of state, beneath those unearthly pictures, was a constant terror to me. Never a night passed in which I was not a prey to the most horrible ghostly visions, and my dread would leave me in a bath of perspiration.

The fact that Wagner could enjoy such splendour even briefly in raises the question why were the fatherless Geyer family staving off destitution while Adolf, the brother of their mother's first husband, lived in comparative affluence? The answer may be that it was difficult to call on Adolf because he had disapproved of Geyer as an actor, a known fact, and may have disapproved even more of Geyer as his dead brother's cuckold, but this is only a hypothesis.

It was in 1827 when Wagner returned to Leipzig to be reunited with his mothers and sisters that his peculiar uncle Adolf took to him. Wagner was now fourteen and his interesting uncle enjoyed his company on afternoon walks, because he listened eagerly and entered into his uncle's literary passions. Adolf had already presented Wagner with his father's books and he now opened his own library to Wagner. Through Adolf, Wagner was able to share the German passion for Shakespeare and the rediscovered genius of Dante. Adolf could recite Shakespeare by heart, and they discussed Sophocles' *Oedipus Tyrannus*, which Adolf had translated into German, as well as Schiller and Goethe. Goethe had given him a silver goblet. Adolf influenced Wagner decisively with his 'blunt contempt for modern pedantry in State, Church and School; and he produced on me the effect of a free-thinker,' exactly the opposite of his religiose mother, and Wagner found himself treated by a man much older than himself on terms of equality at a time when he had a singular need for sympathy and encouragement. He was then a disaster at school, and an outcast, but Adolf was an authority figure who gave Wagner the courage of his convictions and permission to think independently.

At a different level, this uncle was one of the people who seemed an outrider from a fantastic, parallel dimension of dreams, the theatre and myth which would increasingly become a real world for Wagner, and which his works would make real for us. Wagner himself described the three occupants of the Thomä House as exactly the personalities to 'actualise the ghostly impressions of the house in a reality that resembled some strange fairytale'. Its strange cast list began with Jeanette Thomä, who had inherited this vast, palatial building, but was herself very small and stout. Then there was her companion, Wagner's aunt Friederike, remarkable for her height, her extreme leanness and her exceedingly pointed chin. Above all there was uncle Adolf, whom Wagner had first seen in a darkened room, 'surrounded by a great wilderness of books, and wearing a strange felt cap which was very tall and pointed'. The behaviour of all three was apparently wayward and bizarre, but Wagner only provides detailed information about his uncle, for instance the circumstances of his uncle's marriage. His uncle had made some money from his literary activities, and 'found it irksome to have to perform various little duties at the Thomä House which had come his way'. So one day, 'without saying a word, instead of going for his usual afternoon walk, he went to church with his bride, and it was only on his return that he informed us that he was leaving and would have his things removed that very day. He managed to meet the consternation and perhaps the reproaches of his elderly friend with quiet composure, and continued his daily visits to "Mam'selle Thomä" to the end of his life.'

He was a misanthrope and an eccentric, but a cultured and interesting man, and it was probably due partly to his impact that Wagner gave up the name Geyer and from now on became Richard Wagner. Wagner always remained full of gratitude to his uncle, and much later went to determined lengths to acquire his portrait from the servant girl who had inherited it, a determination born of simple affection.

His uncle was not Wagner's first literary influence. He had been only six, a boarder at the country clergyman's school, when 'the newspaper accounts and monthly reports of the Greek War of Independence stirred my imagination deeply.' (How many children of six are normally aware of anything in the newspapers?) 'My love for Greece, which afterwards made me turn to the mythology and history and ancient Hellas, was thus a natural outcome of the intense and painful interest I took in the events of this period. In after years, the story of the Greeks' struggle against the Persians always revived my impression of this modern revolt of Greece against the Turks.'

And subsequently at the Kreutzschule in Dresden, 'Greek particularly attracted me, and because the stories from Greek mythology so seized on my fancy I tried to imagine them speaking in their native tongue.' Later in life, he recalled that he had then made translations of the first twelve books of the *Iliad*,[91] and he had a young teacher, a Herr Sillig, who took to him and played a part in spurring on his literary enthusiasms. It is not always easy to keep track of dates and time frames in the zigzagging course of Wagner's life, especially in his younger days when Wagner's account darts about and interlards different phases, but Sillig belonged to his second stay at Dresden after his year at Eisleben was over, and after his first brief stay with his uncle Adolf. Wagner began at the Kreutzschule in 1822 when he was nine. Herr Sillig at some stage arranged for him to recite Hector's farewell from the *Iliad* and Hamlet's monologue. Sillig also invited him home, went over his translations and his original verses, and helped to improve a poem commemorating a fellow pupil after his sudden death. It was published and circulated, and it convinced everyone, including Wagner himself, that he was born to be a poet. Something which may come as a surprise is that as an adult he possessed an overweening assurance in his capacity as a poet which was utterly unlike his hesitation and uncertainty as a composer. He went on later to describe *The Ring* to his friend Uhlig as the greatest poem ever written, a claim more far-fetched than any he ever made for his music. In a letter of 8 May 1858, the man who had in less

91   This claim is not as far-fetched as commentators allege when they note that Wagner later had to read Aeschylus in translation and argue consequently that he could never have translated Homer so young. However Homer's Greek is easy, and I can still enjoy dipping into *The Odyssey* almost fifty years after finishing classics at Oxford. The Greek of Aeschylus is very different, and very difficult. Supremely great though it is, it is like a Greek mix of T.S. Eliot and Gerard Manley Hopkins; and it always needed utter concentration and virtually a wet towel round the head, to come to grips with it. There is no incompatibility between Wagner's claims about translating Homer at school and his need later on to read Aeschylus in translation.

than five years completed *Das Rheingold, Die Walküre* and most of *Tristan und Isolde* was telling Liszt, 'I cannot tell you too often how miserably weak I feel as a musician. I know in the depth of my heart, that I am an absolute blunderer ... You ought to watch me when I am at it; now thinking, "It must do after all," then going to the piano to puzzle out some wretched rubbish, and giving it up again in a state of idiocy. Oh how I feel then! How thoroughly persuaded of my musical wretchedness!' Cosima's *Diaries* chronicle repeated occasions throughout his later life when these self-lacerating doubts still plagued him.

It was in December 1827 when he was thirteen and a half that his time at the Kreutzschule ended and he returned to Leipzig. The immediate cause for the move was that he was threatened with a punishment which he considered unjust. In his outrage he engineered his immediate discharge and his departure to Leipzig, claiming a sudden summons from his mother (which duly materialised) to go and join his family which was gathering together again. His mother, worried about his unruly life in a Dresden garret, concurred with his manoeuvrings, but although the move gave him much-needed harbour, it was bad for his schooling. The Nicolaischule at Leipzig demoted him to a lower grade than he had achieved at Dresden, and he grew bored and resentful. 'My disgust at having to lay aside my Homer from which I had made translations of twelve cantos, was indescribable. It hurt my feelings so deeply and so influenced my behaviour that I never made a friend of any teacher at the school.'

However, his literary interests still developed and deepened owing to his uncle Adolf, and it was at this point that he again became 'specially attracted to the classical period of Greek history. Marathon, Salamis and Thermopylae composed the canon.' These were battles of Greeks against Persians and against overwhelming odds. His early political awareness was encouraged by his brother-in-law, Friedrich Brockhaus, the Leipzig publisher. Brockhaus employed him to read the proofs of Becker's *Universal History* and did Wagner two separate good turns. First, he paid Wagner real money, eight groschen a sheet, and Wagner later wryly commented, 'I thus found myself in one of the rarest position in my life, actually earning money.' Second and more important for Wagner's development, the proofs gave him an 'acquaintance with the middle ages and French Revolution' which 'filled him with sincere hatred for its heroes … my human sympathy was horrified by the cruelty of the men of that day'. In 1830 (his third year in Leipzig) the boundaries between history and life seemed to dissolve with the news of the July Revolution in Paris; 'The king of France had been driven from his throne; Lafayette who a moment before had seemed to me like a legend was again riding through a cheering crowd in the streets of Paris.' Paris was beginning to take on the visionary glamour that was to draw him there later in 1839. Thanks to the reports in the *Leipzig Gazette* Wagner developed an awareness of the interpenetration of myth and history with life as he was living it, which would suffuse his own creations. He became caught up in 'the struggles of the young and hopeful against the old and effete'. He was excited that in Dresden, some forty miles away, the political shock-waves resulted in 'fighting in the streets, and produced political change – the granting of a Constitution'.

It is not easy for people from an Anglo-Saxon background to grasp the momentous significance of these events for the populations of central and eastern Europe, notoriously in Prussia and Russia, where the monarch with his cabal of aristocrats was often an absolute ruler. Sometimes the monarchs were relatively benign, but they were often autocratic reactionaries who accepted no constitution and regarded the law as an instrument for keeping the better classes, i.e. themselves, wealthy and powerful. Such rulers often suppressed the modest attempts by ordinary people to advance their own welfare or allow freedom of speech, a contrast to England where there has long been a *Magna Carta* [92] and a Habeas Corpus Act. In England, royalty itself

---

92   *Magna Carta*, AD 1215. 'No free man shall be taken in custody, or imprisoned, or disposed, or outlawed or exiled, or in anyway destroyed, nor will we go upon him, nor send against him except by the lawful judgment of his peers or by the law of the land. To no man will we sell,

has long been subject to limitations under the law, even if royalty has sometimes honoured those limitations more in the breech than the observance. Wagner was later presented with disturbing proof of the despotic power of the monarchical state, and the relevant section of *Mein Leben* is so revealing of so many important things, that it is worth quoting in full. It refers to events of August 1834[93] concerning Heinrich Laube, an influential novelist in his day, and one of the leaders of the Young Germany movement, which had affected Wagner very positively.

> The serious side of life at once confronted me in the form of significant experiences. At Leipzig I had to take a furtive leave of Laube. At the instance of Prussia he had been warned off Saxon soil, and he half guessed at the meaning which was to be attached to this move. The time undisguised reaction against the Liberal movement of the early 'thirties had set in: the fact that Laube was concerned in no sort of political work, but devoted himself merely to literary activity, always aiming simply at aesthetic objects, made the action of the police quite incomprehensible to us for the time being.

Heinrich Laube was also an old family friend, who was to help Wagner financially in Paris, but over the next twenty-five years they grew they more and more distant and out of sympathy, and by 1870 when *Die Meistersinger* was first staged in Vienna Laube was Wagner's implacable enemy, and he reviewed it very negatively. Back in 1834, Laube's Young German doctrines of 'free love' were important to Wagner for two separate reasons. First, Wagner was always uncertain whether he could 'attract the attention of pretty girls' and inhibited about being allowed to try, and he discovered a quasi-therapy, a semi-resolution for his inhibitions in the Young German ideology. He was soon to put into practice its ideals of 'free love', as it was once quaintly described. Second, Wagner had taken these ideals and made them the

or deny, or delay right or justice.'

93   *My Life*, i., p. 107 et seq. (translation slightly amended).

subject of his youthful opera, *Das Liebesverbot*. Now however Laube himself was in trouble over what he promoted. By the time Wagner wrote his account of these events in *Mein Leben* Laube was no friend, and Wagner was openhearted in recalling

> The disgusting ambiguity with which the Leipzig authorities answered all his questions as to the cause of his expulsion soon gave him the strongest suspicions as to what their intentions towards him actually were. Leipzig, as the scene of his literary labours, being inestimably precious, it mattered greatly to him to keep within reach of it. My friend Apel owned a fine estate on Prussian soil, within a few hours distance of Leipzig, and we conceived the wish of seeing Laube hospitably harboured there. My friend, who without infringing the legal stipulations was in a position to give the persecuted man a place of refuge, immediately assented, and with great readiness, to our desire, but confessed to us next day, after having communicated with his family, that he thought he might incur some unpleasantnesses if he entertained Laube. At this the latter smiled, and in a manner I shall never forget, though I have noticed in the course of my life that the expression which I then saw in his face was one which has often flitted over my own features. Laube took his leave, and in a short time we heard that on the grounds of his having undertaken proceedings against former members of the Burschenschaft (Students League) he had been arrested, and had been lodged in the municipal prison at Berlin.

Laube had committed no crime, but the Prussian authorities did not like his attitudes, and that was enough for them to get a neighbouring country, Saxony, to make him an outcast and hound him. These were events of significance for Wagner, and these happenings and other events concerned with human rights through which he lived in his late teens influenced both his stance politically and his ideals as an artist. As we have seen, he had long sensed the interpenetration of myth and history with life as he was living it, and now it was happening right in front of his eyes. Myth, drama and life germinated in his imagination and from their fusion a new organism would one day grow, a drama that would express, predict and mould history.

It helped his development that his return to Leipzig in 1827 had afforded him renewed access to live performances in the Leipzig theatre. It put him back in touch with the entire theatrical world, because it was a world to which his theatrically gifted sisters emphatically belonged. His affinity for that world went back to his earliest childhood. Even then, 'What attracted me so strongly to the theatre, by which I also include the stage, the rooms behind the scenes, and the dressing rooms, was the fascinating pleasure of an entirely different atmosphere and a world that was purely fantastic. Thus to me a scene, even a way of representing a bush or some part of it, seemed to come from another world, to be as attractive as an apparition, and I felt that contact might serve to lift me away to a delightful region of the spirits. Everything connected with a theatrical performance had a charm that bewitched and fascinated.'

Now that he was back in Leipzig, the theatre brought him enticements and fulfilments in parallel to those from literature. Through their fusion he was enabled to sublimate his negative experiences in drama, but the effect on his schooling was disastrous. He was already resentful about the demotion, and now he neglected his schoolwork entirely, and concentrated on his drama, his stupendous, blood-curdling tragedy, *Leubald*. He wrote most of it under the desk-top. When his family eventually found out they were aghast, especially when it emerged that because of his lamentable academic showing, he had burnt his boats at the Nicolaischule; 'I had to leave at Easter 1830 as I was too deeply in disgrace to hope for any promotion to the University from there.' It seems that he was actually expelled. Somehow he transferred to the Thomasschule, the Leipzig's other famous school, famous above all because J.S. Bach had been its Cantor. Wagner still did no work, frittering away his time in student clubs, 'above all a sham association called The Freshman's Club; and at the end of half a year the masters of St Thomas's were of the opinion that I had not given a thought to their institution, and nothing could persuade them that I had earned the title to academic citizenship,' i.e. a place at the University. Music then came to his rescue, because his lamentable academic performance did not disqualify him from enrolling at the University as a musician. His *daimon*, his destiny as a musician, was starting to assert itself. *Daimon* is an entity taken from Greek thought which resists translation because it has no real equivalent in our thinking, and although it crops up in Wagner's writings again and again, he never defined it. He evidently saw it as the individual force that controls and compels each one of us. It has about it something of a primordial impulse from the subconscious, as it might be described today, something of a guiding star, and something of an angel of destiny or sent from the gods, although as Wagner envisaged it it could sometimes be far from angelic.

Perhaps his *daimon* strengthened him through his struggles as an outsider, which were a regular part of the Wagner family myth. Ferdinand Avenarius, son of Wagner's half-sister Cäcilie Geyer later gave two descriptions of Wagner trying to do something worthwhile for everyone involved, and of other boys wrecking his efforts, something which helps explain 'why he took so little pleasure in their company and spent more and more time with his sister'.[94] The first occasion was 'a sort of shooting competition':

A great summer festival was to be held for Richard's friends, with the competition as its high point. But they did not have enough money so a kind of club was set up to achieve this ideal aim; the subscription was set at three pence and everyone who contributed could advise on, and take part in, the pleasures in store. The treasures accumulated and when all the paint and wood and brass foil and nails had been received, the master proceeded to plan the festivities by first consulting his

94   Avenarius, Ferdinand, 'Richard Wagner als Kind', *Allgemeine Zeitung*, 14 and 15 March 1883, in Spencer, Stewart, ed. *Wagner Remembered*, London, 2000. Apart from Wagner's autobiography, this brief account provides one of the few sources for Wagner's childhood. Avenarius' account was evidently based on family lore passed on by his mother, and is consistent with other sources wherever comparisons are possible.

attendant, Cäcilie, on a suitable site for the festival. After all manner of arguments with their landlady, who had no time for such noble pursuits, they finally obtained her permission to hold the contest in her garden. Here was erected the pole that normally served as the shaft of a cart, and with his own hands Richard fashioned the proudest eagle from the meanest fire-wood, a bird which, festooned with trophies, soon cast its colourful lustre far and wide. The festival was due to take place the following day, but when the impresario stepped outside the next morning with his sister, his face radiant with happiness, in order to see his handiwork – it lay there in a pitiful heap on the ground. The other boys had brought it down with stones, and now stood there grinning contemptuously. 'We've paid our three pence, we can do what we like,' was their response to his anger and remonstrations. Of course he and his sister dissolved in floods of tears.

What is interesting for us is that it shows Wagner already, at this early (if unspecified) date, being determined to do something, and pursuing it with all the energy and the sound, practical plans that would see it to its completion, even if the result was spoilt by malice and envy. 'Today as I write these lines,' wrote Ferdinand Avenarius, 'I feel only a sense of undeniable disgust. It was Wagner's first experience of this kind. It was not to be his last.'

Avenarius' second story goes back to his childhood in Dresden, describing how

Richard liked to mount amateur theatricals in his room, and as soon as he saw *Der Freischütz* he absolutely had to stage it. It goes without saying that it was the Wolf's Glen scene that struck him as the most suitable in this regard. Pasteboard and glue were pressed into service to make the necessary props. His school friends had to help. Scenery, curtains, fireworks and animals – everything was produced, and my mother particularly admired a large boar with enormous tusks that was rolled along on the board and looked horribly like a Prince of Darkness in person. The performance was to be given at a friend's house. Richard played the part of Caspar, but the Max had not learnt his part, and when Richard indicated his disapproval, he first laughed, then called him names, and the others laughed and jeered too. This was the second of the bitter experiences.

It was Wordsworth who wrote 'The Child is father of the Man', and the man Wagner was to discover in adult life many variations on these sorry themes from his childhood. Whenever he sought authority and position, what he wanted was not 'power over' but 'power to do'. He was to discover and rediscover endlessly the sad fact that anyone who tries to achieve something worthwhile provokes opposition as much as assistance and hostility as much as support. This was always a feature of the circumstances and the culture surrounding Wagner. For example it was in 1873, five years after the premiere of *Die Meistersinger* had established him not just as a genius but a popular genius, that a Munich psychiatrist, Theodor Puschmann, did what he could to create a climate of opinion that was malign towards Wagner. Without meeting Wagner or examining him, he 'diagnosed' Wagner's disorders and used his status as a medical authority to attack and defame him. Puschmann published *Richard Wagner: eine psychiatrische Studie*, and claimed that Wagner's essay *Das Judenthum in der Musik* (1850, 1869) 'offered the psychiatrist a deep diagnostic insight into the private workings of Wagner's soul-life'. It did indeed, as we shall see in a later chapter, but not in the way that Puschmann understood it. Puschmann's other 'evidence' was Wagner's bad behaviour, notably his affair with Cosima (he had actually married her by then), but this was enough for Puschmann to diagnose 'moral insanity' and megalomania. This was not only misdiagnosis but barely disguised slander, because megalomania was then relatively common, a real medical condition which develops only in the late stages of syphilis.[95] Puschmann wrote 'It is well known that at the outset of medical illnesses there is an

95   Mercifully with the advent of penicillin which is lethal to *treponema pallidum*, the germ that causes syphilis, megalomania has become vanishingly rare.

unnatural increase in sexual desire which stands in starkest contrast to the physical and psychological impotence which establishes itself ever more definitely,' and this sentence nudged any reader who knew anything about syphilis into assuming that this was the illness affecting Wagner. Puschmann's treatise had a wide readership, especially in Munich, and the consequent climate of opinion was yet another reason why Wagner could not bear Munich, preferring a small town like Bayreuth where his personal magnetism could work its spell.

The magnetism could almost always work that spell with women. Wagner was strangely attractive to women, even though he no belief in this attractiveness. In return he always loved femininity. Even as a child,

> The elegant costumes of my sisters' wardrobe exercised a subtle charm of my imagination, and my heart beat madly at the touch of one of their dresses. The fact that I was brought up among feminine surroundings must have influenced the development of my sensitive side, and the characteristics of women and womanhood, especially such as were connected with the imaginary world of the theatre, created in me feelings of tender longing.

In early adolescence, when he was back in Dresden and lodging with the Böhme family, he had begun 'to experience the influence of the gentler sex in a manner hitherto unknown, as the daughters of the house and their grown-up friends filled its scanty narrow rooms'. There were occasions when he pretended to be too sleepy to move, so that he was carried up to bed by these girls, a subterfuge that he frequently repeated 'because I was thrilled with the closer and more gratifying proximity' that this entailed. 'Indeed my first experience of boyish love dates from this period. I remember a very beautiful girl coming to call on Sunday. She was charmingly dressed and her appearance as she came into the room literally struck me dumb with amazement.' On his return to Leipzig his reason for fancying himself 'in heaven' was because he was back with his beautiful sisters. The contemporary forms which femininity assumed in his sisters constantly invaded his imagination, and he found them intoxicating. Wagner seems to have been a bit of a Cherubino, young enough to have the freedom of the girls' rooms and old enough to exploit it. His sisters' personal attractions are confirmed by the ease with which they made excellent marriages, even though they had neither wealth nor connections. They were sufficiently his seniors to signify something reassuringly maternal, but graceful and beautiful enough to enchant him, and he adored them. Moreover, they had been separated from Wagner long enough for him not to develop that genderless, childhood familiarity that often nullifies any awareness of physical attractions in a sibling, but also long enough for him not to develop the inhibitions against erotic sentiments which develop if siblings share their childhood closely.[96]

This was significantly the period when Wagner's archetypes of the feminine, of 'woman', were stirring, and it was his sisters who filled out the expectant spaces with palpable images. He was particularly drawn to Rosalie and his half-sister, Cäcilie Geyer, and they all set the cultural stage for Wagner's vision of women as exotic, wonderful creatures in their own right during an era when women were more often appreciated if pretty, but still regarded as chattels to serve men's interests. Wagner was to some extent locked in the traditional outlook of women as utilities, but he could also switch to an attitude that was adoring and even worshipful; and his sisters' presence hovers over Loge's great paean in praise of women in *Das Rheingold*. The same sense of wonder wells up both in Siegmund's address to his lover-sister in *Die Walküre*, '*O süßeste Wonne! Seligstes Weib!* Oh sweetest joy! Most blessed [or holy] woman!' and again in Parsifal's mistaken amazement at Kundry, whom he imagines to be his lover-mother. These sentiments of adoring wonder supercharged his music and, thanks to his sisters at Leipzig, women's loving-kindness was a real experience for Wagner. Even so, Wagner's nurturing sisters reappeared on the scene too late to rewrite the imprints of deprivation engraved in his mind. The same was not true of Wagner's wife Minna

96   See Lieberman, D., J. Trooby and L. Cosmides, 'The Architecture of Human Kin Detection', *Nature*, No. 445 (2007), pp. 727 et seqq.

whose amazing role in Wagner's life and imagination is the principal subject of Chapter 7.

⁊

Two further crucial essentials towards Wagner's growing identity were his natural sensitiveness to sound, and the particular musical culture which surrounded him. From his earliest youth,

> The mere tuning up of the instruments put me in a state of mystic excitement. Even the striking of fifths on the violin seemed to me a greeting from the spirit world – which I may mention incidentally, had a very real meaning for me. When I was still almost a baby, the sound of these fifths which has always excited me was closely associated with ghosts and spirits ... When I saw the well-known picture in which a skeleton plays on his violin to an old man on his deathbed, the ghostly character of these notes impressed itself with particular force upon my childish imagination.

Possibly, this reminded him of the scene when his stepfather, Ludwig Geyer, died. That had been on 30 September 1821. Even then, at the age of eight, Wagner had picked up enough ability at the piano to serenade the dying man and bring him some comfort. His account of music and its effect continued:

> When I used to listen to the Zillman orchestra, one may imagine the rapturous thrill with which I drew in all the chaotic variety of sound that I heard as the orchestra tuned up: the long drawn A of the oboe, which seemed like a call from the dead to arouse the other instruments, never failed to raise my nerves to a feverish pitch of tension, and when the swelling C in the overture to *Der Freischütz* told me that I had stepped, as it were with both feet, right into the magic realm of awe.

It was also when Wagner was still a child and still at Dresden that he had experienced the *Freischütz* performances which he tried to copy. It was because of his sister Clara's burgeoning career as a prima donna, that the composer of *Freischütz*, Carl Maria von Weber, became a welcome family visitor and made an impression on the young Wagner: 'Weber's refined, delicate and intellectual appearance excited my ecstatic admiration; even the bad limp, which I often noticed when he was making his way home past our house, stamped the great musician on my imagination as an exceptional, almost superhuman being.' Much later Wagner discovered the Mozart Requiem and *Don Giovanni*, which persuaded him to include Mozart in his hallowed spirit world. When he heard a Beethoven symphony, the seventh, 'the effect was indescribable. To this must be added the impression produced on me by Beethoven's features which I saw in lithographs. I soon conceived of him as a sublime and unique supernatural being with whom none could compare.'

He went on to Beethoven's Ninth Symphony which became 'the mystical goal of all my strange thoughts and desires about music'. The Romantics reckoned that the boundaries between inspiration and insanity often blurred and overlapped. Both inspiration and insanity went beyond reason, beyond normality, and Wagner was first attracted to Beethoven's Ninth Symphony

by the opinion then prevalent among musicians, not only in Leipzig but elsewhere, that this work had been written by Beethoven when he was already half mad. It was considered then to be the *non plus ultra* of all that was fantastic and incomprehensible, and this was enough to arouse in me a passionate desire to study this mysterious work. At the very first glance at the score I felt irresistibly attracted by the long sustained pure fifths with which the first phrase opens; these chords which had played such a supernatural part in my childish impressions of music seemed to form the spiritual keynote of my own life. This, I thought, must surely contain the secret of all secrets, and accordingly the first thing was to make my acquaintance with the score by a process of the laborious copying.

He also transcribed it for piano and sent it to Schott's to publish. (Schott turned it down, but sent him two Beethoven scores in acknowledgement.) In all these instances, Wagner reveals both the stirring of music in the depths of his being and the impact of the particular musical culture of his surroundings. Thus Beethoven's open fifths sing again in the first work of his maturity, *Der fliegende Holländer*.

Mein Leben makes it clear that it was particularly because he wanted to provide music for his *Leubald*, just as Beethoven had done for *Egmont*, that he was first 'filled with the desire to compose. However, this presented greater difficulties than I had met in writing verse;' and 'it was these difficulties that drove me to adopt a career that bore some similarity to a professional musician, whose future distinction would be to win the title of conductor and composer of operas.' These events illustrate once more the further workings of Wagner's *daimon*, which seems to have propelled him firmly towards the lyric theatre. It was in order to compose music for *Leubald* and future dramas as yet unimagined that he began to study the subject in earnest. Writing *Mein Leben* many years later, Wagner deliberately gave the impression that as a music student he had been a lazy tearaway, but the very different picture which emerges between the lines is confirmed by various letters and other contemporary evidence demonstrating that he was industrious, methodical and tenacious about becoming a musician, and Wagner could muster a ferocious resolve when he wanted. He was no untutored genius, natural, untamed and untaught, but as Heinrich Laube later recalled, 'He had received the sort of current musical education that had been popular in Leipzig since Bach's day.'

In his enthusiasm he acquired *Logier's Thorough-bass*[97] (or, just

---

97 Johann Bernhard Logier was one of those many intriguing characters who float across Wagner's biography. He was a composer, pianist and teacher, and though German, lived and worked in Ireland from 1791; in 1818 he published *Logier's Thorough-bass*, in English and in London. The German edition came a year later and was followed in 1827 by his magnum opus, his *System der Musik-Wissenschaft und der praktische Composition*, which appeared simultaneously in German, English and

possibly, his larger work, his *System of Music-theory and Practical Composition*). He rented it from Wieck's library (that same Friedrich Wieck who was Clara Schumann's emotionally abusive father and superlative teacher) but was too attached to this teach-yourself-tutor to return it and ran up huge fines, an augury of things to come. In the autumn of 1828, he approached the musician Gottlieb Müller for lessons, secretly at first, but they became official and lasted almost three years. Wagner described Müller ambiguously as 'the most sincere and strict of teachers; my lessons proved to be a series of almost oppressive demonstrations of an almost pedantically strict sincerity.'[98] At the time, Wagner admired Müller enough to be seriously disturbed at the possibility that he would show him the door after the first hilarious performance of his youthful *Drumbeat* Overture by Heinrich Dorn. He had accidentally-on-purpose forgotten to mention to Müller that it was taking place, sensing that he would disapprove, and he wrote him a fulsome apology afterwards.[99] 'You will accuse me of having acted deceitfully towards you as my teacher and having insulted you in the most grievous fashion ... All I can do now is to ask you most sincerely for your forgiveness ... Be assured of my continuing, most affectionate obedience; and please forget this act of folly on my part.'

In October 1831 or thereabouts, Wagner went on to more intensive study with a musical mentor of real authority and distinction, Theodor Weinlig. Weinlig was J.S. Bach's successor as Cantor at the Thomaskirche, and Wagner described him as 'the greatest contrapuntist now living'. As Cantor, Weinlig was a busy man with many responsibilities and claims upon him, but he was still willing to find time for Wagner, building on the grounding of Müller. It is clear that Weinlig took to Wagner because he was enthusiastic, receptive and talented, and Wagner in turn described their relationship as 'loving and productive'. He told his sister, Ottilie, that he was 'so excellent a

---

French.

98   *Selected Letters of Richard Wagner*, letter of 1834 to Franz Hauser, Leipzig critic.

99   Ibid., letter of 25 December 1830, to Christian Gottlieb Müller.

man that I'm as fond of him as of a father. How fond of me he is you may judge by this; that when mother asked him to name his fee at the end of the half year's tuition, he replied that it would be unreasonable of him to accept any payment for the delight of having taught me.'[100] Wagner knuckled down eagerly and learnt to write fugues and canons and other contrapuntal pieces, and as a reward he was 'allowed' to compose a piano sonata and various overtures. Wagner also gained a sobering slant on life as a musician, even a successful one. Years later he recalled in *Mein Leben* how Weinlig's treatise on vocal exercises had been such a lucrative success for one publisher that it lad led a rival firm to ask for another on the same lines. Weinlig explained that he had nothing suitable but offered the rival a new mass instead, only to be turned down with a gratuitous insult: 'Let him that got the meat gnaw the bones.' Weinlig's music is still performed at the Thomaskirche in Leipzig at the Saturday afternoon concerts; and in the company of Bruckner's motets and of works by Schütz, Mozart, Mendelssohn and even J.S. Bach himself, it holds up well. It meant a lot to Wagner to win Weinlig's good opinion; for instance, Wagner's Piano Fantasy in F sharp minor 'gave me intense satisfaction because it won praise from Weinlig'.

He also had some violin lessons from a Leipzig orchestral player, a Herr Sipp.[101] Sipp's lessons seemed to give Wagner a sense of what strings could do and his first ideas of how to write for them. Wagner's best and most lasting creation from that period was his Symphony in C major which still comes over as beautifully put together and is very likeable.

As the account of Laube's arrest makes clear, life experiences and historical events were as important as culture, religion and literary examples in the development of Wagner's moral sense, which originated

---

100 *The Family Letters of Richard Wagner*, letter of 3 March 1832 to Ottilie Wagner.

101 Sipp was seven years Wagner's senior, and was a guest of honour at the original Bayreuth *Ring* in 1876. He outlived Wagner, and was tracked down in his 90s by Mrs Burrell, a great nineteenth-century Wagner collector. He described Wagner to her as his worst pupil.

in his sense of compassion. He had experienced the unforgotten anguish over the drowned puppies at Eisleben, and he was soon to react against his own want of compassion, which afflicted him when he 'entered into all the dissipations of raw manhood'. He was initially drawn into these by the outsider's urge to belong. Although he did not get on with schoolboys of his own age, he became the mascot of a rakish student fraternity which he was really too young and too small to join. To prove himself he threw down insane challenges resulting in three senseless and dangerous duels, but providence or his *daimon* stood by him in that none of his three antagonists turned up. One had severed an artery in his arm in another duel, one was actually dead, already killed in a quite different duel in Jena; and one had got drunk, attacked a brothel, and been so badly beaten up that he was out of circulation. Otherwise Wagner might easily have gone to an early grave.

Another of his dissipations which generated a reaction against his own callous brashness was gambling, part of his general addictive tendency. If what he says in *Mein Leben* is true, gambling was such an addiction that he once gambled away his mother's entire pension. Some bizarre legal quirk had given him control over that pension, and he was within a hair's breadth of losing it all. Perhaps providence was again with him when he gambled away his last thaler, and already 'visualised myself in the grey dawn, a prodigal son, fleeing from all I held dear'. He staked the money against impossible odds – exactly the pattern of his life to come – and won; and staking it again, won again and again until he won back all his mother's pension money and more. These duelling and gambling experiences turned out to be a do-it-yourself aversion therapy and fortunately produced a revulsion. He never duelled again, and we only know of one other brief period of gambling with money, even though his entire life was, in a sense, a similar gamble against impossible odds. He was seized with another revulsion after another 'dissipation', mob violence against a 'certain house of ill fame ... I recall with horror the intoxicating effect that this unreasoning fury had on me, and I cannot deny that without the slightest personal provocation I shared in the frantic onslaught like one possessed.'

Wagner was unusual because his major reaction to such boorish, disagreeable behaviour came early and decisively. What struck home was the battle of Ostralenka (Ostrołęka) in 1831, when the Poles were defeated and devastated by the Russians. After the defeat, Wagner was horrified that instead of joining in his sympathy for the Poles, 'my boon companions scoffed at me for it. The terrible lack of all fellow feeling of comradeship amongst the students struck me very forcibly.' He was now part of a group where he did *not* want to belong, and he describes coming to loathe the whole fraternity and its fatuous mentality, where 'to get drunk with deliberate cold bloodedness, without a glimpse of humour, was reckoned almost as brave a feat as duelling,' and 'any kind of enthusiasm had to be smothered or turned into pedantic bravado, which showed itself as affectation and indifference.' He realised too that he was someone who he did not want to be, and such things as the plight of the Poles ignited his capacity for compassion and led, slowly and fitfully, to his developing a powerful conscience. There was another personal experience later on when he was chorus master at Würzburg, that ratcheted up his ethical principles several notches further. In *Mein Leben* he tells us of a wanton attack on a certain André. André had never done anything worse than want to be a friendly part of the company, in the same room as the others, but his presence was irksome to another friend, a certain Fröhlich. 'One evening, Fröhlich lost patience. He tried to chase André from our table, hitting him with a stick. The result was a fight, and a mad longing to join the fray took possession of me. With the others, I helped in knocking our poor victim about, and I even heard the sound of one terrible blow which I struck André on the head, while he fixed his eyes on me in bewilderment. I relate this incident to atone for a sin which has weighed very heavily on my conscience ever since.' As it happens the same mad intoxication would sometimes come upon him again, as happened during the Dresden uprising of 1849. His morality only slowly coalesced, but took shape definitively after he had discovered the philosophy of Arthur Schopenhauer with its emphasis on compassion. This was in 1854, but compassion for Laube had already twenty years earlier made Wagner want to find him a safe haven.

All his life experiences and cultural influences were fused and transformed in the spring of 1832, when Wagner first beheld Wilhelmine Schröder-Devrient on the Leipzig stage. The date and exact occasion are uncertain. Wagner's recollections in *Mein Leben* do not quite square with the records: he reported her as performing Leonore in Beethoven's opera *Fidelio*, whereas the theatre archives suggest otherwise. How important is it? What matters is that she changed his life. She was

> at the zenith of her artistic career, young, beautiful and ardent, and whose like I have never again seen on the stage. If I look back on my life as a whole, I can find no event that produced so profound an impression upon me. Anyone who can remember that wonderful woman at this period of her life must to some extent have experienced the almost satanic ardour which the intensely human art of this incomparable actress poured into his veins.

Wagner was moved to write to her: 'After the performance I rushed to a friend's house and wrote a short note to the singer, in which I briefly told her that from that moment my life had acquired its true significance, and that if in days to come she should ever hear my name praised in the world of art, she must remember that she had that evening made me what I then swore it was my destiny to become.' She was evidently touched by his avowal and startled him at Dresden almost fifteen years later by reciting back his letter almost word for word. She meant so much to him that not even her later vindictiveness over his unpaid debts could canker his assessment of 'that wonderful woman'.

Wagner's heavenly powers or his *daimon* showered upon him a profusion of experience allowed to few, and the drastic and negative features of Wagner's younger years were balanced against much that was enriching. I can barely hint at the wild profusion which whirls past in the first hundred pages of *Mein Leben*. Cultural and life events come so thick and fast that it is difficult to take them in. In 1834, there was the riot in Nuremberg after an amateur singer with an elevated self-regard had twice made a fool of himself with his appalling performances. In 1831, there had been four weeks in Vienna 'whose hot summer air was absolutely impregnated with *Zampa* and Strauss'. Wagner further recalled, 'I shall never forget the extraordinary playing of Johann Strauss ... At the beginning of the new Waltz this demon of the Viennese musical spirit shook like a Pythian priestess on the tripod, and veritable groans of ecstasy raised the worship for the magic violinist to almost bewildering heights of frenzy.' Whether consciously or no, Wagner absorbed the sorcery of Strauss, the sensuousness of his harmony, and the sweetness of his orchestration as resources which he would one day make his own. This trip to Vienna was the upshot of a friendly invitation from the Polish count Tyszkiewicz, who had taken to Wagner because of his sympathy for the Polish cause. It was part of the bizarre cluster of impressions that came from this friendship that the count had confided 'a terrible calamity that had once befallen him. He had been married before, and while staying with his wife in one of his lonely castles, in the dead of night he had seen a ghostly apparition at the window of his bedroom. Hearing his name called several times, he had taken up a revolver to protect himself from possible danger and had shot his own wife, who had the eccentric idea of teasing him by pretending to be a ghost.' Travelling part of the way together, Wagner had to part from the count at Brünn (Brno), and he had a dreadful night there because he was convinced that he had fallen victim to an outbreak of cholera. 'When I was shown into a very lonely wing and left by myself in this wilderness, I hid myself in bed with my clothes on, and lived once again all the horrors of ghost stories as I had done in my boyhood. The cholera stood before me like a living thing; I could see and touch it; it lay in my bed and embraced me. My limbs turned to ice, I felt frozen to the marrow. Whether I was awake or asleep I never knew; I only remember how astonished I was when, on awakening, I felt perfectly well and healthy.' The exotic Polish count, his sad and lunatic story, the ride in his stately coach, the lonely room in the hotel, Wagner's nightmare embrace by the demons of cholera, the high life of Vienna and then Johann Strauss: this hectic kaleidoscope was entirely typical of Wagner's youth; it was pure Wagner.

These great panoplies of experience included the sweetness of the feminine, the kindness of strangers, and much else that was treasurably enriching, both from culture and from life. These things and his strange personality structure enabled him to make of himself what he uniquely became. They also gave rise to the phenomenal experience which he bequeathed to us.

SIX

THE CHILD IS FATHER
OF THE MAN

III. Faces of a Genius

An absolute shit.

   W.H. Auden

Not only a great, but a profoundly good man.

   William Ashton Ellis

*What I learn and see there, what I see and understand is
indescribable ... Schopenhauer and Goethe, Aeschylus and
Pindar, are still alive, believe me.*

   Friedrich Nietzsche

Probably the greatest genius of all time.

   W.H. Auden

Wagner was a being of discrepancies and conflicts. We have seen
that as a child he had never been able to form a lasting allegiance to
anyone who could set consistent patterns of conduct and decency for
him to follow. He had no permanent preceptor to teach him caring
behaviour or even an ordinary idea of 'do as you would be done by'.
Life had been a struggle and his existence fitful and arbitrary. As a man

his character reflected the incoherence of an upbringing where bad things materialised undeservedly, and good things, if they came, were sometimes warranted, sometimes the result of chance. This allowed him to form only random associations between doing something good and receiving any reward or acknowledgment. It was impossible for him to learn that when he helped someone, his act deserved recognition, or that other people deserved recognition if they helped him. Nothing established an inner conviction that he was valued, nor that he should value others if they did good things for him, even to the point of making sacrifices.

Nor had he the opportunity to assimilate negotiating skills, and consequently the process of meeting his needs often led to more conflict. He had to make his way on his own, through charm or aggression. He tended to get things by grabbing them; achieved rewards by taking them; gained support by seizing it. He later did work out stratagems that enabled him behave as if he were charm and persuasion personified, but he always remained prone to backsliding into the pattern of grabbing and seizing.

He never escaped a compulsive tendency to be self-centred to the point of narcissism. Narcissism is self-interest that has become pathological. It can sometimes go with an uncanny perception of other people, but without any warmth or concern for them. Narcissists are often aware of exactly how different people work and how they are likely to respond, but exploit this awareness overwhelmingly for their own interests. This was mode of his personality into which Wagner could always relapse. Because it was not natural for him to enter into other people's mindsets, it was always hard for him to sympathise with any point of view but his own. He could not feel consistently that other people might have rights as well as responsibilities. Even though he could be utterly charismatic, he never developed simple tact. He would often hurt people as if under a compulsion. As late as 1881, he and Cosima were still puzzling together over that 'curious and demonic habit of his, of wounding people without the slightest evil intent'.[102] This discussion took place after he had told Paul Joukovsky (no mean painter: he had enough talent for Wagner to want his sets for *Parsifal*) that he was puny, meaning that his talent could never amount to much! On the other hand, real suffering was almost always writ large in Wagner's imagination, causing him horror and a desperate desire to put things right.

Ultimately he came to possess an insight and feeling for character that was extraordinary, as outsiders often do. Like many narcissistic people, he did later succeed in creating inner worlds of mesmerising conviction, populated by the vital characters of his imagination. Sometimes narcissistic people develop imaginary worlds so satisfying but so remote from reality that they veer off into schizophrenia, but thanks to his phenomenal strength of will (his ego) Wagner seldom lost touch. He could and did flick switches in his mind like the channels on a television, swapping from one channel of consciousness to another, and not always aware of it. It puzzled those around him that he could vanish suddenly from real life into a strange serenity of his own, and then just as suddenly come out of it. He was subject to extreme alternations of mood, states of exaltation dissolving in a sense of persecution and loneliness, and this happened particularly when the personal, interior worlds of his imagination clashed too sharply with reality. An additional reason why Wagner's work (and life) are especially illuminated by Jung's psychology is that Jung was to go through interior struggles similar to Wagner's, similar battles with disunities. Jung forged his integration from psychological self-analysis, Wagner through his supremely psychological music dramas. Jung apparently sensed the affinity because it was 'the prophetic associations of Wagner's equinoctial music which Jung himself, in so far as he allowed himself music, preferred'.[103]

Wagner's shaping of private worlds as dramas cost him huge efforts of intellect and imagination. As he often complained, he had to

---

102 Wagner, Cosima, *Diaries*, tr. Geoffrey Skelton, vol. ii, Wednesday 28 September 1881.

103 van der Post, Laurens, *Jung and the Story of our Time*, Harmondsworth, 1978, p. 67.

absorb his characters and then refract them through his distinctive
identity, building them up from within outwards, as is clear even from
his descriptions of Rienzi and the Dutchman early in his career. It was
only after 'Rienzi set all my nerves a-quivering with sympathy and
love,'[104] that he was able to forge his drama on the subject. In the case
of the Dutchman, Wagner wrote, 'He won a psychic force from my
own plight; from the storms, the billows, the sailors' shouts and the
rock-bound Northern shore, a physiognomy and colour.' It was only
when he absorbed his conceptions so as actually to *become* them that
he was able to bring them to dramatic reality, usually with a mastery
which illustrates the truth that the personal achievements which are
hardest won are often the finest honed. Accordingly Wagner ended up
the supreme artist of dramatic psychology.

Even so, Wagner's understanding of people in ordinary life was
erratic to the end of his days, and he could leave them bewildered
and angry that he could utterly charm them with his quickness of
sympathy, only for them soon to meet a wall of self-absorption and
blank indifference. The conductor Heinrich Dorn, who had helped
him when he was young, later wrote,[105]

104 'A Communication to my Friends' (1851), in *Prose Works*, vol. i, tr. William Ashton Ellis, London, 1892.

105 Dorn, Heinrich, *Aus meinem Leben*, Berlin, 1870-77, quoted in Newman, Ernest, *The Life of Richard Wagner*, London & New York, 1932, vol. i. Heinrich Dorn was another of those intriguing characters who intermittently waft across Wagner's life like vapour trails. Dorn first met Wagner at the age of seventeen, when Kapellmeister at the Leipzig theatre. Dorn was probably trying to do a favour both to Wagner himself and to Wagner's popular sister when he put on Wagner's Overture in B flat major as part of a concert on Christmas Day 1830, but Wagner afterwards thought he was making sport of his inexpert composition and aiming for a laugh at his expense. Dorn next turned up in Wagner's life at Riga in 1839, shortly before his appointment as Wagner's replacement as Kapellmeister there, which was in truth the consequence of Wagner's mountainous debts. The theatre management was acting out of circumspect concern that Wagner's debts would lead to his sudden

One gross and ugly failing, of which Wagner has always been guilty, no one can pardon in him; and this failing is so much the worse because it cannot be granted in a man's character, but because the actions resulting from it were done deliberately, just as by deliberation they might have been avoided. I refer to the cold, heartless ingratitude that Wagner has always exhibited. I will here mention only the names of King Friedrich August in Dresden, Meyerbeer in Paris, Wesendonck in Zurich, Bülow in Munich.

People around Wagner could feel like cast-offs and rejects, a feeling backed up by his compulsion to believe himself a self-made man who owed nothing to anybody. This compulsion made him disavow his mentors and disparage his supporters. However, Dorn was wrong about Wagner's heartlessness, because, although he could indeed exhibit a remarkable ingratitude, his capacity for gratitude was just as remarkable.

A gratitude which he struggled to express adequately is evident in his letter to Liszt dated 20 February 1849. 'At once,' writes Wagner, 'after arriving at Weimar, you set to work so that your much tried friend might get on a little. You did not talk or fuss; you yourself undertook the unaccustomed task of teaching my work [*Tannhäuser*] to the people. Be sure that no one knows so well as I what it costs to bring such a work to light in existing circumstances.'[106] Nor was this just a private matter. In his autobiographical sketch of 1851, Wagner

flight, as indeed happened; but even so Dorn's wife and Wagner's were on friendly terms for much of their time together in Riga. Wagner used to play them large chunks of his new opera *Rienzi*, and even discussed ideas that Dorn's wife should play the opera's crucial role of Adriano. Dorn had made it to Berlin by the time *Tannhäuser* was on the boards there, and then, in 1871, as reported by Ernest Newman, he was nettled when Wagner visited Berlin and stated that Dorn, now one of the three Berlin Kapellmeisters, 'should have learned how to conduct, for he saw me conduct in Riga 30 years ago, but he *hasn't* learned'. It was in 1877, the year after the first Bayreuth Festival and six years after Wagner's withering comments, that Dorn wrote of Wagner's ingratitude.

106 *Correspondence of Wagner and Liszt*, tr. Francis Hueffer, New York, 1889.

told the world, 'I thought everything was at an end with my artistic creativeness. From this state of dejection I was raised by a friend. By the most evident and undeniable proofs he made me feel that I was most deeply understood even by those who were otherwise most distant from me; in this way he gave me back my fullest artistic confidence. This wonderful friend has been to me Franz Liszt.' Wagner's sketch then declares in the most glowing and generous terms all that Liszt had done for him, as was Liszt's due. Liszt had shown unfailing goodness towards the strange genius which providence had thrown across his path, and Wagner soon went on to exploit that goodness ruthlessly. But the most hardened cynic could not justifiably deny the genuine gratitude which streams out from page after page of Wagner's letters to Liszt. It is clear that he adored Liszt; he loved Liszt.

Sadly the relationship was to sour. While Liszt's belief in Wagner's immense genius never faltered, it was blighted by his growing awareness of Wagner's equally immense faults. There were several convoluted reasons why Wagner's attitude to Liszt began to seem like Dorn's 'heartless ingratitude', and they were indeed related to that 'curious and demonic habit of his, of wounding people'.

There was another unwitting compulsion at work in Wagner, and it is instructive to recognise that his situation with Liszt was weirdly similar to the one with Meyerbeer. Ten years separated Wagner's encounters with the two men but he grovelled to both in identical terms. On 3 May 1840, he wrote to Meyerbeer asking him for money and for recommendations of his operas.

I have reached the point of having to sell myself, in order to obtain help in the most material sense of the word. But my head and my heart are no longer mine to give away, – they are your property, my master; – the most that is left for me is my two hands, – do you wish to make use of them? I realise that I must become your slave, body and soul … I shall be a loyal and willing slave, – for I openly admit that I am a slave by nature; it gives me endless pleasure to be able to devote myself unconditionally to another person recklessly and in blind trust

... Buy me, therefore, Sir, ... some fr.2500 will help me to survive next winter; – will you lend this sum to me? ... Here I am; here is the head, the heart and here the hands of your property, Richard Wagner.[107]

Meyerbeer responded by doing everything he could to help Wagner, writing to Baron von Lüttichau, the Intendant at Dresden, 'Herr R. Wagner is a young composer who has not only a sound musical training but also much imagination and the general musical culture; ... Some sections [of *Rienzi*] that he played to me I found full of fantasy and of considerable dramatic effect. May the young artist be able to rejoice in the protection of your Excellency, and find an opportunity to see his fine talent more generally recognised.' The consequent staging of *Rienzi* was one of the supreme triumphs of Wagner's life, transforming his prospects overnight, and Meyerbeer was instrumental in bringing it about. Wagner abased himself before Liszt in the same way; he benefited from Liszt in the same way, from Liszt's money and Liszt's promotion of his works, and he would never forgive either of these two men. Worse, he was never in the end able to forgive Minna, before whom he had also grovelled, in much the same self-abasing fashion. He avenged himself on the hands which fed him by sinking in his teeth into them like a werewolf. He persecuted Meyerbeer, and as for Liszt, who had not only championed Wagner's works but made him extensive gifts and loans which he seldom saw again, Wagner was to abuse him and his music so virulently to Cosima, Wagner's second wife and Liszt's daughter, that it could reduce her to tears. However, such unattractive behaviour was not something which Wagner chose to exhibit deliberately, but the result of the twists and the torsions which childhood and life had forged in him.

If he was erratic and ungrateful, he could be just as erratically generous, for example at Christmas 1863 when he was in Vienna and was paying interest on credit at a disgraceful 300%. Friends who visited him and knew of his dire financial situation found presents of

107 *Selected Letters of Richard Wagner*, ed. and tr. Stewart Spencer and Barry Millington, London, 1987, pp. 68-9.

a squanderous extravagance awaiting them, and they were driven as frantic at his folly as they were hopelessly, irritably touched by it. 'The mad Wagner,' said the composer Peter Cornelius in a letter to his sister Susanne of 11 January 1864, 'had a great Christmas tree with a royally rich table beneath it for me. Just imagine; a marvellous heavy overcoat – and elegant grey dressing gown – a red scarf, a blue cigar case and tinderbox – lovely silk handkerchiefs, splendid gold shirt-studs – the *Struwelpeter* – elegant pen wipers with gold mottos – fine cravats, a meerschaum cigar-holder with his initials – in short, all sorts of things only an oriental imagination could think of.'[108] This was for Cornelius alone; and Wagner treated his other friends just as liberally. In *Mein Leben* he tells us, 'Having very little ready money but solid hopes, I could now greet my few friends with tolerable good humour … On Christmas Eve, I invited them to my house, where I had the Christmas tree lighted up and gave each of them *an appropriate trifle*.'[109]

Wagner never stopped falling into trouble because of his reckless generosity; Cosima's *Diaries* later record her worries over an instance in Naples when he 'rescued a poor boy from a difficult situation – the boy was carrying some pictures on his head and dropped them, breaking the glass.'[110] Wagner gave him some money to help meet the damage, but at first he could not make the boy understand, and by the time he succeeded, a crowd of feral children had gathered, and he was almost mobbed by 'a whole swarm of beggars, so that he had to fight his way out'. It was much the same when the sculptor Gustav Adolph Kietz was at Bayreuth creating twin busts for Cosima and Wagner (the same Kietz as had once enjoyed Wagner and Minna's comic turns at Dresden, as we shall see in connection with Minna). Kietz was out walking with Wagner when they saw a lad running through the wet streets barefoot, obviously too poor for shoes. Wagner said 'I hate this,' and impulsively pulled out a thaler, a lot of money, and gave

108 Newman, Ernest, *Wagner as Man and Artist*, London, 1924, p. 132.

109 *My Life, authorized translation* …, New York, 1911, ii, p. 879 (amended; my italics).

110 Wagner, Cosima, *Diaries*, 18 February 1880.

it away. Cosima's *Diaries* are peppered with descriptions of similar events during their walks round Bayreuth. Ungrateful Wagner may sometimes have been, and lavish, but he was not ungenerous.

He did believe that the world should support him. He held the conviction that that he deserved freely the resources which were conducive to the creation of masterpieces. How otherwise could he achieve the wondrous offerings to humanity which he alone could provide? He was close to ruin in 1864 and staying at his friends the Willes' house in Switzerland when Eliza Wille recorded him as saying: 'Mine is a different kind of organism, I have sensitive nerves, I must have beauty, radiance and light. The world owes me a living! I can't live the miserable life of an organist like your master Bach! Is it such an outrageous demand to say that I deserve the little bit of luxury that I need? I, who can give pleasure to thousands?'[III]

It may have been raging egoism, but it was also the simple truth. As that titan among conductors, Wilhelm Furtwängler said in his essay, *The Case of Wagner: Against Nietzsche*, it was not reasonable to expect ordinary behaviour from Wagner 'because the man who had *Tristan und Isolde* in his drawer was not an ordinary man'. It is poignant that the resources Wagner needed never flowed freely enough, even after his rescue by King Ludwig of Bavaria, shortly after his stay at the Willes.

He still had to fight his way, underfunded, through sloughs of indifference, but also through envy and hostility; and these were very real, not figments of an over-heated imagination. Wagner may have been paranoid, but he had plenty to be paranoid about. For instance, the Belgian critic Fétis may have disliked Wagner, but that was no reason to try and prejudice the French-speaking world by telling everyone, in print, the lie that *Tannhäuser* had been a miserable failure at Dresden and had been taken off after only four performances. And Wagner did not always have the ability to perceive how readily he laid himself open to attack. He gives us an instance when he tells us 'nothing did more harm than a remark which I made in an address to the performers

---

III   In Spencer, Stewart, ed., *Wagner Remembered*, London, 2000, p. 157.

at the beginning of the dress rehearsal [of *Rienzi* in Berlin] when I described the excessive demands made by *Rienzi* as "an art-crime of my youth".' Unsurprisingly, 'the reporters served this to the public steaming hot ... as a work which the composer himself had described as "a miserable failure",' whereupon they all wrote as if 'its presentation in Berlin was an effrontery that cried out for punishment'.[112] The result of such hostility was that Wagner developed hard armour and bitter weapons, a biting pen of his own. As so often with Wagner, adversity gave rise to a talent. It was during his first visit to Paris that the threat of penury taught him to write for publication, but it was the desire to pay back his critics with interest that sharpened his pen later. This was not something that endeared him to the press. After the foundation-stone was laid for his Bayreuth Festival Theatre in 1872, then

scarcely had the report of the occasion been published when a veritable storm burst forth in almost the entire press of Germany and Austria – unbelievable abuse, invective, ridicule, hostility, slander and the like, all aimed at Wagner and his Bayreuth project. The powerful opposition, originating largely in Munich, but soon spreading everywhere, stopped at nothing in the violence of its malicious campaign. It was then that a self styled psychiatrist published the 'proof of Wagner's insanity' – without even meeting him. Others attacked him because of the nature of his morals, his artistic theories, his connection with the King of Bavaria, his music, everything, in short which could be pounced upon as a means of denouncing him and his Bayreuth project.[113]

This account was not from Wagner, displaying the irrational sense of persecution commonly attributed to him, but from Elbert Lenrow, a long-headed American writing in 1932, giving a considered retrospect on far-off events after he had gathered and sifted his facts.[114] Furtwängler,

---

112 'A Communication to my Friends', p. 349.

113 *The Letters of Richard Wagner and Anton Pusinelli*, tr. Elbert Lenrow, New York, 1932 (repr. 1972), p. 252 (commentary by Lenrow).

114 Elbert Lenrow was editor of *The Letters of Richard Wagner to Anton Pus-*

who not only lived close to these events but then investigated them with scholarly rigour, said the same of this press outcry. No wonder that Wagner was a pugnacious fighter; he had to be.

It helps towards appreciating Wagner's great dramas to understand the flavour of his personality, and Nietzsche, the great German philosopher, was one of those who provided some idea of what he was like to meet. Nietszche described him as 'a marvellously lively and fiery man, who speaks very fast, is very witty, and certainly livens up a private gathering.'[115] Nietzsche wrote this in 1868 after his first introduction to Wagner at Leipzig, a meeting which soon resulted in Nietzsche's regular visits to Wagner at Tribschen in Switzerland, about which he wrote the words quoted at the heading of this chapter: 'What I learn and see there, what I see and understand is indescribable.' Twenty years earlier, August Röckel had been just as impressed. Röckel was a conductor from Weimar who was installed as Wagner's deputy in Dresden shortly after Wagner's appointment as Kapellmeister on 2 February, 1843. Röckel wrote of Wagner, 'You cannot imagine how daily intercourse with him develops my admiration for his genius.'[116] For Röckel, Wagner was one 'whose greatness overshadows that of all other men I met'. Eduard Devrient[117] was another Dresden colleague

---

inelli, New York, 1932. His editorial and biographical notes are a model of sanity and objectivity; he could deplore a mixture of condescension and deceit in Wagner's autobiography 'whose chief purpose seems to be to repay everyone he knew for real or fancied wrongs done to him,' but still recognise how when it came to Wagner's ideals and aspirations and press reaction, the response was venomous.

115 Spencer, *Wagner Remembered*, p. 188.
116 Kohler, Joachim, *Richard Wagner: The Last of the Titans*, tr. Stewart Spencer, New Haven and London, 2004, p. 182.
117 *Aus seinen Tagebüchern*, ed. Rolf Kabel, Weimar, 1964, in Spencer, *Wagner Remembered*. A note by Stewart Spencer records that Edward Devrient began his professional career as a singer, and that he took the role of Christus in Mendelssohn's 1829 revival of J.S. Bach's *St Matthew Passion*. He was two years older than Wagner and joined the Dresden Court Theatre in 1844, two years after Wagner, but dissension followed

whose diary records an exasperated respect for Wagner. He was irritated by Wagner's politics: 'He wants to destroy in order to rebuild;[118] I want to transform what already exists.' But he continued, 'There's no doubt that he has the best mind of anyone I know in Dresden.'

Of great interest too is Ferdinand Praeger's description of Wagner's London sojourn in 1855.

Wagner arrived at midnight precisely on Sunday, the fifth of March. If I had not already acquired through the graphic letters of August Röckel an insight into the peculiarities of Richard Wagner's habits of thought, his power of grasping profound questions of mental speculation whilst relieving the severity of serious discourse by the intermingling of jocular ebullitions of fancy, I was soon to have a fair specimen of these wondrous qualities. One of many points at which we found ourselves at home, was his habit of citing phrases from Schiller or Goethe, as applicable to our subject of discussion, as often ironically as seriously. To these he added an almost interminable dictionary of quotations from the plays and operas of the early part of the century. These mental links were, in the course of a long and intimate friendship, augmented by references to striking qualities, defects, or oddities, our circle of acquaintances forming a means of communication between us which might not inaptly be likened to a mental shorthand. Nothing could have exceeded the hilarity, when upon showing him, at an advanced hour, to his bedroom, he enthusiastically said, 'August (Röckel) was right; we shall understand each other thoroughly!'[119]

---

when Devrient moved to a post as Theaterintendant for the Archduke of Karlsruhe and Wagner thought him insufficiently eager to promote either the staging of *Tristan* there or the extraction of money for Wagner from the Archduke.

118 A direct reference to Proudhon's '*Destruam et aedificabo*' which appeared as the motto at the beginning of one of his books. Proudhon was much in the air at Dresden.

119 Praeger, Ferdinand, *Wagner as I Knew Him*, London, 1892. Praeger was listed by Wagner first among his London acquaintances; he was a German composer, pianist, and musical litterateur. Two years younger than

Praeger soon formed a very positive impression of Wagner's qualities as a comedian and mimic, 'a born actor, and it was impossible not to recognise immediately who is the individual caricatured, for Wagner's power of observation led him at all times to notice the most minute characteristics in all whom he encountered. A repast in his society might well be described as a "feast of reason and a flow of the soul", for, mixed in odd ways were the most solid remarks of deep, logical intuition with the sprightliest, frolicsome humour.' Praeger was less enthusiastic about Wagner's 'Vesuvius-like temper', or his 'mad habits' when confronting the London traffic. 'In the matter of crossing a crowded thoroughfare his intrepidity bordered close upon the reckless. He would go straight across the road; safe on the other side, he was almost boyish in his laugh at the nervousness of others. But this was Wagner. It was this deliberate attacking of everything that made him what he was; timorousness was not in his character; dauntless fearlessness, perhaps not under proper control, naturally gave birth to an iconoclast, who struck with vigour at all opposition, heedless of destroying the Penates worshipped by others.' Praeger was quite frank with Wagner over some of his faults; 'He sang and what singing it was! It was, as I told him then, just like the barking of a big, Newfoundland dog. He laughed heartily and kept on nevertheless. He cared not. Yet

Wagner, he settled in London in 1834 and did a great deal to smooth the way for Wagner in London when he conducted the Old Philharmonic Society's concerts season in 1855. He put Wagner up on the night of his arrival, and saw him at least seventeen times during Wagner's London stay, visiting Gravesend and Brighton and going to the theatre together to see the pantomime *Mother Goose*. It is fashionable but wrong to write off Praeger as an unreliable witness. It was Cosima and her Bayreuth acolytes who gained acceptance for this glass-house judgment of Praeger, but they would stop at almost nothing to discredit him (as William Ashton Ellis did in his introduction to his translation of Wagner's letters to Mathilde Wesendonck). They particularly wanted to discredit the picture of real Wagner, the left-wing revolutionary, whom Praeger was preserving, whereas Cosima was posthumously turning Wagner into a right-wing nationalist – and in the long term doing him no good at all.

though his "singing" was but howling, he sang with his whole heart and held you, as it were, spellbound.'

Praeger was more serious in his criticism of Wagner's smoking habits, which he described as barbarous; moreover it was 'a practice, which as he was fully aware, increased the malignity of his terrible dyspepsia'. Praeger was unusually perceptive in grasping how far Wagner's trying idiosyncrasies were tied to his physical condition and bad health. 'There was in Wagner a nervous excitability which not infrequently led to an outburst of passion which it would be difficult to understand or explain, were it not that there existed a positive physical cause. First, he suffered as I have stated earlier from occasional attacks of erysipelas.'

Then his nervous system [Praeger continues,] is delicate and sensitive, nay, I should say, irritable. Spasmodic displays of temper were often the result, I firmly feel, of purely physical suffering. His skin was so sensitive that he wore silk next to his body, and that at a time when he was not favoured of fortune. We went together to a fashionable tailor in Regent Street, where he ordered that his pockets and the back of his vest should be of silk, as also the lining of his frockcoat sleeves; Wagner could not endure the touch of cotton, as it produced a shuddering sensation throughout the body that distressed him. I remember well the tailor's surprise and explanation that silk for the back of the vest and lining of the sleeves was not at all necessary; it was not seen. This last observation brought Wagner up to one of his indignant outbursts, 'Never seen! Yes; that's the tendency of this century; sham, sham in everything; that which is not seen may be paltry and mean provided only the exterior be richly gilded.'

Further revealing impressions come from Edouard Schuré, the French man of letters, shortly after *Tristan und Isolde* had been premiered.[120] His portrait of Wagner is cast in a very literary style, but it is still illuminating and convincing.

120 Schuré, Edouard, *Richard Wagner: son oeuvre et son idée*, Paris, 1933, tr. in Spencer, *Wagner Remembered*.

I opened the iron gate, rang the doorbell and was admitted by a mulatto servant, who ushered me into a small salon decorated with dark wall hangings, luxurious rugs, paintings and statuettes barely visible in the mysterious half-light. At that very moment, a curtain parted, and the Master appeared. A powerful hand gripped mine, and I found myself face to face with the composer of *Tristan und Isolde*. He looked tired, and his smile consisted of no more than a slight contraction of his lips. His words tumbled out, coming in fits and starts. After we had exchanged compliments, his first words were: 'Your letter gave me immense pleasure. I showed it to the King and told him, "You see, everything is not lost."'

'What?' I exclaimed, 'How could everything be lost after the miracle of these performances? The press is against you, but the public is with you …'

'Don't you believe it' he broke in at once. 'They understand nothing. When a Frenchman shows his enthusiasm, good, then there's no stopping him. But the Germans aren't the same. If by chance they are moved, they start to ask if their feelings accord with their philosophy and they go and consult Hegel's *Logic* or Kant's *Critique of Pure Reason*, or else they write ten volumes to prove that they were not moved and could not have been. Ah! This public, this press, these critics, you see, it's unbelievably wretched. It doesn't exist.'

'So you're not satisfied?'

'Satisfied?' he sprang up, his eyes flashing. 'Satisfied! Yes, when I have my theatre, only then will people understand me. But for the present, I feel only exasperation, and you find me in a state of extreme irritation.'

He threw himself on the divan with his head back. He seemed to be genuinely in pain; a yellowish colour and an expression of fatigue suffused his features. But his trembling lips and feverish volubility bespoke an energy and a will that was always ready to reassert itself. The light from the window fell directly on his head and I was finally able to examine it in detail.

Wagner was then fifty-two years old. It was impossible to see this magician's head, evocative and subjugatory, and not retain an indelible impression of it. What a life of bitter struggles and tumultuous emotions lay in these troubled, furrowed features, in this sunken mouth whose thin lips were both sensuous and sardonic and in this pointed chin that signalled an indomitable will. And in this mask that concealed a daemonic drive, this vast beetling brow that told of power and audacity. Yes, this ravaged face bore the traces of passions and sufferings capable of wearing down the lives of many men. But one also felt that this immense brain which laboured constantly beneath his brow had tamed life's baser matter and reduced it to substance for the intellect. In these blue eyes, dimmed with listlessness or flashing with desire, eyes that always seemed to see an immutable goal, there was one constant vision that dominated all others and lent them what I can only call an eternal virginity; it was a vision of an ideal, the pride and divine dream of genius!

To observe Wagner's head was to see one after the other, and in a single face, both Faust and Mephistopheles, the former viewed from the front, the latter in profile. There were other times when he resembled a fallen angel, brooding on heaven and saying; 'It does not exist, but I shall create it.'

In a word, this man impressed me less by his prodigious abilities and astonishing contrasts than by his formidable concentration and his marvellous unity of thought and will that was forever directed at a single goal.

His manner was no less surprising than his physical appearance, changing as it did between reserve and absolute coldness on the one hand, and, on the other a familiarity and unceremoniousness that could hardly have been more complete. There was no trace of the poseur about him, not a vestige of affected solemnity, no sense of deliberation or calculation. As soon as he appeared, he burst forth like a flood-tide that nothing can stem. One was left dazzled by his exuberance and protean nature, a nature, moreover, that was passionate, private, extreme in everything and yet marvellously balanced by his all-consuming intellect. The frankness and extreme daring of a character whose qualities and faults were plain for all to see had the effect of a spell on some, but served only to repulse others. His conversation was a constant spectacle as every thought found a corresponding action. On this vast brow, ideas and sentiments succeeded each other like flashes of lightning, no two of which were the same. He bore within him all his great heroes. Within minutes one could see in the expression on his face the Dutchman's black despair, Tannhäuser's unbridled desire, Lohengrin's unapproachable pride, Hagen's glacial irony and Alberich's rage. Oh. what a strange whirl of emotions one felt on peering into this brain. And dominating all these characters there were two that revealed themselves almost always simultaneously, like the two poles of his nature, Wotan and Siegfried! Yes, on the deepest level of his thinking, Wagner resembled Wotan, this German Jupiter, this Scandinavian Odin, whom he created in his own image, a strange god, a philosopher and pessimist, forever troubled by the end of the world, forever wandering and brooding on the enigma of all things. But in his impulsiveness, he resembled Siegfried more than anyone else, the strong and ingenuous hero who knows neither fear nor scruples, forging a sword for himself and setting out to conquer the world. The miracle is that these two different characters were merged as one. The result was the constant union of profound reflection and ebullient spontaneity. With him, excessive thinking had not dulled his vital spark, and whatever life's vicissitudes, he never ceased to philosophise, combining a calculating metaphysical intellect with the joy and eternal youth of a truly creative temperament.

His highest spirits overflowed into a joyous froth of acts of sheer buffoonery and eccentric jokes, but the least contradiction provoked unprecedented anger. Then he was like a caged lion, roaring like a wild animal, pacing the room, his voice growing hoarse, the words coming out like cries, his words striking at random. He then seemed like an unleashed force of nature, a volcano erupting. But, withal, there were outbursts of ardent sympathy, expressions of touching pity, excessive tenderness for the men he saw suffering, for animals and even for plants. This man of violence could not bear to see a caged bird; a cut flower made him blanch, and when he found a sick dog in the street, he had it brought home. Everything about him was larger-than-life.

Schuré's enthralled attachment to Wagner survived the Franco-
Prussian war when he proved as stridently nationalistic for the French,
crowing over their initial victories, as Wagner was for the Germans.

We saw in the Introduction how Wagner altered and evolved, but
his charisma and magnetism were constants. Eduard Hanslick, the
Viennese music critic who was an initial enthusiast and then grew
violently away from Wagner, hit the mark in his obituary:

> He exercised an incomprehensible magic in order to make friends and to
> retain them; friends who sacrificed themselves for him, and, three times
> offended came three times back to him again. The more ingratitude
> they received from Wagner, the more zealously they thought it their
> duty to work for him. The hypnotic power he everywhere exerted, not
> merely by his music but by his personality, overbearing all opposition
> and bending everyone to his will, is enough to stamp him as one of the
> most remarkable of phenomena, a marvel of energy and endowment.[121]

Hanslick's point about Wagner mesmerising people was borne out
by Hans von Bülow (and indeed Otto Wesendonck). Bülow hero-
worshipped Wagner, and never gave up, but no one had greater
experience of Wagner's repellent side. Bülow was Wagner's ideal
conductor and conducted the premieres of *Tristan* and *Die Meistersinger*;
and yet the next chapter presents an account of Wagner stealing the
affections and the person of Bülow's wife (and appropriating his two
daughters). Wagner was fully aware of the damage he did, a damage
so devastating that it eventually caused Bülow a nervous breakdown.
That was in December 1882 and the damage was still fresh even
though Cosima had left Bülow for Wagner in 1868. In 1869, Bülow
had written to her,

> Since you left me, I have lost my sole support in life and in my struggle.
> It was your mind, your heart, your patience, indulgence, sympathy,

---

121 Quoted and translated in Newman, *Wagner as Man and Artist*.

encouragement and advice – last and most especially, your presence, your face, and your speech – which, taken all together, constituted that support. The loss of this supreme good, whose full value I recognise only after its loss, has brought about moral and artistic collapse – I am a bankrupt. My suffering is so great that I may permit myself to express it since I abstain from accusing anyone of being the author of it but myself.[122]

And a few lines later he went on, almost unbelievably, to tell Cosima, 'You have preferred to devote your life and the treasures of your mind and affection to one who is my superior, and, far from blaming you, I approve.' Bülow even asserted later that the nineteenth century had produced only three great men, Napoleon, Bismarck and Wagner, and he made endless tours conducting concerts and giving piano recitals to raise money for the theatre at Bayreuth and the festival. Bülow could never attend it himself, because he never wanted to set eyes on Wagner again.

Ernest Newman was another knowledgeable person who maintained a lifelong admiration for Wagner. Although he maintained a mordant approach to Wagner's faults, he kept a sense of balance. One of his earlier books on Wagner, *Wagner as Man and Artist* (1914, rev. 1924), was a landmark in peeling back the whitewash and exposing Wagner's shabbiness, for example, in the 'Jessie Laussot affair'. This was after the Dresden uprising of 1849 had been put down and when Wagner, deeply disturbed and unstable, had his lunatic idea of sailing off with her to the Orient. Ernest Newman's awareness of Wagner's shabby side – and worse – did not stop him from seeing Wagner in the round; and Newman's final assessment was an admiration bordering on awe:

The stupendous power and the inexhaustible vitality of the man are shown in nothing more clearly than the sacrifices everyone made for him and the tyrannies they endured from him ... There is something titanic in the man who can inspire such hatred and such love, and

122 *Letters of Hans von Bülow*, tr. (from the French) Scott Goddard, New York, 1972; von Bülow to Cosima, 17 June, 1869.

such love to overpower the hatred in the end ... He was indeed, in the mixture of elements he contained, like nothing else that has been seen on earth ... What a man! one exclaims in amazement. What belief in himself, in his strength, in his destiny! ... What a sublime confidence! ... Was there anything like it outside fiction?

We can be critical today, but we have no reason to be ungrateful for the strange qualities which Providence had synthesised in Wagner. Anyone reading *Mein Leben* or Cosima's *Diaries* is bound to recognise that Wagner's virtues included vitality, energy, quickness of intellect and sympathy (albeit fitfully) as well as idealism, passion and courage, all qualities which colour his creations. Along with these went other qualities less glamorous, above all a staggering capacity for sheer, dogged, unrelenting hard work, powered by his restless, obsessive energies. When Wagner was gripped by an idea he could be overbearing and utterly unreasonable, but some of his worst examples, when he drove others without consideration, reflect the extent to which he was then most driven himself. His enthusiasms left him no peace. Ernest Newman provides a helpful example of an enthusiasm turned into an obsession.[123] The year was 1850; Wagner was in Swiss exile, and on 16 September he had taken a 'water cure' for his besetting health problems, which, as Newman reminds us, included fevers, giddiness, physical and mental malaise, chronic indigestion and constipation, bacterial skin infections and non-resolving shingles. His 'murderous cure' as he later described it made him no better, but worsened his problems by leaving him terribly emaciated and weak. Ernest Newman described how Wagner at the time tried to persuade himself and everyone else that his water cure had made a new man of him.

His constitutional reluctance to admit that he could be in error on any subject made him, on his return to Zürich, do all he could to convince his friends (perhaps as the best way of convincing himself) of the

---

123 Newman, Ernest, *The Life of Richard Wagner*, New York, 1937, ii, p. 274.

superlative merits of water as a means to health. On 24th November, he and Minna gave a party to celebrate the anniversary of their wedding. He was very much annoyed at the hearty way in which Sulzer and the others indulged their carnal appetite for wine and beer that evening; and for weeks afterwards, he argued with his friends about the effects of strong liquors, with such vehemence on both sides that they often came near quarrelling. He had, as he says in *Mein Leben*, adopted a sort of new religion – and there is no fanatic like a religious fanatic, unless it be a health fanatic. He could not deny that wine in moderation produces an exhilaration that was well worth having for its own pleasant sake, helps its devotees to bear the burden of existence, and unlocks the chambers of the imagination: but, he argued, as against Sulzer and Herwegh, that for his 'spiritual intoxication, regenerate man should look not to the juice of the grape but to love'.

Ernest Newman then quoted Wagner's words from *Mein Leben*:

The more closely my friends studied my condition, the more occasion they had to be anxious about my strange and obstinate extravagances. I was exceedingly pale and thin; I hardly slept at all, and showed an alarming excitement in everything I did. But although sleep eventually forsook me almost entirely, I stuck to it that I had never been so well and cheerful in my life: I went on with my cold baths on the coldest winter mornings – to the torment of my wife, who had to lead me out with a lantern for the walk that had to follow.

It was only his friend Sulzer's good nature and good sense that prevented a breach between them because of the arguments which raged over Wagner's 'doctrine of salvation by water'. After one of those arguments, Sulzer offered the reasonable view that 'it was useless to quarrel about matters which neither of them understood'. Wagner resented this hotly and even more another remark from Sulzer that he, Richard Wagner, was inclined to dogmatise about matters where he had no professional knowledge. Wagner wrote that he feared that

Sulzer's obstinacy could lead to a rupture. He, Wagner, 'would be unable to exchange the completest and most sympathetic relations which they had previously enjoyed for a mere acquaintance,' and if Sulzer could not see the matter Wagner's way, it 'must lead to the final and serious consequence of my leaving my Zürich refuge'.

Ernest Newman pointed to this episode as a perfect example of 'Wagner's inability to understand how anyone sensible could think differently from him on any subject and the intellectual tyranny he tried to exercise over others'. However it was because of these uncompromising aspects in Wagner's make up that he won in 'the most terrific conflict that any artist has ever had to wage with the world', as Nietzsche aptly described it when still sympathetic to Wagner. Without his exuberance, his obdurate conviction and his determination to get his own way in the matters small and great, he could never have achieved what he did.

The odd thing was that Wagner's 'self-will run riot' must be set against the dimension of compassion, quietism and serenity which found expression in *Parsifal*. He never lost his egoism and his manic belief in himself, but his growing interest in denial of the will and compassion were in contrast to the hedonism and instant gratification which had been his battle-cry when a Young German in the Laube mould, and which he never entirely gave up. This opposition and tension of opposites was why he could tell Liszt, 'I can live only in extremes – great activity and excitement and – most perfect calm.'[124]

It was not any injunctions from parent-figures or others in authority that brought his sea-change to compassion and quietism, but his own growing awareness that the unbridled unleashing of the passions created pain and suffering for others and even for the unleasher. In his art he formulated morality as a resource which could both resolve the internal conflicts in a new integration, and also create a better social order. It was a morality which only slowly coalesced, and it formed part of a long road, the road that ended in *Parsifal*.

----

124   *Correspondence of Wagner and Liszt*, i, p. 269, letter of 4 March 1853.

This summary view of Wagner's character would be incomplete without something from his son Siegfried about Wagner as a parent and about family life with Wagner. Both Wagner himself and Cosima were such driven, damaged personalities that it is remarkable that they could avoid the common phenomenon of repetition compulsion. Instead of visiting the same mistakes on their offspring from a belief that their own damage had made him the fine figures that they were, they provided happy childhoods for their children, allowing them mental space and creative freedom. This enabled Siegfried to grow up into a benign and non-obsessive personality, quite unlike his parents. Wagner thought he might become a surgeon or an architect, but he grew up to be a musician and an opera composer like his father. He was a lasting testimonial to all that his parents gave him, and he has left us a simple and uncontrived description of his life as a child.[125]

Happy the man who has a carefree childhood. No frost or tempest in later life can dispel the warmth that the sunbeams of a happy infancy can bring to a human soul. Such a childhood as that was enjoyed by myself and my sisters, and for that we are eternally grateful to our parents. Their aim was to bring us up as happy, true human beings. Sombre faces were not allowed. If my sisters had to slave over written homework and the sun tempted them outside, I was soon sent to my parents: 'Papa', I would call, 'I am all on my own and have no one to play with. Can't my sisters come into the garden?' And within moments all five of us were romping in the garden. In this way, the educational principles of my mother, who had been brought up entirely according to the rules of the *ancien regime*, were often thwarted by those of my father; but genial by nature, she finally acquiesced in these disruptions to her plans. Even afternoon visits to the cake shop – our greatest pleasure was to go to Lavena's famous coffee shop in Venice – even these she agreed to when she saw what pleasure it gave my father to treat us with sweets. As a result we were not unduly troubled by lessons. Our beautiful garden at

125 Spencer, *Wagner Remembered*, pp. 271 et seq.

Wahnfried was our school, our school friends were dogs, hens, canaries and also, I think, salamanders and frogs which, hidden in cupboards, were supposed to feel at home, though they would no doubt have felt even more at home in water.

I have only a vague recollection of the first important event of my childhood, the laying of the foundation stone at the Festspielhaus in 1872. My family told me that I had been exceptionally well behaved. When I was asked what I had understood of the festival address, I answered: 'German men, good men!' ... Of decisive influence on my whole development were our repeated trips to Italy. Tired of the everlasting grey skies of Germany – I remember my father shaking his clenched fists at the clouds and shouting 'Those damned potato sacks!' – he crossed the Alps with his whole family and with the generous support of King Ludwig II, in order to forget his cares and troubles, even if only for a time, and to enjoy the sun, the visual arts and the carefree life of the Italians. Our first such journey was made possible not only by the King's help, but also by the fee for his Festival March which had just arrived and which was very generous by the standards of the time. Following the first [Bayreuth] Festival, which although a brilliant artistic success, proved a financial disaster, our journey took us via Verona, Venice and Bologna to Rome and Naples ... My happiest memory of this period was the performance of my father's early symphony to mark my mother's birthday. It was the third time I had seen him conduct. A few years previously, also on my mother's birthday, it had been Beethoven's A Major Symphony and movements from the F Major, which he conducted at Wahnfried with the Meiningen Orchestra.

The portraits in this chapter make it easier to comprehend Wagner, and confirm the maxim that a man may be known by his friends. No friends reveal as much about a man as his women friends, and no other woman revealed as much about Wagner as his first wife, Minna. She did more; she partly created him, and to explain why her impact was so drastic and extensive, she and her successors need the next chapter to themselves.

SEVEN

FEMME INSPIRATRICE, FEMME FATALE

Minna Wagner and her Successors

Of all the experiences which went into the making of Wagner, Minna Planer was the most far-reaching. Normally the foundations of personality are set fast at a younger age than Wagner had reached when she first blazed into his consciousness, but she had such a drastic effect, creating such a meltdown of his values, his outlook and his way of feeling, that she virtually configured him anew. The importance of her role is impossible to exaggerate, and yet it goes unrecognised. With too few of her letters in existence to colour in her personality, and fewer pen-portraits, the accepted view of Minna is strangely indeterminate. Alexander von Otterstedt's picture included in this book is appealing but too stylised to convey a real sense of what she was like. The prevailing impression of her in the Wagner literature is half misty, half negative; but then it mostly derives from Wagner's autobiography which is often unreliable, and from his published correspondence with her which has further reliability problems of its own. What undermines confidence in the idea of Minna presented in his autobiography is that he mostly composed it after she was dead; that it contains discrepancies with the few other sources which are available; and that he cannot quite hide how painful and embarrassing he found it to admit to his secretary that Minna had ever amounted to much. That secretary, sitting there and taking his dictation, was Cosima von Bülow, his latest romantic attachment and destined to become his second wife. There is something not entirely pleasant about the idea of Wagner declaiming disparagements of his dead, discarded wife for the ears of his approving, righteous mistress.

Wagner's official published correspondence with Minna is unreliable for different reasons, first because Minna's contribution is meagre. A one-sided correspondence is always less enlightening than something more balanced, as becomes very clear when we compare Wagner's published correspondence with Minna to that with his doctor, Anton Pusinelli.[126] Because this includes letters from Pusinelli as well, Wagner comes out of it not only more exposed but more interesting and likeable. A worse problem with Wagner's letters to Minna is again Cosima, because she acted as editor and censor of all Wagner's correspondence after he was dead. In this capacity she destroyed many letters and made cuts in others, so as to vilify Minna and sanctify Wagner as they were published.

We have too little that provides independent access to Minna's predicaments and inner worlds. There is nothing that enables her to 'stand before us' as Wagner does, and the notion of the tepid *Hausfrau* presented in *Mein Leben* is nutshelled in his words, 'I do not believe that Minna ever felt any sort of passion or genuine love for me … Her feeling for me was one of heartfelt goodwill, and the sincerest desire for my success and prosperity … without ever betraying any desire or ardour herself.' Fortunately for the truth, there *are* a few documentary sources over which Wagner and Cosima had no control. Above all there is the vital collection assembled by Mrs Mary Burrell, a Victorian collector of extraordinary determination, who sensed cover-ups and misrepresentations from Bayreuth and had a passion for the truth at all costs. Her major collection was eventually published[127]

126 *The Letters of Richard Wagner and Anton Pusinelli*, tr. Elbert Lenrow, New York, 1932 (repr. 1972). For Pusinelli, see below, p. 191n.
127 *The Letters of Richard Wagner, The Burrell Collection*, tr. Hans Abraham,

without tampering and it proves that 'tepid' was not precisely how it had been between Wagner and Minna.

That was not how it had been at all. Even from *Mein Leben*, it is plain that where they first met at Bad Lauchstädt in 1834, Minna dazzled him. He was there trying for a job. He had finished his studies with Weinlig in the spring of 1832, and begun to compose a large opera, *Die Feen*, completing it on 6 January 1833. Eleven days later on the 17th, he began a post as chorus master at the opera in Würzburg, where he stayed almost exactly a year, leaving on 15 January 1834. Back in Leipzig, he fell under the influence of Heinrich Laube, and early in that same summer, he made plans for his next opera, *Das Liebesverbot*, which reflected Laube's hedonism. In July he tried for the conductor's job with the theatre company of Magdeburg which put on both opera and straight plays. The company was giving a summer season at the spa town of Bad Lauchstädt, where Wagner duly applied, whereupon he discovered that his first task would be to conduct *Don Giovanni* the very next Sunday. To make matters more difficult, the regular orchestra were working to rule and refusing to play on Sunday, and he would have to make do with a scratch group of instrumentalists who had never played together before. Worse still, he would be doing it without rehearsal, and he decided to turn down the offer. What made him change his mind was the sight of Minna coming out of the lodging where he was to stay the night, and her membership of the Magdeburg company was the sole reason why he changed his mind, signed up for *Don Giovanni*, and took the Magdeburg directorship. His assurance is almost beyond belief, a 21-year-old who had never conducted anything before and was now cutting his teeth on one of

---

Henry Lea and Richard Stoehr, ed. John N. Burk, London, 1951. This volume does not consist exclusively of Wagner's letters but includes a great deal of invaluable background, such as the testimonies supplied by Natalie, Minna's daughter, to Mrs. Burrell herself. After Mrs Burrrell had gained Natalie's confidence and become her friend, Natalie talked a lot about what it was like to grow up as a child in Wagner's household.

the supreme achievements and challenges the operatic repertoire, and was doing so under such inauspicious circumstances. The date of that performance was 2 August 1834, and it was the prospect of Minna Planer that made him do it. Later he recollected her from that period merely as 'looking very charming and fresh,' but this does less than justice to her loveliness and style.

Minna was eye-catchingly beautiful, a sensation, far more stunning than any idea of her that Wagner himself provided, or any known portrait. Friedrich Pecht[128] first encountered the couple five years later in 1839 at the Louvre, and he described Minna's impact. He explains that in spite of Wagner's bizarre proportions, 'in spite of the fact that his legs were much too short,' he had 'such an extraordinarily pretty woman on his arm that she alone would have sufficed to make the couple interesting.' At Dresden in 1842, she made a similar impression on the ten-year-old Marie Heine[129] who later recalled: 'His wife, who was then very beautiful, conquered my heart with her friendly ways.' Further testimony to her beauty comes from an unlikely source, Eduard Hanslick, that same Hanslick who later became Wagner's most unrelenting critic. One of Hanslick's earliest forays into journalism was an interview with Wagner at Marienbad when Hanslick was barely twenty.[130] When Hanslick commended Wagner on Minna's beauty, Wagner said, 'Ah, she's scarcely recognisable now; you ought to have seen her a few years back! The poor thing had to go through much trouble and want with me in Paris.' In *Mein Leben* Wagner at least admitted that the young actress's 'general manner and

---

128   Another German artist trying his luck in Paris, where he became one of Wagner's most loyal companions.

129   Marie Heine, who became Marie Schmole after her marriage, had been ten when Wagner became a friend of the family. Her father was Ferdinand Heine, costume designer at the Dresden Court Theatre and one of the first to have faith in Wagner at Dresden. He rapidly became an early and a loyal friend, and was with Wagner at the premiere of *Rienzi*. When Wagner was almost in hysterics about its reception and his own fate, it was Heine who calmed him down.

130   Ellis, William Ashton, *Life of Richard Wagner*, London, 1902, ii, p. 93.

movements were full of a certain majesty and grave assurance … She always looked very much like a fairy … This fair actress differed from those around her in her unaffected soberness and dainty modesty.' According to Wagner, it was 'with a friendly serenity and composure that had something almost motherly about it,' that she was soon to nurse him through an attack of erysipelas. That was in the early stages of their mutual attraction. The impression of her that Wagner draws together is pleasant enough, but of a woman too prim and petit-bourgeois to grasp and support his great ideals. Above all he presented her as anxious to erase the one solitary lapse of her youth with its legacy of an illegitimate child, and so concerned for her reputation that by the time he knew her she had turned rather prudish and dull.

In fact Minna Planer was no brown mouse but an Alma Mahler of her time, a bewitching force who made men, including a man of genius, lose their heads, and she reconfigured Wagner's outlook, his aspirations and his whole being. Before meeting Minna, he had been full of his Young German ideas of 'unbridled licentiousness' which he had taken from Laube and promoted in *Das Liebesverbot*. This is the story of a heavy-handed German viceroy who tries to impose restrictions and punishments on the harmless, pleasure-loving Sicilians for their enjoyment of 'free love', as it was known in the past; but when the viceroy fails to practise what he preaches, he meets his nemesis for his hypocrisy. Wagner's experience was the very opposite of the viceroy's, and in Minna he met a kind of nemesis not for hypocrisy and inhibition but for his 'unbridled licentiousness'. The changes she created were momentous, as his letters to a close friend, Theodor Apel, made clear. They demonstrate that prior to falling for Minna, he had played the field, the field in question being the ladies of the Magdeburg theatre troupe. He had been having the time of his life and indulging himself sexually, helped by his authoritative position as music director. Minna, leading actress of the troupe, was entirely the reason why he took the job at Magdeburg, but for a time she receded into one conquest among many. There is a letter from Wagner to Apel that is crucial to our understanding because it makes the position clear.

The letter explains airily that he is really too busy for love affairs but he mentions a lady called Toni (otherwise unknown to us), and also the 'Planer girl', *who had brought him moments of 'sensual transfiguration'*.[131] The letter goes on to suggest that Apel should come and visit so as to try her out too, and this establishes three things: first, Minna was 'hot stuff' erotically; second, she was generally available; third, Wagner was not bothered about her general availability, and was even advertising her services to a friend.

All the available evidence confirms that everything then changed, utterly and totally. Minna destroyed all Wagner's previous ideas of 'free love'. It was the experience of Minna that reshaped his thinking into a belief in the one grand passion, and it was she who symbolised as well as creating this new ideal of one single wonderful woman as life's ultimate fulfilment. This ideal infused all his later operas except *Parsifal*. Under Minna's impact he became 'mad with passion' as he himself put it, a passion that really did amount to a kind of madness. Part of the insanity was that he seemed to erase from his mind any unwelcome facts that might contradict his wishful thinking about her, particularly all his awareness of her previous promiscuity. He idealised her, set her on a pedestal, and achieved this through the extraordinary force of his imagination and by twisting out of focus all evidence to the contrary. Before he married Minna, his sister Clara Wolfram had showed him a letter from her husband, then away in Berlin, with news of Minna. Minna had chanced to lodge at the same hotel as Clara's husband, and he had witnessed her behaviour and reported it as perfectly scandalous. As a result Wagner wrote to Clara's husband explaining his passion, his intent to marry Minna, and his consequent need to know the truth about Minna's behaviour. Wolfram acted diplomatically and wrote a hasty retraction, telling Wagner that he must have been mistaken; whereupon Wagner eagerly convinced himself of what he needed to believe, as he so often did.

He needed to believe in Minna, because something had had

131   Spencer, Stewart, and Barry Millington, ed., *Selected Letters of Richard Wagner*, London, 1997, p. 23 (my italics).

happened that is surprisingly common among people in 'open' relationships: these relationships come to grief unexpectedly because one of them falls madly in love with the other, discovering an agonising need for exclusive possession and belonging. With this change goes a determination to slam down the portcullis against any former 'openness', decisively and forever. The fact that this happens so often stands on its head the common notion that romantic love is merely a sublimation of unsatisfied lust, and that love begins to evaporate once lust is satisfied. This notion lay behind the pessimist Schopenhauer's recommendation that a bit more familiarity with the love-object and some regular sexual intercourse would soon disabuse anyone of romantic love and its trashy inanities.

What Schopenhauer did not realise was something which Wagner discovered and demonstrated, that things can just as easily go the other way. It was familiarity with Minna that turned her from being one available sex object among many into Wagner's great and exclusive passion. He became utterly infatuated with her and neurotically jealous. His blistering intensity is obvious throughout the entire series of his early letters to her which was acquired by Mrs Burrell. When Minna is away, Wagner truly suffers, and he writes huge, maudlin, manipulative letters, day after day, telling her he is in anguish and miserable whenever she is not there. He weeps, he implores, he is in agony; he cannot live without her; she must, must, must agree to be his forever because he needs her so desperately. She alone 'can bring him peace, redeem him from his turmoil and anguish;' she must meet his needs. What is disarmingly impressive is the truth of his feelings and his commitment; 'I love you too much to be able to breathe and live except in you, who are the breath of my life!' he wrote on 3 June 1836.[132] 'I do not want to be diverted or disturbed by anything from the image of Minna; any other thought seems unholy to me … To be yours, yours with every breath, to be never, nevermore separated from you, I forsook all my family ties, all relationships; in short everything that had bound me before'. And on

132 This letter to Minna and those that follow are all found in *The Letters of Richard Wagner, The Burrell Collection*, pp. 43–84.

6 June: 'Oh my wife, where are the words to express how I worship and adore you? It's a religious, holy sentiment. Each part of your being is a god to me to whom I am fervently praying.' There are so many pages of this that he could barely have found time for anything else but to write, and it is all more extreme than anything in his operas, anything from Lohengrin to his Elsa or any homage to Sieglinde from Siegmund as his '*seligstes Weib*', more tumultuous than Wagner's own later passions for Mathilde Wesendonck or Cosima von Bülow. Planning out his future with Minna (30 May 1836), he aimed that as soon as he was secure in Berlin in 1837, he could have her totally for himself and she would then leave the stage. 'My reputation as a composer will have grown so much that I hope then to take you away from the theatre. You will see what a good husband I will make. Oh let the future be my care, for united with you, I am confident of finding my highest powers.' As he explained (3 June 1836) 'I know those accursed attentions an actress has to encounter; that you will continue to be pestered by troublesome gallants.' And (4 June) 'Where you are, there are said to be some handsome men. Don't look at them. Do you hear? ... Minna, *you* surely do not doubt *my* fidelity for a moment. You never thought of such a thing, even in your dreams, you could not think of your Richard as faithless.' Not with Mathilde Wesendonck, not with Cosima Wagner, his second wife, or anyone else was Wagner ever so obsessed and besotted.

He married Minna on 24 November 1836, but the obsession lasted and there were reasons for it. There was more to the matter than Minna's beauty and her sexual prowess. Anything concerned with Richard Wagner tends to be strange and fascinating, and fascinating too were the immense forces that drew him and Minna together and 'grappled them in such hoops of steel'. To understand these forces requires a sympathetic insight into Minna's poignant past, insofar as we can perceive it. She was like several others in the cast list of Wagner's life, a shadowy figure until she drew near enough to shine with reflected light. Our knowledge of her early years is sketchy, and comes from *Mein Leben*, but there is no reason to question Wagner's account of Minna's origins and life before she met him.

She had been born at Elberfeld on 5 September 1809, which made her three and a half years older than he. Her parents were poor; her father was a *Mechanikus*, and a native of Oederan in the Erzegebirge. He had invented an improved card for the carding of wool, and a manufacturer in Chemnitz had given him a large order for these cards, only to go bankrupt. As a result Minna's father was also utterly ruined. He was left unpaid for the goods already delivered and used, but was also burdened with large quantities of the wire he had bought for his invention. He went to Dresden with his wire, and the ten-year-old Minna had to start hawking it around, mostly among milliners who used it to make artificial flowers. Minna's exceptional beauty as she walked the streets soon attracted attention, not all of it benign; she was seduced by a Herr von Einsiedel when barely seventeen, and as a result produced a child. This child, a daughter Natalie, was always passed off as Minna's sister; but the secret was entrusted to Wagner at an early stage of their relationship, and except for telling it to King Ludwig in *Mein Leben* (and to Cosima who took down his dictation), he kept it to himself. Even Minna's father and Natalie herself were kept in ignorance. Ernest Newman stated that this ignorance caused trouble in the Wagner household later, because Natalie resented what she took to be an unwarrantable tendency by her 'elder sister' to regulate her conduct, but Ernest Newman was apparently unaware that children generally resent being regulated anyway, even when it is their real parents who do it. It was from Natalie that Mrs. Burrell was able to purchase Wagner's revealing letters to Minna.

The important point is that Minna's young days were as fractured and insecure as Wagner's, if not more so. Her father had been bankrupt and destitute. She had needed to wander the streets of Dresden selling wire. She had then been desecrated sexually, at the core of her identity as a young woman. She had been through the painful, terrifying loneliness of a childbirth shrouded in secrecy and shame. Most of her biographers and Wagner's seem not to have any inkling of the shattering impact of a pregnancy so shocking and so disgraceful that she collaborated with her mother to pass off her daughter as her mother's, even deceiving Minna's own father.

To Minna adult life brought insecurity, emotional deprivation and abuse, traumas which were branded into her being. A person so damaged risks a permanent, frightening sense of emptiness, and the events themselves had taught her a harsh and unpalatable lesson; that her face was her fortune, and her person. Her great beauty could lead to gifts, financial benefits and windows of opportunity to a better life, but also to false promises, abuse of her body, and comprehensive disasters. There were also other lessons more inward and darker, that the only real security comes from being wanted or needed, on whatever terms it takes. Women in this situation are often unaware of developing the conviction that it is only in this, in the finding of someone who needs them and in the satisfying of those others' needs that they can discharge the gnawing anxiety and annul the emptiness within. The sad fact is that even abuse, sexual and emotional, can bring to damaged women a peculiar sick security and a sense of being needed, however poignant and misguided. For Minna, the contracts with theatre directors, the acclaim of audiences, and above all the admiration of men wanting her and her body gave her a release from insecurity.

Additionally she existed within a climate of opinion in German society where the justification for women and consequently their accepted role was to provide for men and meet their needs. It was in fulfilling this role that women were expected to fulfil their destinies; and Dieter Borchmeyer has pointed out that in the early nineteenth century many women took up this idea so completely they were literally willing to die for the men they loved in order to redeem them.[133] Wagner's hopes for a commitment true unto death, as expressed by characters in his dramas, were not some bizarre aberration expressing his personal arrogance but a reflection of the times. Borchmeyer

---

133 Borchmeyer, Dieter, *Richard Wagner: Theory and Theatre*, tr. Stewart Spencer, Oxford, 1991, p. 200. Borchmeyer gives as an example the case of Charlotte Stieglitz, 'who hoped that the shattering experience of her death would free her weak and sickly poet husband from his "writer's block" and set him on the road to literary creativity'. It didn't.

comments aptly that this situation presupposed an appalling egoism in the men concerned, but this was an era where many people regarded it as the natural order. It was another element in the matted tangle of assumptions that engulfed Minna as she grew up.

She possessed a combination of qualities which was irresistible to Wagner. She was not merely pretty, but beautiful. All the independent evidence goes to show that she must have been more than competent as an actress. Wagner's later disparaging assessment, that she had no talent, does not square with her success in finding engagements at many theatres and keeping them. She was reliable, a real trouper and a true professional. The order and calm she brought to her own world was something to enthral the rootless, rudderless conductor-composer.

> Early in the morning she got up to attend to the household; then at half past eight, she hastened to the rehearsal in theatre, and returning, not before half past twelve or one o'clock, from the ice cold, cavernous theatre, she had to hurry back to prepare dinner. For the winter that year was very severe. Right after dinner she sat down to sew and make ready her wardrobe for the evening performance, always memorising a new part at the same time. Often her hands trembled in her anxiety to have her wardrobe ready in time. She did everything tastefully and even with assiduity, and as the sewing machine was not yet known at that time, every stitch had to be done by hand.[134]

Even with all this going on and with Wagner often behaving like a maniac, sometimes ranting all night with rabid jealousy, she still managed to captivate people onstage; they loved seeing her. There was evidently a real 'something' about her.

She was an excellent and economical household manager. Natalie described how well she managed in Paris.

> She well knew how to make the small household cosily neat and clean,

---

134 *The Letters of Richard Wagner, The Burrell Collection*, p. 91.

by meticulous order and tidiness. Calmly and quietly she worked like a maidservant, sweeping, washing, cooking, cleaning his [Wagner's] suits and shoes since they had no money to give those chores to hired people. She always looked rosy, fresh, neat, and exceedingly clean, so that nobody would guess that she did all his menial work. How she enjoyed buying a few cigars or a screw of snuff for her beloved Richard when marketing at a distance since it was cheaper to buy the needed victuals there, enabling her to save money and so surprise Richard. He always welcomed this love offering like a child, and could not thank Minna enough with kisses, for what she had done.

She brought order, stability and loving kindness both to Wagner's physical surroundings and to his restless spirit.

She was also fun to be with, and analysts of relationships often miss the importance of fun. Even after the upheavals of Riga and Paris that almost destroyed their marriage, Wagner and Minna still went on to have fun again, once they settled in Dresden. Gustav Kietz, their sculptor friend, offers a vignette from his Dresden visit in 1845:[135]

I arrived to find him and his wife still in a state of helpless mirth at a dubious pleasure they enjoyed almost every lunch time when the local military band passed beneath their windows. In order to give me a better impression of the musical delights provided by the Riflemen's battalion as it passed the house, Frau Minna took up her position and imitated the sound of the clarinets, while Wagner, laughing all the while, accompanied her on the piano. She was such an excellent mimic, her performance so virtuosic and the effect so comical that in the end we all collapsed in a heap of laughter. On such occasions they were both as happy as sand-boys.

Minna did have one affair, deserting Wagner briefly for a businessman shortly after their marriage. Perhaps this was not surprising. The pair

135   Kietz, Gustav, *Richard Wagner in den Jahren 1842-49 und 1873-75*, quoted in Spencer, Stewart, ed., *Wagner Remembered*, London, 2000, p. 48.

had literally no money, and Wagner's behaviour was unbearable; but once Minna had decided that the marriage was for good, she was amazingly loyal and faithful, any promiscuity consigned to oblivion. Her loyalty was tested and proved at Riga, then part of Russia, where Wagner had become musical director of the Opera, beginning on 1 September 1837. Naïve trust and his usual improvidence had resulted in unmanageable debts, compelling him to flee the town in secret and cross the border into Germany illegally. Minna consented to his flight, even though she was more of a realist than he, and whatever he thought later about her never having loved him, at the time he wrote, to Apel again, that Minna 'who was never given to cherishing ardent hopes, and had a presentiment of the misery we were in for, agreed out of love for me.' It was from love and loyalty that she went along with his fantastical plans to storm the Paris Opera with the unfinished *Rienzi*. Their journey was ghastly, a staggering test of any woman's commitment. They were shot at by border guards and their coach overturned into a ditch which was probably a cesspit. Wagner himself emerged a stinking mess, and because of her own fall, Minna had a miscarriage.[136] Her hormones must have been thrown into chaos, and women in this situation commonly become acutely depressed and unstable. The accident almost certainly caused her childlessness afterwards. On their voyage from Pillau in East Prussia to London, their little vessel, the *Thetis*, seemed at one point close to sinking in the tremendous storms that swept over them, and it was then, on this voyage, that she begged Richard to lash her to him because she wanted them to drown and perish together out of love for him. So much did she go through for love of Wagner! Staid and passionless indeed! Minna really did symbolise '*treu bis zum Tod* (true unto death)',[137] the ideal which Wagner, in the guise of his Flying Dutchman, would seek in Senta, his heroine in the opera of the same name. Minna's fears for the *Thetis* and its safety were fully justified; later this vessel *did* sink in another, similar storm, sadly with the loss of all hands.

136 Minna's daughter Natalie revealed this in full to Mrs Burrell.
137 See Chapter 10, *Der fliegende Holländer*.

The 'sensual transfiguration' described by Wagner indicates that Minna was good at 'bed': obviously as important for Wagner, and as satisfying, as Constanze had been for Mozart. She evidently liked and wanted sexual intercourse, and must have gone on doing so, since there is a letter that Wagner wrote to his Dresden doctor, Anton Pusinelli, indicating his concern that she would still expect it in 1861, 25 years after they married, when she was 52. This letter belongs to the period after the Dresden uprising and his 1849 exile from Germany, for which Minna blamed Wagner. She had also been angry with Wagner over his passion for Mathilde Wesendonck, and they had been separated for some months. The plan was that they would try being together again, and that she should join him in Paris for his staging of *Tannhäuser*, but from a convoluted mix of motives he did not want her to expect 'intimate physical relations'. Wagner wrote to Pusinelli in advance of Minna's arrival, 'A great reason for my wife's disquieted condition lies in the discontinuance of my sexual relations which gradually came about entirely of itself, simply as a result of her poor state of health … I do not believe that I have to accuse her of a passionate sensuality (although I cannot judge to what extent her extremely overexcited nervousness has influenced her in this respect also) … Nevertheless I consider it important for you, as a physician, to impose a strict prohibition in regard to this.' The only reason why it might occur to Wagner that the discontinuance of sexual relations would disquiet her was if past experience had established the belief that she would expect them; and his suggestion that it was her over-excited nervousness that 'influenced her towards a passionate sensuality' bears out the idea that whatever the reasons, she was indeed passionately sensual. We can obviously never know whether she found sexual activity intrinsically pleasurable, or whether she needed it simply as a prop emotionally, as happens with many women who desperately want this proof of their value and attractiveness; but it seems clear enough that she had counted on sexual intercourse until its 'gradual discontinuation' threw the matter into question.

The whole dimension of sex, love and loyalty stood supercharged in Minna's psyche because she was a deeply damaged person, just as Wagner was, and it is worth emphasising that Minna was damaged in ways that perfectly interlocked with his. There were very good reasons why Minna should love Wagner. He was gifted and able; he was tough and colossally intelligent; he was frequently witty and amusing and always had something to talk about; he was a prodigious worker; he was a genius, even though this was not yet fully manifest; and he was fun. There were equally good reasons why Wagner should love Minna. She was very beautiful; she was successful and gifted as an actress; she was highly efficient as a manager, and economical as a home-maker; she was tough; she was loyal; she too was fun; she was a sensually transfiguring lover; and she adored him. It seems clear that she fitted and matched the preconceptions of woman in Wagner's psyche; after all she created them. He too fitted and matched her needs.

However, the two of them were co-dependent. This means that they were locked in a mutual addiction to each other. For all his own cord of steel, Wagner's fractured childhood rendered him emotionally dependent and needy. He needed Minna. She for her part needed to be needed. She was 'a woman who loved too much', to quote the title of Robin Norwood's landmark text.[138] She was a poignant example of those women, summarised in another landmark text by the feminist guru, Sheila Kitzinger[139] as women who are 'trapped by their longing to be valued and necessary to those they serve … Deep down these women derive satisfaction from other people's dependence. And all too often there is the fear that without their dependents needing them like this

138 Norwood, Robin, *Women who Love Too Much*, London, 1986. A superb and timeless analysis and self-help tract revealing the mental processes that create addictive, co-dependent relationships, and setting out strategies for bettering them. Though the book is addressed to women, addictive relationships are no respecters of gender, and the principles and suggestions in the book apply just as cogently to men.

139 Kitzinger, Sheila, *Woman's Experience of Sex*, London, 1985, p. 125.

they would crumble away and be nobody at all.' Additionally there was in that era the crucial issue of financial security; women were largely dependent on men for money. Thus Minna and Wagner needed one another addictively, and their needs interlocked in a co-dependency of extraordinary strength. Sometimes a co-dependent relationship can be very durable. Even if its emotional basis is unhealthy, the result can be a very binding force. However, a co-dependent relationship remains fragile and precarious, because any shift in the balance of needs can upset the forces holding the relationship together.

Addictive relations additionally contain built-in pressures and forces that work against them, because, as Sheila Kitzinger said, 'it is not only the woman who feels trapped ... all those whose needs she serves are trapped with her, too. They begin to resent her, and the more she tries to make them happy, the more stifling the relationships can become.' Wagner began to feel that Minna was a restriction, and the bonds which held them together began to loosen in other ways as well. *Rienzi* had been accepted by the Dresden Opera and this altered the balance of their needs. After the Paris years, living hand-to-mouth in poverty, Wagner and Minna moved to Dresden in the hope of relative success and security, but Minna must already have been thinking of leaving him, because there are letters from Wagner imploring her to abandon all thoughts of separation; why does she think of this now of all times? As Wagner wrote in July 1842:[140]

You speak of the necessity for our being parted still longer, perhaps! – *Where* is the necessity? When, to pursue my soaring plans and hopes (which you did not even share with me), in circumstances that might well have scared the stoutest hearted man, I prepared to set out from Russia; when amid perils of every kind I embarked at Pillau, to commence a fearfully uncertain journey that was to bring me to a still more doubtful goal – did you then speak of any necessity to leave me? By God, I should have been obliged to agree with you then!

140 *Richard to Minna Wagner: Letters to his First Wife*, tr. William Ashton Ellis, London, 1909, letter of 28 July 1842.

But it never entered your head. When storm and danger were at their greatest, when you saw a hideous death before you as a reward for all the hardships you shared with me, you simply begged me then to lock you faster in my arms, that we might not sink into the deep separately! When we were hovering on the brink of starvation in Paris, many an opportunity was offered you to save yourself: one word and Frau Z, who was so heartily fond of you, would have taken you with her to Gotha ... Why did you not speak of a necessity then for us to part? You see, I could have found nothing to reply to you then. But now that I feel I have my future more and more in my own hands, I ask you, why you are talking now of this necessity?

Thus Wagner was still desperate for her and we now can only wonder along with him about her conscious reasons for wanting to leave. Maddeningly we have no letters from Minna to explain and nothing to show why she changed her mind. Perhaps she was persuaded to stay by Wagner, deploying what she later described bitterly as his '*vortreffliche Suade*': his outstanding gift of the gab.

Soon there were new attractions to make her want to stay. Wagner's staggering success with *Rienzi* on 20 October 1842 meant that she had become the wife of a famous man. While she had gained psychological security from being the needed wife of a needy man, there was an alternative, material security from being the wife of a famous man with glowing prospects. His success had also made him the object of envy and malice, but on 1 February 1843, he was given a lifelong appointment at the Dresden Opera which signified esteem, success and a permanent supply of money, 1,500 thalers a year. Minna was thrilled with him. Her status as his wife allayed her deepest fears of penury and fulfilled her need for status. Incidentally Wagner's annual salary was a large sum, considerably more than the 1,000 thalers which Liszt would soon be paid for an equivalent appointment at Weimar. As for status, Wagner was lionised to such an extent that Minna wrote to Cäcilie, Wagner's sister, that 'in many a week we scarcely dine at home twice.'[141] Unfortunately for their marriage, Wagner wrecked his prospects six years later in 1849 through his leading role in the Dresden uprising. He had been a prominent revolutionist, as they were called in those days. He delivered rousing speeches, arranged the forging of grenades, helped direct military strategies and participated to the full in the provisional republican government. The uprising failed because the king's emergency premier, Count von Beust, called on Prussia, which responded with troops and suppressed the uprising. There were atrocities on both sides but particularly from the Prussians, and Wagner had to flee to exile in Switzerland to escape trial for his life. He and Minna lost everything that they had won, including his irreplaceable library. Glory, position, income and security, they all went up in smoke, almost literally.

Even without this disaster the mutual attraction between Minna and Wagner had been loosening its grip, a gentle weakening which began after his Dresden appointment. Both Wagner and Minna were changing. There was his staggering development. Because he was evolving so far and so profoundly both as artist and man, Minna was ceasing to understand his aspirations and no longer fulfilled his wish-fantasies as she once had. It had always been an 'I need you and therefore I love you' relationship, not an 'I love you and therefore I need you', and the psychological forces that made them need each other were relaxing their hold. With his success, Wagner's frantic need for Minna had been calming down. So too had his gratitude to her for meeting that need, and various other forces which had once kept his love aflame were burning lower. Minna was starting to lose her looks and her charming ways as her heart disease was beginning to take hold. On the other hand Wagner no longer fulfilled Minna's need to be needed. Because he was no longer obsessed with her, he no longer supplied her with security and self-worth as he had formerly, and this in turn made her need him and love him less. In sum, he needed her less, gave her less, and loved her less; she was needed by

141 Letter of 5 Jan 1843, quoted in Ellis, William Ashton, *The Life of Richard Wagner*, vol. i.

him less, gained less from him, and likewise loved him less. Even so, the subterranean forces which held them together were mighty yet, and their deep need and at some levels their deep love would still hold for many years longer.

It held after the failure of the Dresden uprising, when their altered material circumstances furthered the downward trends in their relationship. Her insecurity made Minna antagonistic and chronically angry with him for wrecking their good fortune in Dresden for the sake of mere, fatuous politics. Through his folly he had compelled them to return to the deserts and anxieties they had known in Paris. At first she had refused to leave Dresden. She only joined him in Switzerland six weeks later, and from time to time her suppressed anger would resurface. When they were together and established in Switzerland, it outraged her afresh that, as she saw it, he felt it quite in order to leech off hard-working friends like Liszt while he sat around mostly writing and publishing useless tomes of artistic theories. His work revitalising the musical and concert life of Zurich brought him no money. It was even worse in 1850 when he might have capitalised on this achievement by welcoming the real possibility of the Zurich Opera directorship, but instead displayed a determined lack of interest; this was now a contemptible joblessness of his own making. It is easy and even common to combine love with pity and compassion; it is very rare to combine loving someone with despising them.

What then made matters worse was that Minna was ever more losing her looks and style. Wagner did accept some responsibility for this and explained to his friend and doctor Anton Pusinelli,[142] 'The ever increasing shattering of her nerves dates from the many violent and grievous incidents in our life.' Wagner also commented that Minna's organic infirmity had been developing from their time in Dresden onwards, and that Minna's mother had actually died of what we would now know as congestive cardiac failure. In those days heart conditions like the disease which affected Minna were untreatable, and painful,

---

142 *The Letters of Richard Wagner and Anton Pusinelli*, p. 90.

and in letter of 1858 to his friend Jacob Sulzer, Wagner referred to 'the worsening of her very painful heart condition'.[143] This kind of pain is not sharp, but deep, looming and shapeless. People affected with failing hearts do lose their looks, and there is a rare letter from Minna herself, which declares, 'My poor heart is still is thumping violently. I look so wretched that my acquaintances do not recognise me.'[144] We have no picture or photograph of what she eventually became, but such disease as hers commonly results in a bloated appearance, a discoloured, purplish hue, and a tendency to gasp and wheeze. The remarkable advances in medicine during the mid twentieth century mean that the phenomenon of untreated heart disease has become uncommon in the Western World, so that it is easy to forget how it altered looks and personalities. In Minna's condition the body pours out more and more adrenalin to try and force the failing heart to work harder and keep up the circulation. High levels of adrenalin result in feelings of anxiety at the same time as flogging an already damaged heart. The consequences include pain from the heart, as mentioned in Wagner's letter (angina); a racing, sputtering heartbeat (palpitation); and fear. Another consequence is to turn its victims inwards; they come to feel dominated by a premonition of imminent personal dissolution. Minna, like others in her situation, became an insomniac, and started taking laudanum for sleep. This would have lessened the pain as well but soon turned her into an addict, with all the heated imagination and bizarre thinking that goes with addiction. Taken together, these afflictions would be enough to produce paranoias in the most balanced people, but Minna was damaged by her own past and married to the unreliable Wagner; and there was his 1850 escapade with Jessie Laussot, which provided every reason why Minna should worry about her marriage and her future.

As for Wagner himself, after his exile his entire life, every aspect of

143 *Richard Wagner to Mathilde Wesendonck*, tr. William Ashton Ellis, London, 1905, introduction, p. xvi, letter of Wagner to Jacob Sulzer, Venice, 3 Dec 1858.

144 Ibid., p. xxvi, letter from Minna to an unidentified recipient.

it, was destabilised; and this created his volatile frame of mind for his encounter with Jessie Laussot. As described already, the circumstances and plans surrounding Wagner's passion for Jessie were fantastical, and they were short-lived. He returned to Minna, and she remained, because she and Wagner still matched each other's needs at many levels. In some senses, they still loved each other dearly, and he long continued to set great store by her. It was five years later in 1855 when he was in London conducting the concert series for the Old Philharmonic Society, that he wrote her a letter (6 March) which was part of an affectionate series, and which shows that although the fires of passion were fitful, the relationship was still a rock. He wrote,[145]

> Believe me, dear Minna; even if we don't quite think alike in some respects, and express ourselves differently about this and that from time to time, yet neither of us can survey our life without seeing how near we stand to one another through what great proofs of love and staunchness in the most difficult and often the most appalling circumstances. Only think of the memories thronging my mind as I retread this London where we roamed in such distress and fearing sixteen years ago! What you have had to pass through with me really has been hard! And truly, if I could make things altogether smooth and smiling now, it would gratify my innermost soul. But my not quite understanding how to do so and actually continuing to cause you worry and distress has come to be my singular fate, which I often heartily lament for your sake. It touched me a great deal how hard our parting was for you ... it gladdens me that you expect no more than honour and success for my artistic efforts. Rich my art will never make me; and nothing but the consciousness of finding a few devoted souls can constitute my riches; for them alone can I go on labouring in this world. In this sense I hope to be able to give you nothing but good accounts of myself; but even that will depend on my having to keep an eye on nothing else. I am only glad to know that you now think exactly the same with me on this point.

---

145 *Richard to Minna Wagner*, i, p. 169 et seq.

The next real insult to their marriage was indeed Wagner's famous passion for Mathilde Wesendonck. Though the period of her influence is difficult to date, she was certainly more than an episode, even though she did not eclipse Minna. She was an illuminating presence in Wagner's life between 1853 and 1861, and a flickering, fading presence long beyond. Wagner behaved with her as deludedly as many people do in this situation; he told Minna that she would be just as much married to him as she had been before, and expected her to accept his relationship with Mathilde, simply because he had not been technically and physically unfaithful.[146] He did not face the obvious truth that no love-relationship can survive for long when one partner conceives a rampant passion for someone else and indulges it emotionally. Wagner's relationship with Mathilde was emotionally adulterous, and I have encountered no example where a person could go on living for long with a significant other who was obsessed night and day with the thought of somebody else. Wagner expected Minna to behave as if nothing had changed, but for her everything had changed. She knew all about it; she herself had been there; she had once held the charmed position in Wagner's imagination which Mathilde now occupied. Like anyone in the same situation, she found it intolerable and Wagner despicable, and yet part of the reason for his obsessing with Mathilde was that after Minna, he idolised every woman with whom he was afterwards involved in the same way as he had idolised Minna. No free and easy erotic come-and-go after the New German manner advocated by Laube could be satisfying, because of the way

---

146 Anyone surprised at the degree of self-deception involved has only to recall the historic example of US President Bill Clinton, who denied on television that he had sexual relations with Monica Lewinsky, because he had not literally experienced genital sex with her. Whatever the case for literal truth, the intentional falsehood here was stark. With Wagner and Mathilde it is similarly unlikely that there was any carnal contact. A close reading of Wagner's letters to her, taken together, creates the clear impression of a mutual pact, in a distortion of Schopenhauer's principles, to abstain from sexual intercourse.

that Minna had conditioned him. He was always hoping and believing that each new attraction would bring him that same heightened state of mind and being which Minna had brought him.

At the same time Wagner also continued to demonstrate his singular ability to make any woman believe and feel that she was loved uniquely and beyond measure. To Mathilde Wesendonck he wrote 'i.l.d.g.' in the sketches of the music he then was composing for *Die Walküre*, and this she later deciphered as just that: '*Ich liebe dich grenzenlos*: I love you beyond measure.' Nevertheless, for all that Mathilde became his muse for *Tristan und Isolde*, she was not a great deal more than an episode. The peculiar progress of her role in Wagner's existence illustrated what Jung would one day describe, that Eros or romantic love is often made to serve some distinct, separate purpose:[147] 'Have we not seen countless people who love and believe in their love, and then, when their purpose is accomplished, turn away as though they had never loved?' It bore out Jung's account that once Wagner had accomplished his purpose and completed *Tristan und Isolde*, he 'turned away from Mathilde as though he had never loved'. Additionally, Cosima records him much later as explaining more than once that his feelings for Mathilde had been trivial, and that it was nonsense to believe that anything like genuine passion for Mathilde had played any part in *Tristan und Isolde*. It is easy to assume that Wagner was merely being 'economical with the truth' to sweeten Cosima, but there is the realistic alternative, suggested by Jung's analysis, that Wagner had simply forgotten. He could never forget Minna and what he had felt for her like this, because she had shaped his very foundations and was branded into them; but Mathilde was more lightly impressed. While in the thick of his affair with Mathilde it had called for some bizarre psychological manoeuvrings for him to deny to Minna that his feelings for Mathilde had any importance, and he righteously based his denial on the fact that his actions were 'pure'. For Cosima later he denied that he ever possessed any real feelings for Mathilde, and there

147 Jung, Carl, 'On the Psychology of the Unconscious' in *Two Essays in Analytical Psychology*, tr. R.F.C. Hull, New York, 1956, p. 48.

are various other mentions and references later which add force to the likelihood that he really had forgotten.

It remains a testimony to the immense forces that still bound Wagner and Minna that after he 'turned away from Mathilde', Minna still made some big efforts to come back, and that he too made a big efforts to take her back, first in September 1860, at Paris for *Tannhäuser*, and later at Biebrich on the Rhine. The *Tannhäuser* performances finally took place in March the following year and they were deliberately wrecked, after which Minna returned to Dresden, while Wagner went through a restless period travelling widely, but principally between Paris, Germany and Vienna, where he tried to arrange the premiere of *Tristan und Isolde*. In March 1862 he settled on Biebrich as somewhere cheap and secluded, where he could settle down and concentrate on composing *Die Meistersinger*, and Minna joined him once more. Unfortunately for their relationship, the chance arrival of a gift from Mathilde[148] convinced Minna that Wagner was lying when he claimed that the relationship with Mathilde was over. Ironically it was genuinely no more than a few dying embers, but it seemed to Minna to brandish in her face that Wagner had no need for her. Their wish-fantasies had long diverged; she was dominated by fears, and hopes of security and respectability; he was driven by his art and ideals, his *daimon*, and his hopes of changing the world.

So it was that after an explosive, venomous quarrel at Biebrich, which lasted for days, Wagner and Minna parted. Financially he supported her ever after, and was not ungenerous, however straitened his circumstances might be; but sadly he also conceived against her a deep bitterness. There was no other woman before whom he had humiliated himself as he had before Minna, and so there was no other against whom he ever felt so bitter. Additionally *he* blamed *her*, as ex-lovers often do, for the fact that he loved her no more. Such disturbing

---

148 This had actually been a Christmas present for 1861, but had been sent this way and that through Europe as a result of attempts to run the migrant composer to earth and deliver it. Now it reached him in March the following year.

RICHARD WAGNER

Wagners Jugend:

1. Erste Kompositionsversuche 1821.

LIEBIG'S
FLEISCH-EXTRAKT.

Nachdruck verboten.

Erklärung siehe Rückseite.

1. Wagner plays to his dying stepfather

RICHARD WAGNER

LIEBIG'S
FLEISCH-EXTRAKT.

Wagner als Student
nimmt Unterricht bei Kantor Weinlig
in Leipzig 1831.

2.

Erklärung siehe Rückseite.

2. Wagner as a student

RICHARD WAGNER

LIEBIG'S
FLEISCH-EXTRAKT.

Das Asyl:
3. Villa Wesendonck bei Zürich 1858.

Nachdruck verboten.

Erklärung siehe Rückseite.

3. The Asyl (Villa Wesendonck, Zurich)

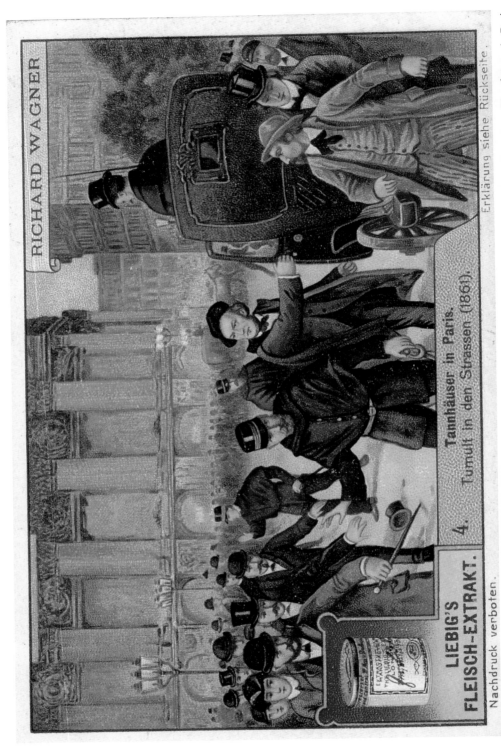

RICHARD WAGNER

Tannhäuser in Paris.
4. Tumult in den Strassen. (1861).

LIEBIG'S
FLEISCH-EXTRAKT.

Erklärung siehe Rückseite.

Nachdruck verboten.

4. *Tannhäuser* in Paris

RICHARD WAGNER

LIEBIG'S FLEISCH-EXTRAKT.

Nachdruck verboten.

5. Die Insel der Seligen - Triebschen.
Wagner dirigiert das Siegfried-Idyll an der Haustreppe 1870

Erklärung siehe Rückseite

5. Wagner performs the *Siegfried Idyll* for Cosima at Tribschen

RICHARD WAGNER

LIEBIG'S
FLEISCH-EXTRAKT.

6. Wagner mit Kaiser Wilhelm I. in Bayreuth,
bei der Eröffnung des Festspielhauses 1876.

Nachdruck verboten.

Erklärung siehe Rückseite.

6. Wagner with Kaiser Wilhelm I at the opening of the Festspielhaus, Bayreuth

Richard Wagner at home
with Cosima, Franz Liszt
and Hans von Wolzogen

The Festspielhaus at Bayreuth

The following pages contain eight photographs of productions by Wieland Wagner at the Bayreuth Festival

Das Rheingold – Wotan before Valhalla, photograph signed by Hans Hotter (1958)

Das Rheingold – The gods before Valhalla (1958)

Die Walküre – Brünnhilde's plea (Hans Hotter and Astrid Varnay, 1958)

Die Walküre – Wotan's farewell (Hans Hotter and Astrid Varnay, 1958)

Tannhäuser – Tannhäuser prays for his salvation (Wolfgang Windgassen, 1960)

Lohengrin – Lohengrin's first appearance (Jess Thomas, 1960)

Parsifal – The Grail scene, Act I (George London as Amfortas, 1962)

Tristan und Isolde – Tristan drinks the love philtre (Wolfgang Windgassen and Birgit Nilsson, 1962

and negative feelings were commonly due to guilt, a guilt so great in his case that he could not bear to go to Minna's funeral. She died suddenly at Dresden in 1866, and Wagner has been blamed, unjustly, for missing the funeral. It seems that he could not cope with the confused and unbearable feelings which he sensed the event would unleash.

It was not until he met Cosima von Bülow, the daughter of Liszt, that he found another woman who needed and loved him in the same way as Minna, and even more so. Minna sculpted into Wagner the expectant spaces, which would always need an ideal woman to fill them, and ingrained some ideas of what the ideal should be like. This was not a matter of looks and appearance. The women in Wagner's life did not look like one another. It was a matter of their personalities, the cast of mind, and their psychology. Wagner had found in Minna a mentality that fitted into his own, a collection of qualities and needs which he would always hope to find in any woman who came after. It was not until Cosima that he discovered another perfect fit. Like Minna, Cosima had been subjected to damage in her upbringing, and this meant that Wagner would likewise be the perfect answer to her own conflicted needs. But this also meant that Wagner would see Minna in Cosima, sometimes almost literally, which created challenges of its own.

Some depth of information about Cosima is necessary in order to appreciate why she fitted so perfectly into the place where Minna had once held sway. The essential point is that Cosima too had been shaped by an injurious and chaotic childhood, the consequence of parents who parted and remained in a state of mutual hatred. Those parents were Franz Liszt and the French countess, Marie d'Agoult, a brilliant, somewhat unstable woman who wrote novels under her pseudonym of Daniel Stern, novels which are still read, enjoyed and studied today. Cosima was born on 24 December 1837 at a villa on Lake Como in Italy, one of the Italian love-nests between which the countess and Liszt moved about, but which were making him feel increasingly imprisoned. With the countess it was much the same. They both found their three children, Blandine, Daniel and Cosima a burden, and in one sense it was better for them when Liszt sent them to be with his mother, old Anna Liszt, who was living in Paris. This separation of the children from their parents took place in 1839, and Anna Liszt was 'a simple, uneducated, unworldly, but warm-hearted woman ... and for the first time they [Liszt's children] knew what it was to be touched by love. For the first time, they were truly hugged and kissed.'[149] Liszt and Marie finally parted in a vicious break-up in May 1844. Their romantic fairy-tale of bliss and rapture ended with Liszt writing to Marie, 'I want neither to speak to you, nor to see you, even less to write to you.' Cosima now grew even closer to her grandmother, pinning on her pillow a note, 'Dear Grandmother: Whom have I to thank for life's delights? Who is it who views me loving tender looks? I feel it and will not forget it. You are all my happiness. Love Cosima.' Her elder sister Blandine was known as the beauty and Cosima as plain and clever, but she admired and loved her sister, sharing a room with her and sharing their secrets. When Liszt had Blandine sent to an aristocratic girls' boarding school to make her genteel, Cosima was so miserable and missed her sister so much that Anna sent her there too. Increasingly all three children took to visiting their mother in the exotic salon she had set up in Paris, enjoying her sweets, cakes and other enticements.

Franz Liszt too was a distant, dazzling figure, and he was generally a byword for generosity and greatness of heart. He helped countless young musicians, slaved to raise funds for the relief of a disaster in his native Hungary, and showered benefits and kindness on Wagner; but as a father he was appalling. He was physically remote and emotionally absent, haughty, uninterested and uncaring. He was also righteous and sententious, expecting from his unfortunate children exalted levels of education. He also demanded standards of manners and duty which he did nothing to deserve and which were the very opposite of his own behaviour to them. In 1847, he fell for his weird new love, Princess Carolyne zu Sayn-Wittgenstein, who was a sort of Polish-Russian

---

149 Marek, George R., *Cosima Wagner*, New York, 1981, p. 7.

Georges Sand, tough, plain, opinionated, and full of herself, an avid smoker of cigars and eventually the author of a 24-volume history of the Roman Catholic church, *Des causes intérieures de la faiblesse extérieure de l'Église*. This was no piece of common-or-garden piety but a work of polemical criticism about the 'weakness' of the church. In 1848 she deserted her husband, an adjutant to the Czar, and fled west to be with Liszt, taking over his life with masterful determination. In her view his children were spending far too much time with their indulgent grandmother and the novel-writing mother, whose output included one book, *Nélida*, where Liszt himself is presented, in only the thinnest disguise, as a fickle, shallow cad.

As a result Liszt now uprooted his daughters from his mother's home to a new address, causing the normally submissive Cosima to write to him, 'I tell you frankly that I felt great pain to have to part from grandmama who has shown us all so much kindness.' The princess imported for them her own, formidable, aged ex-nurse, Madam Patersi, bringing her out of Russia to join their existing governess. Madam Patersi was a martinet with a personality of flint, who taught Cosima responsibility, self-effacement, and religious devotion at its most subservient and self-lacerating. However she also taught Cosima that she must always 'do that which is right'. The chapter on Wagner's childhood provided an idea of the special stresses confronting children who are brutalised and yet commanded never to be angry, and yet further commanded never to tell a lie. Cosima was not wrecked by this unfulfillable combination, because she managed to ignore the last of them. She began to dissemble. She followed to all appearances the dictatorial regimen which forbade the children even to mention their mother's name, but she and her siblings extended their secret visits to their mother to savour her interesting books and edible delicacies. Soon there were even visits to the Louvre, and Cosima later described such occasions as visits to the 'realms of the Blessed'.

On the other hand, Madam Patersi was in some ways an excellent educator. She trained the two girls brilliantly in how to behave like princesses, and as a result Cosima could always hold her own with aristocrats; while Blandine was equally at home in public life, marrying the lawyer and politician Émile Ollivier, who subsequently became Prime Minister of France. She and Cosima learnt how to alight from the carriage, how to enter a drawing room, how to greet a duchess as distinct from an ordinary person, how to eat without appearing hungry, and how to dissemble her feelings when hurt. She was also taught, 'You must be strong – tears are useless water … You must pray, but not be humble. God loves the proud.' Cosima became proud and strong but equally she absorbed self-denial from Thomas à Kempis' *Imitation of Christ*. Cosima also absorbed the history, the literature and the languages taught by Madam Patersi, and her excellent English and German would stand her in good stead. When Cosima conceived a passion for Wagner, she knew as much about Shakespeare as he did. George R. Marek tells us how Madam Patersi also taught the children human history, and that she gave the credit for man's progress to 'heroes', such as Peter the Great and Napoleon.

It was not until 6 years later, in October 1853, that the princess, who now vicariously dominated the children, actually met them. She had instigated a visit to Paris with Liszt and Wagner, and it was the first time that Liszt had seen his children for eight years. The princess herself broke any tension and constraint by embracing them and kissing them; she said nice things about them, gave them miniature gold watches, and told them she hoped they would all now stay together. In January the following year, Cosima's mother countered by giving each girl a dowry of 100,000 francs.[150] In furious retaliation, to nullify their mother's influence, Liszt and the princess determined to relocate the children far away. Liszt had a favourite pupil, a minor aristocrat, whose home was in Berlin; this was of course Hans von Bülow. It was to Berlin that Cosima and Blandine were now abducted, or virtually so, as their mother did not so much

---

150 At a time when the normal wage for a Parisian who working an eleven-hour day was 3.81 francs: Steen, Michael, *Enchantress of Nations: Pauline Viardot, Soprano, Muse and Lover*, Thriplow, 2007, pp. 110 et seq.

as know of the plan until she returned from the country and found them gone.

The Prussian family of Hans von Bülow belonged to a most rigid, unbending tradition, but although his parents wanted him to be a lawyer, he fought them just as unbendingly. He was a pianist prodigy of such brilliance that his father came round, but his mother Franziska fought on, not only against her son but against the new music of Liszt and Wagner. His father divorced and remarried, and it was into this second female martinet's fatherless household that Cosima and Blandine were now transported. Like Wagner, Cosima and her sister had been punted around like unwanted parcels, 'orphans with their parents still alive', and they were now in an unknown Prussian city, forbiddingly different to Paris and a place where they knew nobody. Part of the new arrangement was that Hans would help the girls with their musical education. In fact Cosima and Hans were courteous and friendly, and each was able to expand the other's cultural horizons: she opened up for him the pages of de Musset, Victor Hugo, and Georges Sand, and he fired her with his enthusiasm for German romanticism. In October 1855, when the girls had been at the Bülows' for approximately six weeks, Hans conducted a concert which ended with the *Tannhäuser* Overture and the 'Venusberg Bacchanale'. The audience whistled, hissed, stamped and booed at Wagner's music, to such an extent that Hans fainted on returning to the conductor's room. Liszt had come to Berlin for the occasion and brought him home, but Cosima had also been there, and she stayed up all night comforting Hans. When he told her at dawn that he could not manage without her, she answered, 'Then I will remain.' They were married eighteen months later on 18 August 1857, at St Hedwig's Cathedral in Berlin. Liszt been very doubtful about Hans as a potential husband, until Marie d'Agoult opposed it, writing presciently that circumstances had pushed Cosima into a marriage where there would be happiness for no one.

At least the marriage offered Cosima a position where her wishes could carry weight, with no Patersis, princesses or capricious fathers to overrule them. Prussian women were subservient to their men, but the prospect of being mistress in her own household, the hope of security and the idea of belonging imparted a potent appeal to her relationship with von Bülow. Moreover, Patersi had instilled in Cosima an overwhelming sense of duty to every cause that she undertook, and being a good wife to her husband was her new cause, no matter what it cost. They were genuinely fond and respectful of each other, and he seems to have gained a new courage, relegating his grim mother to a remote apartment where he seldom saw her. He was occupied with assuming the position of a leading light in Berlin's music, conducting concerts and giving recitals, and their home became a salon that echoed Cosima's mother's in Paris. She wrote for the *Revue Germanique*, but above all, she tried to support and assist her husband as a composer. Because he expressed an interest in Merlin, she secretly sketched out a Merlin scenario and gave it to him as a Christmas present, and she even worked on the project of a Bülow opera on the *Oresteia*. Nothing came of these plans. Although Hans's orchestral piece *Nirwana* won Wagner's unstinting praise and even provided him with the rising chromatic scale which permeates *Tristan und Isolde*, Bülow's talent as a composer never blossomed.

There have been worse marriages, but the ongoing stress in this one was that Hans was in some ways very Prussian, and yet another martinet for Cosima. He brought more of the parade ground to the relationship than any sense of warmth and affection, needs which her emotionally starved childhood had etched into her as surely as Wagner's childhood had etched them into him. Von Bülow would even raise his hand against Cosima, how often we do not know; and she was so terrified of his disapproval of her second pregnancy, for which he was after all responsible, that she even concealed her labour until it was almost over. It was a labour that was difficult, painful and frightening, the very occasion when she most needed his support. There were stresses and unhappinesses enough to make reasons why she did not simply contemplate suicide but even made definite plans.

Her attitude to Wagner, whom they visited in Switzerland on honeymoon, was initially antagonistic, but gradually she fell under the strange spell of his personality. It was on 28 November 1862, when she was five years married, that she was taking a ride with Wagner through the Tiergarten and, as Wagner described in *Mein Leben*, 'We fell silent and all jocularity ceased. We gazed silently into each other's eyes, and an intense longing for the fullest avowal of the truth forced us into a confession, requiring no words, of the immeasurable misfortune which weighed upon us. With tears and sobs we sealed a vow to belong to each other entirely,' and though he does not include this in *Mein Leben*, they became lovers that night, and always celebrated its anniversary once they were together.

Thereafter Cosima and Hans, who at this stage was still in the dark, continued to meet Wagner intermittently at Biebrich and elsewhere, and we owe to Wendelin Weissheimer, a composer whom Wagner was then promoting, the rare vignettes of Cosima's relationship with Bülow and of her duty-driven, compassionate character.[151] Wagner and a group of friends including the Bülows were visiting the famous church of St Apollinaris on the Rhine.

Both sides of the road were lined with cripples and habitual beggars of the kind inseparable from any kind of religious festival. I accompanied Frau von Bülow [Cosima] while Wagner and her husband went on ahead. On both sides Frau von Bülow eagerly distributed alms, and when her purse was empty, she asked me for mine. This placed me in a ticklish situation, as I knew that Hans von Bülow had quite different views on the subject from his lady wife, and that, if I were to accede to her request, both of us would be placed in an unpleasant position – he in repaying what his wife had demanded and I in my refusal to accept it. And so I preferred to do all I could to discourage Frau von Bülow from any further acts of charity. Of course she became quite cross with me and asked with some irritation; 'So you won't give me your porte-monnaie?' 'For any other purpose, I would do so with pleasure,' I said calmly, 'but for this, to my intense regret, no!' She now hurried away

---

151   Quoted in Spencer, *Wagner Remembered*.

up a fairly steep path, hoping to catch up with the others. Once or twice I heard her calling out breathlessly: 'Hans! Hans!' but Hans did not hear and even quickened his steps somewhat, turning off into the church with Wagner as soon as they reached the top. Frau von Bülow, too, disappeared inside. I followed slowly after them, telling myself; 'Now you're really in for it!' I had just reached the top of the hill when Hans von Bülow emerged from the other side of the church and came quickly over to shake my hand, saying: 'I can't tell you how grateful I am, thank you!' We descended by a different route, in the course of which I set about attempting to restore Frau von Bülow's former spirits.

It was on 3 May 1864 that Wagner's impossible, ruinous life was transformed by the eighteen-year-old King Ludwig II of Bavaria's fairy-tale summons to Munich. We owe Ludwig an immeasurable debt, because his support, however variable, made possible the completion of the Wagner Experience for us all. Without the king Wagner might have died a debtor in a German jail. Would anyone then have tried to perform *Tristan und Isolde*, or would it be a forgotten curiosity in a drawer somewhere in Stuttgart? Wagner might have been known to posterity simply as the composer of three romantic operas, the series which ended with *Lohengrin*. Although the King never remodelled the composer's identity, he is just as responsible as the three remarkable women at the centre of Wagner's life for his legacy as we know it. It is certain that Wagner genuinely loved the King, even if it was the king's money that he had loved first. The King likewise first loved Wagner's dramas, but was then magnetised by Wagner's extraordinary charm, and he too loved Wagner. Wagner's dramas probably gave the King the greatest happiness he ever knew, and even before they met, the King had determined to look after Wagner and give him every resource needed to complete his works, assuming naturally that he would stage them in Munich.

The King first installed Wagner at a villa on the Starnbergersee, the Villa Pellet, thus unwittingly making it possible for Wagner to summon Cosima. Wagner had no certainty that she would respond and even made alternative plans, but respond she did. She arrived on 29 June 1864, and again she abandoned herself to him body and soul, conceiving their daughter Isolde. Many years were to follow in which she vacillated between Bülow and Wagner, often staying for months with one or the other, sometimes with both, mostly with her children in tow, mostly at Tribschen overlooking Lake Lucerne, but keeping up a sham appearance as a model wife with Bülow whenever he was in Munich. A major obstacle to her marrying Wagner unexpectedly disappeared with the death of Minna, on 25 January 1866. Wagner had long transformed any positive feelings for Minna, but Cosima actually had mixed feelings, as she had liked Minna more than Wagner when they had first met in Switzerland. Cosima took forward the relationship with Wagner another stage on 16 November 1868, when she arrived at Tribschen and told Wagner that she was his forever, and would never again leave him. Their next major event together was on 18 June 1869 when she bore Wagner a son Siegfried, and Bülow, after years of opposition to her divorce, suddenly agreed to it. Bülow in fact expressed his consent in a letter of great nobility, but he never saw or wanted to see Wagner again. On 18 July 1870, the divorce was final and absolute. The other obstacle to Cosima's marriage with Wagner had been her Roman Catholicism, but she had agreed to renounce this in anticipation. Thus it was that on 25 August 1870, at the Lutheran church in Lucerne, Cosima von Bülow married Richard Wagner.

Cosima's *Diaries* had already begun to document her life with Wagner from 1 January 1869, and she continued them until the day he died. Their opening pages are particularly moving. They launch a document intended for her children after her death, and they show how desperately eager she was to explain and prove that she had acted out of high principle in deserting Bülow for Wagner. After she finally responded to Wagner's great need for her, Wagner had become Cosima's second great cause. She had acted under a '*Zwang*', a compulsion of her conscience, which was nonetheless incompatible with every ordinance in that same conscience. The fact that she was motivated by high principle did not absolve her from 'mortal sin' in leaving her husband and giving herself to Wagner. In spite of some bumpy passages related to Wagner's attraction to Judith Gautier, his relationship with Cosima was immensely strong. Judith was the fiery Frenchwoman who first visited Wagner and Cosima at Tribschen with her husband. Her quicksilver vivacity first confused and then captivated them both, and she later became his muse for *Parsifal*. She was utterly different from his first muse for *Tristan* and from both Minna and Cosima; and yet she was complementary to their joint, merged image.

At the root of Cosima's passion for Wagner was a sense of duty, reinforced by her enthralment to Wagner's ability to make her feel that she was truly and utterly loved. In March 1871, after going through some old letters from her father, she wrote: 'they show me once more that I had neither mother nor father. Richard is everything to me. He is the only one who has given me love.' Her desperate, starved desire for love, and her need to be needed as Wagner needed her, would complement and interact with his needs just as Minna's had done. Wagner and Cosima were both under the spell of romantic passion as well, and part of it was their need for sex and their mutual physical fulfilment. My reading of Cosima's *Diaries* follows that of George R. Marek in his *Cosima Wagner*, that the joy of sex was theirs until shortly before Wagner died, even though they were major problems following Siegfried's birth and she then wrote that she feared 'the approach of passion'. The reason for her fear was not that her libido had died but that sex in those days was inexorably liked to pregnancy, childbirth and its great dangers, something readily forgotten today. Cosima had terrible deliveries. They were blindingly, blisteringly painful, and her last one, resulting in the birth of their son, was dangerous. Her diaries reveal that after his delivery she had recurrent post partum haemorrhage and lost a lot of blood. Blood loss after childbirth could be lethal in times when there were no blood transfusions and no easy medical solutions, no quick 'D & C'. Cosima only recovered very slowly and was weak for months. In addition to the obvious threat to her own life, she had actually lost her much loved elder sister Blandine through pregnancy and another related complication, puerperal fever. She had good reason to be afraid of more pregnancies, and with no contraception, she had reason to be wary of sex, in virtue of which she needed time to overcome her dread of its consequences.

She possessed capacities and strengths far beyond Minna's. To be sure, she was too starchy to replicate Minna's sparkle and ideas of fun, but her marriage to Wagner was one of minds, as she was far more of an intellectual equal, better able to connect with Wagner's immense mental powers. She could be wonderfully diplomatic, crucially so in Wagner's dealings with King Ludwig, although she could be tactlessness itself, and in this they understood one another. She was a brilliant manager and organiser. She had a cord of steel as strong as Wagner's, and an equal ability to bend others to her will, although differently expressed. She invigorated Wagner and his creations while he was alive and she maintained the Bayreuth Festival after his death. Whereas poor Minna sickened in her thirties, Cosima at that age grew constantly more beautiful and elegant.

As for Wagner, it was not only sex but the imprint in his psyche of Minna, the cautious, pragmatic bohemian, which led him and bound him to Cosima, the cast-caution-to-the-winds idealist-ascetic. Minna had set up the niche or rather the great empty arch in his mental gallery, which Cosima filled so well and so productively. Without Minna there might not have been the lasting presence of Cosima in Wagner's life. When Cosima was absent Wagner pined for her as he had once pined for Minna, but unlike Minna, Cosima went on giving him unconditional love. She was one of two people who saw Wagner through and through, and knew him exactly as he was, and yet treasured him unconditionally, the other being Wagner's Dresden doctor, Anton Pusinelli.[152] In July 1869, when Wagner planned an

---

152 Anton Pusinelli was already Wagner's doctor when after the triumph of Wagner's cantata *Das Liebesmahl der Apostel* in 1843, Pusinelli made Wagner a formal offer of friendship, which Wagner warmly accepted. Elbert Lenrow, who edited their correspondence (publ. Knopf, New York, 1932) commented, 'Thus began what seems to have been the long-

adventure for his visitors to Switzerland and they were dubious, she
told them quietly, 'Do not refuse: he would be angry. And let him
manage it all; let him take the lead.'[153] She understood when it was
important to pamper him like an eager child.

She had another advantage over Minna because her upbringing had
imprinted in her the ability to endure anything, and she sometimes
needed it. For all his great need and his consuming love, so bountifully
expressed, there were times when Wagner did cast amorous glances
elsewhere and times when Cosima's prim and proper righteousness,
her 'not amused' attitude would drive him to distraction, and he would
rage at her. When the disease which had ruined Minna's personality
was encircling Wagner's own heart with its deathly grip he could at
times be mean, petty and simply horrible. Today a man in Wagner's
state of health, or at least a lesser man, would have long been in a
care home, but Cosima endured his bizarre and hurtful behaviour
without knowing the cause of it. No medical person of today could
read Cosima's descriptions, all unwitting, of Wagner's coronary artery
disease, his worsening chest spasms and their relentless progression,
without feeling amazement at his strength of will, as well as heartache
for them both. There was also the other things already mentioned, his
irritable bowel syndrome and his rheumatism, and in Bayreuth, the
return of his erysipelas. It is impossible now to conjecture the state

---

est and most enduring friendship in Wagner's life.' Wagner confirmed
it in writing, 'Let us be friends ... for life!' They were. Pusinelli came
to know Wagner through and through, all his awfulness, meanness and
dishonesty as well as his greatness, nobility and integrity. He could say
'Yes' to Wagner, and he could also say 'No' without loss of warmth and
mutual respect. In 1877, Wagner could write, 'Dear good old friend! I
am looking back over my years, and there, again and again, I encountered the most friendly man who ever found his way to me!' He died
before Wagner, on 31 March 1878, and when Wagner learnt of it, he got
up and walked out, his body heaving, simply unable to bear it. Wagner's
grief plunged him into a depression, and he declared that he had never
had another friend so sincere, faithful and firm.

153 Spencer, *Wagner Remembered*, p. 195.

of his renal function. He must certainly have been steadily poisoned by the detritus of his metabolism which his kidneys could no longer handle. The circulation to the poor man's brain must have been more and more fitful and toxic, and it is not surprising that he could be irascible and hurtful.

An example of his hurtfulness came in December 1882, in his way of informing her that her ex-husband was now in a mental asylum.[154] This was less than three months before he died; Cosima describes how Wagner, haunted by demons of premonition, burst in on her; 'he throws out the news which even now, after its harshness has been softened, I cannot bring myself to write down! I cannot stay within any longer, I flee to my room and see Hans before me, alone in that institution, and I feel like screaming, screaming to some God to help me!' She coped somehow as she had a few days earlier, when Wagner jumped 'angrily out of bed with the remark that I honestly think I am virtue itself ... his remark about my opinion of myself seemed at first a bitter and painful punishment, but in the very next moment, though still in tears, I accept it with all my heart – if it is just, as a salutary punishment, if unjust (I am not aware of having any good opinion of myself for I have never felt myself to be above anyone else), then as a blessing! May the blessings of suffering prevail!' In this same vein a few days later, 'I struggle to find comfort, to find God – oh children, may you never go through hours such as these!' This was the chasm between Cosima and Minna. Minna was the weaker but grew implacably angry when Wagner behaved badly; Cosima was made of sterner stuff but submitted with bowed head. Ludwig Strecker, who had inherited Schott's music publishing firm, spent two days with the Wagners at Bayreuth in January 1876, and recorded, 'She is a clever, interesting woman who can be utterly charming, as she proved in the course of the evening and the following day.'[155] He also described, 'She worships the master to distraction, following his every movement and hanging on his every word – he rewards her with exceptional and,

154 Wagner, Cosima, *Diaries*, 18 December 1882.
155 Spencer, *Wagner Remembered*, p. 237.

as it appears, sincere gallantry and attentiveness.' It was Cosima that made possible what is for me the most extraordinary achievement of Wagner's life, the fulfilment of *Parsifal*, down to its staging, within a year of his death.

Even so it was Minna who remained most deeply ingrained. It was Minna who became the source and the paradigm of all the heroines in Wagner's dramas, which each new generation admires and loves. What other front-rank opera composer has created so many appealing women? Mozart has given us Susanna and the Countess and perhaps Zerlina; Beethoven of course Leonore. Strauss added the incomparable Marschallin, Sophie and perhaps Arabella; Puccini perhaps Tosca, perhaps Mimi. But what are these in comparison with the irresistible appeal of Elisabeth and Elsa, of Sieglinde, Brünnhilde and Isolde? Venus, Senta, Eva, and Gutrune are also very sympathetic, and we owe them all to Minna. It was Minna who created in Wagner the romantic mindset which gave us these ideals and then made them so real. Cosima, and briefly Mathilde, would reinforce that mindset. They would re-invigorate the paradigm of woman as life's ultimate fulfilment which Minna had instilled in Wagner. But it was Minna who had forged it in the first place.

With his severance from Minna, Wagner was cut off from part of his very own self, leaving a gaping wound which not even Cosima could heal. No other woman ever supplanted Minna. Even after she was dead – *especially* after she was dead – Minna rose up in Wagner's dreams. With his sense of guilt he projected onto her his feeling that she was eternally vengeful, and this gave him nightmares. Paradoxically, in those nightmares he behaved to her like a needy, deprived child, still afraid that she would leave him. Cosima mentions in her diaries at least thirty nightmares on the theme of Minna threatening him or deserting him, or of Cosima doing the same. Because his imaginings had been formed by Minna, he saw Minna in Cosima, and confused them in his imagination. In his dreams, the images of the two women floated into each other interchangeably and sometimes merged. In October 1881, when he had less than eighteen months to live and had been with Cosima for almost eighteen years, she made a diary entry: 'Richard dreams about *me* during the night, that *I* leave him, but he calls out "*Minna*". [My italics.] He gets up, talks about it and then dreams again, this time he says, "It was you after all."' Wagner was never at peace with himself; it was not only in the *Oresteia* of Aeschylus that he became acquainted with avenging furies.

All these people, now long dead, still have the power, across the gulfs of time, to call up a poignant sympathy for the picture of a handful of immensely courageous women and men, whose claims all seem proper and reasonable but were simply incompatible. It was entirely reasonable of Minna to expect Wagner to earn a decent living and provide her with stability and security in return for all that she endured and did for him. It was equally reasonable and right for Wagner to pursue his ideals so single-mindedly and selfishly, both in politics and in art. It makes no sense to judge them. We should be grateful to the damaged Minna for looking after him so well for so long, and she still remains a crucial element in the Wagner Experience for us now. We should obviously be grateful that Wagner himself followed his genius. We should also be grateful to the starchy, but infinitely noble Cosima for contributing so much towards his stability and his triumphs, most of all throughout the desperate end-game of *The Ring*, Bayreuth and *Parsifal*. Without her and the King, the Wagner Experience would only be a fragment of what we now have. We owe an immense debt to this gathering at the vortex of Wagner's life-drama, since it is we who enjoy the rewards that were only possible because of their heroic endeavours, their sacrifices and their suffering.

EIGHT

The Miracle of the Music

The music lies at the heart of the Wagner Experience and without it Wagner might have been forgotten. It is the music which makes the dramas what they are. The music bathes individual scenes with their distinctive light and aura. The music also creates for each drama a complete world that is unique, and the music is responsible for defining its character. Wagner's texts do not do this, although he sometimes believed that they could. When he declaimed them they made a great impact, because of his own gifts as an actor, but he told his friends that he only came to understand his texts from composing the music. On their own they are like the line drawings of an architect, and it is the music which converts these into colourful realities, for him as for us.

The texts of *Tristan und Isolde* and *Die Meistersinger* illustrate this. *Tristan und Isolde* is generally viewed as the ultimate monument to romantic passion, but not many people would realise why from simply reading the text. The discussion of the opera is the place to expound the story in detail; the text on its own is well-written and interesting, but nothing more. For anyone who does not hear the music in his mind's ear, the text of *Tristan* is not extraordinary. It is the music that converts the text into a romance to end all romances by penetrating it, enfolding it and filling it out. It is the music which defines *Tristan und Isolde* as an enthralment about the passion of passions and about mysterious states of the soul. *Die Meistersinger* is generally regarded as a complete contrast, establishing the values of real life and bright day, but the text on its own is not so very different in tone from

Tristan. In fact, *Die Meistersinger* has been described by Lucy Beckett as Wagner's most Schopenhauerian work,[156] and as a text it is closer to Schopenhauer than *Tristan*. What defines *Die Meistersinger* as immeasurably different is the music, the 'C major of life' instead of 'the wonder-realm of night'.

The music is the foundation of everything else that Wagner offers us, and Ernest Newman was not unreasonable in claiming in his first book on Wagner, that Wagner's greatness *was* his music. He did a drastic *volte face* later, but at that time (1899), Newman concluded

> The purely musical effects, which Wagner was so apt to disparage and mistrust, have been the secret of his enormous hold upon the public mind for the last quarter of a century. He who desired not to be listened to as a musician has made his way to the stars on the wings of his music alone. And with the immortality it has won him he may well rest content; for music such as his must surely lie close to the secret heart of men as long as the race remains responsive to beauty.[157]

The point of Newman's claim was that Wagner's music does everything that other great music does, and more. First it is superb in terms of form. Much of Wagner stands among the peaks of music even if evaluated and judged by the stringent criteria of, say, Stravinsky. The reason for bringing in Stravinsky is that he was another of music's great theorists, and even though he belonged to a very different aesthetic, some of his ideas can be applied to Wagner with revealing results. Stravinsky asserted that musical form and purely musical standards were all that mattered to make music work, and his own later music exemplified his 'attempt to erect certain kind of architectural constructions. My objective is form.'[158] He argued that music is incapable of representing anything but itself; that any claim to the contrary involves a category

156 Beckett, Lucy, *Parsifal*, Cambridge, 1981, p. 134.
157 Newman, Ernest, *A Study of Wagner*, London, 1899, p. 393.
158 Stravinsky, Vera, and Robert Craft, *Stravinsky in Pictures and Documents*, London, 1979, p. 193.

mistake, even perhaps a deception. 'I have never made applied music of any kind. Even in the early days in *The Firebird* I was concerned with a purely musical construction.'[159] This may seem perplexing from the man who composed *The Rite of Spring*, but the point of importance is that Wagner's music succeeds even within Stravinsky's restrictive ordinances, as impressive edifices of sound, even if they were at first too original for people to understand; and some people still have difficulty with appreciating their structural quality. Hanslick, who was to become the most fashionable of Viennese music critics and a notable disparager of Wagner, had begun by admiring *Tannhäuser*. However it was on the basis of *Tannhäuser* that he questioned whether Wagner was really cut out for symphonic music, music where structure is particularly important (this of the composer-to-be of *Tristan und Isolde*!) But Hanslick could not see that the Overture to *Tannhäuser* is a demonstration of symphonic principles because its novelties eluded him; and this is the common fate of musical forms that are new and unfamiliar. Weber said of Beethoven's Seventh Symphony, a pinnacle of formal perfection, that it showed its creator as ripe for the mad-house. Deryck Cooke, who created the performing version of Mahler's Tenth Symphony, had earlier described the first movement of his Third as a total formal failure, even though the youthful Egon Wellesz, himself a compser, had fallen for Mahler because of the mastery of form he discerned in this very movement. So too with Wagner; the novelty of his forms often resulted in the failure to recognise their quality because they were too mould-breaking. Their formlessness only existed in the eye of the beholder. Hanslick, now turned hostile, called *Die Meistersinger* a 'boneless tonal mollusc', but this simply demonstrated how far Wagner's forms and musical architecture had forged ahead of contemporary understanding. In fact the same mistaken criticism sometimes greets Wagner's forms today.

The gift of form and order is something which Wagner offers as generously as any composer, and it is one of the benefits that music

---

159 Ibid., p. 195.

in general confers on humanity. Great music, or at least the music of Western high culture, has the ability to reshape the world as we experience it through its organisation. It can percolate the mind and reconfigure not only its software but even perhaps the circuitry supporting it. Throughout life we accumulate a jumble of thoughts, feelings and personal history; and the mind works unceasingly to shape them into patterns. It attempts partly to discover a structure, partly to impose it. It performs this process of arrangement and ordering both as a conscious endeavour and unconsciously. This is one reason why we sleep and dream, so that the mind is free for this important work undistracted by conscious activity and its diversions. It is often in sleep that the mind orders its contents and resolves predicaments, which explains the common experience of waking up with answers to problems that seemed intractable the night before. Carl Jung often spoke of the wisdom of the unconscious, operating to create order in the deepest recesses of the mind. A special benefit of great music is that it can help to create that order.[160] As Yehudi Menuhin expressed it, 'Music creates order out of chaos: for rhythm imposes unity upon the divergent; melody imposes continuity upon the disjointed, and harmony imposes compatibility upon the incongruous.'[161] Pablo Casals, the immortal cellist, and András Schiff, pianist and conductor, are two of many who have described the importance for them of beginning the day with great music, in both cases with something from Bach's '48'.[162] Pablo Casals said, 'For the past eighty years I have started each day in the same manner. It is not a mechanical routine but something essential

---

160 See Storr, Anthony, *Music and the Mind*, New York, 1992; Sacks, Harvey, *Musicophilia*, New York, 2007.

161 Menuhin, Yehudi, *Theme and Variations*, New York, 1972, p. 9.

162 Bach's '48' consist of two complete sets of preludes and fugues in all the major and minor keys. Their purpose was ostensibly to demonstrate the importance of a tuning system that allowed freedom to compose in all keys and greater possibilities of modulation that resulted, but their claim to greatness is as George Bernard Shaw commented; 'Bach was able to express in fugue everything that has ever been worthily expressed in music.'

to my daily life. I go to the piano and I play two preludes and fugues of Bach. I cannot think of doing other. It is a sort of benediction on the house.'[163] The sense of order and purpose which great music can discover or bestow is one reason why it can be transforming, and people attuned to Wagner often find that his music and its structures are among the most ordering and transforming of all.

The question how music achieves this result is one which is immeasurably interesting, both for music in general and for Wagner's music in particular. We have already seen that Wagner modelled himself partly on his idol, Beethoven, and it is time for some detail about Wagner's approach to Beethoven's forms. Wagner did not simply mimic Beethoven and copy his symphonies, but they did give him the basis for his own approach, particularly their development sections. In the development sections of his symphonies and sonatas, Beethoven took the tunes, the two main themes which he had set out at the beginning of the movement, and worked them up. He would repeat them at different pitches and in different keys and with different modulations and varied instrumental colouring, above all with different emphases, now forceful, now relaxed. I knew someone once who liked to count how many times Beethoven used the main theme of the Eroica Symphony in the opening movement,

Allegro con brio

Fig. 8.1: Beethoven, Symphony No. 3, 'Eroica'

but the number is not the point. What mattered was the way Beethoven could arrange the repetitions as building blocks within the structural format of Sonata Form. Sonata Form is based on a set sequence, classically a bold theme first, generally followed by a gentler second theme, which together make up the *exposition*. The first theme is set in the main key, the tonic, and the second is usually in

---

163   Quoted in Exley, Helen, ... *And Wisdom Comes Quietly*, Watford, 2000.

the dominant, pitched five notes above the tonic. After the exposition both themes are worked up with great variety in what is known as the *development section*. This leads to the *recapitulation*, which repeats the original themes more or less as they were in the first place, but with the second theme now in the same key as the first, the tonic. This leads to a final section, the *coda*, which is both another development and also a rounding off of the whole.

A large number of classical composers have followed this format, from Carl Philipp Emanuel Bach onwards, and the genius of Mozart and Beethoven was not simply that they used the format but in the way that they used it. Beethoven had the ability to put his musical material together in such a way as to build it up into something monumental. He could spin unlimited music out of the repetitions, but the outcome does not sound like short segments endlessly repeated but a single melody coursing onwards. Trenchant and vigorous Beethoven's melodies may be, but even when assembled together like building blocks, the result is a fiery, singing line.

Beethoven was particularly effective in arranging his ingredients in a way which built up his structures, and this was one of the gifts that Wagner took from him. In addition to creating lines of music, his structures too would maintain a balance between faster passagework and the slow and lyrical, between lightness and weight, minor and major, relaxation and tension. As Wagner explained in his late essay, 'On the Application of Music to the Drama', the main difference between himself and Beethoven was that his structures were dictated by the requirements of developing drama, rather than by any abstract formal principle; but it is form that makes the music of both composers more and more satisfying at repeated hearings, because it is only by repeated hearing that we can grasp its balance and proportion.

Wagner's music is not Beethovenian, but at times he echoed Beethoven quite directly, for example with his repetitions and developments of the 'Day' theme from *Tristan und Isolde*:

Fig. 8.2 'Day'

Again, Wagner used repeats of a theme with a magnificent kick in it,

Fig. 8.3

to shape the 'Ride of the Valkyries'. As happened with Beethoven, Wagner repeats themes and builds up longer episodes from the repeats, and the repetitions build up musical edifices with their own specific character. In Act I of *Die Walküre* Wagner builds up something beguiling and expressive, a melody of melting perspectives from the great central love theme of *The Ring*.

Fig. 8.4

In these instances, both Beethoven's and specially Wagner's, the music is effectively an organic, self-contained world evolved from its own inner resources. However, Beethoven's were not the only forms that Wagner took over; he absorbed almost as much from the great polyphonists of church music and from his particular mentors as a Leipzig student. We have seen how he was a pupil of Theodor Weinlig, one of Bach's successors and a master-teacher of counterpoint in his own right. Through him, Wagner had an exposure to ecclesiastical music and the open forms often used by Bach, Schütz and Palestrina. To be sure, their music also included ritornellos, rondos and strict fugue, closed forms, but also polyphonic and contrapuntal masterpieces where music is not modelled in this way. Polyphonic and fugal music has complex formal requirements of its own, and its forms grew partly out of the ebb and flow of their own their intrinsic resources, their particular melodic lines, rhythms and harmonies. This was something entirely different from the prescriptive blueprint of Sonata Form as it had solidified in Wagner's time. Polyphonic choral music is moreover framed to reflect the rhythms and accents of the texts and their sentence structures, but also their meanings. Wagner was not an ecclesiastical composer and no church polyphonist, but it is significant that at the time of writing the Prelude to *Lohengrin*, an ever-evolving, ever-replenishing structure, he was busy arranging and performing Palestrina's *Stabat Mater*, and Wagner's forms do at times reflect the evolutionary forms of church music. The crescendos developed by Rossini also gave something to Wagner. The imprint of Rossini's *William Tell* Overture contributed to the great burgeoning crescendos of *Tristan und Isolde*, a populist effect transformed for an exalted purpose. All these were among the models that Wagner merged to develop his own distinctive forms, and the result was always a new vision, never a mere stitching together of other men's ideas.

Wagner's prose works explain how he based his own formats on Beethoven's, and this unwittingly invited charges of formlessness through encouraging the idea that his music was a replica of Beethoven's, but a very poor one, with structures that fell short of Beethoven's. This idea was a mistake, and it never helps to try mentally to force Wagner's forms into procrustean frameworks, whether of Beethoven or any other model. As it happens, the formats of classical music themselves were originally conceived as resources and not as straitjackets. Sonata Form as I have described it offered a framework to Haydn and Mozart which enabled them to compose with a new freedom. They used it freely and varied it freely, and Beethoven used it as freely as anyone. It was only later in the nineteenth century that frameworks petrified into dogmas and yardsticks against which new music was judged, often to its disadvantage. In his own music, Wagner made deliberate efforts to break free of straitjackets. He had to revolutionise the abstract ground plans of Sonata Form because his aims were different, above all the need to serve and express the drama.

He devised new ways of structuring his music and new methods of ordering his themes; and from *Das Rheingold* onwards both the overall structure and the arrangement of his themes were dictated by the drama. In his late essay already referred to, 'On the Application of Music to the Drama', Wagner said, 'The new form of dramatic music must demonstrate the unity of symphonic writing, a unity which it will achieve if it extends over the entire drama;' but this unity comes from 'a web of root themes pervading all the drama, themes that contrast, complete, re-shape, divorce and intertwine with one another as in a symphonic movement, except that *here the needs of the drama* dictate the laws of parting and combining.'[164] From the very beginning, Wagner carefully crafted his texts to allow him to build up effective musical structures and he learnt from the mistakes of others. When only twenty, he wrote to his sister Rosalie criticising *Hans Heiling* by Marschner in a way that expressed his own convictions.

In no other opera by Marschner have I come across such a complete lack of any overall effect ... – and what weak endings to each of the acts! – What an absence of melody in the choruses! In the finale to the second act he treats the culmination of the whole work – 'he hails from the realm of gnomes and dwarfs and is the mountains' spirit lord!' and gives so little weight to the climax that one assumes that something quite insignificant is taking place! In a word not a single number can really hold the listener's imagination!

Wagner set out to achieve everything which he found wanting in the

---

164 'On the Application of Music to the Drama' (1879), in *Prose Works*, tr. William Ashton Ellis, London, 1897, vi, p. 183 (amended; my italics).

Marschner. His dramas conferred a consummate structural integrity on his musical materials, and later he was justly proud of his new methods of building structure from his new style of musical themes, which came to be known as 'leitmotives'. He always hoped that someone from his circle would analyse the purely musical structures which 'I had won by my own artistic labours' with as much acumen as they had applied to the labelling of the leitmotives. Alfred Lorenz famously performed this analysis between the two world wars and wrote compendious analyses of the 'secrets of form' in Wagner's works, to try and call a halt to the tendency, still prevalent even now, to judge Wagner's novel structures against the standards of Sonata Form and find them wanting. Alfred Lorenz intended to refute such negative judgments by a minute analysis of Wagner's works in terms of pre-existing musical forms, largely classical (e.g. ABA, ABAB, ABACA, etc.), and above all Wagner's own bar form as it is described in Act III of *Die Meistersinger*, where Sachs is instructing Walther how to write a prize song. Lorenz does not explain so convincingly why a sequence of segments and sub-segments and groups of segments, which he envisaged as the essence of Wagnerian form, should build up into edifices of a seamless, organic unity with their compelling sense of balance and rightness. The most compelling analysis of all has already been mentioned, Roger North's monumental study of *Tristan und Isolde*,[165] although its 700 pages are so demanding that it taxes concentration. However they are analysed, certain of Wagner's musical edifices register in practice as some of the most perfect ever created. Act II of *Die Meistersinger*, Act III of *Die Walküre*, and the central duet of *Tristan und Isolde* come to mind.

At the detailed level, almost of individual bars, Wagner's innovations were just as far-reaching. He devised a new freedom of metre and a new independence of phrase length, so that from *Lohengrin* onwards the pattern of his melodies and the micro-structure of his music changed. Specialists have identified these developments as an aspect of his new 'open forms' and his 'musical prose', as they have come to be known.

---

165 North, Roger, *Wagner's Most Subtle Art*, London, 1996.

Perhaps these concepts make best sense if explained by an illustration. The song 'Happy birthday to you' is an instance of closed form. Its opening tune 'Happy birthday to you' is balanced by another that has the same rhythm and a very similar tune, to make two foursquare sections. This is then balanced two more sections, 'Happy Birthday dear Richard, happy birthday to you', which neatly round it off. But imagine instead that the second 'Happy birthday to you,' had been changed to 'Much happiness too to all those present,' so that the rhythm and length of the line were changed, breaking up the metre; this would then be a move towards the musical prose and to the open forms that Wagner created. In *Das Rheingold*, Woglinde's first utterances

> Weia! Waga!
> Woge, du Welle!
> *(Weia! Waga!*
> *Wandering waters!)*

are metrical. Her second,

> Mit Wellgunde
> wär' ich zu zwei
> *(With Wellgunde,*
> *I would be two)*

is less so. Wagner set these asymmetrical sequences of words in his text to musical phrases that match their asymmetry, so that these too were asymmetrical. Still more unmetrical, and even jagged, is Alberich's,

> Wie gern umschlänge
> der Schlanken eine mein Arm,
> schlüpfte hold sie herab.
> *(How gladly I would*
> *embrace one of the slim forms*
> *if she would float down to me.)*

The genius of Wagner consisted here in his ability to create a satisfying balance in spite of using natural speech rhythms with their variety and irregularities. This naturalness formed part of his general determination that art and artifice ought to disappear in the actual experience.

The same distinction of closed and open form is just as relevant at the levels of larger structures, and here an analogy with literary forms may help to explain. In literature there are closed forms, such as the sonnet or the ballade. There is also ode and epic poetry and the novel, which last is a very open form, but people do not disparage these as formless simply because they are not as precisely regulated as the sonnet. A form can be free but still a compelling form, and it is wrong-headed to find fault with the Prelude to *Tristan*, as used to happen, as a failed and incompetent attempt at closed Sonata Form. Act III of *Die Walküre* is also not in a classical form, but in due course I shall explain why it seems one of the most perfect musical structures in existence. Like all good forms, it creates in the mind a sense of order through its musical structure alone, quite apart from any dramatic content.

It goes without saying that Wagner's music offers us more than form and organic structures. Above all it offers feeling, and Wagner's music is second to none in its depth of feeling. For all Stravinsky's commitment to form, he too as a composer had in practice no use for empty, mechanical forms, and he even said, 'The machine man is possible, of course, but only where there is no soul.'[166] Any music worthy of the name has soul and stirs feeling, even though the feeling may be of an individual and unemphatic kind. It is not necessarily a feeling of excitement or arousal, let alone an intense sensation. It may be a feeling of calm receptiveness, or of concentrated suspense. The feeling can be strangely passionless, as the feeling evoked by Stravinsky's *Apollon Musagète*. Or rather differently, it may be as Albert Schweitzer said of Bach's *The Art of Fugue*, that its theme does not brighten and it does not gladden; the feeling it evokes is absolute and indefinable, but it is not less a feeling, a feeling of considerable

---

166   Stravinsky and Craft, *op. cit.*, p. 196.

intensity. At the other extreme the feeling in music can be overtly and floridly emotional, overwhelmingly so in Mahler or Britten, and Wagner's music like theirs has been faulted for too much feeling, for emotional temperatures that run too high.

What is important about good music is that it can impart structure, even a narrative structure, to feelings and their evolution, and this takes further the earlier point about music's ordering of ideas and experience. Its command of order is one reason why music, even when as openly emotive as Mahler's Sixth Symphony, is not like the raw stuff of everyday emotions. However intense the emotions it expresses, good music still creates a sense of order and balance. This is partly due to a singular feature of the brain; the interpretation of sound and the function of hearing extends and permeates widely throughout the cerebral cortex instead of being confined to a single area. This helps to explain why music intertwines with our other mental processes and affects them, and also why music can bring order and balance to the mind as a whole. It means that music can reach out to old memories and emotions, and that it can extend back into the far distant and atavistic past. It helps the mind in its task of drawing these diverse elements into a new synthesis, to establishing a mode of consciousness that is positive. The quotation from Pablo Casals about beginning every day with something by Bach continues, 'But that is not its only meaning for me. It fills me with an awareness of the wonder of life, with a feeling of the incredible marvel of being a human being.'[167]

The patterning process instigated by great music is the reason why we do not necessarily feel the same emotions as the music expresses. However strongly we respond, sad music does not necessarily make us feel sad, any more than passionate music make us passionate, or martial music makes us militaristic. Sometimes it does. People who sing Purcell's *Hear my prayer, O Lord* can find that they are drawn

---

167 For anyone wanting to learn more about these things, and particularly about the psychology of music, among a number of revealing books on the subject I would particularly recommend the two mentioned already in the footnote above, by Anthony Storr and Oliver Sacks.

into it, into the contrition, the desperation and the anguish that it expresses. Music played at public occasions can draw together the feelings and unify the emotions of the people gathered together. After the funeral of Princess Diana, it was largely music, and not always music of high culture, that created the strange unity of a national grief. Likewise, the rousing sound of a first-class brass band can strike cheer and communal enthusiasm into a gathering. In these instances the feeling of the music is infectious, and people do feel directly what the music expresses. There are other situations where the music makes us feel something different from what it expresses, because it not only puts the stuff of emotions in order but alters them. It reinterprets them and transforms them, taking sadness and passion and other emotions and reconfiguring them. The 'Confiteor' from Bach's Mass in B minor, the Marcia Funebre from Beethoven's *Eroica* Symphony, Chopin's Fourth Ballade all reconfigure deep feelings in new patterns, and they leave a sense of equilibrium and adjustment, and not pain, misery, or disunity, not the emotions and sensations to which the music gives overt expression.

The application of all this to Wagner is that his music achieves all these things to an exceptional degree. The adjustments which it instigates and the new dispensations which it confers convincingly explain why Wagner's music uniquely empowered Anton Bruckner, as we saw, to become his true self. It was not the Wagnerian music drama but the purely musical experience that changed him. He had no interest in the Wagnerian aesthetic, the fusion of the arts; and his favourite place in the opera house was in the upper circle, at the end of the horse-shoe, close to the stage where singers and drama were all but invisible but where he could look down with a matchless view of what really mattered: the orchestra. The music must have represented something that Bruckner had no words to describe, new feelings and orderings that unlocked the wellsprings of his own creativity. This was not simply a matter of its formal perfection or of Bruckner's response to its forms and symmetries. Even without any knowledge of its programme the 'Overture and Venusberg Music' from *Tannhäuser* is an emotional roller-coaster that eventually leaves a sense of completeness and repose. The Prelude to *Lohengrin* is emotionally satisfying in its own right as a journey through ethereal soundscapes of blue and gold. The Overture to *Die Meistersinger* seems emotionally charged from its own 'C major of life'. Even *The Ring* initially owes its emotional impact to its music. Many people begin their Wagner experience with the first notes of *Das Rheingold* as recorded by Decca, and its sound, dark, warm and golden.[168] There is exhilaration – the Valkyries' 'Ride'; loveliness – the 'Forest Murmurs'; and cosmic surge – Siegfried's 'Rhine Journey'. No one needs to know anything about music drama or Schopenhauer or the plot of *Tristan und Isolde* to be emotionally affected by the Prelude with its milestone harmony, its structural coherence, and its disturbing force of expression. It is the music itself that traverses an unprecedented sequence of form and feeling. I am not suggesting that the feeling in Wagner's music always alters and changes people, let alone as drastically as it changed Bruckner, but Anton Bruckner and C.S. Lewis were quoted early in the book because they have expressed a common experience, that of being affected profoundly affected by Wagner's music – as music.

On the other hand, Wagner's music does convey more for people who go further. For people willing to see with their ears, it offers visions, visionary views of river depths, mountain heights, caverns and stifling murk, mists and clouds, midsummer magic, thunder and lightning, rainbows and sunsets, the surge of the sea, dark forests, radiant forests, magic fire. It also offers personal characterisations on a heroic scale, a cobbler poet of rare and generous spirit, knights of shining righteousness, Rhinemaidens in the depths, gods of creation taking their ease in the heavens, giants with their brazen stamping, slaves toiling in the heat, a hero running for his life through forests and the rain, Valkyries riding the storm, giant serpents, dragons that crawl and heave. The characters have emotions which Wagner also

168 According to Decca's publicity in 2007 its recording of the *Ring Cycle*, conducted by Sir Georg Solti, was said to have sold over seventeen million copies worldwide.

defines in music, the joy of the Rhinemaidens hymning the gold, the ironic hauteur of Loge, the panic of Mime, the raw fury of Alberich, Brünnhilde's confusion and tenderness for Siegmund when he refuses her offer of Valhalla, Wotan's calm authority and his mounting disquiet as he listens to Fricka, and the beatitude of his reconciliation with his daughter. There is the illimitable agony of Tristan's yearning, the marmoreal joylessness of Hagen, the gentle ecstasy of Parsifal as he surveys his surroundings on Good Friday. Situation, character, and emotions: it is the text which provides the outline, the blueprint for these; but it is the music which awakens them to life. Nor are the features depicted in music simple and unchanging, like tableaux; Wagner makes them evolve, with scenes, characters and sentiments developing as the dramas develop.

What it about Wagner's music that achieves all this? What is the source of its spell? Part of the answer seems related to the fact that all spells, including Wagner's – and they have this in common with more conventional chemistry – need and require an exact blend of certain specific elements in order to work. More, the elements need to be assembled in an exact proportion, and an exact sequence. The same applies to Wagner's music if it is to cast its spell. His music has to be an exact synthesis for it to work, a synthesis comparable with the synthesis of molecular compounds in biochemistry. Most people know from school that atoms exist on their own and in combinations, and that molecules are units composed of different atoms and different kinds of atoms fused together. Molecules can be complex structures made up from thousands of atoms, and they are three-dimensional arrangements. In a molecule the raw materials, the atoms, are fused into a something that is new and possesses completely new properties, new characteristics that are different from those of the original atoms. Their exact positioning in the molecule is crucial for those new features to be present and express themselves. The new properties may even go beyond the inanimate; and it is then the exact positioning that makes all the difference to the ultimate leap, the transformation from something inanimate into the miracle that we call life. A difference in degree turns into a difference in kind, a quantum leap, and the transformation can sometimes depend on the position of just one atom. It is only when the final atom is in the right place that the spark ignites and life takes fire.

It is the same with the components, the 'atoms' that make up Wagner's music, and it was part of his genius that he could get everything just right. Change one harmony in an extended phrase and its effect is sabotaged. Take away one repetition in a sequence of repeats, and the proportion goes awry. Do as Stokowski did, and repeat the Rhinemaidens' lament at the end of *Das Rheingold* one more time because it is just so beautiful, and its beauty vanishes. Its beauty is too fine yet too complex to withstand tinkering, and the magic easily disappears. It is the exact constitution of a passage in Wagner which enables it to conjure up imaginary worlds.

Another ingredient of Wagner's spell is the thematic richness at his beck and call, and this is another resource which he shared with his idol Beethoven. Wagner's themes sound like no one else's because he too was gifted with an extraordinary aural imagination, and because those themes 'poured from his innermost soul'. Wagner was not above thematic 'borrowing' and we shall come upon several instances, but as they passed through his own imagination they were refracted so decisively that they became his own. His mature works are largely created from themes known as leitmotives. The music for his dramas, starting with *The Ring* (but even with much of *Der fliegende Holländer*), is a tissue built up from these leitmotives, which were fragments of music, often short, incomplete phrases, elements of rhythm, or turns of harmony.

From *Das Rheingold* onwards, Wagner's music is mostly constructed from leitmotives. The leitmotives are symbols, fragmentary yet complete, which represent many things in Wagner's dramas, and in leitmotives, he created themes that go straight to the heart of the matter. They represent objects and ideas with a vividness and conviction that is as extraordinary as their range. Some represent specific entities, like 'the Rhinegold' or 'the Curse of the Ring', and these almost never change their melodic shapes. Others, like 'Valhalla' or 'the Giants', change and evolve as the action goes ahead. Some of the themes represent movement, like the galloping theme that runs through the 'Ride of the Valkyries', or the hammering of the Nibelungs, or Siegmund running for his life. Others depict feelings and emotions like the theme depicting Wotan's rising anxiety in *Die Walküre* during his argument with Fricka, or his yearning and loss as he bids farewell to Brünnhilde. There are themes representing 'the Will to Power', 'Fate', 'Nature', 'the Hero Siegfried', 'Day', 'Perjury', 'Weariness', 'Brünnhilde's New Womanliness', 'the Grail'. These at least are the verbal labels that have become attached and these labels can be useful pointers to their meanings.

The leitmotives represent many of its features of the drama, but this was not their only function; they were also the fundamentals of Wagner's new musical structures. Wagner announced in print that it was wrong and unhelpful that 'one of my younger friends only viewed what he calls my "leitmotive" in the light of their dramatic significance instead of their bearing on musical construction.' Wagner valued the leitmotive idea as much for its structural potential as for its evocative capacity. It was possible for other composers to evoke atmosphere and 'illustration' without leitmotives, and so could Wagner. He did almost entirely without leitmotives in *Tannhäuser*, and in *Tannhäuser* he had no difficulty in defining character and emotion, sights, movement and atmosphere.

Any labels for Wagner's themes were first listed formally by Baron Hans von Wolzogen, one of Wagner's faithful staff at Bayreuth, and he was the 'one of my younger friends' whose work led to these themes being known as 'leitmotives'.[169] In point of fact, Wolzogen originally

---

169 This is an opportunity to mention another misunderstanding about this leitmotive system, the widely held belief that this system was imposed retrospectively on the music by Wolzogen. Wolzogen had listed, published and labelled the leitmotives in 1876 when *The Ring* was first staged at Bayreuth, and this probably led to the idea that it was Wolzogen who had abstracted the system from Wagner's works and then foist-

gave them the title '*Leitfaden*, leading threads', an indication that these leading threads were only the most important or prominent in a musical tapestry entirely made of such threads; an indication too that there were other less prominent threads which have not been formally defined. In fact Wagner's late works have long stretches where there is hardly a harmony or a line that does not possess some representative function. His late essay, 'On the Application of Music to The Drama' alludes to his own term, 'root themes', and this essay expressed his increasing concern that the labels were too rigid.[170] Labels pin down the meaning of the musical themes too inflexibly; and nothing so simple as a verbal label can cover all that a theme may come to represent. Frequently the scope of their meanings develops as the drama develops. There is a useful illustration of this early in *Das Rheingold*. Scene II of *Das Rheingold* begins with a theme that depicts Valhalla in music of solemn grandeur.

Fig. 8.5

The next scene takes place in Nibelheim, a subterranean world of dwarves and smithies, and the Valhalla theme now widens its meaning to denote Wotan as the occupant and lord of Valhalla. Early in this scene the terrified dwarf, Mime, issues a warning, 'Take care; Alberich is near,' at which point it is this theme that designates Wotan's calm

---

ed it back onto them. This is incorrect. Not only do Wagner's own preliminary musical sketches set out many of the motives with their names, but Hans von Bülow, his favourite conductor, was already using these names in correspondence ten years before Bayreuth, which can only mean that they must have been the common coin of his discussions with Wagner.

170 'On the Application of Music to The Drama', p. 183.

authority as he answers decisively, 'We shall wait for him here.' In *Tristan und Isolde* the themes develop and evolve in new ways. They become like the patterns in a kaleidoscope, constantly changing and transforming, as one musical theme dissolves and evolves into another. It is pointless and misguided even to try and define the exact point at which a permutation becomes a new theme deserving a new label. Trying to give titles to these is like trying to lassoo a cloud; and it limits the open-endedness of what the music signifies. Labels also put paid to any dawning on the imagination of the themes in their own right, as they first materialise. This first dawning can only work properly if we hear them for the first time in context as part of the overall musical picture, and a knowledge of the labels in advance burdens the music with preconceptions. Additionally, Cosima's *Diaries* reveal how labels, even those of someone as close to Wagner as von Wolzogen, could be wrong. The diaries refer to Wagner's special themes at several points and show that Wolzogen mislabelled the last music of *Götterdämmerung*. Cosima records Wagner telling her that this was not 'Redemption', but 'The Glorification of Brünnhilde'. Although there may seem not to be a great deal of difference, because Brünnhilde's glorious achievement is that she does redeem the world, Wagner wanted the emphasis on Brünnhilde, not on an abstract principle, and this distinction was in line with his whole personifying approach.[171]

---

171 Spencer, Stewart, 'A Wagnerian Footnote' in *Wagner*, vol. iv, no. 3, p. 90. The great Wagner scholar Stewart Spencer has invaluably provided the correct rendering of Wagner's words which are given wrongly in Geoffrey Skelton's translation of Cosima's *Diaries* (vol. i, 1869–1877, p. 552). Stewart Spencer's correct rendering of Wagner's words as Cosima recorded them is, 'I am glad that I kept back Sieglinde's theme of praise for Brünnhilde to become as it were a hymn to the heroine.' In the German Wagner was keeping it back for the '*Heldin*' Brünnhilde. It was emphatically *not* intended to be 'a hymn to the heroes (*Helden*)', as it is in Geoffrey Skelton's translation. Skelton had evidently misread Cosima's handwriting. Stewart Spencer's correct reading is supported and confirmed by a letter from Cosima to the chemist Edmund von Lippmann of 6 September 1875: 'My husband requires me to tell you

Many of Wagner's individual motives expressed concepts that were simple, but their weaving into bigger structures creates rich scenarios, whole tapestries of meaning. The French composer Debussy criticised the leitmotives for being like characters popping up and 'presenting their musical calling cards' – a bumptious 'Hello, it's me!' – but he was being facetious and deliberately oversimplifying. Not many leitmotives have the same instant, onomatopoeic effect as 'the Giants' in *Das Rheingold*.

Fig. 8.6

Many more are obscurely suggestive like the strange leitmotive

Fig. 8.7

generally labelled as '*Nibelungenhass*, Nibelung-hatred'.

Even individually the leitmotives work on the imagination and musical motives and dramatic motivations are inseparable in mature Wagner. The leitmotives knot together the threads and establish connections, but the effects of the individual threads are as nothing compared with their effect when woven together. The leitmotives have their individual meanings, but only produce their full meaning in

that the motif which Sieglinde sings to Brünnhilde [in Act III of *Die Walküre*] is the Glorification of Brünnhilde, which at the end of the work [*Götterdämmerung*] is taken up, as it were, by the entirety.'

context, because it is then that their different meanings interact and that harmony and orchestration add their distinctive contributions. They then add up to symphonic constellations which offer a larger picture and describe the psychological development of situations and characters, their motivations, drives, feelings, desires, and states of mind. The closing scene of *Die Walküre* is an example of music where the individual leitmotives do in one sense present their individual meanings, 'Magic Fire', 'Sleep', 'Fate', 'Wotan's Farewell', 'the Hero'. Taken as a whole, however, the scene and its music is focussed on Wotan, and it is the particular combinations of the leitmotives that gives the scene its effect. Another example is the passage in *Das Rheingold* where Alberich wields the magical power of the Ring to make the Nibelungs bring up the hoard for his ransom. The individual leitmotives represent the Nibelung hammering,

Fig. 8.8

and the hoard,

Fig. 8.9

but the musical paragraph as a whole represents the rising tide of Alberich's rage, hatred and pain. As we shall see later, a further combination creates the peculiar fusion of majesty and crisis in the Act I 'Transformation' of *Parsifal* (Fig. 20.15).

  These are some of the ways in which Wagner used the tonal, rhythmic and structural ingredients of music, and particularly the ways in which he used them to express ideas. He took to new limits the possibility of expressing ideas in music, and claimed that music could actually speak. His claim raises issues about music's status as a language. The relationship of music to any ideas it expresses is a complex and interesting one. In the case of most language, the association of words with the ideas that they represent is a matter of convention. Any ideas expressed in words could generally have been expressed just as easily in other words, and in foreign languages they are. Joy in English is *Joie* in French, and *Freude* in German. Is music different? Is the language of music and above all of Wagner's music a matter of convention, or is it more fundamental, rooted in the natural laws? In some ways Wagner's match of music and ideas seems a matter of convention, an arbitrary association as in spoken language, but sometimes his match seems more fundamental. There were occasions when he really did seem to produce a match of acoustical and visual and other phenomena almost to the point of identity. The ideas become music, and they bring the conviction that the relation is absolute. The music of the magic fire *is* magic fire. The music of the Overture to *Der fliegende Holländer is* the storm raging at sea. This identity can hold just as cogently with Wagner's correspondences of music with the other senses, such as touch. He makes us feel the coursing of the water in the Rhine and feel the sulphurous heat of Nibelheim. We are buffeted by the rain at the start of *Die Walküre*. We are wrapped in the otherworldly suspense of Montsalvat. The pleasures of touch in *Tristan und Isolde* are so exquisite that they might be noted by the censor if fully spelt out. Wagner went further and even produced identities of music with experiences that do not belong to the senses at all, thoughts, dispositions and feelings, such as contentment, frustration, joy, slyness, hatreds, aspirations, heroic resolve, deceit, intention, and ecstasy.

I have described how it was part of Wagner's genius to put together the different elements of his music in exactly the right combinations, but this is easier to grasp from some examples of what he did in practice. There is no better example than the Prelude to *Das Rheingold*. This Prelude lasts 136 bars, and it gradually conjures up the Rhine, dawning gradually on the imagination. It also establishes the thematic origin of all the musical elements in *The Ring*, and it sets in motion the entire musical action of its four separate dramas. One element of the music is a rippling arpeggio figuration in the violin line that closely recalls Mendelssohn and his Overture, *The Beautiful Melusine*. This resemblance raises the possibility that Mendelssohn was actually the source for Wagner's arpeggio. If so it was probably a half-memory which had come to Wagner as a new idea, because when he was conceiving ideas, his inner ear often caught tones, harmonies, fragments of melody, sometimes snatches of fully formed music, without him always being aware whether they originated in his imagination or his memory. As we shall see in detail when we come to *The Ring*, its four dramas grew out of Wagner's idea for single work, *Siegfried's Death*, which contains a scene between his hero Siegfried and the amphibious Rhinemaidens, three quasi-mermaids from the Rhine. Mendelssohn's composition, his *Beautiful Melusine*, had also been based on a scenario involving a knight and a (single) mermaid. There is every likelihood that Mendelssohn's composition lay in the recesses of Wagner's memory, and that work on his own creation should have summoned to mind the Melusine music.

Using the arpeggio figure for his own piece, Mendelssohn created something picturesque and evocative, of great charm. In the Prelude to *Das Rheingold*, Wagner took the same elements and conjured forth a new world. He managed it through his precise ordering of its components, their exact positioning. Each of the components makes a separate contribution. There is the matter of key. Mendelssohn uses F major, but Wagner chose E flat, a key with special resonances. E flat is in some way a key that is at the foundation of things. Deryck Cooke, whose book on Wagner remains eternally unwritten, once described in a radio broadcast how E flat embodied something atavistically secure and affirming. He described some unusual research from the late 1950s, which I have not succeeded in tracking down, demonstrating that a sustained low E flat could soothe and settle new-born babies. There is also something epic about E flat, the key of the *Eroica*, of *Ein Heldenleben*, of Bach's 'St Anne' Prelude and Fugue, of Mahler's Eighth Symphony.

Another significant feature is the pitch of the prelude's opening, an E flat for double basses in the very depths. In fact the double basses play two low E flats, one an octave above the other.

Double Bass

Fig 8.10

Wagner specifies that four of the double basses should have their lowest string tuned down specially to E flat; in 1876 they had not yet been developed to include a fifth string which would let them play low enough. Consequently their E flat was a sound deeper than any that had been heard in an orchestral performance before. Furthermore the low E flat emerges from silence and it is held long. It has harmonics, and these play an important role. Harmonics are pitches that sound in sympathy with the main note. They are not always distinguishable to the ear but they add important colouring. They resonate above the main note and there are many of them, a whole series of different pitches. Their relation to the main note is constant; the harmonics of a note and their relationships are absolute, and they are dictated by the laws of physics. Their relationship to the main note is known as the harmonic series. All notes possess these harmonics and it is the different balance of these, which make a violin sound different from a flute or an oboe. Stringed instruments in low registers are particularly rich in the way they resonate; and the harmonics of such a deep note on the double basses are genuinely distinguishable to the ear – just. In the case of the four double basses playing the lower of the two E flats, the first of this harmonic series is the other E flat an octave above, played by the other four. The second is the B flat, the note one fifth above (known as the 'dominant'), and when the bassoons come in, this B flat is the very note which Wagner gives them to play. *Das Rheingold* has so far played the first three notes of the harmonic series, the low E flat, the E flat an octave above, and the dominant.

Fig. 8.11

The bassoons play the B flat along with the continuing E flat on the double basses; and this second note, rising from the harmonics of the first, brings a sense of evolution, of growth and inevitability. Another feature of importance is that the double basses and bassoons hold their notes long enough to prevent us from gaining any sense of rhythm, any feeling of tempo or structured time. In playing the first and second harmonics, they also provide two notes out of the three that make up the major triad of E flat, the E flat chord. The two notes point towards the full chord, creating a pre-echo, an expectation of it which hopes to be satisfied. Wagner does satisfy this expectation. He satisfies it as soon as the horns begin to come in. The eighth horn begins with an arpeggio that fills in the missing note, G, in the E flat chord so that the triad, the chord, is now complete. We first hear it as the last note in the second bar of Fig. 8.12, just an upbeat, an understatement. But the last note of the arpeggio, the G in bar 4, now an octave higher, is held for a whole bar.

Fig. 8.12

Wagner's music has produced the full arpeggio, and brought to it a sense of achievement and fulfilment with that final G. This arpeggio also becomes the first leitmotive of *The Ring*, the 'Nature' motive, from which all the other music of *The Ring* evolves, just as all nature evolves from simple first beginnings. The other horns follow suit, one by one,

Fig. 8.13

and this all contributes to the sense of growth from universal origins, of dawning and burgeoning. Meanwhile Wagner's choice of sonorities adds an effect that is dark and warm. The horns add something else, something luminous and golden, and they are also responsible for initiating at last a sense of rhythm and momentum. Everything enhances the sense of evolution; evolution as a welling up out of the depths, evolution of sound out of silence, of light first dawning out of darkness, of the world from its first origins, of substance from void, of form from chaos, even the evolution of consciousness. The twelve cellos move the process further as they take up the arpeggios.

Fig. 8.14

They start to fill in the notes between them, the passing notes. The music has at length arrived at the figuration which was possibly derived from Mendelssohn,

Fig. 8.15 Mendelssohn, Overture, *The Beautiful Melusine*

and it conveys waves rising and falling, currents flowing and eddying.

Fig. 8.16

Meanwhile low clarinets add something reedy and subaqueous, and the quiet twinkle of flutes begins to bring light from above.

Fig. 8.17

Now the Mendelssohnian string figuration passes gradually to the higher strings and runs faster,

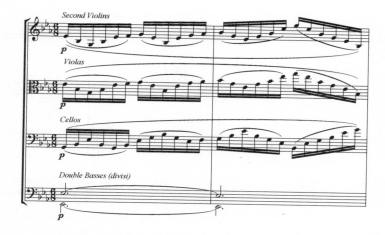

Fig. 8.18

creating a watery swirl. The low voices of the heavier brass add a new depth of sonority, and the trumpets add a soft radiance.

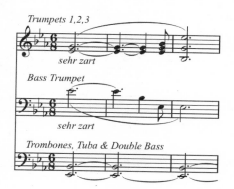

Fig. 8.19

Again the effect is because of Wagner's winning combination; and soon the imagination fills with the currents and counter-currents of the great river.

Fig. 8.20 Page 12 of the full score (1873)

The Prelude to *Das Rheingold* is an organism that is mysteriously alive. It is the river Rhine, and using the terms of Wagner himself, he transfers the Rhine into the souls of others.

A second example of how and why Wagner's music passes into the souls of others comes from the 'Fate' theme ('*Schicksal-Motiv*') in *Die Walküre*.

Fig. 8.21

Again it does this because of the precise arrangement of its components. This music is first played as Brünnhilde appears before Siegmund and tells him that he must die. The Fate theme looms up like an apparition, and it represents destiny with extreme economy and effect. It is very simple, just three notes, starting on a chord of D minor (the minor triad). Its upper tone drops a semitone and then rises by a tone while the supporting harmony modulates to a seventh chord of C sharp major. There is then the matter of its pitch; the music is again set in a low register. There is its measured pace, both stately and inexorable. There is the austere and sombre scoring for the Wagner tubas with their unique, grey timbre.[172] With their defined, dark-metal edge, they

172 Wagner had Wagner tubas made specially for *The Ring*. In German-speaking countries they are known as Nibelungen-Tuben, and consist of two tenor tubas and two bass tubas, and they are not to be confused with the larger instrument which underpins the trombones. To say that their sound is midway between horns and trombones is not right, but it gives some indication as to their tone. They are played by horn-players, but with the bells facing to the right above the players, who do not insert their hands into the bells. Bruckner employed them in his last three symphonies; Richard Strauss in *Ein Heldenleben*, a tone poem, and *Die Frau ohne Schatten*, an opera; and Schoenberg in *Gur-*

sound less succulent than horns but similarly luminous. There is the dynamic; the theme starts softly and crescendos through its semitone drop, only to become suddenly quiet again when it rises to its third note. The effect is extraordinary, a sombre grey which looms up with a feel of menace only to dissolve into mystery. Wagner repeats the theme twice, modulating upwards each time by a tone, and he punctuates each repeat with soft tympani strokes. He creates in music all the forbidding obscurity and strangeness of 'that undiscovered country from whose bourn no traveller returns'.

Wagner evidently associated this music with fate, death and destiny, because it was a kind of thematic archetype. Music with the same 'face' appears again in *Tristan und Isolde*, more explicitly this time as a theme of 'Death'.

Fig. 8.22

This theme is prefigured in the Prelude of *Tristan*. In Act I it is first heard in the depths of the orchestra when Isolde is announcing that she knows of a better draught for atonement than the bromide suggested by Brangäne. Isolde means the drink of death, a poison. In *Tristan* too, the relevant theme consists of three notes, long-held and scored for deep brass, trombones this time. In *Tristan* too there is an ominous crescendo on the first two notes and a *subito piano* on the third. To be sure, there are differences. In *Tristan* the theme is from the first a unison line with no harmony. This makes it more flexible for combinations with other themes and for counterpoint. Then again,

---

relieder. Most surprising of all, given Stravinsky's disapproval, they turn up in *The Rite of Spring*.

its melodic shape is different in *Tristan*. Instead of a semitone drop from first note to second, there is a semitone rise followed in the *subito piano* by a drop of a sixth. Even so it has the same 'face' as the 'Fate' theme of *Die Walküre*, an association of ideas with Wagner that may have been conscious or not.

It helps towards grasping these associations if we realise that in *Tristan* we soon meet another leitmotive with a similar 'face' to a parallel one in *Die Walküre*. Both passages are about ideas belonging to the same psychological group, concerned with death, destiny, and fate. In *Tristan* the particular leitmotive comes at the point when Isolde is virtually consecrating Tristan to his death, the point where she pronounces, as an incantation, '*Todgeweihtes Haupt, Todgeweihtes Herz!*' Wagner set these words, 'O head consecrated to death! O heart consecrated to death!' to a theme that drops an octave and then a third below it, before an upward leap of a major sixth.

Fig. 8.23

It is this theme that blazes out later with devastating power as Isolde throws down the torchlight in Act II, and again in Act III when Tristan extinguishes the light of his life. It is also much the same theme as Brünnhilde sings in *Die Walküre* as she consecrates Siegmund to his death.

Fig. 8.24

There was evidently a musical association in Wagner's imagination between these thematic groups, signifying both an annunciation of death and a consecration to death. It was because such ideas suggested music that came welling up from the depths of Wagner's imagination that it reaches straight into ours. This means too that Wagner's music was 'image-specific'. I explained a little earlier that in his music Wagner often achieved a musical expression that matched the original idea to the point of identity. This is the reason why he had to bring back the 'Swan' theme from *Lohengrin* into *Parsifal* to designate a swan, even though the swan is a different one. He could easily have invented some pleasant, swan-sounding music, but this would not have represented the swan to his mind's eye and ear; and perhaps the image of the swan would not then have 'passed to the souls of others' as it does. Otherwise Wagner seldom repeated himself between operas. At all events, these instances where similar music from different works expresses similar ideas indicate a method of composing founded as much on subconscious intimations as on any cudgelling together of musical ideas.

The Prelude to *Das Rheingold* is particularly illuminating because Wagner described how it evolved in his autobiography. It came to him in a kind of trance, his so-called 'vision of Spezia', which happened to him in August 1854 when he was on solo tour in Italy. He was at Genoa, unsettled and restless.

In consequence however of thoughtlessly indulging in ices, I soon got an attack of dysentery, which produced the most depressing lassitude after my previous exaltation. I wanted to flee from the tremendous noise of the harbour, near which I was staying, and seek for the most absolute calm; and thinking that a trip to Spezia would benefit me, I went there by steamer a week later. Even this excursion, which lasted only one night, was turned into the most trying adventure, thanks to a violent headwind. The dysentery became worse, owing to sea-sickness, and in the most exhausted condition, scarcely able to drag myself another step, I made for the best hotel in Spezia, which to my horror, was situated in a noisy, narrow street.

After a night spent in fever and sleeplessness, I forced myself to take a long tramp next day through the hilly country which was covered with pine woods. It all looked dreary and desolate, and I could not think what I should do there. Returning in the afternoon, I stretched myself, dead tired, on a hard couch, awaiting the long-desired hour of sleep. It did not come; but I fell into a kind of somnolent state, in which I felt as though I were sinking in swiftly flowing water. The rushing sound formed itself in my brain into a musical sound, the chord of E flat major, which continually re-echoed in broken forms; these broken chords seemed to be melodic passages of increasing motion, yet the pure triad of E flat major never changed, but seemed by its continuance to impart infinite significance to the element in which I was sinking. I awoke in sudden terror from the doze, feeling as though the waves were rushing high above my head. I at once recognised that the orchestral prelude to *Das Rheingold*, which must have long lain latent within me, though it had been unable to find definite form, had at last been revealed to me.[173]

This strange source of inspiration sparked off the music of the whole of *The Ring* and was the genesis of its entire thematic growth.[174]

173 *My Life, authorized translation* ..., London, 1911, p. 603.
174 There has been a lot of debate whether his account of the vision of Spezia was historically true, or whether Wagner conjured it up later to give

Whatever the status of Wagner's account as historical truth, there is psychological truth in it, and it offers revealing insights into how his music came into being, which in turn helps us to understand how Wagner's music works, enhancing its meaning for us. When Wagner's imagination was invaded by dramatic ideas, it is true that his inner ear did then catch tones, musical fragments, phrases and tunes. It is also true that the music of *The Ring* is rooted in this Prelude, and *The Ring*'s entire web of motives evolves from it, as does its formal branching structure. The sense of coherence common to Wagner's works is all the more surprising because he did not plan them out in advance as Mendelssohn apparently did, mentally mapping out a ground scheme before beginning to compose. Wagner once said he just went ahead and hoped that something would turn up, but he was doing less than justice to his unconscious and its determination to create order and impose form, and less than justice too to the germinating value of his reflective periods, the years of planning and thought over the design of his dramas in preparation for this eventual 'just going ahead'. The gestation process gave rise to a powerful background sense of structure, upon which he could rely for the shaping of his material.

Accordingly Wagner's achievement resulted from a fine balance of formal constraint and free fantasy. It is in line with Schiller's advice to a friend (Christian Gottfried Körner) who asked why his output was becoming barren and where he had gone wrong, advice which pinpoints exactly where Wagner had gone right:[175]

---

the impression that he composed under the influence of pure inspiration. But ice cream, food poisoning, and dysentery are not normally the stuff of pure inspiration, and at present, as it happens, the balance of opinion has swung back to the view that Wagner's account was genuine; but as so often with Wagner there is a bewildering amount of compelling evidence on both sides of the argument.

175 Quoted by Freud in *The Interpretation of Dreams* (tr. A.A. Brill, New York, 1913).

The reason for your complaint lies, it seems to me, in the constraint which your intellect imposes on your imagination. It hinders the creative work of the mind if the intellect examines too closely the ideas pouring in at the gates ... In the case of the creative mind, it seems to me, the intellect has withdrawn its watchers from the gates, and the ideas rush in pell-mell, and only then does it review and inspect the multitude.

Wagner did allow free play to his imagination, to Spezia-type visions, before embracing them in the hard grind of formal composition. It seems likely that the composition came easily after the Prelude to *Das Rheingold*; he composed the whole work between 1 November 1854 and 25 January 1855. There were other occasions when his composition could be a Herculean struggle, as he described for the closing pages of *Götterdämmerung*.

At some level Wagner always felt inadequate about musical form, and about his musical abilities generally, however imaginary his inadequacies really were. I have mentioned him telling Liszt about going 'to puzzle out some wretched rubbish' in the *Tristan* period, and the same sense of inadequacy was the reason why he told Cosima late in life that he really was not up to much as a pure musician. He was comparing himself disparagingly again with the well-organised Mendelssohn, whereas he relied uneasily on his *daimon*. His account of the prelude to *Das Rheingold* illustrates the belief that mysterious influences were at work in him, part of his general feeling that his existence was shaped by otherworldly, unconscious forces.

In practice Wagner achieved a compelling synthesis in his music, and when the result was as masterly as his definitive version of the *Tannhäuser* 'Overture and Venusberg Bacchanale', it is clear that he did not have much to worry about. He composed this music and put it together over 24 years but there is no music which provides a greater and more ordered expansion, and posterity has no reason to be discontented with Wagner for simply relying on what 'turned up'.

This ordering process was already at work in *Der fliegende Holländer*, in that Wagner had started on the composition of Senta's ballade before he had even together put the text. He went on next to the sailors' chorus of Act I, the music for the Dutchman's spooky crew in Act III, and the chorus of spinning maidens in Act II. He composed the Overture last. This did not mean that *Der fliegende Holländer* was an ad hoc assemblage, the cobbling together of a patchwork. It comes out as a balanced design, a fit of the parts into a matrix which had slowly been evolving in Wagner's mind.

Parsifal provides another example of circumstances compelling Wagner to revisit music and rework something he had finished, with a result that is drastically better. In Act I the effect of the arching span, a massive cantilever, is enhanced by its quotes from the 'Communion' theme at certain salient points. Its essential segment consists of the six bars which come at the very beginning of the prelude.

Fig. 8.25

The first segment (marked with the first bracket below the stave) is transformed into a distant fanfare for onstage brass at the beginning of Act I, and the whole theme comes again at the very heart of the 'Grail Scene', mystically intoned by the hidden choirs. But above all this first segment comes twice at the culmination of the transformation music which links the two scenes of Act I. It blazes out in two mighty statements for onstage brass, six trumpets and six trombones. The second of these reorientates the music towards the entirely new key of C major, the key of the whole of the Grail-temple scene. These two lynchpin statements sound like the outcome of consummate, long-term, strategic planning, and they support immeasurably the arching span of Act I which adds so much to *Parsifal*'s hold on the imagination. The astonishing thing is that these statements were not part of the original design at all; they were late additions from 1881, long after Wagner thought he had finished Act I. He pasted some new pages into his finished score to provide more music, because the original music for the transformation was too short for the time it would need for the panorama to unroll on the stage. In its original form the transformation music had no onstage brass and no 'Communion' theme, and what now seems like inspired long-term planning was due to practical problems over the stage machinery and happy chance. Or was it perhaps inspired after all? Is it excessively fanciful to imagine that Wagner's inspirational *daimon* was at work? This *daimon*, this drive, this organising force was genuinely the reason for his incomparable achievements against impossible odds, and it is not beyond the bounds of possibility that this organising *daimon* was the driving force behind his architectural mastery; perhaps his *daimon* had been waiting in the depths to engineer the masterly shaping of *Parsifal* music.

We have looked at illustrations of similar music occurring in different works to express similar ideas. It was spontaneous and unawares, and it lends force to the possibility that Wagner possessed a form of synaesthesia, mentioned earlier. Synaesthesia, as explained, is a mental cross-talk between the different senses. At its simplest and commonest it involves colour and music, where the experience of hearing particular music gives rise to a sense of specific colours. Wagner's music often suggests that his was a cross-talk not just between sight and colour but all the senses, and that it went further, to embrace every aspect of his thinking and imagination. It is worth recollecting that hearing involves many areas of the brain and not just a localised zone. Wagner's was in any case no ordinary brain, no ordinary imagination. There is a passage at the end of *Das Rheingold* that illustrates well how Wagner could take sights, sounds, and general atmosphere, and translate them all into music. At the end of Donner's summoning of the mists, there is a sudden wind that comes rustling up through the orchestra; it breaks the stillness and rapidly gathers strength. It also characterizes the rising expectations of the bystanders onstage. At its culmination, Donner smashes down his hammer and a flash of lightning goes up, portrayed in a flourish for brass and wind. A split second later comes a cannonade on the drums and thunder machine.

Wagner's music manages to signify wind, hammer-blow, lightning flash, and thunder; and more than this, it conjures up the atmosphere of the entire scene in all its brilliancy. Although it cannot be demonstrated scientifically (or at least there is no way of demonstrating it yet), Wagner seemed to achieve some direct translation of other modalities of experience into music in a way that suggests the possession of unusual neuro-physiological mechanisms. It fits in with this hypothesis that he should have complained often of pains in the 'nerves of his head' when he was overwrought because of creative effort or multiple overloads, that he had such vivid and extensive dreams, and that inanimate things would dance and shimmer if his mind was idle, but none of this is sufficient for us to interpret these symptoms or 'diagnose' them more specifically.

It is intriguing to speculate whether a complex synaesthesia influenced Wagner's desire to create a total work of art where every aspect of the presentation, all the different arts, would fuse and harmonise. This fusion could satisfy all sensory modes with no conflict between them. There would be no clash between the colours evoked by the music and the colours he saw, no conflict between what happened onstage and what he visualised in his creative imagination. This was an ideal he seldom if ever saw fulfilled, not even on his own stage, and the discrepancies between ideal and reality contributed to one of his major depressions after the original Bayreuth *Ring*. He despaired and longed for an invisible stage as well as an invisible orchestra. (The orchestra is covered over by an acoustical cowl at Bayreuth.)

A derivation of synaesthesia may be another reason why Schopenhauer struck such a response in Wagner. Schopenhauer regarded music was the deepest of the arts, a direct expression of 'will', unlike the other arts which were visual or verbal representations. After reading Schopenhauer Wagner became persuaded that Schopenhauer's view was true, and he revised his thinking so that his ideal work of art was now musical in essence. He came to believe that this was a truth which he had always sensed intuitively. As already mentioned, he redefined the staging, the acting, and the representation as 'deeds of music made visible', and all other aspects were reinterpreted as stemming from the music.

Music was always running in Wagner's mind, germinating in that amazing ferment of ideas. Music could well up at unexpected times and sometimes his imagination would throw up an idea at random. He explained to Mathilde Wesendonck (in a letter from Lucerne, of 23 June 1859) how 'while working out the herdsman's merry welcome of Isolde's ship the other day, there occurred to me a yet more jubilant melodic strain. I was on the point of turning the whole thing inside out, when I at last realised that this melody does not belong to Tristan's herdsman, but is Siegfried's to the life. I at once looked up the closing verses of Siegfried and Brünnhilde and saw that my melody belongs to the words;

> *"Sie ist mir ewig,*
> *ist mir immer,*
> *Erb' und Eigen,*
> *Ein und all" – etc.'*

At this point Wagner had barely looked at *Siegfried* for two years, and yet his '*Nibelungen*' was still pursuing a surreptitious course in his mind and germinating there all the while. He was not a composer like Tchaikovsky who would sit down at a set time each morning and expect his muse to wait on him obediently. In 1861 he was in Paris writing the libretto of *Die Meistersinger*, and, as he wrote in *Mein Leben*,

The melody for the fragment of Sachs' poem on the reformation, with which I make my characters in Act III greet their beloved master, occurred to me whilst strolling through the galleries of the Palais Royale. I found Truinet already waiting for me at The Taverne Anglaise, and asked him to give me a scrap of paper and a pencil to jot down my melody, which I quietly hummed over to him at the time.

Later still, on 9 February 1876, Wagner was in Bayreuth, and was trying (in vain) to crank up his muse for a potboiler, the *American Centennial March*, for a $5,000 fee; if ever there were a rock-bottomer by a top-notcher, this was it. Fortunately, his muse or his *daimon* had other, better plans. Cosima found him instead playing a gentle, rocking theme that had come into his mind, and this became his first music for *Parsifal*, '*Komm, Holder Knabe*,' the siren song with which the flower-maidens offer their enticements. Again, the next year, 1877, Cosima's diary entry for 15 August described: 'finally the revelation of "*Nehmet hin mein Blut*". Richard tells me he wrote it down shortly before my return, with his hat and coat on, just as he was about to meet me.' *Parsifal* was always then in his mind, but as happened with the *Rheingold* Prelude, his best ideas often came fortuitously and not when he was consciously trying to summon them up.

There were times when he did more consciously tap into his resources. Decades earlier when composing *Tannhäuser*, he had confided to Karl Gaillard in a letter of 13 August 1847,

> a feeling that a very real spell had been cast upon me. It required the merest contact with the subject matter and I immediately began to tremble with warmth and passion: in spite of long interruptions that kept me away from the score for months on end, I was always ready to re-immerse myself in an instant in the characteristic aura of the work, an aura that had first so exhilarated me when I first conceived the piece.

It was Richard Strauss who asserted that the brain which created *Tristan und Isolde* was ice-cold, but perhaps he was foisting onto Wagner his own mentality, as there is no evidence that Wagner was ever ice-cold about anything. 'Ice-cold' is not what emerged in his letter to Gaillard about *Tannhäuser* nor later from the observations of Wendelin Weissheimer, the fellow-composer who left a description of

Wagner at work on *Die Meistersinger* at Biebrich on the Rhine.

Sitting at the piano, he worked on the introduction to *Die Meistersinger* in the form of a very detailed sketch that looked like a piano score, but already included all the doublings and inner voices as he intended to elaborate them for the orchestra. He said: 'The more detailed the sketch, the easier and more assured the instrumentation.' 'Young people very often commit the mistake of working too hurriedly.' … In order for his sketch to be as accurate as possible, he would invariably consult the piano while preparing it. What mattered to him was the actual sound, not the sound as he had conceived it in his head. That is why he did not commit to paper any chord or modulation until he had properly tested it and was convinced it sounded good. In other words, he needed to be near a piano whenever he was working on a draft. The best way of achieving this was to have the piano lid closed and projecting over the keys, so that he could easily write on it while striking individual chords with his left hand or even trying them out with both hands until he was clear about the phrase in question, which he immediately set down on paper, without having to get up and go over to the desk. This measured approach naturally meant that he did not make particularly rapid progress. But what was written down was now fixed, often so fixed indeed that he rarely had to change it. And when he moved on to the instrumentation, this went all the more quickly and easily. He told me that he was able to complete around six pages in full score everyday without any special effort …

He began work on the first act, attacking it strictly in sequence. The brief exchange between Eva, Magdalena and the Knight simply oozed from his pen (and how delightfully), whereas David proved more problematical. To list and deal with so many modes was no easy matter, but his bubbling good humour helped him through. He was right royally amused by the dancing apprentices and it was a treat to see him perform their comic round in his room, leaping grotesquely and singing their words in the most accomplished falsetto …

Outwardly calm though he seemed, he was inwardly terribly

excitable while working on a piece. If he was elaborating anything that he had already sketched, my presence did not trouble him in the slightest, but if he was in the process of writing something new, he had to be left alone. Twice I interrupted him in the act of creation – on both occasions through no fault of my own, since he had summoned me from Mainz for a particular time. When I arrived, I knocked at his locked door, but he did not answer and so I assumed he had already gone to the hotel for lunch. I was about to go in search of him there when I heard a noise inside. I knocked again. Finally, he opened the door, his features completely altered, almost disturbed. 'I'm busy' he cried and scurried away, retiring to his bed-room where he remained hidden until he was quite calm again. I said how sorry I was that I had disturbed him at such a critical moment – he had run away as though he had committed some terrible crime. He laughed and showed me the pages on the piano, saying: 'Here you can see my terrible crime!' I looked at it: it was Pogner's address, which he had sketched out on a single folio. Once he had calmed down, he was happy for people to come, for then he would play what he had just written and see what impression it made on them. Delightful and alluring as such occasions were, I decided to be more careful in future. When he wrote to me again soon afterwards, asking me to come at a given hour, and the door was not opened to my knocking, I immediately retraced my steps with the intention of waiting for him elsewhere. I had scarcely descended to the street when the balcony door was thrown open above me and he shouted out in utter frenzy: 'Don't interrupt me now – I'm on heat!' An hour later he arrived at the Europäische Hof. He must still have been somewhat agitated as he bolted his food almost unchewed, even though he had been warned not to eat so quickly.

It is beyond this book to try and examine the music with any of the detail that Alfred Lorenz or Roger North have managed, or that Deryck Cooke planned in the book he left uncompleted at his death. Even so what should be clear is why great music affects people, and why Wagner's is both among the greatest and the most affecting of all.

It should also be clearer why Wagner's music acts on the imagination as it does. This in turn promotes and fulfils one of this book's main principles, because the better we can appreciate and feel how and why the Wagner Experience affects us, setting the context for the direct experience, the richer the experience becomes.

NINE

PUZZLES, OBSTRUCTIONS AND OBJECTIONS

> *It is much easier to expose the faults and errors in a great mind's work than to give a complete and lucid exposition of its value. For the faults are single things and finite which therefore can be fully surveyed; but the contrary is true of the stamp impressed by Genius on its works, whose excellence is unfathomable and inexhaustible.*
>
> Arthur Schopenhauer (as quoted by Wagner to Mathilde Wesendonck)

There was something messianic about the man, a degree of megalomania which often approached actual lunacy. As a human being he was frightening. Amoral, hedonistic, selfish, virulently racist, arrogant, filled with gospels of the superman (the superman naturally being Wagner), and the superiority of German race, he stands for all that is unpleasant in human character.

This pronouncement introduces the chapter on Wagner in Harold C. Schonberg's famous book, *Lives of the Great Composers*. It is a book that was widely influential,[176] thanks to the author's colourful vignettes of the composers' styles, idioms and lives. It is generally full of insight, warmth and humour, but not about Wagner. Possibly the pocket biography which follows might justify Schonberg's damning

---

176 Schonberg, Harold C., *The Lives of the Great Composers*, London, 1971.

assessment of Wagner as a profligate, sex-obsessed sponger who was fundamentally evil.

> Aged just 18, he began an eight year affair with Blanche Olivier, wife of a leading (and wealthy) Dresden lawyer. After her, he lived in sin with Ottalie, a tailor's daughter from Chemnitz. He cheated on Ottalie with Mathilde Maiermann, to whom he was briefly engaged, before leaving her for her friend, the fashion model, Rosalie, whom he eventually married. Rosalie clearly had the looks but not the brain to interest Wagner long-term, and she was soon packed back to her father's home when he met the captivating Jessie, the mother of one of his disciples and the wife of a leading banker. Rosalie was so disturbed at being deserted that she shot herself in the chest while standing in the centre of Dresden's main square. Surprisingly she survived this violent suicide attempt, but this was one scandal too many, and he and the now pregnant Jessie were forced to fly to England, although they returned home for the birth of their daughter.

Anyone reading this unattractive record might reasonably think it justifies a low opinion of Wagner, except that some readers will already have sensed a spoof, that I have attributed a true biography to the wrong person in order to make a point; its subject is Debussy[177] and not Wagner. Wagner's private life inflicted less damage and misery than Debussy's, and even if not a racist Debussy was more unprincipled in other respects, but does he attract the same damning assessment from Harold Schonberg as he doled out to Wagner? He does not. Instead of beginning his chapter on Debussy with a character assassination, Harold Schonberg launches it with this eulogy;

> '*A tout Seigneur, tout l'honneur*,' runs the French proverb. Honor to whom honor is due. It is not that Claude Debussy lacked honors in

---

177 This biography is slightly abridged – and with some names changed – from the Cheltenham Festival's *Maestro* Magazine, 4-15 July 2012, p. 9 et seq.

his own day. After a slow start, this *musician français* (so he liked to describe himself) was recognised as the greatest French composer of his time. But today he is more than that. He is considered not only the greatest French composer who ever lived; he is considered the revolutionary who with *Prélude à l'après-midi d'un faune* of 1894 set 20th-century music on its way.

In due course, Schonberg did make some passing references to Debussy's personal imperfections, but shuffled them off instead of highlighting them as the first thing that everyone should know. This gunning down of Wagner's reputation is common, and one of the puzzles of Wagner is why he is the composer whom everyone loves to hate.

Why? Why does it happen? Why give his off-putting features a special prominence? Paraded like this, they make obstacles, because they are bound to distemper impressions of both the man and his works, especially first impressions. Certain off-putting features of the man have already been reviewed and cut down to size, but it seems vital to go further and confront other obstacles head on, and this is my purpose now.

One of the puzzles of Wagner is the hostility which his music itself can call up. When Wagner stirs the depths what comes welling up can be ecstatic and liberating, but it can also take the disturbing form of dark phantoms that come screaming out of the blackness. Wagner's is not the only great music that gives rise to experiences that are disturbing, particularly for those who are disturbed, whether they know it or not. When Vladimir Ashkenazy conducted the Philharmonia Orchestra at a memorable concert in the Festival Hall some ten years ago, there was a particular member of the audience who sat happily through the Mozart Symphony; but when it came to Mahler's 'Resurrection' Symphony, this poor person was reduced within minutes to a fit of uncontrollable shrieking and weeping, and had to be hurried out. It is not only music which obviously disturbing that disturbs people. At that very same location a few weeks later there was the annual Bach Choir performance of the *St Matthew Passion*, and at the ineffable moment when the chorus declare 'Truly, this was the son of God,' a man sitting nearby, who suffered from spastic paralysis, began quietly to sob as if his heart would break. These intense responses from the two audience members came from within, and were not Bach's 'fault', nor Mahler's, and such responses can even be cathartic, but the relevant point is that people often tend to put the blame on Wagner for the disquieting reactions that come from within themselves. There is a poem, if that is the word for it, by Rupert Brooke, entitled 'Wagner',[178] which articulates this particularly well. It has been read in two ways, as a description of the 'spiritual form of Wagner', and as a description of the kind of person who likes Wagner. Either way it is a criticism of Wagnerism and of Wagner's music. Heaven knows what it was in Rupert Brooke's psyche which Wagner's music disturbed at the Queen's Hall in 1908, and which led him to write:

Creeps in half wanton, half asleep,
One with a fat wide hairless face.
He likes love-music that is cheap;
Likes women in a crowded place;
And wants to hear the noise they're making.
His heavy eyelids droop half-over,
Great pouches swing beneath his eyes.
He listens, thinks himself the lover,
Heaves from his stomach wheezy sighs;
He likes to feel his heart's a-breaking.
The music swells. His gross legs quiver.
His little lips are bright with slime.
The music swells. The women shiver.
And all the while, in perfect time,
His pendulous stomach hangs a-shaking.

I have been unable to find out what pieces of music Rupert Brooke

178 Brooke, Rupert, *Collected Poems: With a Memoir*, London, 1918.

actually heard, and it would have been interesting if he had gone on to experience something by Wagner in full; might he have absorbed it and emerged better integrated, as people can? Whatever might have happened, the sense of something dark and detestable in Wagner is a projection of disturbances that originate within. This makes for one of the most difficult and insuperable of all obstacles to Wagner, because not many people are happy to recognise any shadow or disunities in themselves, unless the pain of them makes them want to change.

This is not the only inner problem which people foist outwards onto Wagner. The next common objection to Wagner represents another pathology; it is bound up with the lure that Wagner holds for anyone who is looking for shortcomings in greatness and feels satisfaction from finding them. To do this is the mark of a neurosis, an insecurity, a compensation mechanism for people who cannot accept that others exist who are more significant than they are themselves. People with this disposition may try to cope by targeting the shortcomings of greatness out of a vague feeling that the shortcomings of great people can somehow cancel out the greatness. It is another form of the shadow and another way of projecting the shadow. People so disposed feel more at ease if they can look down on someone great and find a justification for a sense of superiority in spite of the greatness. Comparisons somehow seem less odious; and these unfortunate people come out of it feeling less insignificant. Wagner's towering greatness and his great faults provide these people with a ready target. Hans Keller pointed out something of this kind at work in Wagner's case, and identified it as the 'Polycrates complex'. He wrote of Wagner,[179]

The man has been destroyed by friend and foe and critical referee like, and an objective picture has been created of his personality by critic after critic which is indistinguishable from the image of a phantom. It is not here suggested that there was nothing wrong with Wagner, nor is it suggested that there is nothing wrong with you or me. But you and I

179 Keller, Hans, *Criticism*, London, 1987, p. 96; the term 'Polycrates complex' comes from the psychoanalyst J.C. Flugel.

luckily can't compose like that and so we are safe … [And:] 'Objective' destructiveness has been displaced onto or made to concentrate on the man in order to make things psychologically easy for the observer who can love the music and save his soul, as well as spending his aggression by hating the man.

Keller's Polycrates complex is not a healthy or reliable way to achieve self-worth, first because it necessarily involves resentment, that most corrosive of all emotions,[180] second because it represents a denial of reality. Third it brings no personal integration. Any mental manoeuvrings which deny reality do nothing to resolve a neurosis but only reinforce it.

Poignantly it was Nietzsche who early on provided an outstanding example of how and why such people can be drawn to Wagner. It is absolutely not my intention to belittle Nietzsche, another fractured genius; but Nietzsche illustrates how lonely, disturbed people can get a distressing satisfaction from pouring scorn on greatness. Nietzsche ended by denouncing Wagner both as a fake and as a pernicious influence. In their happier days, Wagner had been a substitute father for Nietzsche, but later Nietzsche had to endure first the dread processes of syphilis burning his brain away, second the warping of his judgment owing to his passion for Wagner's wife Cosima, and then perhaps, in consequence of that passion, the workings of a distorted Oedipus complex regarding Wagner. It makes no sense to take the calamitous Nietzsche as a balanced assessment, but he does help with understanding the reasons why people love to hate Wagner. These are deep reasons, and represent some real and insuperable obstacles.

---

180 See *Alcoholics Anonymous*, AA World Services Inc., 3rd ed., New York, 1976, the so-called 'Big Book' of AA: one of the best books ever written as an adjunct towards emotional health, and that balance which Wagner's works can offer. One of its most therapeutic and influential passages reads, 'It is plain that a life that includes deep resentment leads only to futility and unhappiness.' This book and the AA fellowship has contributed as much to the health of patients as any conventional psychiatry.

Other obstacles are associated with Wagner the man. In this category the biggest and truest obstacle to Wagner the man was his hatred of the Jews, and this was a frightening fact. The next biggest was his Nazi inclinations, a nonsensical fiction, even though some outstanding intellects, such as Thomas Mann, have made the mistake of 'discovering' Nazism and Hitlerism in Wagner. Any attempt to tar Wagner with the Nazi brush flies in the face of historical reality. The oft-repeated assertion that Hitler and Wagner used to breakfast together is obvious nonsense because of their dates, but from everything Wagner said and did, it stares us in the face that he always was, and always remained, a man of the extreme left. (I recognise that applied to politics 'left' and 'right' are vague terms and unsatisfactory, but they are still useful shorthand and can avoid whole paragraphs of irksome explanation.) Hitler's ultra-right-wing use of Wagner was a *mis*-use. It was only possible because Hitler press-ganged Wagner's work to serve his own purposes and distorted his ideas into a complete perversion. Anyone who disagrees has only to remember Hitler's core tenet, that the individual existed to serve the state, and that Wagner held the exact opposite view. For Wagner the only possible justification for the state and its intolerable, stultifying regimentation (what *would* he have thought of Western civilisation today?) was to serve and fulfil the individual. He changed in many ways during his life, but politically he always remained far away to the left, close to Marxism, as becomes clear in *The Ring*. He did dissemble his left-wing beliefs and feelings after the Dresden uprising had failed, first because Liszt and others constantly warned him that he must bury his politics deep or he would never be amnestied from exile back to Germany. Later, after King Ludwig had taken him in, it again seemed politic to play down his past sympathy with revolutionary movements committed to 'making monarchs tremble', monarchs like Ludwig himself. Later Wagner fraternised with aristocracies because he needed their help for Bayreuth, but as a man of the left he always regarded titles, honours and establishment status as fatuous baubles. He can be accused of fraud for dissembling his socialist ideals, but not of giving them up.

He dissembled especially after King Ludwig had proved unsympathetic towards the Bayreuth project. There is a common belief that Ludwig's generosity to Wagner was limitless and that Wagner beggared the Bavarian treasury, but that is a mistake. In comparison with Ludwig's mind-boggling outlay on his fantastic castles and other paraphernalia of Bavarian royalty, his funding for Wagner was not a major expense. His furnishings for his bedroom at Herrenchiemsee, just one single room of the more than fifty in just one of his castles, cost more than everything that he ever gave Wagner; and his lifetime support for the composer added up to less than one quarter of the cost of his royal wedding coach, which was never used. To be sure, there were reasons for the King's penny-pinching. He had idolised Wagner, and he never came to terms with his heartbreak over Wagner's and Cosima's lies about their adulterous relationship. They hoodwinked him into writing to the newspapers and rebutting all the media allegations about their liaison, but those allegations were then exposed by Wagner and Cosima as glaringly true. This made clear to him the painful fact that they had exploited his trust and made a fool of him, when he had thought they revered and loved him, and that they all lived in a happy trio of absolute trust. It also showed him that the genius whom he idolised had feet of clay, and the anguish of discovering this, and that so many ideals were illusions, left the lonely and unhappy King bereft. Accordingly, when he did eventually provide the niggardly minimum which Wagner still needed for Bayreuth, it took the form of loans; and the Wagner family was still paying them off into the twentieth century. The King's bitterness explains why the Bayreuth Festival Theatre was built on the cheap, funded mostly by what Wagner could cajole from the aristocracy and the upper middle classes, until Ludwig came to the rescue with too little and too late. To see Wagner's Bayreuth project in another perspective, the almost contemporary Palais Garnier, the Paris Opera House, cost almost exactly seventy times as much as the Bayreuth Theatre. If Wagner stooped to curry favour with the aristocracy it was from financial extremity, not from aristocratic sympathies or right-wing convictions.

On the contrary, during the period leading up to *Parsifal,* Wagner was desperately disillusioned with the new, right-wing Germany that was taking shape around him, and he was becoming more openly antagonistic to it, to the alarm of his acolytes. It was all so distressingly different from what he had idealised, promoted and foretold in *Die Meistersinger von Nürnberg.* He was in practice like many in England and America who likewise cherish patriotic ideals that are unrelated to reality. He had an inner vision of Germany that was good and splendid, epitomising the noble northern spirit, a new Athens. This was his true Germany, and it made a disturbing contrast to the reality, a Germany of greed, capitalist classes, and wealth-obsession, which he witnessed growing around him. He was also coming to despair of Prussian leadership and of Prussia itself as over-industrialised, warlike, and dictatorial, a clanking, mechanistic, soulless, military machine, with its 'abuses shored up by laws and the constitution'.[181] He wrote these words in the year before his death and asked, 'Who can look upon this world of robbery and murder, organised and legalised by lying, deceit and hypocrisy, without being forced to flee from it at times in shuddering disgust?' The context leaves no doubt that it was close to home that he saw his worst example.

He could discern in contemporary Germany no trace of Schopenhauerian compassion for 'the lower orders' which produced the wealth that made the rich grow richer and richer. The bleak depictions of Käthe Kollwitz are closer to what he warned of in *The Ring;* and his feeling for the less well off was not just theoretical; his unfailing consideration and kindliness to those poorer than himself was one of the documented reasons why his servants adored him. Vreneli, his housekeeper at Tribschen, only accepted a proposal of marriage from her husband-to-be on condition that he was prepared to join the Wagner household and work for Wagner as she did. Similarly in 1881, Marie, a little servant girl at their house Wahnfried,

---

181 '"Parsifal" at Bayreuth' (1882) in *Prose Works,* tr. William Ashton Ellis, London, 1897, vi, p. 310.

was reduced to tears because he was leaving for the sunnier climes of Palermo to try to rescue his health. (He did not succeed.) Wagner's para-Marxist position was strongly opposed to a state controlled by the wealthy, the powerful, and the selfish, and even more to the idea that the individual should be nothing but a cog in the all-important state machine. It beggars belief that Hitler could one day say, 'He who would understand National Socialism must know Wagner.' This could only be true in the paradoxical sense that if we really know Wagner, we can see more clearly everything that is so glaringly wrong with Nazism. Wagner's concern for ordinary individual people was the polar opposite of Nazism.

That said, only a fool would deny that there was one outlook which he did share with Nazism, and that was his pathological anti-Semitism. After originally hoping to produce a book which would concentrate exclusively on other things, I found it impossible not to give time and space to a subject of such importance. The debates continue endlessly about whether the connection between fascism and anti-Semitism was a necessary one or an unhappy chance. However, Wagner did not need intimations of Nazism to make hatred of the Jews his very own. He was genuinely worried that the alien influence of the Jews was distorting the fragile growth of German identity and nationhood. *Das Judenthum in der Musik*,[182] the tract which he published twice, is a vicious attack on Jews as being bad for the German identity. It always seems surprising that a mind as penetrating as his could generate dramas, *Die Meistersinger* and *Parsifal*, about decrepit societies rejuvenated by creative vigour from outside, without seeing how this might symbolise what the Jews could bring to Germany; but as pointed out already, sense and nonsense often sit side by side even in great minds.

The most convincing explanation for Wagner's hatred is related to a common experience, that the greatest revulsion is reserved for those aspects of others which most repel us in ourselves. More technically it

---

182 Wagner, pseudonymously as K. Freigedenk, *Das Judenthum in der Musik*, Leipzig, 1850, repr. under his own name, Leipzig, 1869.

rests in the fact that the Jews were part of Wagner's personal shadow. The shadow represents a locus for coping with tendencies which we regard as bad, such as jealousy, double-dealing, meanness, greed, fraud, hypocrisy, and *Schadenfreude*.[183] A personal shadow is an important mental space where we can size down these unpleasant tendencies and integrate them. If however, we encounter people, places and things which fit the mould of what is sized down, we project onto those people all the antagonism we feel against these features in ourselves. In the words of Carl Jung this is 'transferring to our fellows the injustice and violence we inflict on our own natures,' and the more conflicted we are, the more fiercely this is likely to happen. These features become the personalised shadow, and anything that represents our personal shadow calls up a hatred that feels instinctive, needing no other justification. Wagner described exactly this happening in himself when he described his 'instinctive revulsion' for the Jewish physiognomy. His essay *Das Judenthum in der Musik* presents a ludicrous caricature of 'the normal Jew', revealing that he had parted company with reality and was tilting at a fantasy, at a symbol of his own disunities. Of all the faces he knew, the one that best fitted his caricature was the one he saw in the mirror, but the symbol wielded over him a compelling force, providing a cogent and unhappy example of how and why people become obsessed with what they hate and cannot forget it. People normally avoid and forget things which they dislike, but where the animosity is deeply imprinted and the shadow not accepted, a person is fascinated as well as repelled, and can no more let go than a dog with lockjaw. This is why Wagner was constantly drawn back to his anti-Semitism. His anti-Semitism was very real and loathsome, and it still then raises the question: why was it the Jews that he picked on?

The answers partly lie in history, because history shows both that anti-Semitism had a protracted and discouraging record in Europe long before Wagner came along, and that it was particularly widespread

---

183 *Schadenfreude*, pleasure in other people's misfortunes and satisfaction over their disasters, was identified by Schopenhauer as the worst of all human characteristics.

in Wagner's time. There is a vague notion that Wagner was a special trailblazer for the evils of Hitler, and it suits a number of Germans to believe this. It means that they can scapegoat Wagner.

Wagner's racist shadow was obnoxious but unfortunately it had an impeccable pedigree. For almost two thousand years the Jews have represented a collective European shadow, a negative stereotype, attracting hatred and persecution. It had begun after the conversion of the Emperor Constantine, when Christianity became the favoured and then the official religion of the Roman Empire. Triumphant Christianity destroyed the old Roman religion and all rivals except Judaism, which remained the only alternative to Christianity still allowed, however vilified it might be. Later throughout the Dark and the Middle Ages, the Jews were subjected to marginalisation and persecution, both physical and economic. They were set up as satanic, the Christ-killers, and it is a sad paradox that St John's Gospel, most spiritual of the gospels, played a specially evil role in this. St John's Gospel describes a *Jewish* crowd baying for Jesus to be crucified, and tells that when Pontius Pilate told them that they would have innocent blood on their hands, they brought down God's eternal curse on their race by responding 'His blood be on us and on our children.' This legitimised a general antagonism to the Jews as a righteous doctrine, and turned them into a collective shadow. They were debarred from military activity, owning land, and most other economic activities, and they were excluded from mediaeval manufacturing guilds controlled by Christians. (If Beckmesser had really been Jewish, as is sometimes argued, he would have never had been allowed among the Mastersingers.) Because of their civil disabilities, the Jews were urban and commercial, non-manufacturing and non-military, and so they were branded as cowards, parasites and usurers. In the introduction to *The Origins of the Final Solution*,[184] Christopher R. Browning points out that the negative stereotype was fuelled by far-fetched and demented accusations, fantasies such as the alleged practice of ritual murder and

184 Browning, Christopher R., *The Origins of the Final Solution*, Lincoln, Nebr. and Jerusalem, 2004, p. 3.

of 'torturing the Host', which revealed serious mental pathologies at work in the minds concerned.

During the seventeenth and eighteenth centuries, anti-Semitism became more pervasive. Initially the two crucial revolutions of the era helped the Jews. The French Revolution signalled a new liberalism. The burden of discriminatory anti-Jewish measures soon gave way to equality before the law and to freedom of conscience, even in the autocratic German and Austro-Hungarian territories. After the defeat of Napoleon, all this changed and there was a severe retrenchment. Old feudal aristocracies regained control, and old conservative values, including the vilification of the Jews, returned in full force.

The Industrial Revolution set in motion economic and social changes that were just as far-reaching and initially just as positive for the Jews. They opened up new developments and fresh opportunities for Jews because they were mobile, educated and adaptable, and had little interest or affection for the previous declining economies and the former social structures, where they had been vilified and marginalised. However, it also soon apparent that the Industrial Revolution created a new group of losers, traditional minor elites and small-scale producers, and these perceived in the Jews a focus for their miseries and resentments. These groups came to believe that if Jews were benefiting from the changes that were destroying Europe's traditional way of life, then the Jews must be the cause and engineers of those changes. It was a classic example of the '*post hoc ergo propter hoc*' fallacy; but it carried widespread conviction.

And as the world grew more secular and people looked less to religion for explanations than to science, there arose a new tendency to stop blaming the Jewishness of Jews on their religion, and blame it on their race. Whereas the scope for converting to Christianity had hitherto provided an escape route for the Jews from their position as outcasts, an anti-Semitism based on race and bizarre views of genetics closed down this possibility. In the nineteenth century, anti-Semitic movements were sweeping the world, and Wagner was a marginal player in comparison with the virulent Karl Lueger of Vienna, or the rabid Bernhard Förster who organised a massed petition to the German Reichstag against the Jews.

Leading figures of organised religion in both of its main West European streams gave their blessing to anti-Semitism over many centuries. It was not simply that Martin Luther was as anti-Semitic as any mediaeval pope. Pius IX, the pope who occupied the Vatican from 1846 to 1878, the central thirty-two years of Wagner's adult life, was particularly intransigent. Norbert Greinacher, who contributed 'a theologian's view of Tannhäuser's quest for salvation,' has supplied Wagnerians with evidence that the nineteenth century

> was notable for frequent cases of harassment, for the abduction of Jewish children, and for enforced baptisms. Pope Pius IX had the Jews confined to a ghetto, and in 1858, he ordered the Vatican police to remove the seven year old son of a wealthy Jewish family in Bologna by the name of Mortava and place him in a Christian boarding school, since he had been baptised shortly after his birth by a Christian serving maid.[185]

In 1889, there was even a propaganda book to prove that Jews sacrificed Christian children, and it received the approval and endorsement from the reigning Pope.[186]

There had been Bruno Bauer, lecturer in theology in Berlin the 1830s, who campaigned that the Jews must be baptised before they could reasonably claim civil emancipation. This was all the more bizarre because Bauer had explained away the Gospels as pure fiction

---

185 Greinacher, Norbert, 'How does Tannhäuser find Salvation?', programme for *Tannhäuser*, Bayreuth, 1986, p. 71.

186 This book, title unknown, is described by Charles Godfrey Leland in his complete translation of Heinrich Heine's works. The occasion is Heine's short story *The Rabbi of Bacharach*, a tale describing the vilification of the Rabbi as a child murderer as justification for murdering him. *Complete Works of Heinrich Heine*, i, tr. Charles Godfrey Leland, London, 1891, p. 179.

in his publications, and denied that Jesus had ever existed. Yet Jesus is the central focus of the religion into which he wanted the Jews to be assimilated. All in all, the ground had been prepared for the general antagonism to the Jews, and while it is no part of my intention to deny that Wagner's anti-Semitism was evil, he was not influential in the same way as Karl Lueger or Bernhard Förster. Nor did the Nazis need Wagner to turn the Jews into a hated symbol of their collective shadow; but because Wagner composed operas and dramas of genius and because Hitler liked them, Wagner is the Jew-hater we remember.

What goes round comes round, as the saying goes, and there has been an extraordinary reversal. Just as Wagner vilified the Jews as his personal shadow, a significant number of people now vilify Wagner as the symbol of their own shadow. Hartmut Zelinsky, Robert Gutman and Gottfried Wagner are three among many who may have succumbed to the pathology of the shadow, and projected it onto Wagner. In 1976 Hartmut Zelinsky began a lifetime of torrential and vitriolic outpourings with his *Richard Wagner: Ein deutsches Thema*, ('Richard Wagner: a German Theme'). Joachim Köhler, whose book on Wagner[187] is a brilliant and erratic concoction of marvellous insights, unfamiliar facts and unfounded, evidence-free assertions, announced on television that without Wagner, there could have been no Hitler.[188] This goes beyond reason. Yes, perhaps Köhler's assertion is true in the same trivial way as it is true that if people had never discovered how to build ships, there could never have been a transatlantic slave trade. The difference is that no one is likely to argue that ship-building was directly responsible for the slave trade, but there are many people who hold Wagner responsible for Hitler.

Wagner was partly moved to pick on the Jews by his jealousy of the enviably rich Meyerbeer and the enviably fashionable Mendelssohn, both Jews, and the processes of jealousy were energised by unpleasant

---

187 Köhler, Joachim, *Richard Wagner: The Last of the Titans*, tr. Stewart Spencer, New Haven and London, 2004.

188 Tanner, Michael, *The Faber Pocket Guide to Wagner*, London, 2010, p. 245.

memories of other Jews. There had been the wily Bethmann, the director at the Magdeburg opera who as Wagner saw it, had diddled Wagner over his benefit performance[189] at Magdeburg. There was Dietrich, the wealthy businessman who made off with Minna shortly after Wagner married her, and then deserted her. There was Heinrich Heine whom Wagner knew in Paris, the brilliant star of European literature and just as brilliant as a blackmailer and extortioner.

Issues of Wagner's anti-Semitism are made to cast a dark veil over his dramas with the suggestion that Wagner was so soused in hatred of the Jews that anything that mattered to him so much must dominate his art as well; therefore Wagner's art must consequently be anti-Semitic. Even the basis of this argument is wrong, because Wagner's thinking and prose works are full of ideas that mattered strongly to him and yet never found their way into his stage works. There were other subjects which plagued him just as much as the Jews, above all the question how the artist, i.e. himself, could make enough money to create his works without concentrating on income and compromising his ideals. His correspondence, with his family, with Liszt, Uhlig and countless others is as sad and revealing of how far Wagner spent his life eating his heart out over fees and finances. His letters constantly press their recipients about income possibilities, about the best rates they could squeeze from different opera managements, about his loans and his debts, and about his need for money. These worries dominated his life until his dying day, and as Cosima's *Diaries* show all too poignantly, they consumed energies that might have given the world just one more masterpiece. Even so, Wagner's financial concerns were too petty and dismal to feature in his artistic creations because they warranted bigger themes, and better.

The issue of anti-Semitism in Wagner's art gives rise to the question, what is meant by his 'anti-Semitic Art'? The term seems to turn on the

---

189 Bethmann, as was customary, assigned to Wagner the profits from a performance of his *Das Liebesverbot*, but from the poorly attended second performance instead of from the first night, which is usually assured of good receipts.

assumption that anti-Semitism is not only present in Wagner's output but that it inspires people against the Jews. However, for this to be true there are three essentials, three conditions which must be fulfilled:

1. There must be identifiable Jewish characters in Wagner's dramas.
2. The Jewish qualities of those characters must be visibly objectionable.
3. There must be at least a proportion among Wagner's audiences, his hearers and observers, who are led on by these stage characters to feel and even express antagonism to the Jews in real life.

There are those whose insist that Beckmesser, Alberich, Mime and Klingsor are Jews, and are emblems of anti-Semitism, but it is not clear how they make audiences hate Jews, not least because nobody even noticed that they were supposed to be Jewish until about twenty-five years ago, not even the Nazis who might have sniffed it out and made use of it. Sometimes ingenious writers believe they have found 'proofs' of the anti-Semitism encoded in his works which somehow went undeciphered until the late twentieth century; the absence of visible anti-Semitism is not allowed to be evidence for its not being there, but is twisted into proof of Wagner's stealth in concealing it. Such proofs begin to look fantastical, with as much logical validity as the argument, the false syllogism, 'If there were a ghost in that chair, I should not see it; I do not see a ghost in that chair: therefore there must be a ghost in that chair.' The argument about anti-Semitism in Wagner's output is much the same; 'If there is anti-Semitism in his works I should not see it; I do not see anti-Semitism in his works: therefore there must be anti-Semitism in his works – even though invisible and undetectable.' A person who is convinced of this can be convinced of anything.

∽

There are other, different puzzles and objections that can provide obstacles: 'Wagner was a wanted man, with a reward on his head!' This is an objection that is often stated baldly and simply left, allowing all kinds of interpretation. It has resulted in descriptions of Wagner as a common criminal, whatever that may be – a man perhaps convicted of robbery with violence, or burglary, or fraud, or rape? The reason why Wagner was a wanted man was that he was involved in the Dresden uprising, the left-wing cause supported by most of Dresden's liberal intellectuals, its university academics and large swathes of its business and professional classes. As an instance of what they were fighting, there had been a harsh new law passed, just before the Dresden uprising, which forbade 'thefts' by the impoverished peasantry of decaying wood from the neighbouring forests, wood which they desperately needed not to freeze in winter and which they had previously been allowed.[190] Although the King of Saxony himself was by all accounts a liberal and humane man, respected and loved, not least by a certain Richard Wagner, the political system which he headed was not at all liberal and humane, and apologists who try to show that Wagner was not really involved in the Dresden uprising do him an injustice.

It is worth emphasising again that Wagner's left-wing perspective on society persisted or even grew stronger: for instance one day in 1881 he was in discussion at Wahnfried with his friend, Friedrich Feustel. Feustel was a banker and chairman of the Bayreuth town council, a tower of strength to Wagner and his family, but no pushover. Friedrich von Schön, a factory owner, was another of those present, and he recorded with rare objectivity how they had been arguing about the conditions of factory workers like those von Schön himself was employing. Wagner suddenly lost his temper. 'Yes,' he shouted, 'and they stand there all day in their factories and see and hear nothing but bare walls and noise and pounding of the machines – is that an existence fit for human beings?' Feustel was a man of some spirit, and he tried to bring up new arguments; 'whereupon' says von Schön,

Wagner flared up in a fit of the most profound and painful emotion,

---

190 Berlin, Isaiah, *Karl Marx*, London, 1939, 3rd ed., Oxford, 1963.

summing all that he had to say on the subject in a single exclamation: 'Children, children, have you forgotten Jesus Christ?!!' He uttered those words with so indescribable expression in his eyes and with so shatteringly powerful a sense of fellow-feeling for the darker aspects of our social lives, and with such a moving reverence for the divinity of the name that he had just spoken, that we were all moved to the depths of our being. The effect was as if the master had placed the figure of the Redeemer before our innermost eye: 'I saw him – then his gaze fell on me!' Not another word was spoken. We rose and took our leave, our hearts profoundly stirred.[191]

This account with its reference to *Parsifal* Act II should incidentally give pause for thought for those who insist on maintaining that Wagner had no use for anything Christian.

To sum up so far: any rational view must recognise that Wagner the man possessed titanic faults, as well as titanic virtues, but no-one who examines Wagner's biography in any detail could reckon him as qualified even at entry level for the vast and gloomy gallery of those who have added seriously to the sum of human suffering.

೮

Our next big obstacle to Wagner is another that is submerged, today's climate of instant gratification. There is a common, puzzling belief that anything recreational should give pleasure without effort. Everything ought to have an instant 'hook' to save anyone from getting bored and turning off. This may represent the values of advertising and marketing, which have become commonplace and axiomatic for life in general, and have even acquired a righteous, moral tinge. With it goes an implicit, unspoken ordinance that things not instantly gratifying deserve to fail; the market is master; the market alone is qualified to

191 von Schön, Friedrich, *Eine Erinnerung an Richard Wagner*, Bayreuth Festival Programme, 1924, in Spencer, Stewart, *Wagner Remembered*, London, 2000.

make judgments of value. People should not have to take trouble; indeed people who do so and get something good deserve to be sharply criticised for 'elitism' – except for some reason in sport. Perhaps too there is a hint here of the notion that nobody should expect children to learn music because the effort is off-putting; and it might rein back their natural creativity. This seems almost as debatable as it might be to suggest that children should give up learning to read because this might rein back their natural interest in using the alphabet to craft their own interesting patterns. The idea of not needing to take trouble becomes an obstacle to Wagner as well as an obstacle to classical music generally, because some kind of effort, at least to listen, *is* necessary for music and for Wagner's music in particular.

Another obstacle is the high-flown quality Wagner claimed for his creations, an idea which will not suit anyone who believes that the arts should only be a diversion. '*Musica laboris levamen*: Music that lightens toil' was a maxim that decorated musical instruments in the eighteenth century, and the 'Thunderer' column in *The Times* of 10 July 2012 asserted, 'Art is no good at changing the world. It is at its best when luxuriating in pointlessness or trying to brighten up an afternoon.' There is no answer to anyone who idealises pointlessness, except that it leaves its consumer hungry and dissatisfied. Wagner can certainly brighten up an afternoon, but his art does satisfyingly more. This whole book shows how Wagner wanted his art to change the world, but what causes difficulties is its sheer cargo of meaning. Anyone coming to mature Wagner for the first time, for example to *Tristan und Isolde*, has to grapple with something like a first encounter with Mahler's Fifth, Sixth and Seventh Symphonies, all played one after the another; and there is not just the music, but the text and the drama, layer upon layer, something which could give anyone a serious attack of data overload. For the same reason, its density of meaning, Wagner's music is not ideal as background, not the best thing for 'lightening the toil' of car journeys or kitchen chores. People dedicated to art for its 'pointlessness', will not like Wagner and there is really nothing much that can persuade them.

Yet another obstacle is the sheer diversity, sometimes the conflict, of the ideas and suggestions present in the dramas. This diversity derives partly from the lifelong expansion of Wagner's intellectual base which led him to reinterpret existing works and find unexpected messages and new directions. His reinterpretations should probably not all be allowed the same weight. George Bernard Shaw commented,[192]

> Wagner's explanations of his works for the most part explain nothing but the mood he happened to be in on the day he advanced them, or the train of thought suggested to his very susceptible imagination by his questioner ... We find him taking all manner of positions and putting forward all sorts of cases which must be taken as clever and suggestive special pleadings, and not as serious and permanent expositions of his works.

This goes much too far, but it makes a point: Wagner did put forward some very puzzling ideas about what he meant, one example being his re-imagining of *Lohengrin* as a drama centred on Elsa, 'the woman of the future' who 'who made a revolutionary of me'. Wagner amplified these difficulties for us because of his unorthodox methods of incorporating new information. Sometimes he integrated the new ideas into his existing ones, making a systematic analysis and discarding what no longer fitted, but his other methods were like what happens in rock formations when new strata spread across the old. Sometimes the result of this can be a complete intermingling and fusion, creating a new substance. Sometimes there could be intermingling at the interfaces, with each layer otherwise remaining separate. Sometimes there was no mix, and the different strata remained entirely separate. When this last happens and Wagner's ideas are immiscible, then sometimes the different ideas still often manage to sit well together, but sometimes not. A confusing instance of Wagner altering his ideas has already been mentioned: the Wagner of the middle years believed that music

---

192 Shaw, George Bernard, *The Perfect Wagnerite*, 3rd ed., Leipzig, 1913, p. 202.

drama should combine all the arts equally, but later he adopted Schopenhauer's belief that music was *primus inter pares*. Wagner never abandoned his ideal of drama as an equal synthesis of all the arts, but he suffused it with the belief that some arts, notably music, were more equal than others.

The course of this study shows that Wagner did sometimes put together ideas are incompatible, and that this risks destroying the complex synthesis that was his hard-won achievement. In practice, disintegration does not quite occur even when there are contrary ideas and great tension among them, as happens particularly in *Tannhäuser* and *The Ring*. This is partly because many of his ideas manage to sit side by side in the unconscious, even if they conflict in reason, but more often it is because the music saves the situation. The music embraces the differences; it creates resolutions, transforms disjunctions, and rationalises developments which do not follow logically. Wagner knew it. August Röckel, his musical deputy at Dresden, was serving his prison sentence for his leading role in the Dresden uprising when he wrote to Wagner puzzled about the end of *The Ring*. *The Ring* ends with the gold happily restored to the Rhinemaidens, and from all that has gone before this should lead to the redemption not only of humanity, but of the world and the gods; but instead the gods still meet their destruction, and Röckel evidently told Wagner that he saw no reason why. Wagner's answer[193] explained that the music would make everything clear, and as he demonstrated 25 years later, he was probably right; but people must make up their own minds.

A related obstacle was that Wagner's works do not always mean what he wanted them to mean; even the intentions of a genius can go awry. For instance, writing – again – to August Röckel, he characterised Siegfried as 'pure love', and went on, 'I have sought in Siegfried to represent my ideal of a perfect human being.' In due course it will be clear why it is difficult to discover a perfect being, or pure love, in Siegfried. There is a similar, earlier example of this in the character of

193 *Richard Wagner's letters to August Röckel*, tr. *Eleanor C. Sellar*, Bristol, [1897].

Venus as she appears in the first Dresden version of *Tannhäuser*. He thought this characterisation was remarkable and that her feeble effect onstage was due to his inadequate performer, but later he realised that his feeble characterisation was the problem, and rewrote the role. He also accepted that he could be mistaken about his creations and what they meant; there is his disarming confession (a letter to Röckel yet again) that he was often puzzled at what he had produced: 'the artist himself feels in the presence of his work that he is confronted by a riddle about which he too might have illusions.'

A feature of the Wagner Experience which might have been reckoned problematic or an obstacle is the sheer diversity of what it brings to different people and of what matters most, but this is an added interest, and something positive. For some Wagnerians the theatre is crucial, the different stagings and the range of interpretations placed on the dramas, and there have been conferences and whole books on the subject. Others are enthralled, as Ernest Newman was, by the course of Wagner's life; others by the myths and psychology in his works, or by the political allegory. Others find themselves taken up with technical issues about Wagner's musical language and its forms. The enigmatic *Tristan* chord: how is it to be analysed? Is it fourths or sevenths? Is the form of *The Ring* best understood as a web of interweaving, subdividing classical structures, such as ABA, ABAB, rondos and bar forms etc., as was discerned by Alfred Lorenz?[194] The happy thing about the different aspects is that anyone who widens out his (or her) scope to embrace new angles rarely finds a disjunction. A new interest in the details of Wagner's life or his prose works does not lead to any significant mismatch with the music. A person who starts with the music and then delves into the myth is unlikely to find misalignments.

What can be a real obstacle for newcomers and seasoned Wagnerians alike is the longstanding tendency to revisionist production styles and reinterpretations, a point which harks back to the very opening of the book, and to my concern about the background overwhelming

194 Lorenz, Alfred, *Der Geheimnis der Form bei Richard Wagner*, Berlin 1924-33.

the foreground. Before taking this further, there is one little matter that needs clearing up. Wagner's exhortation '*Macht Neues! Neues! und abermal Neues!* Do something new, new, and once again new,'[195] is often quoted as an endorsement for provocative, innovative productions, but this is misleading, sometimes deliberately so, as when Katharina Wagner printed it all over the Bayreuth programme of 2009 in support of her staging of *Die Meistersinger*. When Wagner wrote these words to Liszt on 8 September 1852, he was specifically criticising his friend for bringing 'old' operas to the stage at Weimar. He was, in fact, objecting to the revival of Berlioz's *Benvenuto Cellini*, ('If I am not mistaken,' Wagner went on, 'this work is more than twelve years old'). He was advancing the claims of new operas instead of yesteryears', not suggesting that 'old' operas (i.e. operas more than twelve years old!) should be given provocative, innovative stagings. Newcomers are probably best advised simply to try and accept producers' opera as a fact of life, and go with the flow, because this is an era which allows relatively few stagings after Wagner's own ideas.

A prevalent problem of many modern productions was succinctly identified by Hugo Shirley in *Opera*, December 2012, when reviewing *The Ring* at Covent Garden. He pointed out that academic discourse and dramatic presentation are different activities; 'the former thrives on uncertainty and flux, but the latter demands a degree of commitment if it's going to keep an audience on-board.' He then made the point that the first *Ring* at Covent Garden in the 21st century had put on stage interesting ideas which were worth discussion but not effective or even meaningful as drama. The producer, Keith Warner had said that heroes never die, they are deathless symbols that endure forever in human imagination. Siegfried therefore did not die after being murdered by Hagen, but made his way to the back, while still facing forwards, and then sidled surreptitiously into the wings. This simply did not fit into the dramatic action, where Siegfried's death is

---

195 *Correspondence of Wagner and Liszt*, tr. Francis Hueffer, New York, 1889, p. 222.

fairly cardinal to the action and meaning of *The Ring*. A fair number of modern productions teem with ideas like this, and often a producer applies these ideas to individual scenes resourcefully, but without building them into a drama that works.

There is a fine exception in the Seattle *Ring* of 2001-2013, and its staging by Stephen Wadsworth which shows how profound and illuminating Wagner can be when done his way, and how great the appeal. Several parts of it had already been performed when I went to it in 2001, and such was its reputation it had been sold out a year-to-the-day in advance of the complete opening cycle. Here in Europe it is probably best to accept constructively what the producers of today, now become directors, are trying to say. Wagner's works are so rich that the most unlikely seams can yield something worthwhile; and the only way of escaping from 'producer's Wagner' is to give up live performances altogether. Some innovative producers (directors) do very good things, for example Götz Friedrich at Berlin and Alan Privett at Longborough. Some of them have a vast knowledge and love of Wagner; Hans-Jürgen Syberberg's extraordinary film of *Parsifal* from thirty years ago shows great depth of insight and imagination.

Yet another different problem arises when a producer devises an alternative drama to Wagner's own. Stefan Herheim produced *Parsifal* at Bayreuth as an 'acting out' of German history from 1882 to the present day. The passage of time itself imparted a narrative structure to the sequence onstage, and Herrheim devised scenes so arresting pictorially that nobody noticed or cared what happened to Wagner's own tremendous drama. Its plot, its tensions, and its own characters simply sank without trace in Herheim's big idea.

A real obstruction comes when producers introduce elements from the sources which Wagner had deliberately modified or eliminated. The problem is illustrated by Colin Davis' description of the reading that he and Götz Friedrich had done for their Covent Garden *Ring* in the 1980s. Colin Davis said for instance that they 'learnt what frightful creatures the Valkyries were – they drank blood, they were necrophiles'.[196] With all respect to Colin Davis, this is not what the Valkyries 'really were' at all, not in Wagner. Davis and Friedrich ended up creating a fine and coherent *Ring* staging, but for the Valkyries, they were false to Wagner, who conceived of them as spirited young women, and beautiful. When Brünnhilde comes to warn Siegmund that he must die, Wagner has him addressing her as beautiful, '*die so schön und ernst mir erscheint*: so *beautiful* and solemn'; and the whole point of offering him eternity in Valhalla with her sisters is that she imagines these 'fantasy-girls (*Wunschmädchen*)' will quite reconcile him to losing Sieglinde. It is clear from their music that the Valkyries can be brash and ebulliently short on good taste, but they brim with energy; they are indeed beautiful; and they are valiant, devoted, and ultimately soft-hearted. To present them as unprepossessing harridans or blood-sucking vampires goes against Wagner. No drama by Wagner is ever a compilation of its sources but a new vision, even if the background sometimes sheds light on moot points. For example anyone uncertain whether Wagner wanted his great opposing figures in *The Ring*, Wotan and Alberich, to be morally indistinguishable, as many producers now make them, could be helped by the first prose draft. Wagner's draft shows categorically that he intended the gods to be noble. The draft tells us 'In high emprise the Gods have planned the world, and devoted themselves to the most careful nurture of the human race',[197] and the music confirms the point. The music for Wotan is heroic and noble, and to make him too much the same as Alberich torpedoes *The Ring*'s tension and dramatic balance.

The alternative to producer's opera is to listen at home to a great recording with a libretto and Wagner's stage directions, and his music on its own can make a more complete experience than Wagner ever realised. For all that he came to believe that music was the queen of

---

196 Osborne, Charles, *The World Theatre of Wagner*, (Preface by Sir Colin Davis,) London, 1982, p. 7.
197 'The Nibelungen Myth considered as a Sketch for a Drama' (1848): *Prose Works*, iv, p. 301.

the arts and described his dramas as deeds of music made visible,[198] he never quite recognised his own music's self-sufficiency, its stand-alone ability to stage the dramas on the threshold of the mind.

In this chapter, we have looked at a welter of obstacles to Wagner, but the list is never exhaustive. In one sense all objections and obstacles are beside the point of particular book, because they are extraneous to its main purpose, and should not affect the impact of Wagner's works; but the fact is that they do; they are obstacles to the Wagner Experience, and had to be addressed. It was also worth addressing them for a positive reason, namely that significant, worthwhile aspects of Wagner have emerged which might otherwise have escaped notice. Hostile prejudice can blight the view of his works, but a balanced understanding, even of the obstacles to Wagner, can give his works a more complex colouring, and actually enrich the Wagner Experience.

The first half of the book has created a good position from which to go into Wagner's ten great dramas and to see clearly their meaning for us.

---

198 'On the Name "Music Drama"' (1872), in *Prose Works*, vol. v.

THE
WAGNER
EXPERIENCE

AND ITS MEANING TO US

VOLUME II

Paul Dawson-Bowling

First published in Great Britain in 2013 by Old Street Publishing Ltd
Trebinshun House, Brecon LD3 7PX
www.oldstreetpublishing.co.uk

ISBN 978-1-908699-43-5

A CIP catalogue record for this title is available from the British Library.

Typeset by James Nunn

Printed and bound by CPI Group (UK) Ltd, Croydon, CR0 YY

PART II

TEN

DER FLIEGENDE HOLLÄNDER

Wagner took the view that *Der fliegende Holländer*, or *The Dutchman*, as it is often affectionately known, was the first of his masterpieces. It was the first that he planned to include in his official canon, and the world has endorsed his opinion; it is the first to hold its own in opera houses across the globe. What gives *The Dutchman* its authentic Wagnerian stamp and its unassailable place in the repertoire is Wagner's ability, fully evident here for the first time, to bring into being a complete new world. *The Dutchman* instantly seizes the imagination. The Overture bursts upon the listener with its shrill open fifths, winds shrieking in the rigging and mountainous seas surging up from the depths of the orchestra. They smash and crash and roar, as real as any reality we can know.

Wagner's mesmerising powers extended to his treatment of the action. His plots were seldom original and the story of *The Dutchman* is no exception. It comes from Heinrich Heine's pseudo-autobiographical *Memoirs of Herr von Schnabelewopski*, a strange piece of writing, ironic and fragmentary, reading like a random sequence of episodes. At an early stage these memoirs describe an erotic encounter between Heine's fictitious author and a Dutch blonde, which Heine frames with the legend of the *Dutchman*. The translation that follows[1] is given in full because any attempt to shorten it takes away the flavour, and

---

1 Heine, Heinrich, *Memoirs of Herr Schnabelewopski*, in *Complete Works*, vol. i, tr. Charles Godfrey Leland, London, 1891; Chapter 7, slightly revised by the author.

Wagner's opera will mean less. A full rendering shows how faithfully
Wagner kept to his source, at least for its storyline.

You certainly know the fable of the *Flying Dutchman*. It is the story
of an enchanted ship which can never arrive in port, and which since
time immemorial has been sailing about at sea. When it meets a vessel,
some of the unearthly sailors come in a boat and beg the others to take
a package of letters home for them. These letters must be nailed to the
mast, else some misfortune will happen to the ship, above all if no Bible
be on board, and no horse-shoe nailed to the fore-mast. The letters
are always addressed to people whom no-one knows and who have
long been dead, so that some late descendants get a letter addressed to
a faraway great-great-grandmother who has slept for centuries in her
grave. That timber spectre, that grim grey ship, gains its name from the
captain, a Dutchman, who once swore by all the devils that he would
round a certain promontory, whose name has escaped me, in spite of a
fearful storm, though he should sail until the Day of Judgment.

The devil took him at his word and therefore he must sail forever,
until set free by a woman's faithfulness. The devil in his stupidity has
no faith in women's faithfulness, and lets the doomed captain land
once in seven years and get married, and so find opportunities to save
his soul. Poor Dutchman! He is often only too glad to be saved from
his marriage and his wife-saviour and yet again return on board.

The play I saw in Amsterdam was based on this legend. Another
seven years have passed; the poor Dutchman is more weary than ever
of his endless wandering; he lands, becomes intimate with a Scottish
nobleman, to whom he sells diamonds for a mere song; and when he
hears that his customer has a beautiful daughter he asks that he may
wed her. This bargain also is agreed to. Next we see the Scottish home;
the maiden with anxious heart awaits the bridegroom. She looks with
strange sorrow at a great timeworn picture which hangs in the hall
and represents a handsome man in the Netherlandish-Spanish garb. It
is an old heirloom, and according to legend of her grandmother, is a
true portrait of the Flying Dutchman as he was seen in Scotland 100

years before, in the time of William of Orange. And with it has come down the warning that the women of the family must beware of the original. This has naturally enough had the result of deeply impressing the features of the picture on the heart of the romantic girl. When the man himself makes his appearance, she is startled, but not with fear. The Dutchman is moved on beholding the portrait. But when he is informed whose likeness it is, he with tact and easy conversation turns aside all suspicion, jests at the legend, laughs at the Flying Dutchman, the Wandering Jew of the ocean, and yet, as if moved by the thought, passes into a pathetic mood, depicting how terrible the life must be of one condemned to endure unheard-of tortures on the wild waste of waters – how his body itself is his living corpse wherein his soul is terribly imprisoned – how life and death and alike reject him, like an empty cask scornfully thrown by the sea on the shore, and as contemptuously repulsed again into the sea – how his agony is as deep as the sea on which he sails – his ship without anchor, and his heart without hope.

I believe that these were nearly the words with which the bridegroom ends. The bride regards him with deep earnestness, casting glances meanwhile at his portrait. It seems as though she has penetrated his secret; and when he afterwards asks, 'Will you be true to me, Katharina?' she answers 'true unto death!'

(At this point Heine's story moves to its main theme, the erotic encounter with a Dutch blonde.)

I remember that just then I heard a laugh and that it came not from the pit but from the gallery of the gods above. As I glanced up I saw a wondrous lovely Eve in paradise, who looked seductively at me, with great blue eyes. Her arm hung over the gallery, and in her hand she held an apple, or rather an orange. But instead of symbolically dividing it each with me, she only cast the peel on my head. Was it done intentionally or by accident? That I had to know! But when I entered the paradise to cultivate the acquaintance, I was not a little startled to find a white soft creature, a wonderfully womanly tender being, not languishing, but delicately clear as crystal, a form of homelike propriety and fascinating amiability. Only that there was something on the left upper lip which curled or twined like the tail of a slippery gliding lizard. It was a mysterious trait, something such as is not found in pure angels and just as little in mere devils. The expression comes not from evil, but from the knowledge of good and evil – it is a smile which has been poisoned or flavoured by tasting the apple of Eden. When I see this expression on soft, full, rosy ladies' lips, then I feel in my own a cramp-like twitching, and compulsive yearning to kiss those lips: it is our elective affinity.

I whispered into the ear of the beauty:

'*Yuffrou*, I will kiss your mouth.'

'*Bei Gott, Mynheer*, that is a good idea,' was the hasty answer which rang with bewitching sound from her heart.

But – no. I would here draw a veil over, and end the story or picture of which the Flying Dutchman was the frame. Thereby will I revenge myself on the prurient prudes who devour such narratives with delight, and are enraptured with them in their heart of hearts, et plus ultra, and then abuse the narrator, and turn up their noses at him in society, and decry him as immoral. It is a nice story too, as delicious as preserved pineapple or fresh caviar or truffles in Burgundy, and would be pleasant reading after prayers; but out of spite and to punish old offences, I will suppress it. Here I will make a long dash ------------, which may be supposed to be a black sofa on which we sat as I wooed. But the innocent must suffer with the guilty, and I dare say that many good souls look bitterly and reproachfully at me. However, for those of the better kind I will admit that I was never so wildly kissed as by this Dutch blonde, and that she most triumphantly destroyed the prejudice which I had hitherto held against blue eyes and fair hair. Now I understand why an English poet has compared such women to frozen champagne. In the icy crust lies hidden the strongest extract. There is nothing more piquant than the contrast between external cold and the inner fire which, Bacchante-like, flames up and irresistibly intoxicates the happy carouser. Yes, far more than in brunettes does the fire of passion burn in many a sham-calm holy image with golden-glory hair, and blue angel's eyes, and pious lily hands. I knew a blonde of one of the best families in Holland who at times left her beautiful chateau on the Zuyder-Zee and went incognito to Amsterdam, and there in the theatre threw orange peel on the head of anyone who pleases her, and gave herself up to the wildest debauchery, like a Dutch Messalina! ...

When I re-entered the theatre, I came in time to see the last scene of the play, where the wife of the Flying Dutchman on a high cliff wrings her hands in despair, while her unhappy husband is seen on the deck of his unearthly ship, tossing on the waves. He loves her, and will leave her lest she be lost with him, and he tells her all his dreadful destiny, and the cruel curse which hangs above his head. But she cries aloud, 'I was ever true to you, and I know how to be ever true unto death.'

Saying this, she throws herself into the waves, and then the enchantment is ended. The Flying Dutchman is saved, and we see the ghostly ship slowly sink into the abyss of the sea.

The moral of the play is that women should be should never marry a Flying Dutchman, while we men may learn from it that one can through women go down and perish – under favourable circumstances!

For his opera Wagner took the frame but threw away the picture. He made full use of the doomed sailor but jettisoned the Dutch blonde, and he fleshed out Heine's story and transformed it. He turned Heine's pallid Katharina into a real character, Senta; he added two sailors' choruses, Daland's crew and the Dutchman's ghostly troop; and for Act II he devised a chorus of spinning girls and Senta's nurse, Mary. These homely girls and Mary provide a foil for Senta, and they provide the audience for her ballad, the song where she tells the story of the Dutchman. Wagner also added a new character, Erik, Senta's childhood sweetheart. After she has sung her ballad it is Erik who tries to browbeat her out of her daydreams of the Dutchman; and it is Erik who triggers the final crisis in Act III. It is his hot-headed remonstration with Senta over her marrying the Dutchman that the latter overhears and misinterprets as betrayal. Senta flings herself into the sea and the Dutchman's ship sinks, as happened in Heine; but then comes Wagner's big change: he has Senta and the Dutchman reappearing in the heavens, redeemed and floating blissfully into the new dawn.

Not for nothing did Wagner style *Der fliegende Holländer* a *Romantische Oper*, a romantic opera. It is its conclusion that epitomises the gulf between Heine and Wagner. Heine's memoir is marinated in irony and made a mockery of redemption through love, but Wagner exploited to the full its possibilities for romantic idealism. Heine was still sympathetic to the Young German ideals of unfettered hedonism and promiscuity which had been spearheaded by Heinrich Laube,[2] just as Wagner himself had been until Minna changed everything. The memoirs of Schnabelewopski amount to a travelogue describing a connoisseur's classification of female charms by nationality. Like Katharina, the women are all cardboard cut-outs, lists of physical attributes, and Schnabelewopski shows no interest in their personalities. In Senta, however, Wagner did envisage a real personality, describing her as a determined Nordic girl, physically hale, emotionally vigorous, and not normally given to mawkish daydreams, even though he could not yet bring her to life in music of such vividness as gave his later heroines their striking identities.

In his fashioning of Senta, Wagner's imagination was influenced by Beethoven's heroine in *Fidelio*, Leonora, and by Wilhelmine Schröder-Devrient, who gave him his youthful ideal of all that drama might be. Wagner's imagination was even more influenced by the ideal of womanhood emblazoned in his psyche by his first wife, Minna. Schröder-Devrient, Leonora and Minna came together in the Dutchman's redemptive angel, Senta. As this implies, he steeped *The Dutchman* in experiences that were very personal. At the time of writing it, he desperately needed to be saved from life's shipwrecks, and part of the reason why the *Dutchman* is so compelling is that he

2   For Laube see above, vol. i, p.115. Heine dedicated his novel *The Rabbi of Bacharach* to him.

poured into it all his experience of the sea and tempests, both in the world and in his inner life. He recreated the crisis and dangers he and his wife Minna had experienced on the voyage that they themselves had made. He had been a 'flying German', flying from his creditors in Riga on the Baltic coast, and after the illegal and terrifying escape described in Chapter 7, they had set sail on the *Thetis* for London.

Instead storms drove them right up to Norway, and the *Thetis* found shelter at Norwegian Sandwike (Sandvika). Wagner described how it was there that they heard the crew, the men, calling out a sharp call of three descending notes which he would recreate in *The Dutchman*. These experiences resonated with him so closely that shortly before the opera's premiere he felt impelled to personalise the action further by changing its location. Sandwike, Wagner's haven on this voyage, replaced Heine's vague Scottish port as the harbour where the Dutchman's ship first comes upon Daland and his crew. His autobiographical sketch just before *The Dutchman*'s first performance emphasised the parallels between his life and his opera in a self-dramatisation, but the parallels were real and continued real. There is a telling letter to Liszt of ten years later – private correspondence, not written for the public – where Wagner describes himself in terms that read like an analytical sketch for the Dutchman. 'When I think back on all the storms that have buffeted my heart and on its tremulous attempts to cling onto some hope in life – against my own better judgment – indeed now that these storms have swollen so often to the fury of a tempest, – I have yet found a tranquilliser that enables me to sleep at night; – it is the sincere and heartfelt longing for death, total unconsciousness, complete annihilation, the end of all dreams, the only ultimate redemption.' (The tranquilliser he had discovered was of course the philosophy of Schopenhauer.)

There is no doubt that he often felt himself as (in Heine's words) 'an empty cask scornfully thrown by the sea on the shore, and as contemptuously repulsed again into the sea himself,' which was a consequence of his rootless, hazardous childhood, and gave rise to the lost, alienated outlook which he poured into the Dutchman, and later into Siegmund. As a child he had summoned up imaginary beings and made them real through the force of his imagination, and in Act II Senta sings a ballad which virtually wills the Dutchman into appearing out of the legend and the old picture on the wall, much as Elsa's prayer in *Lohengrin* would summon up her knight.

The influence of Goethe and *Faust* was also a presence, endowing the Dutchman with Faustian characteristics and drawing in Goethe's '*Ewig-Weibliche*'. It may sharpen the focus of *The Dutchman* to realise that the face, form and ideal of the *Ewig-Weibliche*, a prescient anticipation of Jung's anima, were still those of Minna. Senta, representing Minna, brings the opera to an optimistic conclusion through a supreme sacrifice which cancels itself. She is true unto death but she does not die in the sense of ceasing to exist. Instead she embarks on a new immortality as she draws the Dutchman up towards a sunlit heaven, and this aspiring conclusion, full of wishful thinking, adds to the expressionist intensity of *The Dutchman*. In *The Dutchman* Wagner still experienced Minna as his true, great love, his redemption, his *Ewig-Weibliche*, and he draws all who are sympathetic into his opera's intimations of redemption through romantic love. He had transformed Heine's ambiguous story into something that was personal, romantic and universal.

It was part of his genius to give *The Dutchman* a musical expression of haunting veracity. He had lived the experience of *The Dutchman*, both its wild environment and its spiritual desolation, and what Wagner had experienced he transformed into music, recasting it in the crucibles of his imagination to rekindle it in ours.

The music of *The Dutchman* has a good many 'motives of reminiscence' running through it and these contribute to its unity of mood and symphonic strength. Even if not woven *from* leitmotives, *The Dutchman* is densely interwoven *with* leitmotives, and there are six musical elements or motives that especially run through the work. The first consists of the open fifths which begin the Overture's the first bar, but these came from further back in Wagner's life than from the *Thetis* and its voyage across the North Sea: for they originated his earliest imaginings. In the review of Wagner's formative influences we saw how pure fifths on the violin always seemed to him like a greeting from the spirit world; he wrote in *Mein Leben* that as a baby onwards, he had always been excited by the sound of these fifths which he associated with ghosts and spirits. Although it cannot be demonstrated, there is something in them which mesmerises anyone who hears it receptively, which is why the opening of Beethoven's Ninth Symphony, which is made up of these fifths, is so haunting. They certainly haunted Wagner, and he mirrored them in the spectral world of *The Dutchman*, refracting them through his imagination in a way that haunts our own.

Fig. 10.1 'Storm Wind'

The second musical element is the theme of the Dutchman himself from of those same open fifths, and it is given out forcefully by four horns in unison.

Fig. 10.2 'The Dutchman'

This permeates the work, and in Overture to *The Dutchman* it adds a dark, baying force to the bleak, insistent brightness of the wind and their fifths.

The third musical thread or motive is a phrase for horns which involves a repeated grace note.

Fig. 10.3 'Wind'

It comes again, reconfigured, in the Sailors' chorus of Act I.

Fig. 10.4 'Sailors' Chorus of Mutual Encouragement'

and again in the Spinning Maidens' chorus of Act II.

Fig. 10.5

A fourth thread is the chromatic wave which comes surging up from the orchestral depths and ebbing back again.

Fig. 10.6 'Elemental surge' (cellos and double basses)

Wagner often extended it by taking its rising-descending scales up and down a full two octaves instead of one. It is this theme, a music of wind, rain and high seas, which permeates the score and more than any other confers on *The Dutchman* its stormy, sombre aspect. Wagner also combined it with an accelerated version of the Dutchman motive.

Fig. 10.7

The Dover full score runs in all to 408 pages and Figs. 10.6 or 10.7 appears on at least 58 of those pages in some form, often many times. Only the opening theme of *Tristan und Isolde* dominates a Wagner score more persistently.

In the Overture, there is a powerful opening section built from these four proto-motives which gives way to a new group, the first of the group generally known as the 'Senta' theme.

Fig. 10.8

The second is described as the 'Dutchman's Longing for Oblivion', although this does not quite describe its range of reference.

Fig. 10.9

The third is more straightforward in meaning, signifying the 'Dutchman's Redemption', and there is a strong resemblance between Figs. 10.8, 10.9 and 10.10, especially 10.9 and 10.10, because they are related expressions of the same half-formed aspiration.

Fig. 10.10

There is a sixth thematic fundamental, an element that consists of a three note phrase sung by the sailors, and oft repeated. It was this which captured Wagner's imagination on his North Sea voyage. After the Overture, it first registers during Act I as the Sailors are hallooing and trying to make for port.

Fig. 10.11

This motive is echoed on the horn, the echo being thrown back by the cliff-faces of the Norwegian fjords; and the sailors sing it again a semitone higher, with the same horn echo. These three notes will appear again and again within the texture of the music. They come again in the rowdy chorus that ends Act I, and then immediately again, slowed down, harmonised as in Fig. 10.12.

Fig. 10.12 'Sailors' Rumbustuous Dance'

This whole stretch is later extended and incorporated into the rumbustuous sailors' music that begins Act III.

These proto-leitmotives were forerunners of the leitmotives and the leitmotive forms described in the chapter on the music. Carl Dahlhaus in his penetrating and now almost historic book[3] also draws attention to a forward-looking aspect of Wagner's music in *The Dutchman*, and that is his progressive use of a 'musical syntax' which paradoxically looked backwards. One way in which music achieves coherence is through its so-called 'quadratic constructions'. To return again to 'Happy birthday to you' from the chapter on the music, I explained that the first two bars of 'Happy birthday to you' are balanced by another two of 'Happy birthday to you'. Here $2 + 2 = 4$. Then comes another two-bar segment, perhaps 'Happy birthday, dear Wagner', which is rounded off by another 'Happy birthday to you'. Again $2 + 2 = 4$. Put together they become a $4 + 4$ which makes 8; the whole song adds up to 8. The rhythms and the actual tunes of each segment are closely related, and they build up into orderly 'quadratic' structures. In *The Dutchman*, particularly in the Dutchman's great monologue of Act I, Wagner exploits such four-square *rhythmic* segments to create coherence and structure. However it is only the rhythms that are four-square: the actual tunes in this monologue have broken free from the constraining relationships of 'quadratic construction', because Wagner sets each line of the text to a unique and unrepeatable melody in order to heighten the meaning of the words. It is like following 'Happy birthday to you' with the tune of 'Long live our gra-', from the second line of the National Anthem, and the music would fall apart if it were not that the 'quadratic' rhythms prevent this from happening. As Dahlhaus put it, the schematic system of the (rhythmic) syntax compensates for the melodic anarchy. These subtleties all add to the controlled insistence with which *The Dutchman* impresses its meaning and ideas on the imagination. In its progress the Overture has announced most of the important themes of the opera, with the

3   Dahlhaus, Carl, *Richard Wagner's Music Dramas*, tr. Mary Whittall, Cambridge, 1979.

notable exception of the main melody of Senta's ballad in Act II. It has drawn particularly on certain set pieces, from the rest of Senta's ballad, the Dutchman's great, opening monologue in Act I and the Sailors' chorus in Act III, but the Overture draws its separate elements into a new and compelling unity.

The action of *The Dutchman* begins at Sandwike, a Norwegian bay surrounded by cliffs. It is so dark that it might be night and a violent storm is raging. The sailing vessel captained by Daland is making for shelter. He manages a landing, and he goes ashore to look out from the cliff-top and get his bearings, while his sailors furl the sails and make fast the moorings. Daland returns to comment ruefully that they have been blown at least seven miles off course, even though they had been so close to home when the storm broke that he had glimpsed his house. Anyone who counts on the wind might just as well count on Satan for pity. The storm abates somewhat, and having made certain that his ship is secure, Daland sends the crew below decks for some sleep, and after warning his helmsman to keep watch, follows suit. However the helmsman is himself exhausted, and although he tries to keep himself awake by singing a charming aria, a song about his sweetheart, he soon falls asleep.

The sky grows darker again, and the storm strikes with renewed ferocity. With lightning speed a full-rigged ship with blood-red sails looms up and speeds to a mooring near Daland's ship, where it drops anchor with a great crash. The helmsman starts in his sleep, but does not awake, simply murmuring some more of his song before dropping off again. The storm subsides to leave a deathly calm. The Dutchman, for the ship is his, now comes ashore, and a change comes over the music. The opening section of the opera consists of 'conventional' numbers, a sailors' chorus, a kind of arioso for Daland, and a strophic song for the helmsman. These all speak to us from the familiar forms of mid nineteenth-century opera. Conventional they are, but Wagner revitalised them and turned them into an opening scene of unprecedented energy and realism. Against this, the very music of the Dutchman now sounds like a visitant from another world. Not only are the harmonies dark, the melodies fragmentary, and the orchestration sombre; any build of paired and related tunes is gone, even though Wagner's score describes the scene as an 'aria'. Perhaps it bears a ghostly resemblance to 'recitative, arioso and aria', but he placed these elements in jagged juxtapositions, as distinctive as the character who sings them. The Dutchman begins quiet and almost expressionless, with the words 'Die Frist ist um. The time has come. Seven more years have been struck off. Glutted, the sea has cast me back onto the land.' The music is set in a deliberately vague, wandering tonality, representing his unsettled state of mind, and even formally it is located in the rare, strange key of F sharp minor. At the thought of the sea, he breaks out; 'Ach! Proud ocean! In a little while, you will bear me off again! Your rage is only sporadic, but my torment is ceaseless. The healing and wholeness which I sought on land is something that I shall never find. It is you, the tides of the Earth's oceans that are my home, until your very last wave breaks and last drop of your water dries up. How often have I plunged myself down into the deepest chasms of the sea, but death I could never find. I drove my ship at cliffs where many a ship had met its grave, but my own grave can never close. I threatened pirates with my taunts, hoping for death in some wild combat. "Here" I called, "show your mettle. My ship is full of treasure." But the sea's barbarous sons only crossed themselves in terror and fled. Nowhere a grave! Never to find death! This is the dread decree of my damnation.'

Suddenly he stops shaking his fist at the universe, and his mood changes to one of poignant supplication. The key tilts down from C minor to A flat minor over low string tremolos and a soft drum-roll. The score here is marked *maestoso* for the fragment of arioso which follows, consisting of two far-flung melodies of the kind Wagner later denied himself. They are the only matching melodies of this scene, both aspiring and imploring; 'I beseech you, beloved angel of God, who won for me the terms of my salvation. Was I merely the unholy plaything of your mockery, when you showed me a glimpse of redemption?'

His mood snaps back again to bitterness and to C minor for two recitative outbursts. 'Vain hopes! Dreadful delusions! Is all up with eternal fidelity on this earth?' The aria resumes, still in C minor but now *molto passionato*, for an angry and resolute confrontation with his fate. 'Only a single hope remains, and remains unshattered. The living centre of the Earth may long be active, but must perish in the end. Day of judgment! Ultimate day! When will you break up my eternal night? When will it come to pass, that stroke of destruction, which brings the world crashing in on itself? At last, when the dead rise again, I shall perish into nothingness. You worlds, make an end of your courses! Eternal nothingness, engulf me!' and this sentiment, violently declaimed, strikes a ghostly echo from the Dutchman's crew below decks.

This scene exemplifies why this opera (and Wagner in general) is so involving. It shows how far Wagner enlarged the Dutchman's desire to be free of his curse. He gave to the Dutchman's random act of defiance and its penalty a wider existential dimension. The Dutchman's monologue opens up a main problem at the centre of life's storms, and it describes his attempts to grapple with it. It is his sense of life being blighted, of being hemmed in by some negative characteristic, or error, or failure from the past, and it reflects a widespread human experience. In some instances, the experience is a matter of some binding choice or choices that cannot be unmade, as it is for the Dutchman. He had long ago made a free choice but as often happens it has reared up over him and has him now in an iron grip. Certain aspects of this hemming in are not due to individual choices but are a consequence of the human condition itself. People are born full of aspirations and possibilities, but limited circumstances or restricted opportunities can thwart them. Aspirations are also blocked by abilities which are inadequate to fulfil them. Finally, too, all human endeavours are foiled by mortality. Death sets a limiting term upon life's span, leaving potentials unfulfilled, vistas untravelled, errors forever unresolved. Wagner was perennially fascinated by the stranglehold on life resulting from mistakes and restrictions from the past, and also from the death-grip of the human condition itself. He was just as fascinated by the possibilities of transcending these restrictions. They cannot be obliterated, but if it were possible to nullify their impact and render them innocuous, this would be a part of the *redemption* which is central to Wagner and the Wagner Experience. (Not that the concerns which he addressed were new; these are the problems which lie submerged in the Christian belief that life is vitiated by original sin, and they vitalise Christian aspirations towards deliverance.) The particular sin of the Dutch captain, his determining fault, may seem paltry and meaningless today, his swearing he would sail 'round some cape or other if it took him until doomsday,' but it symbolises graver existential faults and deficits. The penalty exacted, never to escape from his ship and the sea, symbolises the impossibility of escaping the bounds of human nature, and it is from these that the Dutchman hopes for redemption.

At the end of the Dutchman's monologue, Daland comes on deck and is hit by the sight of a strange ship. 'Hey there! Steersman!' he calls, and the steersman, still slumbering, answers, 'All's well, All's well!' before mumbling more of his song in his sleep. Daland shakes him forcefully; 'You keep a fine watch, you booby! That's a ship! How long have you been asleep?' The steersman is instantly on his feet. 'The devil! Forgive me, Captain.' He seizes a loudhailer and calls, 'Who's there?' to be answered only by his own echoes. He tries again, with no better result. Daland comments gruffly, 'They seem just as laggard as we are,' but then he sees the Dutchman onshore. He asks the Dutchman to declare himself, his name, ship, and country of origin. The Dutchman declares quietly that he has travelled immense distances; does Daland mean to deny him safe anchorage and haven from the storm? 'God forbid!' answers Daland. 'Every seaman knows the importance of give and take with strangers. But who are you?' 'A Dutchman,' replies the stranger enigmatically. 'God be with you!' says Daland, and tries to open up a relationship. 'So you too were driven by the storm to this bleak and mountainous shore? My luck was no better. My home is only a few miles away, and I had almost made port when I had to turn back. But where are you from? Has your ship been damaged?' 'My ship is sound: it never can be damaged,' says the Dutchman darkly.

At this point his tone changes from bleakness and fragmentary responses to more extended explanations and the pained lyricism that was a part of his monologue. 'Beaten down by winds and storms, I wander hither and thither over the waters. For how long? I can barely say. I do not count the years any more, and it would not be possible to name all the lands that I have visited. However my own country where I really belong, the only country which I am burning to find, is the one I can never discover.' This has in fact been a self-communing arioso, but he returns to a style closer to recitative as he addresses Daland. 'You will never regret your kindness to a stranger. My ship is richly laden with treasures from every region and zone. If you deal with me, you will certainly stand to gain from it.' Daland is dubious and puzzled. 'This is all very strange. How might I believe you? An ill star has followed your steps until now. I will certainly do what I can to make things better, but may I ask what your ship contains?'

In response, two of the Dutchman's crew bring out a chest, and he tells Daland that it is full of precious stones, and that if Daland takes a look, he will see how much the Dutchman is offering for hospitality. Daland does look and cannot believe his eyes: "Who on earth could pay the price for such a treasure?" The Dutchman answers that he has just named the price, just one night of hospitality. He assures Daland that this is only a minute part of the wealth in his hold, but what use is it when he has neither wife nor child and is doomed never to return home? He would gladly yield all his riches to Daland just to belong to his household. Daland is increasingly bewildered; but before he can sort out his thoughts, the Dutchman confuses him with another question: has he a daughter? 'To be sure, yes, a good girl.' 'She must be my wife,' declares the Dutchman, leaving Daland totally baffled; can the stranger really mean it? However; he tells himself the stranger seems to be speaking from his convictions, and he finds himself increasingly delighted, convincing himself that perhaps his best course is to agree at once before the Dutchman changes his mind. He expresses this in an aria, telling himself that only a fool would pass up such a opportunity, and the Dutchman turns it into a duet by chiming in that in exchange for his daughter's hand, Daland can have the whole of his wealth. Daland announces to the Dutchman that his daughter is his pride and joy, a loyal and loving child, and the Dutchman answers that such a one will be equally loyal to her husband. Daland tells himself he recognises in the Dutchman a noble and a generous spirit, exactly what he would wish in a son-in-law, and he gives the Dutchman his consent to his daughter's hand. The Dutchman asks, will he set eyes on her that day? Daland answers that the next fair wind should bring them home, and the Dutchman cuts in again, 'She shall be mine!'

His thoughts turn inward as he asks whether she will be his angel. That hope was once offered him by another angel: is it one that he dares now to rekindle?

Daland, by contrast, is bluff and breezy as he sings a conventional number (though again brought to new heights by Wagner) expressing his satisfaction that the sea and its chances should have brought him the wealthy husband that every good father hopes to find for his daughter. The steersman breaks in to report that the wind has veered round favourably to the south, and Daland takes the fair wind and the calm seas as a good omen. They can set sail together and soon be at his home. The Dutchman responds that he must rest his men and that Daland should sail on ahead, a suggestion which disturbs Daland; the wind might change again, taking the wealthy stranger with it. However the Dutchman declares with all the assurance of second sight that the wind will not change. Daland has to be content and his crew all take up the steersman's song as they hoist sail. They sing it not as the steersman had, as wishful thinking, but exuberantly and in full confidence of a happy homecoming.

The Dutchman's encounter with Daland has clarified another aspect of his curse. This aspect is *alienation*. It was one of Wagner's achievements to identify and represent alienation in *The Dutchman*, and most people have enough familiarity with a sense of alienation for this to strike chords. It is not simply that the Dutchman's life has become too much for him, that he cannot cope with its storms and frustrations: there is also his isolation. Not only is everything against him; every new acquaintance, as he believes, would reject him if he revealed who and what he really is. He describes a common feature of alienation, the conviction that everyone would detest him 'if they really knew,' that even the pirates are so aghast at him that instead of attacking they make their escape. To gain any acceptance, he must, he feels, conceal his identity.

The Dutchman seems at a loss over how he might escape his alienation, understandably, because people usually are. To be sure, he knows that a woman could redeem him, but what precisely does he hope for? At first sight he seems set on oblivion, nothingness, because he envisages oblivion as the only escape from the tormented, alienated being that he is. The alternative, salvation through a woman who loves him to the point of being 'true unto death', symbolises something which the romantics expressed, albeit chauvinistically, and which depth psychology has confirmed. It is a truth that may seem blindingly obvious, that a chief need towards emotional health, even possibly towards salvation, is for a 'significant other'. The Dutchman possesses and recognises the psyche's romantic need for 'woman' which Jung regarded as just as fundamental as the need for physiological necessities, food, drink, warmth and safety, and was nothing so straightforward as any biological urge to copulate. The psyche's need for another was originally formulated by Jung as the male psyche's romantic need for 'woman' because of the gender stereotypes then prevalent, but it is goes wider, and it is an idea which this extraordinary opera takes forward in the next act when the Dutchman meets Senta.

In Act II, the curtain goes up on a large room in Daland's house, which has nautical objects on the walls. There are maps, and instruments for navigation, and on the back wall a picture of a pale figure with a dark beard and a black, Spanish costume. This mode of dress points to a long-past era when Holland lay under Spanish tyranny. In the room itself are Mary, the nurse supervisor, and her girls, all sitting at their spinning wheels. Wagner's descriptive genius captures both the moderately paced turning of the main wheels with their treadles, and the rapid spinning of the reels onto which the finished thread is winding. They sing two verses of a spinning song chorus which is based on Fig. 10.5, above. It is appealing and conventional, as is Mary's exhortation to keep themselves busy with their singing. Their verses sing about their distant lovers away at sea and the presents they will bring home, but Mary grows annoyed with Senta for sitting there like some dumb outsider, dreaming instead of spinning. She is a naughty child, who will not deserve or get any presents. The other girls retort not very kindly that she has no need, as her sweetheart is never away at sea and does not come home bringing presents. He just brings game, and every one knows what a hunter is worth.

Mary presses her point that Senta is always sitting in front of that wretched picture, and asks Senta how she can dream her young life away in fantasies. Senta asks Mary, if that is her attitude, why did she ever tell them the story of this unhappy man? The other girls make more negative comments; she is in love with the ghost, she will lose her wits; her endless brooding makes her pale: 'Come on, Senta, turn around and stop gazing, otherwise things may end up badly; your lover Erik is hot tempered; he might shoot the picture off the wall or even do violence to you.' They laugh tauntingly, which arouses Senta. She tells them their loonish laughter is soon going to make her angry. The other girls simply embark on the third verse of their spinning song, but Senta suddenly tells them to shut up; their endless 'summ and brumm' is a pain in the ear. If they want to persuade her, they need to sing something better than that. They tell her that she should sing something herself if she is so hoity-toity, but Senta suggests that Mary should do the singing. She should sing them the well-known ballad (obviously a ballad about the Flying Dutchman). 'Heaven forbid!' says Mary. 'Leave the Flying Dutchman out of it.' 'Well then,' says Senta, 'I have heard you sing it so often that I can sing it myself. You others listen, and see if I can sing it so that touches your hearts.' 'Alright, we agree', they say, 'We will even stop spinning to hear better;' all except Mary who says that this is becoming quite absurd, and that she plans to go on spinning.

Now comes Senta's ballad, the central set piece which 'spread its thematic web across the fabric of the whole work as it took shape,' as

Wagner later claimed, even though the chronology of *The Dutchman's* composition is marginally inconsistent with this claim. What is true is that not only the atmosphere and story of the ballad but even its musical themes permeate the opera, although there is the exception mentioned already, the reiterated phrase which begins the first two lines of every verse.

Fig. 10.13 Senta's ballad: opening phrase

'Have you not met that ship on the sea, with its blood-red sails and jet-black mast?' she begins. Her tune with its downward leaps begins very high, and it does not participate in any web-spreading through the opera because it never comes again, before or afterwards. Her ballad has as its Prelude the theme of Fig. 10.2, the 'Dutchman' theme, and of Fig. 10.6, 'Elemental Surge', which both began the Overture. She even sings the 'Dutchman' theme as a kind of warm-up to the ballad, before launching into its three verses, which are exact musical repeats until the refrain of the last verse. The tessitura is so challenging that Wagner had to transpose down its original A minor for his first Senta by a full tone, and G minor is how it is almost always sung today (and in the musical example just quoted). Even in G minor it is very exposed, and the opening drop comes back twelve times. Its difficulty is partly why Senta's ballad often has to go rather steadily, so as to accommodate the singer's technique, but then it has a tendency to stamp and thump. If taken faster and lighter it takes wing. In her first verse, Senta asks if anyone has seen a ship, black with blood-red sails; on the bridge is a pale figure, 'the winds howl around him' (she mimics the winds with Fig. 10.7) 'as he shoots on without aim or rest. And yet', the ballad says, 'there could be redemption if he found a woman faithful to him.' The music softens into Fig. 10.8 as she asks the Dutchman – rhetorically – 'Will you ever find her?' and she goes on to a wistful refrain (Fig. 10.10): 'Pray God to make her faithful in life and true unto death.'

The second verse relates the story of the Dutchman's oath to round the Cape and Satan condemning him. 'But,' says the verse, 'heaven's angel revealed how he might achieve salvation;' and again comes the refrain. In her third verse, Senta describes spiritedly how the Dutchman comes ashore every seventh year to find a faithful bride, but without success. This time the refrain which is sung by the other girls, whose hearts have been so touched by Senta's description that they take over; but before they can finish, Senta herself bursts out ecstatically that she will be the one; she will save the Dutchman; she will bring him salvation. The other girls are all appalled, warned by some sixth sense that her singing might work some occult effect. Apparently it does, as it summons the Dutchman, a summons fortified by Erik's dream which comes next.

Erik is Senta's semi-sweetheart, and he now rushes in on them, over-wrought and angry after overhearing her last words, and he lashes out, 'Senta, do you want to destroy me?' Mary likewise threatens to burn the hateful picture as soon as Senta's father returns. 'Her father's back!' says Erik, and he tells how his ship is now in the bay. Mary tells the other girls that in that case they must hurry and make ready for the men, and they go bustling off. Erik continues, 'Oh Senta, what is to become of me? Your father is back, and before he leaves again, he is going to have it all settled – find you a different husband. If I ask him for you now, he will refuse, unless you speak up for me.' Senta looks at him sympathetically, but asks him to let her go; her father is upset if she is not there to greet him. Erik presses her: will she take his part? When Senta asks what she has done to make him so suspicious, he answers that she never does anything that he asks and breaks his heart day after day. Asked by Senta what on earth he means, he says it is that dreadful picture; her infatuation with it must stop! She answers that it is not wrong to show a little compassion, but he says there is that hateful ballad as well; she has just sung it again. She responds disingenuously that she is only a child, and does not know what she is singing; is he really afraid of a song and a picture? Naturally such a tragic destiny moves her; let him come and look at the picture and take in so much sorrow and grief; then he will understand.

Erik is horrified; it was just as he was warned in his nightmare; Satan has taken over her imagination. She asks what has shocked him so much. He begins to tell her his dream, and she appears to fall into a hypnotic trance so that she dreams along as he tells her. He describes how he lay on the cliffs and watched a strange ship with two men coming ashore. One was her father. Senta breaks in:

'And the other?'

'The other, I knew him too, those black garments and that unusual pallor.'

'The dark expression?' adds Senta.

'Yes, that seaman in the picture!'

'What about me?' she asks breathlessly.

'You hurried down to greet your father, but you threw yourself at the feet of the stranger; I saw you clasping his knees.'

'He raises me up!' adds Senta.

'Into his embrace,' he finishes her sentence. 'You cling to him passionately; you kiss him with wild abandon.'

'And then, and then?'

'I see you sail away together.'

'He seeks me out. I must see him. I would give my life for him.'

'Horrible! You are ruined, lost. My dream will come true.'

He rushes off in dismay as Senta falls back into contemplation of the picture as though mesmerised. 'Oh you pale seaman; if only you can find her! Pray heaven that soon a woman true to him –'

At this moment the door opens to reveal Daland and the Dutchman. Senta chokes back a cry as her gaze falls from the picture to the man. She is transfixed, unaware of Daland waiting for her to come and greet him.

The Dutchman advances towards Senta, his gaze likewise fixed upon her, and Daland also approaches, visibly and audibly put out that she makes no move; 'No embrace? No kiss? What have I done to deserve this?'

'God greet you, father, but who is this stranger?' she answers absently.

'Do you press me? Do you want to know?' laughs Daland, before launching into a cheery aria cast in a conventional pattern, as suits this conventional man. It epitomises the external world of such people with their everyday choruses and arias. When the opera was new, these 'numbers' seemed successful constructions in the forms and styles of the nineteenth century, but they have been stigmatised by the authoritative Carl Dahlhaus for their 'thundering triviality'. This is harsh; over the years they have come to distinguish the everyday world from the legendary one of the Dutchman. Daland's aria is full of the good-natured father who wants to do well for his daughter when he is gone. He asks her to offer a friendly welcome to the stranger who has spent his life wandering in exile and now hopes to settle in a friendly home; moreover he is willing and able to pay. Daland is disarmingly frank, going on both to praise his wonderful daughter to the Dutchman, and to tell her his hopes that she will marry their guest because he is so wonderfully wealthy. She will have her pick of his jewels if they will only exchange rings. Daland gradually becomes aware that his well-meaning chatter is lost in the silence between them, and he is worldly-wise enough to get the message and leave them alone after a final word recommending them each to the other.

The Dutchman's first words seem to well up out of that very silence, and his thoughts seem to rise from realms beyond memory. 'How the image of this girl speaks to me from the distance of ages long gone by; what I have dreamed over long eternities I now see before me. For even in the darkest nights [i.e. of the soul] I would gaze longingly at an imaginary picture of a face like this one. Part of Satan's revenge was to leave me a heart that could still feel and be fully aware of its deprivations. This dark glow which I feel burning within me, shall I identify it as love? Ah no, my yearning is rather for salvation; if only it could come to me in the form of an angel such as this!' His words are some of the most telling and pregnant that Wagner ever put into the mouth of his stage-characters, but because they are also some of the most compressed and allusive, their meaning is not easy. Fortunately their general tenor is clear, and the ambiguities render the Dutchman's psychology more realistic. The Dutchman's monologue in Act I has given him personality and his scene with Senta gives him depth, as indeed it does Senta. Although Wagner never tells us what makes the Dutchman and Senta as they are, this scene tells us a great deal about how they are and about their minds. Wagner charts it all out with all the expressive possibilities of his music. The Dutchman's groping thoughts and his first words in Senta's presence move steadily towards definition, all the more vividly because they begin with hesitant musical lines which take increasing shape, and in an uncertain tonality which coalesces into E major. This key is so remote from any so far in *The Dutchman* that the very key suggests a different world, a new state of being. While the Dutchman is self-discovering and self-communing in his solitary monologue, Senta is pursuing similar solitary thoughts in parallel, asking, 'Am I sinking into a miraculous dream? Is what I see really an illusion? Have I lived 'til now in the halls of childhood, and is this, today, the occasion of my awakening? There he stands, his lines so full of suffering, and he instils in me a sense of his unimaginable sorrows. The burning griefs which I feel within, this longing – ah! How shall I describe it?' Inwardly she now turns to address the Dutchman; 'The healing and wholeness to which your yearnings tend – may you come to it through me.'

In this scene Wagner conveys an awareness that romantic attraction is rooted equally in the rational and the non-rational, in past personal experiences, conscious and otherwise, and in predispositions that are inborn. He conveys the truth that romantic love begins when a member of the opposite sex fits an existing matrix in another person's mind, and he models how the Dutchman and Senta fill out each other's unformed imaginings with real images of one another. The existence of any real romance between the Dutchman and Senta has been questioned, because the Dutchman speaks rather of salvation and because neither the Dutchman nor Senta reveal any clear-cut carnal longings. The point is that their magnetic pull, each for the other, is built on the matching and fulfilling of archetypal expectancies, something more complex than physical attraction. Here, as we saw in Chapter 3, the filling of mental spaces with images from real experience calls up emotions of mind-altering power. Barriers melt away; ego-boundaries dissolve like mists; isolation is no more; even mortality is unreal and meaningless. This is a state of being which appears to redeem the human condition; it seems mystical; it is salvation. Other forms of affection and other human relationships bring other fulfilments; but generally nothing outside the experience of mystics quite matches this. While Senta has been expressing herself, the Dutchman has been repeating his own words, 'How the image of this girl ...' so that their separate monologues entwine in a duet, symbolising what is happening to them. This mutual expression brings the section to a full close, with E major and peace both established.

They both make a partial return from their rapt state to music which reflects their need to engage with the world to take matters forward. The Dutchman asks if Senta is able to accept her father's promised choice; 'Can you give yourself to me forever, and really offer your hand to a stranger? Shall I find in your true love the peace for which I have yearned so long?' Senta makes a declaration that whoever he is (she knows full well), and whatever his fate, she will adopt it as her own and obey her father. The Dutchman is enthralled but baffled at such instant commitment. When he asks, 'So absolute? Are you so steeped in empathy for my sufferings?' she murmurs to herself, 'Oh what sufferings! What consolation I can bring you,' and unthinkingly expresses an understanding and certainty which thrill him all the more precisely because it is unthinking. It makes him sink gratefully on his knees and pray that his salvation may come through her; but at the same time he warns her that only if she is steadfast in virtue and fidelity can she avoid falling back in horror at the enormity of his needs and the consequences of failing him. This warning only has the effect of raising her to a state of exaltation, and she consecrates herself to be 'true unto death'. Their thoughts flow in parallel song and ecstasy, Senta praying and promising to save him, and the Dutchman, both rapturous and precarious, giving conflicted thanks and prayers for her and for his salvation. At this summit of their feelings, Daland enters at the door to explain that he can keep out his retainers no longer.

They are bursting to come in for the party which he always gives to celebrate his homecoming, and this one now could be the most festive of all if it turned into an engagement party as well. Senta instantly offers her hand to the Dutchman, again vowing to be true unto death, and he declares exultantly to Hell, that this true love has put paid to its mockery. Daland takes this as the signal to start the celebrations. Meanwhile the music of the duet has gradually descended from the high places of Wagner's originality to clothe itself in the ordinary forms and conventions of the era, which include vocal cadenzas and even a pulsating (or pooping?) horn accompaniment as Senta declares that she will be true to him whoever he is. It is as if the Dutchman, Senta and their relationship have briefly re-entered the mundane world, and the act ends with the Dutchman and Senta endorsing her declaration to be true unto death while Daland, making up a trio, supplies a bass line which describes his satisfaction. They all adopt a merry, conventional tone which matches and expresses their worldly cheer.

Act III opens with music from an entr'acte, one of the two which bridged the three scenes of what Wagner had originally conceived as a one-act opera. It was purely practical problems of scene-changing which made him divide his work into three for its first production. This is why Act III begins with music that forms a transition from the previous act, instead of following Wagner's more usual practice, where each new act launched forth with music arrestingly different from what went before. So convincingly did he manage his recasting of *The Dutchman*, that never in his lifetime did he try to change it back. (It was first restored to one act in 1901, almost twenty years after his death, when Cosima finally completed the staging of all Wagner's big ten at Bayreuth.) Act III owes almost nothing to Wagner's main source, Heine, and it was Wagner who supplied enough new features and events to ensure that the crisis and the dénouement did not follow too abruptly on Act II.

The opening chorus of Act III does not take the main action forward, and in the full score the first 90 pages of the act are in one sense merely a preparation for the drastic events which lead to the Dutchman's redemption, whereas those events themselves only occupy 33. In the theatre, however, those 90 pages work well; and what the opening chorus also achieves is an additional sense of structure, because this act's opening scene roughly mirrors those of the other two, with a chorus followed by an ensemble and then an aria. This correspondence between the opening formats of each act adds subliminally to *The Dutchman*'s gripping coherence. Wagner presents the sailors' chorus, 'Helmsman, leave your watch! Come and have some fun with us,' as if it were a folk song familiar to the sailors. This music also incorporates proto-leitmotives which are now familiar, Figs. 10.3 and 10.11. They illustrate the point made earlier, that if not woven *from* leitmotives, *The Dutchman* is densely interwoven *with* leitmotives.

Fig. 10.14

Fig. 10.15

'Helmsman, leave your watch! Helmsman, come join us now! Ho! He! Je! Ha! Helmsman, here drink with us!': the sailors' song is a stamping affair which goes with their style of dancing, and they are roundly criticised for their cloddishness by the women when they arrive. The women are laden with food and drink by the basket, but they play hard to get, telling the local lads that it is only polite first to offer hospitality to the newcomers on their strange ship. They call out in a friendly fashion, 'Sailors, are you there? Wake up! We have nice wine for you!' but their calls, oft repeated, are met with an eerie silence. The girls become apprehensive and Daland's men easily persuade them to let them have the food and wine instead. As the men turn tipsy and uproarious, they start to jeer; the strange crew must all be asleep, or perhaps they are dead. Perhaps they are like the ghostly crew of the Flying Dutchman who need no food and no light. 'Let's see what sort of a job you weak and wasted lot can make sailing your ship!' they bellow.

Now things start to happen. The sea, still calm elsewhere, begins to agitate and seethe round the Dutchman's ship, and blue flames to flicker along the masts and spars. Music from the Overture returns as a storm rages in the rigging and the Dutchman's crew start to rise up as ghostly forms. They launch into a spectral imitation of a folk song taunting the Dutchman who, they say, will soon be back at sea after yet another failure. His only bridal march will be the wailing and screaming of the storm-winds. No matter how strong this wind, it does not stop them sailing on without wear or tear, because Satan has fitted the ship with sails as indestructible as the ship itself. This frightens Daland's sailors and their girls, but they make a show of bravado and try to out-sing the Dutchman's crew, unsuccessfully. They are eventually silenced by the ever-wilder uproar, and spontaneously make the sign of the Cross. The Dutchman's crew greet this with a howl of menacing laughter, and Daland's people run off. At once the Dutchman's crew fall silent and all returns to a deathly calm.

The calm is broken by Senta hurrying out of her father's house, hotly pursued by Erik with a barrage of recriminations; 'What am I hearing; God, what am I seeing? Senta, is it madness? Is it true? Is it real?' Senta asks him rather lamely not to ask; she cannot explain; but he continues to take her to task. 'Senta, what unholy power has led you to stray and break this loyal, loving heart of mine? Your father! – He brought the bridegroom with him; I know the kind of thing that passed between them. But you, Senta! How is it possible that you give your hand to this stranger?' Senta tells Erik that she must never see him again; her sacred duty forbids it. This is too much for Erik; 'What sacred duty? Is it not more sacred to hold to the vows of eternal fidelity which you once made to me?' Senta is strangely shocked; she asks: what vows of eternal loyalty? 'Oh Senta,' says Erik; 'do you deny it?'

He embarks on a cavatina, a type of short aria that rises out of a recitative, and it is cast in that maudlin lyricism which has become his hallmark, and which lessens the natural sympathy of the audience for this hapless man. The cavatina also slows the course of the drama, but it provides the Dutchman with plenty of opportunity to overhear and misunderstand Erik's impassioned pleas. Erik reminds Senta of a midsummer evening when she called him down from the heights into the valley, and he laboured to bring her a lovely bouquet of flowers. 'We lay on the grass, watching your father's ship put out to sea after he had trusted you to my care, and you threw your arms around my neck. Then and later when you pressed my hand, was not that itself a seal, your promise of loyalty?'

Senta might very reasonably have answered that he had read far more into the events than was justified, but the Dutchman has appeared unnoticed and takes Erik's pleadings as evidence of a new instant passion that has obliterated Senta's feeling for him. He draws the wild and dire conclusion that Senta is faithless. 'Lost! Lost forever! My salvation eternally lost!' Taking no notice of Senta trying to bar his way, or of Erik trying to hold her back, he commands 'To sea, to sea, for eternity.' He flings at Senta 'It is all over with your faithfulness, and it is all over with my salvation. Farewell; for I will not destroy you.' 'Stop!' calls Senta; 'From this time on you shall flee no more!' but the Dutchman blows a blast on his captain's whistle and tells his crew, 'Cast off. Hoist Sail! Say farewell to the land for eternity.' Senta responds; 'You doubt my word? How could you be so blinded? Do not regret the vow that we have made. What I have promised I shall now perform.' Erik tells her that she is in Satan's power; does she want to be destroyed? The Dutchman continues addressing Senta; 'You have betrayed me and so too has God. Learn the doom that you have barely escaped. I am condemned to a fate so frightful that death would be a happy release, and I can be redeemed only by a woman true unto death. You made your promise of true love to me, but not yet before God, and that has saved you. Eternal damnation is the lot of those who have broken their vows, but you, Senta, shall be saved.'

It is to the Dutchman's credit that even when he believes Senta faithless he wants to save her from her fate, and this contributes to the final impression that he is a man who deserves his own deliverance. Senta is seized with an ecstatic conviction and answers; 'I know you well; I know your doom. I recognised you when I first saw you. Your torment is at an end. I am the one through whose love you are redeemed.' Erik calls for help at the top of his lungs, and every one comes running out to see what is happening. The Dutchman, now on board, tells Senta she is wrong to think she knows. 'You do not know me; you cannot imagine who I am. Ask the seas anywhere on earth; ask the seaman who crosses all the oceans – he knows this ship, the terror of all good people; every one calls me "The Flying Dutchman".' His ship casts off and is heading out to sea with uncanny speed when Senta breaks free and runs up the promontory to call out her final words; 'All praise to your angel and his decree. Here I stand, true unto death.' She hurls herself into the waters, proving that she is eternally true to him because, having perished, it is obvious that she can never be faithless.

The Dutchman's great ship sinks instantly, engulfed by the waves which rear up around the wreckage before collapsing in a whirlpool and fountains of spume. They clear to reveal Senta and the Dutchman, locked in a passionate embrace and floating up towards the rising sun, both transfigured and redeemed. Even if the scene did not show this, the music establishes it, especially in Wagner's revision. In it the orchestra replays the music which Senta had sung at the end of the ballad, announcing that she would redeem the Dutchman. Next comes the Dutchman's own theme, set in D and extended upwards to include the optimistic major third as it had at the end of the Overture. The music now turns all the more mellifluous because there is a harp among its textures, and it is followed by the music of Senta's redemption which soars aloft, enfolding the conclusion in radiance and serenity.

Wagner has enshrined here a strange but beautiful mix of past experience, kitsch, wishful thinking and pure imagination. Having known what it was to be tossed hither and thither on the floodwaters, he presented its main characters as governed by forces beyond their control. Neither the Dutchman's nor Senta's lives are entirely predestined, but their actions are obviously dominated by powerful forces. On the other hand it is by their acts of will that they break free and take control. The Dutchman decides that Senta, of whom he knows nothing, shall be his wife; Senta announces suddenly that she will be the one to save the Dutchman, and she acts yet more conclusively when the Dutchman is heading back to sea. At the point where events could have headed towards disaster, Senta sends them off in a different, happier direction. Wagner's hero and heroine are both creatures of fate and yet alter and rearrange their fates. Wagner prescribes and models for us the paradox, the contradiction by which we have to live, that we are bound by our circumstances and predestined, and yet have free will. It is a free will which we have to exercise, even if the laws of physics and physiology demonstrate that this free will cannot really be there.

Another important point for understanding the Dutchman's message to us is that he does not really want or intend that Senta should die for him. After all, the other women he had attracted had perished for an eternity of damnation, but this had done him no good. What really matters to him about 'true unto death' is the unconditional love and acceptance that it represents. Wagner's ideal, like that of his Dutchman, was a woman who would adore and *be there for him* without limit, and this was the 'true unto death' which he needed for him to feel secure. Senta is so imaginative and compassionate that she is willing to do anything to save the Dutchman from his sufferings, and this eventually does include dying in order to save him. However her suicide is a response to a crisis that is unexpected and not part of her life-plan. It is Erik's appearance in Act III and the Dutchman's instant conclusion that she is faithless which create the crisis. In the general disarray that follows, she grasps with shining clarity that all will be lost unless she demonstrates her love instantly and with utter and unconditional finality, a staged and literal representation of 'true unto death'. This is indeed redemptive for the Dutchman, but it does not bring him the annihilation which he had envisaged as the only redemption possible, because Senta does better. In Wagner, women always do better. Senta draws the Dutchman into a better redemption, a blissful relationship with her forever.

Too many people, too many writers and producers have regarded this conclusion as simplistic and trite, a bolted-on irrelevance, but it is the very culmination of the action, and its message about '*Erlösung durch Eros*, redemption through Eros' brings with it a numinous shimmer. It also possesses a significant truth-value, and to imagine or stage the end otherwise is to misrepresent what *The Dutchman* signifies. Even so there is a real distinction to be made, that redemption comes through Eros and not lust. It is worth affirming that the two are not identical, a point common to Jung and Wagner. Both men were personally acquainted with both experiences, and recognised that while carnal sex could lead to satisfaction and satiation, Eros was different. For Wagner Eros was limitless, looming, all-consuming, overwhelming; and in *Tristan und Isolde* he gave full rein to this idea. The Dutchman and Senta operate at a simpler level, but their ecstatic fusion as they float into the sunset still fulfils archetypal aspirations. Isolation is no more; they are one; and the experience is timeless, deathless, and redemptive.

The idea of redemption may seem meaningless to many people today, and whole cohorts might now go along with Ernest Newman who jeered at it almost a century ago as a senseless Wagnerian folly. Even so, *The Dutchman* addresses an issue which still matters vitally for many today, and mattered still more widely in the nineteenth century. The general importance of redemption was demonstrated by the many dramas and paintings of the period which were deeply concerned with it. Any one doubting the likelihood of this might remember *The Awakening Conscience* and *The Light of The World*, two

famous and different reflections on the redemption theme, or Oscar
Wilde's evergreen plays whose stories are underpinned by this theme.
An Ideal Husband is a redemption story, a play about a politician
with a past. Sir Robert Chiltern, a rising Member of Parliament, had
earlier accepted an immense bribe which led to fortune and political
success, but the revelation of his venality to his idealising wife results
in her rejecting him; later she rises above herself, forgives him and
falls in love with him again. He is another Dutchman redeemed, and
he too is redeemed through a woman's love. Sir Robert's wife is also
redeemed and becomes better and wiser, not a sadder but a happier
person. Hence this preoccupation with redemption was not a personal
quirk of Wagner's but a subject of wide concern. Of course Wagner
had a resource that Wilde did not, the occult power of his music.
Through the music Wagner not only described the experiences that he
promoted; he could recreate them in the minds of his listeners.

What is odd for us of today is that the first audiences missed the
impact of *The Dutchman* and were disappointed. Evidently they were
puzzled about what to make of it, and they were the first in a long line.
The Dutchman has long been a prey to misconceptions, some fuelled by
Wagner himself because of his tendency to reinvent his own works as
his life went on. For the first audiences the problem was that they saw
The Dutchman as a conventional 'Romantic Opera'. Romantic Opera
described a fantastical genre, shadowy, spectral, supernatural, in the
tradition of *Der Freischütz* (Weber) or *Der Vampyr* (Marschner), but
by 1842 this had become 'yesterday's fashion'. Its place was usurped
by Grand Opera which was all the rage in Paris. Grand Opera was
rooted in history, extravagant in spectacle, and rich in resonances for
contemporary society and politics; both *Les Huguenots* by Meyerbeer
and Wagner's own *Rienzi*, which had catapulted him to fame, were
tremendous demonstrations of the new mode. The audiences at
Dresden had hoped for something like *Rienzi*, whereas *The Dutchman*
seemed a throwback.

There was more than this to their disappointment. Wagner himself
rightly pinpointed the opposite difficulty for his audiences, that as

well as being disconcerted by something so seemingly outmoded, they could not grasp something that was really so new. His first audiences were puzzled because they could not see beyond the familiar aria forms and the traditional use of the chorus which were such an intrinsic part of *The Dutchman* to all that was so special and novel in it, and as Wagner said, the ink had barely dried on the score of *Rienzi* when he created something utterly unlike it, a leap so drastic that he was unable to think of anything like it from any other artist.

Eduard Hanslick, later Wagner's most notable critic, was closer to the mark with his complaint that *The Dutchman* was too 'symphonic' to give rein to the fantasy and inconsequence which he enjoyed in opera. Hanslick wanted Symphony to be Symphony with its formal rigour, but in opera he preferred the traditional 'numbers opera' and was attracted to the very discontinuity which let arias, choruses and ensembles follow one another in free association. It made for variety.

Wagner himself was sometimes uncertain what he had created. At one stage he was inclined to call it all a dramatic ballad, because it expanded from Senta's ballad which had come first. He would one day make a different claim echoing Hanslick's objection, that *The Dutchman* was really a 'symphonic opera'. As we have seen, *The Dutchman* does have 'motives of reminiscence' running through it, and its close-knit textures make for a unity of mood and spirit which Wagner barely surpassed, and because it was at least woven *with* leitmotives, it was in some sense symphonic. While he composed many of its numbers separately and then put them together, the result is not a patchwork but more like a mosaic, designed so that the different parts fit in place.

It should also be evident that *The Dutchman* also contains elements of the 'scenes opera' form, a hybrid. 'Scenes opera' was already arriving with mature Mozart, and was common in the early nineteenth century, but it is not sufficiently credited as a specific form. Scenes opera has recognisable arias, choruses and recitatives, but deliberately fused and elided to make scenes or parts of scenes, as Mozart had done in *Figaro*, or as Wagner would do again in *Tannhäuser*; the Dutchman's Act I monologue is a good example of a composite scene.

Because of Wagner's existential insights and his music, the experience of *The Dutchman* as a whole creates an effect far beyond the bare story. The power of *The Dutchman* runs deep. It is more than entertainment, more than opera. It is a work – the first one – where Wagner expands the boundaries of people who relate to it, not as conclusively as in the great works of his maturity, for the lion was yet young; but it is already the voice of the lion and the Wagner effect is unmistakeable. In *The Dutchman* Wagner first displays his astonishing ability to understand inner compulsions, to distil experience from life, and transform it in his dramas. The opera as whole percolates our own consciousness with its message of romantic love as freedom from individual confines. Wagner presents this as a redemptive possibility, and gives substance to it through the music. *The Dutchman* is the first of Wagner's works to offer an actual taste of the experience that it describes, and to some extent it enables us to make the redemption of the Dutch captain our own. The ultimate significance of *The Dutchman* is that it is Wagner's first work to offer anything so extraordinary.

Der fliegende Holländer was first performed on 2 January 1842 at the Dresden Hoftheater. The cast included Michael Wächter as the Dutchman, Wilhelmine Schröder-Devrient as Senta, and Carl Risse as Daland. The performance was conducted by Richard Wagner.

ELEVEN

TANNHÄUSER

A Consummate Drama

Eros is a questionable fellow and will always remain so. He belongs on the one side to man's primordial animal nature which will endure as long as man has an animal body. On the other side he is related to the highest forms of the spirit. But he only thrives when instinct and spirit are in the right harmony. If one or other aspect is lacking to him, the result is injury or at least a lopsidedness that can veer towards the pathological. Too much of the animal distorts the civilised man; too much civilisation makes sick animals.

C.G. Jung (from *Two Essays on Analytical Psychology*)

Wagner described *Tannhäuser* as a 'consummate drama', and how right he was. It is a riveting story with some of the best-loved music in existence, and yet there is something elusive and unsettled about it that challenges this book's very objectives, to explore Wagner's works themselves and to draw out the lessons they offer us. At least there is nothing elusive about *Tannhäuser*'s most striking characteristic, which was to place the realm of the erotic in the full glare of the operatic stage. In doing this *Tannhäuser* gave permission for the erotic phenomenon and even its carnal aspect to be acknowledged within polite society. The idea that these things were not morally repugnant and aesthetically revolting was revolutionary for its time, but many people sense that *Tannhäuser* goes further and surrounds erotic experience, including its sensual aspect, with lustre and a life-enhancing allure. This is still a chief source of *Tannhäuser*'s fascination today. To be sure, the life-enhancing status of erotic experience is challenged in the drama, but many people would agree with Laurence Dreyfus, that although the text of *Tannhäuser* may often moralise against 'wanton sensuality, the dramatic inclinations of the music recommend it without qualification'.[4] As Dreyfus says, the 'musical Venusberg is well-nigh irresistible,' especially in the white-hot Paris version. Perhaps he was exaggerating to make a point, because *Tannhäuser* as a whole does *not* recommend sensuality without qualification. Although it presents erotic experience as rosy, shimmering, and wonderful, both the declarations of several estimable characters and the very action of the opera often repudiate the Venusberg. They condemn everything that it represents, and the opera's fascination is mightily enhanced by its real ambiguities because they make for a peculiar oscillating vibrancy. They also complicate the truths about the erotic phenomenon which it expresses, but this reflects things as they are. The truths which it tells about erotic experience are intrinsically complicated and ambiguous, and in dramatising these complexities Wagner anticipated Jung. Jung was to define his discoveries about 'Eros' conceptually; Wagner had already gone further, and made them real onstage.

It was because *Tannhäuser* proclaimed truths which were previously inadmissible that it sent shock waves through European civilisation. They were as far-reaching as any from the French Revolution, but the shock waves from *Tannhäuser* affected more people and affected them more nearly because it approached head-on the question asked by Wagner's own character, the Landgraf in Act II: 'Can you plumb the true nature of love?' Wagner's operas are full of questions, and much of his meaning comes out in response to characters asking questions. The answers and truths about erotic passion which *Tannhäuser* encouraged overturned the 'denial of man's primordial animal nature' which had

4   Dreyfus, Laurence, *Wagner and the Erotic Impulse*, Cambridge, Mass., 2010, p. 88.

been a life-diminishing ordinance of Western civilisation for almost two millennia. *Tannhäuser* was not the only force behind this immense shift in attitudes, but no other force was so decisive. *Tannhäuser* also examined several other topics which Wagner had considered before and would look at again, such as alienation and isolation, society and the outsider, and the quest for integration. *Tannhäuser* also touches on the relationship between justice and punishment, the fallibility of human law, and the contrast between the punitive regulations devised by man and divine grace and mercy. The opera even contemplates some of the murkier aspects of organised religion, obliquely questioning the extent to which Christ's beautiful ideology had been hijacked and turned into an institution supporting arbitrary authority, a denigration of the body, a rank misogyny, and revolting cruelties against unbelievers and dissenters from orthodoxy.

Opera was always where Wagner presented his ideas and ideals at their best (in contrast to his prose works), and it is easy but pointless to take potshots at Wagner for not living up to the ideals which his stage works promoted. Obviously he did not, and perhaps no one ever has or can, but does this invalidate the ideals, or the value of what Wagner was trying to do? Ideals are guiding stars for navigating when the voyage grows difficult, not easy rules for coasting along the high-roads.

The special difficulty about *Tannhäuser* is the one already suggested, that even as we look at its fixed points and its values they dissolve and its lessons turn hazy. Its unsettled character has intrigued and frustrated people in equal measure ever since its first performance at Dresden on 19 October 1845. Wagner himself directed that performance but he himself was not satisfied, then or ever, and he began making changes the very next day, changes which he continued over the next thirty years. In no other work did he make such wholesale revisions over so long. Almost forty years after its first performance, on 23 January 1883, he was still unresolved and told his second wife, Cosima, 'I still owe the world *Tannhäuser*.' He never gave the world his conclusive version because less than a month later he was dead.

My point of departure now is to describe *Tannhäuser* as Wagner originally conceived it, a direct, straightforward account of the story and the music. I go on to explain how the opera subverts and contradicts any such direct, straightforward idea of itself. The next step is to set out the cultural and religious values of the times, so as set the context for its hero's (or anti-hero's) wrongdoing. Without a grasp of those values, Tannhäuser's wrongdoing, on which the action hinges, will not make sense, and the opera's characters and their motives may look artificial. Its lessons may also seem meaningless because they belonged to a world of values and morals which were different from today's. The fourth step is to describe Wagner's attempts to grapple with the opera's discrepancies as he became increasingly aware of them, and to explain how far he succeeded and how far he added to them. Many of the ideas and suggestions put forward by *Tannhäuser* emerge along the way, but because of those very discrepancies there is a final step, rounding up ideas that have not come out clearly elsewhere.

As often happens with Wagner, the story has begun long before the curtain goes up. It concerns a mediaeval knight of outstanding gifts, the opera's eponymous hero, who is another of Wagner's great outsiders, like the Dutchman, and indeed Rienzi. He had quit the court of Thuringia after finding himself at loggerheads with his fellow knights because of his '*Hochmut*': his high temper, his arrogance, as they see it. He had also created another kind of disturbance, in that his songs of erotic passion have stirred and aroused those who heard them. They had wafted magically to the ears of Venus, and so enthralled her that she adopted Tannhäuser as her special lover, promising him the crown of immortality.

Venus was the ancient Roman goddess of love, a central figure in the Latin or Roman religion with its assemblage of gods under Jupiter. After Christianity had triumphed, she had been driven underground, a telling symbol for the forbidden, subterranean existence to which organised Christianity consigned erotic experience, which she symbolises. The mountain where she lives is called the Venusberg after her, and it is there that the opera begins, with the emphasis very much on love in its carnal, almost pornographic expression.

In its revised Paris version the Venusberg scene starts with a ballet which would have called for an X certificate in the old days of censorship. It includes scenes that are almost bestial, and even in the milder, earlier version, Wagner's stage directions describe

> *A spacious grotto within the Venusberg. In the background a lake is visible where Naiads are bathing; on the shore lie sirens. Venus lies stretched out on a couch, with Tannhäuser before her, his head on her lap. Dancing nymphs; at the sides of the grotto recline pairs of lovers.*

The opera begins arrestingly, with an Overture which almost summarises the action. It was originally in three parts, slow, fast, slow. The slow opening section is the 'Pilgrims' Chorus', a chorale which begins low on the woodwind, apparently dawning out of the distance,

Fig. 11.1

and it is followed directly by an imploring, prayerful passage for lower strings.

Fig. 11.2

The music seems to draw closer as it rises to a powerful statement of the opening music on the trombones, galvanised now by striking string figurations, 'sawn-off triplets'.

Fig. 11.3 'The Pulse of Life'

These create a slow throbbing. After a climax, the 'Pilgrims' Chorus' music recedes, and almost fades into silence when it is interrupted by the fast section, the music of the Venusberg.

Fig. 11.4

The Venusberg is where Tannhäuser has been dallying time out of mind with Venus, the Roman goddess of love. The music takes on a quicksilver, flickering quality as her acolytes perform enticing, libidinous dances. This leads on to an orchestral version of the hymn that Tannhäuser will soon sing to Venus. It is in octave unison high on the violins, rather foursquare and not obviously erotic. The violins then soften and divide, soaring aloft and creating an ethereal shimmer round a solo clarinet playing a truly seductive melody.

Fig. 11.5

Venus herself sings this in Act I during her siren song to Tannhäuser. The darting, quicksilver music returns, and the whole central section repeats and rises to a powerful climax, at which point the Overture reaches a crossroads. Its direction now depends on whether or not it is given in the original version. The original version returns to the strains of the slow pilgrims' chorus, transformed into a thrilling four-four rhythm which clinches its overwhelming effect. Queen Victoria responded to this version in 1855 with an enthusiasm and a perception which eluded the London critics. She heard it conducted in London by Wagner himself, and asked for an encore. Wagner obliged and she recorded in her diary that it 'is a wonderful composition, quite overpowering, so grand, and in parts wild, striking and descriptive'.

In his original version of the Overture Wagner resolved the opposing elements of sacred and profane, at least in the music, a concord which he never established so clearly in the main opera. Wagner's 1852 guide, 'On the Performing of "Tannhäuser"', shows that he intended this final section to describe an integration of the erotic with the sacred, exactly the integration later encouraged by Jung. If the erotic Venusberg is Tannhäuser's shadow side, this first version of the Overture reconciles and integrates it with the sacred, so that 'instinct and spirit are in the right harmony'. Wagner himself described the final appearance of the pilgrims' chorus as 'the exaltation of the Venusberg, redeemed from the cares of sin, as we can hear in the holy hymn. So all the pulses of life well and spring up in a song of salvation, and both the sundered elements, spiritual and sensuous, God and Nature, are enmeshed in the holy kiss of uniting love.' The Overture thus establishes an important position at a tangent to the opera proper, and it conveys a wisdom beyond its time and perhaps beyond ours. Wagner's description contains a view of the Venusberg which was positive, and worlds away from his viewpoint later in Paris, when (more of this soon) he described the Venusberg as a place of horror.

Although Wagner originally intended his Overture to summarise the opera, he increasingly recognised it as so extensive and arresting that he grew unhappy with it as a curtain-raiser. He came to see it more as an independent piece in its own right, like the tone poems being composed by Franz Liszt, who was then his dearest friend. Because the Overture was followed by a substantial ballet depicting the Venusberg, it meant that the opera had two enormous expanses of orchestral music before any of the action proper began. Hence it was that the Overture was the first section which Wagner began revising and trying to shorten. Already in 1852, he was writing from his Swiss exile to his violinist friend Uhlig, still living in Dresden; 'If the decision were left to me I should have only the first tempo of the Overture played. The remainder is too much before the drama.' Later in 1861, he was preparing for a new production in Paris, and at that stage he may even possibly have toyed with the idea of abandoning the Overture altogether. This would have brought *Tannhäuser* into line with his common practice of later, which was to preface each act with music setting the scene for that particular act; and it would explain why Minna Wagner, his first wife, could complain to her daughter Natalie; 'Richard has cut[5] his beautiful Overture and written instead a hocus-pocus of Venus apparitions.' He did entirely rewrite the Venusberg scene, but still could not make up his mind. He formed half-plans to splice the Overture into the new Venusberg music, as he did in Vienna twelve years later, but in Paris these plans were not carried through. To have started with the Venusberg music would have made an indeterminate beginning, and the Overture was given in full. The *Tannhäuser* Overture was so famous and popular that it might have caused a rumpus to abandon it. In the event, *Tannhäuser* in Paris

5   Strohm, Reinhard, '*Zur Werkgeschichte des* Tannhäuser', Bayreuth Festival Programme for *Tannhäuser*, 1983. Strohm's superb analysis of all the changes Wagner ever made to *Tannhäuser* contains an oddity. Strohm says that Wagner planned to abbreviate his Overture, interpreting Minna's word '*gestrichen*' as meaning that Wagner cut his Overture down in size, or shortened it. On 23 August 2010, at Herr Hagen's remarkable guest house in Thurnau near Bayreuth, I was assured unanimously by my fellow-guests, a gathering of German academics and lawyers, that '*gestrichen*' will not bear this meaning; that it can only mean 'cut out', i.e. delete.

caused a rumpus anyway, but for quite different reasons, as will soon be obvious.

As for the new 'Venusberg Bacchanale' which Wagner had composed to replace the Overture in the Paris production and which disappointed Minna, it eventually did replace *part* of the Overture. That first happened at a Viennese concert performance in 1873, but poor Minna never had to witness it because she had been dead seven years. It was then that Wagner finally spliced the second section of the Overture into the 'Bacchanale', cutting out the return of the 'Pilgrims' Chorus' and creating an extraordinary piece of music, even though it sacrificed the concordance of sacred and profane which the Overture had originally expressed. Two years later, in 1875, he repeated his splicing at the Vienna Opera.[6]

The 'Venusberg Bacchanale' is one of those rare occasions where Wagner really did compose at the top of his voice. The size of the orchestra remains unchanged, but the music surges on to a new dimension of weight and power. The 'Overture and Venusberg Bacchanale' has become some of the most famous and successful music that Wagner – or anyone – ever composed, and its energy and dynamic verve are the complete answer to anyone who thinks of Wagner as incurably heavy-footed. Wagner goes on to pile climax on climax, frenzy on frenzy, going so far as to bring in a headlong version of the central motive of *Tristan und Isolde*. Even when the music seems to have reached such a peak that it can go no further, it hurtles off all over again, driven onwards now by castanets. Finally, it really can go no further; and it expires in a kind of post-orgiastic tristesse, where the vitality dissipates slowly in high singing lines for violins of saturated sensuousness. A chorus of sirens enters and entices the listeners to far shores, an Island of Cytherea;

---

6   As soon as Wagner had left Vienna, this version was abandoned and the original, popular Overture was again played complete and followed by the complete Paris 'Bacchanale'.

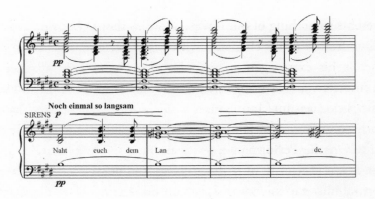

Fig. 11.6

and gradually the music quietens down into something calmer but still gorgeous, a mix of yearning and repose. It is astonishing that such a compelling unity should have resulted from a stitchwork which spliced music from 1845 to music from fifteen years later. With Wagner, apparently, a mysterious integrating principle was always at work, and probably nothing in his creative sphere was ever haphazard.

In order to grasp the story better, it is important to establish Tannhäuser's character and be clear why he should matter to us, because there are those who do not see anything instantly positive or appealing about him. He has been described as a 'broken backed, passive character' and 'an uninteresting man'.[7] In fact, he is active enough, but damagingly so because his activities upset and injure everyone around him. Venus and her court intend him no harm, but after placing them under the spell of his music he enjoys all that they offer until he finds himself sated, whereupon he deserts them. He is in the process of doing this when we first meet him, and soon his actions become so antisocial and damaging to the court of Thuringia that the other knights try and murder him (although this is as much a reflection of their ready belligerence), and he goes on to wound his great love, Elisabeth, and ruin her life. In virtue of this it is reasonable to wonder why he should intrigue and involve us as he does. Perhaps it is that he

7   Tanner, Michael, *Wagner*, London, 1996, p. 72.

represents something of our own shadow, as should become clear.

One feature of his character which is active and obvious from the outset is his extravagance, his extravagance in every possible way. His emotions are extravagant; his reactions are extravagant; and his music is extravagant. Tannhäuser is the Wagner hero closest to Verdi, emotive, emphatic, declamatory, a stranger to reflection. In Wagner's guide, 'On the Performance of "Tannhäuser"' he explained, 'As the most essential feature of his character, I point to the always directly active, almost excessive way in which he is gripped by the emotions of each particular situation. Tannhäuser is never in any circumstances slightly anything, but always fully and to the utmost.'

We meet Tannhäuser as soon as the real action begins, lying in a trance, enfolded in Venus' embrace. Although Tannhäuser's personality is not based on leitmotives, it becomes clear that leitmotives were not essential for Wagner to create characters. He still portrayed Tannhäuser vividly in music, using other means to give him a strong personal idiom. Within thirty lines of his opening words Wagner's music has conjured up his distinctive identity. At first he is asleep, but he starts up with a sudden exclamation; and he is much given to sudden exclamations. 'Too much!' he says, 'it's all too much. If only I could find it all a dream and awaken!' Venus asks him where his thoughts have been, and he explains that he has heard as in a dream the distant peal of bells, and that this has disturbed him with an uneasy awareness of having been absorbed in her fascinations for so long.

The sameness of it all is losing its appeal. It as if he had reached a state of personal entropy. Instead of treacly inertia he wants a sense of progress, or at least some variation – such as comes when night succeeds day – or when the seasons follow one another; he has lost all sense of time and purpose. He even borrows the Flying Dutchman's dark sentiments and tries on his death wish for size as if to emphasise his need to escape this suffocating world; 'Oh goddess, grasp it well, that it presses me onwards towards death'. However Wagner never took Tannhäuser's death wish very far. The music turns unstable and restless along with his thoughts, wandering from key to key with maudlin, self-absorbed undertones, and this represents a distinct side of him. Venus reproaches him, and reminds him what a privilege it is for a mere mortal to have won the love of a goddess, and this goddess above all; she urges him to pick up his lyre and serenade her. He initially responds with a will, and strikes up a song in her praise.

Fig. 11.7

Even so, it is deliberately humdrum music, hectic, diatonic, and strangely passionless. It represents Tannhäuser's worked-up vehemence; but soon he unthinkingly sinks back into a wistful yearning for something more, as he reflects that he is still a mortal; his thoughts drift into an unstable chromaticism as he explains that as a mortal he needs change and wants to leave. When he complains of the stress of having to perform like a god although only a man, the music turns petulant in tone, underlining his resentment that he has never become the god that she promised. His tone grows more determined again as he summons the resolve to demand his freedom. In fewer than seventy bars Wagner has gone a long way towards etching a distinctive identity for Tannhäuser.

Venus for her part is disturbed at Tannhäuser's desire to leave, and initially she cannot take it in; 'What is that for a song?' she asks, 'Is that all that I mean to you?' Tannhäuser responds to her complaint with a second verse where he tries to crank himself up to his past enthusiasm. He only succeeds in cranking himself up a semitone, beginning hectic and strained, and soon trailing off again into wistful thoughts of the simple life, fair breezes, blue skies, green meadows. He repeats his request to leave. Venus grows audibly more distressed and tries a variety of tactics to make him think again, whereupon Tannhäuser responds with a third verse which goes up another semitone. This verse too turns into a demand for freedom yet more urgent. Venus is hurt and angry but renews her attempts at seductive persuasion with offers which he cannot, she believes, refuse. However he does refuse, promising that after he has deserted her he will always remain her bold and loyal champion. Tannhäuser is not being insincere in this; he is desperately sincere, and his avowed determination to desert her at the same time as promising to be loyal represents the 'divided self' of Tannhäuser.

However, no one is impressed when a lover doing a runner promises, provided there is no fuss, to leave glowing testimonials to attract successors, and Venus is furious. She prophesies that Tannhäuser will one day be back; she will see him imploring for mercy, begging her to take him in. He tells her haughtily not to flatter herself; his pride would never let him; he would not degrade himself. She is hurt and says that she herself is not so arrogant; if he were in dire straights she would always be willing to welcome him again; death itself may one day reject him; but she would still happily provide his salvation. To this offer, he simply responds with a great cry: 'My salvation lies in Maria!', in the Virgin Mary, the mother of Jesus. This amounts to an abrupt swing from utter sensuality – life with Venus offers nothing else – to a totally discarnate, sexless state as symbolised by the Virgin Mary. At his cry of 'My salvation lies in Maria!' the Venusberg collapses in ruins and oblivion, and Tannhäuser finds himself alone in a valley near the mountainside.

The disappearance of the Venusberg is one of Wagner's most amazing *coups de théâtre*. It is one of the achievements that make *Tannhäuser* so mesmerising. With Tannhäuser's cry to the Virgin Mary, it is not only the Venusberg which disappears but its whole sound world. It is as though the scenery and the stage, even the orchestra, the very musical apparatus of the Venusberg had all slid down a black hole into utter nothingness, leaving behind an extraordinary stillness. The only sounds come from the stage, a solitary shepherd boy in the meadows, singing a song in praise of Spring and the goddess of Spring.

SHEPHERD BOY

Frau Hol - da kam aus dem Berg_ her - vor   zu zieh'n durch Flur - en und Au   –   en

Fig. 11.8

'Lady Holda from the hill drew near, to dance through woodlands and meadows,' and piping away to himself (cor anglais and then oboe);

Fig. 11.9

This leads gradually to other distant sounds, a chorus of pilgrims setting out for Rome.

Zu   dir   wall'   ich,   mein   Je - su   Christ,

der   du   des   Pil – gers   Hoff - nung_   bist!

Fig. 11.10

'To you the pilgrim's hopes all turn; with love for you his heart must burn.' They hope to celebrate Easter by gaining forgiveness for their sins from the Pope. Their chorale is interrupted, at first touchingly by the shepherd boy wishing them good luck and asking a prayer for himself, and then by Tannhäuser breaking into an exclamation of praise and gratitude, another Verdi-like outburst. Wilhelm Furtwängler was a major intellectual as well as a supreme conductor, and he used this scene to illustrate Wagner's power of synthesis. 'A particularly striking example of the poetic effect he achieves,' writes Furtwängler,[8]

8   *Furtwängler on Music*, tr. Ronald Taylor, Aldershot, 1991, p. 92.

comes in Act I of *Tannhäuser* at the moment when, as Tannhäuser invokes the Virgin Mary, the Venusberg vanishes and the countryside around the Wartburg appears. The music at this point is hardly memorable: – an insignificant tune sung by the shepherd boy, broken into by a characterless ritornello on the cor anglais. On the stage, a set – which consists, after all, merely of cardboard and canvas. Yet it is as though we had never seen so beautiful a May morning, as though God's world had never appeared so glorious. The reason is psychological: we experience the scene through the consciousness of Tannhäuser. And his cry 'Thanks to thee, Almighty, great are the wonders of thy mercy!' must be one of the greatest moments in the whole of literature.

Nobody has to accept Furtwängler's strangely unflattering view of the music to agree with him that it is Wagner's particular synthesis that creates the magic.

Tannhäuser now sinks on his knees in an admission of guilt, and he takes up the strains of the pilgrims' chorus; he too is oppressed by the same burden of sin. The distant hymn of the departing pilgrims is interrupted by horns onstage, twelve of them, heralding a hunting party of Thuringian nobles under their ruler, Landgraf Hermann.

Fig. 11.11

They are puzzled at the sight of a stranger but are all delighted when they recognise Tannhäuser, especially his old friend Wolfram von Eschenbach.

However their pleasure is cut short as they remember his aggression and hostility as he left the court; and they wonder: is he still the same? Wolfram points out that his demeanour now is anything but arrogant, and they readily assent and welcome him among them. They ask where he has been. Tannhäuser is a mixture of confusion and evasiveness;

'Do not ask! Just let me be on my way.' He cannot tell them for fear of the consequences. Nor could he bear a life of denial and concealment, and he makes as if to leave. They almost mob him with an ensemble persuading him back to the court of the Wartburg, but they have no success. Tannhäuser is on the point of hurtling off when Wolfram cuts through the vigorous ensemble and tells him to stay – for the sake of – Elisabeth! This stops Tannhäuser in his tracks, and he repeats her name as if in a trance. Wolfram builds on the impression he has made by telling him that in the old days of their contests, there was one sphere where Tannhäuser was always the victor, Elisabeth's favour; his songs captivated her as did nothing else, certainly nothing by his rivals. Not only that, but when he vanished, she turned into a recluse, a shadow of her former self. Let Tannhäuser come back and she will live again. Wolfram is successful; '*Zu ihr, zu ihr*: to her, to her!' exclaims Tannhäuser, and the act ends with him storming off to find her.

The next act begins with a Prelude setting the scene, the Great Hall of Song at the Wartburg, and it presents us with a beautiful young woman, the princess Elisabeth. The Prelude is all excitement and plainly depicts a lady of passionate animation.

Fig. 11.12. 'Elisabeth's Joy'

When the curtain goes up she sings an aria, her celebrated greeting to the hall unvisited by her for so long, not since Tannhäuser's disappearance.

Fig. 11.13

Wolfram ushers in Tannhäuser who kneels in remorse and clasps her by the hems, reducing her to confusion. She raises him to his feet at once and asks what on earth had become of him. Tannhäuser answers that he was wandering in distant lands and cuts in, 'Do not ask!' This fobs off any further questions, but she barely notices in her eagerness to tell him how his art had affected her, bringing her a peculiar blend of joy and pain. He answers that both this and now his return as well are a miracle from the god of love. They are soon headlong into a duet so passionate and mutual that Wolfram, returning unobserved and seeing them, is moved to remark ruefully that it is all up with his own hopes of Elisabeth.

Wolfram is followed in by the Landgraf of Thuringia, who announces that Tannhäuser's return has prompted him to give a festival. He has invited his nobles and their ladies to a song contest. They are already on their way. Immediately the hall starts to fill with a procession of the competitors and the general populace, set to festive music with blazing trumpet fanfares onstage.

Fig. 11.14

There is soon a large gathering, and the Landgraf sets out the conditions for the contest. The minstrel-knights must attempt to fathom in song the true nature of love. Elisabeth will be the one to crown the victor; and without saying as much the Landgraf manages to leave floating in the air the notion that she herself could be the prize.

The contest takes place, and all the knights except Tannhäuser start from an assumption which seems confusing today but makes better sense in the culture and religion of 1845 or of Tannhäuser's own era, the assumption that a love which contains any element of desire or any carnal expression is automatically unworthy of the name. The knights belong to an elevated ideal world where 'perfect knights in

Arcadian groves die of love for spotless maidens tormented by the sweet agony of passion that only a brute would seek to satisfy.'[9] On the other hand, the status of women seems to have been ambiguous, at the Wartburg as in life. 'Woman' occupied a pedestal where she was to be worshipped, but as in some cultures today, homage was actually a way of subjugating women by confining them to their pedestals, and legally women were chattels, belongings. 'Woman' was too ideal to be allowed any independence or authority, any determinations of her own unless she were royalty, and certainly she was not allowed any erotic sensibility. This attitude sprang partly from what Freud first defined as the 'Holy Mary Complex' but then redesignated the 'Mother Fixation'. His first description is really more illuminating, because it touched on the religious background to an inhibited mental state for men such that 'where they love, they do not desire; where they desire, they cannot love.' The knights have in fact made a romantic principle of denying desire. In line with this denial and inhibition, the knights create well-turned literary conceits and pure abstractions, but they entail serious impoverishments of real life; and Tannhäuser's contemptuous opposition soon reveals more of his personality. His special friend, Wolfram, draws the lot to sing first. Wolfram's song is a fine piece of work, drawing lofty comparisons and likening love to a miraculous fountain that revives the heart, although he would only worship from afar and never presume to taint or soil it 'with wanton mood'. Everyone acclaims it, everyone except Tannhäuser.

Tannhäuser breaks in on the applause, commenting pointedly that there is not much advantage in a refreshing fountain if nobody can approach and drink from it. In this he reveals a capacity for arguing a point, but the other knights do not want to hear it; and the next knight-contestant, Walther von der Vogelweide, continues in Wolfram's rapt and elevated style. The fountain of love is Walther's guiding ideal as well, and he tells Tannhäuser that he has obviously no understanding of its wonder, because its essence is 'chastity. If anyone so much as tries

9   Warner, Marina, *Alone of All her Sex: The Myth and Cult of the Virgin Mary*, London, 1976, p. 173.

to taste it, it loses its magical power.' Tannhäuser breaks in again that this is high-flown stuff and nonsense. He goes straight to the essential objection, that if everyone worshipped from afar and hung round as piously as that, the world and mankind would soon die out. For him, love means mutual joy and joyful union. This brings Biterolf to his feet for what is more of a challenge than a song. 'Who could remain unaffected and peaceable, listening to you?' he bursts out aggressively. What he admires about pure chaste love is its potential to stir up a man's convictions and strength, energising him to grasp his weapons and attack as savagely as necessary. Even though he has trained himself in the art of chaste adoration, Biterolf behaves like a warning of the worst effects of unmoderated, free-wheeling testosterone. Tannhäuser takes a verbal swing at him; 'You foolish boaster, you have no idea of love and its joys; otherwise you could never have sung such a song.'

Hostilities are in the offing, and Wolfram tries to keep the peace by striking up again, but his new contribution is openly sententious. 'May my song ring out to you, O love, O most exalted, as you approach like a messenger of God. I follow you submissively at a respectful distance. You lead us into the lands where your star ever shines.' This meaningless abstraction really fires up Tannhäuser. He is a man possessed. He had vowed to Venus to be her 'bold champion' against the world, and it is as though his vow had laid hold of him like a spell, so that he cannot *not* sing about her. He is another of those Wagnerian characters who first perform an action freely, only to find it rearing up and confronting them like an alien power. He gives us an almost exact encore of his song glorifying her, its third verse, but with the true passion that was missing earlier. He adds for good measure, 'Only the man who has held you passionately in his arms really knows what love is. Wretches,' he says, turning to the other knights, 'If you have never known this, get you away to the Venusberg!'

In German the term 'Venusberg' also refers to that central anatomical focus of female sexuality, the Mons Veneris, and it is no surprise that Tannhäuser causes pandemonium. Even in terms of today's social decencies his declaration is scandalous. The ladies all rush off as if he had leprosy, and the knights go on the warpath, condemning Tannhäuser's self-proclaimed pleasure in Venus' intimate female anatomy, plainly fornication or worse, as a mortal sin worthy of death. Elisabeth flings herself between the oncoming knights and Tannhäuser.

Three times she confronts them. She tells them that Tannhäuser must have been in a state of terrible enchantment to have done anything so appalling as he has revealed, and that if they kill him now, he will have no hope of saving his soul. He must be given the chance to expiate his misdeeds and make amends. She sinks in prayer and beseeches heaven for his forgiveness in a beautiful imploring phrase.

Fig. 11.15 'Elisabeth's Supplication'

Her courage and quick thinking win the day. The knights are not entirely unreasoning; they mumble something uneasily about not being able to forgive the sinner but not wanting to oppose what is apparently heaven's command as Elisabeth expresses it. They develop this idea in the great ensemble that now follows in which Elizabeth's beseeching phrase becomes the central theme. By one of his peculiar, lightning shifts of temperament, Tannhäuser has crumpled and become a broken and contrite heart, and he utters the words that Wagner said later were the key to his character and the axis of the drama. Tannhäuser part pleads, part prays,

> *To lead the sinner to salvation,*
> *God's messenger drew near me,*
> *But I raised my blasphemous gaze to her –*
> *Criminally – to touch her.*
> *O you, high above this earth-realm,*
> *Who sent the angel of my redemption,*
> *Have mercy on me,*

Who was so steeped in sin
That I could not recognise heaven's go-between!
Have mercy on me! Have mercy on me!

Wagner originally put these words at the centre of the ensemble, surrounded by eight solo voices and a huge chorus commenting on the extraordinary situation, forces which swamped Tannhäuser's crucial utterance (we will see how Wagner remedied this in due course). The Landgraf now responds, rising up grandly in judgment. Tannhäuser, he says, has committed a despicable crime. 'A son of sin, loaded with a curse, has stolen among us with a dissembling mask (*heuchlerischer Larve*)!' (The expressive power of the German makes the accusation sound even nastier.) 'We cast you out utterly! Only one hope of escaping eternal damnation awaits you: if you join the pilgrims on their way to Rome for Easter and seek absolution.' The knightly assembly take up a phrase from the Landgraf's arioso and develop it into an energetic ensemble:

CHORUS OF KNIGHTS

Mit ih - nen sollst du wal - len der Stadt der Gna - den - huld.

Fig. 11.16

They insist that Tannhäuser should follow the Landgraf's counsel and not come back until forgiven. Simultaneously Elisabeth presents herself to God in additional atonement for his misdeeds, and at the climax of the choral ensemble, a sudden silence allows the younger pilgrims to be heard through the window singing their chorale down in the valley, as they set off for Rome.[10] Tannhäuser leaves impulsively to join them – 'To Rome! To Rome!' – and as the brass blaze out the ensemble's main theme the curtain falls.

10 Wagner, ever the practical man of the theatre, had cleverly got his courtly ladies, his sopranos and altos, offstage – so that they could now do duty as the chorus of young pilgrims from behind the scenes.

Act III begins with the marvellous Prelude describing Tannhäuser's pilgrimage and its outcome. The version we know had been drastically pruned since the Dresden premiere in 1845, and perhaps it is partly because of this that it registers as a taut, faultless structure. Low tones in the orchestra tell out sections of the pilgrims' hymn from Act I. These are punctuated by reminiscences of music sung by Elisabeth as she made her Act II intercession for Tannhäuser's life, on limpid, pure-sounding wind. The lower strings interject music depicting the dragging weariness of Tannhäuser's journey.

Fig. 11.17

Eventually the 'pulse of life' figurations begin to throb, much as they sounded in the Overture, and the music builds up towards a blazing chorale for heavy brass.

Fig. 11.18 'Easter Joy'

This symbolises Easter and Easter joy, but the mood darkens ominously as the music expresses a damning judgment by the Pope, a judgment which prostrates Tannhäuser. When he regains consciousness, the music of Easter is again audible, high, ethereal and far away, after which everything subsides in a gentle conclusion.

The scene in Act III is the valley of Act I Scene 2, but now it is late autumn and time for the pilgrims' return. Wolfram and Elisabeth are there separately, each waiting anxiously. The pilgrims arrive full of gratitude for their deliverance and singing the pilgrims' chorus as we heard it at the beginning of the Overture. Elisabeth searches among them, looking desperately for Tannhäuser but finding no sign.

The pilgrims depart, bringing desolation to Elisabeth who embarks on her celebrated final prayer. She prays to the Virgin Mary: may she die pure, as she has tried to live! She is not perfect; will the Virgin Mary still accept her through grace? And will the Virgin Mary herself offer up a plea in heaven for Tannhäuser? As she ends, she gently rejects Wolfram's offer of assistance and leaves the scene. Wolfram waits on. He exhorts the evening star (which is incidentally the planet Venus, a bemusing association!) to greet Elisabeth as she passes from the earthly realm to the heavens.

Fig. 11.19

He sings that Elizabeth is to become a new member of the firmament, another star, but in fact she still has a great task to perform. Night falls and a ragged figure enters, leaning unsteadily on a staff, to the accompaniment if an ominous musical strain symbolising darkness on the scene and darkness of the spirit.

Fig. 11.20 'Judgment'

The ragged figure is of course Tannhäuser; but it takes Wolfram a moment to recognise him, just as it takes Tannhäuser more than a moment to realise that Wolfram regards him without rancour or hostility, in fact with rare compassion. Wolfram questions the haggard knight: what has happened? 'Did you not go to Rome?' Tannhäuser describes all that has happened, how he did indeed go to Rome. Throughout the pilgrimage he had gone to extremes of self-denial and mortification in his determination to make amends. He tells how he reached Rome; how he approached the Pope confidently and made his confession; but the Pope gave a terrible response: 'If you have partaken in the wicked pleasures of the Venusberg, you are damned for eternity. Just as this staff in my hand can never flourish fresh and be green again, so your salvation can never blossom forth from among the burning brands of hell;' and the musical strain symbolising judgment comes blasting out like a curse. This had thrown Tannhäuser into a dead faint. When he came to his senses, the songs of Easter joy and salvation were sounding in the distance but, as he sings wildly, '*Da ekelte mich der holde Sang,*' they only filled him with disgust; 'And so now, Lady Venus, I return to you.' He has not after all turned out too proud to beg her to have him back, and Venus materialises as a magical apparition, beckoning him as she promised. Tannhäuser advances enthusiastically, and Wolfram only restrains him by pronouncing again – as in Act I – the name of Elisabeth. Tannhäuser stops again; and again he repeats her name. Wolfram explains that she, the angel who prayed for him on earth, has now made her way to heaven, and is standing above him in benediction. He assures Tannhäuser that he is redeemed, and Venus, finally accepting defeat, vanishes for good. A funeral cortège comes into sight, bearing a bier with Elisabeth's corpse. The mourners are singing that the pure one, Elisabeth, is united with the heavenly host, and that her prayers have won salvation for the sinner. Tannhäuser expires with a prayer to Elisabeth on his lips: 'Saint Elisabeth, pray for me.' And now some younger pilgrims appear back from Rome. They proclaim the opera's redemptive conclusion, Wagner's characteristic *Erlösung*, and they are indeed describing a miracle by which both Elizabeth and Tannhäuser are redeemed. God has proved more forgiving than his vicar on earth, the Pope. What the Pope said could never happen *has* happened. The young pilgrims are bearing aloft the Pope's staff wreathed around with fresh green leaves. A mellow version of the *fortissimo* brass from the Act III Prelude, and the abundant foliage, confirm that Tannhäuser has indeed been redeemed.

Any satisfactory performance of *Tannhäuser* is so profoundly affecting that any criticism seems beside the point, but *Tannhäuser* has come in for a lot of criticism. Some of it *is* beside the point, such as the complaint that Wagner should have created something more like a music drama with more symphonic integration, such as he did in *The Ring*. This applies the wrong criterion, the wrong yardstick. *Tannhäuser* is not like *The Ring*, and is not a music drama. To be sure, the term can mean different things. Today 'music drama' is sometimes used to describe any serious musical stage work which reveals a grasp of personality and psychology. Benjamin Britten's *Peter Grimes* would qualify. However, in Wagner's original formulation, music drama signified something more specific; myth-invoking, symphonic and woven together from leitmotives, as *Peter Grimes* is not. In Wagner's music drama (or simply his 'drama' as he preferred it), leitmotives were essential. Leitmotives make possible the symphonic structures that are a key factor his true music dramas.

Tannhäuser is not a music drama but an opera, and even Johann Strauss's operetta *Die Fledermaus* comes closer to a leitmotive structure than *Tannhäuser*. To be sure, *Tannhäuser* has repeats of music already heard and pre-echoes of music yet to come, but so does *Die Fledermaus*. Nor does *Tannhäuser* begin to represent an intricate symphonic system. Wagner himself confused matters later by trying to reinvent *Tannhäuser* as something other than an traditional opera, just as he did with *The Dutchman*; but an opera it remains, and a wonderful opera, 'opera in excelsis'. It is another scenes opera, more of a throwback than *The Dutchman* because *The Dutchman* did have early versions of leitmotives. The end of *Tannhäuser* Act I is a fine instance of the scenes opera, fusing chorus, recitative and arioso, and it develops a full-blown ensemble-finale out of Wolfram's concluding aria. What Wagner presents here is a purely musical development because the words of Wolfram and the finale have no shared meaning; there are no ideas symbolised in Wolfram's music which carry through to the chorus. Act III of *Tannhäuser* harks back still further, to pure 'numbers opera' where the music is divided up into separate recitatives, arias and choruses.

Another way in which opera differs from music drama is in living for the moment. Before Wagner, the lyric stage was not as a rule concerned with causes and psychological connections (Mozart and Beethoven were exceptions to every rule) and when Wagner abused Meyerbeer as 'effects without causes', he was foisting onto Meyerbeer an irrelevant standard for something which Meyerbeer was never attempting, much as people would do, ironically, with Wagner and *Tannhäuser*. *Tannhäuser*'s abruptnesses were part of the reason why it was a favourite of Hanslick, Wagner's antagonist of later years, and he was much taken with it; 'it made a real impression on me and in places left me quite drunk'. Hanslick did not see that the very discontinuities of *Tannhäuser* bring out the fractured psychologies of its characters. In fact too, Wagner maintained a balance among the constrasts and disconnections that makes for a unity of its own.

This is a good point to return to the character of Tannhäuser himself as he has gone on developing. He has demonstrated his extravagance in the sequence of outbursts which punctuate the work:

1. 'My salvation lies in Maria:' the invocation which obliterates the Venusberg.
2. 'Almighty God, be praised! Great are the blessings of thy mercy:' a thanksgiving for his escape from Venus.
3. 'To her, to her, O bring me to her:' as he charges off to find Elisabeth.
4. 'Alas! Alas for the unluckiest, unholiest of men!' after Elisabeth has warded off the knights wanting to kill him ('*collapsing in fearful contrition*' say the directions).
5. 'To Rome!' the determination at the end of Act II to seek his forgiveness by a pilgrimage to Rome.

This list could go on, but these are enough to illustrate his extravagance and outbursts throughout the opera, which often share musical features. They are all of a piece both with Tannhäuser's energetic hymn to Venus and with his vehement address to Elisabeth. This address is where Tannhäuser's extravagance gains depth because he plainly adores *and admires* Elisabeth, albeit in his excessive fashion. He even briefly shows her some humility, but soon recovers his overweening confidence, telling her airily,

> *You should praise the god of love;*
> *He plucked the strings of my harp;*
> *He spoke to me out of my strains;*
> *He led me to you.*

This passage has exactly the same emphatic quality as his hymn to Venus, and so does his duet with Elisabeth. The tone of this duet confirms both her passionate animation and Tannhäuser's emotional involvement with her. The duet is the lineal descendent of Beethoven's rapturous '*O namenlose Freude*' in *Fidelio*, but more excessive and abandoned:

> *Praise to this hour,*
> *Praised be Almighty God*
> *For bringing his holy Word*

From your mouth.
The sunshine which shines on me
Awakens me to a new life.
I dedicate myself to it,
And in joyous trembling I name
Its beauteous wonder as my own.

As Wagner presents it, it is the extravagance of Tannhäuser's passion for
Elisabeth that sweeps her off her feet, so different from the 'too much
art' expressions of the other minstrel-knights. With their untastable
fountains and other literary conceits they seemed too preoccupied
with style for any real interest in the *real* Elisabeth, let alone real
passion for her. Their troubadour-run-to-seed sentiments are unlikely
to enrich her existence as Tannhäuser does, and his enthusiasm and
conviction even put out of mind any surprise that he has switched
loyalties from Venus so soon. Wagner's picture of Tannhäuser as a
man of extravagance soon gains force from his extravagant remorse
over his damage to Elisabeth from his reckless praise of Venus. His
religious convictions add something further to the picture when he so
extravagantly pleads for absolution, in the words which Wagner's big
ensemble originally overwhelmed. Their failure to emerge clearly led
Wagner to warn,

Unless at this moment and in this place, we have absorbed the intended
impression with the utmost certainty, we are no longer a position to
maintain our interest in the main figure of the drama. If we are not here
at last won over to a feeling a profound sympathy with Tannhäuser,
the whole course of the remaining drama becomes inconsequent and
unnecessary.

Wagner himself only heard his words projected once as he hoped, in
Munich, when his favourite tenor, Ludwig Schnorr von Carolsfeld,
took the role. At the time of the Paris production, he became so
apprehensive that his Tannhäuser, Niemann, would fail to make

the right impression that he did something so dire that anyone else doing it would have been howled out of court as the ultimate Wagner philistine. He simply struck out all the other parts of his ensemble, leaving Tannhäuser singing on his own, but at least this did enable the words to fill out the picture of Tannhäuser in the manner that Wagner felt was so important.

There is a drawback with Tannhäuser's identity becoming more defined, which is that his oddities become more defined as well. He often seems to act not only extravagantly, but without insight or memory. He has a dream about bells and it leads him to quit the Venusberg. He hears a chorale from the pilgrims and he collapses in an orgy of repentance. The huntsmen welcome him but he soon gets smitten with remorse and wants to leave them all. Wolfram brings Elisabeth back to mind, and he instantly forgets about leaving and loses himself in a reverie; and soon afterwards he tears off to find her. So it goes on; he is a bit like Pavlov's dog, conditioned to salivate when the bell rings. If someone rings Tannhäuser's bell, it produces an instant reaction, responding automatically to every new idea – until the next one comes along. He conveys no sense of a mastering consciousness. As a doctor looking at Tannhäuser's peculiarities, he always seems to me a dead ringer for addiction, particularly the addictive pattern familiar in alcoholics and drug addicts; and we come back to this later.

Wagner develops Tannhäuser's personality further in his interactions with Venus and Elisabeth. To extend the point from earlier, a man is known by his friends, his lady friends especially, and so we should now look at his two ladies more closely, both for their own sake and for the light they shed on Tannhäuser. It has often been said that they personify a conflict of sacred and profane,[11] to such an extent that the opera allegedly consists of the warring contrasts between them. At its simplest,

---

11 A conventional view of their status was set out in the Covent Garden prospectus for 2009-10; '*Tannhäuser* is a work in which the composer-librettist presented a conflict between spiritual and sensual love as exemplified in the rival claims on the minstrel hero of Elisabeth and Venus.'

Elisabeth and her world = good: Tannhäuser's relationship with
Elisabeth = sacred and ennobling;

Venus and the Venusberg = wicked: Tannhäuser's relationship with
Venus = profane and debasing.

First then Elisabeth. In Elisabeth Wagner achieved one of his most
striking and appealing creations, and to help fashion her Wagner
resorted to some history. Wagner demonstrated general shrewdness in
situating the action on the Wartburg, a very real castle near Eisenach
in Thuringia. Not only was it home to the historical St Elisabeth,
but it had positive historical associations both old and new. Martin
Luther, the cutting-edge figure of the reformation, had been protected
there, and during the nineteenth century, the Wartburg came to
symbolise political freedom just as it had symbolised religious freedom
earlier. In history the Wartburg and its court were not at all the ultra-
conservative establishment presented by *Tannhäuser*. The Wartburg
had symbolised enlightenment in the popular imagination, even
revolution; and Wagner tapped this iconic association in his alternative
title for *Tannhäuser*, 'The Song Contest on Wartburg', another quasi-
historical event.

St Elisabeth was Wagner's addition from solid history to an opera
otherwise drawn from legends. It was Wagner who turned her into
Tannhäuser's true love, and it is she who brings to the story its
spiritual and tragic dimensions. The real, historical Elisabeth had been
a Hungarian princess.[12] She was born in 1207, and she lived only to
be 24. She was betrothed in infancy to the son of Hermann, Landgraf
of Thuringia. This son succeeded to the position of Landgraf in 1217
when Elisabeth was only ten. Unfortunately he went off on a crusade,
fell ill and died. That was in 1227, when she was twenty. As a widow,
she proceeded to model herself on St Francis of Assisi who had become
world-famous by the time his life ended a year earlier. She deserted

---

12   She is still commemorated by the Elizabeth Bridge or Erzsébet Híd in
     Budapest.

her children, which may not strike us now as entirely admirable, and devoted herself to good works in a way that *was* entirely admirable. She made a tremendous impression in the four years of her life still remaining, so much so that she was canonised in 1235, just four years after her own death. During the nineteenth century, her cult was widespread across the German territories, and Liszt would write a major oratorio, *The Legend of St Elizabeth*, reflecting that cult. It was fairly bold of Wagner to reinvent her, stripping away most of her historical features, turning her into the Landgraf's niece and making her the object of Tannhäuser's romantic passion. She crucially retains her saintly devotion and holiness, and Tannhäuser's last words are a prayer, '*Saint* Elisabeth, pray for me.' The surprising thing is that she does not feature in the Overture. The Overture contrasts a sensual world and a Christian-religious world, but the saintly Elisabeth, on whom the action hinges, does not appear in it. She is often taken as summed up in her Act III prayer to the Virgin Mary, with its purity, flutes and oboes and pastel shades, which emphasise her contrast with the sumptuous and pagan Venus. So do her words, 'May I die pure; as I have tried to live!'

Venus is her opposite. At first sight Venus is not merely oversexed, but a satanic force for human misery, enticing men to do things which result in their damnation. She bears out her origins in the old Roman religion, a religion that had long ago been taken as outmoded and false. Once the Emperor Constantine had chosen in favour of Christianity, the old beliefs were reckoned not merely as untrue but as devilish and evil. Christianity unfortunately been taught appalling practices by the Roman state which had persecuted it, but now the worm had turned and any inclination to the old religion likewise bring down the cruelest punishments in this world and the next. Tannhäuser's situation with Venus can thus dimly suggest a second strand to his transgression, namely apostasy, a reneging on Christianity. In embracing Venus he might have been embracing paganism as well, but this was not something that Wagner pursued with any interest.

The very action of the opera seems on the face of it to confirm

Venus' status as baleful. Tannhäuser's encounters with her in the Venusberg do not present her as particularly satanic, but because she is sex, temptation, and damnation, everything she does is automatically configured as malign. Describing the new Paris Venusberg scenes to Mathilde Wesendonck, Wagner said he had now managed to convey the full horror of the Venusberg, but this was an inconsistency with the past. In Paris he seemed to have lost sight of his earlier vision of the Overture as ending in 'the exaltation of the Venusberg, itself redeemed from the curse of sinfulness'.

At least the plain implication was now that Venus and the Venusberg were sinful and appalling. Venus herself was saddled with the 'full horror' of her carnally seductive kingdom, and for creating a kind of erotic bondage for Tannhäuser. The idea of Venus as baleful is reinforced when Tannhäuser calls on Maria, the Virgin Mary. Because Mary is all that is holy, Venus, her opposite, must be all that is unholy. There are occasions in Wagner when the music tells a different story from the text, explaining that what is really going on is quite different, but in this instance text and music seem all of a piece.

If this seems straighforward, *Tannhäuser* subverts any straight-forward view of itself, and constantly; and this takes us to our second step, which is to explain how it undermines any uncomplicated idea of its principal characters and its values. Perhaps a good way of explaining the point about values is through a comparison, specifically a comparison with *Hamlet*. Hamlet himself is as ambiguous as Tannhäuser, but the play as a whole still leaves most people clearer about its values, right and wrong, wise and foolish, admirable and not so admirable, because the drama establishes its positions as it unfolds. The play itself makes it reasonably clear that King Claudius is a villain; he has murdered Hamlet's father, his own brother, out of ambition, lust and greed. The play also develops a picture of Hamlet as a wronged and essentially commendable figure, however damaged he is; and it establishes that Polonius means well enough, even if he is a 'foolish prating knave'. We involuntarily absorb the underlying values that Shakespeare intends. To be sure, there are times when his characters deviate; Claudius is sometimes sympathetic, and Hamlet can be appalling, as in his disregard for the fates of Rosencrantz and Guildenstern. The good characters in Shakespeare are not simply good; Shakespeare did not go for unrealistic black and white, but he created a climate such that Hamlet calls up a positive regard. We take in unawares how we should regard the other characters, good, bad, or a mixture. *Hamlet* does not subvert its own values.

Tannhäuser does subvert its own values, even though this gives a special richness to the work and a relevance that is both modern and timeless. The contradictions stem partly from Wagner's sources, such as *Des Knaben Wunderhorn*, the collection of myths and legends published in 1805 by Achim von Arnim and Clemens Brentano.[13] This collection presented two stories which Wagner adopted for *Tannhäuser*. The first relates how Tannhäuser breaks free of Lady Venus and her magic mountain where he has spent a year with evil spirits. In the second, the Pope refuses him forgiveness for his sins. These two narratives gave Wagner the beginning and the end of his drama, and he also made use of Venus' fateful farewell, 'Wherever in the realm you roam, my praise shall be your song.' This was Tannhäuser's Act I declaration which returned to haunt him in Act II.

Among Wagner's other sources (and a full discussion of the sources is beyond the scope of this book), there was E. T. A. Hoffmann's collection of fables, *The Serapion Brethren*, and in particular the story, '*Der Kampf der Sänger*, The Singers' Contest'. This tells a semi-scandalous story of Heinrich von Ofterdingen, who is joined by a demon, Nasias, and possessed by him. Their joint songs conjure up 'fragrances breeding erotic desires and pleasures, perfumes where the sweet notes rose and fell like tumbling cupids,' as in the Paris 'Bacchanale'. The idea of joining together the legend about forbidden sensuality with the one about a contest probably came to Wagner from an essay of 1838 by a professor at Königsberg, C.T.L. Lucas, who suggested that the two might have been identified in popular imagination. Whatever

13   This collection famously later inspired Mahler, who wrote many of his songs to texts after *Des Knaben Wunderhorn*.

happened in popular imagination, Wagner followed the professor and did amalgamate the two stories. The point which connected them was at the two fiendish possessions, a demon possessing Heinrich von Ofterdingen and Venus possessing Tannhäuser. In the fusion, Tannhäuser took over Heinrich von Ofterdingen's Christian name, which explains why Tannhäuser is always addressed as Heinrich in Wagner's opera, and also partly why Tannhäuser is a divided spirit.[14]

Wagner's difficulties and doubts over *Tannhäuser* were never to do with the music and its quality as such. He did indeed make frequent alterations to the music but these were always to try and clarify or improve the drama, and his alterations reflected his concern that the music did not carry out his dramatic intentions well enough, not that it was bad music. As was clear from Queen Victoria's response to the Overture, the music of *Tannhäuser* is some of the most cogent and convincing ever created. It is for good reason that, according to BBC statistics, the Henry Wood Promenade Concerts have over their long history played excerpts from *Tannhäuser*, above all the Overture, more than any other work, except for pieces like the National Anthem which are part of the fabric.

The real difficulty was one which Wagner recognised only slowly, that even in its storyline *Tannhäuser* was a drama of unresolved discrepancies, however well they resolve at the levels of myth and psychology. As a narrative, *Tannhäuser* contains non sequiturs between events and their consequences and inconsistencies in the characters and their motives. For all Wagner's genius, ordinary mortals can see this more easily now than he could then, because the passing years have allowed us a degree of critical distance. One and a half centuries' development in many spheres has shed new light on *Tannhäuser*, and as Isaac Newton said, we sometimes see further than the giants of the past simply because we can stand on their shoulders.

14   Wagner also made extensive use of Heine, as he had in *Der Fliegende Holländer*. Heine's parodistic poem, *Der Tannhäuser*, still colours the text of Wagner's opera, although Wagner later disavowed any debt to Heine.

One inconsistency which was positive was that Wagner gave both Venus and Elisabeth features which cut right across any initial, simple impression of the one as profane and the other as sacred. This very ambivalence adds quality to the story, making the characters more relevant and real, more psychologically truthful. This becomes clearer if we look at the two ladies again from altered standpoints. A repeat examination can almost reverse the first impressions. First, Venus. At first sight she is profane and 'horrifying', all sex and selfishness and damnation; but if we set aside the knights' assumption that sex is sinful in itself, what harm has she actually done? It was in the later Paris version that Wagner heightened her allure, but even in the Dresden version she is sympathetic and charming. Her very first words are to ask Tannhäuser tenderly where his thoughts have been. She reminds him playfully what an incredible thing it is for an ordinary mortal to have won her, a goddess, the source of all voluptuousness, and she discloses an affecting softness and vulnerability. When Tannhäuser eventually demands his freedom, Venus merely tries to coax him back with all the engulfing warmth that she can muster. The terms of Tannhäuser's refusal are highly significant, amounting to a manifesto on her behalf, proclaiming that her effect on humanity is positive and life-enhancing. Here, translated, are the actual words:

> *For you alone my song shall ever be.*
> *Your praise alone shall be my theme.*
> *Your sweet enchantment is the source of all beauty,*
> *And every lovely wonder stems from you.*
> *The glow that you light up in my heart*
> *Blazes like a bright flame for you alone.*
> *Against the whole world I shall be your untiring proud*
>   *champion.*

That scarcely represents Venus as horrific, as Wagner envisaged when in Paris. Tannhäuser's praise of the good things which she confers is true. Erotic love and its goddess do inspire so many of the world's wonders, its art, poetry and music, and many of the world's finer feelings. Venus is a positive force, set in opposition to war and man's more destructive instincts. She confers fertility and abundance. With this focus on the positive aspects of Venus the perspectives have at the very least shifted and varied. What never varies is Venus's freedom from malice; and her behaviour, apart from her 'nasty' sexual activity, is never nasty. The worst she does is warn Tannhäuser that if he leaves her, she will one day see him begging her to take him back, and even when he snootily tells her not to flatter herself, she for her part remains gracious.

She evidently adores Tannhäuser and is persistently generous to him. At the end of the opera it is she, the pagan goddess, who is more forgiving than the Christian Pope. None of this fits the idea of Venus as fiendish, and her ultimate loss of Tannhäuser creates a bewildered sense that she gets a raw deal, without any clear impression of whether she deserved it, and if so why.

The initial perspectives slip further when we look closer at Elisabeth. She is anything but a milk and water goody-goody, which is what her prayer in Act III, taken out of context, can suggest. The Prelude of Act II anticipated a lady of vivid identity and passionate humanity. Even in prayer itself, Wagner has her admitting to human longings, which in context seem to be of an erotic kind, and these have worried her because she took them as sinful. (It is not clear whether Elisabeth takes them as sinful in themselves, because her mind should have been on higher things, or sinful because they had not been legitimised and their sinfulness mitigated by holy matrimony.) When Wolfram brings Tannhäuser into the Hall of Song, Elisabeth generously avoids any impression of giving him a hard time for leaving her. Indeed it is rather that she gives herself a hard time after he kneels and begs forgiveness. She raises him to his feet and overlooks his evasiveness. As we have seen, she had missed the 'peculiar blend of joy and pain, feelings that I never knew before, and longings that I never felt before'. She reveals more than she knows or understands about the currents flowing within her, vaguely sensing them but unable to identify or define them. When Tannhäuser explains that this is a miracle from the god of love, she eagerly accepts his answer and all its implications; but Wagner was shrewd in leaving only vague notions regarding the identity of this god of love. Who was it? Was it the Christian God; was it a pagan throwback; was it some Hegelian spirit? Wagner does not say.

Elisabeth's warmth and candour are the mark of a centred person, and she fills out her appealing picture further when she next plays an active role during the song contest. After Tannhäuser has dissented from the other minstrel-knights and told them that love requires every possible expression to realise it in all its richness, Elisabeth responds eagerly, but then falters. As the only lady of royal standing at the Wartburg, whose values are so rigid, she seems to be isolated. She had not intended to step out of line (she feels vulnerable and backtracks on her convictions; we can most of us, alas, relate to that!) However she shows that when it really matters she is very courageous, because she soon throws herself between Tannhäuser and the men advancing on him. '*Haltet ein,*' she hurls at them, 'Stay your hands,' and after a moment of amazement, they are so outraged that there is a real risk of them running her through as well as a scarlet woman. 'What's all this? The chaste Elisabeth standing up for a sinner?' they exclaim in angry crescendo; no wonder that Wagner has her soon needing to assert her status as a pure virgin, innocent of any lascivious involvement with Tannhäuser. She is undeterred: 'Back' she says, 'I count nothing for death. What is a wound from your swords to me compared with the death blow he has struck at my heart?' They come at her a third time; 'Elisabeth! He has done you a terrible injury; how can you stand up for anyone so execrable?' and she parries them a third time: 'Back from him'. She has not a moment to lose before their attitudes harden irrevocably, and Wagner has her toss caution to the winds: '*Grausame!* You horrendous men! You are not to be his judges! Throw down your wild swords, and pay attention to the words of a pure virgin. Hear from me the will of God! The man is in bondage, in the grip of a terrible enchantment, and you are about to kill him in a state of sin. *You* would leave him no hope of salvation. *I* am the one he has wounded to the depths. Mine therefore is the right and the duty

to determine his fate. He must be given a chance to expiate his sin.'
Her nobility of spirit and her heroism are the dramatic centre of this
tremendous scene.

Meanwhile she has indeed been wounded to the very depths by
Tannhäuser; and if the English translation here is old-fashioned, it
is because the ideas themselves are not at ease with today's language,
largely conditioned as it is by economics, statistics, and social
mechanics, and not much by the sacred or the romantic.

> *Look upon me, a maiden whose blossoming shoots*
> *He smashed in a single wanton blow,*
> *Me who loved him so deeply, and*
> *Whose heart he has broken so arrogantly.*

She thus admits to being deeply in love with Tannhäuser, not at all
a prim and proper thing to do, not the conventional mediaeval or
Victorian girl, and she can do it because she is rounded and centred.
Before she was so hurt by Tannhäuser, she seemed to offer him the
possibility of integration, somewhere between the endless sex of the
Venusberg and the total sexlessness commended in the Virgin Mary.
Tannhäuser loves and desires Elisabeth, and she too seems to feel both
'sacred and profane' emotions in his direction, although she cannot
make them out. Facing the Wartburg assembly she also divulges how
she believed that she was loved in return, regardless of her humiliation
at having fallen for a deceitful two-timer. She has confirmed her
force of character, and in this overall context, even her Act III prayer
takes on a new complexion. Its muted tones now suggest *not* that
she is fundamentally feeble and colourless, but that the spirited and
determined person of Act II has changed. She has wasted away over
the months, and it is as though Tannhäuser's behaviour had triggered
off something like *anorexia nervosa*. This was not understood in the
nineteenth century by Wagner or any one else, but was probably the
explanation why ladies *did* then commonly fade away. This possibility
was branded into my memory during my first week as a newly

qualified doctor at St Thomas's Hospital, when a French waif of a girl was admitted in the end stages of this terrible affliction. That situation and the story behind it were weirdly reminiscent of Elisabeth's, and the French waif did fade away and die within two days.

Wagner further complicated matters, but cleverly, by presenting Elisabeth as upholding the same Christianity as the Pope and yet also praying for an outcome based on values that are the exact opposite of the Pope's. Although Elisabeth in some respects stands midway between Venus and the Virgin Mary, Wagner has made her closer to Venus in one respect, that she and Venus are compassionate to Tannhäuser, unlike those stalwarts of religious orthodoxy, the knights and the Pope. At the very least it should now be clear that Wagner subverts any simple idea that 'the composer-librettist presented a conflict between spiritual and sensual love'.[15] The fissures in *Tannhäuser* make it a very modern work, a drama for today. Many people now are fissured about their identities and values, in the same way as the divided spirits in *Tannhäuser*.

The next step is to place the drama of *Tannhäuser* in its cultural and religious context. Not to understand this context means missing what *Tannhäuser* meant for its own time. Not to understand what it meant for its own time means missing what it means for ours. Central to the context is the millennia-long vilification of the body and the conflict between sacred and profane, sex and spirit, throughout the 'civilised world', and central too is the question of how people experienced this conflict in themselves and society. Another key factor was the special power of the theatre in Germany and its ability to produce change in the world beyond. Without an understanding of these things no one could readily appreciate the strength of the attitudes which *Tannhäuser* did so much to overturn, or grasp how a theatrical work could revolutionise these arttitudes throughout the world.

To understand it also calls for an explanation of the ideas and outlooks which prevailed in *Tannhäuser*'s day. They were rooted in Christianity,

---

15   Royal Opera House, Covent Garden, prospectus for 2009-10, as above.

as it had evolved over the centuries. It had become a colossal spiritual and secular force, symbolised in German-speaking territories by Prince-Bishops, rulers who regulated their subjects' outer lives by legal controls and arbitrary power, and their inner lives by ecclesiastical ordinances and spiritual despotism.[16] In place of the godliness, altruism, freedom and active compassion which Christ preached, the religion which took his name would often, not least in Wagner's time, support oligarchy, dogma, religious wars, slavery and wholesale destruction of human life. But nothing in any version of Christianity which Wagner knew drew less authority from its founder than its vilification of the erotic, and nothing rankled with Wagner more. Jesus Christ is not recorded as having said much on the subject of sexuality and the erotic, and Marina Warner's classic study of 1976, *Alone Of All Her Sex*, and to a lesser extent *Eros Denied* by Wayland Young (Lord Kennet)[17] are two incomparable sources of historical information about how Christianity came to vilify sexuality and enshrine that vilification in Christian belief. Marina Warner analyses the extent to which the Early Church Fathers stigmatised sexual expression as the one, true original sin, and explains how this formed a mainspring of the ordinances and rules by which Christians were to live. Early Christianity was a swirling ferment of different cults, but when two main traditions eventually crystallised, it was Roman Catholicism which surfaced as the dominant influence in the West, and Roman Catholicism enforced a morality denigrating the body and mortifying the flesh. Although the Church Fathers had many achievements to their credit, it was from them that originated the poisonous conviction that all the evils of man flowed from sexuality, Eve and 'woman'. Marina Warner herself had been a Roman Catholic, and her book dissects minutely why 'it is almost impossible to overestimate the effect which the Early Church's characteristic association of sex and sin and death has had on the attitudes of our own civilisation,' the very attitudes that *Tannhäuser* did so much to overturn. Wagner created *Tannhäuser* against the 'still unchallenged structure of original sin: the

16   This was true right up to 1803, when Napoleon abolished them.
17   Young, Wayland, *Eros Denied*, Brattleboro, VT, 1964.

rebellion of Adam and Eve against God … When they sinned, death and sex as we know them entered the world.'[18] The idea of women as the embodiment of evil was crystallised by Tertullian in the second century AD where, as Marina Warner aptly describes it, he gave to his rancour the bite of the most accomplished and deadly Latin since Tacitus:[19]

> Do you not realise, Eve, that it is you? The curse God pronounced on your sex weighs still on the world. Guilty, you must bear its hardships. You are the devil's gateway, you desecrated the fatal tree, you first betrayed the law of God, you softened up with your cajoling words the man against whom the Devil could not prevail by force. The image of God, Adam, you broke him as if he were a plaything. *You* deserved death, and it was the son of God who had to die.

This damning assessment remained the basis for the Church's attitude to woman, sex and sin for fifteen centuries. In the early Middle Ages for instance, Cardinal Hugues de Saint-Cher wrote a couplet,

> Woman pollutes the body, drains the resources, kills the soul, Uproots the strength, blinds the eye and embitters the voice[20]

and attitudes like these were reinforced during the period which followed, that of the historical *Tannhäuser*, because of venereal disease. Disease was generally seen as divine retribution for human wickedness, but venereal disease (syphilis) seemed a special punishment newly and divinely crafted to fit the crime, because it was contracted through sexual intercourse, through the sin itself. From this time on erotic deeds and imaginings were more than ever to be expiated with penances, fastings, punishments, flagellations, in the attempt both to suppress but also atone for them, so as to escape the retribution of 'the great pox'. However Eros is not easily suppressed. Eros, as Jung

18   Warner, *op. cit.*, pp. 50 et seq.
19   Ibid., pp. 58 et seq.
20   quoted in Young, *op. cit.*

said, belongs in part to man's primordial animal nature which will endure as long as man has an animal body. The work of Professor Helen Kaplan[21] and Shere Hite (of the *Hite Reports*) was at the forefront of demonstrating scientifically and psychologically what Alberich expressed and represented in *The Ring*, that if the claims of sex and Eros are denied, the result is often 'mutilation emotionally', with the ensuing dire consequences and pathological expression. The equivalence of allure, danger, sin and deadliness were symbolised by Franz Stuck in his picture *The Sin*.

The demonisation of the erotic domain almost certainly gained force from the divided *aesthetic* reactions that often went with sexual activity, even within the sanctified zone of 'holy matrimony'. Before the advances of dentistry, soap and sanitation, sex often smelt bad, in marriage as well as outside it, and not even the grudging stamp of ecclesiastical endorsement could make good the aesthetic aversions. This circumstance probably helps explain why any sense of pleasure of the erotic was for so long blurred, confused and mingled with a sense of disgust, reinforcing the notion of sex as compelling but repulsive as well as sinful and dangerous. St Augustine of Hippo proclaimed, '*Inter faeces et urinam nascimur,*'[22] summing up both an unprepossessing view of childbirth and a misogynistic view of female anatomy and female identity such as moulded attitudes for fifteen centuries. Venus, once a beguiling symbol of sex and 'woman', was recast as a foul fiend to be relegated underground and battened down in her subterranean kingdom, whether in the Venusberg or in the cesspools of Freud's unconscious.

Of equal importance for understanding the action and the effect of *Tannhäuser* is another, countervailing myth, also developed by the Early Church. Again Marina Warner makes it elegantly clear how the myth of the erotic impulse as sinful fed off and into an opposing myth enfolding the Virgin Mary. If sex was sin and if women, provoking lust, were instruments of the devil, then the corollary, through mental

---

21   Kaplan, Helen Singer, *The New Sex Therapy*, London, 1974.
22   We are born into the world between shit and pee.

processes which were not entirely rational, was that the woman who was incomparably good must be an ideal of total sexlessness. The Virgin Mary became the deified ideal of all reputable women, all women who were attempting to rise above their natural, intrinsic sinfulness and become sexless; they were all supposed to follow her example. Accordingly as the feminist writer Sheila Kitzinger expressed it,[23] 'It was assumed for two millennia either that women did not have spontaneous sexual feelings or that they had fallen from grace and from the pedestal on which pure women were adored by their men. The good woman suffered sex for the sake of her marriage.' William Acton, a Victorian genito-urinary specialist (not to be confused with the great historian), whose book, *The Function and Disorders of the Reproductive Organs* operated within an evidence-free zone, pontificated that a newly married husband 'need not fear that his wife will require the excitement, or in any respect imitate the ways of a courtesan … I should say that the majority of women (happily for society) are not very much troubled with sexual feeling of any kind.'[24]

They were indeed probably not much troubled, because as Michel Foucault in France and Shere Hite in America have shown, it is culture which moulds erotic responses and sexuality itself, and women who were indoctrinated with such life-diminishing standards came to metabolise them into their identity and outlook. Ruth Smythers, wife of a Methodist clergyman in New York, wrote a book on 'intimate relationships', and warned young women that 'While sex is at best revolting and at worse rather painful, it has to be endured and has been from the beginning of time.'[25] She advised, 'One heartening factor for which the wife can be grateful is that the husband's home, school, church, and social environment have been working together all through his life to instil in him a deep sense of guilt in regard to his sexual feelings, so that he comes to the marriage couch apologetically

23 Kitzinger, Sheila, *Woman's Experience of Sex*, London, 1985, pp. 17 et seq.
24 Quoted extensively in Young, *Eros Denied*, pp. 232 et seq.
25 Smythers, Ruth, *Instruction and Advice for the Young Bride*, New York, 1894.

and filled with shame, already half cowed and subdued.' The sum of the whole matter was exactly as Laurens van der Post, the great anthropologist, declared;[26]

> This rejection of the feminine and the suppression of sex reached its most omnipotent height in the Victorian era. Although this age carries an English label, 'Victorianism', it was spiritually in charge of culture from Cape Wrath to the littoral of the Mediterranean, the Urals of Russia extending to the remote Pacific coast and across to the New World of the Americas.

This was the matted web into which *Tannhäuser* hurtled like a rocket bomb. The sheer force and extent of *Tannhäuser*'s effect was possible only because it belonged to a period when the theatre and opera house were truly instruments of change. The theatre stage was a chink in the bastions of a growing censorship enforced by Europe's ruling reactionaries in the nineteenth century, because it was a place where liberal intellectuals could still make points that would elsewhere have been censored out of existence. Schiller exploited this possibility consistently in didactic dramas like *Don Carlos*, but by Wagner's time, censorship had tightened its grip. Baron von Lüttichau, Wagner's overlord at the Dresden Opera, was able to comment approvingly that Schiller's *William Tell* would never have passed the censors if it had come out in his day. The reactionary Lüttichau saw this as progress. It was thus entirely understandable why a theatre of contemporary relevance should appeal to the public as a source of freedom. One reason why *Les Huguenots* by Meyerbeer was popular in Paris was that it presented subjects of topical resonance, and he knew that they would register well with large swathes of his audience. In Brussels an opera, Auber's *La Muette de Portici*, was truly an instrument of change, because it *did* spark off

26   van der Post, Laurens, *Jung and the Story of our Time*, Harmondsworth, 1978, p. 138.

a revolution,[27] and these instances suggest how the theatre in general and operas in particular genuinely promoted change.

Another factor for understanding *Tannhäuser*'s influence is what a huge and influential figure Wagner was becoming. Not that his influence can be demonstrated scientifically or experimentally. There were no Shere Hites in the late nineteenth century to research people's intimate attitudes, and nor did people keep notebooks telling us, 'After going to Wagner's *Tannhäuser* my approach to the erotic phenomenon and my way of relating to the opposite sex was reconfigured.' As the American sociologist Charles Tilly expressed it, 'In the world of history, even true love leaves fewer memorials than the price of a sow.'[28] Even so it is possible to study the facts and make rational inferences. One important fact is that no other artist has ever influenced the world so widely with his ideas, and there is plenty of evidence about the extent of his reach. The Emperor of Germany was soon to tune his horn to Donner's '*Hedo, Heda Hedo*' from *Das Rheingold* (Fig. 14.25). In 1876, the year of the first complete *Ring*, Wagner was such a world figure that journalists were vying to use the cable just laid under the Atlantic to telegraph their reports back to America. A certain Wilhelm Tappert, a fringe-figure of the Wagner firmament, was able that same year to make capital simply by collecting the nastiest invective against Wagner into a dictionary of Wagner-hate, a lexicon in which he tabulated all the different modes of ghastliness and awfulness for which Wagner was credited as man and artist. It sold so well that by 1915 it had run to a third edition. Wagner was big enough to sell such a farrago. Could any classical composer

27   It was on 25 August 1830, at a performance at the Théâtre de la Monnaie in Brussels that a riot broke out during the opera's patriotic and revolutionary duet 'Amour sacré de la patrie' and it became the signal for the Belgian Revolution, and thence for Belgian independence. In Wagner's 'Reminiscences of Auber' (1871) he commented that the opera's very representation had made revolutions, and was recognised as an obvious precursor of the July Revolution which meant so much to him; 'Seldom has an artistic product stood in closer connection with a world-event.'

28   Quoted in McPhee, Peter, *A Social History of France, 1780-1880*, London, 1992, p. 4.

today provide any hanger-on with profits from an anthology of attacks against his life and art? Or again there was the firm which made a kind of German Oxo, Liebig's Fleisch-Extrakt, and it exploited Wagner for publicity and advertising. It devised several promotional sets of six cards, beautifully produced, which depicted important junctures in Wagner's life and dramas. (Some of the series are included in this study as whimsical illustrations.) The manufacturer did this simply because he could rely on Wagner to sell the products. Or, to take a literary example, there is *The Experiences of an Irish R.M.*, a literary gem of the late nineteenth century, which was set in the hunting and magistracy world of Southern Ireland. Wagner's influence had penetrated so far that the book's creators[29] could make its fictional English author, Major Yeates, express the hope that even if he were taken for a fool, he might take credit for being 'a pure fool'. The authors, themselves rooted in the fastnesses of Southern Ireland, obviously counted on people picking up the wry reference to *Parsifal*. Long before the first Bayreuth Festival, an awareness of Wagner and *The Ring* had spread yet further, as far as Brazil. The Emperor of Brazil, Dom Pedro had already been so interested that Wagner had once promised him the premiere of *Tristan und Isolde*, and the Emperor went to the trouble of journeying all the way to Europe and Bavaria for the first *Ring* performances. What other artist in the whole of history ever had that kind of clout?

Yet further evidence of his influence is his effect on the cutting-edge poets and cultural elite of France (and even Russia). After the Paris *Tannhäuser* of 1861, *Rienzi* was the only work by Wagner actually to be staged in Paris for 25 years, but this did not stop French Wagnerism from springing up in the 1860s, 70s and 80s. It took the form of a cult, not so much of his music as of his writings and ideas, above all ideas from his operas. His immense French impact was reflected in Emmanuel Chabrier's very Wagnerian opera *Gwendoline*, composed in the wake of his hearing Wagner extracts at concerts conducted by Jules Pasdeloup, Charles Lamoureux and Édouard Colonne, even though

---

29   E. Œ. Somerville and Martin Ross, actually two lesbian ladies.

some French Wagnerians saw Wagner's music as almost secondary to the ideas. Édouard Dujardin, the founder of the *Revue Wagnerienne* looked down on Chabrier because his interest in Wagner had simply been musical. Dujardin complained that the 'insular, backward Chabrier' had never understood a word of the master beyond questions of harmony and instrumentation.[30]

For others like Charles Baudelaire, it was the feelings that Wagner disclosed in himself which enthralled him. The means of disclosing these feelings to Baudelaire, as for so many, was *Tannhäuser*, and simply the *Tannhäuser* Overture. After hearing it in 1860, Baudelaire, the torchbearer of '*la volupté*' wrote to a friend, Poulet-Malassis, that it was fifteen years since he had felt so taken out of himself. Baudelaire also wrote to Wagner telling him that his music was 'the greatest musical joy that I have ever experienced,' and that he had been 'penetrated and overcome by a joy that was almost sensual, like the feeling of rising on the air, or floating on the sea.' Perhaps the author of *Les Fleurs du Mal* was not a typical representative of his era, but as the *Hite Report on Male Sexuality* conclusively established,[31] there is no such thing as 'a normal, typical male'. Baudelaire broadcast far and wide the recognitions and revelations about himself which he found in Wagner, and more 'normal, typical' people soon followed the trail where he had blazed it.

One of the most revealing testimonies about the way Wagner's erotics could infiltrate attitudes and thinking comes from a certain Gustave Stoeckel. Laurence Dreyfus[32] tells us how Stoeckel, later the first Professor of Music at Yale, described an eroticised state which many people first experienced through Wagner's works and consequently recognised as possible for themselves:

---

30 Dujardin later confessed how earlier he and his confederates had had pored over the words of Sachs and Wotan as though they held the answer to the world's riddles.
31 Hite, Shere, *The Hite Report on Male Sexuality*, New York, 1981.
32 Dreyfus, Laurence, *Wagner and the Erotic Impulse*, Cambridge, Mass., 2010, p. 3.

All this scene seems to tremble under the wild glow of sensual love ...
It is impossible to criticise while hearing it. All aesthetics, theory and
morals are chased out of one; one's breath is bated and the beating
of the heart seems to stand still, the whole soul is bewitched by an
irresistible power ... During the performance, all that is sensual in
human nature is wrought up to its wildest activity by the alluringly
tempting music.

Stoeckel was actually describing Act I of *Die Walküre*, but this was just
as true of *Tannhäuser*, and the self-disapproval he felt later on reflection
was just as applicable to *Tannhäuser*. 'It is true' he said, 'that after the
intoxicating enjoyment is over, you perceive the ethical anarchy of the
whole scene, which upsets all the holy emotions of a pure soul, defies
the teachings of morality and is in direct antagonism to established
rules and customs.'

Stoeckel expressed a view that was already commonly acknowledged,
that Wagner's music creates a specifically erotic charge and an
awareness of personal erotic potentials, and even if people's conscious
reactions were negative and angry, they were mightily affected by new
erotic intimations and the fact that Wagner had placed the erotic on
stage. *Tannhäuser* was not of course the only force for change. The
ground had been prepared by the Young Germany movement, but it
was Wagner's music that gave many people their first real experience
of the erotic phenomenon. It is interesting that soon various authors
of world-class stature were depicting the erotic as ecstatic instead of
detestable. In *Salammbo*, Flaubert presented the erotic experience of
intercourse as something worth dying for. The effect of *Tannhäuser*
for ordinary people was more measured, as the opera was gradually
performed more widely and made its way into popular assumptions
and thinking. The climate of opinion was only slowly changing, and in
England it was only much later, in 1918, that Marie Stopes published
her landmark text, *Married Love*, which was the first respectable guide
to making sexual encounters pleasurable and tender. Hers is one of
the mildest and most delicate texts imaginable, but it still unleashed a

maelstrom of hatred and vilifaction against her. The reason for all these changes happening is that they were driven by Wagner in general, and by *Tannhäuser* in particular. More than anyone else, he triggered off the avalanche, and without him and *Tannhäuser*, the irrational mix of denial and suppression might well have persisted longer.

Even so, *Tannhäuser* was inconsistent in its crusade because its creator was inconsistent. He was still partly conditioned by the values he overturned (as was the equally influential Freud). His unsettled childhood and youth gave him an unusual independence, and as a young man he endorsed Young German freedoms in *Das Liebesverbot*, but he always remained pulled in two directions. The old morality that suppressed the erotic dragged him one way, and his own liberated principles in another, and as such he was a man of his time. Accordingly it remains indeterminate whether his Tannhäuser is more of a two-timing cad or a noble, secular Luther leading a life-enhancing crusade. It is not surprising that *Tannhäuser*'s lessons are unsettled.

☙

Wagner gradually came to see that the opera had other problems. *Tannhäuser* was beset by a dramatic imbalance. This imbalance risked swinging the audience's sympathies too far towards the spiritual and sacred. In Wagner the winner is the one with the best music, and it is intriguing that in *Tannhäuser* Wagner, who was then turning into a freethinker, produced religious music of a soaring, high-flown beauty, but that, once the 'Venusberg Bacchanale' is over, its erotic elements, at least in the original Dresden version, are – dare I say it? – slightly dull. That was all to change, drastically, in the Paris version, but initially religion seemed to win the day too easily, so much so that some of his supporters were doing something quite unwelcome to Wagner in 'insisting on reading into my *Tannhäuser* a specifically Christian and pietistic tendency'.

Our knowledge of Wagner's determination to tackle these difficulties comes mainly from three repositories.

1. The descriptions of the five productions in which he took part and which put his intentions on stage.

2. The publication, in 1852, of the guide by Wagner already mentioned, 'On the Performance of "Tannhäuser"'.

3. Other documentary sources, notably *Mein Leben* and Cosima's *Diaries*, and also Wagner's correspondence.

The first of his stagings was the one at Dresden in 1845, and he instantly afterwards began to alter the production and the score. Unfortunately he had already paid to publish the orchestral score using an expensive lithograph process and this not only got him badly into debt, but ensnared him in an out-of-date version. His revisions continued in full spate until the Dresden uprising four years later. After this he was soon at his revisions again, and he continued them until 1860 when the score was properly engraved and reissued. By this time he had made four versions for the end of Act III; three versions for the Act III Prelude, which was pruned by more than thirty bars of its original 135; and three or more versions of the shepherd's tune in Act I, as well as many minor changes. This second published score of 1860 is now the one generally known as the 'Dresden version', but it dates from fifteen years after the Dresden premiere. It is anything but a first ever version; and today the 'Dresden version' would fall foul of any Trade Descriptions Act.

Meanwhile there had been a second staging in which Wagner took a part, at Zurich in 1855, but this did not lead to anything new.[33] His

---

33 Wagner had been asked by the director of the Zurich Opera house to supervise the first *Tannhäuser* there; but he had moved on, and was deeply into *Die Walküre*; so he seems never to have been keen on this waste of his time, as he saw it, and as the various preparations went ahead, he grew even less keen. He described it all in *Mein Leben*; 'With these singers I went several times through their roles, and in consequence found myself obliged to attend the stage rehearsal in order to keep an eye on their performances. This then meant' (I do like this description) 'that, pushed from one intervention to another, I ultimately arrived at the conductor's desk and actually conducted the first performance myself.'

third staging was in Paris, in 1861. This was his big chance because the French Emperor, Napoleon III, had agreed to command a performance of something by Wagner at the Paris Opera under pressure from the Austro-Hungarian Princess Metternich.[34] She was still alive in Vienna

(He actually took over the baton for the third.) 'What particularly remains in my memory is the singer of Elisabeth, a former soubrette, who played her role in white lace gloves to which a fan was attached. But I now I had had my fill of concessions, and when the audience called me on stage at the final curtain, I told my friends very plainly that this was the last time they would get such a thing from me: I should leave it to them to do something for their own theatre, the dire state of which they had that evening been able to judge more precisely for themselves.'

34 There are several ironies about the Paris *Tannhäuser* which are so intriguing that they warrant a full description. The important point is that Napoleon III had come to the throne by means of a *coup d'état* which had utterly appalled Wagner. In the third and fourth decades of the nineteenth century, France, particularly Paris, seemed to Wagner and many of the other liberal intellectuals of Europe to be a beacon of hope and enlightenment; people believed that Paris and France would lead the way to a less authoritarian model of society throughout Europe. Instead of the bigoted, autocratic monarchs of the German states, France represented some kind of enlightened rule involving the people; and it was hoped that democracy would soon spread everywhere from France. Paris was widely seen as a place of political ferment, and Karl Marx, who was in Paris during the 1840s, took many of his ideas from French political theorists. (It was in Paris that he really thought through his principles.) Wagner, leaving Paris for Dresden in 1842, missed him by eighteen months, but he occupied the same intellectual environment, albeit on the fringes. 1848 was the year of revolutions in many parts of Europe, and though the revolution in Paris failed, this did not in itself crush Wagner nor his political associates in Dresden. They pressed on and next year, 1849, they created their own revolution on similar lines in Dresden. This too failed, and as we know Wagner went into exile. However everyone, including Wagner, still believed in liberal France; they believed things would soon change and that Paris would still lead the way to a new freedom; indeed plans were still going ahead in Paris for democratic elections when these hopes suddenly crashed. Napoleon III seized the throne. It was this *coup d'état* that seemed the end of the

when Mahler was at the Opera and it is further evidence of what a universal megastar Wagner had now posthumously become, that she was famous, almost glorious, simply on account of having instigated the Paris *Tannhäuser*. At the time Wagner had been attracted by all the resources which the affluent and splendid Paris Opera could offer. Success in Paris was still regarded as the passport to success everywhere else, and Wagner went all out to wow the Parisians. The Paris Opera was eventually to provide him with 163 rehearsals, and he embarked on a thorough revision of *Tannhäuser* to try and make it mean what he then thought he wanted it to mean. It was his last big push with the work; and the only extensive alterations and additions to his score after its second, 1860 publication were those for the Paris version. This was performed only three times in Paris, and even then it was performed

world. Great expectations were extinguished. Wagner became deeply and clinically depressed; probably the greatest political-existential crisis in his life. The general and artistic conditions of Paris as he found them on a visit there shortly afterwards finally made him abandon all hope of creating a better society and better world; they initiated his turning inwards, away from his 'Hellenic optimism' as he called it, to a world-view that was darker. He even devised a new dating system, a personal calendar that circumvented any recognition of the debacle. And yet in 1861, Princess Metternich, wife of an Austrian diplomat domiciled in Paris, had been badgering this same Napoleon III to command the staging of an opera by Wagner. The Emperor eventually agreed, and the choice fell on *Tannhäuser*, so that the reason why something by Wagner was at last going to be staged in Paris was because the very ruler who had led to the downfall of all his political hopes had taken up his work. Because of this Napoleon, this disaster figure in Wagner's own eyes, Wagner was at last going to be presented in Paris. Moreover it would appear at the very opera house which had been the sole and hopeless object of all his aspirations some ten years earlier. It was he who eventually declared war on Prussia in 1870, in the belief that he would easily crush the opposition, but it led to his defeat and flight, and to the formal establishment of the German Empire at Versailles. There are certainly several of life's little ironies bound up here.

in three different versions, because Wagner made changes for every performance. All three performances became notorious because of the infamous Jockey Club, the young bloods of Paris who expected a ballet in every opera, in Act II. They were still at their dinners during Act I but by the time of Act II they were in the theatre, ready for the ballet where they could eye up the girls and plan selections for afterwards. They were furious with Wagner because *Tannhäuser* did not have a ballet in the right place, and this so far spoilt their notions of fun that they came armed with special screechy whistles which they blew loudly at crucial points until the performances were wrecked. It does seem slightly surprising that the Paris Opera, dominated by the Jockey Club, should have been accepted as the epitome of Parisian civilisation; the Opera played no small part in Paris's claim to be the nineteenth century's cultural capital of Europe.

The next staging involving Wagner, his fourth, did not result in any new developments. This was the solitary performance at Munich, in 1865, of an existing production of the Dresden version, and this was the occasion when Wagner coached and was enthralled by his favourite tenor, Ludwig Schnorr von Carolsfeld, in the title role.[35] The fifth and final staging involving Wagner was at Vienna in 1875; and this was the first time that any opera house heard the first two-thirds of the Overture joined up to the 'Venusberg Bacchanale'. Thus of the five stagings involving Wagner, the important ones were the original Dresden version, the Paris version, and the one in Vienna.

Prior to his Paris rewrite, Wagner had made other alterations by post for stagings that he would never see. He also sent round his guide of 1852 to staging *Tannhäuser* to opera houses throughout Germany. This was seven years after his original performances and nine years before his Paris staging. Operating as an exile in Zurich, he wrote

---

35   Wagner found Schnorr's performance beyond praise. 'With this single performance as Tannhäuser, never to be repeated, Schnorr fully realised my innermost artistic intentions. Never for a moment was the daemonic element in both bliss and pain lost to view.'

the guide because *Tannhäuser* was becoming extremely popular in Germany and he was disturbed at reports of productions which went against his intentions; it was to try and put them right that he circulated the guide. But the guide is also really another attempt to reinvent his opera *post eventum*, and although it is a fascinating and revealing document, anyone who studies it closely will realise that its conclusions do not always follow from the premises that are supposed to establish them, any more than they do in the work that it expounds.

His real main difficulty with *Tannhäuser* was that Venus and her erotic kingdom came across as ineffective, and his guide did acknowledge this, but he put the blame on his Dresden performers, his two principals. He wrote,

> In the scene between Venus and Tannhäuser in the first act I found it necessary to introduce a cut. I took out the second verse of Tannhäuser's song and Venus's preceding words. This was in no way due to any suspicion that the passage itself was dull, unpleasing, or ineffective. The reason was that the whole scene came to grief in the acting, above all because it was impossible to find a completely suitable singer for the difficult role of Venus.

This is one of the most sublime examples in history of a bad workman blaming his tools. Wagner was blaming poor Wilhelmine Schröder-Devrient, his first Venus, instead of accepting that Venus' flatness and indecisiveness, as he described it, might have been the result of his own failure to write a part that even she, *the* dramatic phenomenon of his entire life, could make convincing. He credited her with driving him to near-ecstasy as Adriano in his *Rienzi* and Senta in his *Dutchman*, and the *Tannhäuser* guide's unsporting references are his only recorded disparagements of her colossal talents.

It was not until 1860 when he was beginning preparations for the *Tannhäuser* production in Paris that he came to see where his difficulties really lay. He wrote to Mathilde Wesendonck,

Venus's court was clearly the weakest part of the work. Having no good ballet at Dresden I had to do what I could with a few rough brushstrokes and thereby spoiled a good deal. My Venusberg was completely flat and indecisive, and as a result I lost a significant background against which the tragedy should build up. All the later memories and reminders, which should fill us with horror, lost their whole effect. But I realise that at the time I could never have done what is called for here. I required a much greater technical skill which I have only now managed to acquire. Having written Isolde's final apotheosis, I can now give expression to the horror of the Venusberg.

To create a satisfying dramatic balance, Venus' court needed to be fulsome, and for his Paris rewrite, Wagner readjusted and improved the balance by creating for the 'Venusberg Bacchanale' a music which was overwhelming.

Along with his new Paris Venusberg, he wanted to spice up the role of Venus herself. In the Paris version he significantly filled out her identity; 'The goddess of bliss will herself become touching,' as he wrote to Mathilde Wesendonck, and she certainly became more gorgeous musically. The Paris version decks her song to Tannhäuser with sensuous counterpoints and a new and beguiling orchestration. Wagner altered its square four-four rhythm to a more pliant three-four. He lowered the pitch from bright F sharp major to the rosier twilight of F. At many points in the scene he added a filigree, a new tone-colour, an enrichment of the harmony, and he composed brief stretches of entirely new music, all of which bring extra magnetism and quality to Venus.

Some critics object that the new music is too *Tristan*-like in its chromaticism, but what is interesting is that it represents an area of Wagner's most advanced chromaticism which is not *Tristan*-like at all. It is quite unlike anything else that he ever wrote. It has far fewer echoes of *Tristan und Isolde* than do the Kundry scenes in Act II of *Parsifal*. Our knowledge of Wagner's music is seriously impoverished if we do not know the Paris version of the opening 'Bacchanale' and

'Venusberg' scenes. Again some critics have argued that Wagner's new music goes beyond the style of *Tannhäuser*, and the leading figure among them was a certain Richard Wagner. Cosima and Wagner were at Bayreuth discussing *Tannhäuser* with Anton Seidel in 1878 and Wagner was thinking of shortening the whole Venusberg scene. Cosima urged him to leave it alone, using arguments, even words, which are eerily reminiscent of the very ones which he had used for Mathilde Wesendonck as his reason for expanding it; as she advised 'It casts over the audience the magic spell that causes Tannhäuser's downfall; and thus it makes Act II more understandable.' 'That is what I tell myself,' answered Wagner, 'but it is not right.' Wagner's reservations have resulted in a widespread conviction that the newer music sabotages the stylistic unity of *Tannhäuser*, and that the Dresden version is superior. However *Tannhäuser* never had stylistic unity. In all versions it puts together so many different styles and balances them with such consummate art, that nobody could sensibly regard its stylistic anomalies as a failing. To be sure it is a hotch-potch, but a glorious, compelling, wholly *operatic* hotchpotch, and it has a strange and convincing coherence. It adds to its coherence that the balance between the two contrasting worlds, sacred and profane, works better after the Paris revisions. There was now a believable tension between them, just as Cosima maintained.

However, there was a price to pay because the Paris enrichments increased the imbalance of the *Tannhäuser's* formal structure, of its layout and arrangement over time. The revised opening scenes are so lengthy and momentous that everything afterwards seems tame in comparison. Perhaps Cosima was right that the extended Paris version made a better *dramatic* balance, and Wagner was right that it undermined the long-term *structural* balance. He never resolved the matter.

The next difficulty that he tackled was that he had not made the song contest in Act II effective enough. In his autobiography, *Mein Leben*, he explained;

In the conception of this scene I found myself unconsciously facing the dilemma in which I was obliged to make a decision for all time. Should this singers' contest be a concert of arias or some other poetically dramatic competition? The nature of the operatic tradition demanded that there should be a comparison and confrontation of evolutions in the art of singing, and that, in purely musical terms, the various vocal pieces should set each other off entertainingly, by the use of markedly variegated rhythms and measures in the same way that, for example, in a concert programme care must be taken to ensure that interest is kept alive by continual surprise, invoked by the utmost variety. This was not at all my intention. What I was really striving for, and doing my best to achieve, was to force the audience – for the very first time in opera – to participate in a poetic thought by following it through all the phases of its development. Only in this way can the ensuing catastrophe be properly understood. It arises from no outward course, but has to be achieved through the unfolding of psychological process. That is the reason for the musically very broad, subdued setting, something which would not stand in the way of a clear understanding of the political argument but would in my estimation actually enhance it. It is also the reason for the increasing rhythmic development of the melody, undisturbed by superfluous modulatory and rhythmic twists as the emotional temperature rises; for the extremely economical use of orchestral instruments in the accompaniment; and for the deliberate abstention from purely musical effects, which are only gradually introduced as the situation rises to the point at which emotion becomes more necessary than thought in grasping what is going on.

Wagner was none too thrilled when his wife Minna, present at the rehearsals for the first ever Dresden production, told him bluntly that the singers' contest was in danger of falling flat. Minna tends to be vilified as too small-minded for any genuine interest or understanding of her husband's great flights of imagination, but this remarkable woman was often more perceptive than is credited, and here she was right. Certainly Geoffrey Skelton, the Wagner authority who co-translated Cosima's *Diaries*, shared Minna's opinion when he wrote, 'There is always a danger in performance that the singer's contest is something to be born patiently rather than enjoyed.' When heard in isolation, the individual songs of the contest sound far better than they do in the theatre, and perhaps the reason is their positioning. After the Venusberg scene they sound insubstantial and hold up the action. Minna, at Dresden, did not convince her husband that any ineffectiveness could be due to his shortcomings with the opera itself, but by the time of the Paris production he acted on her criticism and cut out one of the contestants (he also had trouble with the singers). He also made a telling addition, putting in brief reminiscence of some Venusberg music just after Wolfram's song.

The other passage that most troubled Wagner was the great slow ensemble towards the end of Act II. This was where he simply axed all the other vocal parts to ensure that Tannhäuser's *'Erbarm' dich mein,'* would stand out enough, and the musical texture can sound as if the rats had been at it; but he never reworked this scene. There were good reasons why he did not try in Paris: he simply had too much going on. He was beset by problems of casting, problems of scenery, problems of staging, problems of the orchestra, of rehearsals, of the impossibility of getting genuine German horns (the instruments traditionally described in England as French horns) instead of French cornets. He had problems of accommodation and of money, problems of trying to patch up his marriage with Minna, and major problems with his health. As we have seen Wagner's health was often so appalling that it is a wonder how he ever got anything done. It was while in Paris that he contracted typhoid and then some kind of fever akin to glandular fever, which left him overcome for weeks with exhaustion, and he probably suffered from ME or depression as well. He simply could not summon up the necessary reserves of energy, with the inevitable consequence that the Paris revisions went through a sort of petering out. They were tremendous, extensive and splendid in Act I, sketchier and less certain of effect in Act II, and virtually non-existent in Act III.

Thus Act III remains too short, and until Tannhäuser's 'Rome narration' it is too lightweight musically and emotionally to balance the opera's first amazing forty-five minutes or Act II as a whole. After the publication of the 'Dresden version', he never revised Act III nor addressed what had always been a problem, that the conclusion of the opera was too brief and compressed for so much action to be packed in. He had been criticised over this from the beginning, and in *Mein Leben* he provided a description of his attempts to meet the criticism with some early alterations to the opera's finale.

> I had depicted Venus's new attempt to entice her faithless lover back as merely a visionary manifestation of Tannhäuser's momentary madness: only a reddish glow over the distant Hörselberg would be the outward indication of the entire situation. Likewise, the vital information of Elisabeth's death was conveyed merely through a divinatory inspiration on the part of Wolfram. The only attempt to draw the attention of the audience to the distant Wartburg was to be the scarcely audible tolling of the death bell, and the scarcely discernible glow of firebrands. At the very end the chorus of young pilgrims, to whom I had not yet given the sprouting staff, proclaimed the miracle only in words and not through any outward manifestation. This left the issue indecisive and unclear, a failing to which I had further contributed in purely musical terms by providing them with an accompaniment of lengthy and unrelieved monotony.

Although he took no notice of Minna's comments in Dresden, it is wrong to believe that Wagner never did self-criticism. In order to deal with its 'lengthy and unrelieved monotony' as he described it, Wagner tried various revisions. In 1847 he brought back Venus in person onstage. He also brought Elisabeth's funeral cortège onto the scene for the first time, accompanied by the Landgraf. What was odd was that he then also cut out the chorus of young pilgrims which denied his audiences the crucial information about the Pope's staff having blossomed. He tried to justify this bewildering move in his guide.

Only the largest theatres would have the means of staging the whole final scene effectively, and only those that could successfully extend this to include the young pilgrims' chorus could be fully satisfying, since this song with its proclamation of the miracle satisfactorily rounds off the whole action, according as it does with Tannhäuser's description of the events in Rome.

Confusingly, it was in the very same year that he wrote to Liszt strongly asserting the importance of its inclusion. And yet Liszt was at Weimar and Weimar's tiny theatre only possessed meagre resources. (Even for Liszt's world premiere of *Lohengrin* Weimar only managed an orchestra of thirty.) In 1853 Wagner was chopping and changing the end again, cutting out the appearance of Elisabeth's funeral bier. He wrote to Louis Schindelmeisser of Darmstadt,

> You will be receiving from Dresden a further alteration to the ending of Tannhäuser. According to this revised version, Elisabeth does not appear, neither do the Landgraf and the minstrels, but on the other hand the young pilgrims do, as in the first version. The whole of the Venus part remains. The young pilgrims bear the blossoming staff in their midst. Prior to that Elisabeth's death is only indicated by the light of the torches on the Wartburg, funeral bells, and men's voices coming from there.

He did indicate a reason for this;

> All this talk about the appearance of a corpse, about the socio-politico-anatomical impossibility of burying Elisabeth in so short a space of time – (how fortunate that people have time on these occasions to think about time) – have finally sickened me to such an extent that I have decided on this alteration or restitution.

Unfortunately Wagner never revisited the end, and probably he never accepted that his audiences, then as now, might have a point in feeling that the time allowed for it was too short, especially when balanced against the immense time frame for the beginning of the opera. What is more, Tannhäuser himself has in his 'Rome narration' created such an awareness of the distance and labour of his journey that it is difficult not to feel an abruptness when the young pilgrims arrive and the opera instantly hits the buffers. In less than three minutes, Elizabeth's dying intercession has worked and won Tannhäuser's forgiveness; the Pope's staff has broken into green; and the young pilgrims have delivered it all the way from Rome, completing a journey that had taken Tannhäuser six months. It is not that audience members are wilfully over-analytical and pernickety as Wagner complained, but that it just does not feel right. I know too that there are other people who feel as I do, that the pilgrims' chorus at the end sounds sawn-off. The opera has acclimatised us to hearing this music in full whenever it appears, but this last time Wagner gives us just its first bars and then it is all over.

A puzzling feature of his Paris revisions was that he expected Venus' greater appeal to make people feel sorrier for Tannhäuser and more aware of how he must be suffering over leaving such a fiendishly tempting lady, but in fact the opposite happens. Her added appeal makes Tannhäuser seem more heartless, more of a male chauvinist pig. Moreover Venus has been largely reconfigured as a benefactress and the source of beauty: so where does this leave the idea of Tannhäuser's time with her as '*böse Lust*' (evil joy) and of the Venusberg as evil? Similar discrepancies have shown up with Elisabeth, revealing her as passionate and spirited, and no stranger to the erotic impulse. The conflicting claims of the two ladies on Tannhäuser are ambiguous, and ambiguous too is the picture of Tannhäuser reflected in the mirror of the two relationships. This inevitably adds to ambiguity of the *Tannhäuser* messages.

This huge wealth of explanation at last places us in a position to get to grips with central ambiguity of *Tannhäuser*, which is about the sin of its title character. What is it, this sin, this wrongdoing which the opera is warning us to avoid? The first and obvious impression is that it is fornication. This view tallies with the judgments of the middle ages and the nineteenth century, and the events of the opera confirm it. Even so it seems necessary to emphasise it again because there have been articles recently in the widely-read American Wagnerian journal *Leitmotive* arguing that this view is impossible, on the modern-day grounds that sex is no more than healthy self-expression, and that nobody could reasonably have found anything objectionable about Tannhäuser's activities in the Venusberg. This is surprising because as recently as 1974, the American Helen Kaplan had written critically of her own era, 'Unfortunately our society equates sex and sin;'[36] but this only confirm the gulf dividing the outlook of today and the conventional morality of Wagner's time, or even of 1974. It also suggests a common failure of historical perspective and demonstrates why so much explanation is necessary.

Anyone seriously doubting that Tannhäuser's carnal congress with Venus was central to his sin should look at the opera. When Tannhäuser finds himself on the mountainside with the pilgrims, he takes up their prayer and makes it his own, 'Ah how heavily the burden of sin oppresses me; I can bear it long no longer.' The only possible candidate for this sin, as the opera presents it, is his fornication, and shortly afterwards, when the other knights ask him where he has been all this time, his vagueness comes over as a guilty anxiety to conceal the truth because his fornication is not only a sin but harshly punishable. His evasiveness with Elisabeth squares with this anxiety, and it is fully justified by the reaction of the knights when he finally bellows out where he has been. Everyone instantly hates him, and the knights come at him, 'Oh – Wicked! Horror! Frightful! – He has dwelt in the Venusberg!' Elisabeth too makes it clear, at least initially, that she regards Tannhäuser's Venusberg fornications as his sin. When barring the way to his attackers she does not deny his guilt, but argues for mitigating circumstances on the grounds of diminished responsibility; he must be under some evil enchantment to have done anything so dreadful. The Landgraf adopts the same position. When he condemns

36 Kaplan, *The New Sex Therapy*, p. 145.

Tannhäuser as a curse-laden son of sin it is because of his fornication in the Venusberg.

Perhaps changes in these matters have been so sweeping that people today, especially young people, can find it hard to grasp how different was the climate of opinion even in Helen Kaplan's time, the 1970s, let alone Wagner's day. It is difficult for people really to feel their way into a life-pattern radically different from their own. For many people today the idea of sex for its own sake as evil and sex outside marriage as wrong seems to have passed out of memory and beyond comprehension.

Older readers on the other hand may not grasp just what sweeping changes in outlook have talen place over the last forty years. I can best attempt an explanation by reference to the interminable health checks, thankfully abandoned a few years ago, where young people, married and unmarried, would be giving solemn and earnest assurances that they had healthy, regular sex lives with the same quiet pride as if they had announced that they had taken up yoga or given up smoking. Any idea of moral wrongdoing would probably have seemed as incoherent as the idea that the moon is made of green cheese, and perhaps this is one of the unintended consequences of the cultural revolution which *Tannhäuser* energised, but a consequence which its creator would not want. *Tannhäuser* was asserting that man's animal body mattered, but not that the animal body was all that mattered. As Wagner's description of the Overture in its first form shows, Wagner was concerned to achieve and promote a situation where 'instinct and spirit are in the right harmony'.

Today's outlook and values are obviously different from Wagner's, and even more different from those of the mediaeval era he presented in *Tannhäuser*, when the erotic was mysterious and perilous. In those eras Tannhäuser's sin would be regarded as '*böse Lust*', evil joy, the view of the Pope when he consigns Tannhäuser to hell-fire. To take stock, the sequence of events in *Tannhäuser* so far appears to establish two conclusions:

1. That Tannhäuser's sin is terrible and unforgivable;
2. That it consists in his fornication, his lustful enjoyment of Venus.

This was why religious conservatives saw his opera as affirming their own morality, with Tannhäuser framed as a detestable, lecherous, evil fraud who was damned for his sin and should be. Because his forgiveness and redemption at the end are over in a flash, it could seem a bolted-on extra that did not really register. Wagner proclaimed that he was intending no such support for orthodox morality, and thanks to the relative weight given in the opera to the erotic phenomenon and the Venusberg, it is these really register in the end, especially in the Paris revisions. At least Wagner increasingly recognised that the values and lessons of *Tannhäuser* were not coming out altogether clearly. By the time of his 1852 guide he had also begun to see that Tannhäuser himself might not come across as wholly sympathetic in abandoning Venus and reverting to his old love, Elisabeth. This was why Wagner attempted to justify Tannhäuser's action in his guide, stating disingenuously, 'When Tannhäuser forcefully proclaims himself as Venus' proud champion, in his feelings he is solely defending his love for Elisabeth.' This means that, in Wagner's imagination, Tannhäuser had evidently transformed Venus into a disembodied idea, an abstract symbol. Wagner apparently thought that his readers and audiences would swallow this and accept Venus simply as a metaphor for a passion directed to Elisabeth for its real expression.

This just will not do. It does not fit in with the viewpoints which the opera has implanted in our minds, above all about the contrast between two women who are both equally alive and real. Venus is a very carnal reality and not an idea or a symbol. To put the matter bluntly, Tannhäuser had not been copulating with a metaphor. Neither Wagner nor his character Tannhäuser can credibly expect us to switch suddenly to a purely metaphorical view of her. How delusional would Tannhäuser have to be to expect Elisabeth to take his praise of Venus's embrace as a compliment to herself, but metaphorically expressed? How delusional was Wagner in thinking it possible for Elisabeth or us, his audience, to go along with this?

It was bizarre of him to think it for another reason, that it does not square with Tannhäuser's damage to Elisabeth as Wagner immediately represents it in the opera. Wagner makes it plain that Tannhäuser's praise of Venus was an appalling experience for Elisabeth, that it 'crushed her blossoming shoots at a single blow'. And he makes Tannhäuser snap back into a more sensible view of Venus as a very real person. Tannhäuser soon recognises that it was cruel to Elisabeth to praise Venus to her face, because he expresses an extravagant remorse for it. He also beats himself up for a different reason, for daring to think of Elisabeth as desirable, falling back into exactly the outlook of the other knight minstrels who regarded any sensual imaginings as sins in themselves. Tannhäuser's outlook on his sin, his view of what it actually was, is in fact changing as the opera goes on, and so fast that it is hard to keep up. It was first his fornication; but then it came to be his damage to Elisabeth, his blaring out at Elisabeth about his unfaithfulness with Venus; and then it became his disclosure to Elisabeth of his erotic imaginings of her. It must now be partly that he has destroyed her romantic hopes of a life with him. This is complex enough, but the matter is going to become more complex still as he embroils her in his atonement process.

With great generosity of spirit, she has offered to help him pay the price of expiating his primary sin, his fornication. She too will make amends, so as to add extra weight to his chances of forgiveness. Tannhäuser meanwhile seems to have altered his view of his sin again. He now sees it principally as his damage to Elisabeth. It is the 'Rome narration' which makes this clear. It tells us that his object in making his pilgrimage had nothing to do with conventional Christian penance; yes, of course he wanted to earn the Pope's forgiveness, but only as the means for making it up to Elisabeth. His reason for going to Rome was to make amends to her. However, the nature of the damage needing his amends is still undefined.

Perhaps we should take stock again, so as not to get lost in Wagner's labyrinth of shifting perspectives. Tannhäuser's sin began as lechery, a carnal relationship with a witch goddess, Venus; and the Wartburg Court and the Pope held onto this view of it. For us the first jolt away from it happens when the witch goddess emerges reconfigured as a benefactress of mankind. An erotic relationship with a benign deity is a different matter from raunchy carnal knowledge with a rose of hell. The next jolt is when Tannhäuser's sin is redefined as his injury to Elisabeth, in his eyes at least. This redefinition means that his view of his sin has diverged from Elisabeth's. *She* sees his sin as still consisting in his carnal relationship with Venus; for *him* it has become his damage to her. Tannhäuser and Elisabeth are thus operating with two separate ideas of his sin by the time they begin their joint attempts to expiate it.

Wagner makes the perception of Tannhäuser's sin shift again after he fails Elisabeth, as he now does. It is this failure that reduces him to utter despair, his absolute rock bottom. The pair of them had jointly been doing everything possible to win forgiveness for his sin, but this has failed, and it is this failure which becomes his ultimate, catastrophic sin for Tannhäuser. His whole purpose in winning absolution had been to render Elisabeth happy and fulfilled. His aim, not ungenerous, was to 'sweeten the tears of his angel,' but he has failed to achieve it because he has not won his absolution from the Pope. As far as he can see, his penitential pilgrimage has failed to produce the outcome for which he and she have sacrificed themselves. This is what plunges him into despair and self-destruction. What makes it worse is that it is entirely of his own doing. Wagner establishes that even though the Pope's unforgiving attitude makes its own contribution to his woes, there would be nothing for the Pope to forgive if Tannhäuser had not committed his sin.

Herein then lies his final, ultimate sin; it is his failure to present Elisabeth with the gift of his own redemption. This gift would have amounted to a distinctive redemption for her, but he had not achieved it. No wonder that he is full of the self-hatred which Wagner expressed so blisteringly in the 'Rome narration'.

Wagner has Elisabeth managing things better. His drama shows her self-sacrifice and intercessions mobilising all the resources of amazing grace and bringing them to bear on the situation. She is successful and her efforts are rewarded, because her amends on his behalf *do* achieve their intended result; they do save his soul. From her vantage point in the life beyond, she can look down at the world and observe that he has been saved by her self-sacrificing devotion, and it through this that Wagner closes the circle of their mutual responsibility and their loving concern for one other. To try and sum up the conclusion; first, Elisabeth's saving of Tannhäuser makes her happy; second, this happiness of hers makes him happy. The knowledge that she is happy constitutes his release from guilt and his salvation. Her happiness redeems him. The result is that Elisabeth ends satisfied that her efforts were not in vain, while Tannhäuser can be satisfied that his redemption has indeed sweetened her tears, even though it was not of his making. Their reciprocal knowledge that they are both redeemed is their joint, ultimate salvation. This sounds complicated because it is. It is not, I hope, that I have explained it badly, and nor is it likely that you, dear readers, have understood it badly. But while Wagner's drama is complicated, it is not in this confused.

All this tortuous complexity is important and revealing, but in the end the essential message comes to stand out clearly. The dramatic inclinations of the music and the opera as a whole proclaim Tannhäuser's liberating truths and affirm the erotic as life-enhancing. Cosima Wagner was right when she told Wagner that the whole 'Venusberg' scene 'casts over the audience the magic spell that causes Tannhäuser's downfall,' but what really registers in the imagination is the magic spell and not the downfall. What counts is that *Tannhäuser* imparts a spellbinding quality to erotic experience, and even gives an erotic shimmer to Elisabeth and her exalted passion. Tannhäuser's 'Rome narration' likewise arouses sympathy for the erotic values he espouses, whereas the Pope's harsh judgment and menacing dogmatism wins no hearts, and there is a sense of relief when his judgment is annulled and Tannhäuser gains his forgiveness. All these factors add to the opera's subliminal lesson that erotic experience is something to accept and treasure.

Perhaps this is a good point briefly to turn to some of the other lessons of *Tannhäuser*, such as its covert warnings against regression. Tannhäuser himself has this in common with the Dutchman, Lohengrin and later Siegmund and Parsifal, that they all come in from some mysterious 'outside'. This outside is cold for the Dutchman, warm and seductive for Tannhäuser, and glittering for Lohengrin. Venus warned Tannhäuser that he would find the world outside, the world of men, too difficult and bitter, a world too ready to punish deviations from accepted norms exactly, as people do in real life. His escape into the cocooning dream-world of the Venusberg, his being drawn into the seductiveness of its attractions, amounts to regression. Regression is turning back towards an infantile state, instead of continuing to make psychological progress in life. Psychological progress is an ongoing, never-ending process and ideally a person advances steadily through life's different stages,[37] but the advance is often conflicted, and any one who finds the next stage too difficult may try to turn back without even knowing. Calvin Hall[38] explained, 'Having reached a certain stage of development, a person may retreat to an earlier level because of fear. A person who has been hurt by the world may take flight from reality and shut himself up in a private dream world. This is known as regression'.

Regression is an obstacle to achieving worthwhile things. Tannhäuser's flight from the world had taken him to a realm that makes no demands and requires no action, no effort or conscious thought, and as we have seen Wagner himself had found the world a bruising place from early childhood. When he created Tannhäuser, Wagner knew from within exactly what he was doing. The pains of life gave Wagner the periodic inclination to abandon any desire for anything at all in favour of a tepid, resigned inertia. Like Wagner himself, Tannhäuser as Wagner created him broke free of his inertia

---

37   In the wake of Freud, the early stages of that development, involving the first formation of personality, are customarily schematised in four stages: infancy, childhood, adolescence, and adulthood.

38   Hall, Calvin S., *A Primer of Freudian Psychology*, New York, 1954. p. 95.

because his energy and will were stronger than any impulse to regress into a dream-world.[39]

As Hall describes the regressions which people make, he comes close to describing Tannhäuser;

> Even healthy, well adjusted people make regressions from time to time in order to reduce anxiety. They smoke, get drunk, eat too much, lose their tempers, bite their nails, pick their noses, break laws, talk baby talk, destroy property, masturbate, read mystery stories, go to the movies, engage in unusual sexual practices, chew gum and tobacco, dress up as children, drive fast and recklessly, believe in good and evil spirits, take naps, fight and kill one another, bet on the horses, daydream, rebel against or submit to authority, gamble, preen before a mirror, act out their impulses, pick on scapegoats, and do a thousand and one childish things. Some of these regressions are so common that they are taken to be signs of maturity.

The list is an interesting one because Tannhäuser is not the only character among the knights who fits it. It is not Tannhäuser who 'fights and kills' and 'picks on scapegoats', and he is not the only one to 'act out his impulses'. The other knights represent a number of behaviours which are just as common and pathological, above all their scapegoating of their own suppressed urges.

Tannhäuser presents the Venusberg in shifting frames of reference, and from a negative perspective the Venusberg remains an escape whereby Tannhäuser tries to avoid reality. As a doctor, I was sometimes consulted by people for whom the stratagems in Hall's list had not worked and who were still trying to be an escapist Tannhäuser. That is to say, they were hoping to get a fix towards regressing and avoiding reality, instead of trying to make a success of it. Tannhäuser even

---

39   Tannhäuser breaks though it, as happened with Wagner himself. Wagner's years of seclusion at Tribschen were as close as he came to a serene abandoning of the world, but in the end his irresistible impulse to fulfil his life's work drove him out to create Bayreuth.

represents a particular kind of regression with particular psychiatric implications, as anyone who has dealt with it will recognise. He is a dead ringer for an addict, and it is extraordinary that the opera by Wagner should somehow have something important to say on the topic. In this context, the Venusberg ceases to occupy a floating position between allure and horror and inclines decisively to horror. Addiction can take many forms, addiction to cannabis, to gambling, to food avoidance, to sex or television, to anything in Hall's list. All addictions are manifestations of the same basic tendency; and the same mental aberrations are common to them, the same deformed thought processes, the same emotional disturbances and the same disruption of personality. Tannhäuser's particular addiction happens to be sex, but he displays the general features of addicts in that his feelings and actions are marked by an extraordinary impulsiveness and amnesia.

His responses and choices are reckless, and as pointed out earlier he is in bondage to the spur of the moment. His compulsions drive him forth from the Venus and then from the hunt, the troop of the knights. When Wolfram summons the idea of Elisabeth from the deeps of his memory, he forgets in an instant his previous determination to leave the district. When he suddenly starts praising Venus in Act II, it is as if his mind were affected by LSD and was suddenly now erupting on a bad trip, presenting its bewildered owner with a disastrous alternative reality, or several. When in Act III he tells Wolfram that the motivation of his pilgrimage had been to make an amend to Elisabeth, it is only a few minutes later that he has forgotten her and become desperate for his Venusberg fix, until Wolfram again pronounces her name. Tannhäuser then gives the impression that Wolfram has just drawn out the idea of Elisabeth from the remotest recesses of his memory, not that she was the central topic of their discussion only minutes earlier. It is as if memory and forgetting glimmer on and off interchangeably, as happens with addicts. Their minds flit randomly from one mental channel to another, and addicts are all too familiar with these frightening experiences. Tannhäuser attempts to return to reality, to the Wartburg, to re-establish his grip on a life that is out of control, as addicts do, but addictions acquire the force of an insanely controlling spell. In their enslavement to drugs addicts do a lot of damage, mostly unintentionally or unconsciously, just as Tannhäuser does. Part of every addict's best chance of recovery is to make amends and submit to a divine higher power, just as Tannhäuser attempts, calling on the Virgin Mary for his salvation. Indeed the resemblances between Tannhäuser and addicts in early recovery, alternately progressing and backsliding, are mind-boggling and uncanny. How on earth did Wagner know?

As for the way Wagner presents the heroine Elisabeth, she is central to the drama, but she can seem pushed to the margins if the opera's outcomes for her are viewed in terms of today. In a world where scientific and economic materialism are so dominant, Elisabeth risks looking quite simply like 'a woman who loves too much'. As such she stands as a warning against co-dependency and becoming the means to somebody else's ends, particularly if that somebody is an addict or an alcoholic, given to coping strategies that are counterproductive. Co-dependents like Elisabeth can sacrifice everything for their emotionally empty Tannhäusers and never satisfy them, because their hunger and emptiness are insatiable. However in 1845 her sacrificial outcome was more positive, because her transformation into a new star and her immortality as a saint signified something momentous, beyond value, in an age of wider religious belief. Hers would then have been generally accepted as a magnificent reward, enduring for eternity. We are given no idea whether she joins Tannhäuser for life everlasting as Senta joins the Dutchman, but at the very least she wins an illustrious immortality for her own soul.

Many of the topics covered in *Tannhäuser* are important, but its central focus remains the erotic phenomenon, romantic love and the Landgraf's request to define its nature. It should by now be clear why *Tannhäuser* detonated a cultural revolution, and it had other far-reaching effects, one of the most radical being for the status of women. Although the reasons for it are beyond this book, one of the achievements of the magisterial *Hite Reports*, particularly the third, was to demonstrate two-way causal links between women's status in the domain of the erotic and their status in every other sphere of life.[40] Women may still be disadvantaged, even in the 'liberal' Western world, but the status and freedom of women has improved beyond recognition, intellectually, socially, economically, politically and erotically. It is significant that whereas in 1894 the amazing Mrs Smythers was advising women that if the husband 'lifts her gown and tries to kiss her in any place else she should quickly pull the gown back in place, spring from the bed and announce that nature calls her to the toilet,' a hundred years later another woman, not this time a Methodist priest's wife but a Jewish rabbi in her own right, Julia Neuberger, was taking a very different tack. The fact that a woman could be a leading rabbi is itself a measure the enormous changes since 1845. Even more significant is that in her book of 1991, *Whatever's Happening to Women?*,[41] she felt free to complain publicly about 'the general coyness', even in the radical book by Sheila Kitzinger already mentioned, about 'what gives many women by far the greatest pleasure, which is oral sex, or cunnilingus'. (She seemed unaware of the Hite Reports.) A few pages on, Rabbi Neuberger even castigates men, the whole gender, for being too little willing to engage in oral sex. Since the days when *Tannhäuser* had first appeared and because of it, things had changed – and how!

Tannhäuser still has many things of importance to tell us. One of the more equivocal developments of the last fifty years is the closing down of the idea that erotic infidelity might be a bad thing. Marriage, with its trust, loyalties and commitments, is the foundation of society and it possesses an archetypal status; people still feel today that it is some kind of Holy Grail.[42] In the time of *Tannhäuser*, adultery was

40   'Introduction' to Hite, Shere, *The Hite Report on Love, Passion and Emotional Violence*, New York, 1987, p. xxxv. 'Hite's Study showed that sex is part of the whole cultural picture, and that woman's place in sex mirrors her place in the rest of society.'

41   Neuberger, Julia, *Whatever's Happening to Women?*, London, 1991, p. 26.

42   There is a telling illustration of the magnetic power of marriage in jour-

censured in the courts of peoples' minds as well as those of law. As happened in the Wartburg, sex outside marriage was demonised in real life with alarming consequences, as Wagner was to prove for himself, and painfully. There were good reasons for this, and some persist today. First, infidelity is the breaker up of marriage, and the polluter of the Grail. In the *Tannhäuser*'s time, it brought major practical problems, offspring without two parents to look after them or even one. This need no longer be the case, now that contraception is available virtually on demand. However, infidelity is still betrayal. It is not clear why the binding promises of fidelity and the legal contracts made at a wedding seem increasingly to be regarded differently from other legal commitments, and are half-exempted from blame or redress when broken (unless there is the chance to hound a celebrity). As that great and forgotten novelist, Charles Morgan said, there are always good reasons for breaking promises, and they are all bad. However the belief that promises of fidelity between men and women should be kept seems sometimes to be reckoned as positively jejune. On 15 November 2011, that stateliest of newspapers, *The Times* of London, gave a double-page spread to an extended article virtually promoting the 'illicit encounters' website and others like it for people who want furtive sexual encounters which break their marriage promises. *The Times* presented a picture of all this as brightly fashionable, but sadly these encounters often result in misery and anguish. In Elisabeth *Tannhäuser* demonstrates that the inexpressible pain caused by infidelity and betrayal are reality.

Elisabeth's is not the only context which makes sense of *Tannhäuser*'s warning that erotic passion has a dark side. The destructive aspect

---

nalist Tony Parsons' book *On Life, Death, and Breakfast*. He looks back on a great life including 'a decade of married women, German au pairs and assorted crazy chicks,' and 'ten years of multiple partners, strange beds and the loneliness of the twenty-four hour party people,' but finally asks, 'So do I believe that spraying your oats around the hotels of five continents is ultimately no substitute for a stable loving home and a partner for life? – I do.'

of passion has long been recognised; not for nothing did Apollonius Rhodius call love 'the destroyer' in the third century BC. Today as always Venus is a dangerous force as well as a benign one, the demonic goddess who is the potential wrecker of family and society, of civilisation and civilised man. She can impel people to actions that are disastrous for themselves and everyone else, beguiling people to break promises and breach loyalties and generally creating pain and chaos. Wagner's opera illustrates the related truth, that infidelity and betrayal often cause as much pain to the perpetrator as to anyone, and in all this his opera offered wiser advice than he followed in life. Wagner's own 'illicit encounters' provided palpable evidence and a painful example of Venus's demonic side. Several times she nearly wrecked his life, and in this matter *Tannhäuser* is even truer for today than for its own time, because Venus more than ever leaves relationships broken, careers and lives ruined, and children half-orphaned, however people try and defuse and deconstruct her into an exercise bike or a facile amusement. A few years ago there was the well-publicised case of the Canterbury solicitor who arranged for a sexual encounter with an unknown woman at a motel. Sadly the woman's husband found her e-mails and he committed suicide. It is impossible to estimate the damage to the solicitor's wife (a respected acquaintance) and to any children involved, let alone to the man who killed himself, or even to the solicitor. Such enslavement to Venus has an antisocial impact of extreme force, a poignant result of 'the animal distorting the civilised man'. Such immense unhappiness is why such unfaithful activities, Venus-driven, might still reasonably be classified as wrongdoing today.

Accordingly *Tannhäuser* presents and establishes the timeless contrast between passion which enriches life and passion that impoverishes it. Erotic passion with Venus turned Tannhäuser into an inert, ineffective loser, but people thrive when Eros (or Venus) is accepted and integrated, 'when instinct and spirit are in the right harmony'. Elisabeth is a rounded identity who represents a fair amount of the right harmony, and able to confer it on Tannhäuser as a passion that enriches life. The values which *Tannhäuser* proclaimed took more than a century to work through the Western world, but in July 1958, a hundred and thirteen years after Tannhäuser's premiere, the Lambeth Conference of the Church of England, made up of bishops from all over that world, formally revised and annulled the centuries-long denigration of the erotic phenomenon, at least for the Anglican domains. The conference proclaimed, 'The procreation of children is not the sole purpose of Christian marriage; implicit within the bond of husband and wife is the relationship of love with its sacramental expression in physical union.' The lessons of *Tannhäuser* had eventually achieved official, ecclesiastical endorsement. Unfortunately the Roman Catholic Church still remains opposed to any separation of erotic experience from procreation. Its almost-deification of the Virgin Mary as the heavenly champion against Eros and against physical passion for its own sake was re-established at the Vatican as recently as 1950, and it has been periodically reinforced ever since. Even now *Tannhäuser* has things to teach great sections of the world about the erotic phenomenon and about instinct and spirit being allowed to exist in the right harmony.

In the opera *Tannhäuser* all in the end was harvest. Even the fault lines and discrepancies which Wagner left unresolved make it a work very much for our time and for all time. If there is a failure by Wagner entirely to resolve its disjunctions, it is a glorious failure which adds to the opera's peculiar depth and fascination. It is no surprise that this was the work which made Wagner's name, as well as changing history. We can never know whether he might have recast it in a more unified, consistent form had he lived, but even if Wagner still owes the world a conclusive *Tannhäuser*, what he left is both a marvellous experience and an amazing source of wisdom and encouragement for anyone who has ears to hear and the willingness to listen.

Tannhäuser was first given at Dresden, at the Hoftheater, on 19 October 1845. The truly stellar cast included Joseph Tichatschek (Tannhäuser), Wilhelmine Schröder-Devrient (Venus), Johanna Wagner (Elisabeth), Anton Mitterwurzer (Wolfram) and Georg Wilhelm Dettmer (Landgraf). Johanna Wagner was then just 19, and

Wagner still wanted her as a Norn for the original *Ring* at Bayreuth 31 years later. Similarly he imported Mitterwurzer to Munich to be his first Kurwenal in 1865, and Tichatschek specially for Lohengrin in 1867. The conductor in 1845 was Richard Wagner, and it was the third and last time that he conducted the premiere of one of his own operas.

TWELVE

LOHENGRIN

Lohengrin is Wagner's one real tragedy. It is an exquisite, luminous creation, but it ends in pain and loss, without a glimmer of hope or salvation for any of the main characters. For its audiences it registers as positive for many reasons, for its remote, grave beauty and its insights into romantic love, different from those of *Tannhäuser*. *Lohengrin* takes its hero and heroine through some of the disasters which people can bring upon themselves in romantic relationships, even with the best of intentions. In *Lohengrin* Wagner provides insights into things that nurture these relationships and things that wreck them, and he brings to the subject a depth of sensibility that was not always a foremost feature of his own practice.

Lohengrin defies attempts to locate its beginnings in Wagner's own life and experience in any expressionist sense. Generally Wagner's dramas came into being because the scattered particles of Wagner's life and experience collected, rose up and transformed into a distinctive new creation under the compelling force of his imagination. Usually this took place in response to some identifiable set of circumstances. But *Lohengrin* is different. Like the vision in its own Prelude, it seems to exist in its own remote realm, without any silver threads to attach it to the material world of its origins.

The great appeal of *Lohengrin* is that it is *the* ultimate romantic opera. Its sound world casts a spell on the imagination from moment that the ethereal strains of the Prelude first grace the ear. The Prelude is a vision of the Holy Grail[43] appearing in the heavens, gradually descending to earth with a radiance that grows to a revelatory climax, and then floating back into the vistas of blue. It begins with four bars where violins alternate the upper extremes of their compass with weightless harmonics, and the radiance then takes form as the 'Grail' motive.

Fig. 12.1

This is a good example of what Wagner frequently does in *Lohengrin*, which is to compose an extended theme, and then use its beginning – in this case its first seven notes – as a leitmotive. It is interesting that *Lohengrin* has fewer of these than *Der fliegende Holländer* and consists largely of self-contained items with music that has not appeared before and does not appear again. To be sure the 'Grail' motive recurs throughout the score, and there are occasions when a particular theme initiates a section that is closer to a symphonic development. Furthermore one of *Lohengrin*'s greatest choruses, '*Welch ein Geheimnis muß der Held bewahren?* (What is the secret which the hero has to guard?)' is almost as close knit from leitmotives as any ensemble in *The Ring*. (Whether taut developments or loose, stand-alone pieces, the choruses are one of the glories of *Lohengrin*. They have sometimes been criticised for not being progressive enough, but progressiveness is not the best measure of quality, and the choruses in *Lohengrin* are a main

---

43   The Holy Grail is, as we shall see, at the centre of *Parsifal*. It was, in legend, the chalice in which Jesus Christ gave wine to his disciples at the Last Supper, and in which Joseph of Arimathea collected Christ's blood when the Roman centurion Longinus thrust a spear into his side.

reason for wishing that Wagner had created just one more romantic opera before starting out on his new road.) It is not the leitmotives or any web of themes that bind *Lohengrin* together, though, but its balance of keys and orchestral colourings.

Keys and orchestral colourings also tie the music of the Prelude to the music of the opera, and the sound world of the Prelude appears again in Acts I and III, establishing musical connections between the Prelude and the rest of the work. Audiences can still be puzzled as to how the actual subject matter of the Prelude connects with the rest, because it has no immediate bearing on the action which follows. The essential point of connection is that both are about situations where our ordinary, material world is penetrated by the miraculous. The Grail's descent is a miraculous happening from outside time, natural laws and ordinary life; and Lohengrin's arrival in a skiff, drawn up the River Scheldt by a swan, is another.

Lohengrin is such an original work that it is a surprise to find how un-original some of its materials are. The rhyming couplets of the libretto are have long been censured for their conventional quality, and *Lohengrin* has a recurring rhythmic characteristic which is routinely criticised for its monotony (and there is no need to specify it). In practice *Lohengrin* is so luminous and mesmerising that the conventional verse forms and the persistent rhythms go for nothing unless people choose to focus on them. If anything these 'weaknesses' contribute to the stately, formalised mediaevalism of the work. Wagner never had any difficulty in taking so-called faults and transforming them into something special and unique.

The realm of religion and the miraculous always set Wagner's imagination on fire, undimmed by a lifetime of shifts and changes between the different faiths and philosophical beliefs to which he variously lent his allegiance. He achieved his representation of the mystical as ever-present in our mundane lives partly by merging two operatic genres, magic opera and grand opera. It is extraordinary that *Lohengrin* preserves its unity of mood throughout its switching between the mystical and solid history with solid historical locations and events, like those at the beginning of Act I. These are common features of grand opera and are as firmly historical as anything in Meyerbeer's *Les Huguenots*. Wagner represents the historical setting musically through a forthright C major tonality, complete with blazing diatonic fanfares.

Fig. 12.2

This was the framework which Wagner establishes before unveiling the completely different 'other-world' of the Grail's dominion, where the Grail knight appears in all his radiant righteousness, with different keys, different orchestral sounds and a different kind of music that looks back to the Prelude. Human nature has always been attracted to intimations of ordinary life being transformed by something deeper, and this is an important part of *Lohengrin*'s appeal.

The fairy-tale story of *Lohengrin* is about a damsel in distress, a beautiful princess who is rescued by the ultimate knight in shining armour, but the first act takes place on the banks of the Scheldt where a very historical king, Henry the Fowler, has newly arrived from Germany. Henry the Fowler was a significant figure, and at the time when Wagner created *Lohengrin* he was particularly important to Germans everywhere, because he not only signified a heroic past when the German states had been less downtrodden than in recent times, but also their hopes of a German renaissance and the revival of past glories. Many in the audiences for whom *Lohengrin* was intended would have known that Henry was Duke of Saxony, and from 919 to 936 King of Germany. As Ernest Newman tells us in *Wagner Nights*,

He was an energetic upholder of German rights and a fighter for German unity. He set his face against the pretensions of the Roman Church to interfere in German politics, refused to accept his crown from the hands of the Archbishop of Mainz, and reserved to himself the right of appointing bishops. Saxony at that time was the most considerable of the German states. By his wise rule and the power of arms, he made his own duchy internally strong, while externally he fought to save Germany from being overrun by alien hordes, in particular the Hungarians, who at that time were a formidable military power. Saxony was a relatively new state based largely on the village community. Henry persuaded his people to aggregate into towns, and then to fortify them; and to win time for the realisation of these and other plans, such as the building of a number of strongholds, he concluded a nine years truce with the Hungarians in 924, at the cost of an annual tribute. Then he brought in a new system of conscription and national defence and trained his men in the latest developments in the art of war; so that when the truce expired in 933 he was able to face the dreaded Hungarians on equal terms and defeat them, thus saving the German lands from the eastern menace of that period. Secure on this frontier, Henry now turned his attention to the west, extending his rule over the territories round and beyond the mouth of the Elbe.[44]

In the nineteenth-century context of the German desire to resurrect a sense of national identity, Wagner did well to set the solid foundations of his opera in an era of German history which his audiences of the time would be happy to recall.

On the banks of the river Scheldt where the opera begins, the King's herald proclaims that the nine-year truce with the Hungarians is drawing to a close, and that Henry and his armed forces have come to gather support from Brabant against these hordes of the East. As the distant overlord of Brabant he is distressed to find discord and disarray in this outlying province. He questions Count Friedrich von Telramund, a leading noble, as to what has gone wrong. Telramund explains that the old king had died, leaving his children Gottfried and Elsa in his care, with the hope and half-understanding that Elsa might one day

---

44   Newman, Ernest, *Wagner Nights*, London, 1949, pp. 125 et seq.

marry him. It is uncertain whether Elsa turned him down or the other way round, but in any case he had instead chosen to marry Ortrud, scion of a more ancient aristocracy. Telramund goes on to denounce Elsa; she had taken her brother, Gottfried, for an outing to the forest and come back alone; Gottfried was never seen again. Her confusion when questioned revealed her as to blame for his disappearance, and Telramund now accuses Elsa formally before the King of murdering her brother. After a period of shock, king and company resolve that the issue should be settled in a trial by combat. It is to take the form of a fight to the death between Telramund and anyone willing to champion Elsa's defence. The verdict will go to the winner on the assumption, bizarre as it seems today, that divine intervention will somehow skew the event to ensure that justice is done.

Fig. 12.3 'Trial by Combat'

The King summons Elsa to stand forward, and she appears, radiantly beautiful, heartsick and otherworldly, to music suggesting that she belongs to the ethereal world of the Prelude. The company are all touched and concerned because she radiates an innocence which does not square with Telramund's accusation. They wonder audibly whether he is mistaken, and even the king asks him to reflect, but this only results in him turning more aggressive and determined. He says Elsa is a feckless fantasist and he demands justice. The king asks her to speak and defend herself but instead, she embarks on a visionary monologue, '*Einsam in trüben Tagen*: My loneliness and desperation had made me pray for help. Worn out with sorrow I fell into a trancelike sleep where I saw a vision of a mysterious knight appearing, to console and defend me.' Telramund ridicules this as fantasy and hysterics, and as a description of her sinful, secret lover. He presses the King for a resolution.

The King's herald formally issues a summons: will someone come forward to take the lists for Elsa? His appeal is met with total silence, and the situation begins to look ominous for Elsa. Desperately she begs the king to repeat the summons to give time for her champion to make the journey in case he comes from a distance, and she launches into anguished prayer.

Fig. 12.4 'Elsa's Supplication'

It is answered, because this time the summons gives rise to something truly miraculous, as the chorus now exclaim in astonishment. They see a knight in shining armour, standing erect in a boat gliding up the river, drawn by a swan with the boat's chain in its beak. The knight is the hero of the opera's title, although none of the stage characters learn this until the end.

Fig. 12.5 'Lohengrin'

The music takes us back to the Prelude, since the orchestra softly gives out the 'Grail' motive as the knight steps ashore. He thanks the swan and wishes it farewell, to some of the most beautiful and expressive strains ever written for human voice.

Fig. 12.6

Lohengrin salutes the King as appointed by God and deserving of everlasting glory. He turns to Elsa and tells her that he has been sent to answer her call of distress. He is under orders to protect her, but before he can act as her champion, he must establish that she will trust herself and her fate to him. Almost fainting in a confusion of relief and ecstasy, she agrees, and Lohengrin now asks her to marry him if he is victorious in his fight for her innocence. It is not revealed whether this proposal is something required by the Grail, but it must at least be in conformity with the requirements of the Grail, because it is plain that Lohengrin will under no circumstances do anything that goes against his divine sense of Grail-related mission. Elsa, more enraptured than ever, says that just as she lies adoring at his feet, so she will give herself to him, body and soul. Instead of offering a corresponding commitment, Lohengrin lays down an off-putting condition; she must never ask him his name, his origins, or his identity. She must accept him simply as he is.

Fig. 12.7 'The Forbidden Question'

She agrees without a thought, and Lohengrin tries to impress on her how serious his condition really is, adding to his emphasis by repeating it a tone higher (in A minor, as quoted here). She can only respond blissfully that he is her saviour, her beloved; how could she be guilty of anything less than unconditional faith in someone who demonstrates such unconditional faith in her? At this point he cries out, 'Elsa, I love you.' This declaration radically redefines their relationship; even if his actions, his championing of Elsa and his marriage offer, were dictated by the Grail, he has just infused them with a personal passion for Elsa. From this point onwards his life and his sense of purpose are guided by two distinct aims, to obey the Grail and to experience his grand passion for Elsa. The big question is how far these aims can go peaceably together, but there is no reason in principle why they should not, and it is their circumstances that are the problem. For the present the sheer strength and rapture of their passion is all that matters, and Wagner's shimmering music makes it clear that they are ecstatically in love.

Before Freud or Jung formulated their theories about the unconscious forces which led to love at first sight, Wagner had plumbed its roots intuitively, presenting Lohengrin and Elsa as matching each other's archetypes, just as he did with Senta and the Dutchman. Even before setting eyes on each other, Lohengrin and Elsa have had intimations, as they soon explain to one other, and we can perhaps best understand these as ghostly and formless images in the mind which each fills out for the other as a living reality. Elsa had made this point, in '*Einsam in trüben Tagen*'; and during their Act III dialogue, Lohengrin tells how the same had been true for him, 'Although we had never met, each of us had divined the other.' They each describe an urge to give themselves to each other in a total communion, annihilating ego-boundaries in an experience which carries a sense of the mystical. Each recognises the other as uniquely able to provide the experience to the other. Elsa further describes how she hopes that he will take her for every good that she can offer him, and when Lohengrin offers to fight on Elsa's behalf, she repeats, 'I freely give you myself, body and spirit.' When he wins his combat, she goes further: 'In you I must be transcended/annihilated/sublimated.' (In true Hegelian fashion, Wagner believed that man and woman would be '*aufgehoben*' in a complete person, an idea which may hark back to Plato's extraordinary tract, the *Symposium*, although this is conjecture.) In Act III, when Lohengrin and Elsa prepare to mirror their spiritual oneness in the physical consummation of their marriage, they comment that to 'describe themselves as happy would be cold and inadequate;' they are engulfed 'in a bliss that is very heaven'.

Their problem, as Wagner soon makes clear, is twofold, first that their blissful fulfilments are not supported by any matching insights, and second, that the demands of their love and the requirements of the Grail will not in fact run parallel but diverge. Regarding the need for insight, the truth for Lohengrin and Elsa, as for life, is that no real person totally matches the preconceptions. Enduring love learns to embrace the real person regardless of discrepancies between the reality and past ideas. Sadly neither Lohengrin nor Elsa are able to do this. Wagner shows how neither of them has the insight and sympathy which would make it possible to enter into each other's minds. Each consequently fails to appreciate the significance of what is all-important to the other.

However, these problems are yet to arise, and all now seems set fair. Lohengrin turns forcefully to Telramund, tells him his accusation is untrue, swears that Elsa is innocent, and stakes his word and his sword on the combat. Telramund's friends counsel him urgently to stand down, because they can foresee a dire possibilities for Telramund in the strange knight, but Telramund says he would rather die than be taken for a coward. There may be a separate point which Wagner was making here, because he characteristically disparaged honour as a worthless abstraction unless it reflected real achievement, fruit and results. Otherwise he envisaged it as an empty bauble, something like celebrity today. After lengthy preparations, staking out the ground, issuing brutal threats to anyone who interferes, and offering up a prayer for justice to be done, the combat takes place and Lohengrin is the victor. Chivalrously he spares Telramund's life, and his victory results in the jubilation of everyone except Telramund, his party of four disaffected nobles, and his wife Ortrud. The act draws to a conclusion of radiance and coruscating energy.

Act II takes place in the great square at Antwerp, enclosed by the royal palace, the cathedral and other important buildings. It is night. Heralded by an ominous drum roll, the cellos play a restless wandering line symbolising '*Unheil*, Evil'.

Fig. 12.8

In the shadow under the palace walls are Telramund and Ortrud who have met outside the palace and are plotting. The theme just quoted leads into another generally associated with Ortrud, although there are contexts where its labelling as 'Ortrud' barely fits.

Fig. 12.9

It is the eve of Elsa's wedding to the mysterious knight, and from time to time festive sounds drift down from the palace's main hall where there is feasting and celebration.

Defeat is an experience of unbearable bitterness for Telramund, and an argument breaks out between him and his wife Ortrud, which informs us that the king has banished him. Telramund furiously denounces Ortrud for reducing them to degradation and exile, and in essence he declares, 'It was your declaration that Elsa had taken her brother to the woods and drowned him that was my reason for accusing Elsa, but my defeat has proved that you were lying. God's judgment has made this clear.' The eventual denouement will prove that she was indeed lying, and that Gottfried's disappearance was due to her own black arts. Ortrud had transformed him into a swan, the very swan that had drawn Lohengrin up the Scheldt, and Telramund is eventually her worst victim. She now accuses him of cowardice; his cowardice was the real cause of his defeat, not God's judgment. He only just reins back an impulse to kill her, but she merely taunts him with more dishonourable behaviour in threatening a vulnerable woman. With her fiendish allure she mesmerises him again, this time into believing that Lohengrin had won through witchcraft. At the same time she reveals a virulent contempt for the Christian God, which appals and frightens Telramund. He half knows exactly what she is doing, but only says helplessly, 'You wild sorceress, you are again bewitching me with your mysterious spell.' She also plays on his obsession with honour: 'Revenge for your defeat could be sweet to you.' She tells him she knows the way to destroy both Lohengrin and Elsa; 'If you in the fight had cut his finger off, or even a sliver from it, the victory would have been yours!' She explains that the loss of any smallest part of his person would have stripped him of his power; and moreover they can still do it, or rather he can. He himself must arrange to deal with Lohengrin, but he can leave Elsa to her.

Elsa now appears on the balcony to savour the night and enjoy her new happiness. Ortrud makes Telramund fall back into the shadows and calls piteously to Elsa in the first two notes of the forbidden question. Elsa asks 'Who called?' although her troubled tone suggests that she half knows. Ortrud says she is heartbroken that Elsa cannot recognise the voice of her old friend; has her downfall so altered her? She contrasts the splendour of Elsa's situation with her homelessness, exile and degradation; how could Elsa do this to her when all that she had ever wanted was to live quietly in the woods; what harm had she ever done Elsa? Elsa denies responsibility for Ortrud's situation, but she is soon moved by Ortrud's plight and in an impulse of kindness she offers to befriend Ortrud. She goes in from the balcony to come down the internal staircase to a small side door and let in Ortrud. In her absence Ortrud sings a terrifying 'prayer', an incantation to the old gods at full roar. She asks Wodan and Freia to consecrate her

Eight illustrations from *Richard Wagner: 12 Illustrationen von Ferd. Leeke* (c. 1900-10) after original oil paintings by Ferdinand Leeke (1859-1923)

Die Feen

Der fliegender Holländer – The Dutchman and Daland

Tannhäuser – Wolfram takes his farewell of Elisabeth

Lohengrin – Lohengrin defeats Telramund

Die Walküre – Brünnhilde and Wotan

Götterdämmerung – Siegfried and the Rhinemaidens

Die Meistersinger – Walter's prize song

Parsifal – Parsifal's journey to the Grail

Tannhäuser in the Venusberg (1901) by John Collier

Six Scenes from *Tannhäuser*; set of six collectible cards advertising Liebig's Fleisch-Extrakt. 1. Tannhäuser wanting to leave the Venusberg, Act I Scene 1

Tannhäuser: Act I. Scene IV.

Comp.^{ie} Liebig.

Wolfram von Eschenbach erkennt den Zurückgekehrten.

2. Wolfram recognises Tannhäuser, Act I Scene 4

Tannhäuser: Act II. Scene I.

Comp.^{ie} Liebig.   Elisabeth und Tannhäuser im Wartburgsaal.

Siehe Rückseite.

3. Elisabeth and Tannhäuser, Act II Scene I

TANNHÄUSER: Act II. Scene IV.

Comp.ie Liebig. ♪ Tannhäuser singt das Lied von der Venus im Zauberberge.

Scene Rückseite.

4. Tannhäuser sings of Venus, Act II Scene 4

annhäuser: Act III. Scene I.

5

ROMA

Comp.^{te} Liebig.

Siehe Rückseite.

Rückkehr der Pilger von Rom.

5. The pilgrims' return from Rome, Act III Scene 1

TANNHÄUSER: Act III. Letzte Scene.

Tannhäuser stirbt bekehrt.

Comp^{ie} Liebig.

6. Tannhäuser dies, saved, Act III final scene

Franz Stuck, *Die Sünde (Sin)*, 1893

Joseph Tichatschek and Wilhelmine Schröder-Devrient in the first performance of *Tannhäuser*, Dresden, 19 October 1845; as portrayed by F. Tischbein (1845)

The Wartburg, scene
of *Tannhäuser* Act II, today

Following pages:
three illustrations from the
Salzburg Easter Festival,
conductor and producer
Herbert von Karajan, stage sets
Gunter Schneider-Siemssen

Lohengrin Act I, 1976 with René Kollo in the title role. Photographer: Siegfried Lauterwasser

Lohengrin Act III; René Kollo, Karl Ridderbusch, Anna Tomowa-Sintow

Tristan and Kurwenal (*Tristan und Isolde*, Act III); Jon Vickers and Walter Berry, 1971

Lohengrin: a vision of the Prelude as imagined by Henri Fantin-Latour (1836-1904)

Ludwig Schnorr von Carolsfeld, self-portrait as Lohengrin, 1861. The first tenor to sing Lohengrin came from an important family of painters. He was Wagner's first and favourite Tristan but died shortly after the first performances aged only 29

John William Waterhouse, *Tristram and Isolde*, 1916

treachery and wickedness so that she can restore to them the ancient thrones from which Christianity had deposed them. Elsa, reappearing at the door, just misses this fearsome outburst, and when Elsa appears, Ortrud is all misery and charm. To hearten her, Elsa says she plans next morning to ask for an amnesty for Telramund. Ortrud thanks her extravagantly and sensing her advantage, she begins to sow seeds of anxiety in Elsa about the mystery knight's identity. She says that she would love to reward Elsa's kindness and gladly be with Elsa in any of hour of danger or crisis which might materialise in connection with him; after all, his forbidden question is so mysterious; might it not be sinister? Elsa assures Ortrud that her concerns are meaningless and pities her because, not having experienced the love of a man as marvellous as Lohengrin, she can have no idea of the joy and the security that it brings. As she shepherds Ortrud into the palace she promises her rich clothes and a place of honour at her wedding celebrations next day.

Some commentators have found it strange that Wagner has Elsa being taken in by Ortrud, because Ortrud is plainly evil in general and evil to Elsa in particular. Why should Elsa accept Ortrud's kind words as genuine when she and Telramund had been plotting against Elsa's life with a capital charge, and Lohengrin was the one who had saved her? Why should Elsa pay attention to their concern that there might be something threatening about Lohengrin's refusal to tell her who he is, when they themselves were her worst threat? The answer is that Elsa's convictions are all at sea, and she displays Wagner's profound understanding of a mind that is disturbed. Wagner makes it clear that her existence has been transformed by Lohengrin, but in Elsa he created a young woman who is very vulnerable. As happened with the child Wagner, her life has been like a minefield blowing up in her face again and again. Elsa has been repeatedly betrayed. She is an orphan, and there is a common feeling among orphans, however irrational they sometimes know it to be, of having been deserted by parents 'who died *at* them'. Bereavement is confused with desertion and the pain of the loss is often felt as deliberately inflicted. This had been Elsa's first desertion, but Elsa's father had tried to secure her future by entrusting her to a noble guardian, Friedrich von Telramund. Instead of safeguarding her, Telramund had turned against her, a second desertion. To make matters worse, her brother, Gottfried, has mysteriously been lost for dead, more desertion; and worse still, Telramund not only does not comfort her, but denounces her and even threatens anyone who dares take her side, so that the prospect of some nasty mediaeval fate was beginning to loom up menacingly. Wagner creates a character who feels utterly alone after going through multiple betrayals; not all her saintliness can disguise that she is terrified; and Wagner makes her second prayer sound hectic and disordered. With Lohengrin's arrival things turn out unimaginably well, but it all happens so fast that she cannot get her bearings and think clearly. Wagner has etched out a damaged personality who has so far lost her ability to think straight that she gives her worst enemy a hearing. As they go in to the palace together, Telramund reappears and observes equivocally that evil has entered the house. In a telling little monologue, he makes it clear that he half knows that Ortrud is false, but falls in line because he is spellbound and he believes she can restore his honour.

As he ends his arioso, which is firmly anchored in F sharp minor, the far distant trumpets onstage echo its tonality with an F sharp and an A. They then give out a fanfare, in fact repeated fanfares which play on those two notes but reframe them as D major simply by adding a D at the top.

Fig. 12.10 'Trumpets on the Wachtowers'

The day dawns and the trumpet signals from distant watchtowers, calling and answering each other, create a magical effect. They presage a return to grand opera and to a chorus that is splendidly operatic. The rollicking energy of '*In Früh'n versammelt uns der Ruf* (The summons rouses us at dawn)' with which the assembling soldiery hail the reveille shows Wagner's mastery of traditional forms, even if it does not advance the action. The choruses that follow are even finer and do more to take the drama forward. In the processional chorus that greets Elsa with hopes that 'she will walk in blessings (*Gesegnet soll sie schreiten*)', Wagner created melody after melody, all ravishing.

The Herald addresses the assembled vassals and nobles. He informs them that the King has banished Telramund and outlawed him. Anyone who helps him is also banished and outlawed. On the other hand the mysterious knight sent by God will take over the crown and lands of Brabant, but as he does not want to be known as Duke, his title will be 'Protector of Brabant'. His first act is to invite them all to celebrate his wedding that very day, but tomorrow he must lead them to war. Most of the vassals and the nobles respond enthusiastically, but the four felon barons associated with Telramund mutter angrily that there is no reason for them to get involved with in a war against such a distant enemy, except that it is too late to prevent it, and who is there now to stop it happening? Telramund himself comes among them, and tells them that *he* will stop it happening. They are alarmed and warn him of the risk he runs; he has a price on his head; but he tells them he soon intends still greater risks in order to unmask this impostor of a knight. They shuffle him back into concealment as Elsa's grand procession begins to make its way through the crowds towards the cathedral. They do this to a chorus where Wagner again spins one soaring melody after another, and towards its culmination the bass line takes on a significance worthy of J.S. Bach. However the culmination never arrives because to a blistering diminished seventh Ortrud suddenly breaks ranks to hurl scorn and contempt at Elsa. She claims precedence as the wife of a man well-recognised as a great feudal lord over Elsa, who knows nothing of the stranger she is marrying. Elsa is horrified and intimidated and the bystanders are outraged, but they cannot stop Ortrud. 'Although my husband has been falsely condemned and outlawed, his name was honoured throughout the land, but nothing is known of your bridegroom, and you have not even a name for him. You know nothing of his origins. You have no idea when he will disappear. If he were to reveal who he is, it would put an end to the black arts which empower him.' Elsa shows some spirit as she denounces Ortrud in turn; 'You shameless slanderer! You frightful, evil woman! My answer is that he is so pure and rings so true that only an evil person could fail to recognise it.' Unfortunately, the music which Wagner gives Elsa has not the same force and conviction as his music for Ortrud as she jeers, 'He is so pure and rings so true that you dare not even ask him, because you know what the truth would be.'

At this point the King and Lohengrin appear with their own procession, and the King is appalled to find more confusion and contention. Lohengrin is even more appalled to see Ortrud near Elsa, and draws his bride towards him as she begs him, 'My deliverer! Save me from this woman. I fear I went against your wishes, but I found her in such a state at the gates that I raised her up from her misery and asked her to join me. Just see how she repays my goodness, disdaining me and saying I was wrong to trust in you.' Lohengrin turns on Ortrud and tells her to keep away from Elsa, 'Here you will never be victorious!' a prophecy which is sadly far from the mark, as Lohengrin mostly is. For now he turns gently to Elsa, telling her his hope that Ortrud's poison has not infected her heart against him. Weeping, Elsa hides her face against him, and he tells her softly that she should let her tears flow with joy. Once again the procession moves off to music of real glory, but again it is baulked of its tonic culmination, crashing into another diminished seventh, fortissimo on heavy brass, as Telramund rampages onto the scene.

Fig. 12.11

He is arraigned on all sides, but this does not stop him from denouncing Lohengrin; 'O King, you must hear me. I have been robbed of everything by fraud; and it would never have happened if you had only asked the stranger his name. That would have disempowered him. Now because of your failure to ask, I should be allowed to put the question myself.' He turns to Lohengrin: 'Who are you, coming here with your wild swan?' He turns to the company; 'Anyone who resorts to sorcery, puts spells on animals and turns them into his familiars, is not pure and righteous.' His captors have relaxed their hold on Telramund uncertainly, and they look expectantly towards Lohengrin for an explanation. Instead Lohengrin tells Telramund that he has no intention of explaining anything to someone so flagrantly evil, but Telramund is quick with his answer. If Lohengrin considers him unworthy of an explanation, then let the King ask; surely Lohengrin would never refuse the King. Lohengrin tells him, 'Yes, I would even refuse the King and every prince that there is. They can see my good deeds, which speak for themselves. There is only one to whom I must

give answer' – the music takes on a tone of doubt and anguish – 'Elsa!'
Lohengrin pauses in fearful apprehension as he sees her staring starkly
ahead, her breast heaving with conflicting emotions. He continues to
himself, 'I see that she is trembling. Has she been affected by the lies
and the hatred? O heaven, keep her safe in so great a danger.' The so-
called 'Ortrud' motive winds its way sinuously through the orchestra.
It is now that the opera reaches the great ensemble and chorus already
mentioned, '*Welch ein Geheimnis muß der Held bewahren!*' This is
a masterstroke of music and drama, where music really comes into
its own. (Carl Dahlhaus tells us that Richard Strauss particularly
admired this ensemble for what it brought to the action.) In a sense
the action slows to a standstill, and the entire company, except
Ortrud and Telramund, who are describing their own thoughts, muse
anxiously about Lohengrin's prohibition against asking who he is.
With its soaring, shimmering string lines, its sense of mystery, and its
suggestive web of motives weaving contrapuntally amongst its choral
textures, this haunting composition demonstrates how totally Wagner
transformed traditional forms. As Dahlhaus says, it freezes the action
and holds the fleeting moment fixed for contemplation in a way that
is only possible in a drama expressed in music. As Dahlhaus says, the
music also 'becomes the spirit of the narrative,' meaning that this
contemplative ensemble also fulfils a dramatic role. It takes the drama
forwards to an open concern, a half-awareness, both onstage and in
the audience, that Ortrud's poison is indeed percolating through Elsa's
imagination.

The king calls them from their reflections with his personal
assurance to Lohengrin that his actions and everything about them
speak for themselves, and that Lohengrin needs answer no questions.
Telramund has sidled up to Elsa during the ensemble and now assaults
her verbally with promises of assistance and advice how to hold
Lohengrin in Brabant. Lohengrin catches sight of Telramund, orders
him off commandingly, and again draws Elsa close. He tells her that
all their happiness lies in her hands, in her faith, and asks, 'Do you
hold fast your faith in me, or do you wish to ask the question?' Elsa is

so generally disorientated that Ortrud's insinuations have established a foothold, but she ends the act ends by affirming, however frail it sounds, that her love transcends all doubts. The processional chorus again declare their greeting to Elsa and their hopes that she will walk in blessings, this time in C major, *Lohengrin*'s key of historical reality. At least temporarily Lohengrin appears to have descended from the tonalities and colouring of the Prelude to the firmer realities of this world. An organ from within the cathedral and twelve trumpets onstage affirm a radiant optimism with their C major fanfares, but it is undermined by the orchestral brass thundering out the music of the forbidden question in F minor as Ortrud raises her arm menacingly from the far side of the square. The fanfares return and for the time being affirmation wins the day.

Act III begins with a Prelude of roister-doister elation, the staple of brass bands throughout the world before they were largely swept away by amplified drum kits and electric guitars. The Prelude leads without a break into the famous 'Bridal chorus', which is an ambiguous piece.

CHORUS

Treu-lich ge-führt   zie-het da-hin,   wo euch in Fried-en die Lie-be be-wahr'!

Fig. 12.12

'Faithfully escorted, you are now drawn in to this place where love will watch over you in peace.' The words foretell to Lohengrin and Elsa a happiness that is both spiritual and erotic.

However the promise of the words is undermined by the fragile transience of the music, which is worlds away from the *organo pleno* which has blasted out this music at countless weddings ever since. The chorus finally withdraws, and leaves them to a night of erotic bliss. Lohengrin comments happily that they are alone for first time. Their romance has reached full bloom, and ecstatically they discuss their forthcoming union and the prospect of merging in complete oneness. Lohengrin addresses her as 'My sweet wife!' There is only one tiny speck in Elsa's happiness, she says, and that is that she cannot give a name to it, to the man who actualises it. How sweet it would be to speak his name. Lohengrin tries to change her mood by simply responding again, 'My sweet wife!' but Elsa cannot leave the matter alone. Can he not tell her his name so softly that it is virtually unspoken, now that they are alone? It would be like a personal endearment. He tells her he wants no such endearment, but simply to savour the magic of her. She says that confiding his name would be act of trust, and he points out that he had shown absolute trust in her innocence and championed her although he knew nothing of her. Nothing helps with Elsa. His happiness and hers are blighted by the invisible worm of Ortrud, and Elsa simply persists with an altered approach. She says that she would like to make him a return for his trust and his protection. If his name were a dark secret, then she could show how much she loves him by resisting all attempts to extract from her. Lohengrin responds, 'My love!' but Elsa cannot stop herself; 'Prove to me how much you trust me; for that proof I have to be aware of who you are.' Lohengrin declares anxiously 'Oh Elsa, no!' and when she presses him again, he stops trying simply to beguile her, and addresses her with a seriousness that is itself a warning. She owes him everything, he says, because he accepted her unconditionally, and she swore him a solemn oath. She must never waver, he tells her sternly. He softens again at the awareness of her loveliness, and praises her again in glowing terms and at length, trying to calm her and distract her. He tells her that her love and her own self are such a source of joy and fulfilment for him, that everything he ever knew and all the past that he has left behind are nothing in comparison. To make sure that she understands the full extent of his admiration, he goes on to tell her unwisely that this is so even though he left behind a realm of bliss and radiance and not of darkness and gloom as she seems to imagine.

Elsa is unfortunately so out of harmony with herself that this only starts her off on wilder imaginings. She becomes terrified that he will soon want to leave her and go back to his origins of bliss and radiance. How can she ever compete with that, and how can she hold him if she does not even know his name, cannot identify him. She ends up in a state of increasing hysteria. In her imagination she sees the swan returning and taking the knight back whence he came. Lohengrin is in agony as he tries in vain to restrain her; 'Elsa, quiet, no no! Elsa, stop!' But at the height of her outburst she half gasps, half screams the forbidden question, declaiming it word by word and demanding of him his name, origins and nature.

Everything happens at once. Telramund and his knights shatter the door and break in with murderous intent; Elsa rushes to Lohengrin with his sword and he kills Telramund with a single stroke. Telramund's four felon-barons fall before Lohengrin in submission as Elsa faints. Lohengrin revives her and comments sadly that she has put an end to all their joy. He orders the knights to convey Telramund's body to the battle parade which is planned early next day. He announces that he will then formally answer Elsa's question about his name, origins and nature, proclaiming the truth before the world. Attendants lead Elsa away to some of the saddest music ever written in a major key.

The scene changes back to the River Scheldt. A huge chorus with batteries of extra trumpets betokens another glorious dawn, but the rising exaltation of the people of Brabant and the King is suddenly checked when Telramund's body is presented to them by his four barons. The appearance of Elsa, hollow-eyed and unhappy to the point of anguish, does nothing to improve their spirits. The mood brightens as Lohengrin appears, only for him to tell them that he cannot lead them as he intended. He comes not as the protector but as a plaintiff, first to accuse the dead Telramund of his attempted murder, explaining that he had to kill Telramund in self-defence. His plea is accepted, but now he has a second accusation, that Elsa has broken her promise not to ask who he is. He is mystically bound to tell her the truth and proclaim it to the world. They can then judge whether he is worthy and honourable. To the music of the Prelude he tells of his home, the distant Temple of the Holy Grail. He spins a vocal line which exerts its own spell as he describes the Knights of the Grail and their sacred purpose, and the annual descent of the Holy Spirit, in the form of a dove, to replenish the Grail's power. The Knights have power to do great deeds in the world and they bring blessings where ever they are sent, but nobody must know who they are, because the knowledge deprives them of their power and requires of them that they return immediately to the Grail Temple. The King of the Temple is his father Parsifal; he himself is the King's loyal knight, and his name is Lohengrin. If only Elsa had held out for a year her brother would have returned. Now he must return home to the Grail Temple, and must go alone. To the general consternation and Elsa's horror, the swan reappears with its skiff, ready for his departure. Elsa's nightmarish imaginings are self-fulfilling. At this point Ortrud appears on the battlements in triumph, shrieking, 'Go home!' She is apparently unmoved by Telramund's death and points out with horrid joy that the old gods have won. Lohengrin has failed in almost all he set out to do. He has not saved Elsa from Ortrud's machinations. His prophecy that she would never be victor was wrong. His promise that after a day celebrating his wedding he would lead them to victory against the Huns has come to nothing. The old gods have triumphed; Lohengrin and the Christian God have failed.

There is substance in what she says. Although Lohengrin has saved Elsa successfully from her immediate fate, Ortrud succeeds in her determination that Elsa should die, but of a broken heart. However, Lohengrin does now achieve one lasting benefit. In response to Ortrud he advances to the edge of the river, kneels in prayer, and loosens the chain from the swan. It sinks into the water, and a magnificent, heroic young man appears on the surface. It is Gottfried, Elsa's brother, whom Ortrud had transformed into the swan, and he can now take Lohengrin's place as leader of the Brabantine forces. Lohengrin predicts that the King will win a great victory and that the hordes of the East will never be victorious over Germany, and in this he was historically correct, in so far as Henry the Fowler did defeat the Hungarians. (Unfortunately Lohengrin's prophecy has been taken as evidence that Wagner was somehow an advance advocate for Hitler's invasion of Poland and his wanton attack on Russia.) Meanwhile a dove descends from heaven to replace the swan and draw Lohengrin down the Scheldt. Elsa dies, despairing over her irreparable loss, and the crowd cry out a lamenting '*Weh* (Woe)', as Lohengrin, who has to deal with his own despair, is borne away and lost to sight, just as he came.

Wagner did nothing to clarify the lessons and meanings of *Lohengrin* in his publication 'A Communication to my Friends' (1851). In it he provided a male chauvinist interpretation of his opera, which makes no mention of Lohengrin's mission as a servant of the Grail, sent out in response to Elsa's appeal. Instead,

Lohengrin sought a woman who would believe in him, a woman who would not ask who he was or whence he came, but would love him as he was, because he was what he appeared to her to be. He sought a woman to whom he would not have to explain or justify himself, but who would love him unconditionally. For this reason he had to conceal his higher nature, for it was precisely the non-discovery, the non-revelation this higher nature (higher because, to speak more accurately, it has been raised up) that was his sole guarantee that he was not admired or marvelled at, or humbly and uncomprehendingly adored, simply because of that quality. Admiration and adoration were what he did not seek. Only one thing could release him from his isolation, satisfy this yearning: love. To be loved and to be understood through love. All his highest thinking, his most conscious knowing, were filled with no other desire than to be a complete, whole human being, swayed by and received with the warmth of human emotion, to be entirely human, not a god. In other words, an absolute artist. And so he yearned for woman – the human heart. And so he descended from his blissful, barren solitude when he heard a cry for help arising from the midst of humanity, from this particular heart, from this woman. But he is unable to shake off the telltale aura of his higher nature. He cannot help but appear an object of wonder. The amazement of the commonality, but the venom of envy throw their shadow even into the heart of the loving woman. Doubt and jealousy prove to him that he is not understood but only adored, and tear from him the confession of his divinity, with which he returns into solitude, destroyed.

This clarifies what Lohengrin needed from Elsa, but it implies that Lohengrin came to Antwerp mainly or entirely for love, and that he was there to fulfil his own personal yearning for Elsa. This is at loggerheads with the terms and the main action of the opera. The opera itself establishes that Lohengrin has responded to Elsa's call primarily in response to a divine command of the Grail. He is under orders, orders that he should help Elsa and orders not to reveal who he is. In his farewell monologue, he informs the company that the ability of Grail knights like himself to perform deeds of valour and spread goodness throughout the world depends on everybody around them not knowing who and what they are. None of this has anything to do Wagner's suggestion that Lohengrin hides his identity because he is a man desperate to be loved for his own sake. And if this were not enough, Wagner suddenly presents out of nowhere the idea that this desire of Lohengrin to be received unconditionally is the vain aspiration of the absolute artist. From the knight in shining armour following the behests of the Grail, Lohengrin has swerved away, first into being a godlike individual who wants to be loved incognito, then into something completely different, an absolute artist who needs to be understood by his public, something not even hinted by anything in the opera.

On the other hand, it is certainly part of the opera and its mainstream narrative that Lohengrin cries out to Elsa that he loves her. Lohengrin's sudden, headlong involvement in a passionate romance with Elsa in itself creates a new set of motives for his actions, over and above Elsa's defence and the Grail's command that Lohengrin should provide it. But as described earlier, Lohengrin's sudden passion for Elsa is not in itself incompatible with the mission specified by the Grail. The reason why the demands of the Grail mission collide with the romance of Elsa and Lohengrin is because of their circumstances. Elsa's recent history has created the *inner* circumstances of her personal vulnerability and insecurity. There are also the more damaging *external* circumstances created by Ortrud and her pawn Telramund, who are both determined to play on her vulnerability and destroy her happiness and her life.

Whether the action of *Lohengrin* is taken as more about a mission to save Elsa as determined by the Grail, or more about a romance with Elsa determined by Lohengrin, it makes no difference to many of its lessons. Either way, Ortrud's unholy task of destruction is easier because neither Elsa nor Lohengrin can appreciate the needs of the other. Their relationship is like many good relationships that are yet fatally flawed because neither of them is willing to understand the other's inner world and adjust to it. Neither Elsa nor Lohengrin accepts that however irrational the deepest concerns of the other may seem, they are very real and matter terribly to the person who has to live with those concerns. Both Lohengrin and Elsa are faced with each other's failures to understand and make allowances, and the opera is the story of two people who find that they cannot count on each other where it matters most. Act III ends with each of them failing the other. Each of them desperately needs guarantees that nothing and no one matters more to the other than they each do. They present the truth about the importance of coming first. Instead they end up with the conviction that something else will always take first place; their own needs will always come second with the other.

Lohengrin and Elsa possess security needs which are not only different but in the end incompatible. For Lohengrin to feel he can count on Elsa, he needs her to accept him and love him incognito; that is her putting him first. For Elsa to be able to feel she can count on Lohengrin, she needs him to allow her total intimacy and total knowledge of his identity; that is him putting her first. Sadly neither can give precedence to the other. Neither has the flexibility. It is not that their needs are unreasonable or far-fetched, and as the opera tells the story, neither is a free agent. Elsa is swayed by her fears and insecurities and Lohengrin has no say in leaving Elsa. If Elsa asks the forbidden question, the spell will automatically be broken, and he has to go. The extraordinary thing is that while it does not add up logically, and Lohengrin, as a knight sworn to obedience, really has no choice, somehow the lessons that the opera teaches about the necessity of a willingness to meet another's needs, which implies the freedom to choose, still hold good.

As *Lohengrin* warns, so in real life, relationships often fail exactly because of these failures. This lesson from *Lohengrin* is all the more important because it is counter-cultural. In a sense the two protagonists reflect the common contemporary belief that it is unhealthy and feebleminded to want security or expect the satisfying of needs from an intimate relationship. *Lohengrin* passes judgment on this belief, this tenet of popular psychology which holds that expecting to be validated and nurtured by a partner is some kind of sickness or regression. This expectation is commonly disparaged as a childish leftover which properly adjusted adults have outgrown. Wagner has Elsa and Lohengrin do in practice what many people do, not in their time so much as now, and live by the principle,[45]

I do my thing and you do your thing,
I am not in this world to live up to your expectations,
And you are not in this world to live up to mine.

This me-centred outlook grew up in the late twentieth century, and I believe it still persists.

Lohengrin flies in the face of this outlook, and shows how a concentration by either person on his or her needs and a detachment from the other's can ruin a relationship. Elsa's relief at Lohengrin's arrival and her instant passion lead her to promise anything, and this 'anything' includes accepting conditions which deny her deepest necessities. The unconditional love that Lohengrin needs from Elsa, taking him as he stands and knowing nothing of him, is the polar opposite of the total intimacy, the knowing him utterly and being

---

45   in the words of Fritz Perls (1969).

utterly known, which she needs from him. Whether following the dictates of the Grail or his own longing for incognito love, he confides and entrusts nothing of himself to her; and because of her insecurities she is the last person to cope with this. Even in general situations the truth that people need to depend on each other seems obvious. People need the cooperation of families, friends, colleagues, to achieve anything in this life, and two essentials in any successful cooperation are reliability and commitment. This is more true, not less, in a relationship with a 'significant other'.

Admittedly there are certain extreme forms of counting on someone else which are pathological, and this may be the reason for the mistaken idea that dependency on another is in itself pathological, a form of weakness. It is not surprising that there is an element of pathological dependency in Elsa's neediness for Lohengrin. She has been damaged by the traumas of her past, and here too Wagner's opera offers insights ahead of its time. Yet again it is an interesting question: how did Wagner acquire this insight? He had no textbooks of psychology, but he did possess the legacy of his own unmet dependency needs as a child. Perhaps it was because of Minna and his relationship with Minna that Wagner knew from experience about destructive dependency and was able to enshrine in Elsa some of that destructive dependency. He also had the unwitting insight to present Lohengrin as a man of pathological chauvinism in his inability to meet Elsa's need for security, something that past generations, whatever their faults, mostly recognised as a woman's prerogative. After all, Lohengrin was acting for himself when he proposed instant passion at first sight – or at least within three minutes of his first sight of Elsa.

What romantic partners really need from those they love is *interdependence*. Interdependence is not the same as co-dependence with its pathological neediness. Interdependence is not 'clingy', but a free recognition of each other's needs and a commitment to meet those needs. Interdependence enables the partners to embrace the differences in each others' personalities and their separate activities, something represented by Wagner in the relationship of Brünnhilde and Siegfried at the beginning of *Götterdämmerung*. The distinction between a pathological dependence and a beneficial interdependence is the difference between 'I need you and therefore I love you,' and 'I love you and therefore I need you'. It is the absence of interdependence that shears Elsa and Lohengrin apart.

There is something further about Lohengrin's outlook which is all wrong. His expectations of Elsa actually involve an internal contradiction. Real intimacy is intrinsically mutual. Intimacy is by definition two-way. The suffusing of two personalities one with another is what Elsa craves of Lohengrin, and it is also what Lohengrin wants of Elsa – but not really. To be genuine, intimacy must include the mutual sharing of memories because memories and life experience are a large part of who we are. To know someone and know nothing of their past is not to know them. Lohengrin's embargo on Elsa's access to his memories and identity is incompatible with the very fusing and merging that he wants. In life there are a fair number of men, and some women, who hope for this impossible intimacy, this expecting to be loved unconditionally and totally but incognito, intimately and yet not intimately. At times Wagner was one of them. Such fantastic cravings can only be indulged in bogus versions of intimacy, in substitute relationships with computers, work, or addictive substances, or with prostitutes and gigolos. These do offer intimacy-without-intimacy. They masquerade as intimate relationships but ask no questions and are unconcerned with people as people. This was what Lohengrin hoped for, but these relationships are delusional, and unconditional intimacy has nothing to do with them.

Lohengrin makes some other telling points. It demonstrates certain other factors for a good relationship which are missing with Lohengrin and Elsa, such as a willingness to forgive, kindliness, and compassion. Forgiveness is something that is cruelly denied to Elsa, even though her fault, her broken promise to Lohengrin, is not so very dire. It is a strangely virtuous fault, reflecting not only her need but her great love for Lohengrin. It is the intensity of her love that makes her disobey his conditions for it. She is in a double bind. Her intensity makes the love so fulfilling, but the same intensity compels her to do what destroys it. There is no malice about her wrongdoing, no exploitation, no evil intent or fraud, and Lohengrin's failure to forgive Elsa was a mistake that Wagner highlighted as sonething to avoid. Lohengrin's wedding service at Antwerp Minster evidently did not include the promise 'for better, for worse' and the promise 'to love and to cherish', which together amount to a commitment to forgiveness. *Lohengrin* models how things go wrong when people do not observe these commitments.

Lohengrin also demonstrates that an egoistic obsession with honour is a mistake. It is the mistake of Telramund; and Wagner often presented worldly honours as a snare. Telramund persists in the combat against the better judgment of his co-conspirators for the sake of his honour. The same obsession with honour clouds his judgment when Ortrud is plotting, and he pays for it with his life.

Wagner was taken aback to find that a number of people disapproved of Lohengrin as a character. Wagner never gave him enough uncertainties or internal divisions to make him less righteous, in the wrong sense. For all that, *Lohengrin* ultimately demonstrates a remarkable dedication to reality, and in the story as the opera tells it, there is no refusal to oversimplify and make out that Lohengrin's virtuous line is easy. The story does not shirk the difficult matter of pre-existing or conflicting commitments. If the hero of the opera did not show more commitment to be what Elsa needed, then part of the reason was that he was not a free agent. He had made commitments to the Grail long before Elsa's prayers or even the Grail itself had first summoned him up the Scheldt. His shining singleness of mind is part of his appeal to Elsa, but that singleness of mind prevents him from giving her first place, and this is something which spouses find hard to take in reality. Cardiac surgeons are famous for their single-minded selflessness and they are often admired and loved for it, for always putting other people, their patients, before 'everything else'. However it becomes a source of discord when this 'everything else' turns out to include family holidays, wedding anniversaries, children's prizegivings, or even just weekends and ordinary evenings. Such dedicated people, always rushing off to hospital, often leave behind a trail of marriages which came to grief because their spouses could not accept indefinitely this shining dedication, this Lohengrin-syndrome. These situations are genuinely not easy and *Lohengrin* tells it as it is.[46]

Lohengrin does not offer any simple instructions or easy answers, but it rings true, and it is this ring of truth that is so important. Anyone wanting wisdom about a worthwhile relationship would do well to look at this opera. But what ultimately matters about it is that it is so exquisite in its own right, a source of such enchantment. *Lohengrin* is like a jewel, glittering and perfect, and what lingers in the memory is a remote, grave beauty unlike anything else in art or in life.

The opera was first performed at Weimar on 28 August 1850, in virtue of Franz Liszt's enthusiasm and under his baton. The principles were Carl Beck (Lohengrin), Rosa von Milde-Agthe (Elsa), Hans Feodor von Milde (Telramund), Josephine Fastlinger (Ortrud), 'Herr' Höfer (King Henry) and August Pätsch (the Herald).

---

46   I should mention for the sake of completeness that Wagner not only at one stage said that Lohengrin was an allegory of the absolute artist, but at another that the opera was really about Elsa: that she was the woman of the future; and that she had made a revolutionary of him. However, these are ideas which seem to have no basis of expression in the opera itself, and as it is not easy either to make out their value for us, they do not really belong here.

THIRTEEN

DER RING DES NIBELUNGEN

Der Ring des Nibelungen is the name of the four-opera cycle which describes the story of Alberich's Ring, Alberich being the Nibelung dwarf of the title. I will mainly refer to it simply as *The Ring*.

Der Ring des Nibelungen, to start with its full title, is one of the supreme achievements of the human spirit. In its scope and its reach, in its grandeur of conception and abundance of episode, in its universal relevance and its richness of suggestion, and above all in its music, it has no near rival anywhere in art. Wagner enshrined many ideas in *The Ring*, but beyond his explicit intentions, it is a compelling allegory of human existence. It begins virtually with a creation myth, and in common with many other creation myths it narrates not only the beginning of the world but the origins of consciousness. The opening of *Das Rheingold* begins in formless depths and presents a symbol of individuality awakening, an evolution from its first glimmerings to high noon, from formless stillness to animation and energy. From these beginnings, the great arc of *The Ring* takes shape, embracing all the changing phases of life. At the end of *Götterdämmerung* it finally draws to a fulfilling if wistful close.

This immense sequence gives expression to *The Ring's* most positive precept, that whatever twilight and oblivion must fall on all human endeavour, including our own brief span, it is still infinitely worthwhile. Simply to have lived life and experienced its achievements and disappointments, its joys and its sorrows, even its tepid stretches and its dullnesses – all life's richness and variety – is an experience so vital that it is not negated by the fact that it has to end. *The Ring* as a whole represents a compelling validation of human existence. Nobody could sensibly deny that there are people whose lives are so dreadful that no validation could conceivably make sense, but for most of us more fortunate ones, *The Ring* is an endorsement of life on life's terms. The prospect of it ending does stir regrets; but life is so worth living, that even if it must end without trace, it is still worthwhile.

The next important point about *The Ring* is that for all its cornucopia-multiplicity, it has an overwhelming architectonic quality which is all the more remarkable, given the erratic fits and blazes of its creation over twenty-five years and the miscellany of ingredients that went into it. For its plot Wagner went to a wide variety of sources. The mediaeval German epic, the *Nibelungenlied*, the Icelandic sagas and Scandinavian sources were among the many that fed his imagination. As always with Wagner, what he made of it was not a compilation but a vision so new that he was attacked for reworking the grand old stories and for taking unpardonable liberties with the originals. This was unjust. Most of the originals were themselves based on sources still older, and Wagner's own poem *Der Ring des Nibelungen*, as it eventually came to be, gave the myths a unity that they had never possessed before. To be sure, Wagner added new plot material that he devised himself, more than in anything else which he created (except *Die Meistersinger*), but that was pure gain.

The density of meaning that he forged into *The Ring* is phenomenal, and it is concerned with life and the world at so many levels that it is virtually about everything, everything that matters, but it has two main strata. There is an extravert layer to *The Ring*, its ideas about politics and society which included organised religion, and about creating a better world. This extravert layer reflected the same social and concerns as had led to the political theory of Karl Marx. Marx had made an attempt to derive a theory, a political theory, from the material facts of human existence. It was a theory of human relationships rooted in their social and political struggles. *The Ring's* second, inward layer is more concerned with fathoming the psyche and becoming the people we want to be. Its 'fathoming the psyche' was related to the realm of depth psychology which would soon evolve under Freud and his great contemporaries. Freud's new psychology would be another attempt to derive a theory from the material facts of human existence, this time a theory of the mind. Its axioms were derived from the forces which drive people, such as the drive towards safety, food, warmth, shelter, space and sanitation. Both these theories took their origins in man's need to survive, develop and produce offspring, and Wagner presciently enshrined much from both in *The Ring*.

Like Wagner's other works, *The Ring* also explores further dimensions of love, and what is special about *The Ring*'s particular exploration is that it raises big questions about its opposite, and what constitutes the opposite of love. *The Ring* sets out an answer which Jung determined later, 'Logically, the opposite of love is hate; and of Eros, fear. But psychologically it is the will to power'. The conflict of the longing for love and the longing for power is at the heart of *The Ring*, which demonstrates (in Jung's words) that 'Where love reigns, there is no will to power, and where the will to power is paramount, love is lacking'. the Ring also expresses through its action on stage the Jungian idea that it is not a matter of either one or the other, but of getting the right balance.

Wagner's concern with politics and society was the driving force behind his original plans for a Nibelung drama. This concern grew out of his experience as an outsider in Paris, whereas his matching concern with religion derived from his time at Dresden when he had become one of the city's leading intellectuals. The origins of *The Ring*'s second stratum, its inward and spiritual layer, are not so easy to pin down, as will be clear in due course.

Wagner could scarcely have created *The Ring* at all if he had not settled in Paris for two years and drunk deeply of the political and social theories that were circulating during his time there, from 17 September 1839 to 7 April 1842. It was not for the sake of politics that he went to Paris. Then as now, Paris was regarded as a leader of artistic fashion and the arbiter of sophistication in all things. This included fashion and sophistication in opera; where the Paris Opera led, others would try and follow. Even at the one-horse Opera in Würzburg, where Wagner had his first job, the repertoire was dominated by recent successes at the Paris Opera. The Würzburg season's crowning event was Meyerbeer's *Robert le Diable*, which had hit the jackpot in Paris just two years previously. At Magdeburg and Riga it was the same, and Wagner was led to believe that success in Paris would lead to success generally; and this universal success – the opportunity to reach out to all the opera houses in Germany and beyond, and escape being confined to just one locally – was the glittering prize which attracted him to Paris.

In practice Paris took on a different importance for him. What really mattered for Wagner in the end was its intelligentsia, its assemblages of idealists and revolutionaries and their germinating ideas. Part of the reason why Paris was such a beacon of enlightenment in the 1820s and 30s is that these were years of profound political reaction everywhere else in Europe. The French capital represented a centre of liberal intellectual thinking, represented by Saint-Simon, Fourier and Proudhon, and under the relatively tolerant rule of King Louis Philippe and his light touch censorship, it presented a safe haven for exiles. During these years there were in Paris a drove of theorists and reformist historians, ideologues and demagogues, essayists and poets who formed a thriving community of exiles. They came from Italy, Poland, Germany, Hungary, and above all from Russia, because (in the words of Isaiah Berlin) 'The Russian Government throughout the Nineteenth Century represented the greatest embodiment of obscurantism, barbarism, and oppression in Europe.'[47] The exiles spent their time writing, preaching, arguing and discussing, planning and plotting; and Karl Marx was to research crucial facts, form his theories and write the *Communist Manifesto* in Paris. It is important to grasp all this because of its influence on *The Ring* and its meaning for us.

---

47   Berlin, Isaiah, *Karl Marx*, London, 1939, 3rd ed., Oxford, 1963, p. 75.

It is necessary to revise the picture of Wagner's Parisian penury, his social exclusion and intellectual isolation, which he painted in his autobiography. When dictating it, the former Dresden revolutionary was refashioning his life story for his patron, King Ludwig of Bavaria. He had taken to heart Liszt's repeated warnings, which run constantly through the two volumes of their correspondence, that if he was to have any hope of an amnesty for the Dresden uprising, he must avoid politics, above all in his prose works. He must play the artist pure and simple. Just as he therefore chose to play down for the king his revolutionary activities in Dresden, so it also suited him to misremember and shrink the extent of his involvement with the revolutionary ferments of Paris. 1848 had been 'the year of revolutions' throughout Europe; and it was followed a year later by the Dresden uprising where Wagner played a leading and incriminating role. 1848 had also been the year of the *Communist Manifesto*, and Wagner had every reason to be economical with the truth to Ludwig about his association with a movement which still threatened the crowned heads of Europe, even though the real cataclysm, the communist revolutions of the twentieth century, was then as yet unimaginable.

The scattered references to Wagner which crop up in the contemporary accounts of Heinrich Heine, the poet, and Gustav Adolph Kietz, his sculptor friend, suggest that he did occupy a definite position in the Parisian arena, if a very marginal one. He was genuinely poor, far too badly off to be at the centre of things, and too busy, though not poor in the way that artisans and the proletariat of the times were poor. The destitution among the post-industrial working classes of Europe was frightful. In *Das Kapital* Karl Marx analysed in meticulous statistical detail the working conditions in England, not merely of adults but of factory children who might be required to work from six a.m. to nine p.m. for a pittance.[48] In Paris, poverty was such that 15% of babies were left abandoned. 'There were more than 150,000 children aged under fourteen working in the cotton

---

48   Marx, Karl, *Das Kapital*, tr. (as *Capital*) Eden and Cedar Paul, London, 1930, ch. 8.

industry, in terrible conditions. We hear of large numbers of thin, pale women walking barefoot through the sludge, and of a still larger number of young children, equally dirty and haggard, dressed in rags, which are thick with oil that has fallen on them while working.'[49] Later in the 1860s, when Wagner was back in Paris for *Tannhäuser*, it was the same. As explained when describing Marie d'Agoult's dowry for Cosima Wagner, 'The average wage for a Parisian who worked an 11 hour day was 3.81 francs. A skilled laundry girl who might carry on work until three o'clock in the morning was paid three francs and an unskilled one, or a flower girl, 2 francs. A blacksmith might get 7 francs a day, his wage having recently been cut because of the introduction of new machinery.'[50] A day's coal for the stove cost 0.75 francs, and a good shawl seven francs; and it took 30 francs a month to give a child basic education and training, even at a subsidised church school. Throughout his first sojourn in Paris, Wagner saw the depths of poverty and deprivation. He looked into the abyss and teetered on the brink, and was too busy trying to ensure he did not topple headlong to spend large amounts of time with intellectuals. He worked like a madman on musical hackwork to make ends meet, and on the creation of two cardinal works, *Rienzi* which was to bring him prestige, glamour and security, and *Der fliegende Holländer*, his first work to bring him immortal glory.

But if he was not in the centre of things, nor was he an outsider, and the picture in *Mein Leben* of a man isolated from the world by abject destitution was exaggerated. Along with his direct experience of urban poverty, one of the biggest influences towards Wagner's thinking in *Der Ring des Nibelungen* was not Marx or any foreign émigré, but a native Frenchman, Pierre-Joseph Proudhon (1809-65). Proudhon was a utopian socialist, the son of a brewer and a member of the French lower-to-middle classes. He had originally trained as an apprentice printer, a typesetter, but took a leading role in promoting the causes of

49   Steen, Michael, *Enchantress of the Nations: Pauline Viardot, Soprano, Muse and Lover*, Thriplow, 2007, pp. 110 et seq.

50   Ibid., pp. 292 and 513.

the labouring classes. In *The Ring* Wagner was to symbolise Proudhon's labourers as dwarves, Nibelungen, those who 'smelt and smith hard metals'. These labourers were the only classes which created wealth, but they were under-rewarded; after the French Revolution and the overthrow of the Bourbon monarchy and feudalism they felt cheated and bitterly disappointed. They discovered that they had not gained their freedom and a better life, but simply changed masters, substituting the magnates of capitalism for their feudal overlords. In terms of Wagner's early prose sketch for *The Ring*, 'the bondage of the Nibelungen had not been broken'. Alberich, as we shall see, represents the tyrannical exploitation perpetrated by big industrialists; and the Nibelungen were labourers who lived in economic slavery.

Wagner took over into *The Ring* two out of three tendencies which Proudhon identified in his *Qu'est que la propriété?* (*What is Property?*) as inimical to the brotherhood of man and social justice. The first was the tendency towards the accumulation of capital. The second was the selfish deployment of capital to exert economic control. The third was the tendency to combine and unite economic control with political authority, but this is not part of *The Ring*. Like Proudhon Wagner could observe how liberal safeguards against regulation and restrictive practices in fact gave unbridled licence to the industrialists, business magnates and bankers of the day. What should simply have protected constructive free enterprise instead protected the freedom of the industrial magnates and millionaire bankers to exploit the majority. It was unlimited freedom for 'the big guy to screw the little guy'. It was from Proudhon that Wagner first gained his conviction that this freedom amounted to no more than a form of legalised robbery.

Proudhon attempted not only a diagnosis of contemporary ills but a remedy, which was to get rid of competition and replace it with a mutualist, cooperative society. He could countenance limited private property, enough for people to maintain personal independence, but believed, and Wagner with him, that cooperation and 'mutualism' (which Karl Marx later developed into communism) would be the bettter way to organise society. Cooperation and mutualism would avoid the waste and loss both of jobs and machinery which was inevitable when businesses in competition failed, as must always happen in the natural selections of capitalism. Through cooperation and sensible planning, needs could be matched to supplies without waste. Poverty and unemployment would disappear, and people would cease to be forced into demeaning occupations which only resulted from an unplanned society. Cooperation and mutualism would moralise people and make them more civilised, because only injustice and the bitterest poverty had spoiled man's natural goodness and nobility.

Proudhon took the view that the rich were irremediable, and nor he did believe that the benevolent philosopher-king fantasised by his predecessors, the *encyclopédistes*, could never materialise, but Wagner was more optimistic because he was fortunate enough to encounter two kings with a number of the right qualities. At Dresden he had always maintained sufficient genuine respect and affection for the King of Saxony to conceive of him as the first and best of the republicans. In fact, this paradox was not one thought up by Wagner's but general currency of the times. Later he was to recognise King Ludwig as his best financial supporter, and kings always get a good press in his dramas. Kingly figures such as the Landgraf and Henry the Fowler are all sympathetic, and the idea of a patrician ruler who was fundamentally benign found expression in the Wotan of *Siegfrieds Tod*. In *Parsifal* his brotherhood of knights were supervised ideally by a noble king.

Wagner always held fast to the left-wing ideals which he first absorbed in Paris. Even in the final year of his life, he looked back on his staging of *Parsifal* at Bayreuth and reflected on the experience, with only a little wishful thinking, as the realisation and the triumph of an idealised communism, where everyone collaborated instinctively for the common good. Left-wing ideals helped give rise to the *Ring* just as they gave rise to Marxism. Marx just missed Wagner in Paris, arriving just after Wagner had left for Dresden; and by the time the Dresden uprising had failed and Wagner was back in Paris, Marx had been forced to leave and make his way to London.

It is probably not so much a matter of Marx influencing Wagner as two great minds moving in parallel directions after drawing similar conclusions from the facts. *Art and Revolution* was one of the three great essays which do express a consistent worldview as Wagner saw it in 1849 and 1850, and it reflects the influence of Proudhon and Feuerbach more than Marx. In it Wagner attacked the socio-political conditions of the industrial age; 'God is become industry, which keeps the poor Christian worker alive only until the celestial market conditions bring about the gracious necessity of releasing him into a better world.' In its essentials, Wagner's book characterised the ideology of the rich as immoral activity, exploitation, on the one hand, and vicious inertia on the other, two modes of being and behaviour that exactly foreshadow two characters in *The Ring*. Alberich and Fafner exactly personify these two modes. Writing of man's innate need for some kind of artistic expression or aesthetic value, Wagner refers to the 'alienation of labour'. Once the craftsman lost contact with the product of his labour and became a manual worker, all that remained to him was money, the money which his creations and his work generated. The money itself had no aesthetic value for him and brought no sense of fulfilment. He might just as well be a machine; and his creativity could never amount to more than the workings of a machine. The worker became a machine, and his work lost any sense of aesthetic value. 'He regards it as toil, as dismal and bitter drudgery. This is the lot of industry's slaves. Our modern factories present a wretched picture of utter human degradation: ceaseless exertion destructive of mind and body, devoid of love and enjoyment – often – too, almost devoid of purpose.' Wagner never changed. He was expressing the same views to von Schön, a factory owner about thirty years later when he was working on *Parsifal*, and doing it forcefully to his face.

Another phenomenon that was common both for Wagner and Marx was the fantastic, improbable figure of Mikhail Bakunin, and as he fills out Wagner's Siegfried, it is worth knowing something about him. He was a tremendous, colourful person, and a huge man. Originally commissioned in the Russian army, he had left to pursue philosophy at Moscow and Berlin, and rapidly became the prototype of the amoral, bomb-throwing Russian anarchist. He was as fearless as Siegfried, and almost as invincible. After the Dresden uprising had failed, he survived his arrest and several (commuted) death sentences. He would also survive extreme hardships in the Peter and Paul fortress at St Petersburg, hardships so frightful that even Bakunin was driven to begging his brother to smuggle in poison so that he could die. Instead he was exiled to Siberia, and escaped via Japan and the USA to make his way back to Western Europe. He always had a passion for the violent, the gigantic and the sublime, matched with a hatred of order, organisations and institutions, and a total opposition to personal property. Marx incidentally was at first on friendly terms with Bakunin, but then came to detest him for the very extravagance and incoherence which fascinated Wagner. Bakunin was also an orator of natural genius and in Paris and Dresden he roused massed audiences to a frenzy of enthusiasm for the oncoming revolutions. After the Paris Revolution of 1848 had been defeated, he moved to Dresden via Switzerland and became great friends with Wagner. Bakunin joined Wagner in spearheading the Dresden uprising, deploying his speeches, his heroic example and his mesmerising charisma, together with many other qualities which Wagner wanted to put into Siegfried. It is ironic that one of Wagner's prototypes for this blond Aryan hero was a Russian, a Slav. Poignantly, when *The Ring* was finally performed in 1876, Bakunin was not there. He was dead, having perished that very year, in Switzerland.

Politics, the politics of Proudhon, and the inspiration of Bakunin came together and fused in the allegory of *Siegfrieds Tod*, as Wagner's new opera was first called when he drafted it in 1848. Wagner also bound into his allegory elements of the religious philosophy of Ludwig Feuerbach, whose ideas were creating waves during the 1840s and 1850s. Feuerbach is not an easy read, even in translation; but essentially he argued that God or the gods have no independent existence. They are rather a product, a mirror-image of humanity, a humanity which has projected its own nature onto an imaginary divinity, and then worshipped it. In the process of this projection, man has alienated himself from himself and his own destiny; he has mistaken the natural and proper love of human beings for themselves for the infinite love of God. Feuerbach urged that human beings should take back what they had ascribed to the supernatural. Only thus could man's desire for happiness find fulfilment; only thus could human beings reach their true goals. Theology, therefore, was to be reconfigured as a mix of anthropology and psychology; politics and sociology were to replace religion; prayer, which was meaningless, would give way to effective work and common endeavour; and our own beautiful world would take the place of a fictitious heaven.

However there is an important and distinctive quality about Feuerbach, in that he was no advance version of Richard Dawkins, no negative Mephistopheles, and his object was not primarily destructive. Feuerbach's aim was positive, to raise up and glorify humanity. Religion was a benign force, which taught us important truths about ourselves, and was not to be disparaged. But now man had come of age; this was the Age of Man. Man is himself divine; he is godlike, and his institutions, such as friendships, family life and marriage, art and intellect and society at large, are themselves hallowed and sacred and should be celebrated in their own right.

Wagner incorporated a wealth of political and religious theory and life experience in two essays, *Art and Revolution* and 'The Nibelungen myth considered as a sketch for a drama', and afterwards in his Nibelungen drama itself. He wrote the second essay, 'The Nibelungen myth', in 1848, a year previous to the Dresden uprising.[51] In order to help appreciate how *The Ring* evolved from these beginnings and came to mean all that it does, its first fully formed, fully documented beginning, consisting of this 'Nibelung Myth' essay, now follows in full just as it stands (although I have broken up some of its very long paragraphs).

---

51   In *Prose Works*, tr. William Ashton Ellis, London, 1893-9, vii., p. 301 et seq.

From the womb of night and death was spawned a race that dwells in Nebelheim [sic], that is, in gloomy subterranean clefts and caverns: Nibelungen are they called; with restless nimbleness they burrow through the bowels of the earth, like worms in a dead body; they smelt and smith hard metals. The pure and noble Rhine-gold Alberich seized, divorcing it from the water's depth, and wrought therefrom with cunning art a ring that lent him the rulership of all his race, the Nibelungen: so he became their master, forced them to work for him alone, amassed the priceless Nibelungen Hoard, whose greatest treasure is the Tarnhelm, conferring power to take on any shape at will, a work which Alberich compelled his own brother Reigin (Mime = Eugel) to weld for him. Thus armoured Alberich gained mastery of the world and all that it contains.

The race of Giants, boastful, violent, ur-begotten, is troubled in its savage ease: their monstrous strength, their simple mother wit, are no longer a match for Alberich's crafty plans of conquest: alarmed they see the Nibelungen forging wondrous weapons that one day, in the hands of human heroes, will cause the Giants' downfall.

The Nibelungen are industry's slaves, created by the industrial revolution. The Giants represent the old rural and agricultural classes who worked the land and created its buildings, but who are now a fading minority as every new conurbation sucks in more country people and imprisons them in factories.

This strife is taken advantage of by the race of Gods, now waxing to supremacy. Wotan bargains with the Giants to build the gods a Burg from whence to rule the world in peace and order; their building finished, the Giants ask for the Nibelungen-hoard in payment. The utmost cunning of the Gods succeeds in trapping Alberich; he must ransom his life with the Hoard; the ring alone he strives to keep. The Gods, well knowing that in it resides the secret of all Alberich's power, extort from him the Ring as well; then he curses it; it shall be the ruin of all who possess it. Wotan delivers the Hoard to the Giants, but means to keep the Ring as a warrant of his sovereignty: the Giants defy him, and Wotan yields to the council of the three Fates (Norns), who warn him of the downfall of the Gods themselves.

Now the Giants have the Hoard and Ring safe kept by a monstrous Worm in the Gnita- (Neid-) Haide (the Grove of Grudge). Through the Ring the Nibelungs remain in thraldom, Alberich and all. But the Giants do not understand to use their might; their dullard minds are satisfied with having bound the Nibelungen. So the Worm lies on the Hoard since untold ages, in inert dreadfulness: before the lustre of the new race of Gods the Giants' race fades down and stiffens into impotence; wretched and tricksy, the Nibelungen go their way of fruitless labour. Alberich broods without cease on the means of gaining back the Ring.

In high emprise the Gods have planned the world, bound down the elements by prudent laws, and devoted themselves to most careful nurture of the Human race. Their strength stands over all. Yet the peace by which they have arrived at mastery does not rest on reconcilement; by violence and cunning was it wrought. The object of their higher ordering of the world is moral consciousness: but the wrong they fight attaches to themselves. From the depths of Nibelheim the conscience of their guilt cries out to them: for the bondage of the Nibelungen is not broken; merely the lordship has been reft from Alberich, and not for any higher end; but the soul, the freedom of the Nibelungen lies buried uselessly beneath the belly of an idle Worm: Alberich thus has justice in his plaints against the gods.

Wotan himself however cannot undo the wrong without committing yet another: only a free Will, independent of the Gods themselves, and able to assume and expiate itself the burden of all guilt, can loosen the spell; and in Man the Gods perceive the faculty of such free-will. In Man they therefore seek to plant their own divinity, to raise his strength so high that, in full knowledge of that strength, he may rid him of the Gods' protection, to do of his free will what his own mind inspires. So the Gods bring up Man for this high destiny, to be the canceller of their own guilt; and their aim would be attained even if in this human creation they should perforce annul themselves, that is part with their immediate influence through freedom of man's conscience. Stout human races, fruited by the seed divine, already flourish: in strife and fight they steel their strength; Wotan's Wish-maids shelter them as shield maids, as Walküren (Valkyries) lead the slain-in-fight to Walhall, where the heroes live again a glorious life of jousts in Wotan's company.

But not yet is the rightful hero born, in whom his self-reliant strength shall reach full consciousness, enabling him with the free-willed penalty of death before his eyes to call his boldest deed his own. In the race of the Wälsungen, this hero at last shall come to birth: a barren union is fertilised by Wotan through one of Holda's apples which she gives the wedded pair to eat: twins, Siegmund and Sieglinde (brother and sister), spring from the marriage. Siegmund takes a wife; Sieglinde weds a man (Hunding); but both their marriages prove sterile: to begin a genuine Wälsung line brother and sister wed each other. Hunding, Sieglinde's husband, learns of the crime, casts off his wife, and goes out to fight with Siegmund. Brünnhild the Walküre shields Siegmund counter to Wotan's commands, who had doomed him to fall in expiation of the crime; already Siegmund under Brünnhild's shield is drawing the sword for the death blow at Hunding – the sword that Wotan himself had once given him – when the God receives the blow upon his spear, which breaks the weapon in two pieces. Siegmund falls. Brünnhild is punished by Wotan for her disobedience: he strikes her from the role of the Walküren, and banishes her to a rock, where the divine virgin is to wed the man who finds and wakes her from the sleep in which he plunges her; she pleads for mercy, that Wotan will ring the rock with terrors of fire, and so ensure that none save the bravest of heroes may win her.

After long gestation the outcast Sieglinde gives birth in the forest to Siegfried (he who brings peace through victory): Reigin (Mime), Alberich's brother, upon hearing her cries, has issued from a cleft and aided her: after the travail Sieglinde dies, first telling Reigin of her fate and committing the babe to his care. Reigin picks up Siegfried, teaches him smithery, and brings him the pieces of the broken Sword, from which, under Mime's directions, Siegfried forges the sword Balmung. Then Mime prompts the lad to slay the Worm, in proof of his gratitude.

Siegfried first wishes to avenge his father's murder; he fares out, falls upon Hunding, and kills him: only thereafter does he execute the wish of Mime, attacks and slays the Giant-worm. His fingers burning from the Worm's hot blood, he puts them to his mouth to cool them; involuntarily he tastes the blood and understands at once the language of the wood birds singing around him. They praise Siegfried for his glorious deed, direct him to the Nibelungen-hoard in the cave of the Worm, and warn him against Mime who has merely used him as an instrument to gain the Hoard, and therefore seeks his life. Siegfried thereon slays Mime and takes the Ring and Tarnhelm from the Hoard: he hears the birds again, who counsel him to win the crown of women, Brünnhild. So Siegfried sets forth, reaches Brünnhild's mountain, pierces the billowing flames, and wakes her; in Siegfried she joyfully acclaims the highest hero of the Wälsung-stem, and gives herself to him: he marries her with Alberich's Ring which he places on her finger. When the longing spurs him to new deeds, she gives him lessons in her secret lore, warns him of the dangers of deceit and treachery; they swear each other vows, and Siegfried speeds forth.

A second hero-stem, sprung likewise from the gods, is that of the Gibichungen on the Rhine: there now bloom Gunther and Gudrun, his sister. Their mother, Grimhild, was once overpowered by Alberich, and bore him an unlawful son, Hagen. As the hopes and wishes of the gods repose on Siegfried, so Alberich sets his hope of gaining back the ring on his hero-offspring Hagen. Hagen is sallow, calm, and serious; his features are prematurely hardened, he looks older than he is. Already in his childhood Alberich had taught him mystic lore and knowledge of his father's fate, inciting him to struggle for the Ring: he is strong and masterful: yet to Alberich he seems not strong enough to slay the Giant-worm. Since Alberich has lost his power, he could not stop his brother Mime when the latter sought to gain the ring through Siegfried; but Hagen shall compass Siegfried's ruin and win the ring from his dead body. Towards Gunther and Gudrun, Hagen is reticent

– they fear him but prize his foresight and experience: the secret of some marvellous descent and that he is not his lawful brother, is known to Gunther; he calls him once an Elf-son.

Gunther is being apprised by Hagen that Brünnhild is the woman most worth desire, and excited to long for her possession, when Siegfried speeds along the Rhine to the seat of the Gibichungs. Gudrun, inflamed to love by the praises Hagen has showered on Siegfried, at his bidding welcomes Siegfried with a drink prepared by Hagen's art, of such potency that it makes Siegfried forget his adventure with Brünnhild and marriage to her. Siegfried desires Gudrun for wife: Gunther consents, on condition that he help him win Brünnhild. Siegfried agrees: they strike blood-brothership and swear each other oaths, from which Hagen holds aloof.

Siegfried and Gunther set out, and arrive at Brünnhild's rocky fastness: Gunther remains behind in the boat; Siegfried for the first and only time exerts his power as Ruler of the Nibelungen, by putting on the Tarnhelm and thereby taking Gunther's form and look; thus masked, he passes through the flames to Brünnhild. Already robbed by Siegfried of her maidhood, she has lost alike her superhuman strength, and all her runecraft has she made away to Siegfried – who does not use it; she is powerless as any mortal woman, and can only offer a vain resistance to the new, audacious wooer; he tears from her the ring – by which she is now to be wedded to Gunther – and forces her into the cavern, where he sleeps the night with her, though to her astonishment he lays his sword between them. On the morrow he brings her to the boat, where he lets the real Gunther take his place unnoticed by her side, and transports himself in a trice to the Gibichenburg through the power of the Tarnhelm. Gunther reaches his home along the Rhine, with Brünnhild following him in downcast silence: Siegfried, at Gudrun's side, and Hagen, receive the voyagers.

Brünnhild is aghast when she beholds Siegfried as Gudrun's husband; his cold civility to her amazes her, as he motions her back to Gunther, she recognises the Ring on his finger: she suspects the imposture played upon her, and demands the Ring, for it belongs not to him but to Gunther who received it from her: he refuses it. She bids Gunther claim the ring from Siegfried: Gunther is confused, and hesitates. Brünnhild: 'So it was Siegfried that had the Ring from her?' Siegfried, recognising the Ring: 'From no woman I had it; my right arm won it from the Giant-worm; through it am I the Nibelungen's Lord, and to none will I cede its might.' Hagen steps between them and asks Brünnhild if she is certain about the Ring? If it be hers, then Siegfried gained it by deceit, and it can belong to no one but her husband, Gunther. Brünnhild loudly denounces the trick played on her; the most dreadful thirst for vengeance upon Siegfried fills her. She cries to Gunther that he has been duped by Siegfried. 'Not to thee – to this man am I wed; he won my favour.'

Siegfried charges her with shamelessness: faithful had he been to his blood-brothership – his sword he laid between Brünnhild and himself: he calls on her to bear him witness. Purposely, and thinking only of his ruin, she will not understand him. The clansmen and Gudrun conjure Siegfried to clear himself of the accusation, if he can. Siegfried swears solemn oaths in confirmation of his word. Brünnhild taxes him with perjury: All the oaths he swore to her and Gunther has he broken: now he forswears himself, to lend corroboration to a lie. Everyone is in the utmost commotion. Siegfried calls Gunther to stop his wife from shamefully slandering her own and her husband's honour: he withdraws with Gudrun to the inner hall.

Gunther, in deepest shame and terrible dejection, has seated himself at the side, with hidden face: Brünnhild, racked by the horrors of an inner storm, is approached by Hagen. He offers himself as avenger of her honour: she mocks him, as powerless to cope with Siegfried: one look from his glittering eye, which shone upon her even through that mask, would scatter Hagen's courage. Hagen: He knows well Siegfried's awful strength, but she will tell him how he may be vanquished? So she who once had hallowed Siegfried, and armed him by mysterious spells against all wounding, now counsels Hagen to attack him from behind; for, knowing that the hero ne'er would turn his back upon the foe she had left it from the blessing.

Gunther must be made a party to the plot. They call upon him to avenge his honour; Brünnhild covers him with reproaches for his cowardice and trickery; Gunther admits his fault, and the necessity of ending his shame by Siegfried's death; but he shrinks from committing a breach of blood-brotherhood. Brünnhild bitterly taunts him: What crimes have not been wreaked on her? Hagen inflames him by the prospect of gaining the Nibelung's Ring, which Siegfried certainly will never part with until death. Gunther consents: Hagen proposes a hunt for the morrow, when Siegfried shall be set upon, and perhaps his murder even concealed from Gudrun, for Gunther was concerned for her sake: Brünnhild's lust for vengeance is sharpened by her jealousy of Gudrun. So Siegfried's murder is decided by the three. Siegfried and Gudrun, festively attired, appear in the hall, and bid them to the sacrificial rites and wedding ceremony. The conspirators feignedly obey: Siegfried and Gudrun rejoice at the show of peace restored.

Next morning Siegfried strays into a lonely gully by the Rhine in pursuit of quarry. Three mermaids dart out from the stream: they are the soothsaying daughters of the water's bed, whence Alberich once had snatched the gleaming Rhine-gold to smite from it the fateful Ring: the curse and the power of the Ring would be destroyed, were it regiven to the waters and thus resolved into its pure original element. The daughters hanker for the Ring, and beg it of Siegfried, who refuses it. (Guiltless, he has taken the guilt of the Gods upon him, and atones their wrong through his defiance, his self-dependence.) They prophesy evil and tell him of the curse attaching to the Ring: let him cast it in the river or he must die today.

Siegfried: 'Ye glib-tongued women shall not cheat me of my might: the curse and your threats I count not worth a hair. What my courage bids me is my being's law; and what I do of my own mind, so is it set for me to do: call you this curse or blessing, it I obey and strive not counter to my strength.'

The three Daughters: 'Wouldst thou outvie the Gods?'

Siegfried: 'Show me the chance of mastering the Gods, and I must work my main to vanquish them. I know three wiser women than you

three; they wot where once the Gods will strive in bitter fearing. Well
for the Gods, if they take heed that then I battle with them. So laugh I
at your threats: the ring stays mine, and thus I cast my life behind me.'
(He lifts a clod of earth and hurls it backwards over his head.)

The Daughters scoff at Siegfried, who weens himself as strong and
wise as he is blind and bond slave: 'Oaths has he broken, and knows it
not: A boon far higher than the Ring he's lost, and knows it not: runes
and spells were taught to him, and he's forgot them. Fare thee well,
Siegfried! A lordly wife we know; e'en today will she possess the Ring
when thou art slaughtered. To her! She will lend us better hearing.'

Siegfried, laughing, gazes after them as they move away singing.
He shouts: 'To Gudrun were I not true, one of you three had ensnared
me!' He hears his hunting comrades drawing nearer, and winds his
horn: the huntsman – Gunther and Hagen at their head – assemble
round Siegfried. The midday meal is eaten: Siegfried in the highest
spirits mocks at his own unfruitful chase: but water game had come
his way, for whose capture he was not equipped, alack! or he'd have
brought his comrades three wild water-birds that told him he must die
today. Hagen takes up the jest, as they drink: Does he really know the
song and the speech of birds, then? Gunther is sad and silent.

Siegfried seeks to enliven him, and sings him songs about his youth:
his adventure with Mime, his slaying of the Worm, and how he came to
understand bird-language. The train of recollection brings him back the
counsel of the birds to seek Brünnhild, who was fated for him; he tells
how he stormed the flaming rock and wakened Brünnhild. Remembrance
rises ever more distinct. Two ravens suddenly fly past his head.

Hagen interrupts him: 'What do these ravens tell thee?' Siegfried
springs to his feet. Hagen: '*I* rede them; they haste to herald thee
to Wotan.' He hurls his spear at Siegfried's back. Gunther, guessing
from Siegfried's tale the true connection of the inexplicable scene with
Brünnhild, and suddenly divining Siegfried's innocence, had thrown
himself on Hagen's arm to rescue Siegfried, but without being able to
stay the blow. Siegfried raises his shield, to crush Hagen with it; his
strength fails him, and he falls of a heap.

Hagen has departed; Gunther and the clansmen stand round Siegfried, in sympathetic awe; he lifts his shining eyes once more: 'Brünnhild, Brünnhild! Radiant child of Wotan! How dazzling bright I see thee nearing me! With the holy smile thou saddlest thy horse, that paces through the air dew-dripping: to me thou steerest its course. Happy me thou chosest for husband; now lead me to Walhall, that in honour of all heroes I may drink All-father's mead, pledged me by thee, thou shining wish-maid! Brünnhild, Brünnhild! Greeting!' He dies. The men uplift the corpse upon his shield, and solemnly bear it over the rocky heights, Gunther in front.

In the hall of the Gibichungs, whose forecourt extends at the back to the bank of the Rhine, the corpse is set down: Hagen has called out Gudrun; with strident tones he tells her that a savaged boar has gored her husband. Gudrun falls horrified on Siegfried's body: she rates her brother with the murder; Gunther points to Hagen: he was the savage boar, the murderer of Siegfried.

Hagen: so be it; an I have slain him whom no other dared to, what so was his is my fair booty. The ring is mine!'

Gunther confronts him: 'Shameless Elf-son, the ring is mine, assigned to me by Brünnhild. Ye all, ye heard it.'

Hagen and Gunther flight: Gunter falls. Hagen tries to wrench the Ring from the body – it lifts its hand aloft in menace; Hagen staggers back, aghast; Gudrun cries aloud in her sorrow; then Brünnhild enters solemnly:

'Cease your laments, your idle rage! Here stands his wife, whom ye all betrayed. My right I claim, for what must be is done!'

Gudrun: 'Ah wicked one! 'Twas thou that brought us ruin.'

Brünnhild: 'Poor soul, have peace! Wert but his wanton: his wife am I to whom he swore or e'er he saw thee.'

Gudrun: 'Woe's me! Accursed Hagen, what badest thou me, with the drink that filched her husband to me? For now I know that only through the drink did he forget Brünnhild.'

Brünnhild: 'O he was pure! Ne'er oaths were more loyally held, than by him. No, Hagen has not slain him; for Wotan has he marked him out, to whom I thus conduct him. And I, too, have atoned; pure and free am I: for he, the glorious one alone, overpowered me'.

She directs a pile of logs to be erected on the shore, to burn Siegfried's corpse to ashes: no horse, no vassal shall be sacrificed with him; she alone will give her body in his honour to the gods. First she takes possession of her heritage; the Tarnhelm shall be burned with her: the Ring she puts upon her finger. 'Thou froward hero, how thou heldest me in thrall! All my rune-lore I gave over to thee, a mortal, and so went widowed of my wisdom; thou usedst it not; thou trustedst in thyself alone; but now that thou must yield it up through death, my knowledge comes to me again, and this Ring's runes I apprehend. The primordial laws and runes I also apprehend now I know, the ancient lore of the Norns! Hear then, O mighty gods, your guilt is absolved: thank him, the hero, who took your guilt upon him! To mine own hand he gave it to fulfil his work: the Nibelung's thraldom shall be undone, the Ring no more shall bind them. Not Alberich shall receive it; no more shall he enslave you, but he himself shall be free as ye. For to you I make this Ring away, wise sisters of the water's deep; the fire that burns me, let it cleanse the evil toy; and ye shall melt it and keep it harmless, the Rhine-gold robbed from you to forge it to ill-fortune and bondage. One only shall rule, All-father thou in glory! As a pledge of thine eternal might, this man I bring thee: good welcome give him; he is worthy of it!'

Midst solemn chants, Brünnhild mounts the pyre to Siegfried's body. Gudrun, broken down with grief, remains bowed over the corpse of Gunther in the foreground. The flames meet across Brünnhild and Siegfried – suddenly a dazzling light is seen: above the margin of a leaden cloud the light streams up, showing Brünnhild armed as a Valkyrie on horse, leading Siegfried by the hand from hence.

At like time the waters of the Rhine invade the entrance to the hall; on their waves, the three Water-maids bear away the Ring and Helmet. Hagen dashes after them, to snatch the treasure, as if demented. The daughters seize and drag him with them to the deep.

Siegfrieds Tod prophesies that the salvation of Wotan at the end, which comes when Siegfried confirms the eternal power of the gods, will be bound up with the liberation of the Nibelungen from economic and literal slavery. Wagner identified the Nibelungen, the proletariat, as the only productive class. Like the French utopian socialists, he distinguished between productive and unproductive classes, and in *Siegfrieds Tod* the unproductive classes were abolished along with the old feudal system and its self-serving aristocrats, as they were later in *The Ring*; but neither Wagner's dramas nor his prose works suggested that the proletariat, the Nibelungen, might be fit to govern themselves. They are to be ruled by the hero and Wotan.

This optimistic conclusion of *Siegfrieds Tod* was partly a reflection of Wagner's own inveterate optimism, but it is not clear what Wagner expected to teach us by it. The old order would go, but what could best take its place, and how would it work? Unlike Proudhon with his mutualist utopia, Wagner offers no suggestions. He recognised this omission and wrote disingenuously, 'It is far from me to specify that new thing which should arise upon the ruins of a deceitful world as a new political order.' He had no idea what should come next, a common problem of revolutionaries. Thus *Götterdämmerung* does not provide a solution to those questions opened up by *Das Rheingold* which are purely political, and like Karl Marx he was vague to a degree about how he thought society would actually meet its own needs after the dictatorship of the proletariat had been established.[52] Wagner to his credit was in the end better than his word and did provide some guidance and suggestions. However they are not to be found in *The Ring*, but in *Die Meistersinger* and *Parsifal*.

Almost half of Wagner's essay 'The Nibelungen Myth' had been taken up with material which went into *Siegfrieds Tod*. *Siegfrieds Tod* begins at the point in the essay where Brünnhilde gives herself to Siegfried and he gives her Alberich's Ring; this happens just before she sends him off to new deeds of greatness. When the time came to

---

52   The absence of guidance from Marx had devastating consequences in Russia and for the world.

draft the poem, Wagner made some additions, a scene for the Norns at the beginning, and a visit by the other eight Valkyries to Brünnhilde's rock just before the Tarnhelmed Siegfried comes upon her; and also the dramatic scene between Alberich and Hagen at the beginning of Act II. The poem was completed in February 1849, before the Dresden uprising in May, but when he came to compose the music, three years later during Wagner's first Swiss exile, he faltered. After composing a few bars of the opening scene, he broke off, and there were deep reasons for this.

First, the failed revolutions throughout Europe in 1848-9 taught him hard lessons; and Wagner's original conception began to change to reflect his shifting principles. Wagner grew more, not less, preoccupied with politics. The Dresden failure had done nothing to lessen his desire to replace the old feudal, absolutist constitutions. If anything, the mutualist, nearly-Marxist ideas which he took from Paris and fortified with his reading at Dresden began to press their claims more urgently. It is even possible that his exile from Germany which prevented him from any form of political action may have led him to displace his creative energies into dramatic forms, his revolutionary dramas with their revolutionary verse, revolutionary ideas, and revolutionary music. However his personal world had changed since he wrote the text for *Siegfrieds Tod*. As a refugee, an exile in Switzerland, his optimism was beginning to change colour. No longer did Wagner believe in 'the king as best of the republicans', or in the final reconciliation of gods and heroes in *Siegfrieds Tod*, with the glorification of Wotan. He substituted a new conclusion where the gods perish. The altered politics also had a momentous impact on the religious allegory enfolded in *The Ring*, because the end of Wotan and the gods represented not only the abolition of monarchy, but the end of religion. Wotan's death represented the demise of the monarchy, and also of any immortal gods along with belief in them; they ceased to have any existence except as past history. This meant enormous changes to the messages of *The Ring* and what it means, which are best discussed in chapter on *The Ring*'s final instalment, *Götterdämmerung*.

These shifts of principle also represented a decisive modification of Wagner's beliefs and principles about revolution. There were two traditions prevalent in Europe about how revolution should be. The first tradition already mentioned was based on the belief shared by Proudhon that it was only the corrupt order inherited from the past that prevented men from living lives which expressed their natural virtue. The other more pessimistic tradition starts from a view that human beings are intrinsically corrupt, and that until and unless they are themselves reformed, any attempt to reform society is bound to fail. After the failure of the Dresden uprising, Wagner made an involuntary transformation from the first to the second tradition, and *Siegfrieds Tod* as the vehicle of his views had to transform in parallel.

However the most drastic change to his *Nibelungen* idea came about after the *coup d'état* on 1 December 1851 of Louis Napoleon. Wagner had previously looked forward to 1852 as another year of revolutions, and he now refused to acknowledge the new year, dating his letters 32 December 1851, and so on. Exactly a year later on 2 December 1852, Louis Napoleon became Emperor Napoleon III of the Third French Empire, and Wagner regarded him as an utter villain. Even much later in a letter to Liszt of 8 May 1859 he said, 'Do not let that villain L Napoleon touch my dear German confederacy.'[53] The coup had devastated Wagner's egalitarian hopes, and the devastation was soon rammed home by a brief and disillusioning visit to Paris shortly afterwards. The chapter on Tannhäuser explained the supreme irony that it was Wagner's villain who later gave Wagner his chance at the Paris Opera. By then he had long lost his 'Greek optimism', as he described it.

Already Wagner had recognised from a practical point of view that he needed a second Siegfried drama, *Der junge Siegfried*, or *Young Siegfried*. He could then make compelling theatre out of many events that are merely narrated in the *Siegfrieds Tod* and he could also reduce the length of its explanatory narrations, or

---

53   *The Correspondence of Wagner and Liszt*, tr. Francis Hueffer, New York, 1889, ii, p. 296.

so he thought. *Young Siegfried* could make a cheery Prelude and a counterfoil to the sombre drama that would follow. Wagner could weave into it a fairytale idea of the boy who knows no fear. This had recently caught his imagination as an idea for a separate drama, but he suddenly identified this boy with the young Siegfried. He could also bring the gods onstage, making more of them than their ghostly background presences allowed in *Siegfrieds Tod*, where they were brought on simply to be taken off again. He could better explain why they had to go if their failure and decline was presented onstage. Consequently Wagner drafted out plans for this lighter preliminary drama, but his imagination was still swirling with unfinished ideas. He sensed increasingly that in spite of all the new action presented onstage during *Der junge Siegfried*, even the two operas together would still leave too many things unexplained and incoherent. Yet more significantly, he had suddenly become engrossed in the gods and their fate. He admitted to a growing sympathy for the old order which would be swept away and to which he after all belonged, and instead of wishing its members under the guillotine, he was drawn increasingly towards them. He was particularly fascinated by Wotan, still at that stage called Wodan. The god seized Wagner's imagination far beyond the requirements of any socialist allegory, and Wotan filled out in significance until he became one of Wagner's most magnetic creations. Even as Wagner planned *Young Siegfried*, he was still disturbed by a sense that there was still much to explain which would be better acted out onstage, and in virtue of this and his developing ideas, he decided on the third opera or drama. This eventually became *Die Walküre*, where he presented the disobedience of Brünnhilde and Wotan's vain attempts to regain the Ring through Siegmund and Sieglinde.

Another impulse towards his extending the cycle backwards was that he wanted to create a vital drama from the earliest sections of 'The Nibelungen myth considered as a sketch for a drama' so as to explain industrial society and its ills. This would set a clearer context for Siegfried and explain the need for him and his new order so as to remedy those ills. Thus it was that as he worked back through the story to its first beginning, he recognised the need for another drama, and he cast it as his preliminary evening, *Das Rheingold*. This made four in all, representing the whole story as he now had it in mind; and photographs of the flyers promoting its first historic staging at Bayreuth actually show *The Ring* being advertised as a tetralogy.

The strange order in which *The Ring* text came into existence, from the end to the beginning, led to some non sequiturs and features in the plot that never sit easily with each other, as will become clearer as the study of *The Ring* goes ahead. Although the overall coherence of this vast production is astonishing, the dramas which grew out of *Siegfrieds Tod* eventually outgrew it, and the political philosophy of *Siegfrieds Tod* which looms even larger in *Das Rheingold* loses its impetus as the cycle goes forward, and the issues of capitalism and social injustice have faded before *The Ring* draws to its close. Then again Wagner's circumstances, his outlook and his philosophy continued to change while he created *The Ring*, and *The Ring* changed with them. Accordingly a certain 'disconnect' developed between the various elements of *The Ring* which left a structured void at the centre, but Wagner filled this out with the events and characters that lie at the heart of the Wagner Experience.

Opera and Drama (1851) was the essay where Wagner worked up his methods for *The Ring* as well as his formal ideals, and it confirms that he thought everything through to an astonishing degree. When he devised its novelties of words and music he knew exactly what he was doing. The long lines of verse he had used previously in his more 'operatic' operas, were no vehicle for his 'drama expressed in music', such as he now wanted to develop. Instead he employed '*Stabreim*', a terse alliterative verse-form which he claimed to derive from High German models but was really his own invention, and all the better for it. Among its features are two particular devices, similar or related vowel sounds (assonance) and repeated consonants (alliteration). The related vowels create a flowing quality and add bloom, and the consonants make the text sound out more starkly. Consider, for example, Alberich's fine line in invective against the Rhinemaidens:

> *Ihr schmählich schlaues,*
> *lüderlich schlechtes Gelichter!*[54]

When set to music and spat out by a good Alberich, these words sound splenetic, and are clearly audible anywhere in the theatre. *Stabreim* can also heighten characterisation, as in this case. The verse forms of *Stabreim* also had a free, irregular quality which would liberate Wagner from the foursquare rhythms which had previously dominated his work. It made possible the natural and uneven phrase lengths evident in these same lines of Alberich, all of which allow *The Ring* text a new suppleness and plasticity.

Wagner would also exploit for *The Ring* the new compositional possibilities he had adopted from Beethoven's symphonies. We have already seen how Wagner determined to incorporate into his new style of drama all that Beethoven had achieved (although, as we saw, Wagner's music is never really Beethovenian). His music would at least be like Beethoven's in this, that it would 'touch the listener's innermost being' as did no other art. With its particular poetry and its musical presentation, *The Ring* would arouse total sympathy, commitment, and involvement among those who experienced it. Wagner aimed at 'the emotionalising of the intellect', and he aimed too that 'in the presence of the dramatic art work, nothing should remain for the synthesising intellect to quest after'.[55] The music of *The Ring* which performed this emotionalising of the intellect in practice evolved through several distinctive styles. After composing Act II of *Siegfried*, the final title of his third opera in the cycle, he gave up *The Ring* for twelve years, and in the interval created the polyphonic *Tristan und Isolde* and the more contrapuntal *Die Meistersinger*, which he immodestly described as 'applied Bach'. This chronology is partly why he carried

---

54   of which I am rather taken with Frederick Jameson's weird old version (1900):
      Ye shameless, shifting,
      Worthless and infamous wantons!
55   *Opera and Drama*: *Prose Works*, ii, p. 208.

the more overtly contrapuntal style of *Die Meistersinger* into the last act of *Siegfried* and the whole of *Götterdämmerung*, as he renamed the final part of *The Ring*. In spite of its jerky assembly, *The Ring* ends up transcending any disunities. The story itself spins its own continuity, holding the action together, beginning with Alberich's original sin and running through the four evenings to a general redemption. The same personalities return through the cycle even though no one is present in every episode, and they stamp its progress with their consistent identities. There are continuities of ideas, and the four evenings are also held together by the music, its symphonic structure and its web of leitmotives. As we saw, individual leitmotives create symbolic associations, but Wagner had the genius to dispose them in designs of architectural cogency and build up musical structures of immense sweep and balance, sustaining the architectural strength of *The Ring* against all odds.

On 1 November 1853 Wagner entered into a sensational period of creative activity after five years of silence as a composer. The trigger seems to have been that he had fully absorbed the musical language which he created and taught himself, and that had taken hold of his creative imagination. A kettle may be heating up over a long period, but the point where it becomes hot enough to boil is an event, and Wagner now 'came to the boil' after a prolonged period of gestation. Perhaps this critical point had been the vision of Spezia the previous summer, as described in the chapter on the music. Alternatively it may have been some other decisive event which the vision symbolised, but it made no difference to the outcome. By autumn 1854, barely a year after beginning to compose *Das Rheingold*, he was well into Act III of *Die Walküre*.

Then came his introduction to the philosophy of Schopenhauer.[56] This was another of the special, decisive experiences of his life, with

---

56   Arthur Schopenhauer (1788-1860), German philosopher. His best-known book, *The World as Will and Representation* (*Die Welt als Wille und Vorstellung*, 1819), received little recognition for thirty years after publication.

as much impact as Wilhelmine Schröder-Devrient and his first wife Minna. He was introduced to *The World as Will and Representation* by the poet Georg Herwegh, who had played a leading role in the Paris revolution of 1848 and also became an exile in Switzerland after his revolution had failed. It was just as Wagner wrote to Liszt (in a letter mentioned in the context of *Der fliegende Holländer*), 'Schopenhauer's philosophy had come into my solitude like a gift from heaven;' and it was to be as momentous and mind-altering for him as his own creations were to be for Bruckner and C.S. Lewis.

A massive simplification is inevitable in trying to expound Schopenhauer, but essentially he believed that the universe was godless but that it was driven by 'the will', a blind, tumultuous, metaphysical force which galvanised and energised everything. The will is universal, eternal and unchanging. It keeps the planets and galaxies circling on their way; it energises chemical reactions, and drives all living things, including human beings. It may help to bear in mind that the idea of life's blind urge to perpetuate itself soon gained a form of endorsement from Charles Darwin. Darwin's theory of evolution fitted Schopenhauer's ideas of the will, even though Darwin's theory was not published until 1859, later than almost all of Schopenhauer's writings. Something like the will is present in the blind instinct which maintains a species in dangerous and destructive circumstances, and sacrifices happiness and the lives of individuals to preserve and evolve the species. The theory of evolution squared with Schopenhauer's pessimistic outlook because the 'survival of the fittest' required that the less fit would struggle and die in their millions, often in agonising circumstances. In the case of the human species Schopenhauer likewise considered that life for the majority was unmitigated struggle and suffering. The imperious force of the will impels human beings to keep going, replicate and adapt, to plan and strive, whether against environment, circumstances, personal limitations, or other intrusive, predatory agents, both human individuals and human organisations. The ideas of Feuerbach which envisaged mankind as coming to full and wonderful fruition after religion was toppled now seemed to

Wagner shallow and worthless, and Feuerbach appeared to him a self-deluding charlatan.

As the realm dominated by the will is the only realm, there is almost no history and virtually no progress in human affairs, because the blind, mindless, strugglesome urges created in human beings by the universal will are always the same. For individuals the result is a life of endless metaphorical burnt fingers from trying to do things and being frustrated in the attempt; and of bigger sufferings. There is only one way to mitigate them and render life less painful, and that is to stop wanting things, to stop hoping and trying for anything. This 'pacification of the will' can only be achieved by a tremendous effort *of* the will, the individual will which partakes of the universal will. The most useful task which anyone can perform is to use his individual will to pacify and annul itself, in the hope of reaching a permanent state of resignation and a kind of determined mental entropy. In Schopenhauer's scheme an existence without ambitions, hopes or expectations offers the best hope of minimising the pain of life. (It is also a life bereft of much joy, but any joys, according to his bleak philosophy, are quite insignificant.) Part of the remedy for the pain of existence was for everyone to stop having children, so as to cease producing more victims to live life and endure the same pain. The imperious impulses of lust and romantic passion were nothing but snares by which the will impelled human beings to create more human beings, and as contraception was barely invented, the only thing to do was to include love and lust as first among the things which everyone should abolish while pacifying the will. The condition of all things which live and have to endure life is so piteous that it calls for the utmost compassion for them all. Compassion becomes the supreme moral imperative, and to create more suffering human beings becomes an act utterly devoid of compassion.

Wagner came rapidly to see Schopenhauer's writings as the missing link in his life, the revelation which changed it, justified it, and irradiated it. As explained in the earlier chapters, Wagner was himself driven by a mighty ego, an immense will, and the magnitude of aims and his concomitant difficulties in achieving them brought him burnt fingers and agonosing disappointments in proportion. Schopenhauer's great work seemed to supply an explanation of everything, but particularly the reversals and frustrations he experienced. Schopenhauer's ideas affected his life, his work and his identity. They conferred a structure upon the divisions of the world and his own disunities, and they brought him an order and an ordering effect not unlike the one I have described as brought to many people by music itself. Schopenhauer's very making sense of them was a soothing balm for the aching tensions within him, and the sense that he now at least understood what was wrong was liberating, a transforming release that seemed wonderful. In consequence there was no other living individual to whom Wagner felt he owed more. He never ceased to express his unstinting gratitude, declaring again and again, 'I can never thank him enough.'

Wagner's conversion to Schopenhauer had other consequences. If people themselves needed to change fundamentally for any revolution to be a success, but the mass of them mostly would and could not change owing to the unalterable workings of the will within them, then no revolution could ever succeed. Progress in human affairs became generally improbable. Schopenhauer explained why there could be no progress or reform, but then this cast a strange and disquieting light on *The Ring* as a recommendation and an allegory for social progress and political change. After Schopenhauer Wagner came in some compartments of his mind to believe that the way towards a new political and economic freedom led nowhere, and never could; but what in that case was he to do with his great drama? It enjoined precisely the processes of onward change which Schopenhauer's tenets disallowed, but there it was, already half finished. Schopenhauer came to the rescue, and provided Wagner with an alternative view of *The Ring*, a re-imagining of it. In virtue of Schopenhauer, Wagner was able to unearth within his great work a second set of values and ideas that reflected the philosophy of Schopenhauer instead of conflicting with it. For example, Schopenhauer enabled Wagner to discern in Wotan a mighty egoist who becomes determined to pacify his own will.

Indeed Wagner now saw Schopenhauer as present in *The Ring* and his other works all along. He told August Röckel that Schopenhauer had enabled him both to understand himself properly and to perceive what his work was really about.

In this 'new' Schopenhauerian frame of reference, there would be a need for acceptance, wisdom, and the compassion, and people could best learn it from Schopenhauer, and from Schopenhauer as expressed by Wagner in his own reimagined works. In this altered outlook, what anyone could best aim to acquire from his dramas was something personal, an altered state of mind, and this was another form of personal salvation, a theme long dear to Wagner's heart. There will be more about Schopenhauer when we reach *Götterdämmerung*, *Tristan* and *Die Meistersinger*. However the turmoil that Schopenhauer created did dissipate his drive to compose *The Ring*, and the chapter on *Tristan und Isolde* takes up the story of how this turmoil led to the creation of this quite different work. But as far as *The Ring* was concerned, Schopenhauer led to the long gap of twelve years between the composing of Act II and Act III of *Siegfried*. By then the world had changed even further. King Ludwig had rescued him; Minna was dead; he had seen *Tristan* and *Die Meistersinger* given wonderful premieres at Munich; and he was living happily with Cosima at Tribschen, again in Switzerland. His perspective on *The Ring* and what it meant had also developed, and the place to explain this is at the end of the chapter on *Götterdämmerung*.

Such a complicated and enthralling creation as *The Ring* has been a happy hunting ground for analysts of many kinds, and Alfred Lorenz, George Bernard Shaw, Robert Donington, and Jean Shinoda Bolen are only three among many who have written striking commentaries, all different and all true. The commentary by Jean Shinoda Bolen, a self-styled Jungian, was already mentioned in the Introduction,[57] and it seems particularly interesting as it focuses on *The Ring* as a guide for personal development. However her negative view of the will to power

57   Bolen, Jean Shinoda, *Ring of Power: The Abandoned Child, the Authoritarian Father, and the Disempowered Feminine*, New York, 1992.

is not Jungian, and in *The Ring* as in life, everyone needs some will to power. For a balanced and effective personality the will to power is as essential as the will to love. The challenge, as *The Ring* makes clear, is about finding the balance.

Some of what Jean Shinoda Bolen wrote at her most perceptive seems an effective way to draw this chapter to a close. 'Wagner had created a four opera dramatic series whose situations, characters, and words were mythic, with the power of myth to resound in the deepest layers of our psyches ... When a connection is made between a story that captivates us and real life, the truth we perceive in it about ourselves, our families, and society can be transformative ... The evocative power of music and myth to touch deep chords of personal meaning explains why individuals are enthralled by *The Ring of the Nibelung*. When this is experienced, the soul is moved. When psychologic understanding is added the mind also becomes involved.' I heartily agree, except that this is true of all Wagner and not only *The Ring*.

As Catherine Clément said, the end of *The Ring* is never in fact the end. As the close of a live performance of *The Ring* 'we go out into the night with a mind full of figures who are not ourselves but have inhabited our lives during the four days of *The Ring* cycle.'[58] In a sense they never leave. They stay with us for ever, 'acting like yeast in activating the deeper levels of the psyche, raising issues, memories and feelings into consciousness ... The discovery ... may in turn help us know who we are and what is truly important to us.' We can now go on to see how this works out in detail.

---

58   Clément, Catherine, *Opera or the Undoing of Women*, tr. Betsy Wing, London, 1989, p. 156.

FOURTEEN

DAS RHEINGOLD

Das Rheingold has an immediacy and brilliance that sets it apart from anything else by Wagner. *Das Rheingold* draws us wide-eyed into a world of Homeric brightness. As we saw in the chapter on the music, the Prelude is about the origins of awareness and the coalescence of consciousness. It is also about something more specific, the depths of the Rhine, and it conjures up a setting for the three beautiful Rhinemaidens swimming down near the bedrock. It is there that Alberich, an ugly dwarf, soon comes upon them. He is thrilled and fascinated by them, but he is bitterly and brutally rejected by them to the extent of turning on them and cursing forever the love which can never be his. He seizes in its stead the Rhinegold which will bring him mastery of the world. In one sense his action is the rape of nature out of selfishness and greed, but in another he has paid for it, and paid a terrible price.

This opening scene has the appearance of purest myth, shimmering with primordial symbols and truths that we half-knew before we were born; but amazingly it is Wagner's own invention. Nothing could seem more the stuff of myth than the Rhinemaidens and the Rhinegold glinting in the depths, but there is nothing about them in any of the sources, nor about the curse on love which turns Alberich into a monster. These things are pure Wagner, and it is a measure of his insight into myth and the psyche that they speak to the imagination as vividly as any myth or legend from long ago.

The opening scene does other important things. It provides *The Ring* with its central conflict and establishes its crucial tension of opposites, the balance between love and power. Through the Rhinemaidens this becomes an either-or choice for Alberich, and he sacrifices love for power. As we shall see, Wotan, in some ways the central character of *The Ring*, makes the same mistake, bartering away Freia, the goddess of youthful beauty and love, to pay for Valhalla, his fortress and the symbol of his power. As he later confides to his daughter, Brünnhilde, in *Die Walküre*,

> *When Young Love's joys had first disappeared*
> *I longed in its place for power.*
> *Pursued by all kind of unruly longings*
> *I won for myself the World …*
> *But I would not give up love's impulse,*
> *In my power I craved its enchantment.*

The opening scene presents the events that set the whole cycle in motion and hold it together. It is a 'downfall' story, with Alberich's rape of nature and his sacrifice of love for the sake of power as *The Ring*'s original sin, its 'Big Bang' in much the same way as Adam and Eve's tasting of forbidden fruit is the Big Bang for the entire Bible. The curse on love and creation of the Ring is the first fatal splice among the threads which the Norns weave into the rope of destiny. It becomes the rope which binds together everything that follows, the critical event that compels the different characters to try and make good the damage. From this event flowed all the currents of history that course through *The Ring*, opening up so many byways and parentheses, some far flung, that *The Ring* could have ended up as fragmentary as its sources if Wagner had not possessed the intellect and willpower to draw them into a unity. This unity was eventually threatened by *Götterdämmerung*, the very work from which the other dramas evolved backwards, because its action and style are so different from the other three; but in the end the unity remained unbroken.

There is a corresponding unity among the archetypes of *The Ring*, which likewise bind it together. Certain other aspects are less tightly knit, such as its more intellectual ideas. These are both arresting and convincing individually, but they are too many and too varied to form a complete, unitary system. Where it does possess an additional and compelling unity is in the music, and this is extraordinary because the weary, disillusioned composer who completed its final page on 23 November 1874 was a different man from the young firebrand who noted down his first musical ideas in November 1848, and his journey through the intervening years had been improbable and fractured beyond belief.

The last chapter took us into another vital aspect of *Das Rheingold*, its allegory of protest against capitalist society. It was the music which enabled Wagner to make the allegory so compelling and Alberich so real. It is the music that infiltrates the imagination with the conviction that Wagner's slant on capitalism was right. It is the music which gives such a fearsome reality to his picture of post-industrial slave-mines worked by the Nibelungen. In Covent Garden's programme for its *Ring* cycles of 2012, Michael Portillo described *Das Rheingold* as crudely Marxist, and three sentences later he disparaged 'the general crudeness of Wagner's satire in *Das Rheingold*' as a given and accepted fact.[59] It is not clear that there is anything crude about the allegory of *Das Rheingold*, nor about Marxism, but perhaps it tells some truths which dedicated capitalists find inconvenient. Karl Marx in *Das Kapital* gave accurate accounts of British children at their machines, rolling metal all day in temperatures of 80-90 degrees Fahrenheit. Marx provides scholarly chapter and verse and leaves no doubt about the truth and accuracy of his 'satanic' mills, but Wagner actually takes us into Nibelheim, right down among them. Through his music, he brings us face to face with the stifling heat, the sulphurous fumes, the suffocation, and the strange red glare that brings no light. We may never have been down the mineshafts and foundries, but Wagner makes it as if we had; and by the time we leave Nibelheim, he fills us

---

59   Portillo, Michael, 'Politics in Das Rheingold', in *Der Ring des Nibelungen*, programme, the Royal Opera House, Covent Garden, 2012, p. 26.

with an uneasy conviction that after the Alberichs of the world have done their worst, there will indeed be forced labour where there was once free enterprise, and toxic, man-made death-waters where there had once been pristine rivers. In his music's vision of the future it is inevitable that where there had been wide grasslands there will now be slag-heaps; where there had been clear winds from the Atlantic, there will now be smog and suffocation. Without Wagner's music, his allegory of capitalism might never have swayed minds as it did. It still does, anything but crude, and perhaps it still should, now more than ever.

The status of *Das Rheingold* as an anti-capitalist polemic was famously clarified and expounded by George Bernard Shaw in *The Perfect Wagnerite*.[60] His book is such a lucid and penetrating account of *The Ring* and of its take on capitalism, at least as Proudhon and his 'mutualists' visualised it, that I cannot do better than make use of it here. George Bernard Shaw (1856-1950) deserves a word, in fact several, because he was himself a major, larger than life figure. Originally from Dublin, he emerged as a formidable British intellectual from the 1890s and 1900s onwards. He became a leading music and literary critic, an original and didactic playwright as well as a passionate socialist, vigorously opposed to the exploitation of the working classes and women. He wrote brochures and speeches for the Fabian Society, and he became a persuasive orator on behalf of its causes, such as social justice and socialism, equal rights and status for women, state ownership of agriculture and industry, and various lifestyle issues. He was a co-founder of the London School of Economics, and his writings and plays, which often make good theatre, still tell us much of value for today. No commentator has better related *Das Rheingold* to capitalism and no one has told its story with greater pith and vigour. I have based what follows on his exposition, adding to it considerably and supplying musical examples, as well as amending at those rare occasions when Shaw was wrong about his facts.

---

60   Shaw, George Bernard, *The Perfect Wagnerite* (originally published 1898), Leipzig, 1913.

Let us assume for a moment [says Shaw] that you are a young and good-looking woman. Try to imagine yourself in that character at Klondike five years ago. The place is teeming with gold. If you are content to leave the gold alone, as the wise leave flowers without plucking them, enjoying with perfect naiveté its colour and glitter and preciousness, no human being will ever be the worse for your knowledge of it; and while you remain in that frame of mind, the golden age will endure.

Now suppose a man comes along; a man who has no sense of the golden age, nor any power of living in the present: a man with common desires, cupidities, ambitions, just like most of the men you know. Suppose you reveal to that man that if he will only pluck this gold up and turn it into money, millions of men, driven by the invisible whip of hunger, will toil underground and overground night and day to pile up more and more gold for him until he is master of the world! You will find that the prospect will not appeal to him as much as you might imagine, because it involves some distasteful trouble to himself to start with, and because there is something else within his reach involving no distasteful toil, which he desires more passionately; and that is yourself. So long as he is preoccupied with love of you, the gold and all that it implies will escape him; you will soften and civilise him into a benign mentality; the Golden age will endure. Not until he forswears love will he stretch out his hand to the gold, and found the Plutonic empire for himself. But the choice between love and gold may not rest altogether with him. He may be an ugly, ungracious, unamiable person, whose affections may seem merely ludicrous and despicable to you. You may repulse him, and most bitterly humiliate and disappoint him. What is left to him then but to curse the love he can never win, and turn remorselessly to the gold? With that, he will make short work of your golden age, and leave you lamenting its lost thoughtlessness and sweetness.

Here then is the subject of the first scene of *Das Rheingold*. As you sit waiting for the curtain to rise, you catch the booming sound of a mighty river. As the Prelude goes ahead, the music becomes plainer, brighter, clearer: you catch the green light and the flights of bubbles.

Most of the Prelude and the first scene have the running figuration of water flowing and eddying so ceaselessly that the imagination is filled with the swirl of the great river. When the curtain goes up, as Shaw says, you see what you heard: the depths of a river but complete now with three beautiful Rhinemaidens.

They sing music with a lovely lazy lilt,

Fig. 14.1 Woglinde: '*Weia! Wala! Woge, du Welle, walle zur Wiege*'

and give voice to what has been described as the world lullaby, timeless and often wordless.

> It is the golden age: and the attraction of this spot for the Rhinemaidens is the Rhinegold which they value in an entirely uncommercial way, simply for its beauty and splendour.

They love it innocently but they are also its guardians. The first two notes of their theme create an indelible impression, because they are the first accented departure from the chord of E flat, and Wagner deploys them throughout *The Ring*, first for an ecstasy that borders on pain but increasingly for poignancy and pain itself.

> Presently there comes along a poor devil of a dwarf, blundering along the slippery rocks of the river bed, a creature with energy enough to make him strong of body and fierce of passion, but too stupid to see that his own welfare can only be encompassed as part of the welfare of the world, too full of brute force not to grab vigorously at his own gain. Such dwarves are quite common in London. He comes in search of what he lacks in himself, beauty, lightness of heart, imagination, music. The Rhinemaidens represent all these to him, and they fascinate him with their loveliness. They fill him with hope and longing, and he naively asks if he can play with them. He never considers that he has nothing to

offer that they could possibly desire, being incapable of seeing anything from anyone else's point of view. He asks to caress them and effectively offers himself as a sweetheart. But they are thoughtless, elemental, and unthinkingly cruel. The fact that the poor dwarf is repulsive to their sense of physical beauty and their romantic conceptions, that he is ugly and awkward, greedy and ridiculous, disposes for them of his claim to live and love. They mock him atrociously for his ugliness, each of them pretends to fall in love and eggs him on before slipping away, making game of the poor wretch until he is beside himself with mortification and rage.

He is just shaking his fist at them in defeat, an action which tells the whole story of Eros denied, of deprivation turning into violence against the lovely beings that symbolise that deprivation. At that moment the water begins to glitter in the sun, and the gold which had hitherto gone unnoticed begins to glow in the water. Its theme sounds softly on the horn at first,

Fig. 14.2 'The Rhinegold' (solo horn)

but then soon the first trumpet plays it with a laser-like brilliance in a C major that shines out though the waves of sound, reflecting the sunlight, but with a glory of its own. Here is an example of Wagner's perfect artistic judgment; he originally sketched this as C major triads for three trumpets, but then decided on a single line for solo trumpet solo, and the effect is more brilliant and piercing, and does not clutter up the Rhinemaidens' when they now start to sing in triads. The gold sits high on a pinnacle of rock, near the surface, and the three Rhinemaidens sing to it a hymn of ecstasy.

Fig. 14.3 The Rhinemaidens' 'Hymn to the Gold'

By creating such splendour at the outset Wagner throws into high relief the whole tragic action of the remainder of *The Ring*. Alberich is half-blinded by the sight and asks about it. When he hears, he pretends to be unimpressed, telling them that it is not much good to him. His disparagement leads Wellgunde to tell him of its wonders, that anyone who forged the Rhinegold into a ring would gain power beyond measure and the inheritance of the world. Flosshilde responds with a moment of disquiet that this information might lead Alberich to come after the gold which it is their job to guard, but they collectively reassure themselves by recalling the oracle: only who forswears love can seize the gold and then forge from it the Ring which brings world mastery.

Fig. 14.4 'Renunciation of Love'

The Rhinemaidens take the view that they need not fear of the dwarf, because he is convulsed with passion, but they have revealed to him their dark, runic prediction, and they misjudge him and overlook the effect of their cruelty.

They have poisoned his passion by their mockery and denial; and he now knows that life will give him nothing that he cannot wrest from it by the Plutonic power. It is just as if some poor, rough, vulgar, coarse fellow were to offer to take his part in aristocratic society, and be snubbed into the knowledge that only as a millionaire could he ever hope to bring that society to its feet, and buy himself a beautiful and refined wife.

His choice is virtually 'forced on him. He will forswear love as thousands of us forswear it every day,' and forge the Ring, and here for the first time too we hear the theme of 'the Ring' (the theme which Wagner himself described as the 'Will to Power').

Fig. 14.5 'The Ring' or 'Will to Power' (clarinets, bass clarinet, bassoons)

He pronounces the curse and in a moment the gold is in his grasp, and he disappears into the depths leaving the Rhinemaidens in sudden darkness vainly crying 'Stop thief',

whilst the river seems both to swirl up and yet to plunge downwards and sink from us.

As the orchestra meditates on Alberich's act of renunciation, the cloudy blackness begins slowly to clear and the repetitions of the 'Ring' theme brighten over harmonies that are ever more luminous. The clouds lighten and disperse, revealing a lofty mountain landscape with a glorious fortress set in the distant heavens. The theme of the 'Will to Power' broadens and expands into the music symbolising Valhalla, played by brass combinations centred on the Wagner tubas, while the pulse changes from 4/4 to 3/4.

Fig. 14.6 'Valhalla'

It appears and develops both as a complete theme and in chameleon elaborations of the first bar and the second bar of the motive; and at this first appearance there are two important extensions which will pursue independent lives of their own;

Fig. 14.7 (brass choir)

and

Fig. 14.8 (brass choir)

And now [as Shaw asks rhetorically] what forces are there in the world to resist Alberich, our dwarf, in his new character of sworn plutocrat? He is soon at work wielding the power of the gold. For his gain, hordes of his fellow creatures are thenceforth condemned to slave miserably, underground and overground, lashed to their work by the invisible whip of starvation. They never see him, any more than the victims of our dangerous trades ever see the shareholders whose power is nevertheless everywhere, driving them to destruction.

It is the nature of capitalism to create unprecedented wealth but in ways that place it far beyond the hopes of most members of society. Far from any there being any evidence of trickle-down benefits to all as anticipated by romantic capitalists, history shows how wealth polarises. The rich become richer and richer and the poor become poorer and poorer, just as Marx said.

> The very wealth the poor create with their labour becomes an additional force to impoverish them; for as fast as they make it, it slips from their hands into the hands of their master, and makes him mightier than ever. You can see the process for yourself in every civilised country today, where millions of people toil in want and disease to heap up more wealth for our Alberichs, laying up nothing for themselves except sometimes horrible, agonising disease and the certainty of premature death. All this part of the story is frightfully real, frightfully present, frightfully modern; and its effects on our social life is so ghastly and ruinous that we no longer know enough of happiness to be discomposed by it. It is only the poet, Wagner, with his vision of what life might be, to whom these things are endurable. If we were a race of poets we should make an end of the abuse before the end of this miserable century. [Shaw was writing of the nineteenth century, but *plus ça change*.] Being a race of moral dwarfs instead, we think them highly respectable, comfortable and proper, and allow them to breed and multiply their evil in all directions. If there were no higher power in the world to work against Alberich, the end of it would be utter destruction.

Such a force there is, however (according to Shaw at least, and to Wagner); and everything that follows suggests that Shaw would not have accepted Lord Acton's gloomy aphorism to the effect that all power corrupts and absolute power corrupts absolutely. Wagner still in some moods remained a 'perfectibilian', a person who believes in the perfectibility of man. Wagner also somehow clung to a belief in a benign ruling class, characterised for him by King Frederick Augustus

II of Saxony and the Grand Duke of Weimar, and even by Queen Victoria. They were represented in *The Ring* by the gods, although the gods also represent religion.

> From the bed of the river we rise into cloudy regions, and finally come out into the clear in a meadow, where Wotan, the god of gods, and his consort Fricka lie sleeping;

and the Valhalla theme with its solemn grandeur represents aspects of Wotan as its overlord. Wotan has lost one eye. (Shaw incidentally is wrong here; his missing eye was not as Shaw wrote, the price of his alliance with Fricka; he gave it up at the world ash in exchange for wisdom, sacrificing half his outward sight to achieve an inner vision. As Wotan soon tells us, it was his *other* eye that he actually wagered in surety for Fricka, though it is not clear what this means.)

> Fricka in return has brought to him as her dowry all the powers of law. The meadow where they stand is on the brink of a ravine beyond which, towering on distant heights, stands Valhalla. Wotan has not yet seen this castle except in his dreams: two giants have just built it for him whilst he slept; and the reality is before him for the first time when Fricka wakes him.
>
> In that majestic burg he is to rule with her and through her over the humble giants, who have eyes to gape at the glorious castles their own hands have built from his design, but no brains to design castles for themselves, or to comprehend divinity. As a god he is to be great, secure, and mighty; but Godhead, if it is to live with law, must have no weaknesses, no respect for persons. All such sweet littlenesses must be left to the humble and stupid giants to make their toil sweet to them; and the god must, after all, pay for Olympian power the same price the dwarf has paid for Plutonic power.
>
> Wotan has forgotten this in his dreams of greatness. Not so Fricka. What she is thinking of is this price Wotan has consented to pay, in token whereof he has promised this day to hand over to the giants

Fricka's sister, Freia, goddess of youth and love.

Fig. 14.9 'Freia' (a)

Fig. 14.10 'Freia' (b)

Of these themes, (b) is expanded later, in *Die Walküre*, to become the great central love motive of *The Ring*.

Fig. 14.11 'Love' motive (solo and divisi cellos)

The giants are rough, slab-like creatures, mighty artisans.

Fig. 14.12 'The Giants' (trombones, double basses and tympani)

When Fricka reproaches Wotan with having selfishly forgotten his contract, she finds that 'he, like herself, is not prepared to go through with his bargain, and that he is trusting to another great world force, the Lie, to help him to trick the giants out of their just reward'. This force is not part of Wotan's natural endowment but is personified in Loge, one of Wagner's most individual creations. He is the god of intellect, argument, imagination, illusion and reason, the god of fire and lies.

Fig. 14.13 'Loge' (a)

Fig. 14.14 'Loge' (b) (violins 1 and 2)

On the other hand, Loge never deceives himself. The advice that he gives is generally helpful, but generally goes unheeded. As Wotan understands it, Loge has promised to deliver him from his contract with the giants, Fasolt and Fafner, and to find them an alternative for Freia; but now he has not turned up to fulfil his undertaking; and as Fricka bitterly points out, it is only to be expected of such a slippery character.

The giants come soon enough and Freia flies to Wotan for protection against them, calling on Donner and Froh, the gods of thunder and the rainbow for their help.

The purposes of the giants are quite honest; and they have no doubt of the god's good faith. There stands their part of the contract fulfilled, stone on stone, port and pinnacle all faithfully finished from Wotan's design by their mighty labour. They have come undoubtingly for their agreed wage. Then there happens what is to them an incredible, inconceivable thing. Wotan refuses it. There are no moments in life more tragic than those in which ordinary people, trusting affairs to their betters, and envisaging them as worthy of trust, even to the extent of saving them from life's everyday demands, first discover that they are corrupt, greedy, unjust and treacherous. The shock drives a ray of prophetic light into one giant's mind and gives him a momentary eloquence. In that moment he rises above himself and warns the Son of Light that all his power and eminence of priesthood, godhood and kingship must stand or fall with his incorruptibility.

But Wotan plays the politician. He performs a politician's trick of blaming his opponents for the very deviousness, the deliberate misreading of intentions which he is performing himself. Of course he did not expect anyone to believe in his promises; they were just a figure of speech, how sly and dishonest of anyone take him at his word. Even so, he defends the giants against Donner and Froh, who are about to strike them down, ordering them to respect the treaties engraved on the shaft of his spear.

Trombones & Contrabass Tuba

Fig. 14.15 'Wotan's Spear – Wotan's Will – Treaties'

In the murk of recriminations and virtuous indignation the giant's ray of insight is lost. Now begins of a divergence between the wishes and intentions of the giants; the warmer-hearted Fasolt is enchanted at the thought of gaining Freia, whereas Fafner regards her as a pawn in a power game. It is she alone who can nurture the golden apples on which the gods depend for their immortal youth. Fairytale horns intone the music of 'Freia's Apples of Immortal Youth';

Fig. 14.16 'Golden Apples – Immortal Youth' (two horns)

Fafner tells Fasolt *sotto voce* that if the giants deprive the gods of Freia they will age and sicken and die, so that the giants will be rid of them. In the midst of this 'wrangle', Loge at last appears. Wotan finds fault with him for his tardiness but he comments pointedly that he has been busy, engaged on matters of importance, unlike certain others he could name. When pressed to give his mind to the business in hand and extricate Wotan from his dilemma, he has nothing to say except that the giants are evidently altogether in the right. The castle has been duly built: he himself has tested every stone of it, and found the work first class. There is nothing to be done but pay the price agreed upon by handing over Freia to the giants. The lesser gods are furious; and Wotan passionately declares that he only consented to the bargain because of Loge's promise to find a way out of it for him. But Loge says no: he has promised to find a way out if any such way exists, but not to make a way if there is none. He has wandered over the whole wide earth in search of something great enough to buy Freia back from the giants; but in all the world he has found nothing for which Man will give up Woman.

The music blossoms into a rapturous almost-aria as Loge describes the supreme value of women to humanity as harbingers of beauty and civilisation for the brutish world. He expounds the salutary influence of love on mankind. And yet, he says, there was one who gave up love. The Rhinemaidens had complained to him about Alberich's theft of their gold; he had forsworn love for the sake of the fabulous Rhinegold and the mastery of the world that it would bring, giving up love for the sake of the will to power.

No sooner is the tale told than the giants stoop lower than the dwarf. Alberich forswore love only when it was denied to him and made the instrument for cruelly murdering his self-respect. But the giants, with love within their reach, with Freia and her golden apples in their hands, offer to give her up for the treasure of Alberich. Observe: it is the treasure alone that they desire. They have no fierce threats of dominion over their superiors or moulding the world to any conceptions of their own. They are neither clever nor ambitious: they simply covet money. Alberich's gold; that is their demand, or else Freia as agreed.

Somehow Wotan must acquire the gold from Alberich, '*Den Ring muß ich haben!*' he exclaims forcefully, already demonstrating the corrosive effect of power and the lust for power. Alberich has yet to pronounce his curse on the Ring, condemning everyone to want it, but Wotan attests to the fact that there is no need for any formal curse before the obsession with it, the obsession with power, results in an obsessive craving. But how shall Wotan acquire it? With cynical directness, Loge tells him, 'By theft!' The gods, and Wotan with them, are initially taken aback at this suggestion, but the giants force the issue by seizing Freia and carrying her off as hostage, leaving Wotan to consider their ultimatum, that unless he brings them Alberich's treasure by the end of the day, they will stand on the terms of the contract and keep her forever.

With Freia gone and her youth-giving apples unavailable, the gods 'begin to wither and age'. Loge alone is less affected; he is more elemental, and he is also the outsider to whom Freia was always ungenerous with her apples; but for the others these apples, which Wotan so lightly bargained away, turn out a matter of life and death. This is decisive for Wotan; and in a sudden resolve he determines to make his way down into the mine with Loge 'to where Alberich's slaves are piling up wealth for him under the invisible whip'.

Now follows one of *The Ring*'s great purple passages, 'The Descent to Nibelheim'. First one of Loge's leitmotives with its up-rushing scales now suggests smoke billowing out of a cleft in the rocks, and soon great descending chordal masses describe their downwards progress deep into the earth. The music that concludes Alberich's 'Curse on Love' theme comes low on trombones, barely more than a growl, and the strings respond with other mobile, restless music associated with Loge. The trombones repeat the 'Curse on Love', this time an octave higher. Then horns then play it twice more, ever more luminous, but now there is a complete change. The key shifts, oboes apply their acid tang to the sound, and a hectic energy seizes on the music. The leitmotive of Freia, goddess of love, appears in a frenzied, driven form, and the theme of 'the Rhinegold' erupts searingly on the trumpet, its C major glory subverted into B flat minor. Next all the trumpets in unison scream out with measured power the leitmotive of 'Freia', (Fig. 14.10) which is also *The Ring's* central love motive, oppressed and agonised, while the full orchestra pounds it down under the relentless rhythm of Nibelungen hammering.

Fig. 14.17 'Nibelungen Hammering'

The sum effect is a grim, totalitarian picture of love battered down under the brute forces of blood and iron. The entire passage forges on relentlessly over a dominant pedal point which never resolves. Instead the music fades before the acoustical onslaught of Nibelungen slaves hammering at their anvils. The music transports us through the forges to deeper levels, and we are now in the depths of Nibelheim.

This gloomy place need not be a mine: it might just as well be a match-factory, with yellow phosphorus, phossy jaw, a large dividend and plenty of clergymen[61] as shareholders. Or it might be a white lead factory, or a chemical works, or a pottery, or a railway shunting yard,

61   GBS was writing for his time; precious few clergy today are likely to have incomes that enable them to be shareholders of anything.

or a tailoring shop, or a little gin-sodden laundry, or a bakehouse, or a big shop, or any other of the places where human life and welfare are daily sacrificed [for the sake of the plutocracy]. In the mine, which resounds with the hammering of anvils of dwarves toiling miserably to heap up treasure for their master, Alberich has set his brother Mime to make him a helmet,

the Tarnhelm, symbolised evocatively by one of Wagner's most singular motives.

Fig. 14.18 'Tarnhelm' (muted horns)

Mime grasps

that there is some magic in the Tarnhelm and tries to keep it; but Alberich wrests it from him, and shows him to his cost that it is the veil of the invisible whip, and he learns that he who wears it can appear in what shape he will, or disappear from view altogether.

Alberich, now invisible, flogs Mime horribly, [and Shaw comments that the Tarnhelm is a very common article in our streets, the city of London perhaps,] and that it made a man invisible as a shareholder and changes him into various deceptive shapes, a pious Christian, a subscriber to hospitals, a benefactor to the poor, a model husband and father, a practical and independent Englishman and what not, when he is really a pitiful parasite in the commonwealth, consuming a great deal, and producing nothing, knowing nothing, believing nothing and doing nothing except what all the rest do, and that only because he is afraid not to do it or at least pretend to do it.

If things had changed for the better fifty years ago, has not the pendulum been hurled back with a vengeance? Is Terry Eagleton far wrong to say in his compelling book, *Why Marx was Right*, 'Margaret Thatcher and Ronald Reagan together shackled the labour market, let the market rip, strengthened the repressive arm of the state, and championed a new social philosophy known as barefaced greed'?

When Wotan and Loge arrive at the underworld, Nibelheim, they first question the distracted Mime, but soon they are interrupted by Alberich driving his factory slaves to quarry ever more gold for him. When Alberich catches sight of the gods he drives off Mime to join the other Nibelungen. This is extraordinary music, harassing, hectoring, always on at the Nibelungen; nobody had represented anything like this in music before, and nobody has again. They all cower uncertainly for a moment, whereupon he reveals the full power of the Ring by kissing it and brandishing it aloft as an incantation.

It is as if he had struck them, and they all run off in terror and confusion. Alberich turns to the gods roughly: what do they want? Loge tries to ingratiate himself with Alberich as the kindly source of that fire which warms the Nibelungen and makes possible all their smelting and smithying. 'But the dwarf [says Shaw] has no faith in these civil strangers: Greed instinctively mistrusts Intellect, and Alberich breaks out at them with a terrible boast of the power now within his grasp.' Just as he gave up love for power, so shall everything that lives come under the rule of his furious tyranny. When he forswore love and seized the Rhinegold he learnt too the power of exploitation and acquired a talent for enslaving. Psychologically there is a connection between gold (or the obsessive love of money) and exploitation. It is a simple allegorical equation but devastating in its truth. Alberich paints a picture of the world

as it will be when his dominion over it is complete, when the soft airs and green mosses of its valleys shall be changed into smoke, slag and filth; when slavery, disease and squalor, soothed by drunkenness and mastered by the policeman's baton become the foundation of society;

and when nothing shall escape ruin except such pretty places and pretty women as he may like to buy for the slaking of his own lusts. In that kingdom of evil he sees that there will be no power but his own. These gods with their moralities and legalities and intellectual subtlety will go under and be starved out of existence. He bids Wotan and Loge beware; and his '*Hab' Acht!*' is hoarse, horrible and sinister. Wotan is revolted to the very depths of his being: he can barely stifle the [disgust and] execration that burst from him.

Loge defuses the situation by a smooth flow of words pretending sympathy and concern for Alberich. It is clear that he finds it

exquisitely amusing that that dwarf, in stirring up the *moral* fervour of Wotan, has removed the god's last *moral* scruples about becoming a thief.[62] Wotan will now [play the ruffian and] rob the dwarf without remorse; for is it not positively his highest duty to take this power out of such evil hands and use it himself in the interests of Godhead and humanity? On the loftiest moral grounds he lets Loge do his worst.

A little cunningly disguised flattery makes short work of Alberich. Loge pretends to be afraid of him; and he swallows that bait unhesitatingly. But how, inquires Loge, is he to guard against the hatred of his million slaves? Will they not steal from him, whilst he sleeps, the magic ring, the symbol of his power, which he has forged from the gold of the Rhine?

'Loge thinks himself the cleverest, and that everyone else is a fool needing his help', sneers Alberich, and he boasts of having devised the Tarnhelm on his own, without needing Loge or anyone to help. Loge

refuses to believe in such marvels without witnessing them. Alberich, only too glad to show off his powers, puts on the Tarnhelm and

---

62   My italics.

transforms himself into a monstrous serpent [or dragon].

Fig. 14.19 '*Riesenwurm*' (tenor tubas and contrabass tuba)

Loge gratifies him by pretending to be frightened out of his wits, but
ventures the remark that it would be better still if the Tarnhelm could
transform its owner into some tiny creature that could hide and spy in
the smallest cranny. Alberich promptly transforms himself into a toad.
In an instant Wotan's foot is on him; Loge tears away the Tarnhelm;
they pinion him, and drag him away a prisoner up through the earth

to the open country by the castle. The orchestra paints the journey
back upwards from the bowels of the earth, developing further the
motives from the descent to Nibelheim, but in reverse order, past the
Nibelungen at their anvils out to the brightness the world of above.

To pay for his freedom, they make Alberich 'summon up his slaves
from the depths to place all the treasure at the feet of Wotan, along
with the Tarnhelm'. He repeats the incantation heard earlier, (Figs.
14.5 and 14.2).

Fig. 14.20

and the Nibelungen begin to drag up the hoard from the depths. This musical paragraph is a prime example of Wagner's genius for building up a musical representation beyond the ideas associated with the individual leitmotives. The passage is constructed from the 'Nibelung' theme representing their insistent hammering, and from the leitmotive of the hoard grinding up out of the depths. It is all played out over a dominant pedal point, which then switches to the tonic B flat minor, adding a heightened force and concentration; and it culminates in a version of the 'Rhinemaidens' Hymn to the Gold', but subverted. So much for the individual leitmotives; at the same time the passage as a whole is about Alberich as the Nibelungen witness his humiliation. This musical expression of his rage, hate and pain is terrifying and it rises to a devastating climax.

Alberich now demands his liberty; but Wotan must have the Ring as well. And here the dwarf, like the giants before him, feels the very foundations of the world shake beneath him at the discovery of his own base cupidity in a higher power. That evil should, in its loveless desperation, create malign powers which Godhead could not create, seems but natural justice to him. But that Godhead should steal those malign powers from evil, and wield them itself, is a monstrous perversion; and his appeal to Wotan to forego it is almost terrible in his conviction of wrong. It is of no avail. Wotan falls back again on virtuous indignation. He reminds Alberich that he stole the gold from the Rhinemaidens, and takes the attitude of the just judge compelling a restitution of stolen goods. Then Alberich, knowing perfectly well that the judge is taking the goods to put them in his own pocket, has the ring torn from his finger, and is once more as poor as he was when he came slipping and stumbling along the slimy rocks on the bed of the Rhine.

They let him go, but before he disappears, he curses a second time, a curse more terrible than the first.

Fig. 14.21 'Alberich's Curse of the Ring'

This theme and the curse that it symbolises will resonate throughout the whole cycle until it is smelted down and its gold washed clean in the waters of the Rhine a few minutes before the end. Just as it brought Alberich power beyond measure, so now it shall convey death to anyone who wears it. It shall bring joy to no one; anyone who owns it shall be eaten up with anxiety; everyone who does not will be gnawed away by envy. It will become a living death for all concerned until it returns to the hand from which it has been robbed. The expressive force of the music of the curse is strong that whenever it reappears it creates a sense of disaster, and its first instance is not long in coming, but Wotan does not take it in. He is away in a dream of his own, impervious to anyone and anything, so drunk is he with the Ring and the intoxicating sense of power which it brings. Its menace is symbolised by another leitmotive, usually known as 'Nibelung hatred (*Nibelungenhass*)'. It is extraordinary, original, and mysteriously expressive. Where on earth did that come from; how did Wagner conceive it; what were the musical antecedents for it in his mind? Pure genius! This theme too will infiltrate the music and the action of *The Ring*.

Fig. 14.22 'Nibelung Hatred (*Nibelungenhass*)'

Shaw comments that Alberich describes

the way of the world, that in older times when the Christian labourer was drained dry by the knightly spendthrift and the spendthrift was drained by the Jewish usurer, church and state, religion and law, seized on the Jew and drained him as a Christian duty. When the forces of lovelessness and greed had built up our own sordid capitalist systems, driven by invisible proprietorship, robbing the poor, defacing the earth, and forcing themselves as a universal curse even on the generous and humane, then religion and law and intellect, which would never themselves have discovered such systems, their natural bent being towards welfare, economy, and life, instead of towards corruption, waste, and death, nevertheless did not scruple to seize by fraud and force these powers of evil, on pretence of using them for good. And it inevitably happens that when the church, the law, and all the Talents [of the State] have made common cause to rob the people, the church is far more vitally harmed by the unfaithfulness to itself than its more mechanical confederates; so that finally they turn on their discredited ally and rob the church, as happened in France and Italy for instance.

The twin giants come back with Freia, in whose presence Godhead blooms again. The gold is ready for them; but now that the moment has come for parting with Freia, the gold does not seem so tempting; and they are sorely loth to let her go, especially Fasolt. Not unless there is gold enough to utterly hide her from Wotan – not until the heap has grown so that they can see nothing but gold – until money has come between them and every human feeling, will he part with her. There is not gold enough to accomplish this: however cunningly Loge spreads it, the glint of Freia's hair is still visible to the giant Fafner, and the Tarnhelm must go on the heap to shut it out. Even then Fafner's brother, Fasolt, can catch a beam from her eye through a chink and is rendered incapable thereby of forswearing her. There is nothing to stop that chink but the ring; and Wotan is as greedily bent on keeping that as Alberich himself had been;

nothing else matters. This is a disturbing mutation of Wotan's objectives. What was recently at stake is now remote; Wotan who set out to free Freia with the Ring now wants it to be 'the mightiest of mightiest lords'. The decline and extinction of the gods which must plainly follow on the loss of Freia and her apples are of no account. Their pleas and warnings go for nothing. In his lust for power the lord of creation has become like a three-year-old screaming 'mine' when another child shows an interest in a new toy. If all power corrupts, then Wotan is corrupted. He does not yield until he is reached by the voice of the earth-goddess, Erda. She rises mysterious and awe-inspiring from her sleep in the heart of the earth. As Catherine Clément said, 'Wotan himself has no idea who she is. Those broad, sweeping arpeggios, as if the waters of the Rhine ran in slow motion, and that slow, majestic rhythm are not part of the gods' time. Eternity is singing.'[63]

Fig. 14.23 'Erda'

Erda delivers two dark oracles. Everything that exists, including the gods themselves, will one day come to an end; the gods themselves will dissolve in twilight, in their *Götterdämmerung*.

Fig. 14.24 'Twilight of the Gods (*Götterdämmerung*)'

Worse, a terrible and instant danger threatens them; to escape immediate destruction Wotan must instantly give up the Ring. Deeply disturbed, he demands to know more, but she vanishes disquiteningly. After a moment of indecision, he obeys her;

---

63   Clément, Catherine, *Opera or The Undoing of Women*, tr. Betsy Wing, London, 1989, p. 145.

the Ring is added to the heap of gold; and all sense of Freia is cut off from the giants.

But now what Law is left is to these two poor stupid labourers whereby one shall yield to the other any of the treasure for which they have each paid the whole price in surrendering Freia?

While Fasolt is still gazing after Freia, Fafner starts loading the treasure into a sack, and has taken more than half when Fasolt notices and asks for just division between two brothers. Fafner says roughly that he deserves a bigger share, because Fasolt would never have shared Freia equally.

He looks by mere habit to the God to judge for them; but Wotan has had enough and simply turns aside in disgust.

It is Loge, amoral as ever, who yet offers him advice to help, which is let go the hoard and concentrate on the Ring. This Fasolt does, telling Fafner that he was the one who won it demanding it in exchange for the delight of Freia's bright eyes. Thereupon Fafner seizes his great tree trunk of a staff and batters his brother to death.

It is a horrible thing to see and hear, to anyone who knows how much blood has been shed in the world in just that way by its brutalised toilers, honest fellows enough until their betters betrayed them.

Fafner goes off with his booty. It is quite useless to him. He has neither the cunning nor the ambition to establish the Plutonic empire with it. Merely to prevent others from getting it is the only purpose it brings him. He piles it in a cave; transforms himself into a dragon by the Tarnhelm; and devotes his life to guarding it, as much a slave to it as a jailer is to his prisoner. He had much better have thrown it all back into the Rhine and transformed himself into the shortest-lived animal that enjoys a least a brief run in the sunshine. His case, however, is far too common to be surprising. The world is overstocked with persons who sacrifice all their affections, and madly trample and batter down their fellows to obtain riches of which, when they get them, they are unable to make the smallest use, and to which they become the most miserable slaves.

The gods are aghast at the turn of events, and 'Alberich's Curse of the Ring' thunders out twice, on fortissimo trombones supported a cannonade from the tympani. Wotan comments in shaken tones that the force of Alberich's curse now seems fearsome. As he explains to Brünnhilde in *Die Walküre*, this put an end to any lightness of heart that was once his. He must go down to the underworld to find Erda and ask her what to do.

However the other gods do their best to forget Fafner and Alberich. Fricka turns all her melting charm on Wotan, and beguiles him with the prospect of their first night in Valhalla. Wotan still expresses guilt, remorse and responsibility: 'It was an evil wage that I paid for my building;' but Donner, the god of thunder, springs to a rocky summit and calls the clouds: '*Hedo! Heda! Hedo!*' Horns take up his call as he swings his hammer and draws in the mists.

He - da!   He - da! He - do!

Fig. 14.25 'Donner'

They come at his summons; and he and the castle are hidden by their black legions. Froh, the Rainbow god, hastens to his side.

As the mists gather more densely there is a sudden wind running up through the orchestra, the wind that breaks the calm before the storm. At the culmination, Donner smashes down his hammer, and up goes a flash of lightning in the form of a flourish on the brass. Wagner characterises all these different sensory modes in music! There are the mists gathering, a sight, which Wagner described in music. Then the sudden up-rush of the wind, something both felt and heard, described in music. Then Donner's hammer-blow, an actual sound, literally presented. Then the lightning flash, a sight, described in music. Finally the thunder, a sound almost as it is in nature, yet turned into music for the tympani. Wagner includes all these in a single musical sentence, and they become part of a single *musical* experience.

As the air clears, the castle is seen in its fullest splendour, accessible now by the rainbow bridge which Froh has cast across the ravine.

Its theme is related to the arpeggio of the Prelude.

Fig. 14.26 'Rainbow Bridge' (clarinet, bassoon, horn, cellos)

Wotan greets his majestic fortress, now glowing in the sunset, and gives it a name, Valhalla. Fricka asks what it means, and Wotan fobs her off with a profound-sounding answer that means nothing; and yet in the glory of this moment he

has a great thought. [As Shaw says of him now,] with all his aspirations to establish a reign of noble thought, of righteousness, order, and justice, he has found that there is no race yet in the world that might spontaneously, naturally, and unconsciously realise his ideal. He himself has found how far short Godhead falls of the thing it conceives. He, the greatest of gods, has been unable to control his fate: he has been forced against his will to choose between evils, to make disgraceful bargains, to break them still more disgracefully, and even then to see the price of his disgrace slip through his fingers. On every side he is shackled and bound, dependent on the law and the subterfuges of Loge, forced to traffic with the dwarfs for handicraft and with giants for strength, and to pay them both in false coin. [But nature] is not yet exhausted. [Life] has always climbed higher and higher, to its zenith in the gods with their thoughts, with their comprehension of the world, and their ideals. But why should it stop there? Why should it not rise from the god to the Hero?

A race of heroes will join him in defending Valhalla, but he will raise one hero in particular to do what he cannot do, bound as he is by the law, and wrest the Ring from Fafner. This is the significance of the enigmatic blaze of brass in the orchestra, as the trumpets give out the motive of the sword, Nothung. Although this is not revealed until *Die Walküre*, the 'Sword' theme here symbolises the heroes of Wotan's dawning plans.

Fig. 14.27 'Wotan's Great Idea – the Sword Nothung' (trumpet, fortissimo)

For the time being Wotan calls to his wife Fricka cheerfully to come and dwell with him in Valhalla. They are all overcome by Valhalla's glory, except Loge, the realist. He despises these gods with their ideals and their golden apples. Free from self-deception, he discerns the truth behind the façade, and he comments with contempt and irritation, 'They are hastening on to their end. I am almost ashamed to have anything to do with them.' As they set foot on the rainbow bridge, there rises from the river below the lament of the Rhinemaidens for their lost gold.

Their lament stings Wotan's conscience, and he tells Loge to bid them desist. 'You down there in the water,' Loge tells them facetiously, 'If the gold no longer shines on you, what does it matter? Henceforth you shall bask in the splendour of the gods!' They sing back that truth is only to be found in the depths, and then more pointedly, 'False and cowardly are you who find joy up above.'

If *The Ring*'s original warnings were becoming more relevant in the new German Reich of Kaiser Wilhelm, they may be even more relevant now and apply to the whole planet earth. The political dimension of *Das Rheingold* and its warnings have always been worth attention as theories, but the disquieting reality is that they have become more apposite. *Das Rheingold* presents a class of the very rich, and a larger class of the appallingly poor, the division which was maintained and possibly heightened by the industrial revolution. The first seventy years of the twentieth century saw a narrowing of the gap. Forty years ago in a more egalitarian society than Wagner ever knew or than we do now, *The Ring*'s deprecation of capitalism and Wagner's preference for common ownership or mutualism may have seemed naïve and outmoded, a relic of the past swept away by historical progress. Unfortunately the egoism and greed which Alberich symbolises seem to have returned in full force, as unbridled market forces proclaim a lunatic gospel that individual greed is good for everyone. There was in the past, particularly the late twentieth century, a crude and naïve assumption unsupported by evidence, that while the wealth of plutocrats would increase in comparison with that of the poor, the general increase in wealth and a general humanitarian sense of responsibility would ensure that the wealth trickled down through society.

The wheel has turned, and it is clearer that while capitalist society continues to generate wealth, it does it more than ever in a manner that eludes most of its members. *Das Rheingold* calls up a reviving and deepening concern about the chasms of inequality. The widening gap between the stupifyingly rich and the rest may be threatening social consensus and political stability, in Europe and America and certainly in Britain. Assessments like those in *The Times* for 10 November 2010 are increasingly pertinent, that today the United States has inequality so extreme that America's 74 richest citizens receive more income than the poorest 19 million combined. (Apparently since then the ratio of the poorest has since then increased to 31 million.) Marx's prophecy, that the rich would get richer and the poor would get poorer, is proving a reality, and there is no evidence that it causes concern or conscience among the freeloaders, but rather a lofty superiority and a derisive glow of satisfaction. Few people except social workers and those remaining doctors who still do home visits are properly aware of the Dickensian conditions which increasingly prevail in our growing slums, the poverty and the rags, the cold and the hunger, which should revolt us. The blue-collar workers commonly imagined as Marx's proletariat may possibly have diminished in number but sections of the former middle and professional classes have over the last twenty years acquired the essential characteristics of the old working class. Under the impact of managerialism, many professions have been emasculated and destabilised, and social workers, teachers, nurses, hospital technicians are among the many groups who now share the assetless insecurity which defined the nineteenth-century proletariat.

Shaw took his evil capitalist as 'a subscriber to hospitals, as a benefactor of the poor, model husband and father, a shrewd, practical, independent Englishman, and what not, when he is really painful parasite on the Commonwealth'. In Shaw's time, and Wagner's, many bankers and corporate magnates at least felt moved to support good causes for whatever reason, but unfortunately these redeeming characteristics seem to be less in evidence today. The wealthy still include in their number many compassionate philanthropists, but many of today's British super-rich are might more happily squander their millions on buying jet fighters to decorate the front lawn, or arrange a Valentine's Day dinner on an iceberg, as Robert Peston of the BBC has revealed. Even more than in Wagner's time, these people are now, as Shaw put it, engaged in consuming a great deal but 'in producing nothing, feeling nothing, knowing nothing, and doing nothing'.

Meanwhile the gods pass over the rainbow into their new fortress, to music that is Wagner at his most fascinating and equivocal, knife-edged as is it is between empty bombast and real glory. And with the last notes of *Das Rheingold*, *The Ring* softens its socialist emphasis and Wagner's allegory of capitalism gradually recedes and gives way to a *Ring* of myth-related, psychological truths. Already in *Das Rheingold*, psychological truths have shone through the politics, and this second dimension blossoms in *Die Walküre*.

❧

The character of Alberich is not only a political but also a psychological study of trauma and deprivation, and it is the music which gives reality to Alberich's psychotic personality. Through the music, the portrait becomes terrifying. He represents the belief that power over others can compensate for feelings of inferiority. The desire of power over others reflects a misguided attempt to achieve security, but even if it brings a security of a kind, it does not produce fulfilment or serenity. For one thing the possession of power carries with it the fear that it may be lost; 'Uneasy sleeps the head that wears the crown,' and once Alberich has lost possession of the Ring, he turns into a victim of his own curse. Wagner is at his most penetrating when he represents Alberich himself as 'eaten up with anxiety', the anxiety which his imprecation ensures will become general. All the evidence goes to show that the Stalins and Hitlers and even the Robert Maxwells of this world were disturbed, unhappy and even frightened men. In a sense Alberich comes to embody the appalling philosophy of O'Brien, an equally terrifying figure from George Orwell's *Nineteen Eighty-four*. O'Brien expounds the conviction that the only pleasure that never satiates is power, power over others; and that the only convincing and satisfying proof of power is the pain and torment of others. Power that achieves something positive, pleasurable or worthwhile for other people cannot offer its owner the same proof because people would do the things they want of their own accord. Power to help does not afford the same gratifying proof as power to make them suffer. It is only through their torment that they can provide a malignant narcissist like O'Brien with his frisson, and a malignant narcissist is what Alberich has now become.

As Jean Shinoda Bolen suggests,[64] there is something of Alberich in all of us. It is all too true, as she says, that rejection and exclusion are common childhood or adolescent experiences that are wounding emotionally, and Alice Miller maintains the same; that they make a person feel impotent and unlovable. Children who are rejected feel

64   Bolen, Jean Shinoda, *Ring of Power: The Abandoned Child, the Authoritarian Father, and the Disempowered Feminine*, New York, 1992.

that there is something wrong or ugly about them, and have a kinship with Alberich the Nibelung who was 'too dark and ugly' to play with the beautiful people. Such children may grow up to be successful adults in the eyes of others, yet still feel they are Nibelungs – little or fat or otherwise rejectable – underneath the image of power and sophistication that others see. When rejection and ridicule come in adolescence or young adulthood, particularly from the opposite sex, it strikes at the foundations of a personality. To avoid further pain, people in this situation come to deny any desire for acceptance and love, transforming it into a desire for revenge: Alberich shaking his fist in frustration and vengeance. They become abusers of others or obsessed with power, as embodied in O'Brien – or in Jürgen Bartsch, or Adolf Hitler. Power over others is this effort to compensate, part of 'identifying with the aggressor' whereby the individual who wants love and is abused in turn becomes abusive. If he gains power he becomes fearsome, sinning against humanity. Alberich tries to draw a contrast between his own sin, in seizing the Rhinegold and Wotan's doing the same, but it is not true that he sinned only against himself. His real sin was not this theft but his determination to create a world of universal slavery, misery and torment, very much a sin against others.

There are other truths which Wagner sets out in Alberich. One is that disordered emotions wreck judgment. Dealing with Loge in Nibelheim, Alberich oscillates wildly between aggression and vanity, and there is no consistency or balance in his hubristic decision to turn himself into a toad. Another important truth that Wagner didactically represents in Alberich is about resentment. The subsequent course of *The Ring* progressively reveals Alberich's as a life destroyed by resentment, and some of the greatest wisdom on this subject is enshrined in the users' guide of Alcoholics Anonymous:[65] I have already mentioned it in a footnote, but emphasise it, 'It is plain that a life that includes deep resentment can lead only to futility and unhappiness.' Alberich's life certainly becomes one of futility and unhappiness. Whenever we meet

---

65   *Alcoholics Anonymous*, AA World Services Inc., 3rd ed., New York, 1976.

him he is proving the truth of his own prophecy that anyone who owns the Ring shall be eaten up with anxiety; everyone who does not will be gnawed away by envy.

> *All men shall crave it, madly to own it,*
> *But no one who gains it shall ever know joy.*

He spends his entire life in futility and unhappiness, gnawing on his own bones, and is Wagner's genius to create in most people a strange sympathy for Alberich. Most people know something of Alberich from within.

Although there are no literal human beings in *Das Rheingold*, I know of no opera which etches out so many human identities with such deftness and concentration. There are the giants, not so cloddish as Shaw believed, but differentiated vignettes. There is Fasolt, romantic and full of poignant hopes, a contrast to his surly brother, even though they are cut from the same rock. There is Fricka, far more than a nag and a fishwife, the voice of realism and conscience, a deserving consort to Wotan, still hoping to captivate him as her music reveals,

Clarinet

Fig. 14.28 'Fricka's Affectionate Side'

as well to make him see sense. There is Loge with all his ironic hauteur and facetiousness. He enjoys addressing others with descriptions that are the opposite of what they are feeling and turning those descriptions into a jeer. For instance he three times addresses the gods as '*selig*, blessed', always at points when blessed and happy is exactly what they are not. '*Hei Mime, muntre Zwerg*, merry dwarf' is how he styles Mime when he sees Mime whimpering from Alberich's flogging. He blends intellect and arrogance with moral instability, oscillating between candid concern and disdain and lies. He offers good advice without interest in the outcome. Moments after he has been helping Fasolt and warning him to claim the Ring, he is telling Wotan that nothing could be luckier than seeing Fasolt as one of his enemies battered to death by the other, Fafner. He demonstrates a similar want of compassion for the wretched Mime down in Nibelheim, simply laughing at his description of being flogged by Alberich, as indeed does Wotan. Wagner even has the pathetic Mime beginning to reveal a different side, instinctive craft and guile, when not tormented. Loge is a god in whom the Rhinemaidens place their trust, confiding in him about Alberich's theft of their gold, but when they are heard lamenting in the depths, Loge is the one who responds with a callous riposte.

Even the Rhinemaidens are distinctive. They are three gay malicious minxes, but Woglinde has most inhuman sparkle, and Flosshilde is most warm and most thoughtful and wary of Alberich. As for the two minor gods, Wagner makes Froh the more impulsive, and Donner carry more weight. The only cameos which are not rounded out are Erda, who is at this stage more of an archetype than a magnetic allurement for Wotan, and Freia, whose panic-stricken outbursts are too brief and scanty to convey individuality. It is only in Shakespeare and in Wagner's own *Die Meistersinger* that we encounter a gallery of characters modelled so rapidly, so distinctively, and with such understanding.

The cornerstones of *The Ring* are Wotan, Brünnhilde and Siegfried whom we meet later. We have already learnt a great deal about Wotan and his wife. When we first encounter him, he is dreaming of grandeur, literally; he is asleep together with his wife in some rocky but verdant upland overlooked by his new fortress, Valhalla. He is not God Almighty, like the God of the Judaeo-Christian tradition. He represents more of Voltaire's sardonic observation that Man made God in his own image. From Wagner's earliest writings on *The Ring*, his essay on the Nibelungen-drama, it is clear that he conceived of Wotan as a grand but human figure. The music of Valhalla which we hear at his first appearance is noble, even if he proves also to contain a measure of hedonism and ambition as well as principle. He wants a good life, and he wants to be top dog; and he even describes himself later as *Licht-Alberich*; but unlike the real Alberich, he is eager for power not to dominate but to do things and achieve worthwhile results. He has noble aspirations such as Wagner had identified in the kings of his own acquaintance.

Anthony Trollope said of his heroine in *The Small House at Allington*, that we, his readers, must love Lily Dale. Otherwise we cannot enter into the action in terms that make it interesting and meaningful, and so it is with Wotan in *The Ring*. If there is something of Alberich in everyone, there is more of Wotan. Perhaps we do not need to love Wotan, but he must *matter* to us; otherwise we remain on the outside. Wagner told Röckel that Wotan is us, our very selves, and without appreciating the full complexity of Wotan and his impossible dilemmas, we miss a great deal that *The Ring* tells us.

Wotan's character develops. His first, high-flown exordium of his new fortress, Valhalla, has majesty, and he soon proves a personage of ambition, willing to play for big stakes and take big risks for what he considers worthwhile. Later *Die Walküre* will show him doing things that are appalling, but he will be the one who pays the price. In *Das Rheingold* he demonstrates the rash joviality and the easy irresponsibility for which Fricka turns on him. How could he have contracted with the builders, the giants, to take their sister, the lovely Freia, as the price of their labours? Against her accusations of misogyny, and of placing his will to power before love and affection, he banters back that he prizes women highly. After all, having given up one eye to gain wisdom at the world ash, he had wagered the other to gain Fricka as his wife. He pulls her leg none too kindly, suggesting that he is fonder of women than Fricka likes, but reassures her that he had intention of honouring the contract and letting the giants take Freia. He counts on Loge to find a way out. When Fricka turns angry and asks how he could place any confidence in such a double-dealer, Wotan comments calmly that in straightforward and honest dealings he needs no help, but the necessity of keeping treacherous and dangerous enemies under control calls for cunning and guile, and that is where he needs Loge. When Loge does not arrive, Wotan displays a naiveté that is folly, in that he asks the giants affably to name their payment; and when they claim Freia, he acts as if he had no idea that this was coming and tells them roughly to ask for something else. Freia, he says, is not on offer; and he half hopes and expects the giants to submit to his hectoring and give up their well-earned reward. But when the younger gods enter the scene and threaten murderous violence against the giants, Wotan expresses his full authority, stretching out the spear which protects and guards treaties like his one with the giants, and everyone gives way. On the other hand, Wotan has no idea how to resolve the situation and is relieved when Loge finally appears. He spars with Loge briefly, but when the giants tell him 'Stop this delay and simply pay up!' Wotan again exerts his authority and Loge has to take the matter seriously. Wotan is greatly put out when Loge first informs him he has found no substitute for the joy and grace of women. When Loge goes on and tells him about the Rhinemaidens wanting his help against the one exception, Alberich, who has stolen their gold in preference to love, Wotan reacts irascibly. He is not subtle enough to recognise that Loge has dangled in front of the giants the possibility that gold and money might be more desirable than Freia. Soon his own ambition is fired with the idea of owning the Ring and its power, but he and the other gods are still principled enough to stand aghast at Loge's suggestion of simply stealing it until he falls for the smooth sophistry of Loge's arguments. He is arrogant, outraged and disagreeable when the giants hit on the idea that he, Wotan, should wrest the gold from Alberich and use it pay them instead of using Freia. He is irresolute and strangely ineffective when the giants seize the advantage, grab Freia, and go stamping off to their own habitation after threatening to keep her forever unless Wotan has the gold at close of day. It is when the gods sicken and wither and Loge tells them that without Freia they will surely die, that Wotan masters the situation, commanding Loge to go down to Nibelheim with him to help win the gold. When Loge suggests a way through the Rhine, Wotan declines shiftily and evasively.

When they reach Nibelheim, Wotan is wise enough to let Loge

do most of the talking, expressing every confidence in his skill even after they have learnt from Mime the full power of the Ring and the Tarnhelm. In their initial approaches to Alberich, Wotan falls back into the easy good humour which seems to be his default attitude. Even when Alberich begins to describe his dreams of world domination, his response is urbane, until Alberich threatens such brutal and sadistic intentions against the universe that Wotan lunges at him violently, only to let Loge rein him in. He recovers his good humour, or at least appears to do so, as Alberich turns himself into a dragon, laughing with Alberich and congratulating him. After Alberich's arrogance has led to his downfall and the two gods have got him back on the roof of the world, Wotan cannot resist crowing over Alberich and his captive status.

Alberich lets go the hoard and the Tarnhelm, but Wotan of course insists on having the Ring as well. Wotan now reveals a disastrous capacity for self-deception. He will reveal it again in *Die Walküre* with consequences that are yet more disturbing, but he chooses to regard Alberich's acquisition as theft and pillage, not as a price paid, and to regard himself as a law guardian, with a bizarre moral right to take for himself the goods taken by Alberich. His intentions are muddled, a moral muddle of the kind that people find it useful not to clarify. Vaguely floating in his mind is some idea of a restitution for the wrong done to Rhinemaidens, without quite allowing the Ring to feature clearly in this restitution. There is the hazy idea of a ransom for Freia, and the grander, vaguer ideas that he must have the Ring so that he can ensure that the world is really ruled well – by himself. He has to stand firm against the forces of evil which would turn everyone into slaves and change the world into an outsize concentration camp. All this creates a moral smudge. His real problem is the very existence of the Ring. It now obsesses him, and he wants it out of vainglory, but also to add to the smudge, he wants it because he knows that if he does not take it, someone worse, Alberich, will exercise its power. However, he has no idea how far he is himself driven by the will to power; which expresses itself in its most delusional form, so that morally he becomes much less distinct from Alberich.[66]

Because of this confusion, he blusters and rages and undermines his gravitas. He has great physical strength, easily overcoming Alberich and seizing the Ring. He is unaffected by Alberich's anguish, and stands in rapt and idiotic contemplation of himself as the mightiest of mighty lords. He is so bewitched by the Ring and so out of touch with reality that unlike Loge, he is barely aware of Alberich cursing the Ring, something which, given its shattering force, might at least engage his attention. On the other hand Wotan releases Alberich. Whereas Alberich took a sadistic delight in tormenting his fellow Nibelungen, this does not occur to Wotan, a difference which puts some clear water between them.

He behaves disagreeably again when the giants insist that the hoard should be piled up until it completely hides Freia from view. While the other gods are willing to do any work necessary to liberate Freia, Wotan merely tells them to get on with it, because he finds it offensive. And when the giants demand the Ring, he discloses himself as bewitched by power to an extent which closes down all reason. It adds to the impression of his natural authority that no one even now tries to gainsay him. When he finally listens to reason from Erda, he reveals a partial return to the same quest for knowledge and wisdom which once led him to sacrifice an eye. (*The Ring* does not actually reveal this event until the first scene of *Götterdämmerung*.) He makes as if to seize hold of Erda but she is gone before he can act. After a moment's indecision, he lets go the Ring, making light of his dreadful behaviour and allowing the impression that he is Freia's saviour. Now that he has done the right thing, his jovial good nature reappears, and

---

66 There is a revealing fictional analysis of this process in C.P. Snow's novel, *The Masters* (London, 1951). This etches out with the scalpelled precision of a dissector the process whereby Paul Jago, an inspirational candidate for the mastership of a Cambridge college, ends up defeated after wanting it too much and losing his noble ideals, and ultimately recognising that he wanted it simply for the sake of hearing people call him 'Master'.

in their collective jollity, he and the other gods (except Loge) pay no attention to the dispute that instantly breaks out among the giants, not even when Fasolt expects justice from him as the law-guardian. What shakes him to the depths is Fasolt's murder, the turning point in his existence. The very vocal line to which Wotan sings, 'Terrible now does the curse on the Ring appear,' sounds weighed down and indeterminate, and he is no longer so foolish to get any comfort from Loge's comment that he is in luck because his enemies are busy destroying themselves. He faults himself for paying an ill wage for his fortress. For the time being he is swept along as we are, by the glorious demonstration of sight and sound as a bright storm clears the air, and a rainbow bridge arches over the Rhine Valley to Valhalla. Moreover he has had his great idea, presented in the leitmotive of the sword Nothung; as becomes clear in *Die Walküre*, it represents Wotan's scheme for regaining the Ring, and he believes that he can manage it without compromising himself. Wagner has indeed created a complex and fascinating character. *Die Walküre* shows how it all goes wrong, but also how Wotan begins himself to be spiritually redeemed.

Although *Das Rheingold* had already been performed on its own at Munich, it was first given in context as part of the *Der Ring des Nibelungen* at the the first ever performance of the complete cycle. This took place at the Festspielhaus in Bayreuth on 13 August 1876, when the cast consisted of Lilli Lehmann (Woglinde), Marie Lehmann (Wellgunde), and Minna Lammert (Flosshilde), Karl Hill (Alberich), Franz Betz (Wotan), Friederike Grün (Fricka), Marie Haupt (Freia), Albert Eilers (Fasolt), Franz von Reichenberg (Fafner), Eugen Gura (Donner), Georg Unger (Froh), Max Schlosser (Mime), Luisa Jaide (Erda). The performance was conducted by Hans Richter under Wagner's close supervision.

FIFTEEN

DIE WALKÜRE

Die Walküre transports us instantly to a different world. The still, golden depths and the brilliancy of *Das Rheingold* are gone. *Die Walküre* is a drama of storms, storms in the forests, storms in high rocky places, storms on the mountain summits, storms in the lives of Siegmund and Sieglinde, and of Wotan, Fricka, and Brünnhilde. The grey colourings and lowering clouds of *Die Walküre* are central to *The Ring*'s hold on the imagination. Yet in a different sense this is still the same world as *Das Rheingold*, because its style and its methods of composition and its musical procedures are the same; its music is an evolution of all that Wagner had achieved in *Das Rheingold*.

Much has changed since the gods passed over their rainbow bridge into Valhalla. Wotan was already taking leave of his breezy, irresponsible younger self, and he has now become a more sober, thoughtful being. His outlook has darkened. He is aware of the power of the Ring because he has seen Alberich using it to torment the Nibelungen into mining and bringing up the hoard. He is aware of the power of Alberich's curse because he has seen Fafner battering his brother Fasolt to death. As he later confides to Brünnhilde, the daughter who is his adored alter ego and in every sense the heroine of *Die Walküre*, the problem which dominates his existence is how to get back the Ring, a problem that is not entirely of his own making but which he alone can resolve. However, this is bound up with a second problem which is very much of his making. This is that however well-intentioned his own pursuit of power may originally have been, he has compromised his noble ends by ignoble means. He had neutralised most of his enemies and won over dissident groups through a series of contracts engraved on his spear, and these have hallowed it with an authority that is both legal and mystical. But the contract process had been blighted by deception and fraud, and worse, its scope had not extended to Alberich, so as to bring him under control. From a confusion of motives but partly to make the world a safer place, safe from the 'plutonic' Alberich, Wotan was driven to act against the dwarf and seize the Ring, but he gained his objective through a mix of brute force and trickery which has compromised his moral authority and his legal right to rule. He also made the appalling mistake of not returning the Ring to the Rhinemaidens so that it could again be pure beauty forever. Instead Wotan had used it to pay for Valhalla, the fortress from which he now reigns over the world. Even this power was not enough to allay the anxiety that started to gnaw at his spirit once Erda had risen from her subterranean realms and issued her warning. It was a double warning, first that he must instantly give up the Ring to avoid immediate destruction, and second, that everything, including Wotan, must ultimately come to an end. His anxiety to learn more had led him down to the depths to seek her out. He had worked his full charisma on her; and in response to the love which he stirred, she opened to him both her store of prophetic wisdom and her body, conceiving and bearing him the first of nine Valkyrie daughters, Brünnhilde. Brünnhilde and her sisters now do him tremendous service towards the security of Valhalla by carrying out another of his grand ideas, to assemble a host of heroes. The Valkyries scour the battlefields, gathering up fallen heroes and riding through the air with them to Valhalla. These heroes take on immortality and form an ever-growing host which could defeat any force of arms; but there still remains the unsolved problem of Alberich and the possibility that he might recover the Ring. His original curse, forswearing love, would uniquely enable him to wield the Ring's full power. With it he could turn Valhalla's heroes against Valhalla and Wotan himself. It is therefore imperative that Wotan regain the Ring, this time taking it from Fafner, the one remaining giant. After being paid off for building Valhalla, Fafner had used the Tarnhelm to transform himself into a dragon, and he now spends his life brooding joylessly in a cave and guarding the Ring and the gold. Wotan may not play the ruffian again and wrest the Ring from Fafner by force, because it was payment for Valhalla in full accordance with a contract engraved on Wotan's spear. If Wotan were to violate his own contract, the spear would be deprived of its strange power, and all his authority and godhead would melt away. That is his dilemma, as he explains to Brünnhilde in *Die Walküre* Act II. It is *through* his treaties that he is lord, but it is *to* his treaties that he is a slave.

After much pondering, Wotan had devised a way out, or so he believes. If he could create a hero, a being who was not part of Wotan's circle, such a hero would be able to carry out the theft of the Ring from Fafner in his place. An independent hero could regain it without Wotan needing to violate the laws and contracts on his spear, and it could then return forever to the Rhinemaidens. To carry out his plan Wotan returned to the world in human form, with wolf-skin for a disguise, and with the same charisma as had bewitched Erda, he gained the love of a mortal woman. She bore him twins, a boy and a girl named Siegmund and Sieglinde. Wotan had in fact adopted a double disguise, with an inner layer to camouflage himself even from his human wife and children. They have no idea that he is Wotan. For them he is Wälse, a heroic outsider, and they believe that Wälse and his family are to be the first representatives of a new Wälsung line. He has a second disguise, an outer layer, to camouflage the identity of his Wälsung family from the world. In the eyes of everybody, Wotan and the Wälsungs are known and recognised as 'the Wolflings', i.e. children of Wolfe, 'Wolf-lord', taking the title from the wolf-skin of his disguise. (Wagner may have wanted to be readily understood, but he did not always go in for simple and easy.) Wälse had brought up his Wolfling children in the grimmest 'school of hard knocks' and they had grown up as outlaws. As adults they were heroic, inured to hardship and capable of coping with fierce adversity. After a particularly vicious battle, Siegmund had come back on his own to find his home a smouldering pile of ash and cinders, his mother slaughtered, and his twin sister vanished without trace. His father disappeared soon afterwards; and the only sign of him that Siegmund had ever seen of him was an empty wolf-skin.

A belligerent tribe, the Neidings (the Haters or Enviers) had attacked and destroyed their home, carrying off Sieglinde as loot and giving her to Hunding, a grim, dour authority-figure among their leaders. There had been a forced marriage, and while Hunding's guests were half drunk, Wotan suddenly materialised among them disguised as a tall stranger in a grey mantle, before whose terrifying presence they all fell silent. He approached the great tree which was the central support of Hunding's dwelling, and plunged a sword into its trunk up to the hilt.

Just how mired in his means has Wotan become in his anxiety? In order to promote his noble ends, Wotan must inevitably exercise his will to power, but does he not do it to excess? Certainly there seems to be no affection or ethical principle which Wotan will not trample underfoot in order to prevent Alberich achieving world dominion. He wrecks other people's lives and crushes his own humanity. He is faithless to Fricka and hurts her to the quick, as we shall see, in order to gain information from Erda and raise up the nine Valkyries. More dynastic considerations, the need to establish a race of free heroes who can do what he cannot, lead him to more wounding faithlessness, this time in an adulterous marriage with a mortal woman who has no idea who he really is. He reduces this mortal 'wife' and children into a means (Wotan had obviously not read Kant!) Even Elsa's plight in *Lohengrin* is nothing compared with this unfortunate, unnamed woman. The interests of this woman and their children, their feelings, their welfare and even their lives, are secondary to Wotan's great scheme. He allows her to be slaughtered in a state of despair, their house a ruin burning around her, their daughter carried off to become a sex slave after a forced marriage. Again, he stirs up heroes to mortal combat, to kill one another so that his Valkyries can spirit them off to

Valhalla to become his warriors. Everything and everyone is sacrificed to his grand plan for world salvation. It seems appalling.

But that is all too simple. Would any sensible person have any difficulty in deciding whether they would prefer life under Wotan or Alberich? Life with Alberich as absolute ruler would be so frightful that perhaps Wotan is not so wrong to stop at nothing which might prevent the catastrophe of Alberich's world domination, even to the point of his devastating compromises. It is easy to think of Wotan as no better than Alberich and as out for himself, and so he is often portrayed onstage, but *The Ring* presents real and challenging questions: how far it is possible and how far it is right to employ bad means, particularly when there seems no alternative, without fatally contaminating the ends. Part of Wotan's intense interest for us follows from his worthwhile ideals and his failure to achieve them, along with the reasons for his failure. It is all part of what *The Ring* makes real, its lessons which we absorb and make our own.

These are the main events which have taken place and the situations which have arisen since *Das Rheingold*. They have occurred on a time plane that is indeterminate, a few years, a few centuries, or even a few ages, but the creation of Siegmund and Sieglinde must have happened less than a generation before Act I of *Die Walküre* begins.

It begins with a storm. The Prelude does not so much describe a storm; it *is* a storm transformed into music. Unison strings play a relentless drumming D and conjure up heavy rain. The second violins play the same note on two strings at once, an open D and a G string stopped, supported by violas, and this original scoring adds to the relentlessness and the vividness.

Fig. 15.1 'Storm'

Abrupt crescendos and decrescendos are stronger gusts blasting through the torrents of rain, and as so often in Wagner, this nature music also has a human dimension. Its bass line is about a man running for his life, hectic and desperate, on and on and on. The storm increases in ferocity; the 'Donner' theme from *Das Rheingold* rings out in the heavy brass and repeats more and more insistently. The wind rises up as at the end of *Das Rheingold*; and although the atmosphere is utterly different, Wagner establishes a musical bridge between the first and the second part of *The Ring*, and this is characteristic of the musical continuity which extends throughout the whole cycle. The wind rises to a climax, at which the main orchestra suddenly falls silent, except for the timpani. They play thunderous rolls that are another connection with *Das Rheingold*. There follow some explosive developments of the 'Donner' theme before the storm fades. It is soon left behind, but the feeling in the music of a man in flight continues until the curtain goes up, when it reveals a Nordic tribesman's hut.

Immediately the outer door bursts open and Siegmund, heroic but exhausted, staggers in. 'No matter who owns this home, I must stop here,' he says before collapsing. His unsettled existence, and his tragic, uneasy character are all represented by the leitmotive associated with him, an evolution from the Prelude which also recalls 'Wotan's Spear'.

Fig. 15.2 'Siegmund'

An inner door opens quietly and an attractive young woman, Sieglinde, appears.

Fig. 15.3 'Sieglinde'

Thinking aloud she expresses her surprise at finding a stranger there instead of her husband, and she asks who it is that lies by the hearth. As Siegmund makes no response, she draws closer and comments favourably on his appearance, but just then he calls out 'A drink, a drink!' Sieglinde hurries to bring him some water, and as he drinks and consciousness returns, their eyes meet. Each sees there a light like none that has ever shone on either before. The principle cellist and the other solo desks lift up their voices in Freia's sensuous theme, transfigured now into all the dawning sweetness and yearning of romantic love.

Fig. 15.4 'Love'

Siegmund gazes wide-eyed at the vision before him, and asks who she is. She describes herself simply as the belonging of Hunding and the music saddens; and she continues bleakly that Hunding will accept his company if he waits. Siegmund reassures her that her husband has nothing to fear from a weaponless, wounded stranger. The thought of harm to Siegmund makes Sieglinde forget herself, and she cries out, 'Oh show me your wounds at once!'

He tells her that they are not worth a mention; if only his shattered weapons had been as strong as he was, he would never have fled the field. In any case, he says, none of this matters now because she has brought the sun back to his life. Moved but confused, she brings him a horn filled with mead, offering it tentatively, as the music tells us, whereupon he adds to the unspoken tension by asking her to taste it first. The touch of her mouth on the horn which he now raises to his own lips is a metaphor and more than a metaphor for a kiss. He sighs, and tells her that ill fortune pursues him everywhere; he must be on his way so that he does not drag her into it. Sieglinde is instantly and frantically aware of her distress at his intention to leave, and she flies to the door to bar it, telling him that he cannot *bring* ill fortune into this place because it is a house where ill fortune has long made its home. Siegmund stops in his tracks and gazes at her thoughtfully while her glance falters. His growing awareness that she needs help eventually becomes a resolve, and he reassures her; 'Wehwalt (Woeful), that is my name; I will wait here for Hunding.' The music again gathers up their emotions as his gaze fixes on her and she raises her face to his; they gaze into each other's eyes spellbound.

Siegmund is already beginning to tell out some positive ideas about romantic love. These ideas differ from those of the Wartburg in *Tannhäuser* where a disavowal of desire was almost taken as true love's defining characteristic. Tannhäuser's own outlook on the matter was always ambiguous, but in *Die Walküre* Wagner moves on to conceptions of romantic passion that were bolder and incorporated the erotic and desire.

High among the features of Siegmund's romantic feeling is a concern for the welfare, the interest and the advantage of Sieglinde. He puts her first. Although she is already becoming a very special experience, he is willing to leave her, never see her again, if this seems best for her. This ran counter to the male chauvinism that was endemic in Germany at that period, as it is in most places at almost all times; legally they were bits of property, assets or liabilities, but Wagner was bringing forward ideas of women and the erotic which validated and esteemed them. This was more revolutionary than we can readily grasp today, and the fact that Wagner respected women to an unusual degree is another matter that too easily escapes notice. This respect was erratic and conflicted, and Wagner, conditioned by his times, was erratic and conflicted about many things, but his respect was trailblazing as we can recognise by comparing him with Schiller, who had died only nine years before Wagner was born. Schiller is rightly regarded as a standard-bearer of enlightened thinking; but people visiting his house at Weimar can be surprised and disconcerted at the difference between his grand master-bedroom looking south, and the poky little space, barely more than a corridor on the sunless side of the house, which was allotted to his wife for her minimal bed.

Siegmund and Sieglinde are interrupted by the black sounds of Hunding's return, a fierce, energetic theme on the Wagner tubas.

Fig. 15.5 'Hunding'

He bridles darkly at the sight of a stranger, and gives Sieglinde a look of angry enquiry. She hastens to explain that she found the man exhausted by the hearth, and Hunding asks quickly whether she offered him hospitality. The music reveals her desperate eagerness to please as she explains that she only did what custom demanded. Siegmund attempts to placate Hunding, expressing gratitude for the hospitality but asking him not to be hard on his wife. Hunding draws himself up to deliver a kind of threat-plus-imprecation:

Fig. 15.6 'Hunding's Imprecation'

'Sacred is my hearth; hold my house sacred as well.' He tells Sieglinde roughly to get them a meal and embarks dourly on the formalities, asking Siegmund where he has come from and what was his route. Siegmund confesses ignorance; his journey was headlong and he has no idea where he has been or where he is now. Can Hunding enlighten him? Hunding tells that he himself is Hunding and that his house is surrounded by formidable kinsmen who will readily come to his defence. Will Siegmund now return the compliment and enlighten Hunding as to his own name? Siegmund responds that he is generally known as a Wolfling, but the name that suits him best is Wehwalt, Woeful. He outlines the history of his upbringing as far as the point where he lost his father, after which he became a complete outsider. He could never make friends with anyone of either gender. He found that his outlook was always out of line with other people's; what he thought was right, others found wrong; and his standards of good and bad always crossed with those of every society he encountered. Nothing was ever right; nothing turned out well. As Wagner had said of his own youth to Minna, so Siegmund too 'had a pretty miserable time of it'. All that we learn suggests that Siegmund is sensitive, and that like many who are sensitive, he is a man depressed. His ideas of isolation and his sense of persecution seem justified by the facts and not merely a sign of individual paranoia; depressives, particularly reactive depressives, often do have plenty of real grounds to be depressed. However he is truly heroic, in that he follows his principles and is true to himself, no matter how adverse the consequences. This adds to his appeal as someone who knows unhappiness, loneliness and destitution but grapples with it heroically.

Hunding however does not recognise any such appeal in his guest. 'The Norn who dealt you this hand did not love you, and nobody is happy at your arrival.' Sieglinde summons up a moment of unexpected courage and bursts out that only a coward could be afraid of a man who is isolated and wounded. She asks Siegmund how he lost his weapons. Siegmund explains that he went to the aid of a child bride who was resisting an abusive, forced marriage, and that he was violently attacked by her relatives. Her two brutal brothers fell to him (he is no mean warrior), but the girl turned hysterical with grief and threw her arms round their bodies. More relatives came up and launched a fierce counter-attack but he fought on, trying to protect her until his weapons were hacked from his grasp. As he was now both wounded and weaponless, and had no means of preventing her relatives from killing the girl, presumably an honour killing, he fled. Hence it was that he could only call himself 'Woeful'. And the orchestra gives out in full the sombre, poignant motive symbolising the tragic destiny of the Wälsung race.

Fig. 15.7 Wälsungs

Hunding has been listening intently, and now rises to his feet, his face black with anger. 'I know of a wild race. What others hold sacred means nothing to them. They are hated by all, and by me. I was called out because of an attack on my kin, to take vengeance. I arrived too late, but now come home, to find that the fugitive has tracked his way to my own house! My house shelters you, Wolfling, today. For one night I tolerate your survival, but get yourself some weapons for tomorrow, because I name it as the day for our meeting in battle. That's when you pay with your death!' As the music tells us, Sieglinde flies across to Siegmund in horror, but Hunding catches her and hurls her off in the direction of their room. 'Get out of here! Leave us at once! Fetch me my drink for the night. No rest for you, 'til I come!'

Perhaps Siegmund's presence has lent her courage, because she does not leave immediately, but busies herself with the drink and casts meaningful glances at a point on the tree-trunk. Hunding grows increasingly angry and menaces her until she leaves. He then fastens all the exit doors, and with a leering comment about Siegmund's about his defenceless state, he too leaves and bolts him in. Siegmund sinks to the floor near the fire and broods in silence. Then he breaks out in growing agitation that his father had once promised him a sword in the crisis of his life; instead he is now left unarmed. Worse, there is an enchanting woman who tears at his heart but is held captive by the same man that jeers at him for being defenceless. He calls to his father, 'Wälse, Wälse, where is the sword?' As if in answer the fire collapses, sending up sparks and flames, which enable him to see something glinting up in the tree-trunk. He imagines fancifully that it must be a remnant glance from the woman's bright eyes which she has left there. The fire burns down again, the radiance fades, but an afterglow of her lives on within his memory, and he settles himself to sleep a little more happily.

The inner door opens quietly and to his amazement and delight Sieglinde reappears. She tells him that she has drugged Hunding, and that he must escape. Further, there is a sword waiting and destined for him. She tells the story of her wedding and the mysterious stranger burying the weapon in the trunk for the one man who can draw it forth. None of those present could manage it; no visitor has subsequently achieved it, but now she has found the one who, she knows, is destined to succeed and transfigure all that she has suffered. Siegmund embraces her and tells her that she is sacred. He swears to her that he is hers forever; all that he ever yearned for he recognises in her. They will avenge what they have suffered as surely as he now holds the glory of her in his arms and feels the beating of her heart. At that moment the door flies open, terrifying Sieglinde, but the moonlight floods in and Siegmund reassures her; it was the Spring bursting in. He sings his 'Spring Song', *'Winterstürme wichen dem Wonnemond* (Winter's storms now yield to the light of the moon)', and tells tenderly that Spring breaks down all barriers. 'Love that lay deep in their hearts has called to his sister, Spring, for a bridal embrace,' a example that Siegmund follows as he embraces his sister as his bride. They glorify each other, and glory in each other, in the sweetness and rapture of each other's presence. Each calls up for the other forgotten memories from the remote past. Finally, although she really knows already, she asks him to confirm for her who his father really was; and on hearing that he was Wälse she identifies him as her lost brother Siegmund. At this, Siegmund grasps the sword and announcing that he is indeed

Siegmund he makes a mighty effort and draws it from the tree. The leitmotive of the 'Sword', which has woven its way throughout their discussion, blazes out in full radiance, followed by an electrifying triad fanfare. This is the climax to which the music of the whole act has been leading. Siegmund offers his sword to Sieglinde as a bridal gift to his sister, and she in turn confirms that she is Sieglinde and tells him that he has won her with the sword. They fall together in a rapturous embrace, just as the curtain comes down, and not a moment too soon, as George Bernard Shaw archly commented.

In some ways it seems peculiar that Wagner gave such emphasis to the incestuous aspect of their relationship. Although it really does not ultimately matter, there no evidence that Wagner 'did' incest or even engaged in incestuous fantasies, and the outstanding characteristic of Siegmund and Sieglinde and their romance is a weird innocence. This pair does not belong to the further shores of eroticism where bored roués aim to stir their jaded appetites with something ever more off limits, such as incest. Instead we are nearer to the world of first beginnings which we met in *Das Rheingold*, this time the first beginnings of romantic love, conveyed with an accuracy and brilliance beyond any other representation in art. Siegmund and Sieglinde are a light-filled pair who are breathless with the wonder of it.

It may be that the reason for the emphasis on incest is in part related to the nature of sibling relationships in the past, often more intense than we can readily appreciate now. There is an example of this sibling intensity in the lines which William Wordsworth addressed to his sister Dorothy in *Lines Written above Tintern Abbey*. Many people now evidently see these as virtually erotic, as emotionally incestuous, but is there any evidence that their relationship was physically incestuous? Nothing is impossible, but it was not very probable. Equally surprising for us of today is there was no comparable strength of feeling evident in Wordsworth's sentiments for his wife, although their relationship did possess a physical aspect.

Wagner adored his sisters as much as Wordsworth did Dorothy. We have seen that they intoxicated him, and that he also loved them dearly. Adoration, intoxication, and love; they were three different but fused experiences, and his sisters must additionally have started to give pictorial form to the shapeless ideas of 'woman' which adolescence was creating in his imagination. It was not a big step for Wagner to bring his half-sentiments for his sisters into his dawning awareness of erotic experience; *Mein Leben* leaves no doubt that Wagner identified Minna with his elder sister, Rosalie. In his late teens he had cherished for Rosalie a 'tender, almost adoring affection'. In the unstable circumstances of his home and family life, Rosalie had been a certainty and steadying influence and a refinement. She mothered him. She was kind to him, and Minna was another Rosalie. Like Rosalie she was an actress, and in his unstable theatrical life, Minna too was certainty and refinement; she too mothered and nursed him tenderly, kissing him on the mouth even when he was disfigured by facial erysipelas. All this confusion of sister-wife brother-lover feeling and Wagner's overwhelming passion for Minna became the basis for the passions which he gave to Siegmund and Sieglinde and which they feel for each other.

In *Die Walküre* Wagner registered advances towards sanctifying erotic love and resolving the Victorian separation of lust and worshipful regard, a gulf which can still persist. He confers romance on the erotic; and portrays the erotic as being at the heart of romance. With incredible rapidity the relationship of Siegmund and Sieglinde encompasses admiration, commitment, taking trouble, common interests, quickness of sympathy, correspondent wish fantasies, respect, wonder and spiritual affinity, and Wagner presciently conveyed that there was nothing more important within the mix than tenderness. Tenderness is kindness in an erotic context, and kindness and tenderness play a more important role in romantic attraction than people often realise. Paul Bloom, the Yale professor already mentioned, tells us that in the largest study ever made of 'human mate preferences', which looked at people in 37 cultures, the most important factor for both men and women was not good looks, power, income, or sexual performance but simply kindness.[67] As so often, Wagner was again penetratingly accurate in creating a relationship where kindness gives rise to romance, admiration and wonder. Consequently Siegmund tells Sieglinde that what they have is holy ('*heiligster Minne*'); and that she is sweetest bliss, ('*süßeste Wonne*'), a blessed, sacred woman ('*seligstes Weib*'). At the same time his words at the end of Act I and Wagner's stage directions make it plain that all the other elements of their romance are suffused by an overwhelming physical attraction. 'Be bride and sister now to your brother, from us shall the Wälsungs evolve!' is how Siegmund finishes. The erotic expression of their romance is represented as sacred and glorious in Feuerbach's sense, and even today and any day, this is one of the most radical and important prescriptions of *Die Walküre*. Through Siegmund and Sieglinde Wagner permeates the imagination with an example that is truer and more compelling than any exposition in intellectual terms. They present us with the experience as a reality, and they pattern it for us. Their relationship brings them something further: it alone makes it possible for them to fulfil themselves. *Die Walküre* models erotic love as a safe haven for the expression and development of self, safe at least in the terms of the relationship and their inner selves. The external circumstances of Siegmund and Sieglinde are anything but safe.

In Act II the music takes up where Act I had left off. The exuberant mood continues, and the takes up the same tonalities G and C, as ended Act I. The musical themes, the leitmotives are the same: the 'Sword' and the central 'Love' motive in its most agitated, turbulent form. However the 'Hunding' motive begins to hammer its rhythm into the textures until they darken towards C minor. The whole passage contains some of the most colossal scoring in *The Ring* so far, and minor turns to major in a simple and arresting shift. The from the depths the leitmotive of 'the Valkyries' comes riding out on fortissimo trombones.

---

67   Bloom, Paul, *How Pleasure Works*, London, 2011, p. 82.

Fig. 15.8 'Valkyries' Ride – Brünnhilde'

The tumult falls away and the scene reveals Wotan in exuberant mood. All his plans are going well. He summons Brünnhilde to saddle Siegmund, ready for his fight with Hunding. Her task is to bring victory to Siegmund, a prospect which adds to Brünnhilde's high spirits. She is a beautiful and appealing young woman, and she now sings her famous battle cry for the sheer joy of it. She plainly has a tremendous feeling for Wotan and from her high position above the ravine she is able to warn that she can see Fricka raging towards them. She declares that his battles with Fricka leave her cold, but even though she tells him she is leaving him to his fate, her confident teasing leaves no doubt of her affection and assumption that everything will turn out well.

Wotan himself is less happy, commenting wearily that it is the same old trouble and strife, but that he must make a stand. The goddess Fricka sweeps in, very much the great lady and a beautiful one. She informs Wotan that she has at last run him to earth and she claims the right to his assistance. Wotan asks her with stately decorum to explain what troubles her, and she asks him outright for revenge. She has acknowledged Hunding's plight, and she needs to punish the guilty pair who have committed adultery against him. They must pay for their outrageous lawlessness. Wotan asks her disingenuously what harm they have done. Spring has united the pair and the power of love has intoxicated them; who can resist that power? Fricka comments acidly how stupid it is to pretend not to understand, when he knows perfectly well that she has come, as she must, to avenge the sacred oaths of marriage which have been broken. Wotan answers that he does not hold sacred any oaths that bind lovelessness. There is an ambiguity here which extends to Wagner's own outlook, something disingenuous which often materialises in real life. There is a difference between a forced marriage where promises were made under duress, as happened with Hunding and Sieglinde, and a marriage where promises were freely made but where one party is now bored with the relationship. In a forced marriage the promises have no force of justice to warrant their enforcement, but in the case of marriage promises freely undertaken there is nothing to warrant breaking them simply because they have become boring. Perhaps it suited Wagner to avoid distinguishing these two very different situations, and perhaps the self-deception in the drama represents his subterranean wish to deceive himself in life.

Fricka does not give the distinction a thought, but Wotan cannot and will not take action as she asks. His heart, as he explains, is always with the bold and the brave and the outsider. Fricka, referring obliquely to his serial infidelities, explains that she has every reason to be bitter in that he himself acts as an outsider as far as the laws of marriage and its promises is concerned. However as she sings it her music tells us that she is something other than bitter.

Fig. 15.9

The whole phrase carries repeated echoes of the great central love theme of the *The Ring* and Fricka's words '*klag' ich um Ehe und Eid,* ([why do] I complain about marriage and vows)' quote it directly, but tinctured with pain. Underneath her accusation, there is still love for him, but hurt and damaged, an example of Wagner's musical-dramatic powers. She declares that what has finally left her reeling is his condoning of sibling incest, which goes beyond anything she has ever known. Wotan tells her that in that case she can know it today. It has happened; let her bless a genuinely loving bond. 'So it is all over with the gods and their eternal laws?' she demands, flaming with anger. Do these things mean nothing to Wotan since he went and engendered the race of the Wälsungs? It is not surprising that he thinks nothing of this latest desecration, having already gone off elsewhere to procreate his lawless Valkyrie daughters. They were illegitimate and yet he still had the effrontery to pass them on to her as handmaidens. He had then pursued a carnal relationship with a mortal woman, and is now throwing down his lawful wife at the feet of these illegitimates who in the divine order are no better than dogs.

Wotan remains untouched and tries to reason with her. 'You were never willing to learn what I tried to teach you. You only grasp the familiar, but I have to deal with what has never yet happened; and I have to plan for a new and dangerous situation.' The bass trumpet plays the sword motive, hinting at his great idea, at everything described in the opening paragraphs of this chapter. 'We need a hero who can act free of all help from the gods and thus acts free of the restraints that hamper the gods. Only a free hero can regain the Ring.' Fricka retorts that it is nonsense to argue that heroes can do anything which the gods cannot, because heroes are nothing but robots. Siegmund is a personification of Wotan's intentions, an automaton. Her attack is half logical, half personal aggression as she asks of the heroes, 'Who breathed life into them? Who lit up their eyes with vital fire? Without you to inspire them, what could they achieve? I see through your tricks, but you are not going to work this latest one and trick me out of this Wälsung; in him I only find you; and it is only through you that he dares anything.' Wotan answers with feeling that he grew up entirely on his own, forged his identity from his own loneliness and suffering. 'My protection never shielded him.' 'In that case do not shield him today,' Fricka rounds on him; 'Take back the sword.' Wotan is thrown off balance. 'The sword?' he asks, audibly shaken. 'Yes,' she answers, 'that magic-sharp, all-winning sword, that you, O god, gave to your son!'

Wotan explodes; 'Siegmund had won it himself,' but his tone turns to quiet anguish as he adds 'in his need'. Fricka counters inexorably; 'Who devised the need, and the sword to meet it? You were the one who plunged the sword in the tree! You were the one who led him to find it. You were the one who promised him help.' During her onslaught the music takes us into Wotan's state of mind, his rising tide of unrest, disjunction, and distress.

Fig. 15.10 'Wotan's Unrest' (signified by this extended musical section, repeated on occasion in full, significantly in the Prelude to *Siegfried* Act III)

Fig 15.11 Central core element of the above (often appearing indepently and likewise signifying 'Wotan's Unrest')

The music begins to develop this theme, Fricka senses her advantage, and presses it. Siegmund, she says, is just a vassal, in a position of bondage, and he must be punished like a vassal. Otherwise this vile creature will render contemptible not only herself but the entire governance of the gods, their very legitimacy. She presents a mirror of the situation concerning the Ring and Wotan's inability to break the laws of the gods, that is to say his own laws, to regain it. He cannot break the divine laws and condone adultery without bringing down the whole mystical structure of laws by which he rules the universe. He prevaricates, and his tone is cold and weak; 'What are you asking?' 'Let go the Wälsung!' she tells him fiercely. 'Let him go on his way,' is his muffled, meaningless reply, but she continues to be specific and tie him down; 'You will not shield him!' she enjoins. 'I will not shield him,' he mutters vaguely, but again she pins him down; 'Look me in the eye! Don't try deception! Withdraw the Valkyrie from him!' 'The Valkyrie chooses for herself,' says Wotan vaguely, but she cuts in with a simple '*Nicht doch.*' The sense of this is untranslatable: her simple, withering and total put-down, and she tells him that as the Valkyrie Brünnhilde is the another personification of his will, he must give her plain orders. 'I cannot destroy him, he found my sword,' explodes Wotan again, desperately driven to a meaningless argument. 'Then simply destroy its magic, so that Hunding finds him unarmed,' says Fricka, and just then they hear the jubilant sounds of Brünnhilde returning, preparing, as Wotan comments in gloomy aside, to set Siegmund on horseback. Brünnhilde calms down and falls silent when she senses the uneasy tension. Fricka demands that Wotan supports and safeguards the immortal gods by doing her bidding; he must swear it on oath; does she have his oath? Wotan, now leaning on his spear and staring blindly up at its tip, assents; 'Receive my oath.'

Fricka has won and knows that she has won, and again the music that follows tells us what words cannot. It suggests no jubilation or even real satisfaction for Fricka, being something lyrical and yet hollow, expressing the truth that in domestic battles, all victories are pyrrhic. The ostensible winners are often as shredded and worn as the losers. Fricka's music is not happy, and her parting shot to Brünnhilde, now back on the scene, is cutting and elegant, but utterly without joy.

> *The father of hosts awaits you,*
> *Let him now tell you*
> *How the lot has been cast.*

As the music of 'Alberich's Curse of the Ring' rises up balefully on the trombones, Fricka departs, leaving behind an atmosphere of profound unease. Brünnhilde catches the mood and adds a disquiet of her own, evident in the music, with the motive just quoted increasingly prominent. She tells Wotan that she fears for any encounter where Fricka laughs at its outcome. Wotan answers that he is caught fetters of his own making, the least free of all living. Brünnhilde is yet more disturbed, telling him that she has never seen him like this before; what is it that troubles his spirit? Wotan gives vent to his feelings in a rising tide of fury and self-hatred;

> *Oh sacred shame!*
> *Oh shameful grief!*
> *Crisis of the gods! Crisis of the gods!*
> *Endless the rage! Eternal woe!*
> *I am the saddest of all beings.*

In this passage, the music of Alberich's curse is fully and most unusually incorporated in the thematic texture as it rises to a mighty and exhaustive climax. Very significantly it ends with Wotan recapitulating the music of Alberich's despairing exclamation, '*Der traurigen traurigster Knecht*, the saddest of all sad slaves,' as he tells Brünnhilde that '*Der Traurigste bin ich von allen*: I am the saddest of all beings!' Brünnhilde is horrified, as the impulsive, incoherent music of her response makes clear;

> *Father, father, tell me what is it,*
> *You are frightening your child to the depths.*
> *Just trust in me,*
> *I am so true;*
> *See, Brünnhilde begs you.*

The tone of her last words is a telling amalgam of compassion and daughterly wheedling, and so is the orchestral music that follows in the key of B flat, a key Wagner uses to express secret warmth. (And Wagner was as yet childless; how on earth did he know?) Over a soft pedal point in cellos and bases, the bass clarinet gently intones *The Ring's* great central love theme; this mutual love is something quiet and understated for Wotan and Brünnhilde but it is at the foundation of their being. She kneels with her head affectionately on his knee,

and he strokes her hair as he looks into her eyes with an unseeing gaze.
Thinking aloud, he asks;

> *If I spoke it openly*
> *Would not I lose then*
> *The mastering power of my will?*

to which she answers;

> *It's only Wotan's will itself that you address*
> *When you reveal to me your will.*
> *What am I if I am not your will?*

Wotan assents in muffled tones;

> *What I never say aloud then*
> *Shall always remain as unspoken;*
> *I only commune with myself*
> *When speaking with you.*

Brünnhilde as already mentioned is his eldest daughter, his conscience,
and his better self, but she is also increasingly a woman in her own
right, as Wotan has later to accept, and with overwhelming difficulty.

One of the most magnetic scenes ever conceived in any form of
art now follows. There are the same muted colours as before but the
tonality slides down a semitone into A major, more inward than ever,
and Wagner's double basses take us down a falling scale to the innermost
depths of Wotan's soul. He begins to give expression to thoughts that
he can hardly bear to think. His words come in a muffled, secretive
tumble, summarising the history and his grievous mistakes from the
very beginning of *Das Rheingold*, half eager to get it all explained, half
not wanting to hear it, as if speaking it made it more real. He does it
over muted pedal points while the orchestra paints in faint allusions,
revealing echoes, of the relevant leitmotives. He leads up to a point of

something like animation as he describes Valhalla and his plans to fill it with an army of fallen heroes gathered by his daughters. Brünnhilde joins in supportively, reminding him that this plan has been a success; she herself has brought in many a hero. Why should he worry since they never lacked spirit or results in their work?

Wotan explains darkly all that Erda had warned him at their second encounter. It was Alberich and his dark hosts who could and would achieve his downfall if ever Alberich should regain the Ring. He must therefore take it himself again, but is debarred from by the very laws on which his authority rests. Only one being can encompass the deed, a hero acting on his own and outside the sphere of the gods, but all that Wotan creates turns out to be replicas of himself. His creations are no more free agents than he is. Brünnhilde does not understand; Siegmund, she points out, has been deliberately brought up as an outsider and acts entirely on his own. Wotan tells her that Siegmund's upbringing and his very independence were all created and devised by himself. How could he possibly have hoped to deceive himself? How quickly and easily Fricka has unmasked his self-deception! To his shame, she had seen right through him. Now he can only do as she wants.

Brünnhilde still cannot take it in; is he taking back victory from Siegmund? Wotan breaks out again; he has handled Alberich's Ring; its curse now haunts him. The horns bay out a contorted version of *The Ring*'s great love theme as he says that he must destroy his own son, Siegmund, who has gone through so much and is now destined to endure betrayal and abandonment by his own father. In a fit of self-hatred he calls down ruin on the gods, all is vanity, nothing; there is only one thing he seeks: 'The end – the end!' In a calmer moment, he reflects that this, the end for him, is in any case the sole object of Alberich's actions. Erda had warned him that when 'the darksome foe of love' (Alberich) produced a son, the doom of the gods would not delay for long; and he has recently heard that Alberich had purchased the sexual services of a woman whose womb now bears 'the fruit of hatred'. His self-loathing returns as he gives a blessing that is also an imprecation to this 'Nibelung-son'; let him inherit the gods' glory in all its empty charade, and let him enjoy it to the dregs.

Brünnhilde still cannot trust herself to understand; what is he asking her to do? Wotan answers blankly that she must fight for Fricka and her values. He uses the music of Hunding's '*Heilig ist mein Herd* (Sacred is my hearth)' to explain this, and here Wagner somehow transforms it from power and menace to weariness and bitterness. What Fricka has chosen, Wotan now chooses. His own will means nothing. He cannot bring a free spirit into existence, and she must fight for Fricka's vassal. Now beside herself with distress, Brünnhilde begs him to recant. Wotan loves Siegmund, and for the sake of Wotan's love, Brünnhilde will protect Siegmund. Wotan turns audibly sterner, telling her to bring down Siegmund, and adding with anguished pride that it will take all her strength and courage; it will be no weakling or coward that she encounters. Brünnhilde now opposes him directly. Wotan has taught her to love Siegmund; the orders of such a divided spirit as he has revealed will never constrain her to act against Siegmund.

She might as well have stuck a firebrand in the face of a wounded tiger. All Wotan's self-hatred bursts out at Brünnhilde. 'Ha, insolence, you! Sacrilege to me! What are you but a thing, the blind, choiceless means for my will. When I confided in you, did I sink so low that I am now the butt of my own creature's scorn? Do you know my anger? Your courage would fail if a single ray struck you. Within my heart there lies rage enough to turn to dust and waste a world that once laughed for me in joy. Woe to the one whom it strikes! I warn you; do not provoke me. Do what I ordered; Siegmund's downfall! *That* is the Valkyrie's work!'

He rages off, and the orchestra winds up to a tempestuous climax that is devastating in its sheer blast and blackness. At every stage Wagner has taken us right to the heart of Wotan's tormented progress, and it is a draining experience, even at home listening to a recording or watching a DVD. Brünnhilde speaks out what most people are now feeling, sad and weary over an aspect of Wotan she had never imagined, let alone thought possible. Her very armour drags her down, although it felt light enough when she fought in better circumstances. Today's fight is an evil one and in her foreboding she can barely make herself attend to it. 'Alas, my Wälsung, to my grief I, the faithful one, must act faithlessly and forsake you!' As she slowly makes her way from the scene, the orchestra embarks on a counterpoint between cor anglais and unison cellos and basses which looks blunt and dry on paper, but is the height of expressive poignancy when actually heard, even on the piano. It ends in a menacing growl from the trombones with a reminder of 'Wotan's Spear'. The central love motive of *The Ring* begins a soft answer in the strings, love as opposed to law. Gradually the motive gathers momentum. It moves towards agitation and then to crisis and anguish as it is counterpointed by the Hunding rhythm; and Siegmund and Sieglinde come rushing onto the scene. 'Stay here awhile; give yourself rest,' he tells her; 'Further, further,' she flings back, nearly hysterical. 'No further now, sweetest of women,' he tries to calm her. 'You sprang up from our magical rapture and dashed onwards with such speed I could barely keep pace with where you had gone. Speak to me. See; your brother embraces his bride.' He leads her to a low rocky ledge and sits her there. She gazes with growing ecstasy into his eyes, but then starts up again. 'Away, away; I am desecrated and disgusting. When I lay in your loving embrace, you woke in me the purest, holiest ecstasy, a sacred rapture.' The orchestra here melts into a sweet eroticism that fully matches her sentiments, but she continues, saying virtually, 'Shudderings and tremblings and shameful terrors came over the treacherous woman who had previously let herself be possessed carnally without love. I am worthless; I am rubbish. I can never belong to you, to such a wonderful man. I can only bring shame on you, my brother; desecration on my adoring friend.' Her tone has risen to frenzy, and once again it raises the amazing question: how on earth did Wagner know? He has here described minutely and exactly the desecration, the befouling of inner citadels, the misery and self-loathing that women who have been raped and abused often describe, and until the last fifty years the magnitude of the psychological damage was seldom recognised as Wagner has managed here. Even today it sometimes is not. Was it that Minna had in her glory days with Wagner told him things about Herr Einsiedel and what he did to her of which we know nothing; or was it that Wagner's hard-won powers of empathy and his delving down into his own imagination had led to such insights? We shall never know, but even today women generally seem to experience this scene differently from men; and perhaps they are right in feeling that men still do not really understand.

Siegmund responds by telling her that her shame will be annulled in vengeance as his sword pierces her abuser's heart, but Sieglinde is not listening. In her demented state she imagines, correctly as it turns out, that Hunding has awoken and is gathering his kin and his hounds. They are baying to heaven against the breaking of the marriage bond. She grows more and more hysterical, shifting between sobbing entreaties not to reject the kiss of a lost woman, and frightful visions of Siegmund being torn to pieces by the hounds. Horrors from the past flow into present imaginings as she sees in her mind the ash tree splitting and Siegmund's sword splintering. She loses consciousness, and falls limply in his arms. For a moment he fears that she is dead, but reassured by her breathing, he lets her sink sleeping into his embrace. Cradling and supporting her as they sit there, he gazes at her lovingly.

The scene grows darker as the music about the depths of their affection gives way to the 'Fate' motive,

Fig. 15.12 'Fate'

which, as we have already seen in the chapter on the music, is a telling example of Wagner's musico-dramatic genius. Sounded principally on Wagner tubas, it speaks of all that is dark and ominous in that unknown realm, the future. Brünnhilde materialises before Siegmund like an apparition, solemn and sibylline. She warns Siegmund that he must soon follow her. 'Who are you that stand before me, so beauteous and stern?' he asks. She tells him that her gaze only falls on those consecrated to death; she only appears to warriors on the field of their final battle, before they become hers. In answer to his questions, she tells him that she bears her fallen heroes to Valhalla and to Wotan, and that a host of fallen heroes will greet him and acclaim him. Yes, he will find his own father there. Yes, he will find women there; Wotan's own daughters, the embodiment of every man's wish-fantasies, will serve him at the feasts. Siegmund tells her respectfully that he accepts her as high and holy; but let her tell him just one thing, the only thing that matters. Will his bridal sister accompany her brother, will Siegmund embrace Sieglinde there? His voice rises in an impassioned plea; but Brünnhilde's response is cool; Sieglinde must linger here on earth a while; Siegmund will see Sieglinde no more.

'So,' says Siegmund, 'you can greet Valhalla, greet Wotan, greet my father, the heroes, and the fantasy girls; but to go with you I now refuse! Wherever Sieglinde lives, in joy or woe, there too shall Siegmund remain. My encounter with you and your gaze has not unsettled me. You shall never compel me away from Sieglinde.' 'You have looked upon the Valkyrie,' replies Brünnhilde, 'and you have no choice. You might not be coerced in life, but death will compel you.' 'Who then is the hero to whom I shall fall?' asks Siegmund; and when she tells him that it will be Hunding, he scoffs; she will need stronger threats than that, as he can easily deal with Hunding. He has now an all-conquering sword, which will ensure his victory. Brünnhilde disabuses him in a rising tide of emotion; 'He who once planned that, now plans for your death!' Siegmund, accepting instantly the truth of what she says, is horrified; he cries out, 'No more: do not frighten my slumbering love.' He continues, distraught with pain, 'Woe, woe, loveliest wife, you saddest of all loyal beings; against you rages the world in arms, and I, whom alone you could trust – may I not shelter you, must I betray you in the battle? Shame upon him who planned the sword for me and victory, but now plans mockery instead! If I have to die, I shall never go to Valhalla! I will see myself in hell first!'

Brünnhilde is shaken to the very depths, and the orchestra turns inward; 'Are you really telling me you that eternal joy means so little? Is that poor woman everything to you, who so miserable and tired hangs there in your arms? Is nothing else sacred to you; does nothing else matter?' Siegmund rounds on her bitterly; 'You may look young and beautiful, but I know how hard and cold is your heart. If you can do nothing but make sport of me, you can take yourself off; but if you want to feast yourself on my misery, then go ahead; go on, glut your pitiless spirit! But you can just give up blethering to me about Valhalla's dismal joys!' Greatly moved, Brünnhilde asks him to trust his wife to her care. Siegmund retorts that he will trust her to none but himself. If he must die, he will kill her first in her sleep. (After all, he has just discovered every reason to distrust the pledges of divine beings.) Brünnhilde responds hectically, 'Wälsung, madman, listen to me. Trust your wife to me, for the sake of the living symbol she gained from your loving embrace.' Siegmund answers blackly as he draws his sword; 'This sword, which a false man gave to a true one – this sword, it may be useless against the foe, but it can turn against the friend. If there are now two lives here, then Nothung, terrible steel, take them in a single stroke!' Overcome by compassion and moved beyond enduring, Brünnhilde strikes the sword from his grasp. She tells him she has recast his destiny; 'Sieglinde shall live and Siegmund with her; I have changed the conclusion. Trust to your sword, and wield it well, and I will truly defend you. Farewell Siegmund, most sacred of heroes. We meet again on the field.'

She leaves in a whirlwind of emotion, leaving Siegmund heartened, surprised and grateful. The music gradually subsides from its tempestuous high-water mark, and sinks back into the prevailing sombreness. Grey clouds again descend as Siegmund looks down at Sieglinde. Thinking aloud, he wonders whether the Valkyrie had cast a spell so that Sieglinde slept through the turmoil; perhaps she may manage to sleep through the horrors of the battle itself. Despite forebodings in the orchestra, he tells himself that a sweet dream is charming this saddest of beings. The cellos steal in with the secret glow of Siegmund's 'Spring song', as he lays her gently on the moss; but now Hunding's motive blares out offstage, all the more biting because it is now a bare brass unison. Siegmund leaps to his feet and goes to find Hunding. Unfortunately, Sieglinde now begins to stir. Again past and present come flooding together and she talks in her sleep; 'Is not my father yet home? Is he still hunting in the woods with the boy? Mother, who are those strangers, they don't look friendly or kindly. Those dark vapours! Swirling mists! Fiery tongues are licking everywhere! The house is burning. Help me, brother! Siegmund! Siegmund!'

She awakens suddenly from one nightmare into another. Everything is veiled over in black clouds riven by lightning. Hunding's brassy call sounds close by, as does his voice;

> *Wehwalt, Wehwalt,*
> *Stand where you are;*
> *Otherwise my hounds will hold you.*

They miss each other in the mists and greyness. Siegmund challenges Hunding with the sword, telling him that he has drawn it from the tree; and in a flash of lightning Sieglinde sees them in mortal combat. 'Stop you madmen, kill me first,' she shrieks, but then staggers back before a closer, brighter flash. In it Brünnhilde becomes visible, protecting Siegmund with her shield, and telling him, 'Strike now Siegmund; trust to the sword'. But just as Siegmund is doing her bidding, an angry red glow shines through the clouds with Wotan at its centre, and Brünnhilde recoils at his words, 'Back from the spear; in splinters the sword!' He stretches out his spear against Siegmund, and Siegmund's sword shatters on it. Hunding plunges his own spear into the defenceless man, and Siegmund falls dead to the ground. Sieglinde screams and collapses in a terrified heap of hopeless sobbing, but Brünnhilde hurries towards her, realising that there is not a moment to lose and telling her, 'To my horse, for me to save you,' as she gathers up Sieglinde. She vanishes, and the clouds divide again, revealing Hunding smirking dourly as he draws his spear from Siegmund's body. Wotan also becomes visible, leaning on his spear and gazing down at Siegmund in illimitable agony. Quietly and totally turned in on himself, he clenches out to Hunding the words, 'Go hence, vassal, kneel before Fricka. Tell her that Wotan's spear has avenged the slight to her pride. Go! Go!' Before his fulminating whisper and the contemptuous wave of his hand, Hunding falls dead, and this is one of those rare moments when we see the sheer power of Wotan the god. There is a long hollow silence. And then he remembers! Brünnhilde! 'Woe to the guilty one! Fearful indeed shall her sentence be, when my horse overtakes her in flight!' The orchestra erupts as Wotan storms off in pursuit, a tempest of the purest Wotan music set in the blackest D minor. It brings the act to a shattering close, so shattering that it often leaves audiences too drained for anything but the vaguest, thinnest applause.

Before we take leave of Siegmund and soon Sieglinde, they can still tell us something more about romantic passion. Today there seems something of a downgrading of romance in preference to ideas of man-woman relationships that are more practical and serviceable, but *Die Walküre* is majestically opposed to this downgrading. Sheila Kitzinger, the feminist guru already mentioned, set out reasons for being opposed to it which still hold true. She wrote the angry book mentioned in connection with *Tannhäuser, Woman's Experience of Sex*.[68] Along with the even more influential book, *The Mirror Within*, by Ann Dickson,[69] it launched bitter protests that the debunking of love merely suited male orthodoxies, which were little concerned with loving sensitivity and romantic passion. At the very beginning of her book, Sheila Kitzinger states,[70] 'I am, quite unashamedly, writing about love. Even though now it may be difficult to show love in a way that has meaning for the other person, I explore some of the

---

68   Kitzinger, Sheila, *Woman's Experience of Sex*, London, 1985.

69   Dickson, Anne, *The Mirror Within: A New Look at Sexuality*, London, 1985.

70   Op. cit., pp. 13, 17.

forms in which love can be communicated.'[71] It is significant that with her claim to write about love unashamedly she felt she was pushing out the boundaries and had to be defensive. The climate to which she was reacting was the one unintentionally bequeathed by Freud, which reduced romantic passion and the erotic to lust, the urge to copulate. But equally important for a romantic relationship as for any other is the fit or at least the match of two personalities, one with another, and the better the match, the better the relationship is likely to work. Jung envisaged the romantic relationship as supremely important, not least because he saw it as a central part of fulfilment and individuation, of becoming who we really are. For Siegmund and Sieglinde their relationship alone makes sense of the rest of their lives and they briefly become who they really are. Most people are luckier than Siegmund and Sieglinde, who only had a few hours together, and long relationships with significant others are obviously more important for enabling people to become themselves. All these are precepts that Siegmund and Sieglinde affirm. And as I emphasised already, Siegmund and Sieglinde not only affirm the life-enhancing value of romance and romantic passion; they actualise it and the music instils it.

The third act of *Die Walküre* has long seemed to me the most perfect that Wagner ever created. It begins with 'The Ride of the Valkyries', which is their first experience of Wagner for many people, even for a fair number a first experience of 'classical music'. Some then reach a point of finding it vulgar, only to recognise and love it again as they rediscover it as a mesmerising feat of musical imagination, and I have passed through this sequence myself. With its tempestuous wild beauty, its exhalations whizzing through the air and its barely controllable energy, it captures and haunts the mind. It depicts the Valkyries, beautiful, spirited young women, riding the stormy skies and bearing heroes killed in battle across their saddles.

71   The same point as was expounded by Jean-Luc Marion in *The Erotic Phenomenon* (Chicago, 2007).

Fig. 15.13 'Valkyrie Horse's Kick'

They are assembling just under a mountain-top before returning with their heroes to Valhalla. Generally they are fearless and thoughtless, but they share a mutual, sisterly affection.

Some of them are on the lookout for the others, but they all break out into heartless mirth when their horses kick and attack one another, infected by the mutual hatred of the heroes they bear. Eight of them are soon gathered, and they are about to ride off when they realise that the ninth, Brünnhilde, is still missing. At that moment they see her in the distance, towards them riding for her life.

As she draws near, they realise to their confusion that it is no hero but a woman that she carries. On her arrival she leaps from the saddle; and to their horror she tells them that for the first time she is herself pursued and fleeing; Wotan, father of the hosts, is in pursuit. They cannot believe their ears. 'Are you out of your senses? Pursued by Wotan? Trying to escape him?' Responding to her terrified appeal, some of them return to the lookout, only to report the distant storm clouds billowing rapidly towards them with Wotan at their centre. Brünnhilde asks her sisters to protect her and to shield the woman. 'What is it with the woman?' they ask, and Brünnhilde gives them a breathless summary of all that has happened, and again asks them for help. They break out distractedly. 'You mad, mad sister, what have you done? Brünnhilde – broken her father's orders?' She asks each one of them for the loan of a horse; but they all turn their backs; their horses have never before gone against Wotan; nor will they now. Their tumult calms down suddenly as Sieglinde begins to stir. She has heard them, and tells them to forget their concerns; all that she wants is to die. She rounds on Brünnhilde, 'Who asked you to save me when I might have died with my love, my Siegmund? Unless you want me to curse you, then at least now do what I ask and plunge your sword into my heart.'

Brünnhilde exhorts her to live for the sake of Siegmund and

for the sake of the living symbol which she received from him; a Wälsung lives in her womb. Sieglinde is instantly transformed, both ecstatic and terrified for her unborn child, and it was Wagner who taught me aged sixteen what this situation must mean for a woman. Sieglinde cries out, 'Rescue me brave one, rescue my child! Shelter me, everyone with your mighty protection.' Except for Brünnhilde, the Valkyries dare not help, and Sieglinde throws herself on Brünnhilde's mercy; 'Save me! Save the mother!' Brünnhilde makes a sudden resolve, and this is another of the great turning points of *The Ring*. Raising Sieglinde to her feet, she tells her that she must flee but make her way alone; she herself will remain and draw on herself the wrath of Wotan while Sieglinde makes good her escape. Sieglinde asks frantically where she can go, and the other Valkyries relent and do their best to help. They quickly suggest a tangled forest away to the east; Fafner the dragon lurks there guarding the hoard, and it is dangerous, no place for a woman, but Wotan abhors it and never goes near; and so it is there that she should go. Wotan draws ever closer, and Brünnhilde tells Sieglinde to flee for her life and endure every hardship, secure in the certainty that her womb shelters the world's greatest hero. Brünnhilde hands over the splintered sword, and predicts that this hero will one day refashion it and wield it, and that his name will be Siegfried. Rising to an ecstasy and a matching predictive insight, Sieglinde hails Brünnhilde: 'O holiest wonder, glorious Maiden;

Fig. 15.14

I thank you for being so true. For the sake of him whom we both have loved, I shall save the child. One day far into the future he will reward you to the full and bring you joy.' This is the music which will eventually end *The Ring*.

She leaves in violent haste and Brünnhilde in terror asks her sisters to protect her, as the tension and energy rise ever higher. Wotan appears on the wings of the storm, to the same black, D minor 'Wotan' music which ended Act II. 'Where is Brünnhilde? Where is the guilty one? Do you think you can hide her from me?' Beside themselves, they answer like tiny girls, 'Father, you terrify us. What have we done to stir such rage?' 'Do you dare to make a mockery of me?' he throws back; 'Take care; I know; you are hiding Brünnhilde from me; stand back from her, she is lost eternally, cast out for all time, she has thrown away all that gives her value.' The other Valkyries implore him to temper his rage in a short ensemble of astonishing beauty, but he rounds on them with withering scorn, '*Weichherziges Weibergezücht*: You feeble-minded bunch of females! You never acquired that pathetic spinelessness from me, such that you snivel and whine when I pass judgment on the guilty! Listen to me! Nobody knew my innermost thinking as she did. She carried out what my will had designed; but she broke the bond between us by defying my designs. She turned against me the very intentions that I had devised. Do you hear me, Brünnhilde, you who gained from me all that you are, your weapons, your name and even your life! Do you think to hide from my accusation like a coward, and thus escape your sentence?'

It is important to realise that even in this Wotan is more than an angry, bullying father letting fly at a defenceless daughter, though he is all this. He is once again caught up in the constraints of the very laws by which he rules the world. He is bound to apply them to all without favour or discrimination because any social order and legal system that is maintained in a patchy, piecemeal fashion rapidly collapses. A city that is divided against itself cannot stand.

There is a moment of silence before Brünnhilde stands forward and answers. 'Here I stand, father; pronounce your sentence.' Her meekness seems to enrage Wotan afresh. 'The sentence is not mine to determine; you have defined it yourself.' He had formed her very identity, as he tells her, and he describes how she has herself effectively destroyed that identity. In breaking his orders over Siegmund, she has cancelled her character as Wotan's alter ego, and she is left only with whatever remains. Once again, Brünnhilde cannot believe her ears. 'Are you casting me out; do I really understand you?' Wotan lists aspects of her role as a Valkyrie which she shall never again fulfil, such as bringing him his mead, and the music takes on a wistful, mournful undertone as if he were just beginning to recognise all that he himself will lose. However this only serves to add to his rage and pain, and as the 'Spear' motive stalks down a full octave and a half, he tells her that she will be forever cast out from his presence. 'You are really taking from me everything you once gave me?' she asks in anguish, but Wotan has worse to come. 'Not I, but the man who takes you and dominates you; he will take it from you; I shall lay you down asleep and defenceless, and you will be there for the taking by the first man to find you.' The other Valkyries break out in renewed horror; they implore him to desist; he cannot do it, not least because the shame by association would attach to them; but Wotan forges on inexorably; 'Do you not hear what I ordain? She is cast out from the Valkyrie fellowship. Her youthful bloom will decay. Some man will enjoy her, and she will sit and spin by the hearth, a butt and a target for everyone to mock.' At this, Brünnhilde falls with a cry to the ground, and Wotan turns his rage against the other Valkyries: 'Does her destiny make you tremble? Then leave her forever. Any of you foolish enough to stay here or come back to help her will share her fate! Go from here now! Stay far from this mountain; otherwise doom will overtake you!' No decree in Stalin's gulag, no fiat of Pol Pot could be more devastatingly effective. The Valkyries are helpless before this all-powerful tyrant which their father has now become and which they never before knew possible. In a turmoil of confused feelings and abject terror, they rush from the scene, leaving the god and his daughter alone. They remain motionless as the storm calms and the clouds gradually lift and clear.

In the gathering twilight there follows the scene which contributes so much to making this act and the whole *Ring* extraordinary and sublime. There is a slowing of the tempo and fall in the dynamic, and there might have been a lowering of the emotional temperature, a decline in the dramatic interest. Instead there is if anything a heightening, because of this scene's expressive intensity, and no other act of Wagner has such a continuous arching span from beginning to end. Wotan has knocked the bottom out of Brünnhilde's world. Musically there is a thematic transformation of the motive of 'Wotan's Unrest' (from early in Act II) which is itself a derivation from the 'Wotan's Spear' motive.

Fig. 15.15

Introduced by the fate motive, the plangent tones of bass clarinet, oboe and cor anglais reveal Brünnhilde's inexpressible sorrow and her tears behind the eyes, but she does not weep. She takes up and develops the motive above as her own in her first utterance. With extraordinary courage – but then she is, after all, her father's daughter – she starts to reason with him. 'Was it so shameful, what I have done, that you must inflict on me so shameful a sentence? Father, tell me, I beg you, look me in the eyes, soften your anger. Explain how it was so wrong, what I did, that that it leads you to cut yourself off from your most loved and loving child.'

Fig. 15.16

Wotan's muffled, gloomy response initiates a dialogue. 'Consider what you did; that will then make it clear why it was so culpable.'

Brünnhilde: I carried out your command.

Wotan: Did I tell you to fight for the Wälsung?

Brünnhilde: That is what you told me as lord of battles.

Wotan: But that instruction was one I took back.

Brünnhilde: Because Fricka divided you from your innermost convictions. In following hers, you went against yourself.

Wotan: I thought you understood me, and that I was punishing a deliberate act of defiance. But you simply thought me stupid and cowardly. If I did not have to respond to treason, you would be too trivial for my anger.

Brünnhilde: Perhaps there *was* much that I did not grasp; but the one thing which I *did* grasp was that you loved the Wälsung. I knew of your inner divisions, the constraints that made you deny this truth. No matter how bitterly you suffered, you only faced up to the other truth, that you must deny Siegmund your protection.

Wotan. You knew that full well, and still thought to give him support?

Brünnhilde: Yes – because I kept one thing in sight, that other truth which you put out mind. Recall that when Wotan is at war, I guard his back; and I had to witness what he did not see; I had to look upon Siegmund. As I was foretelling his death to him, I had to look into his

eyes, hear his words, watch the terrible anguish of his boundless love.
I stood there, bashful, astonished, and ashamed. I could only think of
one thing, how to serve him, how to share victory or death with him;
this became the only destiny I could choose. And only one being had
breathed this love into my heart; it was you, it was your will!

And as she tells him it was he who had inspired this emotion in her,
the strings transform the music of her pleading into an expression of
radiance and love.

Fig. 15.17

'Your will had drawn my sympathies towards Siegmund, and it was in
obeying your will that I disobeyed your command!'

Wotan: So you did what I so eagerly wanted to do, but what twofold
necessity made impossible. You thought it so easy to come by the bliss
of love while I was in turmoil, when appalling frustrations had roused
me to insensate rage. In the misery of my powerlessness, I even turned
against myself. I was overcome with the terrible desire to end my
sorrows in the wreckage of everything, including myself and my world;
and that was just when you were wreathed about with intoxicating
sensations. You were overcome by a rush of emotion. You were moved
to a state of bliss, at exactly the time when this terrible crisis had brewed
a draught of absolute bitterness for me to drink. Well, let your light-
heartedness lead you now, because you have broken with me. I must
avoid you for as long as I live.
Brünnhilde: So then does it make no difference that your daughter, in
all her naiveté, was baffled by your orders and could not understand

your reasoning? We are so close that my own reason told me only one thing, to love what you loved. We are also so close that if you insist on forsaking me, you will cut yourself off from part of your very own self. You cannot want to shear off and dishonour something that will always remain part of you. Indeed if you inflict such degradation on me, you effectively bring that same degradation on yourself.

Wotan, at a tangent to her argument replies, 'You were happy to follow the power of love; now you will belong to someone whom you *have* to love.'

Brünnhilde: If I must part from Valhalla, then at least do not give me to a coward to boast over me.
Wotan: You cut yourself off from the father of the hosts; he cannot make further choices for you.
Brünnhilde (recalling Sieglinde's prophecy): You gave rise to a glorious race; no coward can arise from it, but only the highest of heroes.
Wotan: Do not dare to mention the Wälsungs; cut off from you, I am cut off from them; envy had to destroy them.

This is a most revealing sentence. Brünnhilde has made Wotan aware in some distant corner of his psyche that the Wälsungs and all that they signify could be a potential threat. First of all there was her sudden, overwhelming rush of feeling for Siegmund that has come between the god and his daughter. Additionally, the freedom of spirit that the Wälsungs enjoy is a new element erupting into his world and challenging it; and it is entirely beyond his control. This spirit of independence might even lead to a new order, a viable alternative to his sovereignty. His first reaction to these developments is only a destructive envy, but other thought processes are unconsciously at work.

Brünnhilde presses her point: 'In shearing myself off from you, I saved them. Sieglinde bears within her the holiest of fruit; and she will bear it forth in sorrow and pain.'

Wotan: Never ask for me to protect that woman, nor the fruit of her womb.
Brünnhilde: She still has the sword which you arranged for Siegmund.
Wotan, in a sudden, towering rage: – 'and that I smashed in pieces!'

His rage collapses again, and continues in withdrawn, muffled tones. 'Do not attempt to weaken my resolve. I must be gone; I have stayed too long; I may not choose for you now. I must simply fulfill the sentence.' In response to Brünnhilde's request to know what he means, he tells her, 'I shall bind you in sleep. The first man to wake you can simply take you for his own.'

Brünnhilde, again falling on her knees: 'If I am to be fettered in sleep, then this one thing you must allow me. Surround me with appalling terrors, so that only the most noble may gain me.' Wotan is still inflexible; 'You are asking for too much, too great a favour!' Brünnhilde: 'This one thing you *must* allow me. Annihilate your child as she clasps at your knees; let all trace of her body be destroyed by your spear, but do not condemn me to such a cruel disgrace. At your command let a magic fire spring up to encircle the rock, so as to frighten away anyone but the bravest.'

This is another of the supreme turning points of *The Ring*. Suddenly Brünnhilde has won. What follows immediately is the music of her triumph as Wotan undergoes a complete and utter change of heart. It now becomes clear that he has been far more affected by the course of their confrontation than he allowed himself to feel; and he discovers that he has come to a momentous decision. His reason for dealing with her so relentlessly was, as we saw, that he was once more caught by the systems of law and ordinance by which he rules the world. It would fall to bits, if he did not uphold it. But now he has come to a decision *not* to uphold it. It is not until later in *Siegfried* that he reveals more plainly and factually what is expressed in *Die Walküre* mostly by the music. He has decided to overturn Brünnhilde's punishment, turning it into blessing for her and an act of self-sacrifice for him. It will ensure that his sovereignty will fade and end.

Wagner makes us aware that something ineffable is happening, as Wotan declaims; 'Farewell, you dauntless, glorious child; you who are the highest pride of my heart; farewell, farewell, farewell!' He now takes leave of his daughter, and makes it clear that he is giving her everything that she asked, and more than either can yet know. This passage is known as 'Wotan's Farewell', and whatever the leitmotives may represent individually, and whatever subjects are told by the text, the opera from this point onwards is about Wotan. He continues, painfully at first, 'If I must part from you, never again give you a loving greeting – if you will never ride with me again – if you will never again hand me my mead – if I must leave you, you I love so, you laughing delight of my eyes! – then a bridal fire shall burn for you such as never burnt before! A flaming radiance shall surround the rock. Its biting terrors shall frighten the timid; the coward shall keep far away.' As he describes the magic fire, the music flashes and flickers, and then broadens for the leitmotive of 'the Hero' as he declaims, 'For one man alone shall win you as bride, one freer than I, the god!'

Now the music recapitulates the phrases which Brünnhilde had sung as she explained to Wotan how he had inspired her with his love of the Wälsungs, Fig. 15.17, but now it is mightily expanded. It diverts at first into an alien tonality, but then gathers itself steadily towards the same apex as before, and instead of ending in an abrupt staccato as earlier, it leads on to a radiant second inversion chord which is both climactic in itself and looks onwards. (It is the chord which precedes and looks forward to the cadenzas in classical concertos such as Mozart's.) After the last words of Wotan, the pair had turned aside, each too deeply affected to meet each other's eyes, but now all else is flooded out by absolute love, and they are drawn into each other's arms while the music speaks a matchless fusion of poignancy and beatitude.

It is a moment where time should stop, but time never stops, and the music moves on to the figure which had previously expressed Brünnhilde's agitation at her fate. It now acquires the gentle rocking character of magic sleep, as Wotan reflects that he must now close her laughing eyes (*'Der Augen leuchtendes Paar'*) which had so often brightened his life on dark days. He sings 'May they gladden me today this one last time, as I kiss them again in this last farewell,' to the music of the ineffable theme known as 'Wotan's Farewell'.

Fig. 15.18

He tells her that their beauty and brilliance will one day shine on a happier being than the immortal on whom they must now close forever. The cor anglais steals in with a rare full statement of the leitmotive which had first appeared early in *Das Rheingold*, the 'Renunciation of Love' (fig 14.4). Wotan kisses her eyes closed, and kisses Brünnhilde's godhead from her. The rapt, remote and eerie music of 'Magic Sleep' descends first in the wind instruments,

Fig. 15.19 'Magic Sleep'

then the strings, and leads on to full restatement in the orchestra of the music of Wotan's '*Der Augen leuchtendes Paar*', but transcribed upwards now into the relative major. To the accompaniment of the rocking motive this melody wends its way seamlessly onwards, as Wotan places Brünnhilde's spear alongside her and then her helm on her head. Finally he covers her tenderly with her huge shield. The music passes through various orchestral colourings, but concludes on horns and cellos in the specific theme of 'Wotan's Farewell'. Not Tchaikovsky, not Mahler ever conveyed such intense yearning and loss as Wagner did here.

But still time does not release its hold. Wotan draws himself together, takes up his spear and pronounces an invocation, calling up Loge in his original form of fire, the shape in which Wotan first tamed him. Wotan strikes his spear-point three times on the rock, and at the third stroke, a rivulet of fire gushes forth. Wotan directs it to surround the sleeping Brünnhilde, and soon the mountain top is encircled by a rampart of flame, a scene where only Wieland Wagner (in my experience) fully presented to the eye what the music presents to the seeing ear.

Wotan pronounces a final incantation; 'No one who fears my spear-point, shall ever pass the fire!' The orchestra surrounds the scene in glory, the music of magic fire, and through it the heavy brass sound out the theme of the hero, a prophecy. As a whole this is a music of timeless majesty. In Wieland Wagner's production, at Bayreuth in 1958, Wotan made his way slowly through the sea of fire, pausing for a last look, and then turning back to look again, before disappearing through the flames. The leitmotive of 'Wotan's Farewell' is played again, and the act comes to a close with the leitmotive of 'Fate', appeased and softened by an enchanted modulation into E major. It is as if any Jungian shadows of destiny had been incorporated into the overall glory, at least for a while.

With this mention of glory it is time to review again just what Wotan has done. It is plain that he has abdicated in favour of Brünnhilde and the hero that is to come. By encircling Brünnhilde with magic fire, he has established that Sieglinde's offspring, the hero Siegfried, will indeed be the one to win Brünnhilde. He has done more, setting things in motion towards handing over his entire sovereignty to a new order, the new age represented by Brünnhilde – and Siegfried. Brünnhilde and Siegfried will inherit the earth and he will decrease. It will be clear later in *Siegfried* that he comes to see that the unplanned line of the Wälsungs will achieve something that he could never manage by design. Siegfried will be the free hero so remote from the gods that he can regain the Ring without Wotan or any one in his entourage breaking his own laws. Siegfried will fulfil for Wotan what Siegmund could not; but Wotan does not expect Siegfried to do it for his sake. He does not expect Siegfried to reinstate the gods, but to initiate the new age of man.

Finally even this expectation turns out differently. It is Brünnhilde and not Siegfried who will finally redeem Wotan and the world, and the paradox is that it only happens because she has disobeyed him and separated from him. We shall see that in *Parsifal* the magician Klingsor tells Kundry that the one who rejects her sets her free, and in *The Ring* it is Brünnhilde who similarly rejects Wotan's ordinances and sets him free. It is a woman, and not any hero, who proves to be the free spirit needed by Wotan. All the time he was lamenting that he had failed with Siegmund and could only create bondsmen, he was telling it to the person who really *was* his free creation, but whom he would first try and punish for exercising that freedom.

Die Walküre has presented further essential lessons. One of the major challenges facing most people is about the difficulty of separating and letting go. We have to do this, for example as parents, but we must all let go of many things and people. Life gives us much but it also separates and strips us again. Wotan finds this difficult. He resists Brünnhilde separating. He resists losing a relationship which had become too important, and emotionally incestuous. Brünnhilde adored being her father's favourite, his little princess. She could bask in his approval, but it only worked because she had suppressed her own burgeoning development and continued being an outreach of his identity. He likewise had been able to bask in her approval, knowing that they shared a special oneness; but they were both stuck. This situation arises between parents and offspring, between teachers and pupils, between leaders and pastoral figures and those that they lead and care for, between doctors and their patients. In *Der Rosenkavalier*, the Marschallin confers an almost universal significance on the way to bear separation when she tells herself that she must lightly hold and lightly let go.

As often happens in real life, so in *Die Walküre* the force which blows apart the special closeness of parents and offspring is a major shift, a sudden step towards a new independence or the onset of the erotic. Sometimes it is both at once, as it is for Brünnhilde. It can be hard to accept that offspring are now independent, pursuing ideals and life-plans that are different from parental intentions; and it can also be hard for parents to accept their offspring as libidinous. In falling for Siegmund and defending him against her father's orders, Brünnhilde acts out something of both. Wotan first does what often happens, and displays a paroxysm of fury. How dare Brünnhilde betray him by separating and negating all that he has made of her? How dare a favourite son (or daughter) go into the voluntary work or the teaching profession instead of the family business, 'when I have spent my life building it up for you'? How dare children fall in love, and prefer someone else to their parents? 'You can leave my house!' 'Don't expect a penny from me.' 'After all I have done for you!' Unfortunately these things really happen. Where Wotan is remarkable and presents a constructive lesson is in his ability to change. Even at first, he gives Brünnhilde a hearing, and goes on listening when she says things he does not want to hear. It seems as if nothing is happening, and yet he is changing. The ice is quietly melting, and suddenly it breaks and he accepts Brünnhilde's new freedom. He does more than accept; he affirms it and promotes it.

Brünnhilde had at first done better than he, because she immediately accepted the change in him. She copes with the shattering recognition that he is not the all-wise, ever-rational father that she believed. Like most children, she had seen him so because she had endowed him with features taken from children's innate expectations of their parents. She then filled them out with the reality of the benign, adoring father which she had hitherto experienced. Then came the destruction of her idol. By the end, when he has softened, she seems to understand him as he really is, with all his aspirations, achievements and failures, and she again embraces him lovingly, but with a love that is different.

Die Walküre illustrates how after people accept change and let go, everyone can gain, but this does not mean that the sense of loss is not very difficult. The bereavements that we undergo throughout life can be excruciating, but unless we embrace them and make peace with them they will drain us away. Sometimes, as can happen with successfully letting children go, everyone benefits. At the end of *Die Walküre* Wotan patterns for us his liberation from anger and resentment. He has been released from his isolation, because he regains a relationship which is real and special, even if it can no longer continue in its outmoded form and he never sets eyes on her again. Things are not as they had been, because children, pupils, trainees, patients, clients and circumstances all change. If we can accept this then what follows is often a new dimension, and in modelling this *Die Walküre* is again redemptive. It is redemptive to embrace necessary changes, not least for the benefit of the bystanders, who get fall-out that is positive instead of negative. If we embrace change as *Die Walküre* subliminally commends, we can be happier people living better lives.

Like *Das Rheingold*, *Die Walküre* had already been performed on its own at Munich, but it was first given in context as the second part of *Der Ring des Nibelungen* at the first performance of the complete cycle, which took place at the Festspielhaus in Bayreuth on 14 August 1876. The cast consisted of Albert Niemann (Siegmund), Josephine Schefsky (Sieglinde), Joseph Niering (Hunding), Franz Betz (Wotan), Amalie Materna (Brünnhilde), Friederike Grün (Fricka), Marie Haupt (Gerhilde), Marie Lehmann (Ortlinde), Luisa Jaide (Waltraute), Johanna Jachmann-Wagner (Schwertleite), Antonie Amann (Siegrune), Hedwig Reicher-Kindermann (Grimgerde) and Marie Lammert (Roßweiße). The performance was conducted by Hans Richter under Wagner's supervision.

Johanna Jachmann-Wagner (Schwertleite) was that same Johanna

Wagner has had created the role of Elisabeth in *Tannhäuser* 31 years earlier at Dresden, and she created the role of First Norn in *Götterdämmerung* three days later.

SIXTEEN

SIEGFRIED

The third part of *Der Ring des Nibelungen* contains Wagner's plainest example of a universal myth. It is a hero myth, a genre familiar to Westerners from the fairy tales of childhood, but found in almost every culture where information is available. Hero myths are purposive, inscribing in young minds the example of the hero who originates in obscure and adverse circumstances, receives the call to adventure, and leaves home to confront difficulty and danger. He must do it with courage, and in many versions of the myth, he is 'the boy who knows no fear'. His reward is a throne and a beautiful bride.

Hero myths symbolise the life and psychological experiences common to people throughout the world. We all begin as helpless children, to be chiselled and moulded in a manner which is at best nurturing and empowering, but fraught with friction and frustration as we become crafted to make a success of life and educated to fit in with other people and society. The hero myth instils an awareness that to make our way in the world, we have to leave home and go forward to meet life's challenges on our own. We free ourselves of parents and their demands, and of other childhood authority figures, but at the same time we have to sacrifice their protection. Everyone has to find his own way through the forest and confront the unknown and its dangers. To live a fulfilling life, a person must vanquish a monster, generally a dragon or some other mythical beast, and anyone who cannot succeed in this risks being unable to achieve a throne (establish a worthwhile position), and win the beautiful princess. The throne and the princess are commonly reckoned as the first essentials for fulfilling ourselves and becoming the people we want to be. Some people never manage it because they have been injured by their parents, by their damaging education or other destructive experiences, the dragons. Sometimes it is simply the consequence of parental diffidence and confusion rather than viciousness, or the effect of uncertainty about adult standards and an ambiguity of their expectations, which can block the progress of their offspring.

Hero myths are the same in different climes and eras because human beings' material and psychological development is basically the same, whether they are born and brought up in Saxony or Saskatchewan, and whether it is 2013 AD or 1500 BC. Throughout the ascent of man from his first grey glimmerings, his anatomy and physiology have not changed much, and the same myths express and mould human experience as they have ever done. In consequence the same didactic myths are eternally relevant. The striking similarities in hero myths go some way towards supporting not only Jung's belief that these myths are inherited but also his theories of inherited archetypes and the collective unconscious. Nothing can prove that these theories are true, but it is a reasonable hypothesis that these myths confer a survival advantage, and that natural selection engraves them ever deeper in the minds of successive generations.

The particular hero myth of *Siegfried* takes its rightful place in *The Ring* because its events follow on from the story of Sieglinde. Sieglinde had made her way the forest while Brünnhilde stayed behind on the Valkyries' rock to face Wotan. Sieglinde had somehow survived her pregnancy, and was discovered in childbirth by another refugee to the forest, Mime, whose brother Alberich had been brutalising him down in Nibelheim (during *Das Rheingold*). All this becomes clear from the discussions and recollections of the main characters in *Siegfried*, as does the fact that Sieglinde died in childbirth or shortly after, having first entrusted her newborn to the care of Mime. Mime had brought up the child in a dwelling he had created in the forest, half cavern, half hut, which he had established as a forge, but his motives had not been pure. Mime is fully aware of the whole history of events so far, and as Siegfried's origins predestine him to be an invincible hero, Mime's plan is to raise him in ignorance, so that he can somehow be induced to murder Fafner and enable Mime to seize the Ring for himself. So it comes about that Siegfried is the hero in this hero myth segment of *The Ring*.

Hero myths are generally happy stories, and the precepts which *Siegfried* conveys are positive. *Siegfried* seems to radiate a special, personal energy because Wagner invested its hero with all the force and success of his own childhood struggles against chaotic circumstances and his own fitful carers. However, Wagner invested Siegfried's particular struggles against Mime, his carer, with considerable harshness which gave the story a chequered complexion. The harshness reflected the scars from Wagner's own childhood, and mottled his carefree youth who knows no fear. In Act I he behaves more like a particularly vicious adolescent than the flawless, irresistable young man which Wagner by his own account intended.

The first music of *Siegfried*, the Prelude to Act I, is extraordinary, and like all Wagner's Preludes it is unlike any other Prelude to any opera anywhere. It begins almost inaudibly with an ominous drum roll in the depths, and its first harmonies are the strange oscillating chords on two bassoons in a low register, symbolising Mime's ruminations. These sink down to Stygian depths where the contrabass tuba intones the 'Hoard' motive. It is the depths of Mime's consciousness and ours but it is he who begins the drama, onstage and alone, brooding on events from *Das Rheingold*, a circumstance which enables Wagner to recall one of *Das Rheingold*'s most significant episodes. The slow, dark beginnings of the Prelude gain form and rhythmic pace from the theme of the Nibelung hammering, and the music develops into a repetition of passage the where Alberich compels his Nibelung slaves to bring up the hoard. Thus the first music of *Siegfried* connects back to the very heart of *Das Rheingold*. Only the devastating climax from the passage in *Das Rheingold* is missing, and instead there are whirling repetitions of the 'Ring' theme, and the Ring dominates

Mime's consciousness as we first see him. He is sitting at an anvil, trying to forge an effective sword and complaining of his drudgery. He has a Sisyphean task because Siegfried has grown up to be immensely strong, as heroes are, and simply breaks and throws out every normally satisfactory sword that Mime can make. Mime approaches his task with an obsessive mediocrity which Wagner portrays on lower strings, endlessly, monotonously repeated.

Fig. 16.1 'Mime'

Mime's motive derives from the Nibelungen hammering:

Fig. 16.2 'Nibelungen hammering'

Mime muses on the one sword that Siegfried could never break, but alas he has not the strength or the skill to weld its fragments together. That sword is Nothung, whose fragments Brünnhilde once gave to Sieglinde. Mime knows that if Siegfried had Nothung reforged, he could kill Fafner.

At that point Siegfried comes bounding in, driving a large bear at Mime, threatening to let it loose on him unless he has a new sword ready, and telling Mime that even the bear was better company than he. Siegfried is temporarily mollified when Mime produces the new sword, and he shoos off the bear, only to fly into a rage at the sword's pathetic quality. He smashes it on the anvil, telling Mime that he should have smashed it on his skull. Mime, he says, burbles about giants and battles, and great swords that he can forge, but he only produces trash. It is only contempt which prevents him from flinging the smith and all his works into the central fire of the forge. Siegfried's first appearance does not leave an impression of unmitigated charm, let alone the 'pure love' which Wagner believed his Siegfried expressed. Mime tries to reason with him, reminding him of all that he has done and offering him a cooked meal, but Siegfried only knocks it to the ground. Mime wailingly points out how he swathed Siegfried as a baby, made him fine toys and a splendid horn, plus a warm bed to sleep. Siegfried replies that none of this taught him to love Mime, who seems only ugly and evil, and whom he would often like to murder. If Mime is as clever as he is always claiming, then let him explain why in spite of loathing him, Siegfried always comes back. Mime says it is because of the natural love of every child for its parent, but Siegfried denies this possibility. He says that he has seen how the animals go with their young, always two by two, but that Mime is on his own, with no wife. When the dwarf answers that Siegfried is not an animal, and that he, Mime, was both his father and mother in one, Siegfried grows angry again. He has seen that offspring are like their parents, but he has seen his reflections in streams and knows that he is no more like Mime than a fish is like a toad, and that no fish ever had a toad for a parent. It now occurs to Siegfried that this must be why he comes back, to learn who his father and mother really are. Mime is evasive and will not tell him until Siegfried half throttles him and threatens worse unless he tells the truth. This makes Mime tell how he found his mother, Sieglinde, in the forest, and how she died in childbirth there in his smithy. Siegfried is much moved and disturbed at the idea that his mother died to give him life, a glimmering of finer feelings. Mime goes on: as she died, his mother had pronounced that her baby should be named Siegfried, and had handed over the fragments of a broken sword. Siegfried demands evidence for this unlikely story, and Mime produces the fragments, whereupon Siegfried insists that Mime instantly refashion the sword. He can then take it and go out into the world, never to return.

He storms off in high excitement, leaving Mime agonising over his conundrums: how can he stop Siegfried leaving; how can he bring him to Fafner's cave; and above all how can he refashion the broken sword, which alone would be strong enough to strike down Fafner?

At this point a visitor appears. It is Wotan in his guise of 'Wanderer', and sonorous brass intone the grand theme symbolising this imposing stranger with his long blue cloak and broad-brimmed hat, pulled down low over a missing eye.

Fig. 16.3 'Wanderer'

He asks Mime with jovial firmness for hospitality as he explains who is, how he is known across the world as Wanderer. Mime tells him rudely that if he is Wanderer he can just wander off. Instead the stranger sits himself authoritively by the hearth, and tells Mime to question him; he stakes his head that he can offer valuable advice on any three questions that Mime may put. Thinking aloud but *sotto voce*, Mime warns himself to ask subtle, cunning questions that will get rid of the stranger. He asks Wanderer who lives in the bowels of the earth, who lives on the earth's broad back, and who lives on the glorious heights. The answers are satisfactory and very full, Wagner's way of telling the audience the events of *The Ring* so far, but they are more than that, as we see in Act III. As Wanderer answers the third question and describes the gods, Valhalla and Wotan, a clap of thunder reveals to the quaking Mime who his unwanted guest really is. He makes as if to show the way out to his unwanted guest, but now the guest turns the tables. He tells the dwarf that his own failure to offer proper hospitality now entitles him also to ask three questions, and that it is now Mime's head which is forfeit if he cannot answer on any point. The first question is what race is worst treated by Wotan, even though he loves it the best, and Mime, beginning timidly, recounts the history of the Wälsungs, Siegmund and Sieglinde. The Wanderer next tells Mime something which he knows well, that a wily Nibelung looks after Siegfried, in the hope that Siegfried will slay Fafner, and he asks Mime what sword Siegfried must use, whereupon Mime, more confident, provides the history of Nothung. Wanderer now asks his third question, who will reforge the sword, and this strikes a fearful apprehension into Mime. A reforged Nothung is essential to his plan, but he cannot do it, and if the wisest of smiths cannot manage it then who can? Wanderer points out that Mime should have asked him the really difficult questions to which he did not know the answers instead of wasting his opportunities.

This question-and-answer sequence explains the prehistory of *Siegfried*, and Wagner devised it before he decided on *Das Rheingold* and *Die Walküre* to present that history onstage. The questions and answers in *Siegfried* eventually acquired a different purpose, and different too from the purpose of Wotan's explanatory monologues in *Die Walküre*. Those monologues make use of the story of *Das Rheingold* to ensure that Wotan will *matter* to us. The sequences of *Siegfried* are part of Wotan's way of creating a personal narrative, a narrative whose significance cannot be clear until after his Act III scene with Erda. Meanwhile the dialogues do contribute to the identities of Mime and Wotan. Mime reveals all kinds of things which he told Siegfried he did not know, thus revealing himself as a liar, and Wanderer on his side reveals that he finds it amusing to strike fear into a miserable, downtrodden little dwarf. Perhaps this is Wotan acting like Wagner himself and 'gratifying the pettier feelings that great beings have in common with small ones'. For now, he goes off laughing as he announces that only one who has never learned fear will reforge the sword, and that he leaves Mime's head forfeit to that one.

What this scene also usefully achieves is a motive, a reason why Mime needs to instil fear into Siegfried; it is to prevent any possibility that Wanderer's prophecy could be fulfilled. Wanderer's departure plunges Mime into a state bordering on frenzy, the feeling of terror which was familiar to Wagner from his own childhood, and which he now etched into music with lacerating precision. Mime imagines Fafner thundering through the dark forest to get him, and turns into such a gibbering, screaming wreck that he falls behind the anvil and is almost relieved when he sees it is Siegfried who springs into the cave, just as Wagner was when he was beaten by his stepfather for his noisy nightmares. Siegfried demands the reforged sword. He seems in better humour than when he left, and he responds constructively to Mime's suggestion about teaching him fear as his mother asked (or at least as Mime now tells him she did). To teach him fear, Mime gives him descriptions of some things that he himself has found terrifying, such as the forests in twilight murk, and Wagner expresses this in music of hallucinatory vividness. Siegfried however feels no pulsating heart, no sweats and shivers, and so Mime instead hits on the idea of a practical lesson which can serve two purposes. He will lead Siegfried to the dragon to teach him fear, so that he ceases to be a threat and kills the dragon, allowing Mime to seize the Ring.

Siegfried is eager to begin, and when Mime declares that he is unable to refashion the sword, Siegfried determines to do it himself. He throws back in Mime's face the suggestion that he should try and solder the pieces together, telling him that if he followed the same principles as his useless instructor, he would produce the same useless result. Instead he takes a metal-file and to Mime's horrified fascination he grinds down the pieces of steel into shreds, places them in a melting pot and sets it on the forge. He asks Mime the sword's name and embarks on one of the great set pieces of *Siegfried*, the first of two forging songs. With its massive orchestration and its brazen harmonies, this song has clear-cut verses. A song was allowed here because it fell within the ordinances of realism which Wagner had set himself; it was included because the drama required it, and it was not simply an aria battened onto the drama for vocal display. Siegfried's song is an expression of brute strength, as he pulls mightily on the bellows and fires up the forge to its brightest heat. His song addresses the sword, admiring the metal turning to liquid in the white heat, and it recalls the great tree which Siegfried felled to provide its charcoal. The charcoal, he sings, was once black but now it is white hot and sends up fountains of sparks. Mime begins to realise that Siegfried is going to kill the dragon without learning fear, and hatches a new plan to foil Wanderer's prophecy. He concocts a poison for Siegfried to drink when he is hot and thirsty from his victory over the dragon. Siegfried has meanwhile reached the point of pouring the white-hot metal into a mould for the sword, and now plunges it into the water to temper it, sending up great billows of steam. At the same time he throws out contemptuous comments at Mime's cookery without suspecting its lethal purpose, and soon thrusts the sword back into the fire. Once it is red hot he positions it on the anvil so that he can hammer it into its definitive shape and beat its blade to cutting sharpness.

He now embarks on his second great forging song, striking massive hammer-blows to the music. He imagines that its red glow and its sparks make a kind of reverse parallel to its past when its cold steel drew hot blood (Siegfried is wrong, as Nothung has only as yet struck Wotan's spear). Mime meanwhile is dreaming of the world dominion which will come to him with the Ring. Thinking aloud, he makes it clear that he is only interested in the worst possible kind of power, 'power over', not 'power to do'. He sees in his mind's eye Alberich and the other Nibelungen helpless, grovelling and agonising under his tyranny. Meanwhile the sword is soon finished, and there is now another reverse parallel, this time to Siegfried's earlier shattering of Mime's sword on the anvil. Siegfried tells Mime that this is how Siegfried's sword does it, and smashes Nothung down on the anvil. This time it is the anvil which shatters, breaking apart from top to bottom with a tremendous crash. Siegfried holds the sword aloft and is gazing up at it radiantly as the curtain falls.

The Prelude to Act II conjures up an atmosphere of nebulous murk in the depths of the forest. This is formless, brooding music. It is night. A vague shimmer in the strings, without rhythm, is the background for the theme of 'Fafner the Giant', now 'dragonised'. Soft, ominous drumbeats have replaced the massive sonority of the trombones, and the low note of the theme has slipped down a semitone. The contrabass tuba stalks the depths with the theme of the dragon, which now has none of the rearing energy of the dragon into which Alberich transformed himself in *Das Rheingold*, but still registers as powerful, even in inertia. The being who has taken on dragon form in *Siegfried* is not Alberich, but Fafner; and yet this dragon is still created by the Tarnhelm, and this may be why both dragons have the same music. The motive of '*Nibelungenhass*' alternates with the theme of the 'Ring' and leads to an extended passage, reprise of 'Alberich's Curse of the Ring', from *Das Rheingold*, only slightly abridged. The Prelude to Act II has summoned up for the imagination the scene of Neidhöhle, the domain of the forthcoming action, but musically it has reached straight back to a pivotal point of *Das Rheingold* where Alberich curses the Ring, the point from which the present events take their origin.

The curtain goes up on Alberich, lurking there in the hope that he can regain the Ring. That is how he spends life, waiting, eaten up with envy and resentment. It is the darkest hour just before dawn, but the strange luminescence which rapidly approaches is not that of dawn. It puzzles Alberich briefly, and fades to reveal Wanderer, whom Alberich instantly recognises as Wotan. Alberich hurls abuse at his arch-enemy, condemning him as a robber without shame, bent now on more tricks and lies. Wotan tells him he has come only to watch events, not to perform them. Alberich says he sees through this fraudulent talk to Wotan's real intentions, and knows his weakness: the laws which give Wotan his authority put him under a binding obligation not to break those laws, as he would like. Wotan retorts that he had achieved Alberich's subjection by the power of his spear, and that he was under no obligations to Alberich, legal or otherwise. Alberich mocks him; he looks so strong, but he is wracked by anxiety; Fafner is doomed under the curse of the Ring, and who will inherit it then? Alberich reminds Wotan that if it comes back to Alberich, he will use it very differently from the foolish giants. Wotan replies calmly that he neither knows nor cares what Alberich plans; the Ring shall belong to whoever can win it. Alberich says he knows Wotan's hopes for a hero to pluck the fruit that Wotan may not. Wotan answers evenly that Alberich has the wrong target; he should pay more attention to Mime. Mime is bringing a lad who knows nothing of Wanderer (Wotan); but for Wotan's part Alberich can do what he likes. Alberich asks desperately, does that mean Wotan will not try and lay hands on the hoard (and the Ring)? Wotan replies obliquely but tenderly that he must allow the one whom he loves to fend for himself; he must stand or fall on his own. Alberich asks whether it can possibly be that he is only competing for the Ring with Mime, and Wotan leaves it open, commenting cryptically much as before, that the Ring will go to whoever takes hold of it. Wotan goes on to suggest that Alberich could take the initiative. There is Fafner; if Alberich warns the dragon of its death, perhaps it will give up the Ring to save itself; he, Wotan, will even call the beast and awaken it for Alberich. To Alberich's excitement and confusion, Wotan calls down to Fafner; and from the depths, the cavernous voice of Fafner asks sluggishly who is there. Wotan announces that it is a friend come to warn of danger and suggest a plan; will Fafner repay him with the treasure? Alberich adds desperately that a mighty hero is on his way to pit himself against the dragon. Its only response is to comment darkly that it is hungry, and Wotan begins to explain the scale of the danger. Alberich weighs in frantically, urging Fafner simply to let go the Ring and live a long life in peace. With a long yawn, the dragon declares, '*Ich lieg' und besitz, lasst mich schlafen*': it has and holds, and wants only to go on sleeping! Wotan laughs, but tells Alberich he should stop abusing him and listen to his advice instead. Everything is of its own nature, and Alberich can do nothing to change it. He must deal with Mime, whom Alberich should understand better, as made of the same stuff as himself; but Alberich will soon have to learn how different other natures can be from his own. With this Wotan departs. The storm again rises briefly, the glimmer breaks out and speeds away into the forest, leaving Alberich confused, dejected, and furious. He calls after the departed Wotan that laugh as he may, Alberich will yet see the immortal gods fade into oblivion, and the music reiterates his curse on the Ring, amplifying and heightening it. His final utterance is almost another imprecation; that as long as the gold sees the light of day, he will be a sentinel on guard, awaiting his chance. He slips into a rocky cleft, and the music sinks back into the same brooding silence as in the Prelude.

Dawn soon appears and with it come Siegfried and Mime. While Neidhöhle in the far background remains in the shadows, the new arrivals find a sunlit area further forward, and Mime announces that they have arrived. Siegfried says that if this is the place for learning fear, then he needs Mime no longer and wants to be on his own. Mime says that if Siegfried cannot learn what fear is now, he never will, because there is a dragon of immense size and brutality lurking in the cave behind them. In its raging anger, it will open its jaws and gulp him down in a single mouthful. Its slaver is so poisonous that a single drop would be enough to shrivel up Siegfried's body and bones. Its mighty tail could catch him in its coils and crush him like glass. Siegfried hears all this attentively and makes plans to deal with the different hazards in turn. He asks if the beast has a heart, and on being told that it has, a grim mercilees heart, he says he will thrust Nothung into it, and asks Mime if this is what he meant by fear. Mime tells him; just wait until he sees the dragon and he will think lovingly of the dwarf who brought him there. Siegfried answers that he cannot bear this talk of love; just let him go away. Mime assents and says he will wait for Siegfried by the stream, and Siegfried answers that in that case he will send the dragon along there to find Mime. Mime shuffles off, muttering, 'Fafner and Siegfried; Siegfried and Fafner; oh – if they only could each destroy the other!'

Siegfried settles down under a tree and begins the long soliloquy which reveals new and attractive aspects in his personality. He comments to himself on the beauty of the forest, and like other orphaned children, he also wonders about his parents. 'What was my father like? – Oh, like me of course! A child of Mime would have looked just like Mime.' Through Wagner's music, the whole forest thrums increasingly with rapturous life. Siegfried goes on to reflect how his mother might have been, and the music begins to develop the leitmotive of 'Siegfried's Longing for Love'.

Fig. 16.4 'Siegfried's Longing for Love'

But his mother? 'That is something I cannot imagine. But why did she have to die when I was born? It would be terrible if all human mothers had to die because of their sons. Oh how I would love to see my mother, a woman and a human being like myself.' He falls into a reverie until his ear is caught by the sound of a woodbird singing in the branches above.

Its main song, quoted shortly, is a refashioning of that other unspoilt voice of nature, the song of the Rhinemaidens, the first words of *Das Rheingold* (Fig 14.1). After listening a while, Siegfried is captivated and becomes convinced that some of the song has meaning; and he asks it directly if it has something to tell him. He recalls being told that it was possible to learn the language of the birds, and he cuts and shapes a reed for a pipe, and tries to play it and speak the bird's language. He only produces a very sour imitation. He whittles at his pipe and tries again but with no better result, and after a third try and a worse result, he gives up, announcing good-naturedly that he is put to shame by the enchanting rogue above. He announces that he does better on his horn, and hopes that his horn will summon up more company as friendly as the woodbird. He embarks on a two minute display passage that has become the joy and the bane of horn players everywhere. Included in it are two leitmotives of cardinal significance, 'Siegfried' (the opening phrase of Fig. 16.5) and 'The Hero' (the closing phrase), both symbols of himself.

Fig. 16.5 'Siegfried's Horn Call'

As if roused by these exuberant sounds, the music of Fafner seems to rear up from the depths, and a monstrous dragon emerges into the clearing. Siegfried is startled, but comments cheerfully that his horn seems to have summoned a really attractive playmate. The dragon pauses to ask who is there. Siegfried is surprised that the dragon can speak, and asks the same question as he put to the woodbird: can it teach him what he has come there to learn, the nature of fear? The dragon bellows mockery at this show of arrogance and threatens Siegfried, which provokes him into threatening the dragon in return, unless it can teach him fear. The dragon says it came out for a drink but now finds fodder as well, and it bares its array of teeth. Siegfried only jeers that that dreadful maw is gaping too wide and needs closing. Swapping threats, the dragon says that its maw will make a meal of Siegfried more readily than go on with this senseless chatter. Siegfried retorts that as he has no intention of making a meal for the dragon, and that he must dispose of the threat on the spot. 'Come on, then, you boastful lad,' it roars. 'Watch out, roarer; the boastful lad is coming!' answers Siegfried, whereupon the orchestra blazes up in some of the best 'fight music' that Wagner ever wrote, only surpassed by Siegmund's fight in *Die Walküre*. The Wagner tubas bellow 'like Stygian bulls' as George Bernard Shaw put it, and Siegfried in turn avoids the dragon's jaws, its slaver, and its tail. Then as the dragon rears up to crash down on him and crush him utterly, he leaps forward and plunges his sword into its heart, before hurling himself aside to escape from beneath its mountainous collapse.

Fafner now lies dying, and asks Siegfried who he is, and who it was who stirred him to such a murderous deed. Siegfried says he does not know who he is, but that it was the dragon's threats which stirred him to the deed. The dragon now acquires second sight and a strange, crude dignity, and reveals that it does indeed have something to tell. It explains that its death spells the end of the giants who once dominated the earth. As a giant he had done to death his brother Fasolt for the sake of the accursed gold which the gods gave away as payment. He had guarded the gold as a dragon, but that dragon has now fallen to a youthful hero. The dragon warns Siegfried to be on his guard, because the one who plotted for Siegfried to bring death to the dragon is now plotting for the death of Siegfried himself. Siegfried is affected by the pathos of the situation; in dying the dragon strikes him as wise; if he tells the dragon his name, can it explain who his father was; his name is Siegfried. 'Siegfried!' sighs the dragon, and falls back dead.

Siegfried can only comment with rueful nonchalance that the dead can tell him nothing, and that aided by his sword, he must embrace life. As he draws forth the sword, some of the dragon's blood splashes out on his hand, causing a burning sensation, and unthinkingly he puts his fingers to his mouth and sucks them. Immediately the woodbird's song takes on meaning and Siegfried realises that it must be due to tasting the dragon's blood. He takes us with him because we too understand what the woodbird sings.

THE WOODBIRD

Hei!_____   Sieg-fried ge-hört nun der Nib-lung-en Hort!

Fig. 16.6 'The Woodbird'

The woodbird tells him that the Nibelungs' hoard in Fafner's cave is now his own. If he finds the Tarnhelm, it will help him do great deeds. If he finds the Ring, it will make him master of the world. Happy to learn this Siegfried thanks the woodbird, takes its advice, and enters the cave.

Mime now sneaks on, making sure anxiously that the dragon is dead before nearing the cave, at which point Alberich rushes from his cleft and bars the way; where does Mime think he is slinking off to? Mime curses his brother for being there, and each calls the other a thief, Mime asserting that he has earned the Ring by years of hard labour bringing up Siegfried, Alberich arguing venomously that it was not Mime whose sacrifice won it from the Rhine, and that not even the mangiest of dogs has less right to it. This virulent discussion goes at a tremendous pace, 'patter song' taken to unprecedented heights, but it slackens when Mime tries cunning instead. Yes, Alberich can keep the Ring, but let him treat Mime as a real brother with some sharing; let Mime at least keep the Tarnhelm. This provokes Alberich to further jeers and fury: share the Tarnhelm with a crafty thief like Mime? Never! He would never sleep safely again! Mime starts to scream, also in fury; 'Am I to have nothing, while you get everything?' 'Not a single nail for you!' shouts Alberich. Mime says he will set Siegfried on Alberich; Siegfried's sword will pay him out; but at that moment Siegfried appears, bearing not the trinkets and toys which the dwarves tell each other he will choose, but the Tarnhelm and the Ring. They slip back into hiding as Siegfried tells himself that he has no idea what use these new possessions can be. Apparently he has not taken in the woodbird's description of their extraordinary powers, and is happy with them for their own sake and because of his affection for the woodbird. They also make a memento of his defeating Fafner, even if he still had no success in learning fear.

Siegfried's gaining the Ring is one of the hinge-points of the cycle, as it brings together the fairy tale about the boy who knows no fear and the story of the Ring. It is interesting that some authorities, most eminently Carl Dalhaus,[72] draw stark distinctions between fairy tales and myths, and Dahlhaus insists that the fairy story of Siegfried, the boy who knows no fear, is not really a myth, and that this somehow sets it completely at a tangent to the myth of *The Ring*. However, his distinction between fairy tale and myth seems mistaken. The story of Siegfried is a fairy tale, but it is also the very paradigm of a didactic, constructive myth teaching important truths to young minds. At all events the fairy tale and the *Ring* myth entwine and fuse, and this brings the Ring itself back into the story after one and a half operas where it was off the scene and far away.

As Siegfried emerges from Fafner's lair with the Tarnhelm and the Ring, the woodbird sings again and tells him not to trust Mime, but that because of the dragon's blood he will be able to hear the murderous intentions behind Mime's ingratiating words. The woodbird's words turn out true about Mime, but it is one of the inconsistencies of *The Ring* that Mime's nephew, Hagen, soon lies and dissembles far worse, and yet Siegfried never hears *his* murderous intentions.

Mime greets Siegfried with wheedling, and asks him if he might have learnt fear from the dragon, even in slaying it. Siegfried says that fear is still an unknown quantity, and that the dragon's death gives him no pleasure because there are worse scoundrels still alive, like the one who led him there. Mime now unwittingly begins to reveal to Siegfried

---

72   Dahlhaus, Carl, *Richard Wagners Musikdramen* , tr. (as *Richard Wagner's Music Dramas*) Mary Whittall, Cambridge, Cambridge University Press, 1979.

(and to us) that he had always loathed Siegfried and only nurtured him as a means to getting hold of the Ring. He adopts coaxing tones as he describes his current plan to drug Siegfried and hack off his head. Mime boasts about it at tedious length until Siegfried is suddenly overcome by revulsion and strikes him dead with his sword. Alberich's mocking laugh (some brother!) is audible in the background.

An instinct leads Siegfried to drag Mime's corpse into Fafner's cave, and with an effort which taxes even his prodigious strength, he drags Fafner's gigantic form after Mime, to block off the entrance. He comments that now at last they can both rest in peace, sharing jointly together what they coveted separately in life. He finds that he is hot from his efforts and the noonday sun, and seeks shelter under a tree, relaxing and looking up into its branches. To his joy, he discovers his particular woodbird among the others in its branches, and asks it to sing to him again. He comments that he is alone and lonely and says that he envies the woodbird for so much company. His mood darkens as he takes his loneliness for real and recollects that his father and mother died without his knowing them; his only companion had been a dwarf; there was never love between them; and he had been forced to kill him. He addresses the woodbird; can it help find him some company; he has often called for a friend without success; so far the bird has advised him well; might it be successful in this as well? If it sings again, he will follow its advice.

The woodbird does indeed sing again. 'Now that Siegfried has destroyed the awful dwarf, he must awaken the glorious bride. She sleeps high on the mountain summit, surrounded by fire. If he passes through the fire and awakens the bride, Brünnhilde will be his!' At this Siegfried leaps up, and thanks the woodbird for this hope and purpose. He asks it to say more, and it turns enigmatic: 'Joyful in grief, I sing of love. I weave a happy song from sorrow; only those who know the yearnings of love can understand.' Siegfried says that this fills him with eagerness; he will away from the forest to the mountain. 'But one thing tell me, dearest singer. Will I break through the fire; will I be able to awaken the bride?' The bird sings a reassurance; 'The bride can be never be woken by the timid, but only by one who knows no fear.' Siegfried laughs happily. 'The stupid boy, who does not know fear; why, dear woodbird, that is me! Today I tried to learn it from Fafner, but my heart burns at the idea of learning it from Brünnhilde instead. Only, how shall I find my way to the mountain?' The bird flutters from the branches, and hovers over Siegfried, who exclaims, 'That is how my way will be clear. You shall fly ahead, and I shall follow!' He goes happily after the woodbird, but it teases him for a while by fluttering hither and thither. Then it takes a definite direction and flies off with Siegfried following, and a sforzando brings the act to a happy and decisive end.

Wagner finished composing the music of this act in 1857 and completed its orchestration in 1864, but it was only in 1869 that he took up the composition of Act III. This twelve-year gap provides a good point for taking stock. Siegfried thus far can present different faces. In performance, it can emerge as a dour drama of grisly caves, storms, and forest gloom, and orchestration that often sounds like crude metal ore. It can also come out completely differently, as something which sets the senses swimming with Wordsworthian loveliness, all forest murmurs and dappled sunlight; and the particular version we hear depends on the conductor's shaping of the design and on the way he plays Wagner's 'colour organ', the orchestra before him in the pit. The first two acts also raise certain doubts, mainly about Siegfried himself. It is true, what is often said, that no other character by Wagner comes with such good references and such high expectations. As the chapter on *The Ring* explained, its first two segments set the scene for *Siegfried* and its hero. *Das Rheingold* had presented an allegory of existing society, its achievements and its failures, and even as Wagner located its action in a mythical past, he was intentionally promoting his vision of a utopian future. However Wagner was vague to a degree about how that future should work out, and *The Ring* does not model a better version of society. Its answer for society's problems turns out simply to be Siegfried, and Siegfried is the future towards which the mythological past was pointing. Wagner proclaimed his belief in Siegfried as the utopian future in the words of Wanderer, and Siegfried is also set up for this role by all that has happened so far. The entire course of the *Ring* story and the promise of *Die Walküre* and its music, above all in those great statements of the hero theme near the opera's end, have added to the anticipation of a sublime and extraordinary being. Wagner's prose writings show how he believed that he had created this in Siegfried, 'a perfect human being, O my King!' (he was addressing King Ludwig), a hero on the lines of Nietzsche's Superman, measureless in his powers, charismatic and fearless, joyous and untrammelled, invincible and naturally so tremendous as to be 'beyond good and evil'. He was to be 'pure love', 'a man who never ceases to love'.[73]

It does not work. The idea that Siegfried could be both this perfect human being and a universal solution to the problems of mankind is fantastical. Siegfried has many positive qualities, more than his detractors allow, but the distance between expectations and reality simply emphasises the contrast between them. As happened with the original Dresden Venus in *Tannhäuser*, Wagner had created a character who failed to express all that was in his imagination. *The Ring* also fails to present convincingly what matters most about the utopian future that Wagner was promoting, what it would be like, and how it would work. *The Ring* is so great that its stature is barely affected by these shortcomings, and Wagner did actually go on to create two works, *Die Meistersinger* and *Parsifal*, where he *did* model theories for better forms of society and better human beings. However, he never revisited the character of Siegfried. What might have happened if Wagner had achieved the same critical distance with this hero as he had with Venus? We know that Georg Unger, his original Siegfried, disappointed him; but this may have been a displaced disappointment over his own failure to create the 'delightful, joyous mirth of youth' in the role itself. Homer was not the only supreme genius who sometimes nodded.

Perhaps Wagner nodded again when he fashioned Mime, because

73 *Richard Wagner's Letters to August Röckel*, tr. Eleanor C. Sellar, Bristol, [1897].

Mime by contrast turned out too sympathetic. Wagner made repeated efforts to make him more sinister and detestable. Initially, as 'The Nibelung Myth considered as a sketch for a drama' demonstrated, Mime, who was still then named Reigin, demonstrated features that were still more sympathetic, and Wagner blackened him progressively as he developed the drama, sensing somehow that Siegfried would put people off unless Mime did more to justify his unpleasantness towards him. Mime's plans to gain the Ring had always entailed the murder of Siegfried, but when Wagner came to write the text, he made Mime more openly nasty, a snivelling hypocrite, a coward, and an insidious, compulsive liar with homicidal longings. Wagner filled in his unpleasantness still more vividly in the music, but Mime still did not become detestable enough for the balance of the drama. His stunted, pathetic, vicious personality seems so inevitably the consequence of his awful life that he mainly arouses pity and compassion. This risks making a tangle of the lessons which Wagner planned for *Siegfried* to present, but perhaps the drama is richer for it. Even so, given the choice of sharing a lifeboat with Mime or Siegfried, the decision would not be as obvious as Wagner might have liked to think.

Fortunately Wagner was Wagner, and it was quite within his power to create a compelling, mesmerising music drama out of unpromising ingredients, partly because of his interesting plot and the amazing music, and partly because of his extraordinary way of putting them together, his power of synthesis.

Tristan und Isolde and *Die Meistersinger* intervened beween Acts II and III of *Siegfried*, and it is received wisdom that there is a gulf between their musical styles. This seems based on hindsight. The Prelude to Act III of is one of Wagner's great achievements, but it is not a sudden jolt forward after Acts I and II. Wagner wanted the third acts of all his last six masterpieces to be culminations, and the heightened focus of the Act III Prelude is an impressive feature which *Siegfried* shares in common with *Die Walküre* and *Götterdämmerung*. But taken as a whole Act III of *Die Walküre* has a sweep that the final act of *Siegfried* does not quite equal. A particular feature specific to

Eight illustrations for *Das Rheingold* (1910) by Arthur Rackham (1867-1939)

The Rhinemaidens at play

The Rhinemaidens enticing Alberich

Alberich seizes the gold; illustration (1922) by Franz Stassen (1869-1949)

The Rhinemaidens complain to Loge (Rackham)

Alberich flogs the Nibelungen (Rackham)

Loge: 'Spare me, Dragon!' (Rackham)

Erda's warning (Rackham)

Fafner murders Fasolt (Rackham)

The Rhinemaidens' lament

Sieglinde succours Siegmund

Brünnhilde in the joy of youth

Fricka rides out in fury

Brünnhilde dazed and confused by Wotan's orders

Brünnhilde prepares to tell Siegmund he must die

The sleep of Brünnhilde

Eight illustrations for *Siegfried* (1911) by Arthur Rackham

Sieglinde in the forest

Mime at the anvil

Siegfried learns what love is like

Nothung reforged

Wanderer with Mime

Siegfried slays Fafner

Siegfried tastes the dragon's blood

Siegfried overwhelmed by Brünnhilde

The Norns at the world ash, illustration (1932) to *Götterdämmerung* by Franz Stassen

Siegfried, and a very effective one, is that each act begins in darkness and ends in light. Through each act, and throughout the drama as a whole, the hero myth pursues an upwards trajectory.

Even though Act III is not some great leap forward, the first scene of Act III is momentous, 'the centre of the world tragedy,' to quote Wagner. The the short, concentrated Prelude is one of the great things of *The Ring*, and it illustrates how cogent the combined associations of leitmotives can be. It begins with the opening arpeggio from the *Das Rheingold* which symbolised universal origins and the dawning of nature and consciousness, as well as conjuring up the Rhine itself. Later in a minor key, it represents Erda, goddess of nature. In *Die Walküre* Act II, this motive also attaches to Wotan, where it joins up with the motive of his inner unrest to convey a growing disquiet. Accordingly it brings to the Prelude of *Siegfried* Act III some rich associations: nature, Erda and Wotan's disquiet. This Prelude is also permeated by a derivative of the 'Valkyries' Horse-kick' motive, but now it is Wotan as Wanderer whose celestial steed courses through the spaces, and nature is itself in a state of storm in keeping with his spirit. Knit together symphonically, the music of the Prelude is about nature in turmoil and Wotan rocked by inner tempests. Because of the arpeggio's particular association with Erda, it also heralds Erda and her appearance. At the beginning of the Prelude, the arpeggio motive surges up and falls back repeatedly. The music passes by way of the 'Wotan's unrest' motive to the familiar theme of 'Wotan's Spear'. This theme repeats several times, forming accelerating counterpoints with itself, as the music rises towards its first major peak, a peak that turns out a plateau and a grander terrain. The leitmotive of 'the Wanderer' dominates that terrain, mightily augmented, a solid wall of brass standing proud through the orchestral turmoil, within which the 'Nature' theme continues to rise and fall. The arcs of sound rise higher and higher, increasing to the mightiest, most elemental climax in *The Ring* so far, perhaps of the whole cycle. It is derived from the climax in *Das Rheingold* where the Nibelungen bring up the gold, and Wagner now creates from it a blast, a crisis and an intensity that are cataclysmic. Great rolls of thunder sound as the crisis falls away in music which combines features of 'Magic Sleep' and 'Twilight of the Gods (*Götterdämmerung*)'. They herald the scene which plays out Wotan's final encounter with Erda, and their strange harmonies subside into 'Fate' set in contrasted with the 'the Spear' motive, Wotan's will. This is the key opposition in the scene, between destiny and free will. The music pushes towards to a new, if lesser, climax as Wotan storms on towards a cavernous entrance at the foot of the mountain, and delivers his incantation to summon Erda. He commands her to awaken and appear, '*Wache, Wala, Wala, Erwach*, Awaken Wala, Wala, awake!' The music for '*Wala, erwach*' is specially significant because it is yet another evolution of *The Ring*'s great central love theme.

Fig. 16.7 'Wotan's Spell over Erda (Erotic Love)'

Wotan soon tells Erda that he is still mighty in the magic by which he had constrained her, and the music confirms what he had told Brünnhilde in Act II of *Die Walküre*, that it was '*durch Liebes Zaube*, through love's magic' that he had cast his spell upon her. He had made her fall in love with him, and it is love's magical hold, its '*Zwang*', that enables him to constrain her now.

His first words had begun an incantation to Erda, and it continues with ritual utterances and repetitions, and with music which develops further the leitmotives of this scene so far; 'I call you from the depths, from your perpetual sleep. Erda! Erda! Woman of eternity! I sing the strains that work your awakening, you who know everything, you whose wisdom stretches back before the world began. Erda! Erda! Woman of eternity! Awaken Wala, Wala, awake!' The turmoil of Wotan's summons subsides in a development of the leitmotive of

'Magic Sleep', not now Brünnhilde's but her mother's, and of 'Fate'. The cave begins to glow with a faint blue light in which Erda materialises. She appears to be covered with hoar frost, and both her hair and her apparel give out a luminous shimmer. Her responses are formal, and sacral; 'Strong comes the call. Mighty are the spells which arouse me. I am awakened from my all-knowing sleep. Who now frightens away my sleep?'

Wotan answers what she must already know; 'It is I who speak the summons of your awakening. I have gone through the world, seeking wisdom and gaining tidings. But no one is as wise as you. You know what lies hidden in the depths, what wends its way through hill and vale, through the air and through the waters. Wherever things come to life, your breath is felt. Wherever minds are thinking, you stir their thoughts. Everything is known to you, and it is to seek your counsel that I summon you from sleep.'

Erda replies that her sleep is an endless dreaming, her dreaming is thinking, and her sleeping thoughts are the source of her wisdom. On the other hand, her daughters, the Norns, are always awake, awake even as they weave their cord and spin into it all that she knows in her sleep. They can better provide the answers that Wotan wants. Wotan counters that they are in thrall to the world's events as they spin them in. They can change nothing, but Erda's wisdom is more fundamental. He needs her counsel and her wisdom on a burning question which reveals to us just how much he does still hope to change the course of events. He asks 'How is it possible to stop the rolling wheel?' She does not answer him directly, but states in oracular terms that the deep pools of her all-womanly wisdom had been stirred and muddied forever by the one who prevailed over her, Wotan himself, but that from his conquest she had borne him a daughter who is valiant and wise. He would do better to ask her. Wotan gives Erda a brief account of Brünnhilde's disobedience over Siegmund and the punishment of her magic sleep, and asks Erda: could any questions now addressed to Brünnhilde produce any satisfaction, any useful result? Erda tells him obliquely that these were exactly the unnatural events which led to the dimming of her wisdom such as she describes, and that this dimming was furthered by his intrusion into the depths of her being. How without such dimming could it have happened that Brünnhilde was punished by him while her all-knowing mother slept on *unknowing*? How can Erda be wise about the nature of things when people and things are so false to their nature; when the one who taught defiance condemns it; when the one who spurred on the deed punishes it; when the guardian of right and truth rules through injustice and betrayal? Let her descend again, and let forever her set the seal upon her wisdom.

Wotan is not ready to let her go. He now accepts the implication that she cannot help him to change the course of events, which is what he would dearly like, bending them to his will; but his very acceptance makes him follow his first question with a different one. Referring to them both in the third person, he tells her, 'It was Erda who long ago drove the thorn of anxiety into Wotan's dauntless heart; it was she who filled him with fear of ending his existence in shame and catastrophe. If he now accepts his powerlessness to stop the rolling wheel, then can Erda at least tell him: how can he lessen his distress over it? How can he cope with the inevitable? How can she help him endure his destiny?'

She tells him harshly, 'You are not what you say of yourself. Why do you come so disturbingly to plague my dreams? He counters, 'You are not as you think yourself. Primordial wisdom, rooted in the eternal feminine, is coming to an end. Your wisdom must bow before my will! Do you know what Wotan does will? I will call it straight into your ear, you unwise one, so that you can sleep on throughout eternity, forever free from care. My distress over the end of the gods has ceased to overwhelm me since I willed it. What I once conceived in a state of conflict, anguish and despair I shall now conclude in joy as freely willed. I once vowed the world to the Nibelung in a state of rage and self-loathing, but now I bequeath it in elation to the Wälsung. This mettlesome lad has never known me, and has never had my help. He does not know the meaning of envy. His loving nature and his freedom from fear make him truly free, and even the Ring and

Alberich's curse of the Ring can have no power over him.' (Wotan is wrong). 'Brünnhilde, the daughter whom you once bore me, will awaken to this hero, and she will achieve the deed which redeems the world. So return to your sleep! Close your eyes again! Observe my downfall in your dreams, knowing that the god gives way in a state of joy.' The theme of 'Sleep' sounds again, now infinitely sad and noble, but resolves in the theme, dignified and bounteous,

Fig. 16.8 'Wotan's Bequest of Power to Siegfried'

of his abdicating his power in favour of Siegfried. Wagner said that this motive must sound like the founding of a new religion. 'Descend then, Erda, feminine spirit of dread, spirit of primal anxiety. Descend, return to eternal sleep.' The 'Magic Sleep' theme sounds again, as he declaims another incantation, releasing his hold on Erda. The theme of his love for her, as in '*Wala erwach*' (Fig. 16.7), is heard subsiding in the deep bass, as Erda slowly fades into the darkness.

This scene, the centre of the world tragedy as Wagner called it, is momentous in effect, and there are deep reasons why. In one sense Erda has done nothing for Wotan, having failed to answer his questions, but in a deeper sense, she has helped him immeasurably. Her presence and her responses have enabled him to describe his situation and shape it in a form that enables him to make sense of it and determine it. People sometimes make fun of Wagner's characters for going back over previous events, but his sessions with Erda are anything but superfluous. At the very least they fill in some important history, while at a deeper level Wotan's descriptions enable him to make sense both of what has happened, what is happening now, and what is still to come. It allows him to sort out the welter of confusion, and gain a new understanding, an inner order and a new balance. He has come to terms with the impossibility of resolving the past and shaping the future, but in the course of the scene, Wotan remodels his own narrative decisively. Erda's presence has enabled him not to reach answers but to render the questions transparent, and through her he arrives at a serenity which she did not possess herself. In retrospect the need to work towards a narrative is partly what drove Wotan to visit Mime and encounter Alberich at Neidhöhle. That Wagner presented these things in *Siegfried* is, as so often, extraordinary. He has effectively set out Wotan working his own way through the practices and therapeutic methods which the best counselling services, such as the Samaritans, now practise with such lifesaving effect. It is a matter of going over the chaos and describing it again and again, until it gradually coalesces into a narrative with order to it. After this a release and a new freedom begin to be possible. But how did Wagner know? Did he instinctively understand? It is interesting that he himself often practised something like this in his huge repetitive essays, his letters, and above all in his visions for society and in his dramas, where the same narratives are repeated and reconfigured in each repetition. Even Wagner's different autobiographies were virtual reassessments of his life.

Thus it is that Wotan emerges from this Erda scene a second time redeemed. He has enhanced and extended what he achieved spiritually at the end of *Die Walküre*, and become reconciled to the world, his circumstances, and himself. He can face and accept his own mortality and his failure to achieve so much of what he hoped, because he can bequeath it to Siegfried – or at least, so he believes – Siegfried the grandson whom he loves and who can make a better job of it all. There is something about him of Oedipus at Colonus (as in Sophocles' play), where Oedipus, who blinded himself after discovering the truth that he had murdered his father, married his mother, and produced children through incest, has reconciled himself to the pain and turmoil of his circumstances and his emotions. Both Wotan and Oedipus have had to leave behind past struggles and hopes and move on to a remote place of the mind, where there is some serenity and a gentle form of happiness. There is a strange discrepancy between this encouraging picture of Wotan and the very gloomy one of his total misery and hopelessness, soon painted by the Norns and Waltraute, in *Götterdämmerung*. I have never seen or worked out a convincing explanation why Wotan should change heart so pessimistically, and Wagner never explains. Perhaps the best that can be said is that his scene with Siegfried which now follows brings him up sharply to the realisation that this really is his downfall, that his end is happening right now: but is this really enough reason why this immense, titanic figure with such will and such a mighty ego should collapse so abjectly and in such misery?

With Erda's departure, the exalted, epic level of the action turns more prosaic as Wotan sees Siegfried approaching. As he waits, the woodbird comes flying towards him, but then stops, flutters, and flies hither and thither before vanishing entirely. Siegfried enters and comments, puzzled, to himself, 'My bird has gone! It led the way with its fluttering flight and its sweet singing, but now it has left! Oh well, I can find the way forward for myself now because my sweet little guide has pointed me so far in the right direction.' Wanderer now asks, 'Tell me lad, what is the way you are trying to find?' Siegfried notices him for the first time and sees him as someone who might help him; 'I am searching for a mountain surrounded by fire with a woman asleep on the heights; I have to awaken her.' Wanderer asks how he knew this, and Siegfried tells him that it was the woodbird's advice. Wanderer asks how he understood the woodbird and Siegfried tells him about the dragon's blood. Wanderer inquires how he came to kill the dragon, and Siegfried tells about Mime inciting him and about the dragon's own threats. Wanderer asks who forged the sword that was strong enough for this great deed, and Siegfried says he did it himself from its broken fragments. Wanderer asks him who created the fragments, and Siegfried answers that he has no idea; he only knows that they were no use until reforged. 'That I well understand!' answers Wanderer, and laughs contentedly.

Siegfried mistakes his laughter for derision and becomes markedly less agreeable. 'Are you laughing at me with your questions! Just stop, and don't keep me chattering here any more. Speak if you can tell me the way forward; but otherwise shut your gob.' (Wagner deliberately uses an expression of arresting vulgarity.) Wanderer is pained but tries to reason; 'Lad, if you think me old, then perhaps give me a little respect.' 'Respect for the old!' answers Siegfried; 'That is all I want to hear! All my life has been spoilt by having someone old in the way; and at last I have got rid of him. You take care that the same does not happen to you.' He goes closer. 'How strange you look! What is that enormous hat? Why do you pull it down over your face?' Wanderer tells him it is his way as he goes against the wind. 'But I see you have lost an eye! Someone must have knocked it out when you got in the way. If you do not let me pass, you might lose the other.' Wanderer comments, still equable, that Siegfried seems to know how to get *his* way, and then offers one of the more obscure observations of *The Ring*, that with the eye that is missing, Siegfried himself is now looking at the one which is still left. Siegfried comments, as well he might, 'That stuff is at least good for a laugh, but listen, I am not taking any more; so hurry up. Show me the way, and then push off; you are not much good for anything else. Say something now or I shall slap you down.' Wanderer is now hurt but still answers softly, 'If only you knew me, you might have spared me that dig. Your harrying me troubles me as one so devoted to you. Take care not to awaken my ill will against you today; it would be the end of you – and of me.' This exasperates Siegfried; 'Still no help, you obstinate fool; stand back, because I know from the woodbird that this is the way to the sleeping woman, even if it has now fluttered off.'

Wanderer at last begins to be nettled; 'It flew off for its own safety. It recognised the lord of the ravens here; and it will be the worse for it if one of them catches it; and the way to which it led shall never be yours.' Siegfried is astonished, but he does not change his stance, and asks Wanderer who he is that he thinks he can rule the highway. Wanderer tells him straight that he is the guardian of the rock, and that his is the power that keeps the woman bound in sleep. The one who awakens her will render him powerless forever. Pointing to the heights Wanderer warns of the sea of fire which encircles the rock and will destroy Siegfried if he does not stand back. Siegfried tells him to stand back himself; he plans to pass through the fire. Wanderer says that if Siegfried does not fear the fire, then at least he shall yield to his own spear. Siegfried's sword has broken on it once, and it will happen again. Siegfried answers; 'My father's enemy! Revenge at last! Wield your spear; see it break on my sword!'

With a single blow, he strikes the spear in two, sending up a flash of lightning and a blast of thunder that quickly fades away. The broken pieces of the spear fall at Wanderer's feet, and he picks them up before disappearing into the shadows with the words, 'Go forward. I cannot prevent you.' Siegfried simply comments that with his weapon broken the coward has escaped, and he lets the matter go because there are more important things. Clouds and fire come rolling down the mountain, and Siegfried, recognising that his way to Brünnhilde lies through them, greets them ecstatically. He puts his horn to his lips and after announcing that his horn will at last bring him a companion, he plunges into the flames, continuing to play his horn as he goes.

He strides through the fire, which leaps up and fills the scene entirely for some time. At length it begins to subside in clouds and smoke, and Siegfried emerges unscathed into the new world which Wagner's music paints for the imagination. Siegfried finds himself surrounded by dawn and an azure stillness and by distant mountain peaks. Above are infinities of blueness, and the sun is just beginning to rise. He comments on it in wonder, and sees a horse asleep, a little lower down. As the sun rises higher, he notices it glinting on the armour and weaponry of a figure lying there on a ledge, also asleep. Siegfried goes closer, and lifts the great shield covering the sleeper. It then strikes him that the closed helmet must be oppressive, and thoughtfully he loosens it and removes it. A sea of blonde hair comes cascading down; and Siegfried finds himself stirred. He is still more stirred in a way that he does not understand by the sight of the face. He has never before set eyes on a woman's face, and does not recognise it as feminine, but he finds something about it which tugs at his heartstrings. The breastplate now looks to him as restrictive as the helmet, and he attempts to loosen it to make breathing easier. He cannot find a way to undo it, but his sword makes short work of the chain-mail fastenings, and when he lifts it, he sees a form enfolded in beautiful draperies. Suddenly he takes in her very feminine contours, in particular her breasts which make him gasp and exclaim that this is no man. (Audiences are always supposed to snigger, but I have never heard it happen.) Siegfried is overwhelmed with the intimations of the feminine which well up within him. He says his senses are swimming, almost blinding him to what he is seeing; and responding to instinct, he calls out, 'Mother, mother! Help me!' before falling in a faint. He surfaces and asks himself how he can awaken this sleeping figure, knowing that if her eyes open, it will add further to the dazzling vision already before him. The unease, the racing pulse and palpitation, the desperate yearning for – he knows not what – all these things fill him with something he identifies as fear. He feels pathetic, unmanned, and yet thrilled and joyous, and his gaze now falls upon the beautiful mouth. Bending close, he feels the warmth of her breath, and he calls out to her to awaken. It has no effect. He does it again, but still nothing happens, and he determines that he will place his lips on hers and draw life from them even if he dies in the doing of it. The very absence of reason in this heightens its truthfulness, and closing his eyes he leans down until fully prone, and kisses her long on the mouth, wholly intoxicated.

Slowly now she opens her eyes, and Siegfried starts back and gazes as she rises and surveys the splendour around, from the roof of the world. The music of Brünnhilde's awakening is at once some of the simplest and most astonishing that Wagner ever created, a supreme example of his genius for taking basic materials and transforming them. The two chords which symbolise Brünnhilde's awakening are essentially the chords of an ordinary full close, the commonplace cadence that ends many recitatives. Wagner alters just one note, and by reason of this and its musical positioning and its scoring it becomes extraordinary. Wagner leads up to the crucial chords with long upwardly spiralling melodies over a succession of harmonies rooted in a B pedal point. This music seem to be heading towards E major, but Wagner suddenly converts the B into the upper note of a two chord cadence which affirms C major. It is awe-inspiring in its simplicity and its power over the imagination. The first chord is scored for wind but at its centre are horns placed very high. The second is spread to the heights and grounded in the depths, and the effect is sublime, especially as it shimmers aloft in high string trills and a response by the harps. The scene also has a personal dimension. It expresses Brünnhilde's elation at what she sees as she awakens to life. 'Hail to you, sun; hail to you, light,' she sings. She also hails the hero who has awoken her and asks who he is. Siegfried is utterly enraptured at and tells her that he is Siegfried who has passed through the fire. She formally hails the gods, she hails nature, and she hails the world that her long sleep is over. She hails Siegfried who has awoken her. He hails his mother for granting him life, so that he could enjoy anything so marvellous as this, and she shares his gratitude, knowing better than he what his mother went through to give him that life. The first great paragraph of this scene ends in a blaze of glory. The theme of the Wälsungs, which was often so unsettled and unhappy in *Die Walküre*, now becomes the sonorous foundation for the orchestral peroration to this first great paragraph, conveying a C major radiance and a joy that are at once steadfast and dazzling.

Brünnhilde breaks their mutual, rapt contemplation by pouring out to Siegfried how she had always loved him; even in his mother's womb, she had shielded and protected him. Siegfried misunderstands; 'Does that mean my mother did not die, but was only sleeping?' His misunderstanding enchants Brünnhilde; 'Oh Siegfried, you darling child!' she says, stretching out her hand to him, 'I am not your mother come back; you will never see her again, but I am your own very self, for you beatify me with your love. I act for you and I know for you all that you do not know; but all that I know myself comes only through your love for me.' She even expounds Wotan's deepest secret, which she says she alone sensed and nurtured, and which was his unacknowledged love for Siegfried; but Siegfried, as he tells her, cannot make head or tail of this. He can only think of the brightness of her eyes, the warmth of her breath, the sweetness of her voice. He cannot concentrate and take in anything as remote and obscure as what she is saying when he has the intoxicating reality of her so near. In a state of rising excitement and agitation he tells her she has bound him in fetters of that fear which she alone could teach him; with looks of yearning he begs her, he implores her to give him back his freedom. This has an unexpected, sobering effect on Brünnhilde. Her first fine careless rapture is passing, and she now observes her horse Grane, and comments that he has also awakened and is now feeding and grazing. Siegfried says with all the immediacy of un-poetry that his eyes can only feed on the sight of her mouth, and his lips burn to feed their longing where his eyes have fed.

They continue in the same vein. She laments the loss of her shield and her unguarded availability; he answers that for her sake he made his way unguarded through the fire. She comments diffidently on her severed breastplate; she is utterly defenceless; he answers that he had no defence at all against the fire which set light to his own passion; she has kindled it and she alone can quench it. With which words, he makes a grab for her from which she breaks free in horror: 'Not even a god ever dared approach me. In the presence of my virgin authority the heroes of Valhalla were respectful and deferential.' She had been sacred when she last left Valhalla, and she cries out in anguish at her shame and humiliation now. Siegfried who has awoken her has destroyed who she was and what she was; she is Brünnhilde no more. Siegfried listens courteously, but then tells her she is still asleep; he has not yet broken the spell which holds her in thrall. 'Awaken!' he says, 'Become a woman.' She begins unwittingly to respond; 'My senses are swimming; is all my wisdom dissolving?' Siegfried reminds her that it was *her* claim that his love bestowed her wisdom upon her, but she describes herself sinking into chaos. A welter of dark feelings and fears seize her, and Wagner borrowed the music for this from *Die Walküre* Act II where it symbolises Wotan's existential turmoil. The cross-reference now is slightly confusing; to be sure, there is turmoil for both, but is Brünnhilde's turmoil also related to the 'Curse of the Ring' as the music implies, and as Wotan's was? It seems to stretch parallels a long way; and the parallels work better when Wagner presses this music into service a third time, as he does in *Götterdämmerung*, in the Waltraute scene. At least in *Siegfried* it shows Brünnhilde as shaken to the fundaments of her being, and she covers her eyes instinctively with her hands.

Siegfried gently uncovers them and tells her that her fears can depart now that she can hail this day of days, but she answers that what she hails is the day of her disgrace; 'Siegfried; see my distress;' and he has the sensitivity to give her some space. Her gaze then softens and she looks at him more tenderly. 'I was always as I am and always will be, eternally devoted to your wellbeing. But Siegfried, my treasure, you life of the world, leave me in peace. Do not compel me with a compulsion that is destructive, and do not shatter something so true and eternal. You have seen your face reflected in a stream, but if you disturb the water, the picture breaks up and is gone. So in the same way disturb me no more, and let the pure picture of yourself which you see reflected in me go on shining back at you in pristine form. If you truly love yourself, then do not wipe out the true self which is mirrored back, by destroying me who am the mirror.'

Siegfried has no taste for these strange, convoluted processes. He loves her wildly; all that matters is that she loves him in return. He feels surrounded by seas of magic, and he is conscious only of the currents and billows of bliss associated with her. All that matters is to plunge into them and immerse himself utterly, becoming engulfed in the floodwaters. 'Awaken Brünnhilde! Be happy and alive, you utter joy! Be mine! Be mine! Be mine!' She responds seriously that she has always been his; and he tells her passionately to be his again now. He says it is when he holds her in his arms, with their hearts beating as one, with them breathing as one, eye to eye, mouth to mouth, that he can then feel certain that she truly belongs to him. That alone will end his anxiety whether Brünnhilde is really his. At this point he folds her in his arms again, and this time she moves swiftly towards him. She tells him of wild changes taking place within her. 'Siegfried, Siegfried. When my gaze sears through you, are you not burnt? When my arms hold you close, are you not set ablaze? Are you not afraid of this mountain woman's furious wild fire?' Siegfried finds that her abandon restores his confidence. He announces that with her growing passion his terrors and uncertainties have already disappeared like a dream which he can barely recall.

They are now both so intoxicated with joy that they break into laughter of the purest exhilaration, and their intoxication and laughter galvanises the finale. As they state, nothing else matters, and Brünnhilde reverts to *The Ring*'s roots in Feuerbach as she tells the gods that they can rejoice as Valhalla goes down in the dust, knowing that the world has been transformed and uplifted by the power of such human love. She and Siegfried are the pattern of a new order where humanity has come of age and transcends the gods and religion. She and Siegfried are the driving force for bringing the new order into being, because she models an existence lived by the bright star of love, Siegfried's love. No such abstractions affect Siegfried's delight in Brünnhilde, and he hails the day, the light, and the world which is made wonderful because she exists in it. He says that now she is really awake, she is really alive; and each of them answers laughter with laughter. They both sing that each exists for sake of the other, eternally and joyously. Each is the other's one and all, a light-bringing love, a laughing death ('*lachender Tod*'), permeated and made intoxicating by joy. As she throws herself into his arms, the act ends.

The music has become brassy and rumbustuous. Its C major has a brash, furious vitality at the remotest end of the spectrum from the intense mystery and chromaticism of *Tristan und Isolde*. The loves of Tristan and Isolde can only find expression in death. The loves of Siegfried and Brünnhilde can only find expression in physical union, an annihilation of self so vital and a form of death so contrary, as to strip the idea of all force and meaning. Their individuality dies, but does not vanish into oblivion and Nirvana. Their individuality dies because they become a delirious oneness that vibrates with life and energy, a oneness that comes over as joyful and deathless. In their ecstasy they are unapproachable and untouchable, like the saints in glory.

Siegfried was first performed as part of the original *Ring* cycle put on at the Festspielhaus in Bayreuth. The performance took place on 16 August 1876. The cast consisted of Georg Unger (Siegfried), Max Schlosser (Mime), Franz Betz (Wanderer), Karl Hill (Alberich), Lilli Lehmann (Woodbird), Luisa Jaide (Erda), and Amalie Materna (Brünnhilde). The performance was conducted by Hans Richter under Wagner's close supervision.

SEVENTEEN

GÖTTERDÄMMERUNG

Götterdämmerung! For many admirers Wagner's Everest, his *summa musices*. Ernest Newman maintained that not since J.S. Bach worked on the *St Matthew Passion* had a musical brain functioned at such a sustained level of intensity. On the other hand *Götterdämmerung* was criticised by George Bernard Shaw, avid Wagnerian that he was, as an impossible mix of ill-matched ingredients only worked into a convincing whole by a supreme effort of Wagner's intellect – and *not* his imagination. Shaw declared that he could not find in it a single bar that carried the same conviction and immediacy as the earlier parts of *The Ring*. Personally I find it overwhelming in its conviction and immediacy, sustained by great flights of imagination that absorb and annul the discrepancies; but discrepancies there are, and the challenges which *Götterdämmerung* posed for Wagner were many and great. It reveals its riches most liberally to people who are aware of the challenges, aware of how he transformed them into achievements, and aware of what he wanted *Götterdämmerung* to tell the world.

The chapter on *The Ring* explained how Wagner was really still saddled with his idea for an opera, *Siegfrieds Tod*, when he came to compose *Götterdämmerung*. Its matrix and form remained those of *Siegfrieds Tod*, resulting in a mismatch with the three other parts of the cycle which it had called into being. In form those reflect and extend the principles of Wagner's treatise, *Opera and Drama*, but *Siegfrieds Tod* was planned as an opera, a successor to *Lohengrin*, and 'grand opera' was what the libretto still remained when he developed it into *Götterdämmerung*. It offered scope for operatic numbers, a duet swearing oaths of loyalty, a trio plotting vengeance, one almost-aria for Hagen and another for Waltraute. There are processions and a chorus of vassals at full throttle, and these were all features which *Opera and Drama* were supposed to consign almost entirely to the past.

Then again, *Götterdämmerung* occupies a different world from the rest of *The Ring*. It disturbs the unity and continuity of the cycle that the sublime myth, which easily absorbed the human scenes of *Die Walküre*, comes down to earth for the human world of *Götterdämmerung*, bumping roughly into civilisation and its discontents. From now on the real action continues in the human world, and the realm of the divine fades into the background. Siegfried himself downgrades from a mythical hero into a more ordinary being. His heroic ability to see through fraud has evaporated. The text itself adds to the disunity because it does not equal the dramatic penetration of the other parts of *The Ring*. Wagner still had a superb libretto, but even the wonderful figure of Brünnhilde becomes simpler and starker, and more operatic. Hagen, the son of Alberich, is relatively two-dimensional, unalloyed envy and '*Neid*', and Gunther and Gutrune, Hagen's half-siblings, are sketchy creations compared even with the giants in *Das Rheingold*, let alone Loge or Fricka.

Wagner's responses to the challenges of *Götterdämmerung* simply awaken renewed admiration and amazement. He eventually accomplished a unity with the rest of *The Ring* so flawless that all the difficulties are lost to view in performance, and most people are not even aware of them. He succeeded in fusing the earthier, human world of *Götterdämmerung* into the mythical world of *The Ring*'s first three parts, and the supreme means and resource for his achievement was the music.

The music does three particular things. First, it transforms the libretto, subtilising its characters, conferring on them a colour and depth which were missing in the text. It is because of the music that the papier mâché Gutrune, for example, becomes beautiful, poignant and tragic. Secondly the music enabled Wagner to do again what he had already done in *Die Meistersinger* and fuse opera and symphonic music drama. Nothing could have transformed *Götterdämmerung* completely except a radical reworking of the text and plot, and trying to work this out would have been daunting even for Wagner. Instead he converted a problem into a triumph by supplying the operatic numbers of *Götterdämmerung* with an orchestral 'accompaniment' which was supremely symphonic. He composed music which gave to *Götterdämmerung* many features of music drama as he had conceived it, drawing it back into the dramatic cycle as a whole. A third provision of the music is the lattice of unifying connections that comes from the leitmotives. It adds brand new leitmotives for Gunther, Gutrune, 'Magic Deceit', 'the Vengeance Pact', and for 'Siegfried's Funeral', but it rejuvenates many old ones, such as the Rhine, 'the Hero', Valhalla, 'Fate', the Tarnhelm, Siegfried's 'Horn Call', and 'Alberich's Curse of the Ring'. Leitmotives from earlier parts of *The Ring* sing again in this final instalment and create a network of cross references which holds the cycle together. Old and new react in new elaborations, new harmonies and counterpoints, new symphonic developments. Sometimes the result is then a symphonic transformation, as happens when the first beginnings of *Das Rheingold* reappear, more resplendent than ever, in the entr'acte known as 'Siegfried's Rhine Journey', or when the music from *Siegfried* which expressed the hero's ascent through the fire returns at the end of *Götterdämmerung* Act I. This is the point where a drugged Siegfried bursts through the flames and brutalises Brünnhilde, and for this terrible event, Wagner made alterations to his music to create a devastating effect. On the other hand when Siegfried is later speared by Hagen, the music of 'Brünnhilde's Awakening' from *Siegfried* Act III comes back in its original glory. This reprise repeats the notes, the scoring and the atmosphere, exactly as they had been, except that half way through the radiance suddenly peters out and the passage ends.

As well as the music, there was another resource, a second mechanism by which Wagner connected *Götterdämmerung* back to the rest of *The Ring*, in that he prefaced each of its acts, all firmly located in human society, with mythical scenes which he rewrote for the purpose. At the outset, there is a myth-soaked scene for the Norns which binds *Götterdämmerung* into all that has gone before. In Act II there is the dream-apparition of Alberich that links that act back to *Siegfried* and *Das Rheingold*. In the first scene of Act III, the Rhinemaidens, those supremely mythic creatures, appear for Siegfried and establish a further connection back to *Das Rheingold*. Still further connections come from the story itself. The arena for the action of *The Ring*'s fourth opera is different from those of the first three, but the story courses on continuously from *Siegfried* into the prologue of *Götterdämmerung*. The brief time lag between *Siegfried* and *Götterdämmerung* is very different from the indeterminate ages which separate *Das Rheingold* and *Die Walküre* or even the eighteen years or so which elapse between *Die Walküre* and *Siegfried*.

For the two opening scenes of *Götterdämmerung* known as the Prologue, the setting remains as at the end of *Siegfried*, the Valkyrie's rock, and the first music of *Götterdämmerung* consists of the two chords which described Brünnhilde's awakening. However it is now the following night and the music is subtly and drastically changed. Instead of modulating from E minor to C major, the two chords move now from E flat minor to C flat. The effect could not be more different. Instead of glory and brilliance, the music now sounds veiled and drained, and there rises up within it a ghostly memory of the arpeggio waves which began *Das Rheingold*. Their effect in C flat is very different from the E-flat of *Das Rheingold*, and instead of gathering momentum, the music spirals upwards and peters out.

Fig. 17.1

This sequence is now repeated, bringing in the second pair of chords from Brünnhilde's awakening. The music continues as if was about to introduce the third pair, but instead it dissolves into the 'Fate' motif from *Die Walküre*. At a stroke the music has bound *Götterdämmerung* into *Siegfried*, *Das Rheingold*, and *Die Walküre*. Soon there is additionally the sound of Loge's fires, burning low round Brünnhilde's rock but leaving enough light to make out three strange women, eerie and half transparent, the Norns. They are spinning the fateful rope of destiny as they have from the dawn of time. The opening music has additionally established that the atmosphere of *Götterdämmerung* is one of Northernness. The Northernness which marks much of *Die Walküre* and *Siegfried* and even parts of *Das Rheingold* expands to dominate *Götterdämmerung*, and there are two new leitmotives that add to it;

Fig. 17.2 'The Rope'

Fig. 17.3 'Valhalla in Decline'

The Norns weave the history of the world from the rope and into it, declaiming incantations as they spin. They describe the past, present and future ages of *The Ring*, and because Wagner put so much of this onstage in the earlier *Ring* dramas, he has been criticised for not pruning out the Norns' scene. However it is not superfluous, and far from getting rid of it, he rewrote and extended it to tell new and different things. The First Norn describes how she would long ago spin the rope under the world ash. That was a time when she would sing for joy under its green shade by the spring which rippled from its roots. There was wisdom in the murmurings of the spring; but then a dauntless god, Wotan, discovered it and disturbed everything. (It is interesting that in northern mythologies it was usually male macho that ruined paradise by some act designed to achieve wisdom and a knowledge of good and evil, and that the blame was not shuffled off onto some Nordic Eve.) Wotan paid one of his eyes to drink wisdom from the spring, and broke a great branch from the ash to fashion a spear. Over the ages the tree sickened from the damage until it eventually died. After that the spring also stopped running, and the Norn's song of joy turned to sorrow.

The First Norn passes the rope to the Second, who takes up the story and describes how Wotan went on to establish laws and treaties, enshrining them in the runes of his spear. This enabled him to rule the world until a hero shattered it, destroying the rule of the law. After this, Wotan had made his heroes cut down the world ash, both its withered trunk and its branches, while the spring finally dried up. Because they no longer have the ash to secure the rope of destiny, the Norns, as they tell us, must attach it to a rock, in spite of their concerns about its sharp edges. The Third Norn continues, describing how the entire fellowship of gods and heroes is now assembled with Wotan in the fortress of Valhalla, surrounded by the timbers of the world ash.

The day will come when they are set on fire and consume Valhalla, and that day will witness the end of the immortal gods; how might that come about? The Third Norn casts the rope back to the First, who asks if she sees the light of dawn or only firelight; sorrow has dimmed her sight, and she can scarcely recall the exalted past ages which Loge had illuminated with his fiery brilliance; what had become of him?

The Second Norn winds the rope round another rock as she declaims how Wotan had subdued Loge through the power of his spear, so that Loge gave council to Wotan. However in his longing for freedom, Loge's flames gnawed at Wotan's spear like teeth, leading Wotan to subdue him again, harnessing him to surround Brünnhilde's rock with fire. The Third Norn grasps the rope and predicts that the day will come when the god will thrust the splintered shafts of his spear deep into Loge's chest, sending sparks and flames leaping up from the burning spear which the god will hurl into the branches and timbers heaped round Valhalla. (In the event, the flames that consume Valhalla do not require anything so brutal, and as far as I know nobody has explained the discrepancy.) The Third Norn passes the rope to the Second who tells them that if they want to know how everything will turn out, they must spin out the rope further. However the First Norn warns that the rope is fraying even as she tries to make it fast, and sings that a hideous sight has set her senses spinning, a vision of the Rhinegold stolen by Alberich. The Second Norn now sees with dismay that the threads of the rope are fraying on the sharp edge of the rock, and that the misery and envy unleashed by Alberich's Ring are swirling all around them. Now his curse tears at the strands, and to the strains of 'Alberich's Curse of the Ring', the rope breaks. The Norns start up in horror and huddle together. They sing in unison that their wisdom is now at an end, and as the 'Fate' motive sounds, they warn that the world will hear of them no more. They vanish into nothingness and the firelight fades completely, leaving the greyness of morning just before dawn. Wagner largely rewrote this scene when he turned *Siegfrieds Tod* into *Götterdämmerung*. In *Siegfrieds Tod* it had sketched in the story of what became *Das Rheingold*, but in *Götterdämmerung* what the Norns tell us is new. The rising sense of crisis which in *Götterdämmerung* culminates as the rope breaks was missing in *Siegfrieds Tod*, and at the end the Norns simply embraced and departed, with none of the doom-laden effect of *Götterdämmerung*.

The Norns and their picture of Valhalla contribute to the darkening of this final instalment of *The Ring*. This is due to the mood of their own scene, and to the altered state of mind which they describe in Wotan and which is confirmed by Waltraute when she tells Brünnhilde (and us) of it, later in Act I. The background of Wotan's gloom gives an ashen hue to the whole work. Wagner never made it known why Wotan had changed so drastically since the end of *Siegfried*. There is another inconsistency with the end of *Siegfried* concerning the timescales. The Norns' scene comes at the end of the day when Siegfried awakened Brünnhilde, and so it is barely twenty-four hours since Wotan encountered Siegfried, but the Norns create the impression that much time has passed since then, time enough for Wotan to return to Valhalla with his spear broken, command his heroes to fell the world ash and pile the wood round Valhalla, and take his place on his gloomy throne to wait for the end. The Norns also give the impression that these events are not new. Myths often contain discrepancies of time, and they do not matter unless they create a jolt, a mismatch between separate timescales in different strands.

In this instance, the 'Rhine Journey' which Siegfried makes between the end of the Prologue and the beginning of Act I lessens the sense of inconsistency because Wagner left vague the length of time which Siegfried takes to make the journey. Wagner intended *Götterdämmerung* to conform to the unity of time, as do the other parts of *The Ring* and *Die Meistersinger*, and they do each roughly take place over twenty-four hours. In giving the name of Prologue to the first two scenes, Wagner was separating it off so as not to spoil the unity of time within the main work. The great dawn duet of Siegfried and Brünnhilde in the second scene of the Prologue was not part of Wagner's original conception at all. It was Eduard Devrient, Wagner's close friend from his Dresden period, who advised him that without a scene to display how spectacular their relationship had been, the tragedy of its destruction would miss its effect.

Dawn breaks to an extended, wandering line for the cellos, which leads to a fully-harmonised version of Siegfried's horn call, the 'Siegfried' motive low on the horns:

Fig. 17.4 'Siegfried'

It is set over an F pedal point which it establishes as the dominant of B flat, and it is followed by a new leitmotive symbolising Brünnhilde's loveliness and melting generosity.

Fig. 17.5 'Brünnhilde's New Womanliness'

It is the music which helps create the *Götterdämmerung* Brünnhilde.

The music establishes B flat, apparently as the new tonic, but then instead turns B flat into another dominant, over which Brünnhilde's new theme is developed in a sequence of crescendos leading up to an elemental statement of 'Siegfried' on the heavy brass, fortissimo, in E flat, the true tonality for the whole scene of Siegfried and Brünnhilde. The brass symbolises Siegfried, but also the day. It is a day of golden fulfilment quite different from the azure brilliance of Brünnhilde's awakening. It symbolises the realisation of their romantic passion. They sing a duet which is one of the most moving things in *The Ring*, but whose words, all-important for a sympathetic understanding of

Siegfried, are easily lost in the floods of Wagner's orchestra. They are both radiant with gratitude for the miracle of loving and being loved. Already their relationship has some hallmarks of a good marriage, and Brünnhilde has the wisdom to recognise that while marriage can be the great aim and fulfilment of life, it also functions as a base camp, a safe haven from which to set out and achieve important things outside it. She tells Siegfried she never wants her love to limit him; he must be free to go on to new things, new successes in the world beyond. Her only concern is that she can never repay him for all that he has given her. She has just bestowed on him all the lore and wisdom that were hers as a divine being. Her wisdom is now shared and her power has now gone from her; but because he has made her so infinitely rich through his love, she wishes she could bring him yet more in return. 'You utter wonder,' answers Siegfried, 'I can never repay you for what you are to me, and what you give me, yourself and all your wisdom. However, just for something in return, however inadequate, I give you this ring. Everything that I have so far achieved and been has gone into it. Keep it as a sacred greeting, a symbol of my trust and devotion.' In return she gives him her horse, Grane, to help his worldly achievements, and he responds that his achievements all stem from her. He wears her colours now, and all his past and future successes are vested in her. He says that he is simply an extension of her identity, and he acts for her just in the same way as her arm does. She says she wishes that he were her soul as well, and he says that it is her soul that confers his courage on him; and the pair of them are both present wherever he is. 'Does that mean my mountain hall is deserted?' she asks, suddenly uncertain. 'How could that be?' answers Siegfried, 'It holds us both here eternally as an indivisible one!' Almost drunken with happiness at this, they call upon the gods to feast their eyes upon their joy. They sing: when separated, who could divide them; when divided, they are still utterly one. The wisdom and idealism which they jointly express is a wonderful, didactic example. The one thing that neither of them emphasises sufficiently is the 'base camp' and the importance of maintaining it. People who spend their entire lives at the base camp find in the end that it becomes barren, but those who spend their energies entirely outside come back to find the base camp deserted and ruined, and find that they have missed what was most precious of all. This is a path to disaster, as Siegfried soon demonstrates.

Meanwhile, both heroism and Siegfried and Brünhilde's heroics are reflected in the orchestral writing which comes close to tub-thumping as Siegfried leaves the rock. The orchestra has already by then embarked on 'Siegfried's Rhine Journey', and the music broadens out in warmth and empathy for Brünnhilde as she finds herself alone. Just as her emotions are settling down, the sound of Siegfried's horn causes her to look down the valley. They see each other and wave gaily as the orchestra launches into a fugue in F major built from Siegfried's 'Horn Call' and from the music of 'Loge's Magic Fire', through which Siegfried must pass in his descent. The fugue takes in various other themes from Siegfried's youth and reaches towards a point that is unexpected musically but wholly right dramatically, the music of the Rhine and its surging arpeggios, now set in the remote key of A major. Siegfried the iconic hero has linked up with the most iconic of rivers, and the tides rise higher and higher until they flood over into the key of E flat. This is as far removed as can be from the recent A major, and yet it is the music's predestined goal, as a return to whence it all began, to the beginning of the 'Rhine Journey' and, traversing a far greater distance, to the Prelude of *Das Rheingold*. The *Rheingold* Prelude music now takes on a new opulence, and leads to a massive reprise of the 'Rhinemaidens' Lament' in full, and again there are suggestions of tub-thumping. The 'Ring' theme reappears in its original form as in the Rhinemaidens' scene, but its bright major turns abruptly into a minor version, and the whole scene rapidly darkens. The 'Rhinegold' theme takes the music to the subverted version of the Rhinemaidens' 'Hymn to the Gold', and the leitmotives for the Gibichungs and Hagen make their first appearance, heralding the start of Act I, and the beginning of the opera proper, beyond the Prologue.

Fig. 17.6 'The Gibichungs'

Fig. 17.7 'Hagen'

The Gibichungs are a people who dominate a large section of the Rhine, and the name 'Gibichungs' refers both to the whole population and to its ruling dynasty, consisting of King Gunther and his sister, Gutrune, who are seated on thrones in the great hall of their rule. Nearby at their banqueting table is their half-brother, Hagen, whose father Alberich had seduced their mother with the aphrodisiac of gold, wealth. Alberich's intention in begetting Hagen was create a grey parallel to Siegfried, someone to carry out his purposes as Siegfried carries out Wotan's. The difference is that Wotan was eager for a free spirit to replace him, whereas Alberich wanted Hagen to be himself reincarnate. Alberich discovers, as other fathers have done, that his offspring has developed a striking independence that was not part of the plan. The trio onstage are engaged in a strange colloquy as the act begins. Gunther is asking if he occupies a dominant position on the Rhine, one worthy of his ancestry. Hagen replies that Gunther's position is indeed an enviable one, not least for Hagen, who is excluded; their mother had enjoined this fact upon him. Gunther comments that Hagen has no need for envy. Gunther may be the elder and more imposing, but cleverness and intellect had been his preserve. Never, says Gunther, had the conflict between half-brothers so well resolved itself, and it is Gunther's recognition of Hagen's quality which made him seek his advice now. Hagen says that he faults his own advice and counsel after all, because on reflection he must judge Gunther's position as poor. He knows of things which Gunther has not yet managed to achieve. Gunther says that if Hagen keeps his knowledge to himself, he too will fault Hagen's counsel. Hagen replies that both Gunther and Gutrune are in their prime, but that neither is married, and when Gunther asks who would make him a worthy wife, Hagen tells him of the noblest woman in the world, living on a mountain summit surrounded by fire. Only a man so fearless that he can break through the flames can win her. At this point, the music conjures up a vision of the magic fire surrounding Brünnhilde and even echoes of the woodbird's song, with the implication that Hagen has learnt about them from his father. To Gunther's question whether he is up to the task, Hagen answers bluntly that it is for someone stronger. Who is there that can be stronger, asks Gunther petulantly, and Hagen explains that there is the son of Siegmund and Sieglinde, who was brought up to be strong in the forests. His reputation as a hero comes from vanquishing Fafner, the dragon who had guarded the Nibelung hoard, but he is the right man for Gutrune.

Gunther comments that he has heard of the hoard and its treasure, and Hagen continues that the man who can exploit it is master of the world, and he alone can win Brünnhilde. This annoys Gunther, who asks Hagen in some agitation why he is stirring up stress and envy about things which can never be his, but Hagen is unperturbed. He asks how it would be if Siegfried won Brünnhilde, but then made her over to Gunther. Gunther cannot see why Siegfried would do this for him, but Hagen says that it would be easy enough to persuade him if he married Gutrune. Gutrune accuses Hagen of making fun of her with this suggestion, as Siegfried must have had the pick of the world's loveliest women and found someone better, but Hagen suggests that they exploit a drug, a potion in their possession. This could make Siegfried forget all other women and fall in love with Gutrune. At this point Wagner brings back the theme of the Tarnhelm and extends it into something further, paired chords with a strange slippery sweetness which provide the leitmotive known as 'Magic Deceit'.

Fig. 17.8 'Magic Deceit' (muted horns)

The deceit lies in this shabby subterfuge, which Gunther adopts with enthusiasm, his only concern being how to inveigle Siegfried into visiting them. Hagen says it will happen automatically as Siegfried makes his way through the world, and on cue the sound of Siegfried's horn comes up from the river. Hagen goes to a lookout point where he can see Siegfried in a boat with his horse. He is driving his boat upstream with a single oar, using it like a paddle. Anyone who has ever seen the torrential flow of the Rhine will realise that this is quite a feat, and Hagen hails Siegfried, addressing him by name. Siegfried is soon at the moorings and comes towards them. All is brightness and humour until Hagen welcomes Siegfried to the 'Curse of the Ring' on trombones, fortissimo, a disturbing shadow which casts doubt over the belief expressed by Wotan and Alberich, that Siegfried's whole nature cancels the power of the curse to do him harm. The 'Curse of the Ring' materialises at critical points of *Götterdämmerung*, demonstrating its power to do him plenty of harm.

Siegfried offers Gunther friendship or a challenge at arms, and Gunther brushes the challenge aside and offers him a real and genuine welcome. Siegfried asks them about looking after his horse, a commission which Hagen agrees to undertake, and the music tells us that Grane, wiser than his owner, kicks out defensively, aware of something to be resisted in Hagen. Siegfried's attention is taken up with Gunther's formalised welcome, declaring him a partner in all that he has and is. Wagner's music now and later describes Gunther as experiencing an uneasy fascination and fondness for Siegfried, as Wagner again fills out a personality and subtilises a relationship through the music. Siegfried says that he possesses nothing which he can share in return, but that his sword and his courage are always available. Hagen queries this, saying he had understood that Siegfried owned the entire hoard of the Nibelungs. Siegfried agrees and explains that he had quite forgotten it because it meant so little. 'So you took nothing from it?' cuts in Hagen. 'Only this piece of metalwork,' answers Siegfried, producing the Tarnhelm, 'though not knowing what use it can be.' Hagen recognises it instantly and explains that it is a consummate creation; with it Siegfried can change into anything he likes and wish himself anywhere he wants to be. Hagen presses Siegfried, 'You took nothing else?' and Siegfried tells him, 'Yes, just a ring which is now in the hands of a wonderful woman,' Hagen comments 'Brünnhilde',' in an aside which the others miss. Gunther tells Siegfried with unaffected generosity that his Gibichung possessions would be like toys in comparison with Siegfried's hoard but that he needs and wants no share in it. He only wants the chance to do well by Siegfried. At this moment Gutrune brings in a drinking horn for Siegfried containing a potion of oblivion. He takes it, but in drinking it he first names Brünnhilde. He says that if he forgot everything else which she had taught him, there is one lesson to which he will always hold fast, to think lovingly of her. He drinks to her and as he lowers the horn, his eyes fall upon Gutrune, whose enchanting, poignant music tells more about her than any words.

Fig. 17.9 'Gutrune' (pastel winds: flutes etc.)

Siegfried becomes a man possessed, bursting out, 'You whose eyes set my heart on fire, why do you drop your gaze before mine?' She raises her eyes timidly to his, and he tells her, 'Ah, loveliest of women, your gaze sets me on fire!' Turning to Gunther, he asks, 'Gunther, what is your sister's name?' and on learning that she is Gutrune, he asks in one of those puns which Nietzsche found so execrable in Wagner's life and work, 'Do I read *good runes* in those lovely eyes? I wanted to forge a bond of service with your brother, but he declined. Will you also decline a bond with me?' She blushes and lowers her eyes, ill at ease, and as much bewitched with Siegfried as he is with her. Siegfried asks Gunther whether he has a wife. Gunther explains that he has not yet tried, because he has set his heart on one who is beyond him. Siegfried asks what could possibly be beyond Gunther with Siegfried at his side. Gunther repeats Hagen's description, in both words and music, of the woman on the rock surrounded by fire, inaccessible to all but the bravest. By the end it is clear that this calls forth no hint of recollection in Siegfried, who tells Gunther that he fears no fire; his courage is at Gunther's disposal to win his bride, provided Siegfried can thereby win Gutrune. Gunther is willing and eager, and Siegfried now sinks unexpectedly low. He tells Gunther that it should be easy to deceive Brünnhilde because of the Tarnhelm. He can take on Gunther's form with it.

Gunther says that before doing anything else they should swear to be brothers, blood brothers, an idea which is somehow familiar to Siegfried, although Wagner does not make it clear why he knows what to do. He cuts his arm with his sword, holding it so that his blood runs into a horn which Hagen has half filled with wine. Gunther does the same, and they both lay two fingers on the brim. Wagner pushes the ranging associations of leitmotives to their limits when he punctuates their oath with the majestic motive of 'Wotan's Spear'. This has gathered a wealth of associations, a generous nimbus of meanings, ideas and feelings, but none of them seem to relate to these conspirators roaring away in sixths like operatic brigands. Each of them then drinks half the concoction and swears eternal loyalty to the other, after which Hagen splits the horn with his sword. Siegfried asks Hagen why he took no part, but accepts Hagen's meaningless explanation that his blood is too meagre and sluggish for oath-making; that it would spoil the process. So soon and so totally has Siegfried lost the second sight conferred by the dragon's blood. Gunther simply tells Siegfried to leave Hagen to his gloom if that is how he wants it, but

Siegfried is already on his way back to his boat; no, he does not want to stop and rest; he can do that after he has collected Brünnhilde and come back. Gunther scrambles hastily after him, telling Hagen to keep watch while he is away. Gutrune has heard the commotion, and returns to find Gunther and Siegfried already on their way back to the river. Hagen tells her they are on a voyage to win Brünnhilde. Gutrune gasps: 'Siegfried?' Hagen answers tantalisingly, 'Yes, he was so eager,' and then relents and admits that Siegfried was eager – to win Gutrune as his reward. 'Siegfried! Mine!' says Gutrune faintly as she leaves, and the music describes something pathetic and fragile about her happiness as she wafts away in a star-struck fantasy.

There is suddenly a complete swing of focus onto the ominous figure, Hagen, now seated on Gunther's throne. He is insubstantial in build, but the music now confers on him a marmoreal joylessness and an infinite menace, in the passage known as 'Hagen's Watch'. This music develops a version of the '*Nibelungenhass*' leitmotive, on the strings now, instead of its usual low wind.

Fig. 17.10 (violins I & II and violas in a low position)

This motive soon passes through an extended version of the 'Tarnhelm' modulations. The textures are periodically invigorated by 'Siegfried's Horn Call', set low in the orchestral texture and in an unusual minor version.

Fig. 17.11 (solo horn)

However the dominating element is the 'Hagen' motive (Fig. 17.7) which Ernest Newman aptly described as dour and irreconcilable.

These elements fuse together as Hagen begins to think aloud. There he sits, left on guard to protect their homestead, while Gunther is off having a good time.

Fig. 17.12 'Hagen's Watch'

With Gunther goes Siegfried, another joyous individual, who will guard him from danger. 'The son of Gibich,' Hagen continues, 'will soon bring back a bride to the Rhine, but to me he will bring – the Ring!' The music rises to a climax, both threatening and anguished, before falling away in a plangent derivative of 'Alberich's Forswearing of Love' (Fig. 14.4). 'You sons of freedom,' continues Hagen, 'Enjoy your voyage! Though you hold him in contempt, and yet you are slaves to his purpose, slaves to the Nibelung son!' The music repeats a particularly haunting, tense version of what was once the Rhinemaidens' 'Hymn to the Gold'. There is a muted repeat over an ominous drum roll, and everything seems about to fade further, when the orchestra jolts back to its powerful portrait of Hagen, complicated now by the theme of the 'Ring' which dominates his thinking. As the scene again begins to fade in mist and darkness, a great postlude broods on the themes of the hero and Wotan's spear before recalling Hagen's vocal line, 'You sons of freedom!' The textures increasingly thin out, and from near-silence the music gathers itself and begins to bring back fragments of the dawn duet from the Prologue, now spun out to immense lengths and wistful effect. The music also recalls the theme of 'Brünnhilde's Womanliness' and the end of the first great paragraph from 'Brünnhilde's Awakening' in *Siegfried*, but with something drained, as it was in *Götterdämmerung*'s opening measures. Through his extraordinary powers of musical imagination, Wagner conveys something strangely lost about Brünnhilde even as she sits there in an apparent idyll. The music describes her cherishing her love for Siegfried, but also that she is isolated; that she is there alone at the base camp, without purpose, company, or anything much to do. It makes sense that she should be glad of a visit from her sister Waltraute. This episode has been quite changed from its counterpart in *Siegfrieds Tod*, where it consisted of Brünnhilde's meeting with her eight Valkyrie sisters and sketched in the events which Wagner elaborated in *Die Walküre* instead.

The first that Brünnhilde knows of her sister's visit is a rapidly gathering storm in the distance, of the kind which recognisably surrounds the Valkyries as they ride through the air. Then comes the sound of thunder, and several themes from the 'Ride of the Valkyries'; and Brünnhilde takes in these long-familiar sounds. Soon she catches sight of a great horse ranging through the sky, and hears Waltraute calling to her. She is thrilled, and gives her sister a welcome, signalling a spot in the glades lower down where her horse can wait. 'You have come to see me; such a brave thing to do, coming to see how I am.' She is too carried away to notice that Waltraute is not responding to her excitement and her embrace, but remains grey and withdrawn, even though she admits that this visit to Brünnhilde was her sole reason for leaving Valhalla. Brünnhilde is touched: 'So then, for love of me, you dared to break Wotan's command! Or even – can it really be that he himself has changed? When I protected Siegmund, I know I was doing what he secretly wanted; and I know that he ceased to be angry with me. He originally bound me in sleep for the first man who found me, but then granted my request and surrounded me with magic fire, so that none but the bravest could attain me. What began as a punishment turned into something glorious, and now the most magnificent of heroes has made me his wife? Enfolded in his love, I lead a life of bliss. Have you come here to share in my good fortune?'

'Share in the frenzy that has raddled your wits!' answers Waltraute in a furious irritation. 'Can you not see that it is anxiety and terror that have made me break Wotan's orders?' Brünnhilde is suddenly crestfallen as Waltraute's mood comes home to her, and she asks if Wotan after all remains implacable; is his anger still a source of fear for Waltraute? Waltraute answers that if only it were still a source of fear, everything would be less awful. She now really frightens Brünnhilde by telling her to hear how utter dread, the same dread as drove her from Valhalla, will drive her back again. Brünnhilde herself is now caught up in Waltraute's distress; she sounds almost frantic as she asks, 'What then afflicts the immortal gods?'

'Listen to all that I have to tell you,' answers Waltraute and launches into her long narration. She explains to Brünnhilde that after Wotan parted from her, he deserted his heroes and battlefields, and roamed the world as Wanderer, until he finally returned home, holding the fragments of his spear which a hero had broken. 'After that,' she continues, 'he directed his heroes to hew down the great world ash, and pile up the logs and branches around Valhalla' (the scene described by the Norns). 'Wotan sits enthroned in the great hall among his gods and heroes who all wait in fear and trembling.' Waltraute describes a scene of unalloyed gloom, and continues; 'Wotan only learns about the world now from his ravens. If only they were to come back with the news he longs for, then once again, and once only, the god might smile. He is deaf and blind to our entreaties, his Valkyries, his daughters. We were all grouped around his knees, pleading, until in my sorrow I pressed myself up to him and wept. The frozen mask of his face melted because this made him think of you, and then he sighed and closed his eyes. In a whisper he said: "If only she would give back the Ring to the Rhinemaidens, then the god and the world would be redeemed and saved from its curse." Then I understood everything and stole out through the serried ranks. In secret haste, I took to my horse and rode straight here. Dearest sister, I beg you now, you alone can reverse the disaster and stop this endless torment.'[74]

Brünnhilde does not understand where Waltraute's description is leading or what she wants. 'My sad sister, what are these strange and unhappy tales which you are telling me? Now that I am separated from the gods and their heaven among the clouds, I can make no sense of your story. You sound so distracted and wild. What do you want of me?' Waltraute can barely resist grabbing Brünnhilde's hand, as she declares, 'There it is! On your hand, the Ring. For Wotan, cast it away.' Brünnhilde is aghast, 'My ring, cast it away?' 'Yes give it back to the Rhinemaidens!' Waltraute tells her. Brünnhilde cannot understand; 'The Rhinemaidens? I? the Ring? The measure and promise of Siegfried's love? Are you out of your senses?' Waltraute implores her, 'Brünnhilde, hear my anxiety and pain. The whole world's undoing may come from that ring. Fling it away, throw it far into the Rhine. For the sake of ending Valhalla's torment, throw that damnable and evil thing into the depths.'

Brünnhilde now becomes angry and contemptuous; 'Do you know what this is to me? How can you grasp it, you loveless virgin who cannot know what feelings are! This ring means more to me than all

---

74   The narrative creates so much hopelessness, misery and gloom, that Wagner seems rather have lost momentum in composing it. One of his gifts was normally an ability to produce a narrative which described events and situations vividly, but at the same time maintained the atmosphere and situation of the narrator. When Alberich down in Nibelheim described his picture of the gods and their glorious life up on the summits, the musical picture is different from the reality of those summits as Wagner sets them directly before the imagination, in the two scenes in front of Valhalla. The music makes it clear that Alberich's description is not the real thing, but in Waltraute's narrative the music offers only the dirgelike stillness and gloom of the situation she is describing, and Wagner conveys no sense of two Valkyries on the mountain and no sense of any urgency between them.

the joys of Valhalla and all the glory of the gods. A single glance at it matters far more than their eternal happiness. It is from the Ring that Siegfried's love shines out to me! How could you understand what this means! Get back to your gods, and tell them this; that just as I shall never forego my love, so my love will never forego the Ring. Valhalla's glory can tumble down in ruins first!' It is now Waltraute's turn to be angry and disbelieving. 'Is this what you have come to, is this is the Brünnhilde that I trusted? Have you so little love that you abandon your sister to her destruction?' This means nothing to Brünnhilde, who says, 'Take yourself off; fly away as far as you can on your horse! You will never have my ring!' and Waltraute departs in anguish and despair and with thunder and lightning, leaving Brünnhilde still infuriated, and telling herself; 'She need not come back – now or ever!'

Meanwhile evening has fallen. The fires below start to burn brighter, as the music of 'Magic Fire' begins to sound and strengthen. As Brünnhilde says, the flames have again leapt up to form a wall of fire, and she asks herself why this should happen, to be answered by Siegfried's horn call. She starts up as the orchestra recapitulates the festive music of Siegfried's ascent through the fire, and she sings of her own joy at his return. 'Soon I can throw myself into the arms of my hero, my god!' she sings ecstatically; but this time the trumpet takes up the horn call theme, and crescendos it mightily towards a climax of brazen dissonance, rammed home repeatedly, as Siegfried, appearing as Gunther, bursts through the flames.

Brünnhilde screams; 'Betrayed! Who forced through to here?' and then falls into a shuddering. The main orchestra falls silent, leaving only the tones of 'the Tarnhelm' – those sinister muted horns – and the motive of 'Magic Deceit' to work their extraordinary effect on the imagination. The horns continue as Siegfried begins, gracelessly and heartlessly. 'Brünnhilde, someone wants you who is not deterred by your fire. I claim you as my woman, so now – obey me willingly!' Brünnhilde starts to tremble more violently; 'Who is the man who dares what was destined only for the bravest?' 'A hero, who will subdue you if you resist his strength.' Brünnhilde declares, 'No, it was no hero but a freak and a monster who landed on the rock; has he come to tear me to pieces? Who are you, so terrible before me? Are you human, or are you from the dark hordes of hell?' Siegfried states flatly that he is a Gibichung, and that Gunther is the name of the man whom she must henceforth obey. Brünnhilde totally misinterprets what is happening, and breaks out in wild accusations against Wotan; 'Grim, merciless God. Now I understand your whole idea, how you are condemning me to shame and sorrow.' Siegfried presses on, 'Night is almost here! Your cave is where we can be united.' The implicit threat to her person rouses her; 'Stand back! Beware of this talisman! You cannot reduce me to shame, so long as this ring is my shield.' Siegfried grows more obnoxious by the moment; 'Your arrogance is the very thing that teaches me, persuades me to take the Ring from you'. He is accompanied by all eight horns, muted, playing 'Alberich's Curse of the Ring'. He adds brutality to boorishness as he grapples and wrestles with her. Meanwhile leitmotives of 'Struggle' and the subverted version of the Rhinemaidens' 'Hymn' alternate with shreds from the dawn duet from the Prologue, and with further statements of 'Alberich's Curse'. At first she tries to wield the Ring against him and initially breaks free, but this does not stop him. He comes at her again, more viciously than ever, and seizes the Ring from her finger, while the monster-music of 'Alberich's Curse' blazes out again. As Siegfried completes this sorry performance, she half faints, but then meets his eyes. There is a flicker of recognition and she collapses completely. As she begins to come round, he completes her disaster and despair, by commenting complacently, 'Now you are mine, Brünnhilde, you are Gunther's bride; so give me access to your cave.' This leads to her despairing capitulation, outwardly broken, inwardly bleeding, 'What can you do; how can you resist, wretched woman?' Siegfried thus completes his frightful personal decline. He behaves like a malignant narcissist: absolutely no remorse; utterly unaffected by Brünnhilde's misery; utterly without compassion. He ends the act by addressing his sword complacently, 'Now, Nothung, bear witness that I "wooed in fetters",' by which he means he does not instantly possess her person sexually. He does not actually add a literal rape to the assault and battery and the psychological damage which he has already inflicted.

'What a guy!' as I heard someone exclaim. This scene seems to be *the* miscalculation of Wagner's entire existence as a dramatist. It is perplexing that such a genius should have etched out Brünnhilde's dire situation with all the incisive draftsmanship of an Albrecht Dürer and the insight of Shakespeare, without seeing how damaging it would be for Siegfried's position. As for the defence of Siegfried commonly put forward, it simply will not do. It is no good saying that these are mythical times when people and standards were different, because Wagner recast his myths into intense psychological dramas that are utterly of the here and now, and his long letter to August Röckel dated 25 January 1854 makes it clear that he knew exactly what he was doing. The motivations and sensibilities which he ascribed to Brünnhilde in this scene are so in tune with today's ideas that we relate to her as if she were of today, and it is a mark of Wagner's dramatic immediacy that we quite unthinkingly make estimates of Wagner's characters as if they were familiar individuals, as real as any that we will ever know. How was it possible for Wagner not to see that Siegfried is even less now that 'perfect human being, O my King!', and even less 'pure love' than in the opera that bears his name, and that he is anything but 'a man who never ceases to love,' as he told Röckel? Wagner's disaster with Siegfried goes beyond leaving a black hole in *The Ring*, because Wagner's appropriation by the Nazis resulted in people seeing Siegfried in particular and Wagner in general as emblems of all that is worst in human nature, and this scene and Siegfried's scenes with Mime paved the way for misapprehensions that still continue.

In fact Wagner did realise his mistake in one room of his strange and wonderful mind, with its intermittent capacity for compartmentalisation. Almost fifteen years before he composed the music of *Götterdämmerung* his imagination was beginning to dwell on a different hero, Parsifal, a different 'glorious human being', as strong and invincible as Siegfried, but with one crucial difference, the capacity for compassion. Compassion became the central virtue of Wagner's final masterpiece. The interesting thing is that Siegfried dents *The Ring*, but not really; as I explained, *The Ring* is so immense, marvellous and profound, that even the serious flaws of Siegfried lose significance, if not completely.

Writing to August Röckel on 23 August 1856, Wagner also commented that he had not hitherto made clear in *The Ring* what the nature of love is, 'which in the development of the myth, we find playing the part of destructive genius'. However, the action of *The Ring* does not bear out the idea of love as a destructive genius, and he wrote these words at a later time when overwhelmed by the influence of Schopenhauer (which is best approached in connection with *Tristan und Isolde*). What *is* destructive is love's suppression and the formidable oppositions to it and pathological behaviour which it chances to provoke, but these are not of its making. In the earlier letter to August Röckel already referred to (25 January 1854), Wagner himself had insisted, 'The poison that is fatal to love appears under the guise of the gold stolen from nature and misapplied,' but is the gold that poisons love and makes it destructive and not love itself that is necessarily so. It is only in one instance, in Brünnhilde's rejection of Waltraute's request, that love – her own love – becomes most nearly destructive. Another passage in his same letter makes it clear that love itself was positive and redemptive for Wagner: 'For what is love itself but the eternal feminine?' and 'it is woman, suffering and willing to sacrifice herself, who becomes at last the real conscious redeemer.'[75]

75 Loge in *Das Rheingold* appears to be another mouthpiece for Wagner's real view of women, which was admiring and validating. Loge tells every one that nothing matters in life so much as 'woman', because of the balance, the leavening, and the completeness that the eternal feminine brings to the world, and because of her softening effect on the male-macho world order. In all Wagner's stage representations until *Parsifal* it is, with the exception of Ortrud, man who is aggressive, self-centred and given excessively to the 'will to power', whereas his stage women were generally redemptive. It was the eternal feminine which drew humanity upwards, and in this Wagner followed Goethe. In *Das Rheingold* Loge asserts '*Weibes Wonne und Wert*' as a force for human creativity and joy,

Act II of *Götterdämmerung* is set in a large open space between the hall of the Gibichungs and the Rhine, with Hagen himself still there as he had been for 'Hagen's Watch', but now repositioned outside. He is still half asleep, half in a trance. The orchestral Prelude takes up the leitmotives of '*Nibelungenhass*' and 'the Tarnhelm' from the end of Act I and reworks them with the grey harmonies and clouded orchestral colouring that characterised 'Hagen's Watch'. This music soon blends with references to the postlude of that monologue, but instead of fading out as before, there is a sudden sforzando, bleak and strident, which dissolves into flitting versions of the 'Ring' theme. Hagen is no longer alone, but assailed by the nightmare presence or the literal nightmare of his father. Wagner made Hagen himself more nightmarish in this scene than he had in *Siegfrieds Tod*, and shortened the scene considerably. He discarded Alberich's account of events now described in the preceding operas, and he concentrated on what Alberich and Hagen have become. Their discussion of events is designed not to relate those events but to allow Wagner to create a strange, diseased dream-world, and colour in what his two characters have now become. The music depicts Alberich as wasted away by obsession and hatred, but he still reveals strong feelings for his son, while still seeing him as a means to his ends. Hagen on the other hand makes it plain that he has no love for his father, no affection for his deceased mother for her gift of life, and no liking for himself.

The wraith-like form of Alberich is hovering round the throne where Hagen sits, and his words tug at Hagen; 'Are you asleep, my son?' Hagen answers, 'I hear you, evil being, what have you to tell me in my slumber?' The exchange draws a contrast between the deathly chill of Hagen and the energy of Alberich, although that energy now sounds spent and brittle. Alberich exhorts Hagen to be mindful of the mettle and courage which he inherited from his mother, but

---

although this casts women as means to ends defined by men instead of existing in their own right with the object of fulfilling themselves. (Like Wotan, Loge had not read Kant!)

Hagen answers sombrely that he owes her nothing for succumbing to Alberich's gold; she produced a son who is old before his time, gaunt and pale. He feels only hatred at the sight of anyone happy, and has never known happiness himself. Alberich urges him to nurture his joylessness and hatred; it makes him one with his father. He must be courageous and cunning, because this will enable them to destroy the forces of light. Wotan's power has already been reduced to nothing by one of his own heroes. At this point Alberich becomes anxious that Hagen is asleep again, but Hagen has been listening, and now asks who will inherit absolute power. 'Me,' says Alberich, and instantly tries to change it by adding, 'and you! We shall inherit the world. Provided I can trust that you share in my sorrow and anger.' He explains that by slaying Fafner and taking possession of the Ring, Siegfried has acquired its power, so that Valhalla and Nibelungs are both subject to him. However because he does not care for it in the slightest, this makes him immune to its curse. (Alberich is wrong about this.) This means that if they are to succeed, they must take active steps to destroy Siegfried. Alberich again becomes concerned that Hagen is asleep, and Hagen answers as if from a dream, that Siegfried is even now a slave to his purposes and is working towards his own destruction. Alberich still gives vent to his obsession, 'the Ring is all that matters, and so have a care. Siegfried loves a wise woman, and if she advises returning it to the Rhinemaidens and they recover it, it is lost forever.' (Is it possible that Alberich is unaware of recent events at the Valkyrie's rock?) 'You, Hagen, must act with the hatred which I bred into you to avenge my wrongs. You must win the Ring! This will make a mockery of Wotan and Siegfried and put an end to them! Swear it to me, Hagen my son.' In *Siegfrieds Tod*, Wagner now had Hagen saluting Alberich and promising, 'Prince of the Nibelungen, you shall be free!' but in *Götterdämmerung*, Hagen has become more ambiguous, and there is something withdrawn and unyielding in his reply; 'the Ring – *I* shall own it; be still,' especially when it is followed by the 'Curse of the Ring' in low tones and low registers. Alberich says frantically, 'Swear to me, Hagen, my hero,' but Hagen only answers, 'I swear it to myself.

Silence your anxieties,' while a repeat of the 'Curse' theme suggests the curse turning on Alberich himself. Still declaring, 'Be true Hagen! My son! ... Trusty hero! ... Be true! ... True!', Alberich fades into nothingness as the Norns had done.

Now as in the Prologue, the flags of dawn begin to appear, but a different kind of dawn. Almost for the first time since the Prelude of *Das Rheingold*, Wagner gives distinct counterpoints to all but one of his eight horns, and he also manages to suggest that while dawn is still dawn and positive, there is something muted about this particular dawn, a B flat dawn, not a C major. With a sudden eruption of energy, Siegfried materialises from nowhere; 'Hoiho, Hagen! Weary man, did you see me arrive?' 'Ha, Siegfried,' answers Hagen, 'back so soon; where did you come from?' Siegfried explains that he has come from Brünnhilde's rock, so quickly that it was on the rock that he drew the breath for his greeting to Hagen. The other two are following by boat and will soon be there. Hagen enquires whether he subdued Brünnhilde, but Siegfried is only interested in whether Gutrune is awake, and Hagen calls her out to join them. She offers Siegfried a formal greeting: may Freia smile upon him, most favoured by all women; but Siegfried answers gallantly that the only favour he wants from her is to be his wife. However, she wants all the details of how Siegfried managed Brünnhilde, and she takes some persuading to be convinced that the Siegfried did not have sexual intercourse with Brünnhilde during his night by her side. Finally satisfied, she shows her kind heart by suggesting that they all give Brünnhilde a splendid welcome and make her glad among them. Hagen should call vassals while she summons the women to prepare a celebration. As she makes as if to leave, she asks Siegfried archly, 'Will you take some rest now, you naughty hero?' but Siegfried answers that to help her is his idea of resting.

Hagen seizes a steerhorn, and in one of the great set pieces of *Götterdämmerung*, he blows a set of blasts on middle C, following them up with a call to arms: 'Hoiho! Hoihohoho!

Fig. 17.13

Men of the Gibichungs! On guard! Weapons! Danger! Danger is here! Arm yourselves for the crisis!' He blows on the steerhorn again, and it is answered by others and C flat and D sounding simultaneously, to create an uncouth dissonance as the vassals rush out into the open space from all directions. Horns intone the wedding summons.

Fig. 17.14 'Gibichung Wedding Summons' (four horns, cellos and double basses)

In music of prodigious energy they thunder out that they are all armed and ready to fight; what is the crisis and where is the enemy? Is Gunther in danger? Hagen tells them to be ready to cheer and congrulate Gunther because he has successfully acquired a wife, and they ask what then is the matter. Are there furious kinsman in pursuit? Hagen tells them that there are none, which puzzles the vassals; what then is the danger? Hagen tells them that the dragon-slayer was with Gunther to ward off all danger, and they ask again why he has called them out. He tells them amidst exuberant interruptions and repeated enquiries, that they must make ready for the wedding, sacrificing oxen on Wotan's altar, a boar for Froh, a goat for Donner, and several sheep for Fricka. They carry out his instructions with lightning speed, and ask what next, whereupon he tells them to take their drinking horns to the women who must fill them to overflowing with wine and mead, and then they should drink until they can drink no more. They all break out in uproarious laughter; good times must really have come when even grim Hagen can enjoy the fun. The Hagen-thorn/Hawthorn (the pun is untranslatable) has lost its bite in his new role as wedding-herald. In reality Hagen has remained sombre throughout, and he tells them now to be serious and prepare to receive Gunther's bride. It is their job to be loyal to this lady and quick to avenge her wrongs.

The boat bearing Gunther and Brünnhilde approaches the banks, and the vassals hail them as they come ashore. Here Wagner has allotted to the vassals a kind of nineteenth-century wedding march which is tinged with militaristic bombast, as well as a certain savage strength. 'All hail, Gunther! All hail to you and your bride!' Gunther addresses the gathering in a formal speech. He displays a mastery of ceremonials which helps explain why he is King. 'Today I bring you Brünnhilde, most exalted among women, as my fair bride. No man ever won a nobler lady. The gods have once again shown favour to the Gibichung people, and raised us today to new heights of glory!' The vassals clash their weapons enthusiastically, and repeat their enthusiastic greeting, while Gunther leads Brünnhilde towards the hall. She remains miserable and gloomy, her eyes cast down. At this point Siegfried emerges with Gutrune, and Gunther resumes his ceremonial style, 'All hail, dear hero! All hail, lovely sister! It is with joy that I see you at the side of the hero who has won you as his wife. Two happy pairs are standing here, Brünnhilde and Gunther, Gutrune and Siegfried!' At the sound of Siegfried's name, Brünnhilde looks up, sees him, turns radiant, and rushes over to be with him, but then finding that he looks at her unresponsively and slightly puzzled, her face changes and she passes through confusion to pain and horror. The Gibichung men and women know nothing of the background, but have been exhorted to do their best by their new Queen, and they are concerned; why she is so distraught? Almost fainting, she can only say, 'Siegfried ... here ... Gutrune?' Siegfried takes it upon himself to explain to her, 'Gunther's gentle sister, married to me, as you are to Gunther,' at which something snaps in Brünnhilde. 'I ... Gunther ...? You lie!' But again she is overcome, and Siegfried catches her as she falls to the ground. She looks up into his face disbelievingly and says faintly, 'Siegfried ... does not know me!' Siegfried calls over Gunther, telling him that his wife is unwell, and tries to make her surface from her faint: 'Wake up, my lady!' He points at Gunther: 'Look, there is your husband!'

Brünnhilde now catches sight of the Ring on his outstretched finger. 'Ach, the Ring! ... there on his finger! He ... Siegfried?' This is a moment which Hagen has been waiting for, and he tells the vassals to mark carefully what the lady accuses. Brünnhilde, trying to recover herself and make sense of it all, addresses Siegfried. 'I saw a ring upon your hand. It does not belong to you; it was seized from me' – she points to Gunther – 'by this man! How have you acquired the Ring from him?' Siegfried answers that he did not acquire it from Gunther. Brünnhilde now turns on Gunther, and tells him that if it was he, Gunther, who looted the Ring from her when he took her as his wife, then he should claim his rights to it and make Siegfried give it back. Gunther, confused and out of face, says he did not give Siegfried any ring; does she know it? Thereupon Brünnhilde asks him what he did with the ring which he took from her. He does not reply, and with a sudden insight, she pronounces, 'Hah! Siegfried stole it! He was the one who seized the Ring from me. It was Siegfried, and he is the treacherous thief.' Siegfried now indicates some crossed wires in his own head, 'the Ring did not come to me from the hand of any woman. I won it myself at Neidhöhle when I slew the dragon.' This is the next cue for Hagen; 'Brünnhilde, honoured lady, can you truly identify the Ring? If it is the one you gave to Gunther, then it is his and Siegfried has acquired it through treachery. He must pay the penalty as a traitor.'

Brünnhilde breaks out and storms, 'Treachery! Treachery! Shamefully betrayed! Double-crossed! Worse than any thought can conceive!' The music of the 'Vengeance Pact', evolved from Hagen's call to the vassals, begins to sounds ominously in the orchestra.

Fig. 17.15 '*Rachebund*, Vengeance Pact' (initially muted horns in octaves, over cellos and double basses)

This music sets the atmosphere, grey and relentless, such puts off people who are not on the wavelength for Wagner, particularly if they come upon music like this and hear it out of context. Gutrune, the vassals and the women are angry and baffled by Brünnhilde's accusation; 'By whom, by whom?' they ask, but Brünnhilde is too disturbed to explain. Instead she looks up to the heavens and calls on the gods, and principally Wotan, 'Is this what was decreed for me? Are you bent on teaching me to know a shame and suffering such as no one ever has ever known before? So then you must teach me rage and vengeance such as were never known before. You gods may break my heart, provided I can destroy my betrayer!' Gunther tries to pacify her, but she will have none of it; 'Away, you deceitful wretch, yourself deceived. Hear me everyone; I proclaim it: not Gunther but Siegfried had me for his wife!' As her listeners cannot take it in, she spells it out as plainly as was then permissible, 'He wrung from me love and ecstasy,' and the orchestra, sounding a sad memory of a phrase from their glorious duet in the Prologue, makes it achingly clear that she mournfully remembers her erotic experience as truly ecstatic.

Siegfried asks her how she can possibly defame her honour as a woman like this. Because she is doing it, he at least will defend it, even if it means showing her up as a liar. Let everyone now learn how he remained true to the blood-brotherhood which he had sworn to Gunther. Nothung, his sword, ensured the integrity of his oath. Its shining steel had divided him from this unhappy woman. This must have confused the vassals yet further, because they know nothing of the Tarnhelm and the deception on Brünnhilde's rock, and Brünnhilde must confuse them further when she counters, 'You slippery hero, see how you lie, calling on the sword as your witness. I know all about its sharpness; I also know all about the scabbard where it rested against the wall, while its owner possessed me as his own true love.' The vassals are beginning to become roused, and Siegfried is their natural target, a stranger whom most of them have never seen before, and they take up Gunther's cause. Gunther tells Siegfried that he, Gunther, now stands dishonoured unless Siegfried can give the lie to Brünnhilde's claim, and he is supported by Gutrune and the vassals, who weigh in and assert that Siegfried must swear an oath. Siegfried readily agrees, and he somehow seems to know the form for it since he asks which of the vassals can provide the spear.

This is another cue for Hagen, who comes forward and says that his spear is at his service. Siegfried now pronounces his oath with all due ritual. He lays his hand on the spear-point and addresses it. 'Shining steel! Sacred weapon! Be now the symbol of my oath! On this spear I swear to the truth; spear-point, witness my word. You shall strike me and bring me my death if this woman's word is true and I betrayed my brother.' He has barely finished when Brünnhilde advances and hurls his hand from the spear, placing hers on it instead, for an oath of her own; 'Shining steel! Sacred weapon! Be now the symbol of my oath! On this spear I swear to the truth; spear-point, witness my word. I consecrate you to striking him down! I vow and devote your cutting edge to killing him, because he has broken all his vows and sworn perjury.'

This is a situation for which none of those present have any plans or resources. The vassals call to Donner send down a storm to douse and extinguish the disgrace, and it is Siegfried who unexpectedly takes control and attempts to improve matters. He advises Gunther to look to his wife; and tells him that with a little time and rest, her frenzy will settle. He then turns to the vassals, asking them to give Brünnhilde some space and telling them that when the battle is one of words it is best for men to play the coward and quit the field. As the vassals fall back, he turns to Gunther confidentially for what is almost an apology; he says it grieves him more even than it must grieve Gunther, that his ruse worked so badly. It seems that the Tarnhelm only half disguised him. But in any case, the rage of women soon calms down, and she will still end up thanking Siegfried for acquiring her for Gunther. Siegfried now turns to the vassals again and encourages them: now is the time for joy and happiness, and they should follow him in to the feast. He addresses the women in similar terms; this is for him the happiest of days, because he is blessed with a wonderful bride, and he wants his own happiness to spread through to every one. Embracing Gutrune, he makes his way into the hall. The vassals and their women, enthused by his example, follow him, and the commotion subsides.

Only Brünnhilde, Gunther and Hagen are left outside, and there is a long silence, broken by Brünnhilde. Wrapped in thought, she asks half rhetorically, 'What infernal cunning is lurking here? What use is all my wisdom for resolving these riddles?' She breaks out into an impassioned lament, one of the most beautiful phrases in the whole of *Götterdämmerung*, '*Ach Jammer, Weh ach Weh!* Alas! Alas! Oh misery! I have given him all my wisdom, and he holds me now in bondage as though by cords. Who will give me a sword to cut them through?'

Hagen has come up behind her, and he tells her, 'You have been betrayed, but trust in me. I can avenge your betrayer'. Brünnhilde looks at him in weary disbelief and asks whom he means, and when he tells her 'On Siegfried', she says with open contempt, 'On Siegfried? – You! A single glance from those flashing eyes which I recognised, even through his lying disguise, and your courage would turn to nothing.' Hagen argues that Siegfried swore perjury on his spear-point and this makes him vulnerable, but Brünnhilde, with a surer sense of *Machtpolitik*, comments, 'Oaths and perjury, what do they signify? It will take something more than these to fortify your spear for this task.' Hagen says he well knows that Siegfried cannot be beaten in open conflict, which is why he needs her to whisper how he can put an end to Siegfried. This makes Brünnhilde burst out and complain of Siegfried's ingratitude because she had held back no spell that could protect him, everywhere and in any way; but when pressed by Hagen, it comes to her that she had not thought to protect his back, because he would never turn away from an enemy. 'And there' says Hagen, 'is where my spear shall strike!'

He turns to Gunther, sitting stricken, and addresses him with a bogus bonhomie; 'Up, Gunther, noble Gibichung! There stands your stalwart wife! Why such inertia?' Gunther continues to dwell on his own misery; 'What shame! What disgrace! I am the most miserable of men!' Hagen communicates a certain satisfaction as he comments to him, 'You lie there in disgrace, quite true!' and now Brünnhilde rounds on Gunther as well, 'You coward! You miserable fraud! You held back behind the hero, happy for him to make over to you the prize which his heroism had won. Your high-born lineage has sunk very low if it spawns such cowards as you.' Gunther has to wrestle both with his dishonour in the eyes of the world and an inner sense of moral degradation; 'Yes, I am betrayer and betrayed. Help me, Hagen! Help for the sake of our mother, who after all bore you as well.' Hagen answers that he cannot help, nothing can help, except only – Siegfried's death. This brings up Gunther short. 'Siegfried's death,' he repeats pensively, unhappy even to contemplate it. Originally, these words were a direct expression of the opera's title. Hagen tells him insistently, 'Only his death will purge your honour'. Gunther starts looking for reasons not to murder Siegfried, first that it would run counter to their oath and bond of blood-brotherhood. Hagen answers that Siegfried has broken the oath and annulled the bond. Gunther asks in what way Siegfried has broken his oath; and Hagen answers that he broke it through his betrayal. 'You think he has betrayed me?' asks Gunther, and now Brünnhilde weighs in, 'He has betrayed you, and you have all betrayed me. If there were any justice, then all the bloodshed in the world would not atone for your guilt. But the death of one must atone for all; Siegfried's death shall atone for his crime and yours.'

Here Wagner gave Brünnhilde an idea that is bizarre, indicating by his dissonant harmonies how far her state of mind is disturbed. In this bloodthirsty outburst he has created a complete contrast to her once generous altruism, which he had led Sieglinde to praise her as 'the highest wonder'. Equally bizarre, at least initially, is Wagner's import of the idea of 'atonement' because atonement (*Sühne*) in the sense of reconciliation (*Versöhnung*) is a Christian concept from outside Nordic mythology.[76]

Hagen meanwhile keeps up the pressure on Gunther, adding that Siegfried's death would add to Gunther's wellbeing and standing. 'Power of a monster (*ungeheure*) magnitude' would come to Gunther, if he gained the Ring, but only Siegfried's death would make this possible. 'You mean Brünnhilde's ring?' asks Gunther. 'The Nibelung's Ring!' answers Hagen. Gunther sighs deeply, and asks if there is really no other way, and Hagen argues that it would benefit them all. Gunther, fundamentally weak rather than evil, has further scruples, 'But what of Gutrune; I gave him to her. If we condemn her husband, how can we stand before her and look her in the face?' Brünnhilde starts up in a fury; 'What use has my wisdom been? What use is my insight? At least they tell me this much, that Gutrune was the magic which charmed away my husband.' She sings this to another phrase of ravishing beauty from the 'Gutrune' motive, and she adds, 'Make her suffer!' Hagen softly suggests a further low trick. When they go hunting next day, Siegfried will forge on ahead, and they can pretend to discover him 'gored by a wild boar'. Gunther finally caves in, so that he and Brünnhilde agree with Hagen.

---

76 It is a main tenet of Christianity that Jesus Christ sacrificed himself and atoned for the sins of the whole world, past, present and future, and one of Wagner's objections to Christianity was over this very tenet. He could not understand or believe in a God who could devise a form of existence where anything so bizarre and cruel could ever be necessary. In practice the foisting onto Siegfried of some Christlike aspects becomes less bizarre in the context of his 1840s-50s essays, tracts like *Die Wibelungen*, where Wagner drew parallels and connections between Apollo, Siegfried, Jesus Christ and Prometheus. Insofar as these essays present Wagner's quasi-anthropological theories of racial migrations from the East, they are tendentious, but they also present his insights into myth which are profound. Where Wagner has Brünnhilde perverting the whole idea of atonement is that she sacrifices Siegfried with him unknowing instead of him doing it willingly of his own accord. This is not atonement but scapegoating.

Wagner has these three conspirators merging in a trio, with Gunther and Brünnhilde calling upon Wotan, as guardian of oaths, law, and justice, to sanction and bless their redress against Siegfried. They cannot hear (and nor, usually, can we), that Hagen is invoking not Wotan but Alberich, telling him that the hoard is virtually Hagen's; that it must pass to him, and that Siegfried will soon be stripped of the Ring. 'Nibelung-father! Fallen prince! Guardian of the night! Alberich! Hear me now! You will soon again command the hordes of the Nibelungs, and they will obey you once again as lord of the Ring!' Events now follow so thick and fast that there is barely space to stage them during the music which ends the act, especially when conductors race through it at breakneck speed. Wagner ends the act with a wedding procession which comes streaming out of the hall. There are not only men and women, but boys and girls with garlands, and they carry Siegfried and Gutrune on thrones in their midst. The men take their horns and blast out the leitmotive announcing the wedding, familiar from Hagen's summons. The women smile happily at Brünnhilde and beckon her to join Gutrune, and Gutrune also greets her with a welcoming smile. Brünnhilde returns it with a bleak, cold stare, and is plainly about to leave in an aggressive show of non-cooperation when she is forestalled by Hagen who brings her round to Gunther, and by Gunther, who seizes her by the hand. The procession moves on to general acclamation. In the orchestra Wagner achieves an incomparable tour de force, half-blending and half-alternating music of a near-hysterical joy with music of grey death in the hearts of the principals. It is this, symbolised by the leitmotive of 'Rachebund, the Vengeance Pact', which has the final word. Did even Wagner ever create another action of such pace and drama? Even as a piece of purely musical structure this act is extraordinary.

It is time now to say something more of Brünnhilde. It is becoming ever clearer how she too is the source of continuity in The Ring. Wagner establishes her as increasingly central in exactly the degree that he makes Wotan recede. The golden heroine seems rather tarnished in this second act, where she stoops to fraud and hatred. I have more than once seen it argued, not least by a legal knight, that she becomes a deliberate liar. For the sake of *The Ring*'s meaning to us it seems as well to address and resist arguments that she set out to perjure herself and mislead her Gibichung listeners. She has supposedly done this by swearing on the spear that Siegfried had sexual intercourse with her at the end of Act I, which was *after* he had sworn blood-brotherhood, whereas she knew full well that their intercourse had happened on a different, earlier occasion. Accordingly she was deliberately perjuring herself when swearing that Siegfried lied, and that Siegfried was entirely innocent. This legalistic line reveals an absence of human understanding. Here is a woman who has just experienced a double catastrophe, her body invaded by a brutal stranger, and the love of her life acting towards her with rude indifference. Worse, he is in raptures over another woman. Her mind is all to pieces, and the real point is not the legal quibble whether or not Siegfried had reneged on his sworn blood-brotherhood technically, but the plain fact that he promised eternal loyalty and immortal love and has gone off with somebody else. She even has to accept that it was Siegfried, masquerading as Gunther, who desecrated her at the end of Act I. She is almost breaking down from the bewilderment and the impact of it all, as Wagner portrayed so well. No wonder that she is irrational and cannot think clearly, and there is nothing far-fetched or deliberately mendacious about her behaviour.

Indeed, I once had a real patient reminiscent of Brünnhilde. She is necessarily modified somewhat to avoid identification and offence, but the picture is true in essentials. She was an academic, a company director and a warm-hearted wife who was a leading and popular figure on educational boards, and was embarking on a political career when her husband left her for another woman. My unfortunate patient fell to pieces in every way except for her single-minded concentration on vengeance. She cut up her husband's suits, put milk in his petrol tank to wreck his car, daubed his suits, shirts and underpants with her excrement, and made a fair success of ruining him. She did not plot her husband's murder like Brünnhilde, but she did on impulse run a carving knife from his right groin to his left shoulder, half disembowelling him. He only just survived emergency surgery and intensive care, and she pleaded guilty to manslaughter and after a finding of diminished responsibility, she went on to a special hospital. In her revenge she swung completely, degrading herself and wrecking everything, her own mental health included.

No, there is nothing far-fetched about Brünnhilde's violent swing, nor about her second volte-face, her subsequent switch back to redemptive wisdom. This takes place when the Rhinemaidens tell her that it is all a terrible mistake, that Siegfried was guiltless, that he was deceived by Hagen's evil and fraud; and only reasons of space prevent the inclusion of another weird parallel from life. The intensity of Brunnhilde's remorse and suffering brings her a mystical serenity, but the final scene of the opera presents more of the serenity than the anguish which led to it, so that Brünnhilde's enormous psychological journey can easily pass by and fail to register.

The beginning of Act III seems at a stroke to cancel the greyness which has been shrouding *Götterdämmerung* since the Prologue. Four horns in unison sound Siegfried's exuberant horn call. They are answered from the stage by the sound of Siegfried himself, repeating it. The lower strings run down on a scale to a low F sharp, a stark, dissonant intruder into the cheer of F major, and there are grim echoes of 'Hagen's Summons', but only for a moment. An upwards string rush brings back Siegfried's horn call and the bright tonality of Siegfried at his best, as he was in the scene with the woodbird. Within this framework *Götterdämmerung* now reaches back to the first beginnings, recapitulating the very opening of *Das Rheingold*, but in F major, which was Mendelssohn's original key in the *Beautiful Melusine*. This time Wagner is kinder and gives the initial arpeggio, so exposed, to the first horn instead of the eighth, and the long evolutions of the *Rheingold* Prelude are compressed into eight bars. It leads to a radiant version of the 'Rhinemaidens' Lament' which is punctuated by more horns offstage, and to a new song for the Rhinemaidens.

Fig. 17.16

In mood it is similar to their first song of *Das Rheingold*, and yet so different. These immortal creatures are unchanged since the first scene, perhaps centuries ago, perhaps thousands of millennia. They are even now circling and swimming on the surface of the Rhine, which is visible nearby through a clearing in the forest. In a trio of ravishing beauty, they are asking the sun to send down light into the darkness where the Rhinegold once shone.

They are interrupted by Siegfried's horn playing again, and it launches then into a second 'verse'. This time they ask the sun to send them the hero who will return the gold. They break off when Woglinde hears his horn still closer, and they disappear under the surface to decide what next.

Siegfried appears. The hunt planned by Hagen is well under way, and as Hagen predicted, he has run on ahead of the others. He is complaining humorously that an imp must have led him astray and made him lose track of the creature he was pursuing. He is demanding rhetorically what rocky cleft is concealing his quarry when the Rhinemaidens appear. They address him by name in a sudden, unmodulated shift which is one of the most beautiful things in all Wagner. They ask him facetiously why he is scolding the empty air in front of him, whether some goblin has upset him, or some gnome. He begins to banter; perhaps it was they who enticed away the shaggy creature he was pursuing; perhaps this creature was their sweetheart, in which case they are welcome to him! The Rhinemaidens ask him what he would give if they found his quarry for him, and Siegfried says that he has caught nothing, so let them ask what they will. They answer, 'The golden ring on your finger; give that to us!' Siegfried stops short, and points out that he had overcame a gigantic dragon to gain the Ring; it does not make sense to give it up for a mere bearskin. The Rhinemaidens taunt him; is he so mean, so grudging; he should be open-handed with lovely girls. His reply, that his wife would be annoyed if he wasted his wealth, leads to more taunts; is she difficult; is she hard on him; has the hero felt the force of her hand? This ruffles him, and he tells them that they can laugh if they like, but they will not get the Ring. They only laugh again; he is so handsome; so strong; so apt for love; how sad it is that he is so miserly. They dive below the surface, and Siegfried goes right out to the water's edge, commenting to himself, 'Why should I put up with this derisive praise? If they reappeared, they could have the Ring.' He calls out, 'He! You lovelies in the water! Come back! I will give you the Ring'. He takes it off and holds it aloft, ready to throw it to them.

The Rhinemaidens reappear but they now tell him it to guard safely until he has learnt of the evil that lurks in it, the curse. He will then be even happier to give it up. (If people reading this wonder why Wagner made the Rhinemaidens do this, they will not be the first.) Siegfried's response, whether heroic or simply obtuse, is to put the Ring back on his finger and invite them to tell him what they know. All their music is beautiful, but their calls of 'Siegfried! Siegfried!' – set to the music of their original 'Hymn to the Gold' in its subverted version – are almost unbearably lovely. They tell him quickly of the Ring's origins, of Alberich's curse, manifest in the death of Fafner, and they warn him that it will soon bring death to him unless he gives it away; they alone can purge and purify its gold in the Rhine. Siegfried now demonstrates that heroic freedom from fear is sadly no substitute for judgment. He tells them to say no more; if their attempts to charm him had no effect, then even less is he affected by their threats. The Rhinemaidens now become genuinely concerned for his welfare and try to warn him again; the Norns wove this ending into their rope of fate. Siegfried suddenly displays an astonishing grasp (where did Wagner mean this to come from?) of how his actions impinge on the myth and alter its course. He says his sword has shattered the spear, and his sword can also cut through the eternal rope of the Norns, but nothing as yet has taught him fear. He would gladly have given them the Ring for love, but their attempt to frighten him is the last thing that would influence him. The idea of a threat to his life matters so little that he would happily throw it all away like this. He picks up a clod of earth and hurls it behind him.

The Rhinemaidens give up, and exhort one another leave the fool to his fate. 'He thinks he is strong and intelligent, but he is blind and stupid. He has sworn oaths and taken no account of then. He has been granted wisdom' (by Brünnhilde) 'but made no use of it. He was allotted the greatest blessing imaginable' (they again mean Brünnhilde) 'and simply threw it away. And yet the Ring which will lead to his death: that he clings to as something precious. Farewell, Siegfried, farewell! A wonderful woman will inherit from you today, poor fool, and she will give us a better hearing. To her, to her, to her!' They swim away swiftly. Their last words create a vital link in the story of *Götterdämmerung* but they sing at such a pace and the music itself is so beautiful, that what they are singing can easily flit past unnoticed. It is the Rhinemaidens with their second sight who now go on to explain to Brünnhilde what has really happened, how Siegfried had selectively lost his memory owing to Hagen's mind-altering drugs, how this led to Siegfried's entanglement with Gutrune, and how he is morally blameless; how his real self is still true to Brünnhilde. Because none of this happens onstage it is easily overlooked, but this alone explains Brünnhilde's second change of outlook, why she transforms into an icon of universal understanding, wise through suffering, all-knowing and all-forgiving. It happens because of the crucial truths she has learnt from the Rhinemaidens.

Siegfried, now alone, brags to himself that he knows all about women and their ways, how they first try to get what they want by charm, but if that does not work, they try again with threats and viciousness. 'And yet,' he reflects, 'if I were not true to Gutrune, I would have taken one of these enchanting women for my own.'

The 'Curse of the Ring' sounds softly in the orchestra, and the music shifts focus to the people and events now emerging from the forest.

Gibichung steerhorns call from the distance, and Siegfried answers, first with his own horn, and then by hailing the huntsmen. Soon the stage is swarming with men and their stock of game, and Siegfried encourages everyone down to the shaded, pleasant spot. Hagen agrees that it is a good place for their meal, and after giving instructions for food and drink, he turns back to Siegfried with the suggestion that he tell them the wonders of his own hunting. Siegfried explains that he has so far caught nothing, even though he almost bagged three wild waterbirds who sang that he would be struck down that very day. Gunther is appalled, but Hagen picks up Siegfried's mention of water-birds to ask him if he really understands birds' language, as he had heard tell. Siegfried says that it is a long time since he noticed, but seeing that Gunther looks gloomy and disturbed, he tries to cheer him up. He mixes up his wine and Gunther's, spilling it and telling Gunther that this is their joint offering to mother earth. Gunther looks gloomier than ever and tells Siegfried that his cheerfulness is excessive, leading Siegfried to comment quietly to Hagen that Brünnhilde is still causing him grief. Hagen comments, 'If only he understood her as well as you understand the birds!' Siegfried says again that since he heard the singing of women, he had forgotten about birds, but the mention gives him an idea.

He turns to Gunther; 'Poor, unhappy Gunther, would it cheer you if I told you the story of my young days?' Gunther says that he would like that, and Siegfried begins with his upbringing by Mime, his forging of the sword Nothung after Mime had been unable to do it, and his fight with Fafner. It was then that he tasted the dragon's blood and began to understand the singing of the birds as if it were human speech. There was one bird whose song told him to take the Tarnhelm and the Ring from Fafner's treasure. Hagen, knowing the answer already, asks him if that is what he did, and Siegfried, confirming it, says that he now heard the woodbird again, warning him that Mime meant to murder him. Hagen asks if the woodbird's warning stood him in good stead, and Siegfried says that after Mime had done everything to prove the truth of it, he put an end to Mime with his sword Nothung.

Hagen comments with cheerless mirth that although Mime could not forge the sword he still had a taste of it; and several of the vassals ask Siegfried to continue: was there anything more from the woodbird? At this point Hagen offers Siegfried a special drink, to help him remember the past more clearly, and gives him a potion which reverses the effect of his first one. The theme of 'Magic Deceit' sounds in the orchestra, followed by the theme of 'Brünnhilde's New Womanliness', which reveals that Siegfried is now beginning to remember her. He describes being instructed by the woodbird that he must now go and awaken a glorious bride. He was told that she slept on a mountain fastness, that she was encircled by fire; and that she would belong to the man who had the courage to pass through the fire. Hagen asks him if he had done as the woodbird advised, and completely unaware of the implications, Siegfried recollects eagerly how he did not stop until he reached her mountain summit. There she was, this wonderful woman in shining armour. He removed her armour; she awoke to his kiss; and soon he was engulfed in Brünnhilde's miraculous embrace. Gunther leaps to his feet in horror, and at that moment two ravens fly out from the bush, circle round Siegfried, and make off up the Rhine. Hagen asks him if he can make out what the ravens are saying, and Siegfried, turning round to see better, presents his back to Hagen. Hagen stabs Siegfried with all the force of his spear-thrust, shouting that he interprets the ravens as calling for vengeance. Siegfried turns round and tries to crush Hagen with his shield, but his mortal wound has already weakened him, and dropping the shield he falls forward onto it. Gunther has made a move to seize Hagen and restrain him, but too late. The vassals, ignorant of the circumstances, are aghast; 'Hagen, what is that? What are you doing? What does that mean? Why did you do that?' Gunther also asks, and Hagen, unrepentant, shouts out 'Vengeance for perjury!' He then leaves the scene, walking off on his own and leaving the vassals numb with shock, and Gunther stricken with grief.

Siegfried now has a dying vision of Brünnhilde. Adopting the formal style of ritual, he greets her as wondrous bride, and asks her to awaken. 'Who bound you in slumber so dire? One has come to awaken you, to kiss you awake. He breaks the letters that bound the bride, and now she enfolds him in her joy and happiness. Ah, her wonderful eyes, now open for ever! Oh her breathing, its sweet, soft rise and fall. Wonderful dissolution! Sweet intimations! Brünnhilde bids me greeting.' His exaltation fades suddenly as the music of 'Brünnhilde's Awakening' gives way to 'Fate'. Unless Brünnhilde told him more than we are told during their first period together, he dies knowing nothing of who he is, or of his crucial and disastrous contribution to the story of the world. When he tells Gunther the story of his life, he does not create a revealing and redeeming narrative for himself as Wotan did with Erda. Symbolically a mist rises from the Rhine to cover the scene as the vassals raise Siegfried on his shield, and form a procession which makes the journey back to the domain of the Gibichungs.

As the scene fades into the mist, ominous drumbeats begin 'Siegfried's Funeral Music'. This is one of the greatest things that Wagner ever composed. It celebrates Siegfried as he always remained in Wagner's imagination, the ideal figure who set the pattern for the future of humanity, both in *The Ring* and in our own real world. This 'Funeral Music' is bound together by a characteristic rhythmic figure running through it, its own special leitmotive.

Fig. 17.17 'Siegfried's Funeral Music'

The music begins quietly, but soon fortissimo trombones give out 17.17 as chords of the blackest C minor, a part of this leitmotive. Wagner tubas and horns respond by intoning the tragic leitmotive of 'the Wälsungs'. Woodwind recall the themes symbolising Sieglinde and the love she shared with Siegmund, and they do so over a grinding bass line which consists of the Wälsungs' other leitmotive. This forms the foundation for further developments of the 'Funeral Music' theme, and drives forward a powerful crescendo towards C major and then to the stabbing brilliance of the 'Sword' theme, played as it mosly is on the trumpet. C major is the musical context for a yet bigger crescendo towards the first of three supreme climaxes, made up from the 'Funeral Music' theme. It is followed by the theme of 'the Hero' on four horns and bass trumpet, stately and elegiac now in C minor, and the hero theme leads into to the second supreme climax, a development of the first. Two trumpets now repeat the theme of 'the Hero', and this time it modulates into E flat and into another major climax on the theme of 'Siegfried'. This is scored for the whole choir of heavy brass, fortissimo, and leads straight into the third of the supreme climaxes. The 'Siegfried' theme blazes out again, but this time its conclusion fades. The theme of 'Brünnhilde's New Womanliness' emerges over darkening harmonies, indicating her tragedy. It is repeated, and stopped horns and woodwind in their lowest, most acrid registers give out the 'Hymn to the Gold' in its subverted version. 'Alberich's Curse' rises soft and menacing from the depths and takes the music back into C minor, and four horns, no longer stopped, play a rare minor version of 'Siegfried', fully harmonised.

It is a mark of Wagner's genius that this music casts the spell that it does. Although the theme of the 'Funeral Music' binds this great passage together effectively, it is at one level nothing more than a procession of themes marking aspects of Siegfried's existence, with some very loud climaxes. Except that it is not; it is everything more. It is a profound celebration of human life, great and small. Not for nothing is it regularly played at the funerals of the great and the not-necessarily-good. It was played at Lenin's funeral almost twenty years before it was played for Hitler's obsequies. It is played for great musicians, great artists, and great scientists – sometimes the genuinely great and good – all round the world. In a sympathetic performance it scales the heights of exaltation and is immeasurably moving, and perhaps it touches the hearts of everyone because it is about everyone. It puts in a nutshell the central message of *The Ring* and draws people into its lesson that life is mostly an experience infinitely worth celebrating.

Sadly there are people whose lives are so frightful that they are impossibly difficult to celebrate. A hint of this is provided now by Gutrune, who becomes visible in front of the Gibichung hall as the mists lift and reveal the open space between the hall and the Rhine. It is now late at night and Gutrune senses it rustling with unfamiliar sounds. Wagner poured into this brief scene all his sympathy for women. Gutrune believes for a moment that she hears Siegfried's horn, but the rustling silence descends again and she tells herself, 'No, he hasn't come home. Nightmares have driven away my sleep; or was it those neighings from his horse? ... Did not I hear Brünnhilde laugh? ... Who was the woman I saw down by the banks of the Rhine? ... This Brünnhilde is frightening. Is she still at home?' She goes to one of the side doors of the hall, and peers in. 'Brünnhilde, Brünnhilde are you awake? ... No, her place is empty. Then it must have been Brünnhilde down at the Rhine.' With these words, Wagner is explaining, obliquely, that Brünnhilde has encountered the Rhinemaidens; and Brünnhilde will later confirm this and establish that they have told her the truth about Siegfried. Something again makes Gutrune start; 'Was that his horn? ... No. It's all deserted. Oh if only I could see Siegfried soon ...'

She begins to make her way back but stops short at the sound of Hagen's voice, his familiar 'Hoiho', as he shouts to everybody to wake up, 'Bring lights; light the torches. Torches! We need torches. The huntsmen are back with their game.' Maliciously, he calls to Gutrune; 'Get up Gutrune, your mighty hero is coming home.' Gutrune is now terrified; 'What is happening, Hagen? I cannot hear his horn.' Hagen continues, now openly cruel, 'The mighty hero will never sound his horn again, nor hunt, nor pursue pretty women.' Gutrune still cannot take it in, but now the vassals arrive, and place the shield with Siegfried's body on it in full view. Hagen, that virtuous avenger of falsehood and perjury, now perjures himself, 'Here is the victim of a wild boar, Siegfried, your dead husband.' Gutrune screams and collapses over Siegfried's body. The gathering crowds join in the general horror and mourning, and Gunther, whose heart was never in the plan to murder Siegfried, tries to comfort Gutrune. She turns on him, and with a wife's sixth sense she denounces him; 'Get away, you treacherous creature. It was you who murdered my husband. Help me, help me!' she shouts to every one vaguely as she looks round. She turns back to Gunther; 'You struck down Siegfried.' Gunther tells her not to accuse him, but Hagen; he was the wild boar that tore into Siegfried.

Hagen looks at Gunther blackly; 'Are you angry with me?' and Gunther answers, 'I hope that distress and disaster wreck your life.' Hagen brazens it out; 'Yes then! It was me; I killed him; I, Hagen, did him to death. I did it rightly, and with the spear on which he swore perjury. I now claim my divine right to the spoils and lay claim to this Ring.' He asks the vassals to support his claim, but Gunther tells Hagen, 'the Ring belongs to me, and you shall never have it. Gutrune should inherit it.' Hagen counters, 'It is the heritage of its Nibelung lord, and passes to his son!' and the 'Curse of the Ring' sounds as Hagen attacks Gunther, takes him by surprise, and murders him. He turns to the dead Siegfried, ready to seize the Ring, but Siegfried's corpse raises its arm menacingly, and Hagen gives way to an unexplained weakness and falls back.

This is the point where Brünnhilde sweeps in, having learnt the truth about everything from the Rhinemaidens, those wise sisters as she soon describes them. She begins by telling everyone else to put a stop to their feeble laments. She announces that there has been no lament that does justice to Siegfried; so far it has been no more than children whining over their spilt milk. Gutrune, heartbroken and furious, fights back, 'Brünnhilde! You hateful, envious creature! You created all this havoc and misery. You stirred up the men against Siegfried. It was an evil day that brought you here.' Quietly Brünnhilde tells her to be silent, 'because you, poor woman, were never really married to Siegfried. You were only a physical plaything, but I was his second self, and he swore oaths of deathless devotion to me before he ever beheld you.' Gutrune flies at Hagen; 'Damn you Hagen, how I hate you! It was you who advised the poison which made him forget. Now I have nothing left but anguish; I see that Brünnhilde was the true love, and he only forgot her because of the drink.' Brünnhilde's new wisdom and universal compassion were tellingly expressed in Harry Kupfer's Berlin production, where he had Brünnhilde gently embracing and comforting her weeping sister-in-law.

Brünnhilde now turns to Siegfried and embarks on the great panegyric which rounds off the meaning of *The Ring*. That at least was Wagner's plan. The difficulty is that it had many meanings. This complicates what it finally tells us – but as so often enriches it. As mentioned in the chapter *Der Ring des Nibelungen*, part of Wagner's intention had been to follow Feuerbach and show how the gods (and religion) were outmoded and transcended by man in his humanist maturity. However, the conclusion which he first gave to *Siegfrieds Tod* followed the same line as his prose draft and by no means showed the gods as outmoded. Instead it re-established them. Wagner made Brünnhilde join Siegfried on his funeral pyre; but after they had perished in the conflagration, Brünnhilde was to reappear fully armed as a Valkyrie and lead Siegfried to Wotan and immortality. Brünnhilde was to tell Wotan, 'I lead Siegfried to you. Give him your loving greeting, for he sets the seal on your power and authority.' It appears that when he hammered out his ideas into the drama of *Siegfrieds Tod*, Wagner replaced his 'Feuerbach' intentions with the conclusion expressing his distinctive brand of republicanism: 'All that we ask is that the King should be the first and truest of republicans.' This was why Wotan took on the mantle of the Saxon king, reigning with his republican heroes as symbolised by Siegfried and Brünnhilde. Brünnhilde's address conveying this idea was to last 53 lines and be followed by Siegfried's funeral procession, made up of two groups, men and women, who would conduct a ceremonial dialogue. The women would chant questions, 'Who is the hero?' and 'What was his fate?' and the men would chant back the answers. This plan eventually became the model for Titurel's funeral procession in *Parsifal*, but in *Götterdämmerung* Wagner deleted it.

A number of things had changed for Wagner that caused his first serious revision of Brünnhilde's final address (actually his second, as the first revision, one of six in total, was virtually unaltered from the original). One of the most important changes was in his outlook on death. In *Siegfrieds Tod*, death is not the end but a transforming gateway to a better life. Brünnhilde and Siegfried both move to immortality as they ascend to Wotan, and the idea of death as transformation was one which Robert Donington even tried to discern in *Götterdämmerung*.[77] However, it is not for nothing that even people who know nothing of Wagner use the term '*Götterdämmerung*' to describe an utter, total and irrevocable annihilation, and this was the idea which went into Wagner's second revision of Brünnhilde's address. Wagner lost interest in preaching his special kind of republicanism, and he did now make his finale express the ideals and ideas of Feuerbach. Feuerbach believed that there was no immortality, and so instead of affirming that immortality and presenting it onstage, Brünnhilde's address did away with it.

In this new version Brünnhilde absolves the gods from their guilt for all that they (and religion) had imposed on mankind. She pronounces for them a blessed redemption, a release from existence, because they had only ever been figments of human imagination, and now that they have ceased to exist in people's minds, they have ceased to exist outright. She still expresses this by addressing them allegorically; 'You may depart now because your guilt has lifted. Your guilt gave rise to a happy hero whose action, freely performed, atoned for your guilt. You are released from the fearful struggle for your vanishing power. You can fade away in joy before the deeds of man, before the hero, to whom you pointed the way. I proclaim that in death you will find redemption from your existential anguish.' Man's outgrowing of religion spells the gods' annihilation. However this annihilation means not just that is there no immortality for the gods, but that there is none for Siegfried, Brünnhilde and mankind either. In this

---

77 Donington, Robert, *The Ring and its Symbols*, London, 1963.

new frame of reference all transcendental worlds and all immortality is no more than a invention of religion, and they are all false. The release from the oppressive beliefs of religion does away with any possibility of man's own immortality, in real life as in *The Ring*. The exact date of this immense shift is uncertain, but it probably dates from early in Wagner's first Swiss exile when he was in close and admiring contact with Feuerbach. Wagner revised the closing scene again in 1852, on similar lines, but now he wanted to make it even clearer that Wotan had met his doom, and so the new revision staged his destruction in the sky as well as declaring it though Brünnhilde.

Partly as a result of Wagner's alterations, Brünnhilde's concluding address or 'Brünnhilde's Immolation' as it is known, expanded to about 142 lines (the exact number depends on how they are divided up). Eventually Wagner omitted 30 lines, but for us the great thing is that his eventual 112 lines produced a great flight of musical inspiration. The address as Wagner eventually set it begins with Brünnhilde taking control and organising the vassals into building the funeral pyre ('*Starke Scheite*'). She commands that Grane be brought to her, because she and the horse are to join Siegfried in the blaze. For some people, including me, the whole idea of Brünnhilde's immolation, her suicide, strikes a jarring note which does not seem to have troubled Wagner. Perhaps the reason was that her death was originally allegorical; she did not really perish but moved on through it to life in Valhalla as an immortal. Once death became real, with no resurrection, dying itself became starker and more forbidding. Death by burning takes on an agonising realism that is horrifying, and it strikes a great red gash across the final pages of *The Ring*. The thought of Brünnhilde's unthinkable pain mars and confuses all the positive messages and precepts. Perhaps Wagner acted more wisely when he allowed Isolde to transfigure and Elsa and Kundry to expire gracefully, in mythical, allegorical conclusions which do not blacken the message; but it is a mark of Wagner's mesmerising powers that he draws the imagination beyond Brünnhilde's destruction to a final, lasting appreciation of all that is most life-enhancing about *The Ring*.

In the version of Brünnhilde's closing scene which Wagner eventually gave to the world, he had her making ready her horse and organising the funeral pyre, and then gazing at Siegfried with an expression of infinite tenderness. She describes the radiance she feels streaming from him and affirms her faith in his absolute integrity, even though he betrayed her. She bewails the contradictions involved in his second appearance at her mountain fastness, and the paradox that he was barred by his sword from embracing the wife who loved him, and was yet at the same time betraying her. Hence, 'He was at once the truest of men, and the most treacherous. Do you know why all this had to be?' She lifts her eyes upwards and tells the gods, 'O you eternal guardians of oaths, look down at my burgeoning despair and recognise in it your guilt. Most exalted of gods, Wotan, listen to me and hear my accusation. It was through his most valiant act, so desperately desired by you, that you sentenced him to fall to the curse by which you are doomed.' She tells Wotan that the gods offloaded their guilt onto Siegfried, and continues, 'Siegfried, truest of all men, was destined to betray me so that I might become all-wise. I hear now the beating of wings, of your ravens hovering near, and at last I send them home to you with the tidings you so fear and desire. Rest, and be at peace at last, O god!' She sings this to a luminous, low-toned reminiscence of the music which so long ago formed the Rhinemaidens' 'Hymn to the Gold', and the degree of awareness into her insight and compassion for Wotan which this music instils, and the poignancy of it all, is extraordinary.

She turns to Siegfried again and proclaims, 'My inheritance ... I now claim it for myself. Accursed charm! Terrible Ring! I grasp your gold to cast it forth for ever. You sisters of the watery depths' (here she addresses the Rhinemaidens) 'I thank you for your wisdom and your counsel. I give you now what you so long to own. Take from my ashes that which is yours. The fires that destroy me shall purge the Ring of its curse. In the depths of the waters you shall henceforth guard in safety and forever the gold whose theft brought so much misery and evil into the world.' She places the Ring on her finger and again addresses the ravens; 'Tell your lord all that you have heard here by the Rhine. Take your flight past Brünnhilde's rock, where Loge's flames still burn, and send him to Valhalla, for the end of the gods is now dawning. Thus ... do I cast the flames into Valhalla's great fortress.'

Wagner's plan in his Feuerbach period, was for her to declaim, 'The race of the gods is vanishing, and I leave a world free of its old despotic rulers.' She was to continue, 'What matters is not wealth nor gold, nor the splendour of the gods, not vapid treaties, nor contracts with all their implicit treacheries, nor the bondage of tradition. It is love that counts, love alone that is sacred, whether in joy or sorrow.' This is Feuerbach speaking, and not a bad prescription.

However, Wagner and his outlook changed again because he turned his back on Feuerbach (or half did so) when he fell in love with the philosophy of Schopenhauer. Wagner consequently reworked the meaning of *The Ring* to embrace and preach resignation, pacification of the will, and universal compassion. Brünnhilde was now to declaim, 'I go forth from the home of longing, and I fly forever from the home of delusion' (or 'will'?); 'I close behind me the doors of eternal becoming. Free from reincarnation, I, who am made wise, go to the sacred, chosen land, the destiny of all our sojournings on the earth. Shall I tell you how I won it, this sublime goal of all existence? It was the deepest suffering from sorrowing love which opened my eyes; thus it was that I saw in my mind an end to the world' (that is, to all future existence). This is not a straight translation but an attempt to draw out Wagner's meaning into a less obscure form; and anyone who tries to translate passages like this learns to feel a certain sympathy for the predicaments of William Ashton Ellis. Wagner's German is so compact and yet so discursive, and so allusive, that a straight translation into English barely makes sense. One difficult point about this post-Schopenhauer peroration is that it takes for granted both that there is reincarnation, and that achieving an end to reincarnation is an ultimate goal of existence and the ultimate freedom. These ideas are wholly new to *The Ring*, and do not connect with anything in it otherwise. Even Wagner's most goggle-eyed admirer might suspect him of wishful thinking when he declared that the drama had already expressed these ideas so clearly that it would be otiose to spell them out in words in Brünnhilde's peroration. But if either version of her peroration crystallises the meaning of the drama, it is actually the 'Feuerbach' version, which was integral to it. The 'Schopenhauer' adaptation was bolted on afterwards, even though Wagner may at some stages have felt that it expressed the true but unconscious direction of his thinking.

Eventually he set to music neither the 'Feuerbach' or the 'Schopenhauer' ending, even though he composed music for the 'Feuerbach' version for King Ludwig privately. At the time of writing the *Ring* text, the 'Feuerbach' version did do something very positive, advancing Wagner's friendship with Franz Liszt because it appealed so strongly to Princess Carolyne zu Sayn-Wittgenstein, Liszt's almost-wife. Liszt told Wagner in a letter how he heard her repeating these lines happily to herself as she was going up the stairs. (She became very hostile to Wagner later.) In the final version which went into the completed *Ring*, Brünnhilde does almost no philosophising, but simply greets Grane, her horse; 'Do you know, dear friend, where I must lead you? There, shining in fiery brightness, lies your master, Siegfried, my sacred hero.' At this point Wagner brought back the great melody with which Sieglinde glorified Brünnhilde in *Die Walküre*. This is the leitmotive of 'Brünnhilde's Glorification', as Wagner himself described it.

Fig. 17.18 'Brünnhilde's Glorification' (The form given here is in fact from the great orchestral peroration at the end of the opera.)

She continues, 'Are you neighing with joy to follow him, dear friend? I, too, long to join him. Bright fires have seized on my heart as well.

Soon to embrace him, absorbed within him in an ecstasy of passion, utterly one with him – *Heiajoho* Grane! Greet now your master – Siegfried! Siegfried! See! Your wife now greets you in bliss!'

With the Ring on her finger she spurs Grane into the flames, and this initiates the ultimate catastrophe of fire and flood. The music symbolises the flames leaping up with an intensity which rapidly consumes the pyre and those who are on it. Then the themes of 'the Rhine' come surging up as the Rhine bursts its banks. The 'Rhine' music completely floods over the 'Fire' music and the inferno itself, leaving only clouds and steam. Riding on the crest of the waves come the three Rhinemaidens, and in the orchestra there sings again the music with which Woglinde began *Das Rheingold*. Hagen sees the Rhinemaidens surging forward with the waters, realises that they are on the verge of recovering the Ring, and acts like a madman. The orchestra is already celebrating the Rhinemaidens' recovery of the Ring and playing their 'Hymn to the Gold' when Hagen hurls aside his weapons and plunges into the waters, roaring 'Back from the Ring!' The 'Curse' theme rings out over its last victim as the Rhinemaidens entwine Hagen in their arms and drag him into the depths to drown. The 'Curse' theme is in fact shorn off midway, its force destroyed forever by the Ring's final return to the Rhinemaidens. The waters retreat, and the 'Valhalla' theme, its inherent nobility transfigured as the leitmotive of the 'Rhinemaidens' Primal Innocence' and the one previously known as 'the Redemption of the World by Love' swathe it in counterpoints and optimism. This optimistic title for the leitmotive reflects the influence of Feuerbach, and signifies the fact that she has made the Ring safe forever with the Rhinemaidens, because no new Alberich can ever work the spell again. Perhaps in the end Wagner was not so wrong when he said that the meaning of *The Ring* would become clear in a good *musical* performance. High above, in the distant sky there is the glow of more fire as Valhalla becomes visible, engulfed in flames. The 'Valhalla' theme begins to shine out with fierce brilliance, high on fortissimo trumpets and all the heavy brass. The gods and heroes also become visible, assembled as Waltraute had described. In the river below, the radiance from Valhalla reveals the Rhinemaidens circling in the waters. They are sharing and adoring the Ring, even as Valhalla is entirely consumed by fire; but Wagner gives the last word musically to the 'Hero' theme, and to 'Brünnhilde's Glorification', soaring out on all thirty-two violins. It establishes that Brünnhilde is glorious; she has purged away all misunderstandings and imperfections, and the music affirms that she is a redemptive example to humanity of forgiveness, generosity, compassion, altruism and ultimately, real, true love. In the end it was she and not Siegfried who redeemed the world by her 'vital deed', by her returning the Ring to the Rhinemaidens, and her theme, 'the Glorification of Brünnhilde', brings *The Ring* to its end. Perhaps in the end the conclusion does come very close to the idea once attributed to this music, 'The Redemption of the World by Love'.

The end of *The Ring* also sets the seal on the affirmations which have gradually gained force from the beginning, to the effect that whatever twilight and oblivion must eventually fall on all human endeavour, it is still immeasurably significant. *The Ring* as a whole is a compelling validation of human existence, a secular redemption. Simply to have lived life in all its richness and variety is an experience of such value that it is not negated by the fact that it must end. The prospect of it ending does create a degree of regret; yes, that is there in *The Ring*'s final eight bars; but it still establishes the conviction that to have lived life is an experience so worthwhile, that not even the prospect of total, eternal oblivion can detract from that worthwhileness.

Götterdämmerung was first performed as part of the original *Ring* cycle at the Festspielhaus in Bayreuth. The performance took place on 17 August 1876, and the cast consisted of Johanna Jachmann-Wagner (First Norn), Josephine Schefsky (Second Norn), Friederike Grün (Third Norn), Georg Unger (Siegfried), Amalie Materna (Brünnhilde), Eugen Gura (Gunther), Gustav Siehr (Hagen), Mathilde Weckerlin (Gutrune), Luisa Jaide (Waltraute), Karl Hill (Alberich), Lilli Lehmann (Woglinde), Marie Lehmann (Wellgunde), and Minna Lammert (Flosshilde). The performance was conducted by Hans Richter under Wagner's supervision.

EIGHTEEN

TRISTAN UND ISOLDE

Nothing Wagner had done had hinted at the operatic miracle named *Tristan und Isolde*. Never in the history of music had there been an operatic score of comparable breadth, intensity, harmonic richness, massive orchestration, sensuousness, power, imagination, and colour.[78]

Not a bad recommendation, especially coming from Harold C. Schonberg, whose assassination of Wagner's character we saw at the start of Chapter 9. Wagner's masterpieces are all extraordinary, but there is something special and different about *Tristan und Isolde*. Nietzsche fell under its spell in his teens after learning it in Hans von Bülow's piano transcription, and even after he had turned to a confused, conflicted hatred of Wagner, he remained enthralled by its 'fifty strange delights', in comparison with which he found that even Leonardo da Vinci faded into insignificance. D.H. Lawrence and T.S. Eliot paid it the homage of writing it into their own creations, *The Trespasser* and *The Waste Land*, and it was its 'heaven-born ravishment'[79] that consecrated Bruno Walter to his life as a conductor.

There I sat in the topmost gallery of the Berlin Opera house, and from the first sound of the cellos, my heart contracted spasmodically. The magic, like the terrible potion that the mortally ill Tristan curses in the third act, 'burst raging forth from heart to brain'. Never before had

---

78 Schonberg, Harold C., *The Lives of the Great Composers*, London, 1971, p. 262.
79 Walter, Bruno, *Theme and Variations: An Autobiography*, tr. John Galston, London, 1946, pp. 41 et seq.

my soul been deluged with such floods of sound and passion, never before had I been consumed with such yearning and sublime bliss, never had I been transported from reality by such heavenly glory. I was no longer in this world. After the performance, I roamed the streets aimlessly. When I got home I did not say anything and asked not to be questioned. My ecstasy kept singing within me through half the night. When I awoke on the following morning I knew that my life was changed. A new epoch had begun; Wagner was my god.

These are just a few examples from the many that illustrate the impact of *Tristan und Isolde*. John Culshaw, the moving spirit behind Decca's *Ring* recording and much else, wrote that *Tristan und Isolde* was the closest thing in music to a drug, and that the *Tristan* 'Rausch (rush)' made *Tristan* the most intoxicating thing that Wagner created. Not that its effect is narcotic, but more on the lines of Aldous Huxley's experiences with mescalin, bringing a widening of perceptions and a mighty expansion of meaning, even though it is a challenge to put that meaning into words. Reginald Goodall, greatest of English Wagner conductors, had devoted a lifetime to Wagner when interviewed in a famous television programme.[80] He was asked what he thought *Tristan* was about, but simply shook his head and said he did not know. Wagner himself gave a description of the meaning which he first intended in an undated letter to Franz Liszt,[81] 'As I have never in life felt the real bliss of love, I must erect a monument to that most beautiful of all dreams, in which from beginning to end, that love may be satiated. I have in my head *Tristan und Isolde*, the simplest, most full-blooded conception.'

The action, the story and the events on which *Tristan und Isolde* turns are few and brief; instead Wagner (in his own words) 'plunged into the inner depths of soul events, and from the innermost centre of the world fearlessly built up its outer form'. Before embarking on the story there are three important points to make, two about

80 'The Quest for Reginald Goodall', *Omnibus*, BBC2, 1984.
81 *Correspondence of Wagner and Liszt*, tr. Francis Hueffer, New York, 1889, ii, p. 55.

its genesis and origins, and one about the music. *Tristan und Isolde* broke into Wagner's composition of *The Ring* on 9 August 1858, and the important question is why. He had not only welded together its action, but completed the poem and the music for more than half of it. It was not that he was led away by suddenly discovering the story of *Tristan*, because he had read it in Gottfried von Strassburg's version in Dresden ten years earlier.

What had changed was that he was becoming increasingly pessimistic about the prospect of an amnesty allowing him back to Germany, because it kept repeatedly fading instead of brightening, and with it went any real prospect of staging *The Ring*. Worse, events in France and elsewhere had shaken his belief in his ideas and ideals for *The Ring*, and his certainty that they could ever be realised. Worse still, after discovering Schopenhauer, he was uncertain that it was even sensible to try. In such an unsettled state of mind, he was open to the idea of a simple popular work which could be staged easily everywhere (that was not precisely how *Tristan* turned out), and might make him some money, and he therefore grew susceptible to the dawning possibility that *Tristan* might supply what he wanted. Its subject matter was newly present to his mind because two of his protégés had taken it up. Karl Ritter, the son of his benefactor Julie Ritter, had written a play whose faults, as Wagner saw them, filled him with the desire to do something better on the same lines. In 1854 Hans von Bülow, another protégé, had sent Wagner his symphonic poem *Nirwana*, intended as the Overture to Ritter's play and which impressed Wagner so much that he told Bülow that after an achievement like that he could do anything he wanted. Wagner even took over from *Nirwana* the rising chromatic scale which haunts *Tristan und Isolde* from the second bar of the Prelude onwards.

Another factor was the feeling which he developed for Mathilde Wesendonck. The idea that she inspired the 'unhappy love story' of *Tristan und Isolde* is erroneous, even in its premisses about the nature of the work, but she certainly lit up Wagner's imagination, and the intense, conflicted feeling that she did inspired made its own contribution to his general, febrile excitability, and to the unsettled state of mind that made him readier to detach from *The Ring*. The reasons why Otto and Mathilde Wesendonck had settled in Zurich remain slightly mysterious, as their business base for trading silks to America was situated hundreds of miles away on the north German coast, but whatever the reasons, they had eagerly attended many of the concerts which Wagner conducted in Zurich with such stellar success. The Wesendoncks rapidly became generous supporters of the musical scene at Zurich generally and of Wagner in particular. Eventually they installed him and his household at the Asyl, apparently a charming dwelling close to their own newly built villa, for a reasonable but not a negligible rent. Mathilde's significance for Wagner has already been evaluated in the chapter on Minna Wagner and her successors.

Another reason for taking up *Tristan und Isolde* was as Ernest Newman expressed it, that 'the whirling nebula of incandescent dust from which the *Ring* music was being generated spontaneously threw off a mental and musical world entirely different from itself.' Accordingly it happened that from the end of 1854 onwards, the continuation of *The Ring* began to jostle increasingly in Wagner's mind with the possibility of embarking on this different drama. By 19 December 1856 Wagner was writing to Princess Marie Wittgenstein, the daughter of Carolyne, Liszt's long-term attachment, that while trying to work on music of *Siegfried* he had fallen unawares into the *Tristan* subject. It had come between himself and *Siegfried*, even presenting him insistently with some music. His mind was increasingly flickering from one creative channel to another, and matters came to a head in June 1857 when he wrote to Liszt, 'I have led my young Siegfried into the beautiful forest solitude again; there I have left him under a linden tree, and said farewell to him with heartfelt tears.' However, the following August, he told Princess Marie that he had just sat down to sketch the poem of *Tristan*, when he was overcome by a pitiful longing for *Siegfried*. 'I took the score out again and decided to complete the second act at any rate. This has now been done … so now I know that my hero is all right. Yet all this has been a great strain on me, for while I was working at *Siegfried* once again I could get no peace from *Tristan*. I actually worked simultaneously on both, the *Tristan* taking more and more definite shape, and I being so passionately occupied with it that the double labour was a perfect torment to me.' *Tristan* now won and it was twelve years before he again took up the composition of Siegfried in earnest, although he did some orchestration in the mid 1860s.

The second point for the genesis and nature of *Tristan und Isolde* is related to Schopenhauer and his philosophy, which played a far more positive role in its creation than simply leaving the way clear by compelling Wagner to throw his ideas for *The Ring* back into the melting pot. Schopenhauer provided the terrain for *Tristan*, because *Tristan* is a drama situated entirely in the landscape of his philosophical ideas and principles, and *Tristan* takes it for granted that those ideas and principles are true. As we saw in connection with *The Ring*, Schopenhauer believed that the universe was godless but driven by 'the will', a blind, tumultuous, metaphysical force which galvanised and energised everything. Wagner gave 'the will' his own gloss and redesignated it as '*Wahn*'. As for the translation of '*Wahn*': my plan is not to translate it. Although *Wahn* was a German word for 'illusion' and 'delusion' both for Schopenhauer and generally, Wagner somehow identified it partly with Schopenhauer's 'will'. There is no good English word for *Wahn* in Wagner's special sense, because the idea itself is alien to our thinking.

Wagner's encounter with Schopenhauer's philosophy and its distinctive pessimism remodelled his outlook and his way of experiencing everything, including the erotic phenomenon. However, the renunciation of life's erotic dimension essential to Schopenhauer went against Wagner's whole cast of mind and against his conviction that the erotic dimension largely gave life its meaning. It remained an open question for Wagner whether Eros generated more joy or misery, and whether this weird god or goddess was ultimately more demonic or redemptive. Perhaps his core position was described almost in passing when he was making a point about music in *Opera and Drama* and took as an illustration the text 'Love brings both joy and pain, but even in its pain it weaves rapture.' His position throughout *Tristan und Isolde* is divided, and reflected the shifts and disunities of his own outlook. Although he sometimes shied away from knowledge which life threw in his face, his experience did show how destructive the erotic impulse could be, damaging loyalties, wrecking plans, and ruining every possible security. For example, there was the real risk that Wagner might have sunk himself if it emerged that Cosima and he had hoodwinked King Ludwig into publicly proclaiming and defending the untruth that their very erotic and adulterous relationship was actually platonic and beyond reproach. The King might have cut off his allowance and his support to Wagner, because even if Ludwig had been unwilling, the public outcry might have compelled him; but fortunately by the time the truth became openly known, Wagner had married Cosima and the façade of respectability was patched up, if not restored.

Although the philosophy of Schopenhauer provides the framework in which *Tristan und Isolde* is located, it is not a dramatisation of that philosophy any more than *Parsifal* is a bio-drama of Christianity and Jesus Christ. *Tristan und Isolde* is music drama set at a tangent to Schopenhauer, and in it Wagner aimed to reveal how it was possible to experience the erotic phenomenon without paying the inevitable price identified by Schopenhauer, the bringing of children to these stony shores and the feeding of an appetite, which as Shakespeare said, could only grow by what it fed on. In *Tristan und Isolde* Wagner generalised from his own conflicted experience, that the erotic aspect of life was both the main cause of life's worst privations as Schopenhauer held, but also that it redeemed life; and in either case he represented erotic passion as spellbinding. He establishes in *Tristan und Isolde* that fame and fortune, pride and position, the good opinion of others and a sense of duty are all tawdry baubles in comparison with the glory of love. Although *Tristan und Isolde* additionally gave expression and weight to a view that was diametrically opposed, it primarily establishes love as something so precious that it is worth sacrificing everything for it. For both Tristan and Isolde, their mutual passion is the fulfilment of their existence, and its supreme value, but a romantic passion so absolute makes demands which are impossible. They are impossible because they are incompatible with the inalienable demands of society and ordinary living, the very necessities of life.

This impossibility is one main reason why Tristan and Isolde want to escape from life into an infinity of isolation and togetherness. This is no ordinary togetherness, and there are illogicalities about it as there are about other aspects of their passion, but as should also by now be clear, the actions and attitudes of the mind are not always logical, particularly where it matters most. Isolde and Tristan also want to escape for another reason, that their passion is unbearable in its intensity, so that it brings no lasting serenity even in its fulfilments (that at least was the real Schopenhauer), and the longing of each for the other is something which no satiation can satiate. For them the only way out of their anguished longing is escape into the 'wonder-realm of night', fusing their identities at exactly the moment when they enter into 'divine, eternal, primordial oblivion'.

The third point is about the music. The music of *Tristan und Isolde* has often been described as on the verge of atonality or even going beyond the verge; but in atonality music casts itself loose of all its moorings in conventional harmony. The ideas of harmony developed in Western music over the centuries are so deeply ingrained in our awareness that they seem second nature, but the atonal system of music devised by Schoenberg was intended to forge a new road, and not to register at all in the terms of this normal, centuries-old harmony. Atonal music is meant to be heard with different ears, but *Tristan und Isolde* is absolutely *not* meant to be heard with different ears. It is set very much in a tonal framework and makes the most of that framework. One reason for the music's amazing impact is that Wagner exploited the framework to its ultimate degree. It is the tremendous tension between the music's clear-cut tonal framework and its chromatic extremes that helps to create its intensity. Reams have been written about the 'Tristan chord', the work's very first harmony, and about the tensions within it, but the chord itself was not new to music. What was new was Wagner's way of making it lead on to other chords that do nothing to resolve the initial tensions but stretch them out endlessly. His way of extending the process on and on and on was unprecedented, and is still unique. This description may sound academic and dry, but there is nothing academic about the music of *Tristan und Isolde*. In no other work does Wagner's orchestra so much represent a wizard's cauldron from which heady vapours swirl into fill the air and intoxicate the imagination. If ever music were witchcraft, this is it.

The opening of the Prelude establishes the style of *Tristan und Isolde* and its status as a landmark for music. I give its opening bars in full score,

Fig. 18.1

as well as a more playable piano reduction,

Fig. 18.2

because the piano version conceals the fact that there are two interlocked phrases, separate leitmotives here, (a) for cellos and (b) for wind, although they frequently appear joined together. (a) is a strange, apparently inconsequential sequence of four notes given out by the cellos. (Incidentally, this opening cello motive appears as it is here only once again, at the end of Act II; in all other cases the opening leap upward is widened by a semitone.) This opening motive (a) emerges from nowhere and leads into leitmotive (b), the rising four-note sequence which Wagner took from Bülow. It begins with a peculiar pang, a sforzando on woodwind which sounds the famous Tristan chord. Wagner gave the Prelude the title of 'Liebestod: Love-death, Death-in-love, Death-through-love, Death-from-love (but emphatically not the Death *of* love)', but by some obscure turn of events this title has become attached to Isolde's final peroration, which Wagner himself entitled 'Verklärung, Transfiguration'. In Tristan und Isolde the labelling of leitmotives brings problems, because there are fewer which can be given a clear designation than in The Ring. In Tristan there is nothing like the 'Sword' or the 'Dragon', no 'Rhinegold', no 'Curse of the Ring', all of which titles have firm connections with particular motives. But in Tristan even Wagner's own descriptions, for example 'the Look' for (Fig. 18.2 (b)), can seem restricting, inadequate to indicate the states of mind, the emotional subtleties and the complex experiences which the music conveys. For this reason very few of the musical examples in this chapter are supplied with names, even when they are leitmotives at their most definite. Significant motives are often simply bracketed in the music without a verbal designation.

Unlike Wagner's earlier Preludes, the Tristan Prelude is not pictorial. Previously, pictorial representation had been as much a part of his Preludes and Overtures as had states of mind, but the Prelude to Tristan und Isolde is purely about emotions, inner worlds and 'movements of the soul'. The musical forms of Tristan und Isolde can at first seem elusive, but the whole Prelude, and indeed the whole opera, derives from its opening leitmotives and those that soon follow.

Fig. 18.3

The music makes its way through hesitancy and tenderness to a melting sweetness,

Fig. 18.4

and then to a mood of high seriousness, as the leitmotive of 'Death' or 'Fate' looms up in the bass at (h).

Fig. 18.5

The Prelude gathers force towards a passage of towering passion, and at the same time it evolves by its inner laws into a tightly coherent symphonic structure. It is so effective as a form that Bruckner half-adopted it, consciously or otherwise, as the template for the adagios of his last three symphonies. All the while the leitmotives draw themselves out like plasticene, mutating into other motives and spinning out their own variations. This evolution of leitmotives has something in common with the patterns of a kaleidoscope, turning into new mosaics, new music, and this pattern of musical evolution plays a major role in the entire work. The leitmotives only reveal their full significance as the opera unfolds, and the paradox of the Prelude, pointed out by Michael Tanner, is that although it is wholly self-contained, it yet needs the rest of the opera to complete it.

If the music of the Prelude is a landmark, so too is what it means, even though there are different ideas about what it *does* mean. In *The Perfect Wagnerite*, George Bernard Shaw's interpretation of *The Ring*, he mentions in passing his idea of the Prelude as a particularly 'faithful translation into music of the emotions that accompany the union of a pair of lovers'.[82] In their responses to this suggestion people unwittingly reveal aspects of themselves, but those excited by a Shaw-derived impression of the Prelude as a sequence of sexual responses during intercourse easily overlook the important point that Shaw described it as translation of *the emotions* of a pair of lovers, and not their tactile sensations. The inability to recognise the distinction, and the related failure to distinguish between love and sex, obscures an understanding of *Tristan und Isolde*.

Tristan und Isolde is an opera set not only in the landscape of Schopenhauer but in the legendary worlds of the early Middle Ages. The framework is Celtic, and as so often, Wagner's opera comes in on the action towards its culmination, near a crisis point. Act I of the opera is set on a ship whose master, Tristan, is ferrying the Irish princess Isolde back to Cornwall to marry Mark, King of Cornwall (and as an afterthought, of England). The curtain goes up on Isolde in a luxurious pavilion on the deck, richly caparisoned with silk curtains and carpets. She has in attendance her servant and confidante,

82   Shaw, George Bernard, *The Perfect Wagnerite*, Leipzig, 1913.

Brangäne. From somewhere aloft in the rigging comes the voice of a sailor singing a strange folksong. Its words do not quite add up, even in the original German. It is without a clear-cut key and adrift without moorings in the tonal framework. Even its rhythm is indeterminate.

Fig. 18. 6

The sailor continues,

> *Is it the sorrows of your sighing*
> *That keeps the ship still flying?*
> *Blow us on, wind so wild!*
> *Alas for you too, my child!*
> *Irish girl!*
> *You wild, irresistible girl!*

At these last words Isolde flings herself up from her couch, both furious and distracted. She recollects herself as she finds herself alone with Brangäne, and asks her how far they have travelled on the voyage. Brangäne tells her soothingly that the journey is going well, and that they should reach land before sunset. 'Which land?' Isolde asks shortly, and Brangäne answers 'Cornwall's meadowy coast.' This unleashes from Isolde an outburst of self-hatred which takes Brangäne by surprise and horrifies her. Isolde storms, 'Nevermore! Not today or tomorrow!' Brangäne, as she tells Isolde, cannot believe her own ears, but Isolde rages on at herself;

> *Degenerate race!*
> *Unworthy of your ancestors!*
> *For what, O mother, did you give me the power*
> *That gives me control over seas and storms?*

The orchestra gives out in high registers a very turbulent version of the '*Frisch weht der Wind*' theme as Isolde addresses her mother, the Queen of Ireland. Her mother is famous for her occult powers which include the power of healing, and which she had long ago taught her daughter, but Isolde berates herself for making such feeble use of those powers as to brew healing potions, and she delivers an imprecation;

> *Awaken again,*
> *O mighty powers;*
> *Forth from my breast*
> *Where now you lie hid.*

The storm winds are to rouse the slumbering seas from their dreams, and she offers them this insolent ship as a prize. The seas are to smash it and swallow its splinters, while she consigns to the winds everything on it that lives. Brangäne wrings her hands; she has long had premonitions of some imminent crisis, and is distressed that Isolde kept such dire thoughts and feelings locked within. She had shed not a tear for her parents and barely said goodbye to her friends. Since their departure she had not eaten or slept, and had been either completely withdrawn or completely distraught. Brangäne had scarcely been able to bear it, seeing Isolde in such a state, but she was doubly distressed because Isolde had not confided in her. Winsomely, to Wagner's winning music, Brangäne beseeches Isolde to tell her what is wrong, but Isolde has the sudden feeling that she is suffocating and calls for air. Brangäne quickly draws back the curtains, revealing the ship's open stern with sailors and knights at their ease on deck and Tristan standing pensively, looking out to sea. His esquire Kurwenal is nearby. Isolde fixes her gaze inscrutably on Tristan while the eerie song of the sailor is heard again from the rigging. Its effect on Isolde is different this time. Thinking aloud, she declaims, as if to herself,

> *Chosen for me,*
> *Lost to me*
> *Glorious and holy,*
> *Courageous and cowardly –*
> *Death-devoted Head! Death-devoted Heart!*

In the original German of the final line, given below with its music, *'geweiht'* has in it a sense of consecration.

Fig. 18.7 'Consecrated to Death'

With a bitter laugh and a toss of her head towards Tristan, she asks, 'What to do think of that object?'

Brangäne is bewildered, and asks who does Isolde mean? Isolde says she means that so-called hero who does not even have the courage to return her gaze. 'Dear lady,' replies Brangäne, 'You cannot mean Tristan, the wonder of all lands, the very image of renown?' 'That flincher from all challenge, hiding as best he can!' is Isolde's withering riposte; 'He brings to his master a bride who is dead! Do you think that my words about him are so hard to understand? Then go; see what happens when you ask him to appear and see me.' Brangäne asks for clarification: 'Am I to ask him to attend you?' Isolde responds imperiously; 'Command him to attend me! – out of homage and submission to his princess, Isolde!' This leaves Brangäne confused and uneasy but she obediently makes her way towards the stern past the men on deck, to the sounds of that eerie sailor's theme again, but now tonally solid, broadened and urbane on four horns.

Fig. 18.8

Kurwenal sees her coming. Sensing trouble he jumps up; 'Have a care Tristan', he warns; 'Legation from Isolde!'

Tristan starts; 'What's that? Isolde!' He collects himself, and launches into a smooth flow of flattering and evasive courtesies designed to manipulate Brangäne and deflect her from the matter in hand, leaving her to respond as best she can. He asks how he can best serve his lady; Brangäne begs him to attend on her. He responds that the exhausting journey will soon be over and he will then willingly fulfil her every command; Brangäne entreats him that he should fulfil Isolde's simple request to see her now. He promises that it shall be exactly as Isolde wishes, that after their landing none but he shall conduct her to King Mark; Brangäne explains that it is right now that Isolde solicits his services. He states that he is providing services to Isolde even as he stands there at the helm, and asks how he could possibly serve her so well if he deserted his post and neglected the safe navigation of the ship. This finally drives Brangäne to address him directly. 'My Lord Tristan, why make such a mockery of me? If you cannot take Isolde's meaning from her untutored servant, then listen to what she actually told me to say: "Command him to attend in homage and submission to his princess, Isolde!"'

At this Kurwenal leaps to his feet, and asks vehemently if he may suggest an answer. Tristan seems to be in a daze; 'What answer would you make?' he says vaguely. 'This is what she should say to the lady Isolde!' says Kurwenal, and he launches into a tirade, to the effect that the man with the power to confer on Isolde the thrones of Cornwall and England and additionally bestow her upon his uncle is not a man she can treat as a chattel. 'I proclaim it; you go and explain it – even if it were to a thousand griping Isoldes.' Horrified, Brangäne starts hurrying off, and Tristan attempts to stop Kurwenal, but he seems carried away and sings on at the top of his voice, incidentally giving the audience further information about the course of events so far. Morold, as Kurwenal now jeers, had been a gigantic Irish hero and Isolde's husband designate. He had visited Cornwall, Ireland's vassal state, to collect a hated tribute of youths and maidens. However, Tristan had challenged the Irish hero to single combat and defeated him. 'His head, returned to Ireland,' jeers Kurwenal, 'was the only tribute that Cornwall sent. Hail to our Lord Tristan; he knows exactly the proper way to pay tribute!' The sailors take up this parting shot, singing it as a familiar, popular song, indicating that its bravado and insult to the Irish are common currency in Cornwall.

Brangäne hastens back to Isolde, wringing her hands and drawing the curtains tightly closed. When Isolde demands to know what happened, Brangäne tries to spare her the humiliation, but Isolde commands her to hold back nothing. Brangäne explains how Tristan had spoken in courteous tones but only to dress up his refusal to comply, and even when she pressed him, he had fatuously asked how he could navigate safely if he deserted the helm, words which Isolde now repeats bitterly to herself. She cuts short Brangäne's description of Kurwenal's mockery, telling her that she heard it all; and as Brangäne knows the extent of Isolde's humiliation she should learn how it came to be. It is as though the floodgates had opened, and to a new leitmotive,

Fig. 18.9 'Isolde's Narration'

Isolde pours out her story. She tells Brangäne how once a pitiful little boat had drifted to Ireland bearing a wounded, dying man, who soon learnt the value of Isolde's occult powers because she had discovered him and took it upon herself to still his pain and cure his wound. He made himself known as Tantris, but she saw through this disguise after she had noted a tiny cleft in his sword, and found that it matched a fragment from the head of Morold which had been sent back to Ireland. She had determined instantly to kill him there, but as she stood over him, her avenging sword poised to strike downwards, he looked up, not at the sword, not at her hand, but *into* her eyes. She tells Brangäne that the anguish of it had touched her to the quick, and the music tells of deeper changes within her. 'That sword;' says Isolde, 'I let it fall,' and instead of vengeance she had continued to nurse her guest to health with the intention that he should leave and his gaze would trouble her no more. Brangäne exclaims in disbelief that she could have missed all this as it was happening. Isolde continues that Tristan swore her a thousand oaths of eternal loyalty, and that Brangäne shall now learn how he kept them. The pitiful Tantris-figure whom she secretly set on his way home had returned in grand style as Tristan, and he had insolently requested that she, heir apparent to the throne of Ireland, should become the bride to his decrepit uncle, ancient King Mark of Cornwall! (As events will show, this disparaging view of Mark is not justified.) She says that if Morold had still lived, the Cornish, Ireland's vassal-subjects, would never have dared presume to the crown of Ireland, and she laments bitterly that it was her action, or her failure to act, which had resulted in this disgrace. She should have wielded the sword. Now she pays for her failure, in being herself subject to this miserable rabble. She is another yet of those Wagnerian characters whom I have described as performing an action freely, only to find it rearing up and confronting them like an alien power.

Brangäne breaks into this narrative in confusion and distress; Cornwall and Ireland had sworn freedom, atonement and friendship amidst general rejoicing; how could she possibly have known that Isolde was so racked by grief? Isolde exclaims that at the time the eyes of all had been as blind as her own heart had been weak; but how different Tristan been on his return. In Ireland she had concealed him in silence and secrecy, but he repaid her by proclaiming openly in Cornwall that as wife for Mark she would be an ideal catch; he, Tristan, knew just how to get her; let Mark give the word and he would be on his way; she was as good as Mark's already; he would relish the chance of such a daring enterprise. The rising tide of Isolde's fury reaches its culmination;

> *Damn you, you traitor!*
> *A curse on your head!*
> *Vengeance! Death!*
> *Death for us both!*

Brangäne instinctively embraces Isolde, and tries to soothe her; 'Isolde, sweetest, dear one, golden princess, sit with me, calm yourself,' as she settles Isolde on the couch. Isolde's sorrows, Brangäne tells her, had blinded her to the facts; Tristan had in reality behaved with great honour and selflessness towards her. He had renounced the crown of Cornwall to which he had been heir himself and had laid it at her feet, and having once himself been heir apparent he would from now on simply become one of her subjects. And to be Mark's wife was itself no small blessing, given his inborn nobility and kindly disposition. With knights like Tristan to serve him, who would not see it as a wonderful blessing to marry Mark? Isolde hears her from within a dark reverie. 'Unloved,' she says, 'while seeing that man near me constantly.' Brangäne gently upbraids her: 'Unloved! Is there a man alive who would not love Isolde?' And if Mark himself were, unbelievably, somehow not drawn to her, Brangäne has the means to bind him in love to Isolde. Has she forgotten her mother's magic arts? Her mother would never have sent her to a strange land without providing 'every assistance which she might need'. Isolde answers that she knows her mother's magic arts full well; let Brangäne produce the casket containing her many mysterious potions. Brangäne brings it and responds, 'Yes, look; here is balm for pain and wounds; for poisons, here is the antidote, and here, yes, here it is; this is the noblest draught of all, the love philtre.' 'Not so!' says Isolde enigmatically, and the trombones sound a leitmotive of unfathomable darkness, not heard since the Prelude, Fig. 18.4 motive (g), as she continues, 'I know one better. *This* is the one which serves my need,' and to Brangäne's horror she takes a vial of black crystal full of poison. At that moment the sailors are heard singing as they furl sail, and to Isolde's mounting distress it is plain that the voyage is coming to an end. An instant later Kurwenal comes blustering in, telling the ladies to be quick; Mark's castle on the cliffs is already visible, and they must robe themselves festively for Tristan to escort her ashore.

Isolde is now at her most formidable. She returns formal greetings to Tristan, but gives warning that if he expects to escort her to King Mark, he must first attend her and seek her grace for an unatoned wrong. Kurwenal makes a scornful gesture, but she insists and asserts that she will not even begin her preparations unless Tristan seeks her grace; she for her part guarantees to grant it. Kurwenal remains defiant, 'Be sure that I will tell him; we shall see what he says!' but it is pure bluster and they all know that Tristan must now appear. Isolde hastens to Brangäne and embraces her; 'Brangäne, farewell; greet for me the world, greet for me my father and mother.' Brangäne is bewildered and asks, 'What do you mean? Where will you go? Where must I follow you next?' Isolde becomes peremptory; 'Did you not hear? Here I stand. Here I wait for Tristan. Do as I say; prepare the cup of atonement. You know the one I mean.' Brangäne still does not really understand; 'Which potion?'

she asks. Isolde takes the phial of poison; 'This is the one! Pour it all into the golden goblet; leave nothing behind.' This leaves Brangäne reeling and asking in horror, 'Can I believe my ears? Who is it for?' Isolde: 'For him who betrayed me!' Brangäne: 'Oh horror! For pity's sake spare me!' Isolde: 'No! You spare me!' whereupon she sings back cuttingly the very words and music that Brangäne had used to try and calm her; has she forgotten her mother's magic arts? Her mother, she says sardonically, would never have sent her to a strange land 'without supplying every assistance which she might need'. However, Isolde's conclusion is different; 'For the deepest pain and the highest grief, she gave me this draught of death!' While Brangäne is repeating it all and trying to make sense of it, Kurwenal strides in and announces Tristan's appearance. With immense difficulty Isolde contains herself, draws herself up and pronounces with patrician hauteur, 'Sir Tristan may approach!'

At this the orchestra embarks on some extraordinary music, terse, pregnant, tremendous in tension, and full of meaning which as so often cannot be put into words.

Fig. 18.10 'Crisis' – 'Tristan's Approach'

Isolde stands there, imperious in royal state, and Tristan makes a formal, chivalric entrance. He states in courtly style, 'Command, lady, what you will,' but from beginning to end Isolde is in command, and Tristan simply cannot keep up. She berates him for failing to obey her earlier summons, and when he says that honour towards her had prevented him, she says she discerned no honour in him but only contempt and disobedience. Put briefly, Tristan's reply is: 'Where I come from, custom demands that the bride-chamberlain should keep his distance from the bride from a sense of honour.' Isolde: 'But if you are so committed to honour and custom, then there is another custom you should observe. You must make atonement with your enemies if you hope that they should become your friends.' Tristan: 'Whom do you see as my enemy?' Isolde: 'Ask your inner fears. Blood-guilt seethes between us.' Tristan: 'It was absolved!' Isolde: 'Not so; there may have been reconciliation between the nations, but this did not go to the heart of the matter, between our two selves.' She says that when Tristan lay ailing and in her power, she had restrained herself from striking him down but had nonetheless sworn a silent oath to avenge Morold. Now is the time to keep her promise. Tristan asks a question, as if puzzled: 'Did that really matter?' This strikes fire and rage from Isolde; 'How dare you? Morold had been my betrothed, he was noble, and he fought his battles under my star. I had vowed that if no man would avenge his death, I would do it myself.' She had not then done the deed, but had healed Tristan so that he could fall victim to the man who won her; but as Tristan is now everyone's friend, who would still do the deed? She has Tristan entirely under her control morally and intellectually, and he can only respond as she intended, that if Morold meant so much, she should again take up the sword (he offers her his sword), and this time fulfil her task.

Isolde turns mock-conciliatory, 'Yes of course, and would it not it be just the thing for the king and my husband to be, if just as I arrived, I did away with his best knight, the man who had not only secured his rule, but delivered me as an emblem of the treaty between Ireland and Cornwall? You were the man who turned me into this emblem to give into Mark's safe keeping. I missed my chance entirely when you lay there planning to make me a bauble for Mark. So let us now instead drink atonement.' She signals to the trembling Brangäne to prepare the cup, and heaps irony on irony, driving it home to Tristan how impossible it will be for them to live in constant proximity at Mark's court, given their mutual past, unless first there is atonement between them. Their intense colloquy is interrupted by exclamations from the sailors outside on their progress towards their imminent landing, and by Tristan's instructions to his crew. Isolde seizes the chalice from Brangäne and advances on Tristan. Tristan mutters a dark aside; 'I grasp the intent of which she is silent; I shall keep silent over those things which she does not grasp', which is to say that he has taken in that she plans a mutual suicide and that the cup contains poison. The sailors reveal by their shouts that they are dropping anchor, and he grasps the chalice. Pledging Isolde for offering him a cure for all woes, he raises it to his lips and hails it as a draught of oblivion.

He makes as if to drain it completely, but Isolde seizes it and rages; 'Half is for me! Traitor! I drink to you.'

She drains it to the dregs, and they stand waiting in a silence of electrifying tension, waiting to die, but the orchestra tells of something different happening. The strains of the Prelude, expanded and developed, reveal that there dawns on them now a mutual passion of exorbitant intensity. Brangäne has substituted a love philtre for the poison. They shudder and their eyes seek one another and meet. The silence and the tension grow, and they each finally bring themselves to speak each other's name, which sets them on fire with passion, even as blazing trumpet fanfares herald King Mark's appearance. As Tristan and Isolde tell each other ever more hectically, they are lost to the world but found to each other, their senses and spirits are uplifted; they know nothing but the ecstasy of love. At this point the curtains are suddenly flung back to show the whole ship swarming with knights and other agents of regal chivalry. All is public ceremony but for the pair of them there is only a confused mix of ecstasy and anguish. Brangäne sees their state of mind and, realising what she has done, wrings her hands hopelessly; 'Alas, alas, alas! Unredeemable tragedy! Eternal, ongoing disaster instead of just the brief pangs of death!' The ladies-in-waiting enter with Isolde's royal robes and begin to array her even as the crowd hails King Mark's arrival. Kurwenal enters in high spirits, praising Tristan for his mission accomplished, and telling him that the king himself is hastening towards them in a skiff, overjoyed to be meeting his new bride. Tristan is a man in a dream. Oblivious to the shouts of 'All hail, King Mark!' he asks Kurwenal what king, and Isolde likewise asks Brangäne in a sudden, brief return to the world, 'What is it? Where am I? Do I still live? Ah – Brangäne, what was that drink?' Brangäne's response, her confession that it was the love-potion, is overheard by Tristan and it leaves them both appalled. She asks, 'Must I still live, then?' and just as she faints in his embrace, Tristan exclaims incoherently but truly, 'Oh joy consecrated to lying; Oh bliss from pure deceiving.' Then as the trumpets ring out again and the chorus once more hails Mark, the curtain falls.

Wagner achieves here an extraordinary amalgam of anguish and excitement. Music of passion and inner worlds is seamlessly integrated into music of prodigious festive energy. He manages it partly by combining four themes, the young sailor's song in the highest register, the fanfares for Mark onstage, and that other music of the sea, from the double basses at the beginning of the act, now in the tenor register. The double basses themselves now play a powerful theme to which no name is normally given, but which is first given out as an octave unison by all the strings as Brangäne tells Isolde, 'Come, look where you are!' It adds up to a contrapuntal tour de force worthy of Bach's Mass in B minor.

The whole act is a masterpiece in many other ways. Irradiated by the music, the laconic, pared-down text glows with new meaning. The act displays a Shakespearian subtlety in establishing the characters as real and fully human, even though they shimmer with an archetypal significance. Isolde emerges as appealing as well as regal, mostly through her interactions with Brangäne. Wagner shows that Brangäne knows her well and yet adores her, addressing her as 'sweetest Isolde', 'golden mistress' or 'loveliest Isolde' and embracing her warmly in her sudden access of sympathy. Brangäne is respectful and deferential, but so affectionate as to show that Isolde is not a hard mistress. Brangäne feels too warmly towards Isolde for intimidation, and we soon learn that Isolde is instinctively compassionate, having saved Tristan's life and nursed him through to health. We discover that she has mastered both medicinal skills and occult powers. We see that she has assertiveness skills of no mean order and a tremendous temper, totally outmanoeuvring Tristan into doing her bidding. She is loyal to her dead suitor Morold and she is confused between her compassion for Tristan and this loyalty until the prospect of death suddenly makes everything clear. The act also tells us a lot about her relationship with Brangäne and about Brangäne herself. Brangäne is herself loving and loyal, and with Isolde she alternates between deference and gentle coaxing on the one hand, and on the other assertiveness and advice that expects to be taken. She knows how to wheedle and is very loving to Isolde. She is so horrified at Isolde's deadly plans, that she disobeys and defrauds Isolde. She acted with quick understanding in doing this, and is equally quick to understand the result.

There are tremendous forces drawing Tristan and Isolde together and it is as much the belief that they are going to die as any magic in the drink that makes all barriers go down. Wagner himself said at one point that the love philtre could just as well have been water. One of the forces for their mutual attraction is their effectiveness as people, their similar strength of purpose. Another is Isolde's pity for Tristan, but pity has two faces. There is one tinged with compassion and close to love, and there is the other is tinged with contempt. As pointed out in connection with Minna's feelings for Wagner, it is difficult for love to exist without respect, and Isolde is torn between at least three emotions towards Tristan, compassion for his sorry state, admiration for his noble nature and contempt for his appalling behaviour to her, as she sees it. However her unrecognised passion is whetted by her *taking trouble* over Tristan, and this is another of the submerged principles implicit in *Tristan und Isolde*. People – patients – often maintain that feelings cannot be made to happen, by which they usually mean that love and romantic passion cannot be made happen by willing them.[83] Possibly these emotions cannot conjured up purely

---

83   The interesting thing is that a different or perhaps not so different kind of love, the love of God, was something commanded to believers over the centuries; it was something that followers of Jesus Christ *were* expected to make happen by willing it; 'Thou shalt love the Lord thy God, with all thy heart, with all thy mind, and with all thy strength.'

and simply by willing them, but what Isolde shows is that by *taking trouble* over Tristan, she does kindle them. She can do it because of the general truth which she instantiates, that a person can often develop an enthusiasm or even a passion for something by taking trouble over it. In taking up a profession, a religion, or a leisure activity whether stamp collecting, golf or charity work, people often start out with a mild interest, but as they take time and effort over the new pursuit they are drawn in. As they learn more and take more trouble, they become enthused. The same can happen with jobs or relationships; and love in all its forms – even including romance – is no different. What happens to Isolde demonstrates that by taking trouble over someone, a person can kindle romantic passion or even rekindle it. There must be a real, heartfelt willingness to take trouble for it to happen, but it is a common experience that it can and does. Thus it is that Frau Minne, the Northern goddess of erotic passion, makes her appearance in Act II. She cannot be conjured up by willing her into existence, but two people taking trouble can create a charmed circle in which she is likely to materialise.

Tristan's situation is different. His passion for Isolde is inspired by her beauty and charisma, the qualities which Brangäne describes when trying to console and hearten her, but also by gratitude. Gratitude for care given can lead to romantic passion, and this is one among the complicated reasons why men often fall in love with their nurses. Isolde has nursed, healed and saved Tristan, and he conceives an inadmissible passion for her. As she makes no secret of her hatred, he could not reasonably hope that any feeling for her would be returned. Love and hatred are linked, even if psychologically the opposite of love is not hate but the will to power. Tristan does try his utmost for her in other ways, but these she misunderstands. Brangäne is correct when she tells Isolde that in gaining her for King Mark, Tristan has done well by her, at least on the plane of conventional worldly values. He has demonstrated the ideals of chivalrous, courtly love by creating for his lady the most brilliant match imaginable. Given that while nursing him she articulated hatred, she must have seemed to him inaccessible beyond hope, and his oaths of loyalty took for granted that he could only worship from a distance and serve her from afar. These oaths had not aspired as far as any romantic possibilities. She has misunderstood his motives in arranging to marry her to Mark. She cannot appreciate that he could never have known of her secret obsession with him, and that he might never have pursued the idea of her marriage to Mark if he had believed it possible that there might ever be any deep relation between himself and Isolde. In its intimations of the immense gravitational forces which exist between them and that each was dry tinder waiting for the spark, the whole act rings true.

The act has incidentally built up the picture of both Tristan and Isolde as high achievers, not the mawkish sentimentals imagined for example by Clara Schumann, who cordially detested *Tristan und Isolde*. Isolde is subtly established as a woman possessing material advantages. She is princess of Ireland, and she he is accustomed to practising with great skill the healing arts which her mother taught her. She is the beloved of Ireland's sensational hero Morold, and she plays a surprisingly significant role in moulding the politics and diplomatic policies of Ireland. Tristan began as an orphan, with all the disadvantages that come with this. He still managed to build on his innate gifts to make a great deal of himself. Having entered service in King Mark's court he has become the perfect knight. Because of his personal charisma and his achievements, King Mark has come to love him like a son. His willingness to risk his life in a duel with the great Irish hero reveals him as a man of heroism. He wins at great personal cost.[84] Because of what he is, he gets results. He does free Cornwall from its subservience to Ireland. He does achieve an accord between the hostile kingdoms of Ireland and Cornwall. Because of his success, Tristan finds himself unpopular, as do most people who try to achieve something worthwhile in this life. Wagner knew.

---

84   This cost is not described by Wagner in the opera, but it is a wound so purulent that nobody can bear his presence. Hence he is put in a boat that drifts through fate to Ireland and Isolde.

❦

The first hour of Act II may be about the most flawless large-scale musical structure in existence, vying even with Act III of *Die Walküre*, except that the latter act sustains its perfection, whereas *Tristan* Act II sags musically after its central duet. The act is set in the garden of King Mark's castle in Cornwall, and it is a beautiful summer night. Isolde and King Mark have now been married for an indeterminate period. The centrepiece of the act is the meeting of Tristan and Isolde for an immense duet, and what they say suggests that this is their first meeting alone since their landing in Cornwall. The act begins with an explosive forte,

Fig. 18.11

which immediately shimmers away into stillness and silence. It is a tense silence of that starts up expectantly with music that soon becomes more mobile:

Fig. 18.12

New leitmotives spin together;

Fig. 18.13

soon an accelerated précis of the Act I Prelude's opening bars, repeated and agitated,

Fig. 18.14

leads to a new conclusion, a full-blooded culmination

Fig. 18.15

This will become very important at several of this act's turning points. Wagner told Mathilde that his supreme achievement was his art of transition, but his capacity for thematic transformation was just as striking. It will herald the music's settling into the sweetest calm

Fig. 18.16 'Nirvana'

before '*O sink hernieder*', the duet's central section. It will also take the form of great waves of sound rolling towards the zenith and catastrophe of its conclusion.

Fig. 18.17 'Nirvana'

Meanwhile as the curtain goes up, six horns, hunting horns, are heard from the stage, which Wagner has marked '*sehr stark geblasen*, always very loud', not the delicate horn tints often found in performances. (In fact Wagner asked that that where possible each part should be doubled, or further strengthened, and Solti's Decca recording did muster 18 horns.)

Fig. 18.18 'Hunting Horn' motive

They are very near at first but fade rapidly into the distance at each of the three occasions when they sound. Isolde, a model of wishful thinking, is arguing with Brangäne whether they have vanished into the night, and Isolde asserts that Brangäne is deceiving herself in imagining that she still hears them. She says that the only sounds still audible are the whispering of the leaves and the murmuring of the stream. These two suggestions draw forth from Wagner two exquisite examples of his art of transition, with the horns melting softly into a string *sul ponticello* as the breeze rustles the trees and then into shimmering strings and clarinet for the stream.

Isolde insists to Brangäne that her worried imaginings are no reason for delaying any longer the signal for Tristan to approach. Brangäne admonishes her about someone who is on the lookout against Tristan – muted horns give a strange sigh – and specifically Brangäne warns her of Melot. Isolde laughs gently, arguing that if Tristan could not be with her, then Melot is the friend whose company he would seek. Brangäne answers that this is exactly what disturbs her, because Tristan is Melot's way to Mark. This hunt by night, and so suddenly set up, has a nobler quarry than Isolde can imagine. Isolde insists that it was out of kindness that Melot instigated the hunt. In spite of *Tristan*'s 'poem' often being inclined to the prosaic, Isolde now requests, in a text of rare beauty as well as in ravishing music, that Brangäne should douse the flaring torch, so that the night may encircle and cloak the world. Brangäne blames herself for Isolde's insanity because it was she who filled the chalice with love instead of death. Isolde rounds on her as a silly girl; she should recognise the effect of Frau Minne, the ancient German goddess of erotic passion. The text here becomes even more poetic and more untranslatable, yielding only clumsy paraphrases as Isolde describes the goddess as queen of bold spirits, holding at her disposal all that the world brings to being. She holds even life and death in her hand, and as Isolde now belongs to her entirely, she must obey her entirely. Brangäne answers that Frau Minne must have done away with Isolde's reason; but Isolde responds by pronouncing imperiously that Frau Minne wills that it should be night, so that she can shine brightly; she will have no more of Brangäne's torch. Seizing it in her hands Isolde commands Brangäne to go and keep watch. Even if the torch were her very life, she would still put out its light. She hurls it to the ground, and trumpets blaze out the '*Todgeweihtes Haupt, Todgeweihtes Herz*' leitmotive with tumultuous force before the orchestra falls back into brooding silence and expectancy.

The music from the beginning of the act is heard again, but with new developments that rise to a frenzy of anticipation. At the peak Tristan comes blazing onto the scene and enfolds Isolde in a '*sturmische Umarmung*, a tumultuous embrace', set to an immense music which carries one of Wagner's very rare *fff* markings. At first they cannot manage anything but broken phrases: 'Isolde!' 'Tristan!' 'My love!' 'Is it true?' 'Is it real?' 'Is it just a dream?' 'Oh rapture of my soul!' 'Unimaginable!' 'Forever one; eternally, endlessly one!' 'How long we were divided!' 'So near and yet so far.' 'So far and yet so near.' Tristan curses the light which, long after the sun had set, had kept him at a distance thanks to its ongoing presence in the form of that glaring torch. Isolde claims credit for daring to defy the day to bring him to her, and Tristan joins her in her revulsion for the day, asking if there is any woe that the day does not summon into fullest being. Even when night had fallen at last, she kept alive a remnant of the day in the form of that torch, and still brandished it at him menacingly. She retorts that although she may have kept the day alive as he accuses her, he had done worse, because he had kept it alive within his own inner self. Was it not his adoption of day's lying values that led him to Ireland to win her for King Mark and thus doom her to virtual destruction? He had been vapid slave to the day. Tristan confesses that at that time he could only see her in the context of 'daylight' and the terms of daylight's or society's values. She was the glorious princess, and honour and the call of duty required him to assign her to King Mark. Isolde reproaches him because this enslavement to the day had made her suffer so much, so that she had longed only to draw him into the night. This had seemed their only escape, the drinking together with him of the draught which would end their illusory values and indeed all illusions.

Tristan tells her that he realised she was offering him death, and she laments their inability to achieve it and their failure to find escape and oblivion. She blames their predicament on the wrong drink, but he hails it on account of its magical, sublime power. It was the means for opening his eyes to the vision of her as she really was, in terms of night and truth. Isolde assents fondly, but then she points out that the day soon had its revenge, condemning him to live by the light of its empty radiance, far removed from her. She herself could not bear it then; she cannot bear it now. Tristan agrees and exclaims that they are now dedicated to the night; and that whoever has once gazed into the night of eternity and learnt its secrets can only know one yearning for ever after, the yearning for that hallowed night-realm where the only truth is the ecstasy of love.

He draws her into a corner of the wonder-realm of night, and they embark on a duet that is also an incantation. They respond to each other by repeating each other, and by intertwining each other's melodic lines with related counterpoints as they invoke upon themselves the night of love. They beg for their release from all being.

Fig. 18.19

They continue that when the stars of joy shine upon them, they are blinded with bliss; and as they mutually assert, 'I then become the world!' they are almost like mystics, one with everything as well as one with each other. In thrall to this level of awareness, they are carried away by ecstasy and passion. Over a tapestry of miraculous counterpoint and almost unbearable beauty, the voice of Brangäne comes floating from her far watchtower, warning them of danger. They surface from their trance to advance further on the same mystical plane as before, asking whether they need ever awaken. Tristan would prefer that day should yield to death and night, allowing them to enter this state of mystical oneness forever. Isolde asks him whether death would not destroy that all-important little word 'and', which binds Tristan and Isolde. Tristan answers that on the contrary the only thing that death would destroy is everything that prevents him from loving her for eternity and living to her forever. If they perished *together* they would never again be separated, but be one, eternally and everlastingly.

Tristan has now assumed the lead. In Act I it was Isolde who tried to arrange their annihilation and oblivion; now it is Tristan who explains the way and Isolde who takes up his suggestions and repeats them assentingly. A further warning from Brangäne about the day soon to return adds urgency to their joint determination. They hail the night, the sweet eternal night of love, and they pray to death as the ultimate fulfilment, their *Liebestod*, untranslatable but signifying, as indicated earlier, Love-death, Death-through-love, Death-caused-by-love, Death-in-love. They tell each other that in this state, Tristan will be Isolde and Isolde will be Tristan, but they will both be nameless, lost in oneness and a supreme communion of love's endless bliss. At that very moment, Brangäne cries out in terror and Kurwenal bursts upon the scene with drawn sword. Mark, Melot, and other courtiers dressed for the hunt enter in great haste and then pause, mostly appalled to see Tristan and Isolde together. The real world, bleak, empty and meaningless, has come in on them again, as Tristan comments in misery and anguish, 'The deserts of day – for the very last time.'

What is extraordinary is that Wagner now goes on to give substantial emphasis and conviction to the real, normal world in the form of King Mark's long address to Tristan. Set to an obligato for bass clarinet

Fig. 18.20

and its subsidiary

Fig. 18.21

his accusation follows after Melot has denounced the lovers. Melot claims that in unmasking them, even staking his life on his veracity, he had loyally averted the King's disgrace. Mark begins by disabusing everybody, above all Melot, of this absurd claim. Did Melot really imagine that his trap for Tristan and Isolde had saved Mark from humiliation and disgrace? Nothing could be a greater disgrace for Mark than this unmasking of Tristan and Isolde. Mark displays some contempt for Melot as he says that if Tristan, the epitome of honour and integrity, had destroyed his world, how could Melot imagine that it could be made whole again through such a creature as him?

Everything that now follows from Mark validates the claims of society, of the 'day'. In life, these claims include all the demands confronting the boy who knows no fear in the hero myth. They cover the need to grapple with the world and achieve results and worthwhile successes, jobs to be done, livings to earn, follies and injustices to put right and above all families to support. There are also the conflicting claims of other relationships; and King Mark justifies the values of the world. Judged against these values, Tristan's actions are not only dishonourable but appalling, and rationally Mark's accusations are unanswerable. Even so, I do wonder in all humility whether Wagner has assigned to him music which makes his case as well as it might. Mark's arguments are compelling in rational terms, but are they as compelling musically? Whatever the answer, Mark asks Tristan how it was possible for anyone who had done so much to promote Mark's interests, honour and prestige, to bring him such ignominy. Did Tristan think that his appointment as Mark's heir was insufficient recognition and recompense? Mark had even avoided marrying again so as to safeguard Tristan's crown inheritance, and it was only when Tristan had threatened to leave Cornwall forever unless given a commission to win Isolde as Mark's queen that Mark had finally given way. The result had been the arrival of this miraculous woman, the jewel of his court. Her presence had softened Mark's nature and as a result he was newly sensitive to the pain that Tristan had inflicted. Mark's worst torment was having to recognise that his relationship with Tristan had been a fraud and a sham. What greater dishonour could there be than that he should be driven to skulking around by night, eavesdropping and spying on his unique and special friend. How was it possible for him to have deserved such horror? Throughout his lament, Mark has displayed humanity and sensibility, but nothing equals his concluding insight as he reflects that there must be some secret and unfathomed reason for it all; he asks gently who could ever bring it to light and expound it to the world?

Tristan himself is wracked with genuine guilt as his betrayal looms in full focus before him; and he admits to the King that his accusation is unanswerable. However he had only spoken the plain truth: anyone to whom the night of death and love had revealed its secrets could only know one yearning, one reality, to escape into it forever. To music that is instantly ravishing and reverts to the heart of the duet, Tristan mirrors back to Isolde the very requests and objectives that she had pressed on him in Act I. He puts to Isolde the question, will she follow him to land where the sun never shines, the shadowy, nocturnal kingdom whence his mother sent him forth? It is darkness beyond the womb, darkness beyond the grave. Isolde replies that he is presenting the way to his own true kingdom, and that she has no future except in following him there. Tristan kisses her gently, which incites Melot to madness. Hoping perhaps to vindicate himself before King Mark, he shouts out, 'Ha! Traitor! O King, will you endure this shame?' whereupon Tristan snaps back into his other identity as a man of decisive, even violent action. He fixes on Melot, and asks who wagers his life against his own. 'That man', he tells Isolde and the company, 'had been my friend; how well and truly he loved me! Nobody urged me on to enhance my reputation as he did when urging me to marry you to King Mark. His difficulty, Isolde, was that the sight of you inflamed his passions as well, and it was from jealousy that that my friend betrayed me to the King – whom I myself betrayed!' Drawing his sword, he suddenly challenges, 'On guard, Melot!' and makes for Melot. As Melot thrusts a parrying blow at Tristan, Tristan drops his guard and falls, desperately wounded by Melot's sword, into Kurwenal's arms, while Mark holds Melot in check. The orchestra takes over a fragment of the second melody of Mark's lament (quoted above) but this time without its modulating conclusion, so that it is it is now set firmly in D minor. It sounds and is an extraordinarily alien key. This fragment is first given out with minatory force by the trumpets and then more sombrely on the horns. The act ends with a D minor bang as curtain falls.

This is the point to review the principles and ideas of the opera so far, because a major change comes in Act III. From now on the focus extends from the trials of romantic passion to the trials of existence itself. Act II has ended with Tristan and Isolde attempting to leave the world a second time. However it is still passion and its extremities and not the whole of reality that they are trying to escape. Strictly, even from the vantage point of Schopenhauer, this escape is an idea that does not make sense. For Schopenhauer, as for Wittgenstein, and perhaps in reality, death is not an event in life. The belief that death is a wonder-realm of mystical experience which someone can enter is not compatible with Schopenhauer's view (as it was for the most part) that death is total extinction, allowing no possibility of experiencing anything.

However it is a fact already mentioned that the truths and realities of the spirit (or psyche) are not the same as those of logic, and nor are they led or bound by reason. Nor is it the truths of reason and the rational aspects of living that matter most. Tristan and Isolde seem aware that their relationship exists in a dimension that is remote both from the tangible, physical world and the world of reason. Nevertheless their relationship is what gives meaning to their lives. Even if their state of mind seems delusional to outsiders, they bring it into being for themselves with full force, as real as anything they can know, and they are able to do so because of the intensity of their imaginations. This is not so far-fetched. People do conjure into existence all sorts of non-physical ideas through collectively believing in them, and there are many examples: the economy, team spirit, or Sharia law, as well as musical theory and charitable giving. These too are not physical realities but dreamt into existence by human minds and yet people still live in them and through them. They too give shape and meaning to life, because people's collective beliefs in them make them real. Even so, romantic passion is a special case. Romantic passion is more than a paradise which people create and inhabit through the force of imagination. Jung (Jung again) has convincingly argued that the propensity for romantic passion is rooted in our biological predispositions, in our animal nature, and that it is part of our identities as creatures inhabiting the real, physical world. We may learn the other man-made ideas just mentioned through being taught them or by thinking them into existence, but it is axiomatic that the predisposition to erotic passion is as inborn and fundamental, with its roots in the archetypes.

It is a matter of cardinal significance that erotic passion and love in all its forms are *feelings*[85] or states of mind dominated by feelings.

85   This is the opposite of Wittgenstein who said that love is not a feeling, part of a general view later elaborated by Gilbert Ryle in *The Concept of Mind* (London, 1951). Gilbert Ryle argued that emotions, intentions and other mental states do not really describe inner feelings but dispositions to behave in certain ways. Accordingly it is a delusion to believe that we describe inner experiences when in fact we are only describing the mechanical ways we behave. Man is a machine and it is a category mistake to imagine that there is a ghost in the machine; the machine itself is the only reality and its behaviour is what we really describe, not some inner realm of mental action.

Hence if somebody falls over in the street and provokes a compassionate impulse to run over and help, the compassion is actually a mechanistic predisposition to act. The perception of the person fallen over and his distress activates circuits in the brain and produces a response, which we might describe as compassionate, but compassion is the predisposition to do the helpful action; it only comes to exist in the action; and it consists solely in the disposition to act, not in any inner mental feelings or actions.

The Gilbert Ryle approach seems to run counter to the real experience of people, who do feel feelings, nor can these feelings be written off as unreal and treated as though they did not exist, when the most essential thing we know is that they do. Moreover it is debatable whether there would be any compassionate action if there were no feelings to drive it. Would a person who felt nothing, no smidgen of compassion or interest, run over to try and help? What would impel him if there were no feeling? We cannot go into all this here but at the very least feelings

Likewise the experiences of Tristan and Isolde are feelings and associated states of mind. To define love as something other than a feeling, as sometimes happens, is to be false to the word, to the idea behind it, and to what it actually means for real people in real life. In its fundamentals this feeling is the same for humanity everywhere. No matter how differently the experience may be moulded by the different cultural circumstances into which people are born, the idea of love that Plato discussed in *The Symposium*, that Shakespeare represented in *Romeo and Juliet* and Apollonius Rhodius depicted the *Argonautica* is not so different from the one that Wagner made so overwhelmingly real in *Tristan und Isolde*.

Love was a feeling which Wagner sought insatiably. The history of his life and works indicates that he was in love with it, for the reasons revealed in Chapters 4 to 6. In *Tristan und Isolde* as in life this feeling is ecstatic. As Act II shows, it is a state of mind where ego-boundaries dissolve, where isolation and separateness are no more, where all is consumed and transformed, '*aufgehoben*' in a oneness and communion with the beloved. Wagner sought this experience insatiably for the sake of an intensity which is otherwise known principally to mystics. However as my précis of *Tristan und Isolde* should have made clear, the text on its own gives only a meagre impression of what Wagner's opera is like. Admittedly there are passages of high poetry, but the words seldom convey the real experience. It is the music which transforms them. Thanks to its music, *Tristan und Isolde* describes romantic love and erotic passion more vividly than any other story or description in existence. Because of the music, *Tristan und Isolde* is more than a description; it creates the actual feeling within us. Through the music it creates the very experience in the imagination. It conjures up all that love might be, even for people who have never known it, somewhat like conferring the gift of sight on someone who has never seen. On

are experienced as counterpoints to action. Whether the feeling is the cause of the action or merely a by-product of mechanical processes may be debatable, but the feelings, the inner sensations and emotions cannot simply be swept aside as unreal.

the other hand, while *Tristan und Isolde* presents an experience which a person may not yet have known, it is also an experience that was always half-known. It was half-known already, because the experience is rooted in archetypes and predispositions. Through *Tristan und Isolde* these become activated, switching on the mind to ecstatic possibilities that may previously be unimagined but are innate, and to the hope that they may be realised.

Romantic passion, which Wagner rightly or wrongly took as the essential form of love, is an emotion of great complexity. There is Eros, even sex in the mix, somewhere near the centre and sometimes even at the centre. There are even people, most recently Laurence Dreyfus,[86] who apparently believe that the music of *Tristan und Isolde* is a portrayal of sexual gratification that is almost pornographic. As it happens sexual activity was one of the ways in which Wagner's *Tristan und Isolde* differed from his main source, the mediaeval poem of Gottfried von Strassburg, which is largely taken up with the lovers' adulterous sex and their cunning in achieving it repeatedly. Wagner however did not present us with the view that love, even erotic love, was the same as sex, and it is in any case a mistake to imagine that there is a *necessary* connection between love and lust. The connection between the emotions generally and the drives of sex is a complicated one, but love is not the only emotion that can be expressed in sex. Envy, loneliness, compassion, the urge to dominate or be dominated, the will to power, even self-hatred, can also stir up sexual urges and be acted out in sexual congress.

Conversely erotic love is not necessarily best expressed in sex, nor inspired by it, and Wagner did not make sex the central preoccupation of Tristan and Isolde themselves. His opera represents romantic love

---

86 Dreyfus, Laurence, *Wagner and the Erotic Impulse*, Cambridge, Mass., 2010, p. 105, stating of the Prelude, 'It is difficult to avoid the impression that Wagner has devised a musical depiction of a male fantasy moving in waves toward an explosive climax.' Dreyfus even identifies detumescence in the music which follows the Prelude's explosive climax which he sees as orgasm.

as larger than the displacement of carnal sensations with which Freud subsequently identified it. About fifty years after *Tristan und Isolde* Freud was to deconstruct erotic love simply as sublimated lust, as essentially an uncomfortable genital itch which was best gratified without a fuss, so as to defuse it.[87] This reductive view, which Freud evangelised to point of obsession because the view and the man were both so strongly attacked, was a main reason for his split with Jung. It was Freud's overemphasis on 'genitality' that ultimately led Jung to polish him off as 'a typical representative of the materialistic epoch, whose hope it was to solve the world riddle in a test tube'.[88]

George Bernard Shaw has been mentioned already for his description of the Prelude, which showed him recognising that the music was about emotions. Natalie Oliveros is an American lady who deserves a singular consideration for her views on the emotions and erotics of the Act II 'duet', because she is not only an opera enthusiast and a vintner but possesses a second, unusual identity as Savanna Samson, a hardcore porn star.[89] She was the special guest on a New York Public Radio programme about the Act II duet, and during the interview she said of the duet, 'It's what we call tantric sex.' Significantly she continued, 'I think that every woman would like to have just once in their life that kind of *passion and emotion*, and experience *that kind of love* that you hear in the music.' (My italics.) It is instructive that a woman whose profession is sex as a visual and tactile commodity should have recognised in *Tristan und Isolde* the 'kind of passion and emotion, the kind of love' that 'every woman would like to have just once in their life'. Perhaps unwittingly she subscribed to a conviction that the duet is very much about feelings and emotions. What she

---

87 *The Art of Loving* by Erich Fromm (New York, 1956) pointed out that if Freud were right then masturbation would be found preferable to an erotic relationship.

88 C.G. Jung, *Two Essays on Analytical Psychology*, tr. R.F.C. Hull, New York, 1950, p. 38.

89 Quoted in J.P.E. Harper-Scott, 'Wagner, Sex and Capitalism', in *The Wagner Journal*, vol. v, no. 2 (2011), p. 47 (my italics).

says also lays bare her inclination towards something beyond sensual commodification or gratification, a longing for the relationship where ego-boundaries do indeed dissolve, where isolation and separateness are indeed no more, where all is indeed consumed and transformed in a oneness and communion with the beloved. This experience of love and of being loved, as presented in Act II, might give anyone's spirit wings. Perhaps tantric sex or an experience of being engulfed in exquisite physical pleasure may sometimes be part of it, but that is not the whole, not for Tristan and Isolde and not for us. (The philosopher Roger Scruton has written an absorbing book[90] where he suggested, with some justice, that Isolde may remain a virgin to the end.) Wagner's position in *Tristan und Isolde* was close to that held later by Jung, that the essential point and purpose of erotic passion is integration.

At the same time one of the services which Wagner and *Tristan und Isolde* rendered was its insistence that sex was an admirable element within erotic passion, and as we saw in *Tannhäuser*, this message was revolutionary, clashing with the prevailing idea that a form of love which included even a bat-squeak of physical desire was automatically disqualified. Even more than *Tannhäuser*, *Tristan und Isolde* rewrote the rules. It integrated sensuality into romantic passion and yet still represented this passion as an exalted experience, and it played its part in refashioning the ideas and expectations of men and women throughout the entire 'civilised world'.

Tristan und Isolde did more than refashion ideas and expectations of love; it remoulded the actual experience for people. The verbal-musical-dramatic language of Wagner forms and moulds us in many ways, and as already indicated, the language of *Tristan und Isolde* shapes and conditions the way that people experience the erotic. This shaping and transforming effect still continues today and is available for each new generation that encounters *Tristan und Isolde*. Its availability is important because a transcendental passion illuminates the ordinary world where people live. As Wagner shows happening for

---

90   Scruton, Roger, *Death-Devoted Heart*, Oxford, 1996.

Isolde and for Tristan, the experience of this passion belongs partly to their private world, the 'wonder-realm' which those involved in this passion will into being. The transcendental passion of *Tristan und Isolde* is exactly that, an ideal willed and imagined into being which transcends ordinary reality. If challenged, Tristan and Isolde might have answered, 'You tell us our reality is an illusion; maybe, but that reality is the only one for us, and that is where we prefer to live.' At the same time, it has a great deal to offer to ordinary reality. From its position in a parallel dimension it can transform the day-to-day world and its sphere of action. The death-devoted form represented by Wagner in his great drama is incompatible with ordinary life, because suicide is incompatible with living life at all, but as asserted already the value of ideals is that they provide guiding principles and standards of comparison.[91] The harder and more remote the ideals, the more worthwhile and important it can be that they should influence life even without quite bringing life into line with them.

Insofar as is feasible within its time frame, the opera imparts ideas about the factors that give rise to romantic passion, the most important being the growing concord of two personalities. Personal appearances and gender naturally play a part in the process. Difference in gender can polarise two members of the opposite sex towards each other, but it takes more than gender-difference for a magnetism to develop, and gender is only one feature among the many which can lead to a romantic attraction. An accord in ideas, aspirations, practicalities, culture, archetypal symbols and many other things are as important. So, as I have explained, is the effect of mutual tenderness as Tristan and Isolde demonstrate, once they feel free to admit and express their emotions. So are correspondent wish-fantasies revealed in the Act II

---

91   The elimination of cancer is an ideal. So is universal democracy. So too is the object of 'making poverty history' and the commitment to end all wars. The realisation of these ideals is as remote as ever, but this does not invalidate them. They still irradiate real-life aspirations, and it is better to achieve them in part than not at all. Ideals are points of reference which help us to steer in the right direction.

duet, not least their fantasies of escaping from day into the world of night. So too are the cultural and intellectual interests which they have in common, such as the nocturnal imagery of the German poet Novalis and the philosophical ideas which Wagner gave them to discuss. So above all does the fact that the two of them simply enjoy talking together. As Wagner dramatised with instructive conviction, people in love talk and discuss everything from trivia to the meaning of life, and Tristan and Isolde do not just talk a little. They do more talking and they go on talking, endlessly; they might never have stopped if they had not been interrupted at the end of Act II. And Wagner shows their thoughts dovetailing, their ideas intertwining and floating in and out of one another. Wagner shows prescriptively how such talk draws lovers towards one another. In Act II he had the insight to make even their disagreements constructive because they exist in a framework of courtesy and respect, such as Tristan and Isolde come to display once the fearsome crossed purposes of Act I are resolved. In virtue of so much affinity at so many levels Tristan and Isolde are shown to achieve a romantic passion of such conviction that their personality boundaries really do become porous and dissolve.

එ

If *Tristan und Isolde* is overall a supreme monument to romantic passion, it pushes its concerns beyond this passion in Act III. This act extends the scope of the work in two ways. First it brings a shift of emphasis from a positive view of romantic passion as making life worth living to a more negative view of it as being a prime source of human suffering. Second, the act expands its scope to cover human existence in general, appraising it and judging it as one made up largely of suffering. It is in Act III that *Tristan und Isolde* comes closest to pure Schopenhauer without Wagnerian gloss, and it is disturbing in the sheer radiance and intensity of its pessimism. Its axiom that consciousness entails suffering is a sombre remodelling of Descartes' '*Cogito ergo sum*' into a '*Cogito ergo patior*', and this was what Wagner meant when he wrote to Mathilde Wesendonck, 'Child, this *Tristan* is turning into something terrible.' Tristan subjects existence in general to his agonised, unflinching gaze.

The setting for this act is Kareol, Tristan's castle in Brittany, now fallen into disrepair. Kurwenal has brought him there, ferrying him across the English Channel to his ancestral home, after his wounding by Melot. There the unconscious Tristan surfaces into a semi-delirious state and pours out his agonies. These outpourings fall into two great sections, related to the act's two expansions of *Tristan*'s scope, and separated by the point where Tristan first believes that he sees Isolde coming to him across the sea. In the first of these sections Tristan is concerned with the torments of love and with his failure to escape them. It is in the second that he rails against the awfulness of life itself.

The act begins with the second leitmotive from the Act I Prelude in a new development, sounding low on the strings, and three times repeated before spiralling upwards on the violins to the heights.

Fig. 18.22

This music differs from the Act I Prelude because of its vivid pictorialism, presenting the dilapidated bastions in a light that is grey and leaden; but it also presents an emotional image, one of desolation. The curtain goes up on the derelict castle; and the sky and the sea, and the breakers surging and ebbing in the distance, are all grey. Tristan is lying unconscious with Kurwenal watching over him. The orchestra falls silent and the only music now is the shepherd onstage, playing a strain on his pipe, strange, haunting, and unending;

Fig. 18.23

Finally he pauses and asks Kurwenal, 'Kurwenal, tell me, my friend, has he not yet awoken?' Kurwenal sadly shakes his head. 'If he awoke it would only be to leave us forever – unless she arrived here first, the only one who can heal him.' He in turn asks the shepherd, 'Nothing to be seen yet? No ship on the sea?' 'If that were so,' answers the shepherd, 'you would hear from me another strain, as cheery as I can manage. But tell me, dear old friend, what is the matter with our lord?' 'Ask no questions,' says Kurwenal. 'You could never understand. Keep your watch and if you see a ship, signal the fact with something bright and cheerful.' The shepherd leaves for his lookout over the sea, and reports '*Öd' und leer das Meer*', the phrase which T.S. Eliot quoted with mesmerising effect in *The Waste Land*, mesmerising at least for those who know *Tristan und Isolde*.

The shepherd takes up his pipe again, and now from the sickbed comes the murmuring, indeterminate sound of Tristan's voice. 'That ancient strain! Why am I awakening to that?' Kurwenal jumps up, scarce able to believe his ears, and when Tristan continues more audibly, 'Where am I?' Kurwenal is overjoyed: 'At last! That voice! His voice! At last! Alive! Sweet life given back to my Tristan!' Tristan looks up vaguely. 'Kurwenal, you. Where was I? Where am I?' Kurwenal reassures him, 'You are at peace, safe and free in Kareol. Do you not recognise the castle of your ancestors? Only look around you.' 'What was that sound?' asks Tristan, still trying to make sense of his floating perceptions. 'You heard the Shepherd's tune again. He is down the hill looking after your flocks.' Tristan; '*My* flocks?' Kurwenal; 'I should say so. They are all yours, and your faithful people have cared for them all ever since you left to go off to strange lands.' Tristan: 'What strange lands?' 'Cornwall! Cornwall is where you found fame and fortune.' Tristan; 'Am I in Cornwall?' Kurwenal keeps up a tone of bluff, jocular tone that is heartbreaking in its depth of affection. The orchestra strikes up a leitmotive generally designated 'Kareol', but it really seems to belong to Kurwenal. It is this motive which sounds, desolate and broken, at the end of the act when Kurwenal dies. It makes no sense there as a reference to Kareol but extreme sense as a reference to Kurwenal. There is something even more that is intriguing about this motive, because it indicates Kurwenal's potential for reincarnation as a Mastersinger. The theme is not given here as presented at its first appearance, but as it occurs a little later in C major, because this makes clearer its close connection with the first theme quoted in the next chapter, the very opening of *Die Meistersinger*.

Fig. 18.24 'Kurwenal'

If the little turn is exchanged for a drop of a third, then the passage from the crescendo onwards contains within it the kernel of the Mastersingers' most characteristic musical emblem.

Meanwhile, Kurwenal answers Tristan's question; 'No, no; in

Kareol.' Tristan; 'How did I get here?' Kurwenal says, 'How did you get here? Well now, it was not by riding a horse. A little old ship ferried you here, but it was my own broad shoulders which carried you down to the shore. Now you are home, your own true home, and our local familiar sunshine will cure you.' He embraces Tristan, who takes a moment to reply.

'Do you think so?' resumes Tristan with a strange incoherence that is wholly coherent; 'I know it otherwise; but yet I cannot tell you. Where I awoke, I did not stay, but where I stayed, I cannot tell you. I saw no sun, nor any land nor people, but what I saw, that too I cannot tell you. I was where I have always been and where I am always going, the vast kingdoms of the world-night. We who belong there can only appreciate one thing: divine, eternal, primordial oblivion.' He now describes to Kurwenal his bewilderment that he ever lost his knowledge of it, and now embarks on the first of his great appraisals of existence, this one biased towards a searingly pessimistic view of romantic passion. 'It was love, passion, that forced me back to the world of day, back to the false and tawdry glare which still surrounds my Isolde. It drags me back still. I rejoiced to hear the doors of death crashing together behind me, but now they yawn wide open again. The sun's beams have prised them open, forcing me to surface again from out of the night. I must now still search for the one through whom alone it is granted to achieve oblivion. But the day is gathering itself and awakening my brain to madness.' His emotions are rising to a turmoil, to a fury. 'Damn you, O light of day! A curse upon your brightness! Will you stand like a dread sentinel over my anguish to ensure that it continues forever? Will your light forever prevent me from joining her? When will the light go out? Will night never fall on the house?'

Kurwenal, who evidently half imagines that Tristan is striving for a return to ordinary health, breaks in with the reassurance that he has sent for Isolde and that she is even now on her way. This news excites Tristan to a new delirium and a hysterical joy. He salutes Kurwenal's loyalty and his willingness to suffer *with* him; but he changes tone as he says that Kurwenal can never suffer *what* he suffers. Otherwise he would be up on the lookout. 'Kurwenal', he bursts out, 'She is on her way; she is arriving; how can anyone not see her?' the music surges up to a frenzied pitch of expectation, represented by a teeming, insistent high A on violins, which suddenly collapses in on itself and turns hollow and cold. The shepherd's strains sound beneath it, and Kurwenal states dejectedly that there is still no ship to be seen. The sad, ancient sound of the shepherd's pipe continues and it works strangely on Tristan's imagination.

It summons to his memory all the torments of existence that he has ever lived, an ultimate existential agony which is the basis for Tristan's second critical attack, this time against the ills of existence itself. These are behind the mournful strain which he had heard along with the dire news, first the news of his father's death and then of his mother's fate. 'That ancient strain pressed on me the question, what fate I was born for, to what end? Nothing but yearning and dying. No, ah no! That is not it. Even in death still there is longing. When I lay dying in the boat, longing sang out in that melody. She healed my wound, but first tore it open again with the sword, but then she let fall the sword. She gave me poison to drink, but instead of bringing me oblivion it proved the most hurtful magic possible, such that I did not die but entered into everlasting torment. That drink, that terrible drink, with what fury it surged through me from my heart to my brain. Now no cure, not even sweet death, can free me from the agony of longing. Never shall I find rest. Night has flung me back into the day, back into the scorching rays of the sun. Oh how they burn my brain with their torturing heat! No shade, no unguent can bring relief. That terrible drink! That drink which condemned me to this torment, it was I, I myself who brewed it! From my father's distress and my mother's misery, from the tears of love – ever and always – from laughter and sorrow, from joys and wounds, I found the poison for the drink. And what I brewed flowed through me, because I drank it down, quaffing it eagerly, ecstatically! A curse upon you, terrible drink! A curse upon myself as the one who brewed it!' There is now a new leitmotive, signifying his curse.

Fig. 18.25 'Tristan's Curse on the Drink'

Tristan's delirium is madness, but how much method there is in it, as he faces life's horrors head-on and draws those who hear him into doing the same! Life has become for him an abyss, the frightful story of his own and universal suffering, just as Schopenhauer viewed it, and perhaps it is wise not to view it from the perspective of Schopenhauer–Tristan too often. Anyone who accepts Darwin's theory of evolution as true must view aeons of suffering, with the deaths of millions and only a few surviving to perpetuate and advance the species. The same grim picture may confront anyone who views human existence and its particular dreadfulness, and not merely because of human want, and natural disasters, plagues, fire, flood and famine, and life's inexorable processes. As Schopenhauer saw it, life is at best a matter of aspirations frustrated from one moment to the next, in things great and small. But then populations of uncountable magnitude are doomed to eke out horrible lives, for instance, in the foetid, stinking slums of the world's tropical mega-cities. Worse is the unspeakable cruelty of human beings one to one another, the endless crucifixions and burnings alive, the millions of innocent Muslims murdered by Genghis Khan after his envoy's head was sent back in a box, the untellable miseries of the Thirty Years War, the hundreds of millions killed in the scramble for Africa, the genocidal murder of the American Indians, the gulags of Stalin, the death camps of Hitler, the killing fields of Pol Pot … on and on and on. And as Schopenhauer would have recognised, such lists of horrors barely scratch the surface. Wagner himself knew all about it because he was always stunningly well informed; for instance he knew more probably about the Peabody housing schemes in central London and why they were necessary than did most Englishmen.

To go with Tristan and gaze into these abysses is only bearable if there is the power to do something. The essential for anyone wanting to do something is to take responsibility, as Tristan exemplifies. He says 'I, it was I who brewed the draught!' – not that he can do much. His suffering and his injury and physical weakness are too great, and he is incapable of action. It was in *Parsifal* that Wagner presented us with a drama which turns wholly on the hero's decision to take responsibility and perform some decisive actions. Tristan's outburst exhausts him, and to Kurwenal's dismay he falls back unconscious. Kurwenal only half understands when he exclaims, 'What fearful magic! What a terrible enthralment to passion!' He half addresses Tristan and half himself as he continues, 'Such passion is the most beautiful illusion in the world, but it has brought you to this. See what a reward it has brought. This is what passion always gains as its reward.' Tristan makes no response. 'Are you dead? Have you succumbed to the curse?' But then, 'Not so. Oh joy. He is stirring; he is alive.' Tristan slowly regains consciousness and asks Kurwenal if he can yet see the ship. Kurwenal reassures him soothingly that it must come soon, today. 'Yes,' continues Tristan, 'and there it is, with Isolde onboard waving. She is drinking reconciliation to me. How sweet she looks, floating over the watery distances to bring me her final consolation. She wafts to me across the waves of flowers. Oh Isolde, you are so beautiful! And Kurwenal, didn't you see her?' He starts suddenly from serenity to agitation. 'You stupid idiot! Up to the lookout post, so as not to miss what I can see so clearly. The ship, the ship, can you not see it?'

At that moment the shepherd is heard, piping a jubilant call on a special wooden 'trumpet' which Wagner had designed for the purpose, and Kurwenal leaps up; 'The ship! I see it, coming from the north.' Tristan, whose mind is here, there and everywhere: 'Did not I say so?'

Kurwenal: Yes, and it is a brave course that the ship is taking as it forges on through the waves.
Tristan: Only Isolde holds me to the world now. Kurwenal, my dearest, most loyal friend, today I bequeath my all to you! Can you see her?

Kurwenal: Not at this moment; the ship has disappeared behind the reef.

Tristan: Behind the reef? That means danger. Who is at the helm?

Kurwenal: The best of helmsman.

Tristan: Might he betray me? Is he Melot's man?

Kurwenal: Trust him like me.

Tristan: You betray me too?

Kurwenal: They are safely through.

Tristan laughs in hysterical joy; 'O dearest Kurwenal, I bequeath to you all that I have and possess.'

Kurwenal: 'They are safely in the harbour.

Tristan: Then down from the watchtower! Stop your empty gawping; go down and help her!

Kurwenal: Trust to me and my strength! I will bring her up safely; but you, Tristan, promise to stay quietly here on your bed!

Without stopping for an answer, he hastens down to the landing point.

Tristan tosses on his couch in feverish excitement, and tears at his bandages. 'Blood bounding forth! Jubilant heart! Joy with no bounds! Mad exaltation! How can I bear it, chained to this bed? The mighty hero Tristan has torn himself free of mortal coils. With bleeding wounds I once conquered Morold. With bleeding wounds, I lay claim to Isolde, who comes bringing me salvation.' Her voice is heard calling his name, and he lurches forward ecstatically, exclaiming, 'Is that still the torch? The light goes out. To her; to her!' This unleashes from the orchestra an immense demonstration of sound. Fortissimo trumpets overblast the remaining heavy brass and the whole orchestra in a reprise of the music with which Isolde hurled down the torch in Act II, the '*Todgeweihtes Haupt, Todgeweihtes Herz!*' motive. This time it is indeed the light of life that is being thrown down. The trumpets give way to the horns surging upwards and baying out the twin motives from the beginning of the opera before descending into the 'Tristan' chord, to the most tragic effect. Isolde appears and as the dying man sinks slowly to the ground, she gathers him into her arms. To a faint, fading version of music from the Prelude (Fig. 18.3 (d)), he utters her name and dies.

She cannot take it in and addresses him; 'It is I, it is I, my sweetest friend!' She too now is half delirious, but delirious with grief because he did not wait for her. In expiring without her and making his way to eternity and annihilation alone he has betrayed her again. Let him awaken, let her heal him once more so that they can become one, fully conscious of their oneness even as their twin consciousnesses fade forever. She imagines that she sees him awaken and sinks down upon him in a swoon, but at that moment, the shepherd reappears and approaches Kurwenal with secret urgency; 'Kurwenal, listen; a second ship!' Kurwenal takes one look and takes in everything. 'Death and Hell! Everyone to battle. It is Mark and Melot. Weapons and boulders, grasp them at once.' A small band of Tristan's men gathers hastily to try and barricade the gates just as Isolde's helmsman comes running in. He tells them that Mark and his soldiers are close behind, and that the defenders are outnumbered. 'Stand here and help!' says Kurwenal; 'So long as I live, nobody comes leering in here.' Brangäne's voice is heard, calling for Isolde, and Kurwenal demands roughly, what is she doing there? She asks not to shut them out, and Melot repeats her request. Hearing Melot, Kurwenal laughs savagely and as Melot breaks through the defences with Mark's soldiers, Kurwenal falls upon him, strikes him to the ground and tells him to die. Brangäne implores Kurwenal to stop and listen to reason, and Mark adds his voice, 'Stop, raging madman; are you out of your mind?' Kurwenal: 'It is only death that rages here, O King; come on if you would choose it.' Mark and his retinue now storm the gates. Brangäne makes for Isolde as Mark exclaims at the *Wahn*, the exorbitant, irresistible, delusional force which he finds at work, and at the terrible mistakes of those resisting him. Where, he asks, can he find Tristan? Kurwenal, himself now desperately wounded, indicates Tristan by staggering towards him and collapsing nearby. He asks Tristan not to reproach him that he follows on so soon. Mark looks around distractedly; 'Everyone dead then. All dead! Tristan, my truest friend, you have again betrayed me, your own true friend!' Brangäne hurriedly explains to Isolde that she had confided the secret of the drink to Mark, who immediately set sail to renounce Isolde and marry her to Tristan. Mark tells how glad he had been that Tristan was blameless, but he is now in the pits of despair because his best intentions had simply added to the harvest of death. *Wahn* had heightened the crisis.

Isolde is still in a trance. Brangäne asks her whether she can hear and understand them, but she is lost to the world. She slowly rises, standing erect and gazing at Tristan. With growing radiance she sings her extraordinary, final transfiguration. By supreme force of will she has forsaken the mundane world for the realm of pure imagination, a realm which had its foundations in romantic passion but now encompasses everything of significance. This realm is now her only reality, and through the power with which she conjures it into being she makes herself see Tristan rising to life, smiling gently, opening his eyes, set in a new radiance and surrounded by the stars. The orchestra takes up the music which concluded the Act II duet, from '*So sterben wir um ungetrennt*' onwards, and develops it as a vast shimmering tapestry that fuses and resolves any incompatibility between her imagination and the real world in a way that music alone can achieve. The music rises gradually to a peak of intensity that some find orgasmic, but I think this misses the point. Isolde's *Verklärung* is more importantly a new and fulfilling version of the unfulfilments of the Prelude and a correction of its ideas and its partial vision of romantic love. It refashions that vision so that it ceases to be an endlessly unsatisfying experience, as Schopenhauer, and later Freud, considered it to be. Instead it views and defines romantic love as the means and essence of completeness, integration and wholeness. It expresses and presents this wholeness as ecstatic. It represents Isolde's a mystical fusion with the world, its all, its everything: all one. Grammar and coherence dissolve for Isolde, but what she expresses is as meaningful as Tristan's delirium earlier, but now wholly positive. 'Is it I alone,' she asks, 'who hears the strange music resounding from him? It streams around me ever brighter; or is it rather waves and purest-scented breezes? How they all surge and flood around me. Shall I breathe them; shall I sip them; shall I submerge underneath them, sink within them? In their surging flood, in this music's resounding call, in its world breath, in its oneness with all – to drink it utterly – to drown in it forever – unconscious – highest bliss!'

Isolde and Tristan expire in a state of awareness that is ecstatic, but it is also an advanced state of *Wahn*-illusion, an exalted make-believe. It has no roots or connections in the ordinary world, even if it is their supreme and only reality. Their objective was to ensure their ceasing to exist at the point of their ultimate ecstasy, and this is what their transfiguration means – and no more. There is no portal to an afterlife, and they do not float off into a new dawn like Senta and the Dutchman. They are simply on the verge of nothingness, and everything depends and fixes on the moment when nothingness comes upon them. What matters is to ensure that this moment occurs when they are in that state of ecstasy which each alone can create for the other. Tristan achieves this by engineering his departure from life while in Isolde's embrace. But by dying first, he makes it impossible for him to do the do same for her and leaves her behind, still alive. She puts matters right by an effort of will that is literally superhuman. She makes herself imagine Tristan returning to life, and then builds on the imaginary consciousness of his presence to think herself into a final oneness with him. She then extends the scope of her imagination to think herself into oneness with everything. She finally sees herself as becoming Tristan and the world, 'I am myself the world', as they sang ecstatically in duet during Act II, but this dissolving of consciousness is not a blackout but a white-out. It is an extraordinary triumph of mind over matter, where everything is overwhelmed with radiance and bliss. At the same time this music and the whole opera seem to sink a shaft into some unknown depth, some charted realm of reality only previously known to the mystics. This is an experience bordering on the paranormal, and no account can do much more than skirt around it.

The psychological and myth-related reasons why Isolde should expire are compelling, especially when irradiated by Wagner's music, but the biological ones are less clear. When we come down to earth and the radiance of *Tristan und Isolde* begins to fade, questions start to surface: what is actually happening here; what does it mean, and what do the deaths of Tristan and Isolde really tell us? It is important to keep in mind that *Tristan und Isolde* is set in the Schopenhauerian landscape where the only escape from suffering is by ceasing to exist. But while Wagner felt unbounded gratitude and allegiance to Schopenhauer, he often and intermittently remained Schopenhauer's exact opposite in his outlook, an erratic but inveterate optimist, which was why he tried to square the circle and reorientate Schopenhauer's pessimistic ideas to positive effect. He attempted to show how it was possible to transform the bleakness of Schopenhauer's negation of life by enfolding it an ecstasy of romantic passion. For Wagner it may barely have mattered if the whole process was a make-believe, completely at a tangent to reality. Wagner had even done something like it himself, wish-fantasising that he swooned ecstatically out of life in the arms of an adoring Mathilde Wesendonck. Obviously nothing like this ever came to pass, but within the closed terms and charmed circle of *Tristan und Isolde* he made the experience believable.

This still leaves the further question what Act III is telling us to do and be. Is it really proclaiming that we can transform life through imaginary, fictitious ideas about it, and should we? Is it telling us that it does not matter whether or not our ideas are true? On our visit to the great monastery of Ettal near Oberammergau we encountered an example of ideas transforming life which provides a fascinating slant on these questions. We were hosted there by a young ordained monk who described both the workings of the monastery and his own part in it. His discussions and his whole approach revealed that he was a considerable intellectual, and knew all about the world and what was happening in it; but when he explained that he spent three or four hours a day in prayer, some of our group were almost impolite in making plain their disbelief that anyone could lead and experience a life so delusional, as they saw it. They saw him as suspended in a world of fantasies and inventions that were unreal; but the point about the young monk's experience was that it was utterly life-enhancing, something which the most sceptical could not gainsay. It made no difference to its value whether his reality was conventionally true or not. What was so arresting was the exceptional level of intensity at which this young man lived life. Even more than with Jung's Mexican Indians with their belief that their efforts kept the sun going, his beliefs afforded this monk an unusually high quality of living, a Tristanesque exaltation such as is known only to a few. If challenged he would of course not have accepted that his reality was an illusion. For him ordinary reality appeared to symbolise a deeper reality, and it was easy to understand why he preferred to live in a way that embraced both. Nor were his transforming convictions simply an interior matter with no practical value; we saw him again as we were leaving the monastery, returned now to productive work that made a very practical difference. *Tristan und Isolde* is not impossible in representing how life can be transformed by the power of imagination (or the spirit?), because spiritual worlds can change and become as anyone wills them, and with them the rest of life can change as well.

There are other reasons why *Tristan und Isolde* is Wagner's most extreme creation. The pessimistic idea of life implicit in the work is itself extreme. The idea of escaping its pain only by ceasing from it altogether is yet more extreme. Wagner's idea of converting this 'ceasing from a life of pain' into something ecstatic is more extreme still. These ideas beat against the boundaries of normal experience and perhaps go beyond them, and people do not expect to lead an existence along the lines of *Tristan*. Even less does it provide effective guidance for about living life by its ideas. Wagner must have recognised this, because he went on to create *Die Meistersinger*, which does suggest how Schopenhauer's ideas might at least in part be incorporated constructively into real life.

Where *Tristan und Isolde* does yield practical applications is in the ideas it instils about the romantic love. As the earlier parts of this chapter have explained, these ideas are illuminating and compelling, and people can fruitfully incorporate these into real life. This is perhaps the reason why an account of *Tristan und Isolde* should end as it began, with simple homage to it as the supreme monument to romantic passion. In the end however, *Tristan und Isolde* remains what it is in itself, shimmering, numinous and overwhelming. No words can ever encompass this still mysterious work of art.

Tristan und Isolde was first performed at the Munich Hofoper on 10 June 1865. The cast consisted of Ludwig Schnorr von Carolsfeld (Tristan), Malvina Schnorr von Carolsfeld (Isolde), Anna Deinet (Brangäne), Anton Mitterwurzer (Kurwenal), Ludwig Zottmayer (Mark), Karl Samuel Heinrich (Melot), Karl Simons (Shepherd), Peter Hartmann (Steersman). The singer of the Young Seaman is unknown. The performance was conducted by Hans von Bülow under the close personal supervision of Wagner.

Anton Mitterwurzer had created the role of Wolfram for Wagner in the Dresden *Tannhäuser* of twenty years before.

NINETEEN

DIE MEISTERSINGER VON NÜRNBERG

Die Meistersinger is astonishing in every way. The Overture instantly establishes its distinctive world with its confident rhythmic stride and its 'C major of life'.

Fig. 19.1 'The Mastersingers'

George Bernard Shaw described this opera, for an opera it is, as lovely and happy. Instead of myth and a nebulous atmosphere of shifting chromaticism, *Die Meistersinger* places us solidly in sixteenth-century Nuremberg. Instead of Tristan railing against the sun as the root cause of all his agonies, there is Eva Pogner launching into the quintet, a musical gem, by praising the day. She sings straightforwardly of the blessed manner in which the sun of her happiness laughs with her, and of a morning of joy awakening her. Nothing, it seems, could be further from the darkness and pessimism of Schopenhauer, and yet Lucy Beckett, in her celebrated study of *Parsifal*, mentions in passing that *Die Meistersinger* is Wagner's 'most fully Schopenhauerian work',[92] and she is right. In fact the observations of Bernard Shaw and of Lucy Beckett are both right, and nothing by Wagner was less simple and straightforward.

When Wagner finished *Tristan und Isolde* he had certainly not finished with Schopenhauer, nor did he waver in his allegiance to *The World as Will and Representation*. He had eventually reckoned on setting out the realities of life as Schopenhauer recognised them in *Tristan und Isolde*. Even though it was a paean to romantic love, Wagner intended increasingly that it should represent Schopenhauer's principles and give an idea how people could live by them. However *Tristan und Isolde* ended up not fulfilling this intention. It does not present Schopenhauer's ideas in a workable form, and it does not model any Schopenhauerian lessons which anyone could apply to life. Its leading characters choose an alternative brought into being by their own imagining, but after Wagner himself had emerged from this realm, which he had brought into being by *his* own imagining, he had to recognise that the ordinary real world was still going on and he was still part of it.

It was in the autumn of 1861, when he was in Vienna trying unsuccessfully to stage the world premiere of *Tristan und Isolde*, that the idea of *Die Meistersinger* came back to his mind. Wagner's first ideas for it dated from 1845 when he thought it might serve as a comic pendant to his more serious opera *Tannhäuser*. Instead of going ahead, he went on to create *Lohengrin* and *The Ring*, and when he broke off from *The Ring* it was for *Tristan und Isolde*. Part of the matted skein of reasons for this was his need to earn some money with an opera which he originally envisaged as a romantic potboiler in a popular Italian style. Because *Tristan und Isolde* turned out so different, Wagner had to look elsewhere for his box office success. It came to him that he

---

92   Beckett, Lucy, *Parsifal*, Cambridge, 1981, p. 134.

should turn out something splashy and popular like *The Barber of Seville*, and this was his intention in taking up *Die Meistersinger* again. In it a dashing young knight would carry off a glamour girl from Hans Sachs, a gruff, ill-tempered old cobbler who fancies himself as a poet. Sachs was to be the buffo contrast to Walther, the knight. His autobiography tells us that it was his meeting in Venice with the Wesendoncks in November 1861 that set him firmly on course for writing *Die Meistersinger*. It is significant that he was then even more than usual an unsettled, fragmented spirit. He was living homeless and wifeless. The year had already inflicted on him the Paris *Tannhäuser* fiasco and the failure of his hopes for *Tristan* in Vienna which gave rise to his thoughts of *Die Meistersinger*. Now too Mathilde Wesendonck was demonstrating in Venice that whatever fantasy realm she had shared with Wagner under the mesmerising impact of his presence, she had now reverted to being Frau Wesendonck, a mother and the wife of an extraordinarily able, successful and wealthy businessman. Mathilde, who was plainly pregnant by her husband, had obviously not kept true to a mutual vow which Wagner believed they had made renouncing sexuality. Wagner now had to carry out an excruciating renunciation of Mathilde that was not a fantasy, but very real and very much of this world. On the other hand the Wesendoncks took him round Venice as an appendage, a tourist enjoying the marvels which he had missed on his previous long stay in Venice, when he had been a hermit composing Act II of *Tristan*. Now he was mostly too numb and unhappy to respond to most of what he saw, but he was overwhelmed by Titian's great picture, *The Assumption of the Virgin*. He wrote later in *Mein Leben* that looking at it, he felt a resurgence of his old powers, and that he thereupon resolved to proceed with *Die Meistersinger*. By his own account he somehow identified Titian's picture with the *Verklärung* of Isolde, but also with the idea that his personal Isolde, Mathilde, had floated out of reach. The necessity of performing an act of renunciation that was somehow redemptive was a galvanising force towards his creation of Hans Sachs, the character at the centre of *Die Meistersinger*.

When Wagner left Venice he returned by rail to Vienna, and writing to Mathilde he said, 'pinned between then and now, I journeyed off into drabness,' but he also tells that it was during this journey that he 'conceived with the utmost clarity the Overture in C major' which begins *Die Meistersinger*. This was before he had written the text; and elsewhere he gave a different date for composing the Overture, January 1862, which was *after* he had written the text. Either way he finished the Overture, eventually renamed the Prelude, before the composition of the opera; and although it contains many important motives, he had not decided how they would function in the opera itself.

Both in Vienna and Venice real life only fitfully followed Wagner's ideas about the way it should go, and more than ever he regarded Schopenhauer's ideas of renunciation and his general world-view as correct. He was thus faced with the challenge: how to reconcile Schopenhauer with real life, and how to dramatise this as possible? *Die Meistersinger* was his answer. It does model believable suggestions for applying Schopenhauer to life. In *Die Meistersinger* Wagner created a drama of very real characters which showed how Schopenhauer's bleak vision might apply to life as people actually live it. This was one of Wagner's achievements in *Die Meistersinger* generally, and more specifically in the very real character of Hans Sachs. Sachs had been a real historical figure, even if Wagner remodelled him in the opera. As usual, Wagner's ideas were to change as the work evolved, because he grew more and more drawn to Sachs, his cobbler-poet, just as he had to Wotan, and although he retained a cantankerous side, Sachs grew beyond recognition. So did the whole opera, and its initial easy-money scenario bore little relation to the searching, moving, life-enhancing, and yet still comic masterpiece that eventually materialised in *Die Meistersinger von Nürnberg*.

Before embarking on its story, there are as ever some points to explain. *Die Meistersinger* is often made out to be nationalistic, Teutonic and militaristic, as if it were an all-conquering, all-bullying advance manifesto for the Third Reich. Before it was rebuilt, the last opera broadcast from Covent Garden was *Die Meistersinger*, and it was sad to hear music director Bernard Haitink using his interval talk to attack the work for insisting to the world the Germans were its masters. Haitink made it clear, as others have done, that he saw Sachs's final peroration as a manifesto for German nationalism which struck him as quite unacceptable; but Sachs's peroration is nothing of a kind. A misconception like this is only possible through a *mis*understanding of the text, and of history. Certainly Sachs's concluding monologue does end by issuing the instruction, 'Honour your German masters', but the first point is that 'masters' does not signify masters of the universe or even of Germany, but masters of the arts and crafts, the skills which they so humbly serve. Second, this is an instruction addressed specifically to Walther von Stolzing who has just behaved boorishly, rejecting the masters and all that they stand for. As for the fudging of historical perspective, Germany was not even a country in 1868 when *Die Meistersinger* was first performed, let alone a country with aspirations towards world domination. At that time the 37 German states still had an appalling history of being the downtrodden, battered victims of the great military powers of Europe such as Sweden and France. Fearsome despots like Gustavus Adolphus and Louis XIV, mired in crimes against humanity, had for centuries inflicted ruinous invasions on the German states, which were mostly small and ill-organised. Throughout most of the nineteenth century 'Germany' was only a remote, hazy ideal which belonged with other hazy visions, of a German democracy and a better, more egalitarian world.

Nor was Wagner an enthusiast for the major military power, Prussian style, which the new Germany would soon start to become. In 1870, after Prussia's victory in the war initiated by France, he was initially enthusiastic about the new, unified Germany, even under Prussian leadership. He seems briefly to have put out of mind his own experiences of Prussian troops in the Dresden uprising in 1849, when those troops and their atrocities had annihilated any democratic aspirations in Saxony.[93] However, the realities of the new German Reich

---

93 '*Gegen Demokraten helfen nur Soldaten*: Against democrats only soldiers can help.' Prussian marching song, quoted in Berlin, Isaiah, *Karl Marx*,

gradually sobered and soured his thinking so that on July 15 1878, to take one instance, Cosima records him saying 'I am so disgusted with the new Germany'. Her diaries make it clear that he saw Prussian-led Germany as ruthlessly anti-egalitarian and starkly opposed to his own convictions. He saw Bismarck, the architect of the new nation state as 'a Prussian *Junker* if ever there was one', above all after Bismarck had passed the Sozialistengesetze, the anti-socialist laws of 1873, and was overseeing the rebuilding of Berlin on lines that disempowered ordinary people. These new laws prevented workers from gathering together for any political purpose whatever, and clamped down on the freedom of the press. Under Bismarck the working classes were cooped up in miserable dwellings described routinely as *Mitzkaserne*, or rental barracks. Workers had become industrial slaves, veritable Nibelungen, the cannon fodder of German capitalism, and they were oppressed both economically and politically by the ruling classes. Reversing his initial admiration, Wagner came to detest the 'Iron Chancellor', and he was horrified when Bismarck's legislation provoked a multitude of denunciations and informers. Martin Gregor-Dellin comments[94] that given the ferocious suppression of press freedom and of political dissent, Wagner was probably only protected from big trouble by his extensive contacts among the Berlin aristocracy. The reason why contributions to the Bayreuth fund ceased after June 1878 was in Gregor-Dellin's view because his newsletter *Bayreuther Blätter* published an article by Constantin Frantz criticising Bismarck. On 13 November 1879, Cosima reports Wagner even as commenting that the present state of affairs – national exhaustion, more and more taxes, and continuing military expansion – was barbarous. 'Conquering new provinces and never stopping to wonder how to win them over, never debating how to make friends with Holland, Switzerland, etc, – nothing at all but the Army.'

This Wagner is not exactly the militaristic, world-conquering

---

3rd ed., Oxford, 1963, p. 158.

94 Gregor-Dellin, Martin, *Richard Wagner: His Life, his Work, his Century*, tr. J. Maxwell Brownjohn, London, 1983, p. 472.

precursor of Adolf Hitler. Even before the 1870s, Wagner had opposed the values of *Machtpolitik* in the violence of Walther von Stolzing; and *Die Meistersinger* ends with Sachs proclaiming that art is the one sphere where Germany could truly lead the world. Sachs tells Walther, 'It is not your ancestors, your castle, your power or your strength at arms, nor your spear and sword' (all those instruments of feudal militarism) 'that have won you your life's happiness; it is the fact that you are a poet. How can you not celebrate an art which has brought you such rewards? It once flourished; but then came bad times, and it was guilds like those of the Nuremberg Mastersingers which kept up standards.' Sachs speaks both for the sixteenth and the nineteenth century as he continues, 'These times now are also difficult. If ordinary Germans and their realm were to succumb to foreign hubris' (as happened in the sixteenth century and the centuries that followed) 'people would lose any sense of German identity unless it lived on, nurtured and cherished among us masters in the form of holy German art.'

Although *Die Meistersinger* is an opera, it fuses Wagner's mature symphonic style and leitmotive textures with stretches of more expansive, freer composition. Passages where leitmotives weave tapestries or act as ostinatos dissolve into arioso or independent orchestral fantasies. *Die Meistersinger* includes some songs composed in the 'Bar' form prescribed by Kothner in Act I, but symphonic elements and leitmotives still shine through them. Its libretto is conventional, at least in form, with many end-rhymes, but the dialogue itself has a point and subtlety that is unique in Wagner, except perhaps for *Das Rheingold*. Its intricacies and turns of meaning are essential for grasping the action, and so the text of *Die Meistersinger* has to be presented in even more detail than with Wagner's other works.

The Overture begins with the music quoted at the outset of this chapter. It is not only an affirmation of daylight and reason, but occupies the key, C major, which Wagner regularly used for solid historical locations, as he did in *Lohengrin*. The music sets before us a picture of sixteenth-century Nuremberg; but it also represents a bold civic confidence which is timeless. It leads to the leitmotive which will symbolise Walther's romantic approaches to Eva.

Fig. 19.2 'Romantic Approaches'

It seems about to come to rest, when it is swept aside by some downward rushes from the strings which herald the 'King David' theme. King David, from the Old Testament, is the patron saint of the Mastersingers, and this music is the emblem of their guild.

Fig. 19.3 'King David'

This splendid theme advances towards to another which more specifically designates the guild as guardians and trustees of poetry and music. The sense of joy, evident from the beginning, expends ever further towards a powerful, spirited climax.

Fig. 19.4 'The Mastersingers' Guild'

The climax dissolves in a theme of romantic yearning, of Walter's feeling for Eva.

Fig. 19.5 'Romantic Yearning'

This in turn moves into a theme which will eventually take its place in Act III as the 'Prize Song' though which Walther will win the heroine, Eva as his wife.

Fig. 19.6 'Prize Song'

More generally it seems to symbolise the happiness of day. It leads straight into the theme of another important song belonging to Walther; this time, it is the song which he will sing as his exam piece to try and qualify as a member of the Mastersingers' guild at the end of Act I. This theme is traditionally designated as 'Love's Crisis' or 'Spring's Command'.

Fig. 19.7 'Love's Crisis' or 'Spring's Command'

Both these last two themes begin in a key that is remote from the one which either will occupy in the opera, and the latter theme is developed in A major before a musical surprise, a sforzando in the distant key of E flat for a perky version of the opening theme of the Overture, going at twice the speed and thoroughly staccato. At the very end of the opera, this will represent the young apprentices, although they mostly have their own music. For the time being, the staccato becomes a subject for a short fugue, suddenly interrupted by the same theme, given out broadly by trumpet and trombone at normal tempo and in its normal C major. Wagner now achieves a magisterial combination of his themes, typically the main 'Mastersingers' theme in the base, an accelerated version of the 'King David' theme in the middle, and the 'Prize Song' theme up above. The result is an intense animation, ever more vivacious, to the point where the 'King David' theme comes stalking through the music again, after which the music surges higher and higher to create a point of enormous climax and exaltation, followed by more chords all hammering home C major.

The final chord of the Overture is also the first chord of an onstage chorale. The congregation at St Catherine's Church, Nuremberg are singing it, and it concludes the afternoon service on Midsummer Eve, to which the Wagner's magic carpet now spirits us. The stage setting of Act I reveals rows of pews at the back of the church. For the first time since *Lohengrin* Wagner returns to a Christian setting which colours and permeates the work. There are its song-baptisms, its references to St John, and Sachs's own paean to Luther and the reformation, which the crowd sings in homage in Act III.

The pews at the back of St. Catherine's are filled with congregation and behind them is a space for meetings. At present this is empty except for a dashing young knight, Walther von Stolzing, who is lurking and darting about surreptitiously, trying to get a better look at one of the congregation. His object is Eva Pogner, an attractive young woman, who is eye-flutteringly aware of his attentions. Snatches of what will become some of the opera's main leitmotives, familiar from the Overture, sound in the majestic pauses that come after each line of the chorale; they suggest an amorous attraction rapidly developing. Because of the conventions of the times Walther must approach Eva circuitously to ask her a pressing question. To give him a better chance, Eva twice gets rid of her maid and chaperone, Magdalena, by sending her back to the pews, first to look for her lost kerchief and then the clasp that goes with it. Walther von Stolzing keeps on prefacing his question with flowery verbiage; Eva's answer will spell life or death for him, one word will be enough; will she be so good as to tell him – , and before he can come to the point each time, Magdalena is back on the scene. Fortunately Magdalena now realises that she has left her own book behind, and while she bustles off to get it, Walther at last manages to carry out his purpose and ask Eva whether she is already bespoke, i.e. married or engaged.

Magdalena is close enough to hear the knight addressing Eva, but not to catch what he says. She matches him in the matter of florid ceremonials as she thanks him for his interest. She asks if she may tell Eva's father, Veit Pogner, master of their household, to expect him at home again later. Walther startles and offends her by bursting out that he wishes he had never set eyes on the place, evidently a reference to Eva and her presumed inaccessibility, although Wagner leaves this and other puzzles still hovering in the air. As Walther has been at the Pogners' house for a night at least and has met Eva, it is slightly curious that he has not learnt if she is single. Magdalena bridles and points out that at Nuremberg and particularly at Pogner's house, he has met nothing but kindness; what kind of gratitude is this? Eva breaks in and explains that he had not meant to offend. He simply wanted to know – can she believe it – whether she were available. Magdalena takes fright; 'Heavens alive; not so loud; we must go home; people might see us!' But Walther will not let them go without an answer and Eva points out that there is no one left to see them. Magdalena says that that only makes it worse, and is about to hurry them off when she sees her own swain, the apprentice David, appearing. He has turned up to arrange things for what follows, and now that she wants to linger herself, she starts to clarify Eva's peculiar circumstances for Walther. She is engaged, but nobody knows who the bridegroom is, not until the singing contest scheduled for the next day when some Mastersinger will win her as his prize. Walther cannot believe his ears, and he now tries to clarify things; is it really a prize-winning song that will determine the choice of her husband-to-be? Who decides on the winner? If it is the Mastersingers, then does the bride herself have no choice? Eva responds ardently that it is the bride herself who will choose and crown the winner, and that she chooses Walther or no one.

Magdalena is aghast at this avowal, such a breech of convention, but Eva presses on with her demand that Magdalena should help win the man she loves. Magdalena protests that it was only the previous day that Eva first saw him, but Eva answers that he had set her heart instantly aflame because she had long known him in his likeness to David. Magdalena, thinking of her own David, is bewildered; and his theme now begins.

Fig. 19.8 'David'

Eva explains she meant the portrait of the Old Testament David in the church, and when Magdalena takes this as referring to the picture showing him in his stately maturity, Eva again corrects her; she means the one showing the young hero going to defeat Goliath with sling and pebbles. Her words make Magdalena think fondly of her David, and he reappears on cue. Magdalena now expresses concern that he has locked them all in the church. 'No, no', says David who has no difficulty with open avowals; 'I only locked you in my heart.' In some asides she reveals that she too is seriously smitten, but she plays hard to get and asks him the meaning of all this nonsense. David remonstrates that this is not nonsense; he is setting up the arrangements and furnishings for a meeting of the Mastersingers' guild, which is holding a qualifying exam that very afternoon. Magdalena tells the knight that he is in luck with his timing as this is his chance to meet the entry requirements in the contest for Eva. She herself must now hurry Eva home. Walther wants to escort them back to Eva's father, but Magdalena tells him to stay where he is, as Eva's father, Veit Pogner, will soon be there and Walther will need Pogner's help towards becoming a Mastersinger. Her own David will meanwhile explain the rules and conditions. Walther recognises aloud that he is dealing with a new situation. He is fully committed and full of passion, but whereas his sword and military skills have hitherto been effective in gaining him whatever he wants, they count for nothing now. It is by his singing alone that he can win Eva, and his passion must therefore be the force that galvanises him into becoming an instant master.

David listens in astonishment; 'Gracious! An instant master? What a nerve!' but he is interrupted by the other apprentices demanding that he come and help them. They poke fun at him as the cobbler's apprentice who is always getting beaten and writes his verses on greasy leather. David pays no attention but suddenly sings out, 'Now begin!' Walther looks surprised and asks, 'What does that mean?' David explains that these are the words with which the *Merker* (in English 'the Marker') tells applicants to the Mastersingers' guild to begin their trial songs. Walther asks: who is the Marker? Again David cannot believe his ears; has Walther never been at a singing trial before? Is he not a poet? Is he a not a singer? Walther answers in the negative, and David suggests that at least he must have been a student or a scholar at a guild. Walther answers that even the words themselves are new to him, and David asks him how then can he ever hope to become an instant Mastersinger. Walther asks if this is such a big problem, and David calls out the name Magdalena like a talisman against disaster. Walther urges David to advise as best he can; and David answers that to become a Mastersinger in a day is out of the question. In Nuremberg the greatest master of the times is Hans Sachs, and he, David, has already been his pupil for a full year, learning how to be a shoemaker and a singer-songwriter in one.

David provides all the information that Walther needs, bringing in details of his own progress, and although Walther rather makes fun of him, David explains the format of the 'Bar'. This is the basic musical form of the Mastersingers, made up of two similar verses followed by an 'Aftersong'. All these must follow a form as set as the form of an English sonnet. Walther again makes fun of the cobbling terms which David uses, and David tries to warn Walther of the huge challenges facing him. He now gives details the different modes and styles necessary for the different sorts of subject matter; there is even a 'writing paper' and a 'hawthorn' mode, a special tone to express 'passing passion', or 'barking' or 'marjoram'. Walther is half-amused, half-appalled at his endless recital, and David points out that these are only the names of just some of the ingredients for a successful mastersong. He gives advice about voice production and melodic requirements, and he warns that any slip or mistake will result in a 'fail'. In spite of all his own great efforts, he has never yet come anywhere near success. Each new failure brings him another beating from Sachs, and whenever Magdalena is not there to comfort and succour him, he is also confined to 'solitary' and has to sing to a bread-and-water strain or go without supper altogether. Let Walther learn from this and forget this mad fantasy about becoming an instant master.

Despite interruptions from the other apprentices who taunt him as work-shy and demand that he helps them, David goes on to explain that if Walther does manage to create an original work on the lines described, then he will have earned the coveted title. The other apprentices again butt in and accuse David of laziness, and he turns round to find that they have set up the furnishings all wrong for the particular kind of assembly which the Mastersingers are holding that afternoon. This is not a 'training' assembly, which is what they have prepared, but an 'exam', a session to assess those hoping to become a master. The apprentices knuckle down and follow his instructions, rearranging things, but they get their own back by laughing at him: 'Here's a great lord of a singer, honed to perfection by sharp knocks, short rations, and hearty kicks.' David tells them that they can have their laugh, but today it will not be at his expense. There is another come to judgment. This candidate is not a scholar, a poet, or a singer, and yet he hopes in a single leap to become a master. They must therefore set things up ready for the Marker to take his stand. He turns again to Walther and asks if the mention of the Marker makes him grow pale. Many candidates fail, because the Marker marks down and rejects anyone making more than seven mistakes. For all that, he hopes that the knight will soon win the accolade of the Mastersingers, the garland of silken flowers, and he sings his good wishes to a tuneful, dancing jingle which the other apprentices take up and repeat as a jibe, this time at Walther.

Fig. 19.9 'Apprentices' Aspirations'

At that moment the door of the sacristy opens and the Mastersingers begin to appear. The apprentices scamper off to their proper places

Seven illustrations for *Götterdämmerung* (1911) by Arthur Rackham

The Norns fade into nothingness

Brünnhilde treasures Siegfried's Ring

Waltraute remonstrates over the Ring

Siegfried with the Rhinemaidens

The Rhinemaidens entreat Siegfried one last time

Brünnhilde rides into the flames

The Rhinemaidens drown Hagen and recover the Ring

Donald McIntyre as Wotan summoning the magic fire, in the centenary performance of *The Ring* at Bayreuth, 1976; director Patrice Chéreau, musical director Pierre Boulez

A Wagner Miscellany:
Seven Valkyries, Covent
Garden, 1935

A Wagner Miscellany: Berta Morena as Brünnhilde, c. 1910

A Wagner Miscellany: The Ride of the Valkyries; by Carl Emil Doepler for a magic lantern projection used in the original 1876 Bayreuth staging, whereby the Valkyries' ride was projected onto the scenery. Doepler was also responsible for the costumes of the 1876 *Ring* cycle.

A Wagner Miscellany: Hans Sachs the cobbler, Die Meistersinger Act II: as portrayed for Liebig's Fleisch-Extrakt

A Wagner Miscellany: Hans Sachs the cobbler, *Die Meistersinger* Act II: as portrayed by Hans Hotter, Bayreuth, 1956; production: Wieland Wagner, musical director André Cluytens

A Wagner Miscellany: *The Annunciation*, Marienkapelle, Würzburg. Wagner found this 'bas-relief of God the Father transmitting the embryo of the Saviour to the body of Mary by means of a blow-pipe' (which he misremembered as being in St Kilian's Cathedral) to be the height of the fatuous 'degradation into artificiality' of religious art.

A Wagner Miscellany: Raphael (1483-1520), *The Sistine Madonna*, 1513. Wagner (who knew the painting from his time in Dresden) believed that 'the painter has revealed here the inapprehensible and indefinable mystery of the religious dogmas, no longer to plodding reason, but to enraptured sight'; the complete opposite of the Würzburg *Annunciation*.

A Wagner Miscellany: Betsy de la Porte as Waltraute (*Die Walküre*, Covent Garden, 1935);
anything but an overweight harridan; the author's mother-in-law

Six Scenes from *Parsifal*; set of six collectible cards advertising Liebig's Fleisch-Extrakt 1. Amfortas tells of the prophecy of the pure fool, Act I

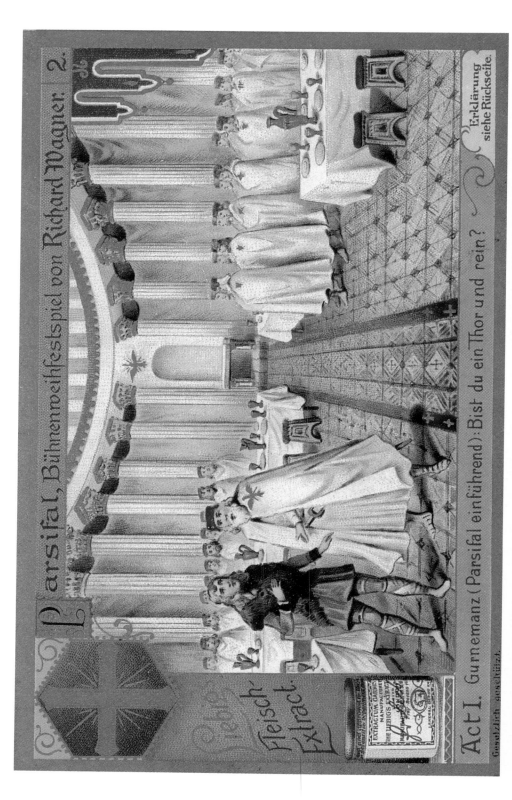

Parsifal, Bühnenweihfestspiel von Richard Wagner. 2.

Liebig Fleisch-Extract.

Act I. Gurnemanz (Parsifal einführend): Bist du ein Thor und rein?

Gesetzlich geschützt.

Erklärung siehe Rückseite.

2. Parsifal and Gurnemanz in the Grail Temple, Act I

3. Parsifal and Kundry in Klingsor's castle, Act II

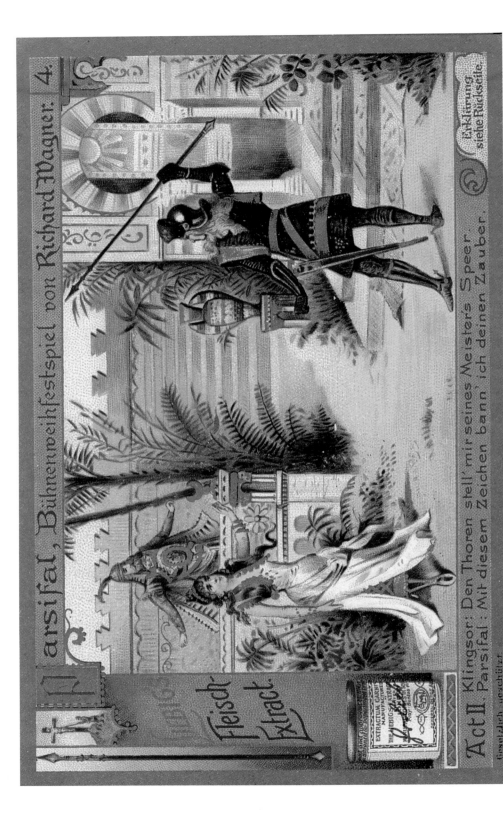

4. Parsifal takes the spear, Act II

Act III.   Gurnemanz: Mittag — Die Stund' ist da :—
Gestatte, Herr, dass dich dein Knecht geleite!   Erklärung
siehe Rückseite.

5. Parsifal robed by Gurnemanz and Kundry, Act III

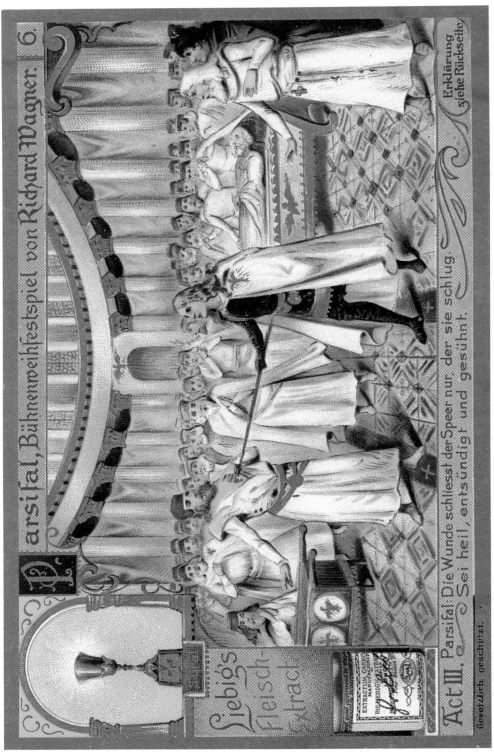

6. Parsifal heals Amfortas' wound, Act III

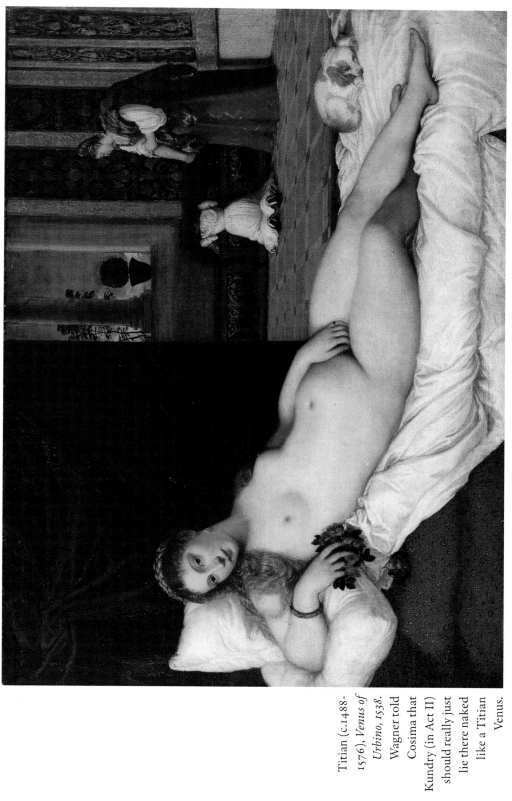

Titian (c.1488-1576), *Venus of Urbino*, 1538. Wagner told Cosima that Kundry (in Act II) should really just lie there naked like a Titian Venus.

Waltraud Meier as Kundry, Staatsoper Unter den Linden, Berlin, 1990s; production Harry Kupfer, musical director Daniel Barenboim

while the goldsmith, Veit Pogner and the town clerk, Sixtus Beckmesser
make their way gravely onto the scene.

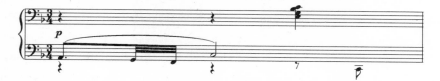

Fig. 19.10 *'Freyung* – contest'

Both men are Mastersingers of distinction, and as they arrive,
the whole tone changes, literally so, since the tonal centre for the
remainder of the act shifts from C to F. The two Mastersingers are deep
in conversation, and Pogner is assuring Beckmesser of his support.
Beckmesser soon makes it clear what the discussion is about, because
he voices his concern that if Pogner allows Eva the power to reject any
competitor, then what use is his mastery against her flibbertigibbet
ideas. Pogner retorts that if Beckmesser is really concerned about the
possibility of Eva rejecting him, then he should really assure himself
of her affections. Should he think of competing to marry her if he
is not certain of them? Beckmesser collects himself, 'Yes, yes; quite
right! But please put in a good word for me. Tell her that I am sweet-
natured and behave properly; and that you thoroughly approve of me.'
'Yes, gladly,' says Pogner, but Beckmesser had hoped for more, and
comments irritably to himself, that 'rubbish flummery' means more to
women than poetry and matters of the soul. He quickly forms a plan
to serenade Eva at night in the hope that a romantic approach will
soften her heart in his direction.

Meanwhile Pogner has seen Walther sitting among the pews and
greets him in some surprise. Walther tells him that he knew that this
singing school was where to find Pogner, and explains diplomatically
that although he had not revealed it earlier, it was purely art and
the love of art which had brought him to Nuremberg. He wants to
become a Mastersinger; so will Pogner therefore enrol him into their
fellowship. The astonished Pogner begins enthusiastically explaining

this to various other masters who are coming up and greeting him; here now is something unusual, a knight attracted to the art of the masters and wanting to join their guild. He tells Walther that the good old days must have come again when an aristocrat supports the arts like this.

At this point Beckmesser catches sight of Walther, and it is dislike at first sight. He does not suppress his exclamations which cut into Pogner's conversation, 'Who is that man? I do not like his looks! What is he doing here with his smarmy smiles and graces? Holla, Sixtus, beware of him.' Wagner does not give Beckmesser his scratchy, dyspeptic character by developing his specific motive, but through the general style of his music. Meanwhile Pogner is assuring Walther that whatever Walther desires shall be his insofar as is possible, and he would be happy to help him join the Mastersingers. Walther thanks Pogner, and asks if the way is clear for him to become a Mastersinger right now. Pogner has to answer that these things are subject to strict rules, but that there is fortunately to be an entry exam that very afternoon, and he can count on the other Mastersingers giving a willing ear to his recommendation of Walther. Beckmesser overhears them and comments disapprovingly; 'Hoho! That's fine! No flies on him!' Meanwhile the masters have now arrived, including Sachs, as Beckmesser fussily points out.

The scene that follows is Wagner at his most extraordinary. As Michael Tanner has said, Wagner succeeds in writing a committee meeting, setting it to music, and making the whole thing an absorbing experience. The proceedings begin with Fritz Kothner announcing formally that they are assembled to conduct a singing exam. Kothner is the newest qualified and is automatically the master of ceremonies. His first duty is to call the roll in order of seniority, beginning with Pogner. Nicholas Vogel alone fails to answer as he is off sick, as his apprentice explains, and Hans Sachs's answer is pre-empted by David jumping up bobbishly and pointing him out, to Sachs's annoyance. When Beckmesser's name is called, he answers unctuously: he is 'always there right next to Sachs, so that his rhymes can bloom and

wax'. Sachs laughs good-naturedly, and the roll call runs its course.
Kothner then moves on in strict order of procedure and suggests that
they should now choose the Marker to judge the candidates, but
Kunz Vogelgesang breaks in and says that they need to discuss the
festival first. Beckmesser responds with an irascible sarcasm; if they
are so pressed for time, of course he would gladly give his proper pre-
eminence to Vogelgesang. 'Not so fast, Masters', says Pogner, 'May I
first broach a matter of importance?' The other masters all rise and
nod assent to Kothner, who asks Pogner to proceed. Pogner's address
makes use of the '*Freyung*' motive, but also another that signifies
Midsummer Day – The Feast of St John the Baptist.

Fig. 19.11 'Johannistag – Midsummer Day'

'Tomorrow,' says Pogner, 'is St John's Day, a day of general rejoicing,
where everyone forgets his problems. Our singing school always
begins it with songs of praise in the church, and we go on to sing a
more secular music as we processes through the town to the meadows.
Everybody enjoys the music of the Masters, and our songs are greeted
with applause and with prizes. But now look: insofar as God has made
me a wealthy man, and insofar as each of us gives as best he can, I
thought what prize I could best give. The background to my thinking
is this, that in my journeys throughout the German territories, I was
disturbed to find how often we good burghers are run down as mean
and selfish, as obsessed with money. We seem to get no credit for
tending the arts, as we alone do, and so I want to demonstrate how we
cherish the good and the beautiful, and the power of art. This then is
my reason for what I have decided; and I hope you approve. My plan
is that whoever creates the best song, the best music at tomorrow's

public festival, will receive from me the best that I can offer, everything which I possess, along with Eva, my only child, as his bride.'

This creates an uproar of enthusiasm. 'What a man, what an offer!' the Mastersingers exclaim, along with some wry comments; some now would rather be single or give up an existing wife. Kothner in particular addresses Beckmesser as their front-line candidate, 'Come on, Bachelor; now is your chance!' Pogner breaks in with a reservation; 'I must point out that I am not presenting an object, something inanimate, and this means that my daughter too must have a say. The prize will go as the Mastersingers decide, but she will have the right of refusal.' This is confusing, and it confuses the masters. Kothner points out that it places them all in the young woman's hands; how could they in that case be free to judge? Beckmesser comments very reasonably that it might be better to let her choose a husband after her own heart and leave mastersinging out of the question. 'No, no!' says Pogner, 'Let me be clear. She can reject the man who wins her, but then she must remain unmarried; a Mastersinger is what her spouse must be, and no one else can win her, but only he.'

Sachs begins to emerge as a figure of consequence. 'You know,' he says, 'I think you go too far. The responses of a young woman's heart are different from those of our masters' art. A woman's ideas are likely to be closer to those of the public. If you want to give the girl her choice and yet still subject the matter to meaningful judgment, then let the decision go to the public, because the choices of the girl and the public will coincide better.' The Mastersingers are instantly against this; they could kiss goodbye to all their rules and standards, and it would be absurd. 'No,' says Sachs, 'please hear me out. Nobody knows the rules better than I do, or has done more to maintain standards, but it would be good once a year to submit our rules and standards to public opinion. This would prevent us becoming too esoteric and out of touch. As our aim is ultimately to bring joy to ordinary people's lives, we would do well to present our ideas for ordinary people to endorse.'

The other Mastersingers are not persuaded. Most of them have sincere objections on grounds of principle, with Kothner worried that

Sachs's proposals will dilute standards. However Beckmesser turns personal, flaring up at Sachs for the grubby doggerel which he writes for the crowds – 'ordinary people' – which has ruined standards already. Pogner gently adds his authority; what he proposes is new, and too much all at once could lead to trouble. He asks the masters simply to endorse his original plan. They agree except for Sachs, who still resists unless the girl is given a free choice. This makes Beckmesser grind his teeth with rage, while Kothner, true to form, is more concerned to tidy up points of procedure: who exactly is eligible; presumably it is only bachelors. Beckmesser asks: what about a widower; should not Kothner be including Sachs? Sachs answers, 'Eva needs a younger man than you or me!' and Beckmesser explodes: 'Than you or me; you vulgar jobsworth!'

Kothner is still trying to sort out the question of eligibility but is cut short by Pogner insisting that they are straying too far from the day's agenda which is to assess candidates for the guild. He himself is proposing one, Walther von Stolzing, a traditional German aristocrat, a knight, who steps forward affably.

Fig. 19.12 'Walther von Stolzing'

(In fact Wagner makes relatively little use of this theme in connection with Walther, colouring in his character more by turns of melody, shifts of harmony, and other means of musical expression.)

Beckmesser mutters that he thought as much; he can see through Pogner's plans; but out loud he argues ineffectively that the time is too late for this. The other masters are puzzled at Walther's unusual application but not hostile, and they reason that Pogner's recommendation is a strong point. Kothner insists that the knight must satisfy the proper conditions and pass their formal singing trial.

Pogner explains that although he wishes the knight every success, he agrees that the rules must be followed; the knight must satisfy the standards of the guild. Kothner then begins by asking whether the knight meets the first condition of being born legitimate, and Pogner cuts quickly in to avoid the row that would ensue if the knight was so much as asked, explaining that the knight is indeed the honourable scion of a venerable nobility, but its last representative. He has just come from his estates to Nuremberg with the specific intent to join the Mastersingers. Konrad Nachtigall says that Pogner's word is good enough for him, and Sachs offers further support for Walther from the guild's articles, which lay down that social position is irrelevant, and that the sole requirement is artistic quality.

Kothner accepts this and moves on: Walther needs to tell them which masters apprenticed him. Walther tells them that he learnt his musical principles from a fascinating old book which he found in his castle by Sir Walther von der Vogelweide. Sachs approves and expresses his veneration for Sir Walther, but Beckmesser asks witheringly what anyone could learn from a master so long dead. Kothner passes on and asks which school of singing Walther attended. Walther answers that after he had mastered his grounding from his ancient book, he went on to absorb all that was revealed by the voices of nature. The music of the moorlands and fells, the nature sounds of fields and forests, and the singing of birds, these had been his school. Beckmesser jeers that if finches and thrushes had schooled him, they can really expect something special, but Vogelgesang points out that in presenting his answer Walther's words have amounted to two well-turned verses. Beckmesser tries to put down Vogelgesang, which in translation means 'Birdsong'. 'You like his stuff, Master Birdsong, because he learnt his song from the birds!'

Kothner is becoming unhappy on procedural grounds. He doubts whether Walther fulfils their requirements, but Sachs retorts that what counts is quality; if the knight produces something of sufficient quality, then what does it matter who taught him? Adjusting his stance in line with Sachs, Kothner asks Walther if he can produce a song worthy of a master. Walther announces in florid and extended terms, that full as he is of both booklore and the voices of nature, he is both glad and eager to produce a mastersong that will meet their rules and requirements. In doing this he is adding a third and a final stanza to the two already sung, but its discursive quality enrages Beckmesser and puzzles the others.

Kothner tries to keep things moving, and declares that it is time to appoint the Marker, the judge, the assessor. Is the knight planning to sing on a sacred subject? Walther answers that for him, *the* sacred subject is love. Kothner says reprovingly that this comes under the heading of 'secular', which calls only for a single examiner. He therefore calls upon the official Marker, Beckmesser, to take up his post on his own. Beckmesser rises with a show of reluctance and a sigh, and says that his is a bitter task, especially today, because he knows that he is going to be busy causing distress with his marking chalk.

Fig. 19.13 'Beckmesser'

His music is a peculiar, darkened mirror-version of Walther's jaunty theme, Fig. 19.12. He tells Walther that Sixtus Beckmesser is Marker. 'Here at his post, he pursues his stringent, exacting task. He allows you seven mistakes, but if you make more than seven, then you have "unsung" yourself, and fail. And yet, so as not to put you off, the Marker sits concealed from you. May God bless your efforts today!' He has made his way into the strange booth set up for the Marker, and drawing its curtains behind him, he disappears. Next Kothner announces the requirements for a mastersong. 'It must consist of two verses which have the same rhymes and the same melody. These must be followed by an Aftersong, which has its own distinct verbal and musical patterns but are still related. So now, take your place, please, in the singer's special chair.' There must be something odd about this chair which is not evident to audiences today because Walther shudders and can only bring himself to sit on it by reminding himself that that this is his route to Eva. Kothner proclaims that the singer is correctly positioned, and Beckmesser, invisible, proclaims loudly 'Now begin!', a kind of starter's orders.

After a moment to reflect, Walther repeats his words, gloriously re-establishing the tonic F major of this whole scene, but creating consternation among the masters. Walther turns the Marker's words into the central idea of his song, which is utterly unlike the music of the guild. As a song about the spring and the goddess of spring, making urgent use of theme of Love's Crisis' or 'Spring's Command' from the Overture, but also another theme, quoted the peaceful form of its appearance in Act II but here sounding urgent and propulsive.

Fig. 19.14 'Springtime'

Walther's song opens doors to a fresh new world. The goddess of spring is a source of new beginnings; she possesses a transforming, replenishing power and a romantic aspect as well, to urgent expressions of Fig. 19.7, 'Love's Crisis'. As Walther sings this, the discouraging sound of chalk scratching away is audible from the Marker's booth along with groans of disapproval. Walther hears and gives his song a personal turn; obliquely referring to Beckmesser, it describes how the winter still lurks in the thickets trying to spoil the spring and its joys. However the words 'Now begin' have set his heart on fire, and he has answered their call and begun his glorious song of love. Beckmesser's scratchings have interrupted Walther's song more and more insistently, and he now bursts out of his booth with a loud 'Well, have you finished?' 'Why do you ask?' replies Walther. 'I've finished with the slate, that's all!' says Beckmesser.

Walther demands that he still be allowed to sing his lady's praises, but Beckmesser tells him he must sing somewhere else because he has unsung himself and failed. Beckmesser turns to the other masters, and asks them simply to look at the slate. He has never heard anything like it. Pogner tries to intervene: 'Just one word; you are overwrought!'; but Beckmesser continues in full cry; 'Anyone who wants the job can be Marker from now on, but I can prove that the knight has failed, even though it is difficult to know how to begin. His whole song was solid confusion. It broke this musical rule and muddled this principle with that. The whole thing was utter nonsense.' The other masters, including Kothner, agree that they could not make head or tail, reinforcing each other's beliefs that it was empty noise. Kothner points out that in any case the knight had broken procedure by rising from his chair. Supported by this apparent show of unanimity, Beckmesser is just about to pronounce the verdict of 'unsung and failed', when Hans Sachs breaks in calmly to say that they are by no means unanimous. He gives them all pause for thought as he tells them that although the knight's song and style were novel, he found them by no means unmeritable. 'It is a mistake to condemn something simply because it does not fit our normal rules and ideas. Perhaps this instance rather calls our rules themselves into question.' At this Beckmesser angrily pours scorn; 'You would like the bunglers of the world to be given their chances everywhere, but here at things are governed by rules and principles.' Sachs asks 'Why all such heat and feeling? You are letting emotion affect your judgment. You might judge more clearly, if you could pay the song a more disinterested attention. It all supports my belief that we must hear the knight to the end.' 'So,' rages Beckmesser, 'The masters' guild and the principles and traditions of the school mean nothing against the idiotic beliefs of Sachs!'

Sachs says that as a man devoted to the Mastersingers' traditions, he is the last person to go against their principles and rules; 'But they state categorically that the Marker must be so chosen that he can judge free from all personal animosity or favour. But when the judge himself goes after the same stakes as the candidate he is set to judge, then what does it really signify when the Marker discredits his rival?' The other masters do not like this, telling Sachs that it breaches their rules and is too personal, but then Beckmesser attacks Sachs very personally; 'It does not matter to Sachs how I go on foot. It would be better if he took more trouble over his cobbling. Since Sachs took to verse, his shoes have grown worse, and I would gladly swap all his plays and histories and his entire farrago of tasteless doggerel for a pair of decent shoes.' Sachs says there is something in this. 'I try to ensure that even the soles of donkey-drivers are marked with some worthwhile moral, and I wanted the Marker at least to enjoy the same benefits as the donkey-driver. Unfortunately I have never hitherto managed to produce anything worthy of him, but at long last I hope to find inspiration after hearing Walther's marvellous song – so far. This is one more reason why we have to hear him to the end.' 'No more,' shouts Beckmesser, 'just make an end!' and he is echoed by the other Mastersingers. Sachs also now turns personal, encouraging the knight to sing on, just to annoy Beckmesser.

What follows is a great ensemble, permeated by Fig. 19.7, 'Love's Crisis', where the individual voices are impossible to make out. Beckmesser continues with his list of Walther's faults; most of the other masters give reasons for supporting Beckmesser; Walther continues his paean in praise of spring, love and woman, while Sachs, who can somehow still hear Walther's song through the mayhem, is enraptured by it. He tries to make the other masters give it a proper hearing, telling them that it is divinely inspired. After trying repeatedly, he sees that his efforts are in vain. The apprentices, delighted at the uproar, add their jingle to the ensemble; and when Beckmesser again asks the masters for their verdict, they declare unanimously – except for Sachs – that the knight is 'unsung' and has failed.

The whole gathering disperses in confusion, and there are different ways of presenting it. One of the commonest is to show Sachs as remaining there on his own, humorously thoughtful as he gazes at the chair where Walther had sung, before he goes off with a chuckle. One of the best was Wieland Wagner's at Bayreuth in 1964, when Beckmesser and Sachs were left onstage together and it was Beckmesser who had utterly dominated the scene. Sachs sat there looking discomfited, unhappy and irascible whereas Beckmesser stood superior, triumphant and contemptuous, relishing the fact that the vulgar cobbler had been humiliated. Beckmesser was holding out his slate to Sachs with a leer, and as the curtain came down, he was laughing in open contempt. He left no doubt that he was a powerful and dangerous adversary, and that it was going to tax all Sachs's ingenuity to devise any way of dealing with him.

The pace of this act is terrific, only slackening a little at David's long recitation of the different modes and styles which candidates must make their own. Act II keeps it up, and is only equalled by *Das Rheingold* in richness of incident and character; and it complements that richness with a wealth and a felicity of musical invention that are just as remarkable. There will be an opportunity to take stock after this act before going on to the third where the pace is quite different.

Act II reveals a street corner in Nuremberg, with the street itself widening out between the two corner houses, one belonging to Sachs, the other, a grander one, to Pogner. Each has a front door opening onto the street, and near Sachs's front door there is an elder in flower. Near Pogner's there is a bench partly hidden by shrubs. It is a beautiful midsummer evening with a balmy night gradually falling, and the Prelude and opening section exploit a long recurrent pedal point which repeatedly promises to resolve in G major but never does, creating a vital expectancy. The apprentices, with David among them, fuse developments of Figs. 19.11, 'Midsummer Day (*Johannistag*)', 19.14, 'Springtime', and 19.9, the jingle for the 'Apprentices' Aspirations', with this last jingle subtly altered for Midsummer Eve, and David is in such a daydream that he does not notice Magdalena bringing him a basket of things to eat. When she catches his attention, she makes as if to offer him the basket, but first asks how it went with the knight and his trial song. David has to give her the bitter news of his failure, which makes her very agitated, and as he reaches in the basket for something to eat she smacks his hand and hurries into Pogner's house, disturbed about the outlook for Eva. The other apprentices instantly adapt their jingle to make fun of David; he has given Magdalena his heart, but she will not even give him a basket. He tells them to mind their own business, but they dance around jeering until he lashes out and starts a fight.

Sachs suddenly arrives, still out of humour, and the other apprentices vanish.

Fig. 19.15 'Sachs as a Cobbler Dissatisfied'

Sachs accuses David of always being in fights. David says that the other apprentices started it by making fun of him, but Sachs tells him not to pay them attention, to lock up and set up a light. David asks if it is time for his singing lesson, but Sachs says irascibly that David must go without because of his bad behaviour, and they go into Sachs's workshop which looks onto the street. At that moment Pogner, with Eva on his arm, comes past on the way home, and Pogner confides to Eva that he might like a word with Sachs if he is at home. Eva says she can see his light on, but now Pogner pauses uncertainly. It was Sachs who had been critical of his great plan when he hoped for his approval, Sachs who said he had gone too far; but then it was Sachs who went further than anyone and supported the knight and his song. He turns from his unsettled thoughts to Eva asking: has she nothing to say?

Eva is a self-possessed young woman and says with a meekness that is not really her style, that a well-brought-up child is seen and not heard. Pogner says what a good girl she is, and asks her tenderly to sit with him. Eva asks whether it is not too cold, but Pogner answers that it is a lovely evening, auguring well for the morrow which is of course her great day. All Nuremberg's populace, great and small, will come to admire her. They will see her as she crowns the prize-winner in the song contest and becomes the bride of the Mastersinger she has chosen to crown. Eva asks if it has to be a Mastersinger, and Pogner reassures her; that it must be a Mastersinger, but one of her own choice. 'Yes, of my choice – ' says Eva tensely, as her confusion prevents her from bringing up her real concerns. She suggests to her father that it is time to go in for formal supper. 'Why formal supper when we have no guests?' asks Pogner with mild irritation, whereupon Eva asks him anxiously whether they are not expecting the knight to join them. Pogner says absently that he hopes not because the knight has just upset him, but then he stops in his tracks, seeing Eva's anxious face with new eyes; he asks himself how could he have been such a fool not to see what was happening in front of him. Eva draws him into the house, a touching mixture of embarrassment and affection for her father. He makes his way in through the front door, muttering about the new thoughts which Eva has set whirling in his mind. Interestingly there is barely a leitmotive anywhere in this scene, but in its brief span it still presents vignettes, relationships and interactions with a subtlety that is specially moving. It conveys Eva's closeness to Pogner and their affection, but also the distances.

Magdalena darts out to ask if Pogner had told her the result. 'Not a word,' says Eva, and Magdalena has to explain, 'David said he was "unsung and failed".' 'You mean Walther,' says Eva; 'Heaven help us; what can I do? I cannot bear it; where can I get help?' 'Perhaps from Sachs,' suggests Magdalena. 'Ah yes,' says Eva, 'He loves me a lot. I'll try him.' Magdalena tells her to watch out for her father noticing her being late. She also has a secret message she must tell Eva. 'From Sir Walther?' asked Eva, brightening up, but Magdalena says no, from Beckmesser, and they go unhappily into Pogner's house. On the other side Sachs, now in his shirtsleeves, comes out with instructions for David where to put the stool and work table, before telling him to get off to bed; 'And sleep off your idiocy and get some sense by tomorrow!' David, setting Sachs's things out, mutters that so many things are puzzling; why was Magdalena so awful? Why is Sachs still working so late? 'What are you still doing here?' says Sachs suddenly. 'Sleep well, master,' says David hurriedly and disappears as Sachs responds with a gruff 'Good night'.

He is still disgruntled at the day's events, but soon the scent of the elderflower and the magic of the evening begin to work on him (and thanks to Wagner on us): Fig. 19.14, 'Springtime'. He is haunted by a leitmotive from the knight's trial song, Fig. 19.7, 'Love's Crisis' or 'Spring's Command'. He feels in the mood for writing poetry, but nothing will come to him, and he turns back to his work and starts hammering the shoes, only to break off as the magic steals over again. 'That strain, it haunts me still. I feel it, but cannot follow it. I cannot forget it, but cannot grasp it. I cannot get the measure of it, but then how could I get the measure of something so immeasurable? It did not follow the rules but it was faultless. It was all so novel, but as old as the hills. It was the behest of spring and its sweet necessity that taught the singer. He sang under its compulsion, but it was that compulsion which enabled him. The other masters may have taken against it, but Hans Sachs has absolutely taken to it.'

These thoughts put it him in a more cheerful mood as he takes up his work again. He does not notice Eva approaching shyly, until she greets him, 'Good evening, Master, still busy?' Sachs looks up with pleasure. 'Sweet Eva, still awake? Perhaps I know the reason; your new shoes?' 'You are wrong', she replies; 'I had not given them a thought, because they are so obviously perfect.' 'So you will be wearing them tomorrow when you are a bride?' says Sachs. 'How do you know that?' says Eva. 'Well, the whole town knows that much,' answers Sachs. 'I thought you knew something more,' says Eva archly; 'I mistook you, and where I thought I saw fine wax, I see there was only coarse pitch!' 'But Eva,' says Sachs mildly, 'both have their place. Wax was right for the thread of the beautiful shoes I made for you, but these need pitch to make them strong enough for a mighty figure.' 'A mighty figure?' 'Yes, a mighty master who expects to win tomorrow; yes, I am making shoes for the great Beckmesser!' Eva flares up: 'Then pile on the pitch, to glue him down and leave me be! A man like that!' 'Well he is a distinguished candidate, and a bachelor,' says Sachs, 'and there are not so many suitable candidates.'

Eva, both wheedling and genuinely tender, asks, 'Could not a widower think of it?' and Sachs, moved more than he is happy to show, answers, 'My child, he would be too old for you.' 'What do you mean too old?' she flashes back, 'What matters is art!' 'Dear Eva, you are putting me in a blue fog,' says Sachs, becoming jocular to hide his feelings. 'No, it is you who are filling me with nonsense,' she answers. 'You are so changeable; God knows whom your mind is set on now! For many a year I thought it was me!' 'That was probably because I used to hold you in my arms when you were little.' 'Just because you had no child of your own?' says Eva. 'There was a time,' answers Sachs with quiet feeling, 'when I had both a wife and children as well.' 'But your wife died and I grew up.' 'Yes, grew up and grew beautiful,' says Sachs. 'I had thought,' says Eva, 'that I might do as a child and wife in one.' 'Oh my goodness,' parries Sachs, 'a child and a wife! I could bid goodbye to most of my life. Yes, yes, I can see how you plotted it out.' Eva pouts at Sachs for making fun of her; 'You would not even care if Beckmesser and his song carried me off tomorrow.' 'If that is how it turns out, what is to stop him? It would be exactly what your father has thought up,' says Sachs with some point. 'Have not you, Master Sachs, also got a head to think with?' asks Eva irritably. 'Would I need to turn to you if I could count on my father for sound thinking?'

'You know, Eva, you are probably right about not having a head to think. It is all full of confusion over this and that. It has been a disturbing day.' Eva becomes all sympathy; 'Ah, Sachs, I wish you had mentioned that earlier. I would not have bothered you with my chatter. Was it something in the singing school that disturbed you?' 'Yes,' answers Sachs, 'It was a knight who was trying to become a Mastersinger.' 'Gracious, a knight! And did it go well?' 'Oh no, my child, there was a heated argument.' 'But how did it turn out?' 'Oh, the knight was hopeless,' says Sachs, 'ignorant and conceited, his exam piece was ghastly, and then too he was all hoity-toity; he knew it all, lording it and telling us all where we were wrong. He was Lord

Arrogance; he can go seek his fortune elsewhere!' Eva has listened in growing distress. 'Yes,' she bites back in sudden, hysterical tears, 'he will find it in warmer hearts than yours. No wonder you stink of pitch, God help us all. Why don't you just set fire to it and it might warm up your soul a bit.' She rushes off into her house, leaving Sachs to comment that he thought as much, and to wonder how he can best try and help her. Magdalena catches Eva on her way in, worried because her father has been asking for her again, and giving her a message from Beckmesser. Beckmesser has made Magdalena promise to bring Eva to the window so that he can serenade her with the competition song he plans for the morning. Eva groans, 'That is all I need! But is *he* coming?' She means the knight, and she is too self-absorbed to spare a thought for Magdalena who is now worrying about having been too hard on David. Magdalena still wants to do her best for Eva, and falls in with Eva's suggestion that Magdalena should impersonate her when Beckmesser does his serenade at her window. At that moment, Walther arrives and Eva rushes up and tells him confusedly that she knows everything, that he is the only real poet, the hero of her prize and her only friend. Walther says bitterly that she is wrong, because the masters have condemned his efforts out of hand. What hope of her is there now? Eva tries to reassure him (and herself) that she alone crowns the victor and that he is the only man that she would ever crown. Walther tells her why he believes she is wrong. Though she might decline anyone else, her father has to keep his promise that she can only choose a Mastersinger, and this leaves him no chance. At the time his hopes had enthused him and he sang like a man inspired, but although he knew his song was good it had meant nothing to these bigoted, rule-obsessed masters. All that he can do is go back home where he is master of his castle. He asks: will she go with him? And now the scene among the Mastersingers comes back to him like a hallucination, haunting him with memories of being unable to strike down their jeering and mockery and their silly grimacing faces. In his confusion he draws his sword in readiness to assault a whole contingent of masters, but the nightwatchman's horn sounds, and he cries out as if it were an attack, and yet there is nothing, only the magic of Midsummer Night, expressed in a theme played softly on muted strings.

Fig. 19.16 'Midsummer Magic'

Eva tries to calm him down. 'It is alright; there is no need to get so excited. Hide here under the linden tree just until the nightwatchman goes past.' 'But you're not leaving?' asks Walther. She does in fact slip briefly into the house as the guardian of law and order goes by singing his song of reassurance, a song that Wagner had derived from an original of the period.

Sachs, who has been watching events from his workshop, opens the door to see better, and has just time to comment that an abduction is under way, which must not be, when Eva reappears and throws herself into Walther's arms. He tells her he has it all planned; they have only to slip through a side street to be at the gates, and he has a man waiting outside with horses at the ready. But at this point a great beam of light shines up the side street from Sachs's shop, and Eva loses her nerve; and now to Eva's disgust, Beckmesser appears, having sidled up behind the nightwatchman. Beckmesser starts to tune up his lute for his serenade, but Sachs, sitting at his work table, takes up his hammer and strikes a loud bang. He then launches into a noisy song of his own, a strange, bittersweet song aimed at Eva, based on Fig. 19.15, 'Sachs as a Cobbler Dissatisfied'. It describes how Eve (Eva) was cast out of paradise for tempting Adam, but also tells how God adored her little feet, and hated seeing them hurting on the stony paths. The result was that he sent down an angel to make her a pair of shoes, and as the angel found Adam in the same state, he made some for Adam too. Eva and Walther are both puzzled at hearing Eva's name pronounced by Sachs, and they are both anxious to leave, but they now have to deal with Beckmesser as well as Sachs.

Beckmesser approaches Sachs with a show of surprise; 'Well, Well, Master, still up? So late at night?' Sachs makes out that he too is surprised; 'Why – the town clerk! Still awake? You must still be worrying about your shoes. That is why I am pressing on, so that you shall have them ready tomorrow.' Beckmesser tells him, 'Devil take the shoes. I just want quiet,' but Sachs is off again into the second verse of his song. 'Naughty Eva, it is all your doing that angels like me now have to make shoes. If only you had only left that fruit alone, I would not be working my fingers to the bone. As it is I sit with my awl and thread, making wretched shoes to earn my bread; and if I weren't an angel too, the devil could make your shoes for you!' The horns add as counterpoint the theme of Sachs's pain and resignation. Walther has gained some idea of Sachs's subtle game, and asks, 'Is he laughing at us or the Marker? Who is he aiming at?' Eva answers that Sachs has all three of them in his sights, and adds that she finds something poignant and distressing about his song; can they not simply leave? 'Yes!' says Walther, 'Even if it means using my sword!'

Eva, horrified, holds him back, and at that moment the window of her room opens, and Magdalena looks out. Beckmesser is desperate to shut Sachs up so that he can sing his serenade and approaches him unctuously; 'Dear Sachs, just one word. Do not trouble about my shoes; I had forgotten about them, but I know you as a fine judge of anything to do with the Mastersingers and I would be glad of your comments on the song I am hoping to sing tomorrow.' 'Ah no,' says Sachs. 'I never want to be the target of your criticism again. You said that since I took to verse, my shoes have grown worse, and I am not wasting any more time now on arty, Mastersingerish stuff. My sole purpose now is to make sure that you have your shoes tomorrow.' Beckmesser tries to make out that he did not really mean what he said, and that he really wants Sachs's advice on his song more than his shoes. Sachs throws back at Beckmesser his words of a few hours earlier, that Sachs' poetry was pure doggerel, and he makes ready to begin his song again. Beckmesser says that it will wake up the neighbours but Sachs says they are used to it. Beckmesser springs at Sachs and almost assaults him while he launches into an extended tirade; Sachs is a mean, spiteful, envious old man, who cannot bear to see anyone doing better than himself. Sachs (he says) envies Beckmesser his position among the Mastersingers and his importance as Marker, but he swears that Sachs shall never replace him. Sachs, who has listened quietly, tells him that if that was his song, well, it was a bit disorderly, but at least it had a certain passion. Beckmesser, beside himself, tells Sachs to go to the devil and shut up so that he can sing; Sachs tells him to sing on: it will not disturb Sachs as he works on at Beckmesser's shoes. Beckmesser says he does not want the shoes; but Sachs answers that in the morning he will tell a different story.

Then a new idea comes to him. He announces that he has just thought of the way both can carry out their plans. It is true that he would like to learn to be Marker, and if Beckmesser sings his song, he can mark it and learn from Beckmesser, no less, how best to do it. However it cannot be with a chalk and a slate as Beckmesser normally does it himself. That would not lead to any progress with Beckmesser's shoes, and so Sachs will be doing the marking with his hammer and his last. Beckmesser is now thoroughly out of countenance. He is further disorientated when it looks as though Eva, really Magdalena, is about to leave her window. In desperation he consents. 'Now begin,' Sachs calls out, issuing starter's orders in the best Marker style. Beckmesser begins a strange, plangent song to Eva, a song whose anxious strains are curiously at odds with its words; 'The glorious daylight dawning brings me pleasure today.' He sings to the strains of Fig 19.17:

Fig. 19.17 Fugue Subject

Sachs strikes with his hammer and Beckmesser starts, but continues,

'My heart takes right good courage, as well I feel it may.' Sachs strikes again and Beckmesser asks him why. Sachs tells Beckmesser that his melody has imposed false accents on the words, and in fact Beckmesser does this persistently. Beckmesser decides that the only thing to do is to keep going, but his faults and the racket of Sachs's hammering are so persistent that he soon leaves his place under Eva's window and crosses the street to round on Sachs again; the day will come, he says, when he gets his own back on the loathsome cobbler. Sachs merely tells him in good-natured tones that the Marker is still ready if only Beckmesser will continue; and Beckmesser presses on regardless. His song makes Overtures to the lady it addresses, but of the most stilted, literary kind. Sachs continues to hammer away through its glaring false accents, and Beckmesser has to sing louder and louder to make himself heard.

After a while Sachs leaps up from his stool to shout, 'Well, have you finished?' 'Why do you ask?' replies Beckmesser. 'I've finished with the shoes, that's all!' says Sachs. This is a mirror image of what Beckmesser told Walther earlier, and Sachs drives the point home by telling Beckmesser ,'I've long finished your shoes! I really call these Marker's shoes, and I have even created my poem and hammered it into the soles.'

Beckmesser can only sing on as loudly as he can, and the combination of Sachs's hammering and Beckmesser bellowing up at Eva's window does now begin to wake up the neighbours, who start to complain. The noise also wakes up David, who looks out and sees Beckmesser apparently serenading Magdalena. Paradoxically what now develops musically is a fugue, one of the strictest and most disciplined of all musical forms, and yet Wagner uses it to express a scene of mounting chaos. David imagines that Beckmesser has drawn away Magdalena's affections and that this was she was so mean with the basket earlier, and he climbs down out of his upstairs window and hurls himself at Beckmesser, laying into him viciously. The other apprentices appear, attracted by the noise, and with the senseless, youthful gusto which Wagner remembered from his own young days, they join in just for the sake of it. Some of their wiser elders appear and attempt to restrain them, but as their only reward is to be attacked, they retaliate and soon are in the thick of it themselves. Irritations long submerged well up, and the opportunity to pay off old scores incites everyone to madness. More and more normally affable neighbours join in and soon there is a scene of terrifying brutality. As the fugue rises in force and momentum, the riot becomes a phantasmagoria. Women, looking out to see what is going on, scream down at the men in the hope of bringing some sense, and when this has no effect, they start hurling down water by the bucket to try and stop them. All of a sudden everything changes. The nightwatchman's horn again sounds through the town, and Wagner with pure genius has the dulcet theme of 'Midsummer Magic' thundering out from the full orchestra, but above all on trumpets in a searing high register. Midsummer Night has a different side; and Walther rushes out with drawn sword from where he and Eva have been hiding. His plain intention is force his way through the crowd, at whatever cost in bloodshed, and elope; but Sachs has been watching from behind his front door and he is too quick for Walther. He races out, taking Walther by surprise, and hurls him through his own front door. At the same time Pogner, appearing at his own door seizes Eva, still disguised as Magdalena, and draws her back into safety. Sachs grabs David with several angry kicks and whacks from his strap which wallop him through the door after Walther. He himself follows instantly, bolting the door. The entire crowd comes to its senses, affected by the watchman's horn, and disappears as if by magic, leaving the square deserted. The tremendous energy and volume of the scene dissolves in calm and stillness as the watchman repeats his song and his horn call. The orchestra takes up the key of his song and soft, muted strings give out the theme of 'Midsummer Night', transformed now into purest enchantment. Above them a solo flute, a sound relatively unusual in Wagner, tells out a sweet, unsteady echo of the riot music. Another echo on solo bassoon, this time of Beckmesser's song to Eva, accompanies the wretched man's broken, humiliated departure as he limps away up the street. Wagner as usual draws our sympathy for any stage characters who are humiliated and defeated, whatever their faults. This leavens the humour and beauty of the conclusion with a hint of sadness before a final chord ends it all with a bang.

This is the point to take stock. Act III is Wagner's longest, almost as long as the first two acts together, and the headlong pace steadies down into something more reflective and expansive. The focus falls increasingly on Hans Sachs, but the character of Sachs is complex. Wagner told Mathilde Wesendonck in a letter that she would fall in love with Sachs, and many other people over the last 150 years have done the same. Sachs can produce an impression of being all of a piece, as he did on Ernest Newman. In *Wagner as Man and Artist* Newman summed up his view of Sachs as 'the last word in mellow and kindly middle age',[95] and thirty years later his book *Wagner Nights* showed that his view had not changed. However, it is possible to look at one of Wagner's characters through different eyes, and I am indebted to Sir Donald McIntyre for a two-hour telephone conversation on 25 February 2011 which shed quite a different light on Sachs himself and on *Die Meistersinger* as a whole. Donald McIntyre sees Sachs as a divided spirit and literally so, a man with a bipolar personality disorder. Bipolar disorder is the condition previously known as manic depression, alternating moods of exaltation with an acute sense of isolation and despair. Throughout Act I and most of Act II Sachs is all energy and action; at the outset of Act III he sinks into a trance so extreme that he has no idea of his surroundings. It is no secret that Donald McIntyre has witnessed this affliction close at hand, and he speaks with authority when he recognises bipolar tendencies in Sachs. With this understanding comes an awareness of how far Sachs evolves. There is a general tendency in many stage productions to envisage Sachs both as mellow and kindly and as fully formed from the outset, even though his character fills out. Donald McIntyre's scrutiny of text and action had provided him with a different view of a man who

95   Newman, Ernest, *Wagner as Man and Artist* (revised ed.), London, 1924, p. 317.

changes. Sachs at first demonstrates abrasive, belligerent traits, much as Wagner originally conceived for him in the 1840s. In the finished opera Sachs still comes across as tough, and in dealing with any challenge or opposition he often starts out combatively. To be sure, there is quite early on his sudden breadth and sanity at '*Halt Meister, nicht so geeilt*, (One moment, Masters, not so fast)' which causes the other masters to pause when they are all bent on rejecting Walther's trial song. This is the hidden, benign aspect of Sachs first showing itself, but Wagner still continued with him as a divided spirit. David's account of his apprenticeship reveals that Sachs's style of instruction is not benign. David is all too familiar with the 'knee-strap mode' and the 'bread-and-water strain'; Sachs evidently beats and starves his apprentice when he is not up to scratch. But Sachs changes. In Act III, as we shall see, David finds Sachs alone in his workshop, and David's first reaction is apprehension, just as it was the previous evening after Sachs had growled 'Why are you still hanging around?' David is surprised now that when Sachs emerges from his trance, he seems to have no thoughts of the brutality which experience has led David to expect. Again it is as a stirrer that Sachs tells Walther to sing on and annoy Beckmesser, and stir up conflict among the masters. It is Sachs whose Act II mockery of Beckmesser stirs up the full-scale riot. It may be an unintended consequence, but its roots are in the combative behaviour which is a characteristic.

There is certainly too a latent common sense and goodness in him, particularly towards Walther and Eva. Until Walther had arrived in Nuremberg, he had half-allowed himself to imagine that Eva might offer a chance of a fulfilling relationship with a glamorous young woman, but Walther's arrival has made him face reality. Common sense dictates that she needs a younger man. Wagner gives Sachs the insight to grasp the immense forces which draw Eva and Walther together, the '*Zwang*' as she describes it, and which Sachs sees as something he should support at every turn. Sachs grasps this not because he is a late twentieth-century psychologist who has read Shere Hite, but because Sachs, speaking for Wagner, has learnt his truths from life and from life's school of hard knocks, better in fact than his creator. Sachs has just been reminded by Eva, minxishly softening him up, that he once had a wife and children enough, but that they are all dead. That was hard knocks.

His common sense is just as plain in his conviction that specialists and experts need sometimes to refer back to the general public; otherwise their esoteric concerns can result in strange ideas of what passes for quality. This is another important truth presented by Wagner in *Die Meistersinger*. If Sachs's convictions had been allowed their head in London and the public had had their say, then Britain's capital city might have been spared many of the strange and unattractive buildings relished by experts who do not have to live anywhere near them. The National Theatre was described with some justice by Prince Charles as a clever way of letting experts build a nuclear power station in the heart of London without anyone being able to object. Other instances are ubiquitous.

Even so Sachs when we first meet him is, as Donald McIntyre had said, not so different from Walther in relying on force to get his own way. The turning point is the riot. In its outward aspects it reflects a violent episode from Wagner's young days, but it says something deeper, warning of the horrors that would come upon the citizens of Nuremberg if civilisation should fall away.[96] As Sachs recognises when he reflects on the history books which David finds him reading, the result is indeed a phantasmagoria, and the experience of the riot makes him reflect deeply on humanity, existence and absolute values. His reflections found expression in the '*Wahn* monologue' of Act III.

---

96 Poignantly *Wahn* was to fall with a vengeance upon Nuremberg at the end of the Second World War. People today are rightly disturbed at the firestorm bombing of Dresden, but the devastation of Nuremberg was far more annihilating. Dresden has at length arisen like a phoenix, but the famous mediaeval skylines of Nuremberg are gone for ever, replaced sixty years ago by a faceless modern city largely made up of box-like buildings and shopping malls; although some rare gems still survive amidst the concrete jungle.

Even more than in *Tristan und Isolde*, '*Wahn*' as Wagner recognises it has in this opera the character of Schopenhauer's '*Wille*', or will. It is blind, headlong, and beyond good and evil, the drive behind everything that changes. *Wahn* compels all living things to survive and reproduce. It can sweep over individuals, societies, and whole nations, inciting a manic and sadistic destruction, but it also supplies the energy which generates all progress. Unchecked *Wahn* is as devastating as a cyclone; but if channelled and directed, it provides the energy for development, discovery, ideas and achievements, artistic creativity. The important thing is to harness it, as Sachs recognises. He seems to be developing ideas fast, but the *Wahn* monologue is only partly about philosophical ideas. It also reveals a major shift taking place in Sachs's identity; and compassion, wisdom and resignation now surface as his foremost characteristics. The bobbish David who had previously lived in apprehension is amazed at the change. Sachs's denunciation of the very violence which he previously deployed is central to his concluding homily, and in the *Wahn* monologue he had even anticipated Jung as well as Schopenhauer in his recognition that *Wahn* is a constant throughout the ages; that as Jung might say, it will persist 'as long as man has an animal body'. From his experience of the riot, Sachs warns that *Wahn* (like libido) cannot be suppressed or eliminated from human nature. If denied it finds alternative channels of expression that are dysfunctional, pathological and devastating, but at the same time it can be assimilated, integrated and harnessed, and thus 'turned to nobler work'.

In the context of Walther's passion for Eva, *Wahn* takes the form of the drive which inspires his prize song, which will win him Eva and a new life in Nuremberg. Unfortunately Walther von Stolzing is not Wagner's most sympathetic main character. He has not a lot of personality and only a little psychology. Even David and Fritz Kothner are more richly drawn, and it is good that the singing actors who portray Walther usually bring to the role a kind of celebrity glamour that fills out his personality. Almost to the end of the opera he seems rather conceited and selfish. He has minimal insight into points of view other than his own and so no negotiating skills, no powers of persuasion. His response to a situation which does not suit him is violence; he simply draws his sword. His hallucinatory sense of being attacked by the masters while out in the street with Eva points to a mind out of balance. Later, while in hiding with Eva, Walther nearly attacks Sachs himself, 'I'll put out his light!' he says. Soon after, when Beckmesser appears, his exclamation, 'The Marker? Here, in my power!' as he draws his sword is plainly a Prelude to cutting down Beckmesser. In Act III, he accepts Sachs's help without thanks or even willingness to cooperate, and after his song has won him the prize, he behaves arrogantly and boorishly to Sachs and to the whole masters' guild. It is intriguing that Walther ended up representing one tendency in his creator, the graceless ingratitude and self-obsession, while Sachs (as he develops) represents the opposite, Wagner's quickness of sympathy, wisdom and generosity.

Then there is Beckmesser. He takes to extremes the Mastersingers' general tendency, illustrated by Fritz Kothner as well, to view the rules as the essential. For him conformity with regulations seems to be the yardstick for quality in all things. Beckmesser is rule-bound in what is often perceived as a very German way. As town clerk, he is steeped in legality and pedantry, and his Act I behaviour has revealed him as an authoritarian temperament which is the very send-up of a German, or perhaps of a Prussian. For this understanding I am indebted to Mr Timothy Philp FRCS and his wife. It was a revealing experience to go to a performance of *Die Meistersinger* at Glyndebourne with two friends of great sophistication, who had nonetheless not previously seen the work onstage. They carried no freight of prejudice, and they observed the action with fresh minds. Their preconceptions came solely from Timothy's youthful experience of surgical training in a German hospital. He had encountered surgical hierarchies German-style, and in virtue of these encounters Beckmesser struck him at once as the caricature of a very German German. For him Beckmesser pillories the German respect for rules. He is an overstated version of the German expectation that juniors should defer submissively.

He is the lampoon of a German unwillingness to revise his thinking when confronted with new information. Timothy Philp commented, 'My goodness, Wagner didn't half have it in for the Germans and the German way of doing things!' For him it seemed obvious that in Beckmesser it was the Germans that Wagner was lambasting.

From this perspective, even the common idea that Beckmesser's Act II serenade is not really German in style seems unsound. At the end of Act II Wagner supplied a fugue. It was and still is a challenge for anyone but Bach to write well in this most exacting of forms, and although fugue did not originate in Germany, it came to be viewed as a form that is particularly German. This was a view exemplified in Sir Thomas Beecham's famous dismissal of J.S. Bach; 'too much counterpoint, and worse, *Protestant* counterpoint,' and fugue was the apotheosis of Protestant counterpoint and a style of music that is very German. The subject, the main tune, of any fugue has to meet the strict rules for its development, and in Beckmesser's serenade Wagner carefully crafted a tune that could became the basis for an excellent fugue, the riot fugue.

The German-ness of Beckmesser's theme (Fig. 19.17, the fugue subject) becomes explicit when it is taken up as an actual fugue by the Nuremberg populace and sung by the whole of Wagner's appealingly German Nuremberg.

Pogner and his decision to marry off Eva to the winner of a song contest both seem like strange leftovers from Wagner's original idea of a opera-farce, sitting strangely in a work where the etching out of real characters and their motives is so delicate and refined. However there are even now cultures where women are bartered off by their fathers like cattle, and it is as well to bear in mind that this was the situation in European society until quite recently. It was just not just among the European royals and aristocrats that women were married for reasons which had nothing to do with personal inclination. A familiar middle-class example is conveniently provided by none other than J.S. Bach. He was trying to succeed Buxtehude in Lübeck but lost interest when he discovered that part of the deal for the successful applicant was that he would have to marry his predecessor's daughter.[97] In the sixteenth century Pogner's idea was not far-fetched, in spite of its intolerably uncertain consequences for Eva, as we perceive them today. What woman could be glad if the choice of the man with whom she will have to share her life and her person should turn on a singing contest? Fifty years ago, that great artist Kurt Böhme helped Wagner out by successfully presenting Pogner as a man of some seniority and very real authority, but also a man with hints of senility, a man who might just do something as dotty as make his daughter the prize in a competition for singer-songwriters.

Act III begins with the Prelude that goes to the heart of Sachs's identity. It begins with the theme which had first came blaring out painfully on the horns during Sachs's song about being condemned to cobble shoes everlastingly for Eva.

Fig. 19.18 'Sachs's Pained Resignation'

It constantly recurs during Act III as a reminder that Sachs is still haunted; however wisely he works at accepting what he is powerless to change, he has not readily achieved serenity. This music has a dark and withdrawn colouring. It is an unharmonised, sombre reflection of Sachs's mood as he surveys the events of the previous evening. It reflects his feelings as the thinker who gazes unflinching at the world, at the meaninglessness of human brutality and its frightful consequences: the Schopenhauer in Sachs. But Sachs, as the music soon tells us, does not conceive that there is nothing else to life, because the music broadens out into a chorale scored in the glowing sonority of horns and trombones. Later this chorale will become the music for a setting of the historical Sachs's poem which Wagner imported into the opera.

97   Boyd, Malcolm, *Bach*, London, 1983, p. 22.

Significantly it is about Luther and the Reformation, the awakening of the spirit and the triumph of reason over irrational forces. When the strings again resume their sober theme, its tone is more reflective and less gloomy, and it soon soars aloft into the highest registers of the strings and wind, where it is tinged with aspiration as well. This leads to a resumption of the chorale for brass in a lower key than before, as though the affirmation was itself in a lower key. It is in any case cut short by the opening motive in its starkest form, darkly harmonised on massed strings as Sachs again gazes into the abyss. The moment passes, and a sense of resignation, more Schopenhauer, steals gently across the music, a calm acquiescence as the act begins. Sachs goes on living on the world as it is. He is now sitting silent and immobile in his workshop and David nervously tiptoes in, holding a basket of food, ribbons and bunting. Initially he is unaware of Sachs's presence.

Sachs is holding a great book and suddenly rustles a page. This brings David up short, 'Gosh, master, here!' He attempts to mollify Sachs, whom he imagines as angry with him for the previous evening, and he starts telling Sachs that he has already been round and delivered Beckmesser's shoes. He comments to himself that Sachs is not even willing to recognise him; from past experience, when Sachs is too angry to acknowledge him it means big trouble. He starts to gabble off a stream of excuses and explanations, slightly incoherent, about his Magdalena; 'She is usually so loving and tender, but then last night she was so off with me, and when I found that blasted fellow singing up at her for all the world to hear, I saw red, and so, yes, I did go for him. But master, don't be cross; Lena has explained it all now and it has turned out for the best! We are closer than ever, and just look at all the flowers and ribbons she has put for me in this basket.' Sachs still says nothing, and David begs him, 'Master, will you not say just one word?'

Sachs suddenly closes his book with a snap, and David, startled by the noise, stumbles, which brings Sachs at last from his reverie. He comments gently on the basket of finery, and asks vaguely how it came to be there. David, puzzled, reminds him that today is the big day, when everyone looks as festive as possible, and Sachs, still perhaps affected by lost hopes and imaginings of Eva asks vaguely if it is 'wedding day', and then comments abruptly that the previous evening had been a stag party. David, thinking that the storm is going to break, begs,

> *Forgive me master, as I pray,*
> *Today is now Midsummer Day.*

'Midsummer Day?' Sachs repeats. 'Well then, sing me your new verses.' David, relieved, launches into his song, but gets muddled and sings it to the strain of Beckmesser's serenade. Sachs startled, brings him up short, and David sings better, about a 'woman who travelled all the way from Nuremberg to the Jordan to see and hear John the Baptist. While there she had her son christened by him, giving him the Baptist's name,' i.e. Johannes. 'She then came home glowing with pride, but found that in her native land, the name Johannes was changed to Hans.' David is suddenly struck by the name he has just spoken. 'Hans! Hans! Dear master, it is your name day!' Name days are celebrated almost more than birthdays in Germany, and with the quick sympathy that makes David so appealing, he berates himself for overlooking Sachs's special day, and offers him everything in the basket, 'flowers and ribbons, and – what else have I got; ah look, try this pastry or this sausage!' Sachs tells him David will need the decorations himself, because Sachs wants him to look good and act as his herald on the festival meadow, though David in the end does no heralding. David says he would prefer to be Sachs's best man, and tells Sachs he really should get married again. 'So would you like a woman bossing and ordering every one around?' asks Sachs humorously, to which David answers that it would certainly make the place more respectable. And, he says, if Sachs were to sing, Beckmesser would not stand a chance; that is the talk of the town. 'You could be right,' admits Sachs; 'But now go and get dressed in your best clothes, and see that you do not disturb the knight.' As David leaves he comments to himself that though Sachs's kindness had surfaced often enough, he had never known him quite like this; it has made him quite forget being belted by Sachs and his strap. He senses some fundamental change, but does not stay to hear Sachs expressing the change.

Sachs does it in the monologue which is the heart of the work. It is really a stream of consciousness, and therefore not entirely orderly or consistent. There are also times where the thoughts Wagner gave Sachs seem too complex and compressed for a simple translation to do them justice, and at these points I have attempted a paraphrase. '*Wahn. Wahn!*' says Sachs; 'Everywhere *Wahn*! Wherever I searched in local histories or accounts of the world I have tried to make out what are its origins and its causes, why men torment and injure themselves in mindless fury. Nobody is ever the better. *Wahn* creates the situation where the hunted imagines himself the hunter. He does not hear the scream of pain – that is his own – as he tears the flesh – that is his own; instead he imagines that he is the one to gain! How can anyone make sense of it? It is always just the same, this same, age-old *Wahn*. Nothing of importance can ever happen without it, but it also mars all that we do and wrecks our best efforts. At times it seems laid to rest, but it only slumbers and is regathering its strength, and when it awakens – well, who can resist it then? And who would have thought these things would be possible here, that they should be visited upon my beloved Nuremberg? Here lies this lovely town, at peace with itself in the very heart of Germany, full of kindly, hardworking people; but then what happens? To check the foibles and follies of a youthful passion, a cobbler in his workshop tries to grasp the threads of *Wahn*, but when he pulls at them, he soon finds he has unwittingly tugged at the only ties holding back *Wahn* itself. He has unleashed it among his neighbours and friends, and they soon rise up. All normal restraints break down, as *Wahn* enters man, woman, and child and impels them to rush into the fray. They misguidedly try to extinguish violence through violence.' The music here rises up to recall the most aggressive sections of the riot fugue, but breaks off abruptly for Sachs's 'God knows how that could be!' He pauses reflectively, as the music transforms into a recollection of the 'Midsummer Magic' motive. 'Did some imp cast his strangest spell? A glow-worm could not find his mate; and he induced that mindless hate! It was the elder that did it – Midsummer Eve! But now there comes Midsummer Day. Let's see what good Hans Sachs can weave, to shape that *Wahn* as best he can, so that it serves a nobler aim. Yes, if *Wahn* is in the midst of us, even right here in lovely Nuremberg, then it must be harnessed and set to work. Nothing worthwhile happens without it; for everything that succeeds needs some *Wahn*-energy to drive it to success.'

His recollections have completed the transformation of Sachs begun by his experience of the riot. He has talked himself through a process of personal integration that mirrors his acceptance of the world and its *Wahn*. If *Wahn* expresses itself in Sachs's own will to power, he has worked his way to absorbing it towards a state of wholeness and integration. He has accepted the awful possibilities and the grim realities of life, its full ghastliness as Schopenhauer discerned it. He has assimilated it along with his own shadow side, and he has resolved his own bipolar tendencies. He is now far more like the centred, balanced source of the wisdom in thought and deed, which is often if wrongly seen as Sachs's permanent, infallible characteristic. Sachs has grown, and is more resigned and more serene. It is not that life's ordeals have ceased, because the remainder of the action is going to throw huge and painful challenges at him, but his disunities are sufficiently resolved for him to stand firm as he is. There may be heartbreak, but there is no breaking now of Sachs himself. Wagner would not have formulated the matter in these terms, which make use of ideas and language which were not yet available, but his uncanny, prescient insights led him to an instinctive understanding so advanced that ordinary mortals are still pressed to keep up with him.

Walther now appears and Sachs enquires after his welfare in the friendliest terms. Walther tells him he slept shortly but very soundly, and that his sleep brought him a wonderful dream. Sachs asks him to describe it, and when Walther says that pinning it down in words would destroy the magic, Sachs tells him two things, that this is exactly what the poet's function is, to express the inexpressible, and that the imaginary experience of dreams yields the deepest truths that mankind can ever know. The whole function of poetry is to put into words the profound truths revealed in dreams. And this particular dream might also become the means for his joining the Mastersingers. Walther is still upset over the events at St. Catherine's church, and says that there is not much hope of him doing that now, but Sachs jollies him along by telling him that things are not really so bad. 'If they had been, I would have been off with you lovers in your flight last night, instead of putting a stop to it. But do not be quite so hard on the Masters. They are actually good men, people with standards and honour, even though they can get things wrong as much as anyone else. Yes, they tend to see everything their own way; their method of doing things is the only one; but that is a very ordinary human failing. Remember that Pogner in particular has made an incredibly generous offer, and it is not unreasonable for the man who gives so much to want some say over the consequences of his gift. As a matter of fact,' and here Sachs turns mock-jocular, 'they have good reason to be concerned about songs like yours, because songs so full of fire might well stir up their daughters into foolish adventures.' Sachs is taking a dig at Walther here. 'However it takes other words and other strains to praise the loving and honourable state of marriage.'

It is now Walther's turn to take a dig at Sachs, and he says that he understands exactly; he heard all those loving and honourable strains bashing out in the streets the last night. Sachs cuts him short. He himself had bashed out time to those selfsame strains, but let that be. Briefly, Walther must turn his all efforts to devising a mastersong. Walther cannot understand why there has to be all this effort and devising; is not nature and natural beauty enough for a mastersong? Sachs explains that in the springtime of life, nature is enough inspire a beautiful result, but spring comes to an end, and life passes on to autumn and winter. Marriage admittedly confers many blessings, but with it come plenty of challenges, the bringing up of children, the dealings of business, contentions and conflicts. This later period of life is when the man who can still create beauty from it all really deserves to be hailed as a master.

Walther is only half listening, but he has taken in Sachs's words about the blessings of marriage. He affirms that his love for Eva has an honourable conclusion as its object (and not, he implies, the elopement of the previous evening). In that case, says Sachs, the best thing is to make use of the Mastersingers' rules to channel your vision into a mastersong. Walther asks him who created these rules, that they should have such an elevated status. Sachs's answer goes straight to the heart of Wagner's beliefs, or one of them, about what art, his art, should be. 'The rules were created by old masters who were worn out with the pains of living and the cares of the world. They determined to create an image, a representation of love, and of all the hopes and promises that are part of being young, with the object of keeping these things pure and unsullied as an ideal.' Walther is unimpressed, and asks what is the point of an image once the reality of youth is over. Sachs answers that the image keeps these things burning and alive, but he is eager to move Walther onwards to the pressing essential, which is to create a prize song. Sachs will teach him the time-honoured forms, and Walther will fill them out with something that is new and inspired. Walther must recall his dream, his inspiration, and then deploy all the poet's art to give it a worthy expression. Sachs takes pen, ink and paper and tells Walther, 'Create your own rules, and then follow them.' With these words, Wagner has made Sachs step out of the world of the Mastersingers and its heritage of rules and regulations, and express the mind of Wagner himself. Sachs is telling Walther to do exactly what Wagner had done in *The Ring*, create his own rules (and language), and then follow them. Fortunately for Walther, he does not do as Sachs tells him, which would cut no ice whatever with the guild in the contest for Eva, but he follows the rules of the Mastersingers as he learnt them the previous afternoon.

Surprisingly Walther's song suggests that he might just have strayed out through the centuries from Tannhäuser's Wartburg. The song is full of the same rarefied conceits and efflorences as were deployed by the knights of Thuringia. Under Sachs's guidance, Walther sings two sections in this Wartburg vein about his morning vision. These sections have identical melodies and metrical forms, and Sachs tells him to follow it with a third section, an Aftersong, which is similar to the first two but not identical. This symbolises a child born to two well-matched parents, or so Sachs says, and this is the section which brings in Fig. 19.6 from the Overture, the 'Prize Song' Motive. The song does not begin with it, but it is the music which Wagner always uses to refer to the prize song, not its opening phrases. Sachs now coaxes Walther into creating a second verse, a mirror image of the first, this time about the evening. It too has a fountain like Wolfram von Eschenbach's 'miraculous fountain that revives the heart' in *Tannhäuser*, though it is unlikely that Walther would follow Wolfram and 'only worship from afar'. Sachs now asks him for a third verse to reveal the meaning of the first two. Walther gracelessly refuses; he has had enough of all this talk. Wagner seems to have described a certain kind of aristocrat very well; he had met examples at Dresden and Munich. Walther seems to think he should take what he wants, and that everybody owes it to him. Sachs merely expresses the hope that the third verse will come on its own at the right time, and gives Walther the news that his manservant has already been home for his wedding attire, and it is now ready and waiting for him. They both leave to dress, ready for the day's great events.

Beckmesser now appears. Wagner seems now to have forgotten the dramatic veracity of the formidable figure in Act I, the town's leading lawyer and a man of standing with his colleagues. He has degenerated into a buffoon, a clown, and *Die Meistersinger* loses something as a result, a degree of balance. Beckmesser is now such a sad figure that his defeat seems predestined and pathetic, and his nemesis too harsh. After he comes in, music from the end of Act II is heard in comic form as he performs an elaborate mime. He limps and hobbles about, rubbing his back and wincing when he tries to sit down. He hallucinates that he is pursued from all sides, and swivels between anger and despair. Finally he notices the paper covered with Sachs's handwriting, reads it, jumps to conclusions and breaks into a fury. 'A Song for Eva, by Sachs! Is it true? Now it all becomes clear!' At that moment, he hears Sachs returning, and quickly hides the paper in his clothes. Sachs, dressed for the festival, pauses when he finds Beckmesser, and tells him that he hopes he has not found anything wrong with his shoes. 'Devil take them,' answers Beckmesser; 'I have never knew such thin soles as you have hammered for these. They make me feel every pebble.' Sachs answers that it was only marking Beckmesser's faults that make them so thin, not an explanation that is likely entirely to ingratiate him to Beckmesser, who has had enough of his cleverness. 'Believe me, Sachs, I know what are up to. Your mean trick last night is something that will come back to punish you. I know how you stirred up the neighbours and got them into a fight, so that that it would draw me in to disaster, and get me out of the way.'

Sachs is still no saint, and he is now at his most disingenuous. He tells Beckmesser breezily that it was a stag night, when everyone celebrates his forthcoming marriage; the cheerier the stag night, the better the wedding. This is the last straw for Beckmesser who launches into a rant which verges on incoherence. 'I know all your venomous cunning. The girl who was predestined for me and was even born for my sake – you, you disgrace to all widowers! – you are after her. You set your sights on Pogner's rich inheritance; and you began your plotting with all that rubbish you were telling us in the singing school yesterday. You set out to turn the girl's head with it, so that she would choose you. Then your hammering ruined my serenade, and finally you stirred up gangs to beat me up. You also made a fool of me in front of the young woman – you really meant to kill me – but I got away – I shall pay you back. Even though you have injured me, my own style of hammer blows will beat you down yet.'

Sachs turns serious and he warns Beckmesser that he is in a bad state of *Wahn*-delusion, a delusion produced by jealousy. He tells Beckmesser that he does not have it in mind to try and win Eva's hand. Beckmesser tells Sachs that he is a bare-faced liar. Sachs asks him what on earth he means; Sachs's affairs are his own, but Beckmesser's

weird idea that Sachs is competing for Eva is pure *Wahn*. Beckmesser
asks Sachs what if he had proof positive of Sachs's intentions. Sachs
immediately takes in what must have happened, and not seeing his
new written text where he left it, he turns to Beckmesser; 'The poem;
I left it here. You took it then?' Beckmesser produces the poem, and
asks sardonically if this is Sachs's writing, so fresh. Sachs, equally
sardonic, says yes, the ink is still wet. Perhaps, says Beckmesser even
more sardonic, it was a song with a religious intention, and Sachs
answers that anyone who thought that would be seriously misguided.
'So then?' says Beckmesser. 'So what?' answers Sachs. 'So that you in
all sincerity are the most consummate of rogues and liars!' 'That is as
may be,' says Sachs, 'but even so, it was never known that I took other
people's things from their tables! But so that no one should think
ill of you – you may have the song.' Beckmesser cannot believe his
ears. 'Good heavens, a song by Sachs!' Half elated, he still haunted by
suspicions; has Sachs learnt it by heart? Sachs reassures him and tells
him he can have the song to use as he likes, even sing it himself, but
warning him of its serious difficulties. Beckmesser makes light of the
difficulties, and says that a song by Sachs is really something. It is all
up with his own song from the previous evening, and he is in no fit
state now to create another himself. Without a song he would have
to give up, but Sachs is making everything come right. This present
from Sachs has made peace between them. Beckmesser suddenly
recoils; or is this perhaps another trap? After all it was only yesterday
that Sachs had been his enemy. Sachs retorts that he had taken the
trouble to sit up late over Beckmesser's shoes. Was that the act of
an enemy? Beckmesser now shows that his wits must be very badly
affected by *Wahn* as a mad driving force, because he instantly accepts
this unconvincing argument. He simply asks for an undertaking that
Sachs will never lay claim to the song if he is successful with it. Sachs
swears with all due formality never to tell anyone that this song is
by him, and Beckmesser is elated; there is nothing else for him to
worry about. Sachs now reveals his good side as he again tries to warn
Beckmesser against the song. It is very difficult, and Beckmesser will

find it hard to choose the right melodies and harmonies for its words as set down in the masters' rules. Beckmesser proudly overrules him; 'My dear Sachs, you are a very good poet, but when it comes to the right kind of melodies and harmonies, let me remind you how they say, "Beckmesser; none is better!" Now I must be off to learn the song. I misread your intentions over the knight von Stolzing. We are better off without the likes of him. You and I will soon meet again, but thank you meanwhile. I will buy everything you have written. You should be our marker, but only do it with chalk; no more hammer blows. Yes, Marker; Marker Hans Sachs! So that Nuremberg should cobblerishly blossom and flourish!' The confusion of his words is matched by his actions. He somehow limps off at the double, only to return in the belief that he has left the song behind. After scouring the table for it, he finds it in his hand. He embraces Sachs and hurriedly stumbles off, while Sachs looks after him pensively. 'I never met any man,' he says, not unkindly, 'who was so full of badness that it held out for very long. The hour of weakness soon comes to everyone, the critical turning point after which he comes to see reason. It leads him on to better things. And the fact that Beckmesser took the song will help my plan along. Ah here is Eva,' as she comes in from the street. 'I wondered where she was.'

She is dressed in dazzling white, but her expression is distinctly muted and her face is pale. Sachs greets her tenderly; 'How splendid, how proud and elegant you look today. You will make them all envious, both young and old alike, when you look so beautiful.' She tells him that things are nothing like so good, because her shoe is too tight. Sachs says it is a naughty shoe to hurt her, but that she should really have tried it on earlier. Eva replies that her faith in Sachs was too great, and he says kindly that he is sure he can soon put the trouble right if she tells him where it pinches. Eva's description is confusing. As soon as she stands up she says it starts to slip, and then when she wants to walk, it stays put where it is. Sachs asks her to put her foot up on the stool, and kneels in front of her to feel, but he cannot find where the trouble is. 'Can't you see; it's too broad,' she says. 'Child,' says Sachs, 'that's simply vanity; the shoe fits perfectly.' Eva: 'Just what I said. That is why pinches my toes.' Sachs: 'Here left?' Eva: 'No, right.' Sachs: 'Here at the heel?' Eva: 'No, more at the instep.' Sachs: 'Really? That place as well?' Eva: 'Oh Master! Do you know better than I where it pinches?' Sachs: I'm simply puzzled if it is too wide, why it pinches you so.'

At this moment, Walther appears, if not quite a knight in shining armour, then very much a matinee idol in his knightly apparel, and before she can stop herself, Eva cries out. The young pair stand rooted to the spot, locked in mutual contemplation, and Sachs who has instantly taken everything in, draws off Eva's shoe and takes it to his workbench where he starts to tinker with it. He soon tells Eva that he has found the trouble and can soon put it right, but launches into a rebarbative, irascible reprise of his cobbling song from the previous evening as cover for unbearable emotions; 'Just blasted cobbling, that's what I do, and it's all that I'm ever fated to do; by night and by day, there is never an end. So listen, Eva, what I now have in mind. My best way forward is still to compete for you. At least a success there would bring me some respect as a poet. Aren't you listening? Come on; say something. After all, it was you who put the idea in my head. Oh well; I see what your silence is saying; "You stick to your shoes."' He collects himself as he realises that the rapt suspense between the pair provides an opportunity to further his hopes for them, and however great his own loss may be, he tells Walther how good it would be now to hear the third verse of his song. Walther obliges, continuing in the same rarefied vein as before, and it holds Sachs and Eva both spellbound. At the end Sachs kneels to put Eva's shoe back on her foot, and glancing up just before he begins to rise, he looks at her full in the face. At this radiant vision, he is suddenly overcome with an unbearable sense of loss, and hides his face in his hands. He collects himself quickly as he stands up and says that that now that mastersongs are being sung, he can finish his labour on her shoe, because he thinks now that it will fit.

At this Eva bursts into tears, and collapses forward onto Sachs, who takes her in his arms to prevent her from falling. She turns it into an embrace, but Sachs extracts himself and flings her arms round Walther instead. He takes up his cobbling song again, and again curses his occupation. His life as a cobbler is nothing but complaints, 'This flaps, this chaps; it nips or grips, and if the cobbler is a widower as well, people take him for an idiot. Young girls expect him to listen to their sob stories when things go wrong with their young men. Whether he understands them or whether he does not; whether he says yes, whether he says no; nothing makes any difference. And if he smells of pitch,' (a special dig at Eva over the previous evening) 'they tell him he is stupid, a rascal, above his station. And the worst thing of all is about that apprentice of mine. He has lost all respect, and Lena has done for any sense in him; she just has him licking out her pots and plates all day. And where the devil is he hiding away now, at this moment?'

At this Eva again turns to Sachs in a flood of affection, and pours out her heart with some depth of understanding. 'Oh Sachs, my friend, my darling man, how can I ever repay your goodness? What would I be without you and your love? Every good thing that I am and have I owe to you, and so, dear Master, don't blame me now. You set me on the right path and if I had any choice, I would choose you alone for my husband and give the prize to you. But now I have been taken over by a power which condemns me to an unimagined torment, and if I were to be married now, I could have no choice. This power has an irresistible force over me. I am powerless in its grip, and you yourself, dear Master, would feel intimidated in the face of it.'

What Eva is describing is barely rational, but she tells it as it is. Wagner meanwhile transforms his yearning for Mathilde Wesendonck and his enforced renunciation into Sachs's willing generosity of spirit and his great-hearted understanding of Eva's thoughts and feelings. Of course Sachs does not blame her. He tells her he knows a sad tale of Tristan and Isolde (which was certainly true of the historical Sachs, as he had written a play on the subject). Wagner's Sachs is wise enough, he tells Eva, not to want to share King Mark's destiny. It was time to find her the right man; otherwise the situation might have run away with him. At this point Magdalena appears, festively dressed, and he shouts for David again. When David joins them, Sachs tells them all that they are gathered to witness the christening of the mastersong newly created by Walther. They need David to act as a witness at the ceremony, and as no apprentice is legally allowed to be a witness and as David has been progressing really well, Sachs will now make him a journeyman. He tells David to kneel, and boxes him on the ear, hitting him hard. It takes no great subtlety of mind to recognise the violence as a displaced expression of his violent turmoil over the loss to which he is resigning himself. He pronounces the song's name as part of the christening; it is to be called 'The Blessed Morning-Dream-Telling-Song', a big mouthful even by Wagner's standards and his habit of piling up words and agglomerating them together.

His pronouncement leads to the quintet which is not only a high-water mark of the opera, but an incomparable operatic ensemble. Eva has forgotten all about unimagined torments as she hails the day of her joy. David and Magdalena are at one in their own elation, barely able to believe the happy prospect of their being so soon married, as is possible now that David is a journeyman, and even Walther reveals unexpected depths. Many of the words are lost in the music, and those which matter most are from Sachs, revealing the conflict between his wish for Eva's happiness and his sense of loss, but they are all submerged in the ensemble. At the end he collects himself and shepherds the others off to the festival meadow, telling Walther to be of good courage. The scene changes to the festival meadow itself where the various guilds are processing to their positions and celebrating their achievements, first the cobblers, then the tailors with their story of a tailor who sewed himself into a goatskin and capered around the walls, terrifying a besieging army into retreating. Then come the bakers, and now a boatload of pretty girls land from the river. They are seized by the apprentices who start to dance with them. David is onstage, and his response is a reflection of conflicting attitudes. He admonishes the apprentices disapprovingly for a simple pleasure in which he has no part, but when nobody takes any notice, he stops moralising and joins in. The others make fun of him, and tell him that Magdalena is watching him. The music which Wagner has created for the dance seems to have been the paradigm for the exquisite 'menuets' of Mahler's Second and Third Symphonies, even to the extent of Mahler's countersubjects for cellos.

A distant announcement that the Mastersingers are nearly there heralds the arrival of their special guild, and their procession brings back the music of the Overture, fortified now by a contingent of trumpets onstage. When all are assembled, the apprentices, now prim and well drilled, admonish the crowds to listen quietly for an announcement, but when they see that it is Hans Sachs who is to address them, they begin a name-day greeting long planned. They sing to Sachs his own hymn to the Reformation, using music from the Act III Prelude, but at the end it dissolves into a welter of acclaim. Sachs is plainly overwhelmed, and says in a voice choked with emotion that he can barely cope. He soon masters the situation and explains the day's plans and the reasoning behind the idea of a singing contest with Eva as the prize. Pogner, very apprehensive now, seeks and gains Sachs's reassurance, and Beckmesser seeks it as well, because he cannot see how on earth to set the new poem to music.

Sachs tells him that he is under no compulsion to use it, but Beckmesser persists, saying that he counts on the obvious popularity of Sachs and his fashionable style (not seen as doggerel now) to work to his advantage. Perhaps Wagner made a mistake in making Beckmesser such a clown and stacking up everything so far against him, above all the hostility of the entire crowd. Wagner even has the wretched Beckmesser stumbling on the mound and demanding that it be firmed up. He has the apprentices laughing at Beckmesser, and although some of the crowd insist that he deserves some respect as a master and the town clerk, the prevailing impression from the crowd is of jeering and disparagement. The musical introduction to his song on his lute is pathetic all senses, and his opening words garble those in Walther's poem.

> Morning I shone in a rosy shine,
> The air goes quickly full of blood and scent.

The same kind of thing happens throughout Beckmesser's attempt, which is punctuated by heckling and threats from the crowd, indicating that *Wahn* as a lynch-mob mentality is still lurking there under the surface. By the time he finishes he has unsung himself and become a laughing stock but nothing worse. As he flees the scene he falls into a sudden fury and denounces Sachs as the real author of this dreadful song; they should all blame him. This confuses and worries the crowds and the other Mastersingers turn to Sachs for an explanation. He tells them that Beckmesser is mistaken, and that he, Sachs, could never have created anything so fine, which makes them all laugh; this is Sachs's little joke; but he insists. The reason why the song sounded so bad was that Beckmesser sang it wrong. However he, Sachs, has been accused and should be allowed a witness in his defence. The crowd lets him call upon Walther, who makes his way forward to a general approval. Before the other masters can recover from Sachs's manoeuvring, Sachs has Walther singing the Prize Song, subtly altered and curtailed to avoid an exact repetition within a single act. It is of course a tumultuous success, grabbing everyone's imagination and sweeping them along. Sachs seizes his opportunity and gets the crowd to reaffirm its enthusiasm, leaving the Mastersingers no alternative but to call upon Pogner to appoint Walther and welcome him as a Mastersinger. But when Pogner tries to place the chain of office on Walther's shoulders, Walther shies away impetuously, and tells them with a meaning glance at Eva that he can be happy without becoming a Mastersinger. This creates total consternation and reduces Eva to tears, whereupon Sachs rounds upon Walther with all the force of his own inner *Wahn*. 'Don't you run down the masters to me!' he says in tones of unopposable vehemence; 'Give them full credit for their art. As for you, it is not your ancestors, your castle, your power or your strength at arms, nor your spear and sword, that have won you your life's happiness; it is the fact that you are a poet that the people recognise.' Walther has just created something which transforms other people's lives instead of destroying them as his raw, unprocessed *Wahn* and his sword would do. As already explained Sachs's monologue has been wilfully misinterpreted but his emphasis is on non-material values. He accepts that the Germans may not have been up to much at matters military, and that the German lands may soon fall under foreign domination (as they often did over the centuries), but he asserts that the essential liberal qualities of the German spirit can still live on because they are enshrined, nurtured and protected in German art, as epitomised by the Mastersingers.

Walther to his credit is persuaded, and accepts the insignia, while Eva, the crowd, and the other Mastersingers all recapture the mood of happiness and celebration but with that extra added edge, because it all so nearly seemed to hang in the balance. The already rich conclusion has been further enriched by a number of penetrating productions. Hans Hartleb's 1980s revival at Covent Garden showed a disconsolate Beckmesser creeping back to an corner of the stage, but then had Sachs going over to embrace him warmly back into the fold, his status restored, to his own obvious surprise and everyone else's delight. Sir Geraint Evans, the Beckmesser of this production and the leading exponent of his generation, was so taken with this addition that he persuaded producers to adopt it all over the world, wherever he played the role. On the other hand, the version at Glyndebourne (David McVicar, 2011) had Sachs making the attempt at reconciliation but meeting only rejection, and at the Deutsche Oper Berlin (Götz Friedrich) Sachs suddenly leaves, unable to cope with any more. This was interesting, but ran counter to Sachs's hard-won integration.

In *The Ring* Wagner had put forward no model of society to replace the feudal and capitalist systems which the revolution would sweep away, but in *Die Meistersinger* he did – to an extent. Interestingly it is a model where there is no king to rule, but then even amongst the feudal kingdoms of old Europe, there had been islets of democracy like the one at Nuremberg, and the model he proposed was his idealised Nuremberg society. Even if Wagner romanticised the mutualism of mediaeval Nuremberg much as he did the Athenian democracy, he it was for him the emblem of Germany's real and democratic identity. It was an identity where ordinary people genuinely had an influence, and Wagner would always remain on the side of *Gemeinshaft*, cooperatives, and mutualism, communism in its liberal form, as opposed to *Gesellschaft*, big business, and capitalism, and he believed that Nuremberg, still in his time almost a mediaeval city, represented his ideals of mutualism in manufacture and democracy in government. *Die Meistersinger* unobtrusively recommends the democratic method distilled in the Mastersingers' guild and presented by the guild, and as usual, Wagner regarded this model as both rooted in the past and as pointing the way to a better future.

Given his known outlook, he would probably view the Western democracies of today as self-appointed oligarchies, wearily rubber-stamped by the electorate at indeterminate intervals but without having any real participation, and on the basis of what he wrote, said, and did, today's democracies of America and Europe would have struck him as a government by the rich and powerful for the benefit of the rich and powerful, much like the Prussian system which he criticised so roundly. Unfortunately, when it comes to practical detail and realistic functioning, nobody has yet come up with anything better than the distorted version of democracy that is with us today. Wagner, who knew both from history and from experience quite a lot about the other forms of government, might even have endorsed Winston Churchill's wry observation, that democracy of this kind is the worst form of government, apart from the various other forms that have been tried from time to time. Even this perversion of democracy is better than the alternatives. But Wagner had something more to say on the subject, and he would say it in *Parsifal*.

Sachs meanwhile has patterned how it is possible to follow Schopenhauer into renunciation and still live in the world. Admittedly Sachs does not possess much of Schopenhauer's pacification of the will; in his own unpretentious style, Sachs deploys plenty of will to power. He is one of the world's movers and shakers, and not a resigned, compassionate observer. *Die Meistersinger* is like *Tristan und Isolde* in that the first impression should remain the last impression, this time the impression of a lovely and happy opera. It represents beyond logic how people can face the disturbing realities of Schopenhauer and yet live lives which are rewarding and worthwhile. The currents of darkness which Schopenhauer sets coursing through life do not have to spoil it; and though this too is not logical or rational, these currents add a chromatic richness to the C major of life.

Die Meistersinger had its first performance in Munich on 21 June 1868. The cast was:

Sachs	Franz Betz
Beckmesser	Gustav Hölzel
Pogner	Kaspar Bausewein
Vogelgesang	Karl Samuel Heinrich
Nachtigall	Eduard Sigl
Kothner	Karl Fischer
Zorn	Bartholomäus Weixlstorfer
Eisslinger	Eduard Hoppe
Moser	Michael Pöppl
Ortel	Franz Thoms
Schwarz	Leopold Grasser
Foltz	Ludwig Hayn
Walther	Franz Nachbaur
David	Max Schlosser
Nightwatchman	Ferdinand Lang
Eva	Mathilde Mallinger
Magdalena	Sophie Dietz

The conductor was Hans von Bülow working under Wagner's supervision. The quality of the musical performance, the singing and the staging went beyond his ability to praise it sufficiently. With the possible exception of *Rienzi*, it was the greatest artistic triumph of his life. He received the storms of applause from his place beside the king in the royal box, and eight other theatres in Germany had staged the work within a year.

TWENTY

PARSIFAL

No other work by Wagner has such radiance as *Parsifal*, and no other is so subtle and rich. There lies the rub; its richness is partly due to the complex influences that went into it over its thirty-five-year evolution, influences so various that they might have turned it into something confused and turgid. Its story is about a fellowship of Christian knights at Montsalvat in the legendary Spain of mediaeval myth. Their ability to fulfil their vocation and benefit the world has faltered disastrously because of the rashness of their king. The story describes how the knights and the king are restored to wholeness along with the 'fallen woman' responsible for the king's downfall, and how this healing comes from two sources, the decisive actions of Parsifal, the title hero and an outsider, and the mystical interventions of a divine higher power. This is straightforward, but many of its ingredients are not. There were philosophical influences: Feuerbach (again), even though Wagner had long since disowned his influence; David Strauss, who similarly deconstructed Christianity and even the historical existence of Christ; Hegel (again) with his intriguing philosophy of historical progress through creative conflict; Schopenhauer with his pessimistic denial of any such progress, his atheism and compassion; Buddhism with its karma and its notion of reincarnation; and Christianity itself. All these influences would have badly affected anything less inalienably radiant than this 'final card' of Wagner's. Unravelling those influences has become a self-contained subsidiary in the light industry now devoted to Wagner, and it raises again the question how much background is really necessary for a meaningful experience of the work itself. Wagner himself had no idea that *Parsifal* would become such hard labour, and that the future would bring such a widespread concern with the elements that went into its making. He imagined as usual that he had smelted them down in the crucibles of his imagination and cast forth something new that would stand on its own. *Parsifal* is a visionary, spell-binding experience in its own right, and if there is one characteristic which marks it as a late work it is economy. This alone sets it apart from everything else by Wagner. Far from being glutinous, it is luminous. It does not insist but casts a subtle, persuasive spell; even Klingsor's magic garden does not fulminate as Wagner's other magic garden, the Venusberg, had done; but shimmers into being before the imagination. Enshrined within the work is a profound didactic purpose. Wagner provides in it his final instruction on how to be better people, how to set up a better community, and how to create a better world; and as usual, he offers a vision of his ideas becoming a reality, how they might work in the world of real life.

Parsifal bears out the principle from the beginning of this book, that a straight view of the work can reveal many riches without excessive digging into the background. At first impression *Parsifal* is Christian, and perhaps this should be the final impression as well, even though it can have an impact without reference to religion. The world-view of Ernest Newman rejected religion, and yet he described the 1951 Bayreuth performance as 'not only the best *Parsifal* that I have seen and heard, but one of the three or four most moving spiritual experiences of my life'. This spirituality goes beyond creeds, which is probably a help for anyone averse to religious belief. *Parsifal* can extend its appeal wider, even to people disinclined to spirituality as such, who see *Parsifal* simply as a drama, and as 'not being about anything but itself'. This outlook was claimed as the right one by Carl Dahlhaus, who stated bluntly, '*Parsifal* is undeniably a document of the nineteenth-century religion of Art.'[98] The difficulty about this,

98 Dahlhaus, Carl, *Richard Wagner's Music Dramas*, tr. Mary Whittall, Cambridge, 1979, p. 144.

as for those who assert the same of his other works, is the internal evidence of *Parsifal* itself, as well as the declarations of Wagner such as his letters to King Ludwig about what *Parsifal* was meant to do and be. All the evidence goes to show that he was more than ever bent on projecting lessons to the entire world, and many people, including Nietzsche at his most perceptive and antagonistic, consider that Wagner was never more of a crusader than in *Parsifal*. Nietzsche objected virulently to all that *Parsifal* crusaded. As for Dahlhaus, there are others who go yet further and do not connect with *Parsifal* as a drama, but only with the music. Debussy described *Parsifal* as 'one of the loveliest monuments of sound ever raised to the serene glory of music'[99] even though its characters and its narrative meant nothing to him – he scoffed at them – and his endorsement of the 'musical beauty of the opera, which is supreme,' is all the more remarkable because it was above all as a musician that Debussy maintained a special love-hate relationship with Wagner.[100] He was always famously on the lookout for signs in his own music that it had been subverted by that 'Klingsor of Bayreuth'. Would anyone argue that there are not rewards enough in the music of *Parsifal*, as Debussy found?

Perhaps not; but those open to its wider dimensions gain more. The status of Wagner's religious beliefs will always be a conundrum, but the account of Count Auguste Villiers de L'Isle-Adam is a revealing one. The count stayed with Wagner at Tribschen in 1869 on his way to the world premiere of *Das Rheingold* at Munich, and this, slightly abridged, is what he recorded;

I passed almost every day and evening with Richard Wagner. One evening, as we sat in the already darkening salon, looking out into the garden, breaking the silence only occasionally, I asked Wagner point-blank if he had succeeded in filling his works – *Rienzi, Dutchman, Tannhäuser, Lohengrin, Meistersinger* as well as *Parsifal*, about which he

99 Quoted in Beckett, Lucy, *Parsifal*, Cambridge, 1981.
100 Debussy abandoned his opera *Rodrigues* from a conviction it had been incurably 'Wagnerised'.

was already thinking at that time – with that elevated mystical spirit which emanates from them in a so-to-speak artificial manner; in short, was he only a Christian to the extent that the material of his lyric drama demanded it; did he view Christianity with the same outlook as he did the Scandinavian myths whose symbolism he had so splendidly brought to life in his *Ring des Nibelungen*?

I shall never forget the look that Wagner gave me as from the depths of his unusually blue eyes. 'If I did not feel the light and the love of this Christian belief, to which you refer, in my soul, then my works, which portray my thinking and experience and which all bear their witness to them, would not they be those of the deceiver, a monkey? Would I be so childish as to be enthusiastic in cold blood for something which seemed to me basically mere superstition? – My art is my prayer. And believe me: every true artist sings only that which he believes, speaks only what he loves, writes only what he thinks; for those who lie betray themselves by the unfruitfulness and worthlessness of their work, for no one can create a true work of art without selfless honesty. As far as I am concerned, you shall know, since you ask, that I am before all else a Christian, and that the emphases in my works that have impressed you are fundamentally inspired only by that.'

That was the exact sense of the reply that Richard Wagner gave me that evening, and I believe that Mrs. Wagner who was present will remember equally well.

It is a pity that the count did not ask Wagner what he meant when he said he was 'above all else a Christian', because his Christianity was of a very personal kind, and difficult to pin down. However it was central to *Parsifal*, and no one can understand Wagner's departures from the mainstream in *Parsifal* without having an idea of what Christianity's mainstream beliefs are. Some people question whether there can be a 'main stream' at all in a religion which runs in so many different channels, but there are enough features common to its principal European variants to make up a central course, and without knowing what that is, it is difficult to grasp how Wagner branched away from it.

It is also necessary to provide some ideas of Christianity because classic texts like *The Death of Christian Britain* by the historian Callum G. Brown[101] show that many people now, in Britain at least, are almost as unfamiliar with Christianity as with Schopenhauer or Buddhism. It is surprising how far people without knowledge or experience of Christianity will pontificate authoritatively about what is and what is not Christian in Wagner and in *Parsifal*, with results that are often wildly off-beam.

The central manifesto of Christianity is the Nicene Creed,[102] and taken as a whole the creed has a compelling completeness. Its different tenets are interrelated and it shapes orthodox Christian believing, even though devoted Christians may baulk at parts of it today, as Wagner did himself. Briefly, and such reductive brevity is rather shocking, Christianity is a religion centred on the belief in the divinity and the eternal invisible presence on this earth of Jesus Christ, the

---

101 Brown, Callum G., *The Death of Christian Britain: Understanding Secularisation, 1800-2000*, Abingdon, 2001.

102 The Nicene Creed affirms: 'I believe in one God the Father Almighty, Maker of heaven and earth, And of all things visible and invisible: And in one Lord Jesus Christ, the only-begotten son of God, Begotten of his Father before all worlds, God of God, Light of Light, Very God of very God, Begotten, not made, Being of one substance with the Father, By whom all things were made: Who for us men, and for our salvation came down from heaven, And was incarnate by the Holy Ghost of the Virgin Mary, And was made man, And was crucified also for us under Pontius Pilate. He suffered and was buried, And the third day he rose again according to the Scriptures, And ascended into Heaven, And sitteth on the right hand of the Father. And he shall come again with glory to judge both the quick and the dead: Whose kingdom shall have no end. And I believe in the Holy Ghost, The Lord and giver of life, Who proceedeth from the Father and the Son, Who with the Father and the Son together is worshipped and glorified, Who spake by the Prophets. And I believe one Catholick and Apostolick Church. I acknowledge one Baptism for the remission of sins. And I look for the Resurrection of the dead, And the life of the world to come.' *Book of Common Prayer* (1662).

embodiment of God in human form. Jesus Christ was born in Palestine around the date from which our system of dating takes its name. 'AD' (Anno Domini) signifies 'the year of our Lord', the year of his birth which occurred 2,000 years ago.[103] Christians celebrate his birth at Christmas, although aware that the historical connections between this festivity and the birthday of Christ are tenuous. He was son of a carpenter, and he grew to be a remarkable teacher and a prophet. He preached otherworldly values, kindliness, wisdom and mercy, the path to holiness. The essence of the historical Jesus' proclamation was the kingdom of God and the concomitant standards of mercy, compassion and openness to God. For three years he attracted huge crowds and a band of twelve disciples, one of whom later betrayed him. He also performed miracles, finding food for thousands from almost nowhere, curing illnesses, calming storms, even raising the dead. At the end of the three-year period he was arrested by the Jewish authorities from a mix of motives: jealousy of his influence and his unsettling charisma, anxiety that his sacrilege, as the Jews saw it, would incite the wrath of God, and concern that his activities would appear seditious to their Roman conquerors and result in general retribution against the Jews.[104] After a show trial Jesus Christ was crucified. He died on the day now commemorated each year as Good Friday.

The cardinal, central tenet of Christian belief is that he rose again the following Sunday, Easter Day. As an Easter carol, paraphrasing St Paul, puts it;

---

103 There are doubts as to whether the venerable Bede, who devised the system, calculated the date of Christ's birth correctly; apparently 4 BC is more probable.

104 That this concern was justified was demonstrated roughly 40 years later in AD 70, when a Jewish sedition of extraordinary bravery was put down by the Romans with revolting atrocities. They destroyed Jerusalem, and razed the great temple to the ground, leaving just one wall still standing, as it still does, remaining one of the most sacred and iconic sites in the world.

Had Christ that once was slain
Ne'er burst his three-day prison,
Our faith had been in vain;
But now hath Christ arisen.

Christians believe that after a further six weeks he 'ascended into heaven,' whence he originated, and to God the Father, but that his invisible presence continues on earth for ever. This presence continues here along with or in that of a mysterious 'third person of God', the Holy Ghost, who descended on Christ's disciples on Whit Sunday. Christ's crucifixion and above all his resurrection open up extraordinary possibilities for those who believe in this miraculous sequence. Believers enjoy the hope of achieving a new freedom, absolution for wrong things done in this life. The monk at Ettal (mentioned in the chapter on *Tristan und Isolde*) was an extreme example of Christian believers' experience of living life in a metaphysical dimension as well as the ordinary world, and also of their hopes for immortality at the end of life on this earth. The value system put forward by Jesus Christ in his teaching was centred on a reciprocal love of God, and on compassion towards our fellow human beings, a compassion expressed in action, and it is best summarised in his most famous teaching, the 'Sermon on the Mount'.[105] Much of his teaching took the form of parables. Parables, as mentioned already already in the introduction, are simple, approachable stories, vignettes of the everyday world with great depths of meaning and spiritual significance. However his programme was emphatically an action programme; he 'walked the walk' as well as 'talking the talk', and he did good things. He fed people when hungry; he made them well; he attacked injustice and was capable of stopping

---

105   The Sermon on the Mount is found in the Gospel of St Matthew. Its Chapters 5-7 form Christ's most sustained account of his ideals, value system and religious fundamentals. It gathered together St Matthew's recollections of Jesus' teaching over a long period in the form of a single address, one of the many he preached to assemblies of those who gathered to hear him.

a vindictive, bloodthirsty crowd in its tracks, when they were on the brink of legalised murder, the stoning of an adulterous woman. He gave people a sense of value, of worthwhileness. He expected his followers to do the same.

Returning now to the description of Wagner's Christianity provided by Count Villiers de L'Isle-Adam, it has to be said that there have been questions as to its veracity. The count's description has been questioned, largely, it seems, because Wagner during his middle period seemed worlds away from any Christian convictions. However the first point is that the convoluted, discursive style of Wagner's answer to the count sounds like the authentic Wagner. More important is the fact, however confusing, that Wagner's Christianity never died in his middle period but slumbered. There was in particular a beautiful spring morning in Switzerland which put him in mind of Good Friday. He was then deep in *Tristan* and at the peak of his absorption in the atheist Schopenhauer; and yet instantly Christianity lit up his imagination and his thoughts turned to *Parsifal*. One of the paradoxes of Wagner is that later he was to tell Cosima, 'Yes, it was Schopenhauer who revealed Christianity to me' – Schopenhauer the atheist!

Both the encounter with Schopenhauer and the revelation of Christianity took place after Wagner had lost his youthful belief in life as an experience of untrammelled joy and hedonism. His 'Hellenic optimism' had gone, and with it had gone most of his hopes for creating a better world through political reform and action. He had come to see these hopes as naïve, at about the same time as he discovered Schopenhauer and something like the four noble truths of Buddha, the first of which is that 'Life is suffering.' Schopenhauer acknowledged his debt to Buddhism, both for truths such as this and for Buddhism's emphasis on universal compassion. There are those who see in *Parsifal* more Schopenhauer or Buddhism than Christianity, but the distinctions are artificial because the different beliefs share so many ideals. Compassion is at the heart of Buddhism. Compassion is essential to Schopenhauer. Compassion is the essence of Christianity, its fundamental moral imperative. Perhaps Christianity is distinctive in demanding a particularly active response. Wagner drew a distinction between Buddhism and Christianity, believing not quite accurately, that Buddhism had degenerated into 'Brahminism' (*sic*), and was limited to salvation for a select few, the wise, the leisured and the rich. For Wagner this was another example of that social and material privilege, mandated by organised religion, which he had found detestable in his Dresden days. He considered Christianity a better faith than what he called Brahminism because it was on offer to everyone, above all 'the poor in spirit',[106] a phrase which Wagner took directly from Jesus Christ's 'Sermon on the Mount'. He admired Christ more than Buddha, because 'Buddha contemplated; Christ acted' – and suffered.

Significant though the Count's description is, there is other evidence that Wagner had come back to Christianity, however idiosyncratically, particularly the evidence of Cosima's *Diaries*. On 11 January 1880, for example, Cosima recorded, 'Wagner flies into a rage' after one of those present, Herr von Stein, had expressed the opinion that after shedding transcendental faith, philanthropy would one day become even more powerful. 'It is always the same,' said Wagner, 'people think only of the church and confuse this with Christianity – the true task is to glorify the figure of Christ so that his example provides an outward bond. Humanity runs in the two parallel lines, he continues; the one is concerned with nothing but plunder and murder, the other can be regarded as a reaction against that; no figure is more sublimely moving than that of Christ, and all the rest who affect us have been his imitators.' This is just one sample from the plethora expressing Wagner's late passion for 'true Christianity' as he contrasted it with institutionalised religion, and this passion runs through Cosima's *Diaries*. Wagner evidently did not appreciate in life a point implicit in *Parsifal*, that without an organisation to support the practice and spread of Christianity, like the fellowship of the Grail, it may sicken and die out.

106 *Religion and Art: Prose Works*, tr. William Ashton Ellis, London, 1897, vi, pp. 214 et seqq.

Even with Cosima's *Diaries* it is still not easy to pin down Wagner's version of Christianity. He once said to Cosima, 'I really must write down my theology one day,' and it is a pity that he never did. Fortunately his writings provide pointers, and they indicate that Wagner's Christianity was centred less on Easter and Christ's resurrection than on his passion, and the compassion for humanity which it expressed. Wagner never set out his views on the Resurrection but in practice he tended to marginalise it. If he believed in Christ's resurrection, it does not feature much among his many affirming references to Christianity in Cosima's *Diaries*. Wagner's Christianity was centred on the Crucifixion where Christ 'acted out voluntary suffering as an expression of limitless compassion, an ultimate negation of the will, the will to live'. It was his example that Wagner most appreciated; but did he appreciate something more? It is difficult to decipher his thinking. It is possible that Christ was for him a purely historical phenomenon, influencing us now as Socrates–Plato influences us, by means of teachings and an example passed down through history. It is also possible that Wagner had a metaphysical belief in Christ as a supernatural and transcendent being outside time and space, and as achieving some redemptive effect for humanity on the level of the paranormal, the miraculous, the mystical, such as he presents symbolically in *Parsifal*.

Whatever the case, for Wagner the heart of Christianity and the essence of *Parsifal* is the message of compassion and forgiveness, a message which is redemptive in itself. As some examples will indicate, compassion is a constant in the Gospels, and Wagner was emphatic about how completely Jesus Christ and his New Testament teaching of compassion had superseded the God of the Old Testament, whom he saw as a grim, narcissistic and terrifying figure, at times demanding mass murder and genocide. Wagner drew a contrast between this fire-and-brimstone tyrant and the Christ who preached a new covenant of love and divine compassion. A few short examples must serve to illustrate the compassion of the Gospels which is at the heart of *Parsifal*.

Jesus Christ was once asked how often it was right for someone to forgive his brother; was seven times enough? Christ answered; 'No! Seventy times seven!' and then told a story to explain his principle of compassion and forgiveness. The story was about a servant who had run up an unimaginable debt, ten thousand talents, with his master and could not repay it. His master threatened a brutal foreclosure, but was then moved to compassion by his servant's abject pleas, and let him off the whole sum. This same servant then went off in pursuit of a second servant who owed him a quite small amount but again could not pay it. Despite his requests for more time, the first servant grabbed the second by the throat and threw him into prison. The master was informed and grew understandably angry; and he now acted with an avenging ruthlessness against his first servant, because he had failed to extend the compassion he had received himself. Such failure of compassion was the one offence for which Christ would countenance no compassion.

Compassion also runs through the story of 'the woman taken in adultery'. She had been caught in the very act, and the intention of the crowd bringing her before Jesus Christ was to stone her to death. He was expected to pass judgment and endorse this frightful plan but instead he gave them a devastating riposte, 'Let him that is without sin cast the first stone!' at which they all slunk off surreptitiously, one after another. Jesus turned to the woman. 'Doth any man accuse thee?' he asked. 'None, Lord,' she answered. 'Nor do I accuse thee,' he said. 'Go thy way and sin no more.'

Perhaps the ultimate compassion story is the Prodigal Son. In St Luke's Gospel, Chapter 15, Christ told the parable of a man who had two sons. The younger asked his father to give him his half share of the inheritance now, without having to wait for his father to die, and his father did as asked. With his gains this son took himself off, journeying to a far country where he spent prodigally, squandering everything on riotous living and prostitutes. After the money was gone, there was a famine and he began to starve, to the extent that he was soon grateful to eat pigswill. Eventually he came to his senses, and reflected that the very servants in his father's house were better off. He said to himself, 'I will arise and go to my father and will say unto him, "Father, I have sinned against heaven and in thy sight, and am no more worthy to be called thy son. Make me as one of thy hired servants."' But while he was still a long way off, his father saw him coming, and came running to embrace him. The son made his confession, but his father would have none of it, providing him with the best clothes and 'killing the fatted calf'. His father made a great celebration, offering unconditional forgiveness and compassion, and the general happiness was something which he expected everybody to share. The father was saddened that his other son was angry over all the fuss for his wastrel brother, and the father tried with uncertain success to draw him into the same mindset of compassion.

It is this Christian compassion that resonates throughout *Parsifal*, even though the seed for it was planted in Wagner by the atheist Schopenhauer. Schopenhauer actually held Christianity in high regard precisely because, however deluded its supernatural beliefs might appear to him, its standpoints on compassion chimed in with his own principles. It was indeed because of Schopenhauer that Wagner had connected again with Christianity; no longer did he see Christianity simply as a conspiracy of the wealthy and powerful to hoodwink the masses with fraudulent promises of 'pie in the sky'. That might be the function of organised religion, particularly, as Wagner rather harshly believed, of the Roman Catholic Church, but pure Christianity was about believing in the divine figure of Christ, learning everything possible about him, and following his example. It is difficult to be clear how far Wagner believed in the possibility of a personal, mystical relationship with Christ as orthodox Christians do.

Whatever the facts, the threads woven into *Parsifal* were all *inter*woven with the stuff of Wagner's Christianity. The action of *Parsifal* takes place against the background of Christian beliefs. *Parsifal* takes it for granted that these beliefs are true and accepted, as much in life as in the framework of the drama. *Parsifal* acts out two Christian sacraments, Baptism and Holy Communion, and its action centres on the Holy Grail, the chalice with which Christ instituted Holy Communion. Its action incorporates divine interventions that are miraculous, the daily rejuvenation of its knights by the Grail; the sudden ruin of Klingsor's castle when Parsifal makes the sign of the Cross; the breaking of Kundry's curse which had prevented Parsifal from finding the way back to Amfortas; the instant healing of Amfortas' wound by the spear which inflicted it; and the ecstasy of all creation on Good Friday in virtue of Christ's redeeming crucifixion. As Gurnemanz explains in Act III, even the meadows and the flowers are radiant with a sense of innocence restored. The Crucifixion took place two thousand years ago, and it is a redeeming event which is both rooted in the deep past and yet reverberates across the gulfs of time, re-enacted in the liturgy and imagination of Christians every year. It is cyclically and miraculously redemptive.

It is not only the action of *Parsifal* which resounds with Christianity; the music of *Parsifal* does the same. And it is probably the music of *Parsifal* which confirms the claim of Bayreuth to provide an experience unequalled elsewhere. Wagner had created the Bayreuth Theatre for *The Ring*; he created *Parsifal* for the Bayreuth Theatre. He always hoped to preserve *Parsifal* for Bayreuth alone. Cynics insist that Wagner only wanted to do this for the money, but his claim that it was only at Bayreuth that *Parsifal* could work its proper effect is borne out by experience, and here is how Felix von Weingartner described it in his memoirs. Weingartner was later one of the twentieth century's great conductors, but when he first heard *Parsifal* he was only nineteen.

The auditorium grows completely dark. A breathless hush falls. Like a voice from another world, the first expansive theme of the Prelude begins. This impression is like unlike anything else, and is ineradicable. I have heard Parsifal at Bayreuth in later performances which were the most bitter disappointment to me, but the solemnity of this beginning was always the same. The inspiration, the instrumentation, the acoustic and, in a negative sense, the optical impression worked together here in a unique manner that is impossible anywhere else.[107]

107 Weingartner, Felix von, *Lebenserinnerungen*, Vienna and Leipzig, 1923, quoted in Barth, Herbert, Dietrich Mack and Egon Voss, *Wagner, a*

Much of this Prelude and the other music of *Parsifal* reflects the church music traditions from two separate streams that Wagner knew well, the Roman Catholic and the Lutheran. This music is also pure Wagner because his alchemy invariably transformed any music which he took over. In the *Parsifal* Prelude, the initial limb of the long theme representing 'Holy Communion' was directly borrowed from Liszt,[108] from another semi-religious work, Liszt's obscure cantata *The Bells of Strasbourg Cathedral*.[109] The Prelude to Liszt's work is dominated by a single musical element:

Fig. 20.1 Franz Liszt, *The Bells of Strasbourg Cathedral*, Prelude

Wagner took it, transformed it, and added to it to create his own arching theme. He recast it in A flat, which is the tonal centre for the first half of Act I where it is mainly surrounded by other keys of similar colour, G, A, B flat. Parsifal himself makes his first appearance in B flat. Although the tonality, A flat, of the opening theme is clear in Wagner's version, he dissolved any clarity of rhythm when he made it his own as part of the long leitmotive known as the 'Communion' theme, and he gave it a timeless, weightless character:

Documentary Study, London, 1975.

108 At one stage, Wagner actually said to Liszt of something in his music, 'I got that bit from you,' and Liszt commented wryly, 'Well at least that means it will now be heard.'

109 Wagner had heard this work at Budapest as part of a Liszt–Wagner concert organised by Hans Richter on 10 March 1875. Wagner had conducted excerpts of the *Ring*; Liszt conducted his own work, a cantata for orchestra, chorus and baritone solo; and it was dedicated to Longfellow, whose poem, *The Golden Legend*, had inspired it.

Fig. 20.2 'Communion' theme

In the second scene of *Parsifal* Act I, mystical choirs will use this music to intone Christ's words from his last supper on earth, slightly adjusted from Luther's Bible to fit the music. Within the span of this theme are some subsidiary motives, somewhat arbitrarily named 'the Spear' and 'the Wound', titles which would almost have been as valid the other way round. The whole theme intoned in unison hints at monasticism and Gregorian chant, but the instrumentation avoids any suggestion of a monastic, masculine timbre. In the first 'Grail' scene, it is sung by mixed choirs, to give it a strangely genderless quality. In the Prelude and again in the 'Grail' scene this long phrase is played four times in all, in two paired renderings. The first pair is in A flat; the second in C minor. In each pair there is first a plain unison; it is then repeated, suspended in a shimmering halo of orchestral sound. As Lucy Beckett sees it, the music has established a sense of grieving aspiration, but Nietzsche was affected by it, and by the whole Prelude, as if by 'a look of Love'. The opening plainsong is answered quietly by the theme of the Dresden Amen, symbolising the Grail,

Fig. 20.3 'The Grail'

which Wagner knew from his Dresden days, believing rather vaguely, and incorrectly, that it had somehow come together at the very origins of Lutheranism.[110] There follows a theme, forte and rhythmically assertive, which Wagner himself described as faith declaring itself, exalted, unshakeable even in suffering:

110 Wagner only learnt in 1881 after completing *Parsifal* that this music probably derived from the composer J.G. Naumann (1741-1801). According to Cosima's *Diaries* he had previously believed that it was much older, having emerged from the uncharted traditions of the early Reformation. Wagner read about Naumann in a musical almanac of the time. In its origins this theme probably *was* older, as it was apparently a setting of a 'traditional melody' by Naumann. (*Grove's Dictionary of Music and Musicians*, ed. Stanley Sadie, London, 1980.) The Dresden Amen and the compositional style that it represents evidently seemed to Wagner dimly representative of the Reformation; and before settling in Dresden, Naumann had held a Lutheran post at Stockholm in Sweden. The Amen has long been familiar in the English choral tradition thanks to Charles Villiers Stanford, who deployed it in his robustly Protestant setting of the Service in B flat. In *Parsifal* itself the theme similarly and increasingly takes on this same robust quality as the drama progresses, and except in Mendelssohn's 'Reformation' Symphony where it represents Roman Catholicism, it generally signifies the Reformation, Lutheran, all things Protestant.

Dresden itself was Protestant and Lutheran, even though Augustus the Strong was king of Saxony at the time when Naumann was Oberkapellmeister, and Augustus had made a strategic conversion to Roman Catholicism in order to enhance his claim to the throne of Roman Catholic Poland. The general population of Dresden was not happy with this religious opportunism and built a Protestant cathedral to counterbalance Augustus's Roman Catholic one. Surprisingly there was in spite of this no big conflict in Saxony, and none in terms of musical styles. Protestant styles were in evidence in both churches, and the Lutheran Bach's most life-affirming religious work was a full Roman Catholic mass written in the hope of appealing to the Roman Catholic Saxon king. Wagner too was ideologically and with increasing assertiveness a Lutheran; and for him the Dresden Amen always represented the epitome of Protestant music, even though the opening strains of *Parsifal* are evidence of his attraction towards plainsong, which is a Roman Catholic tradition.

Fig. 20.4 'Faith'

To English ears it sounds forcefully Protestant after the Roman Catholic plainsong, floating and indeterminate, that precedes it. It expands in variations of itself, and ends up in a remote minor key, whereupon the Dresden Amen softly restores the general radiance.

The 'Faith' theme comes in again, high and ethereal on the woodwind, but soon descends to the central registers of the orchestra, burgeoning and broadening into a climax. This softens and fades, though still keeping up the same embracing warmth. Eventually it gently gives way to a soft, unsettled rustling on the lower strings. Over this the opening limb of the first theme returns, to be borne aloft in a luminous shimmer of sound. The theme darkens as Wagner develops it, but at length it seems ready to settle down into the tonic, A flat, where the Prelude began. Instead, however, the music begins a long ascent and then an ascent within an ascent, winding up to the very highest regions that the strings can manage. It is interesting that the 'Faith' theme reaches its fullest, most solid and emphatic expression in the Prelude, and from now it will generally become ever more airborne and transparent. Contrariwise, the delicate 'Grail' theme from now on strengthens its profile and generates the supreme climaxes in all three acts. The dynamic level of *Parsifal* is generally restrained, especially in comparison with the work that preceded it, *Götterdämmerung*, but such climaxes as there are rock the foundations. This happens particularly with the 'Grail' theme, at its immense C major statements in Act I, at the blistering dissonances at the end of Act II, when Klingsor's magic castle collapses in an earthquake, and at the great B major blaze of

Act III when Gurnemanz anoints Parsifal to be King of the Grail. But more of this after the story.

In Act I, the curtain goes up on a forest clearing in the neighbourhood of the Grail Temple. Gurnemanz, an elderly knight of the Grail, still hale and vigorous, hears a distant fanfare summoning the Grail fellowship to prayer, and he rouses the young esquires in his company, teasing them gruffly that they are better at guarding their slumbers than the forests. Amfortas, King of the Grail Temple, is soon due to make his way to the lake, and Gurnemanz asks his advance party if the herb that Gawain has won has helped relieve the pain of Amfortas's wound. It has not. Gurnemanz is deeply disturbed at the thought that the Grail King is so sick and feeble from his wound that he is incapable of performing his function as king and priestly servant of the Grail, his privilege and his duty. The esquires see the strange wild woman Kundry arriving.

Fig. 20.5 'Wild Energy'

Her horse flies through the air, and when it touches ground she falls off exhausted, and after handing over a balsam for Amfortas' wound, she collapses.

Fig. 20.6 'Kundry'

She has brought the unguent from Arabia, and Amfortas is carried in on his sick bed.

Fig. 20.7 'Amfortas'

In response to Gurnemanz's kindly enquiries after his sufferings he comments that although the night had been very dark and anguished, he was touched and moved by the morning and its great beauty.

Fig. 20.8

He muses on the prophecy that a pure fool might redeem him and intones it to a motive;

Fig. 20.9 'The Pure Fool'

but reflects darkly that the 'pure fool' might be a coded reference to his own death, which he would welcome. Gurnemanz tries to hearten him by suggesting that at least he first try the balsam that Kundry has worked so hard to obtain, whereupon she is presented;

but she protests impetuously against any thanks for it.

Amfortas still gratefully agrees to try the ointment but at Kundry's unexpected, peremptory bidding, he goes on his way. When he has left, the esquires round on Kundry from instinctive mistrust, but Gurnemanz forcefully intervenes. He reminds them that Kundry has often helped them, even though she owes them nothing. To their suggestion that if she is so marvellous they should send her to recover the sacred spear, he responds vehemently that this is beyond her, and the orchestra takes up emphatically the segments of the opening motive representing 'the Wound' and 'the Spear'. This brings to his mind how Amfortas had gone out to attack the Grail's arch-enemy, Klingsor, with the spear, and he muses sadly how Amfortas was seduced by a woman of fearsome beauty; while lay intoxicated in her embrace and distracted from his purpose, Klingsor had seized the spear and dealt Amfortas a terrible wound, agonising and unhealing. Not one of the Grail fellowship realises that this woman is really Kundry. Stirred by Gurnemanz's recollections, the young apprentice knights ask him to tell them more of the fellowship's past history; and he describes how their saintly leader, Titurel, and his band of knights had once been gravely threatened as they fought for Christianity against heathen onslaughts. At the height of the crisis, angels descended from heaven. The orchestra sounds a peculiarly radiant derivative of the 'Faith' theme,

Fig. 20.10 'Faith's Vision of Celestial Radiance'

which becomes especially important at the very end of the opera. The angels were bearing two sacred relics to fortify the endeavours of the fellowship. The first was the Holy Grail, which was in legend not only the chalice which Christ had shared with his disciples at the last supper before he was crucified; it had also caught his blood when he was stabbed on the Cross by a Roman soldier's spear to make sure he was dead. The second relic was this same spear; the wound which it inflicted had sanctified it. Titurel erected a cathedral-like temple[III] to house these objects which possess miraculous powers, and he installed and expanded his fellowship to serve the cause of making the world better, safer and more Christian. Even now the knights of the fellowship are nourished by the Grail. Its radiance fortifies them for their labours and regenerates them spiritually.

This tells a truth about religion as it is. A symbol of divine higher power set among the knights can result in great things, but it can do nothing in isolation. It requires a saintly brotherhood of knights who believe in it to achieve any effect. Human beings are generally like the knights in that they cannot readily achieve anything worthwhile in isolation; they need the fortifying, unifying conviction of the Grail to produce results. It is the combination of a divine influence, as believers perceive it, and their response to it that can create a powerful force for good.

Few people looking at the world today with its corrupt politicians, jihadist mullahs, self-obsessed celebrities and money-drunk financiers, could reasonably doubt that the Grail Temple principles could usefully infiltrate popular thinking now; that they could only improve the world. However *Parsifal* also suggests that the efforts of human beings only fulfil their possibilities if touched by grace or providence, and that this alone renders them fully effective, as is borne out in the action.

Only applicants with faith, goodness, and a dedicated singleness of mind amounting to obedience are suitable for the Grail fellowship, and there was one particular hopeful, Klingsor, who was rejected because he was self-will run riot, the 'will to power' epitomised by his overwhelming libido (something Wagner knew all about; long echoes here too of Schopenhauer's rejection of libido). Klingsor is

---

III Wagner's original Bayreuth staging of the Temple was based on Siena Cathedral in Italy, which he visited in 1880.

characterised by a restless leitmotive:

Fig. 20.11 'Klingsor'

In the attempt to suppress this drive he castrated himself, but this mutilation did not change his character and his self-obsession, and he was again rejected by Titurel and driven out without, it seems, a shred of Christian compassion.

This want of compassion was a departure from Grail principles, a fall from grace that cost the fellowship dear. Klingsor grew determined to win the spear and the Grail for himself. His killing of every capacity for love worked as it did with Alberich; and rage, bitterness and pain gave him superhuman determination and the occult powers by which he was able to conjure up a rival castle in the desert. He filled it with flower maidens, innocent blossoms which he transformed into glamorously seductive girls. With these he lured many knights of the Grail into a world of sensual intoxication, anaesthesia and oblivion, wrecking their sense of purpose and dedication, and threatening the Grail fellowship. Singleness of mind is the ideal of the knights – purity or '*Reinheit*' – and this is not identical with sexual abstinence. As Houston Chamberlain pointed out long ago,[112] there is nothing in *Parsifal* that 'glorifies chastity', as people have often maintained. *Reinheit*, purity, is the ideal in *Parsifal*, not *Keuschheit*, chastity. Act

---

112 Chamberlain, Houston Stewart, *Richard Wagner*, tr. G. Ainslie Height, London, 1900.

II will even show Kundry jeering at Klingsor, '*Bist du keusch?* Are you chaste?' a potent thrust because they both know that his chastity is meaningless, because he still is not *rein*. There is no suggestion in *Parsifal* that the erotic phenomenon is evil as such, but only that it becomes evil if it leads people to neglect the good that they should be doing or to inflict damage in pursuit of it. Amfortas had neglected to guard the Grail; and as we saw with *Tannhäuser*, Wagner's life provided copious and painful illustrations of his neglecting the good and doing immense damage in the service of his libido and his overpowering erotic drive. For Klingsor the failure to achieve *Reinheit* was a staging post in his path to perdition, and as we encounter him, he is wholly negative, a Mephistopheles. His sights are set simply on revenge, on taking something that exists for the general good and wrecking it. He was once a danger to Titurel, just as he now is to Amfortas, who is Titurel's son and his successor now that Titurel has grown old and abdicated the kingship. As the new king Amfortas had seized the sacred spear and gone out with it against Klingsor, but unfortunately Klingsor had a deadlier weapon than the unwitting charms of his flower maidens, and that was Kundry.

Kundry, the submissive handmaid of the Grail fellowship, has a double life; in fact she has had many, and in some ways she is the one raw, unprocessed element of Buddhism and its ideas of reincarnation and the migration of souls into new beings which persists in *Parsifal*. She is also an additional connection between the *Parsifal* story and Christ, because of her cardinal misdeed which was to laugh at Christ on his way to his crucifixion. This was a supreme act of *Schadenfreude*, pleasure in another person's misery, the opposite of compassion. *Schadenfreude* was the negative human tendency which Schopenhauer regarded as the most terrible, and he saw it as infusing all the other bad ones. In the framework of Buddhist ideas, Kundry's cruel deed carries its own curse, condemning her to a detestable immortality; she must repeat life endlessly, atoning for her cruelty with repeated acts of compassion until they finally cancel out, allowing her to escape from the wheel of life into Nirvana and oblivion. Meanwhile she is driven to make repeated attempts at an alternative oblivion, a self-forgetting through eroticism, the brief abolition of identity and ego-boundaries through a blatant carnality.

Fig. 20.12 Kundry's 'Seduction' motive.

Unfortunately her attempts at self-forgetting through eroticism are counterproductive, because from the perspective of Schopenhauer the blind, wanton sex-drive is the ultimate expression of 'the will'. In his view, which still seeps into *Parsifal*, the will, compelling life to perpetuate itself, is totally opposed to Nirvana and to any progress towards non-being. In any case Kundry's brand of eroticism is 'love' at its most predatory and destructive, and so too are the carnal drives of the men she lures in. What she needs is a love that cares for her, and looks to her welfare and her salvation. Even more unfortunately Klingsor gained power over her by his knowledge of her curse and her bondage to carnality, which enables him to manipulate her for his own ends. When Klingsor says in Act II that the man who can resist her sets her free, he expresses a pithy distortion of the important truth that she needs a love that is willing to forego gratification for the sake of her welfare. Her drive towards carnal satisfactions is all the more overwhelming because it is supercharged by two other drives. One of these is a confused impulse of maternal love, which Wagner once described to his own mother as the strongest, truest form of love, but which is part of life's determination to keep itself going. The instinctive impulses of mothering were another thing which Schopenhauer scorned and vilified in his pessimistic belief that the more people there are, the more people there are to experience suffering.

The orchestra sounds – ever so softly – the theme of '*Ur-Mutterheit,*

Primordial Motherhood' at exactly the point where Klingsor is thinking aloud, and this underlines '*Den Zauber wusst ich wohl*,' how he knew full well the magic that compels Kundry to do his bidding as a seductress, that maternal instinct which he has harnessed to his will.

Fig. 20.13 '*Ur-Mutterheit* – The Primal Mother' (often associated with Herzeleide)

As we have seen, Wagner's ideals of maternal love were wishful thinking for him; but his insight was as true as it was profound. In the world post-Freud, it has become axiomatic that maternal relationships are suffused with the erotic, and the poet-seer in Wagner divined something of this. He also divined in Kundry an image of a woman who needs to be needed, the idea first impressed in his mind by Minna, and this is the second of the drives that supercharge Kundry's impulse towards Parsifal. Kundry was the woman whose terrible beauty intoxicated Amfortas. She engulfed him in the folds of an exquisite pleasure and brought him down, but when not needed by Klingsor, her craving takes a better form. She expresses it through serving the knights of the Grail. She has done so ever since Titurel first found her in the forests in a trance half-way between sleep and death, and this version of Kundry as a wild but lowly messenger serving their needs is the only one known to Gurnemanz and the knights of the Grail. Not even Amfortas recognises her as the agent of his downfall. Amfortas' wound from the spear is one that would never heal and it had left him in an agony of despair until the day when he was sent the oracle, '*Durch Mitleid wissend, der reine Tor* – The one made wise through compassion, the pure fool: wait for him, my chosen one.' 'Pure fool' here signifies unsullied innocence, not mental deficiency, as Debussy mockingly suggested.

Gurnemanz's account is interrupted by the new leitmotive of Parsifal, which is, as here, generally scored for horns,

Fig. 20.14 'Parsifal'

to shouts of rage and grief offstage; someone, according to this chorus of outrage, has shot an arrow and killed a swan flying over the lake. The company bring on a youth of heroic strength clutching a bow and arrows; Parsifal, for this is he, is the one responsible, as he boasts. He shows not the least awareness of having done anything wrong, let alone remorse for it, bragging instead that he can hit anything that flies. Gurnemanz, aghast, compels him to consider the swan's point of view, and Parsifal becomes aware of the pain and suffering that his thoughtless action has produced. He breaks his bow impulsively, no mean feat as anyone who has handled a real bow will know, and hurls away his arrows. Gurnemanz, intrigued, moves on from censure to enquiry; where did he come from; who was his father; who sent him this way; what is his name; but each time Parsifal can only answer that he does not know. Gurnemanz then asks him to tell what he does know, and he responds that he has a mother called Herzeleide. (At this the orchestra introduces the motive of 'Ur-Mutterheit'.) Parsifal continues that they used to live together in the wilds. Kundry butts in and explains that Herzeleide brought up her son in a state of general ignorance so that he should escape his father Gamuret's fate, an early, heroic, knightly death. However the day had come when Parsifal had been captivated by some knights riding past and followed them, trying to keep up until he was lost, far away from home. Kundry adds that this tough, warlike lad had soon become a terror to robbers and giants; any malign individuals who tried to harm him learnt that they did so at their peril; he was invincible, a super-Siegfried.

'What is bad, what is good?' asks Parsifal, symbolising an ignorance of any moral sense; at which Gurnemanz laughs gently, telling him that his mother was good, and that she must be worrying and grieving over his disappearance. Kundry bursts in derisively, demonstrating again her inmost difficulty in actually *feeling* compassion, and she tells Parsifal that his mother grieves no longer, because she is dead. Parsifal is stricken and rounds on her; 'Who says so?' Kundry tells him that she herself saw his mother declining, and adds mockingly that his mother sent him her dying greeting. At this Parsifal springs on Kundry as if to strangle her, and he is only prevented by Gurnemanz who drags him off and throws him down, telling him furiously that he must be out of his mind; 'Such violence again!' Parsifal is seized with violent trembling, and nearly faints. Kundry hurries over to a nearby spring and brings back a horn full of water, some of which she sprinkles over Parsifal, giving him the rest to drink. She has developed a rational understanding of what compassion means, and what she has to do to atone; but any feeling for it is still fitful and wayward. It shifts in and out of focus in a way that Wagner well understood from within; there is Wagner in Kundry. Gurnemanz praises her for demonstrating the principles of the Grail; but his assurance that anyone who requites evil with good overcomes that evil is something she brushes uneasily aside. She seems to have come to no harm from Parsifal's attack; and Gurnemanz turns back to him while she, unnoticed, creeps away into a thicket, vainly fighting off the overwhelming urge to sleep, induced by Klingsor and his enchantments.

Gurnemanz has become increasingly interested in Parsifal because of the prophecy about the 'blameless fool'; and the possibility is beginning to glimmer in his mind that it might refer to this uncouth young man. When the royal procession returns, Gurnemanz decides to test out this idea by taking him to the Temple of the Grail and seeing if he relates to it. The scene around them transforms miraculously into the hall of the Grail, to some of the greatest music Wagner ever wrote. It begins built largely from repetitions in canon of a very simple, four-note theme, usually named the 'Transformation' motive or 'Grail March',

Fig. 20.15 'Transformation' motive

and Parsifal comments that although the pace of their procession is measured and stately, they seem rapidly to cover great distances. The forests of the Grail give way to a causeway that narrows through sheer cliffs, and then they seem to be passing through a mountain to emerge in a great hall, circular and domed, with a shrine at the centre. The music has meanwhile passed through a mighty expansion to embrace developments of the 'Faith' motive, riven with searing brass polyphonies that are at once plangent and blistering. They pile up on each other to create an extraordinary amalgam of majesty and crisis, modulating unexpectedly towards a culmination for six onstage trombones. They cut through the textures with a fortissimo summons consisting of the opening limb of the 'Communion' theme, but beginning now assertively *on* the beat. This mighty summons silences the orchestra for a moment, but it picks up the four-note theme again, and develops it to a new high-water mark, at which point the brass from the stage sound again, mightier than ever because six trumpets add their voices, fortissimo and an octave higher, to the trombones. The onstage brass take the music into a new tonal realm: their last note is C, and as this C slowly fades into silence the eerie booming of the bells begins to sound from the distance from the Grail Temple.

Fig. 20.16 'Bells'

The pitch and the intervals of the bells reflects those of the theme which launched the 'Transformation' music, but they add another note, to make C, G, A and E. C major is the key embracing the 'Grail scene', and the 'Grail' theme ratifies it, rising up in C major to create a radiant exaltation as knights begin to enter the hall. They come from either side in two formal processions. They intone ritual sentences, and form a circle around its central shrine, and once they are assembled, the 'Grail' theme and its radiant exaltation come again, bringing a glory that overwhelms the imagination. (And all that Wagner does is to hold out a loud chord of C major over a bass that repeats C, F G and E. Pure witchcraft.) Mystical choirs now come in from the middle regions of the dome, and finally heavenly voices from the heights continue with more incantations. This sublime ritual should lead now to the revelation of the Grail and its miraculous powers. However the music fades into a dark silence, and nothing happens. Amfortas is eventually exhorted by his moribund father to unveil the Grail, because his father will die unless he can gaze daily into its radiance. At this Amfortas bursts into a passionate lamentation, accusing himself of sin and describing both the agony of his wound and a mental agony still worse, his awareness of being both the king and leader of the brotherhood and also its worst failure. At length the knights and voices from above calm him with the words of the prophecy. He prays agonisingly for mercy and forgiveness, and eventually sinks back exhausted. After Titurel has exhorted him a second time, he finally summons the resolve to reveal the Grail and set the seal on one of the most numinous scenes ever witnessed onstage – or anywhere. The voices from above virtually quote the words of Jesus Christ as he first instituted the sacrament of Holy Communion, and the Grail, an antique crystal cup, glows with otherworldly radiance. Amfortas is transfigured, if briefly. Bread and wine generated by the Grail are distributed, and Gurnemanz tries to draw in Parsifal. Instead Parsifal holds back, evidently taking in none of the Grail ceremony.

The knights are replenished by the ritual, and they sing the work's opening phrase with a solid rhythm and an assertiveness that is quite different from the original weightlessness which Wagner had created. Gradually the radiance fades; the king's wound again breaks out as the company disperse, leaving Gurnemanz alone with Parsifal. Gurnemanz asks briskly if he has understood what he saw. Parsifal convulsively shakes his head, and Gurnemanz, bitterly disappointed, throws him out with an irascible parting shot; let him leave swans alone in future; he himself is nothing but a goose. The grizzled knight has a fallible, engagingly human side. It is true that Parsifal did not understand the Grail ceremony, but as Wagner's stage directions tell us he has taken the agony of Amfortas into the very depths of his being. During Amfortas' anguished lamentation, Parsifal has clutched at his heart. As a mysterious voice from above hints, bringing the act to a sublime close, compassion is even now at work within Parsifal to transform him.

Act II moves to Klingsor's magic castle, with Klingsor himself in front of a magic mirror. He has long ago subdued Kundry to his will by gaining control over her curse, and he summons her from sleep, taunting her about her vain attempts, through acts of service, to undo the damage she has done, and reminding her of his power over her, which he somehow won through his self-mutilation. She in turn taunts him that his chastity is meaningless, and Klingsor turns on her furiously with the reminder that his occult powers have given him a control that is by no means meaningless, over Amfortas and the spear as well as her; soon the Grail itself will be in his hands. He asks sneeringly whether the 'hero' Amfortas was to her taste; and she moans that Amfortas was too weak to resist her; oh, if only she could achieve the sleep of oblivion! Klingsor then tells that the one who rejects her sets her free, and suggests insinuatingly that she tries her charms on the lad now approaching. First, he conjures up his fallen knights to do battle with the intruder. These are former members of the Grail fellowship who have fallen victim to his sorcery, his flower maidens. His callousness at the wounds which they sustain from Parsifal is more *Schadenfreude*; their sufferings simply amuse Klingsor. He now summons up the flower maidens to charm Parsifal. Initially they accuse and reprimand Parsifal for the harm he has done the knights who were their lovers, but they soon invite him to join in their flirtatious games. They entice him with a gentle swaying theme which was one of Wagner's first ideas for Parsifal, presenting itself to his imagination when trying in vain to think up some good music for an American commission. The commission was for a march celebrating the USA's Declaration of Independence, at a fee of $5000; instead this came into his mind.

Fig. 20.17 'Flower Maidens'

It has a lasciviousness so sweet, unwitting and simple, as to be almost innocent. For a while they are enchanting, but they fall to quarrelling over him, and this irritates him.

He is about to make off when he is held in thrall by the haunting sound of a woman calling his name, and asking him to stay awhile. This is allurement of a different order from the flower maidens; it is Kundry, transformed into a vision of voluptuous and breathtaking beauty,[113] beside which the flower maidens are insignificant. She gently dismisses them, and they depart, still imploring him, to a motive of supplication to that which will increasingly come to the fore later in this act and in the next.

---

113 Cosima recorded in her *Diaries* how Wagner told her that ideally she should lie there naked like a Titian Venus.

Fig. 20.18 'Supplication'

Parsifal is fascinated; how could she address him by the name that only his mother knew, having once called it out to him in her sleep.

Is this his mother come back to life? Kundry gently puts him right, and explains at length: his mother, Herzeleide had known much joy as the beloved of Gamuret and mother to Parsifal when he was a babe in arms; Kundry had known him through all that period when Herzeleide had tried to protect him from following his father and becoming a knight. But Kundry had also seen her sorrow.

Fig. 20.19 'Woe', 'Anguish' or 'Melancholy'

As Kundry explains, Parsifal had broken his mother's heart on the day he left, never to return; she pined away and died of grief. Parsifal is shaken to the depths, and torments himself; 'Where was I; where am I, that I could do this to you, sweetest, dearest mother?' In a move indicating Wagner's extraordinary psychological penetration, Kundry offers him release into oblivion from guilt even as she enfolds him in her arms and kisses him, telling him, 'A mother's last greeting, love's first kiss.' She cleverly implies that Parsifal has some kind of duty to respond out of filial piety, and that some obscure oneness with his mother or with her embodiment in Kundry will bring him atonement; but as the world fades for him under Kundry's intoxicating impact, the consequence is quite unexpected. Her kiss pierces him with a sense of something both ecstatic and disastrous. The swooning oblivion of it makes him aware of the evil of sex and lust as Schopenhauer believed it to be, which is blind, headlong egoism. Nothing else exists for Parsifal but the kiss, nothing else matters but this. It is intoxication, carnal exploitation, oblivion of others, oblivion of all else. The bliss took over, but at the same time it stabs Parsifal from his trance, and this saves him. He feels instantly that he had ceased to care for his mother, for anyone or anything. He is agonisingly conscious that what had gripped him was obsessive and destructive, stopping at nothing for the sake of itself. Through an insight and compassion that is now possible because of his own new experience, he recognises that the cause of Amfortas's torment as he witnessed it in the hall of the Grail was identical. It was the same self-centred egoism of lust but complicated by the agonising remorse for it which Amfortas felt while still remaining in its grip. The difference between Amfortas and Parsifal is compassion; Parsifal's undeveloped capacity for compassion has been awoken by Amfortas' suffering, whereas Amfortas has not shown any such capacity.

Because of this difference, Parsifal's experience of Kundry's kiss results in a new awareness, the sudden shift of consciousness that can come on abruptly in adolescence. This shift signifies partly an awakening of the erotic, but it also opens the door to other new vistas and new dimensions that are often disturbing. It creates an awareness of time and its boundaries and limitations, an awareness of mortality. It is about separation, the need to desert a family that is itself disintegrating. It throws the world wide open, but each person must go out into it and stand there alone. The new mode of being is opportunity, but also constraint; it is individual talent that is burgeoning, but yet restricted; it is the future opened wide, but also the current of time beginning to run ceaselessly, insistently, time passing relentlessly and closing in. These are some of the dragons which the boy who knows no fear must overcome.

Erotic experience, Kundry's kiss, can also signify wisdom and revelation. If a man is alienated from emotion and instinct, and many men are (and this is not sexist, but an admission that men really are more likely to be so alienated than women), a woman who fascinates him and opens up his humanity can appear to him to possess an age-old wisdom. In this situation erotic experience can lead to a new sphere of feeling and emotion that is not necessarily erotic, a whole new world of understanding.

The kiss has also brought to Parsifal an understanding of two separate experiences in the hall of the Grail. Almost beside himself, he tells out his recollections of Amfortas' agonising distress, and he can now appreciate it and what made it happen. He also experiences a second empathy, an empathy with Christ and his imploring lament, which he had sensed through another more mystical compassion. Parsifal could hear in his mind's ear the appeal that had rung out, 'Redeem me; save me from hands that are flecked with sin.' There is a twofold thrust to the appeal. First it is an appeal about the Holy Grail which is now being protected and revealed by Amfortas who is fallen and sinful, and is demonstrably incapable. Parsifal shows an intuitive sense of Christ's suffering and an intuitive recognition of Christ's presence in the Grail and its contents.[114] There is also another appeal, about the even worse problems attaching to the other hallowed relic, the sacred spear. The spear, which preserves a matching element of that same sanguineous presence as the Grail, is in the evil clutches of Klingsor. All this comes flooding into Parsifal's consciousness.

Kundry listens to all Parsifal's outpourings with their compassionate concern, and she asks Parsifal to extend that same compassion to her. She can barely bring herself to describe the *Schadenfreude* whose

---

114 This may partly reflect the biblical belief set out in Leviticus, that blood is the essence of life. It also partly reflects a wayward notion held quite widely in Wagner's time, that blood was the fluid essence of a person's character. Such apparently primitive beliefs were not uncommon even in the nineteenth century. The beliefs of phrenology, as already mentioned, were another common aberration of the times which explains Wagner's comments, ludicrous as they seem today, on the personality characteristics implicit in Beethoven's skull!

haunting memory has pursued her from world to world, incarnation to incarnation, but she manages to force out 'I saw – him' (Christ on the way to his crucifixion) 'and – I – laughed.' His response, his look of love, pierced her very being, making her aware of herself, and it was unbearable. Laughter and mockery were then branded into her as her only emotional expression available to her; and the memory drives her endlessly from one state of being to another, incarnation to incarnation, hoping endlessly to find Christ again, so that she can atone and experience again that look of love which alone can redeem her. This yearning has become confused in her mind with maternal yearnings of overwhelming force, and with some vague erotic yearnings fuelled by her need to be needed. Meanwhile Parsifal has been empowered by all the insight and understanding kindled by her kiss, and he knows now that he can somehow bring redemption to Amfortas. But she cannot accept the comparable offer of redemption which he promises her, because it is only possible if she denies all the egoism of her instinctive, carnal urges.

He turns down her offer of bodily union but then soon drives her to fury, both for scorning her as a woman and for demanding to be shown the way back to Amfortas. She regards Amfortas as despicable for his failures, condemning her own faults mercilessly when they appear in others; and when Parsifal persists, she goes so far as to curse his way back to Amfortas. She calls up help from Klingsor. Klingsor appears and plans to strike down Parsifal as he struck down Amfortas, but more decisively, because he deploys the sacred spear. He hurls it viciously at Parsifal, but it flies to a point above Parsifal's head and hovers in the air. Parsifal seizes it and pronounces an incantation against Klingsor:

> *Just as the spear shall close the wound*
> *Which you made with it,*
> *So shall it topple your treacherous*
> *Splendour in mourning and ruin!*
> *With this sign I end your magic!*

He makes the sign of the Cross, and as the 'Grail' motive blazes up in blistering dissonance, the whole scene collapses in ruin and nothingness, taking Klingsor with it and leaving a desert where Parsifal and Kundry are alone. He turns to her and tells her she knows where she can find him again.

Many years pass between the end of Act II and Act III. The Prelude to this act is a musical account of Parsifal's conflicted progress, both material and spiritual. He forges on indomitably against repeated adversities, and the way seems forever barred by Kundry's curse. The mood is one of dragging weariness.

Fig. 20.20 'Desolation – The Waste Land'

The constant promise of the Grail's nearness repeatedly proves an illusion as the glowing cadences of the Dresden Amen veer off into dissonance. The curtain goes up on a clearing in the forest of the Grail, with spring meadows in the distance. It is Good Friday, and Gurnemanz, who has become a hermit, is searching the undergrowth for the source of a strange yet familiar groaning sound. It leads him to discover Kundry once again, now dressed as a penitent. She is deathly cold and in a trance. He embraces her to warm her through, and attempts to rub her down and restore her circulation, but she awakens with a scream of horror at finding herself back in the world and still alive. Gurnemanz is somewhat affronted when she neither acknowledges him nor his efforts but says only two words, 'Service, service,' before lapsing into silence. Gurnemanz, still gruff but sad, responds that she will not have much service to do nowadays, because the knights have given up their active role in distant lands.

As he speaks, he sees an unfamiliar figure approaching, a knight

entirely encased in black armour. Gurnemanz makes friendly
Overtures: has the knight lost his way; can he help him; but the knight
makes no response. Gurnemanz, affronted again, tells the knight that
if the knight is vowed to silence, he, Gurnemanz, also has a vow to
fulfil; he must forbid anyone to stand in this holy place fully armed,
especially with his visor down, on Good Friday of all days! He asks the
knight testily: from what heathen realms has he come, not to know
that this is the holiest of all days when our Lord gave himself for
the redemption of mankind? The knight's only response is to remove
his helmet, whereupon Gurnemanz recognises the callow youth of
long ago who once laid low the swan. Parsifal, for of course it is he,
plants in the ground the spear that he is carrying, point upwards,
before kneeling to it in prayer. Gurnemanz is seized with an ecstasy of
recognition as he takes it in as the sacred spear, and identifies Parsifal as
the one who will lead the brotherhood back to health and wholeness.
Parsifal gently hails Gurnemanz in gratitude at finding him again, at
last, and the opening limb of the 'Communion' theme undergoes a
very simple change that somehow brims with significance. Instead of
dropping back in the third bar it lifts and this creates an extraordinary
sense of release. This is the form in which this motive will conclude
the whole work.

Fig. 20.21

Parsifal goes on to explain how he has wandered everywhere in the
world seeking his way back through trials and tribulations, foes and
battles, always hoping to rediscover the Grail. The way was always
closed by a curse until now – or does it still elude him? Everything
looks so changed and decayed. Gurnemanz reassures him: if he was
once under a curse it must be unmade, because he does indeed stand
in the realm of the Grail; and his release from the curse must be due

to Good Friday. But, as Gurnemanz sadly tells him, he is right about the decay. The brotherhood sorely needs the healing that Parsifal can bring; Amfortas has long refused to perform the Service of the Grail, and this has caused the brotherhood to sicken and fade. Starved of the Grail and its nourishing radiance, the knights wander feebly and aimlessly through the woods foraging for greens and roots; everyone fends for himself. Gurnemanz has retired to a remote corner to await his own end, inconsolable now that his own warrior lord Titurel has succumbed to Grail starvation and died.

Parsifal bursts out in an agony of contrition; '*Und ich, ich bin's, der all dies Elend schuf,* It is I, I who created all this misery.' Musically Wagner does so little, and yet the extremities of the Act III Tristan are not more intense than this barely accompanied utterance of Parsifal. Pure genius. In shouldering responsibility for the situation, Parsifal demonstrates his high lineage from Aeschylus' Orestes, who had not created the line of tragic events that destroyed the house of Atreus, but still took upon himself the responsibility for putting matters right. This is one of the prescriptions of *Parsifal*, that no matter who started the trouble, it is only by assuming responsibility that anyone can remedy the situation. Parsifal is the reverse of Amfortas, who could not cope with responsibility. Even Parsifal almost faints, and as happened in Act I, Kundry fetches him some water. Gurnemanz however enjoins that the rites of kingship call for purification from the sacred spring itself. In consequence Kundry begins to wash his feet with its water and then dries them with her hair, and this is such an obvious reference to Gospel references to Mary Magdalene, the woman who did this for Jesus Christ, that it has misled some commentators into identifying Parsifal with Christ. When Wagner was asked about this, on one occasion he answered that he had never given the matter a thought, and on another he said more testily and revealingly that if he had meant Parsifal to be Christ, he would have written the part for a bass! He was creating not a bio-drama of Christ himself, but a work which spelt out the transformation that could take place in a person who took to heart Christ's spirit and his precepts.

Parsifal acknowledges Kundry's ritual and asks Gurnemanz to anoint his head as well. Gurnemanz responds that it must be so, that Parsifal is now forgiven and cleansed of all sin, and is to be crowned king. The orchestra blazes up in a great demonstration of sound and affirmation as Gurnemanz completes the coronation. Parsifal, himself redeemed and ecstatic, casts his gaze upon the distant meadows; he has never seen anything so beautiful as these fields now, bathed as they are in celestial light. Gurnemanz tells him that this is the magic of Good Friday, and Parsifal again bursts out in anguish at all that this means; surely on this day of the Redeemer's agony on the Cross, all creation should grieve and weep. Gurnemanz gently puts him right; 'You see, it is not so!' Nature, he explains, has no immortality and no ability to perceive Christ's terrible suffering, but only an instinctive sense of his redemptive impact throughout all creation. Even the soulless flowers of the field know that today no harm will come to them from any human footprint crushing them down. Wagner has created here an experience that is almost mystical in its loveliness and purity. The music passes from B major to D major, and Parsifal gently makes clear to Kundry that he recognises her as the woman who in Act II attempted to destroy his mission and himself, but that he recognises even more her desire to atone. He baptises her and kisses her gently on the brow, a mutual purification. Kundry, whose punishment had been an inability to respond to to any emotive situation except with mockery and screeching laughter, is at last able to weep and weep and weep, as if her heart would break, and Parsifal recognises her salvation in her tears. He draws her attention to the smiling meadows of early spring, redeemed just as she too is redeemed. The distant sound of the Temple bells breaks in on the scene, reminding them that further action is still before them.

Parsifal's determination to put things right is now confirmed by his motive, blazing out on the brass, after which all horizons dissolve in *Parsifal's* second great 'Transformation' music. The bells come pealing in again but now create an atmosphere that is quite different. It is now the bottom note of the peal, a low E, that literally sets the tone, so that the key is not C major but grim E minor. This is the main tonal context for the music of Titurel's funeral, and the theme of 'Woe' or 'Anguish' from Act II (Fig. 20.19) appears in new developments. This music takes on an immense, gloomy grandeur and conveys a dark night of the soul, such as afflicts the brotherhood and perhaps the world. It leads to the final scene, again set in the hall of the Grail, where Wagner works a further act of tonal wizardry. He discloses that the E minor was all along a kind of springboard for the B flat minor chorus of the knights which begins the final scene. Titurel's funeral rites are under way. They include celebrations of Titurel's life, but also recriminations against Amfortas, whose refusal to reveal the Grail is leading to the death and extinction of the entire fellowship. Amfortas has now acquired an additional burden of guilt because he has in effect murdered his father, and he offers up a prayer to him, now in heaven, to intercede for him and bring him rest. Yet even now, Amfortas fails to act; even now he will let his failures destroy them all. The long-suffering knights finally rise up against him. He responds hysterically telling them to go ahead, yes, to plunge their swords into his wound up to the hilt and deliver him from his torment. They recoil, but suddenly appearing in their midst, Parsifal pronounces that only one weapon will suffice. He touches the wound with the tip of the sacred spear, instantly healing it and at the same time delivering Amfortas from the burden of responsibility which he cannot bear.

Parsifal himself takes office as King of the Grail and encourages Amfortas with the idea that good has come from his terrible sufferings; it is only through them that Parsifal is enabled to bring salvation to them all. They had begun to transform Parsifal from blind destructiveness to a wisdom and compassion which alone can redeem individuals and the world.

Parsifal has even redeemed Christ himself. The two sacred relics are the discarnate emblems of Jesus Christ's continuing presence on earth, and they belong together. Each had been crying out to the other, and this was the subject of the second empathy which Parsifal had described when he was in Klingsor's realm. There he recollected how he had heard not only Amfortas but also another cry, 'Redeem me, save me from hands that are defiled by sin.' Parsifal has succeeded in rescuing the spear from the sinful, defiling hands of Klingsor, and brought the twin relics together. He has freed them from their sacrilegious possession by Klingsor and Amfortas, and this is how he brings 'redemption to the Redeemer', as the choirs mystically intone it from the heights of the dome. There is redemption too for Kundry, released at last from the wheel of life into eternal oneness with everything.

At the end of the work Wagner marshals every symbol at his disposal to create a representation of a circle completed, brokenness made whole. First, *Parsifal* ends in the key where it began, an unusual conclusion in Wagner. Then in the Prelude to Act I, the 'Communion' theme was set in opposition to the music of the Grail. But now at the end, in the last music of the entire work, the 'Grail' theme becomes one with the 'Communion' theme's opening phrase. The 'Grail' theme rises up within the embracing shape of the 'Communion' theme as it has evolved in Act III, and they share their final notes. This is a musical reconciliation of the two main strands of Western Christianity, the Roman Catholic and Protestant traditions. Additionally the spear and the chalice are archetypal symbols of the two genders, and the action of *Parsifal* represents their long estrangement and impoverishment, because they are only half realised when separated. At the end they come together again, a unified whole, oneness, wholeness, integration.[115]

115 *Parsifal* was first performed at Bayreuth on 26 July 1882, the first of a series of sixteen performances, with changes in casting to lighten the load for the singers. Wagner was very concerned that no lesser honours should be accorded to the substitutes, some of whom he ultimately preferred. After the premiere when Hermann Winkelmann performed Parsifal, he shared the role with Heinrich Gudehus and Ferdinand Jäger. Amalie Materna, Wagner's original Brünnhilde, shared Kundry with Marianne Brandt and Therese Malten. Emil Scaria and Gustav Siehr alternated as Gurnemanz. Klingsor was divided between Karl Hill and Anton Fuchs, but Theodor Reichmann sang every Amfortas and August Kindermann every Titurel. The musical direction was shared between Hermann Levi who conducted the first performance and Franz Fischer,

We are now in a position to look deeper into the meaning of *Parsifal*. If Wagner had formulated his theology he might have avoided the confusion produced by the opening lines of his essay, *Art and Religion* (1880);[116] 'One might say that where religion becomes artificial, it is reserved to art to restore the spirit of religion by recognising the figurative value of the mythic symbols which the former would have us believe in the literal sense, and revealing their deep hidden truth through an ideal presentation.' These lines are quoted time and again as indicating that Wagner had fulfilled his mission by transforming and transcending Christianity in a sort of Hegelian process, subsuming its truths into a new religion of Art, such as we saw Dahlhaus maintaining.

People who read Wagner's essay further, instead of stopping after its opening sentence, will discover assertions and beliefs that put a wholly different complexion on that sentence, just as they will if they read Cosima's *Diaries*. They will realise that Wagner was drawing a distinction between symbols which depict a genuine religious truth and those that are nothing but 'an appalling degradation of religious dogmas into artificiality'. His illustration of 'degradation into artificiality' was a picture which he had seen above the porch at St Kilian's Cathedral in Würzburg, which depicted something which struck him as fatuous, 'a bas-relief of God the Father transmitting the embryo of the Saviour to the body of Mary by means of a blow-pipe'. Wagner drew a distinction between such things and art that 'represented true religion … This flagrant example will point up the redeeming effect of true idealising art if we turn to its handling by heaven-sent artists such as Raphael and his *Sistine Madonna*.'[117]

The *Sistine Madonna* hangs to this day in the Zwinger at Dresden, and Wagner described it as being about 'Love divine … this unspeakable wonder we see with our eyes, distinct and tangible, in sweetest concord with the noblest truths of our own inner being, but

---

under the close supervision of the composer, who himself conducted the last part of Act III for the final performance on 29 August.

116 *Prose Works*, tr. William Ashton Ellis, vol. vi.

117 *Art and Religion*, ibid.

lifted high above conceivable experience.[118] The painter has revealed here the inapprehensible and indefinable mystery of the religious dogmas, no longer to plodding reason, but to enraptured sight.' It is clear that Wagner regarded 'the mystery that the painter revealed' as a religious mystery, and that he took the same as true for *Parsifal*. For Wagner, art was the best medium by which inaccessible religious mysteries could become most tangible to the mind, but this did not mean that art itself became a religion or replaced it. Cosima recorded 'the thought he has written down: "The path from Religion to Art bad, from Art to Religion good".'[119] Art was the 'handmaid of religion', not 'religion the handmaid of art'.

Nor did Wagner seem to find the miraculous aspect of religion unbelievable. He made it clear that he regarded its miracles as counter-intuitive, as a mystery going against all preconceptions, but then pointed out that Christ's compassion in dying on the Cross for the sake of humanity was proof that the counter-intuitive and inconceivable *could* happen. Christ's acceptance of crucifixion and the compassion it expressed signified to Wagner a reversal of natural laws just as extreme as – say – the reversal of the laws of gravity. After anything so improbable as Christ's achievement, anything was possible; anything was credible, and any other miracles became believable.

This means that while *Parsifal* is in one sense valuable in the same way as the *Ring* is, because of the ideas and the psychological truths which the *Ring* reveals to us about ourselves, *Parsifal* also operates on a different plane. A belief in the gods of Valhalla is something that Wagner neither held himself nor expected anyone else to share, but the redeemer invoked in *Parsifal* has a different status. Wagner actually wrote to King Ludwig about *Parsifal*, 'It is as though I am inspired to write this in order to preserve the world's profoundest secret, the truest

---

118 We can only speculate whether this was intended as a deliberate riposte to Kant. Kant's argument was that anything which lay outside our senses and our ability to think about it had no reality for us.

119 Cosima's *Diaries*, ed. Martin Gregor-Dellin and Dietrich Mack, tr. Geoffrey Skelton, London, 1981 vol. ii; entry for 13 Jan 1880.

Christian faith, or rather, to awaken that faith anew.' This letter alone
would enough to demand a reappraisal of the notion that Wagner 'was
not interested in glorifying orthodox religion through art'. This view
is often argued with vehemence, as it was by William Kinderman in *A
Companion to Wagner's Parsifal*.[120] This is in many ways an illuminating
and worthwhile book, but he argues; 'Although Wagner assimilates
many Christian elements in *Parsifal*, the name Christus never appears,'
as though this were sufficient reason for thinking that it does not have a
context permeated by the presence of Jesus Christ. As further evidence
against the idea that *Parsifal* is Christian, Kinderman asserts that 'some
aspects of the work draw on pagan and Buddhist traditions'. Indeed
some commentaries press this further and urge that Wagner took over
so many symbols from many other faiths and philosophies for *Parsifal*
that *Parsifal* is a composite affair and that any Christianity in it has
been diluted out of existence.

There are two points. First, it is true that Christianity contains many
ingredients that are common to other religions, as anyone will realise
who is even distantly acquainted with J.G. Frazer's *The Golden Bough*,
that landmark text on the topic. However many religious elements
that were once universal symbols have long ago taken on specifically
Christian associations. Purification through water, for instance, long
antedated Christianity, and is a symbol found in many religions.
However, in Western Europe it has over the centuries acquired a very
Christian significance as baptism. Both friends and foes of Christianity
can hardly escape recognising Kundry's baptism in *Parsifal* as a
thoroughly Christian ingredient. In fact it was because baptism had
become so Christian, and would immediately be recognised as such by
his contemporaries, that Wagner deployed it to confirm the credentials
of *Parsifal* as a Christian myth.

The second point is about another argument, that many aspects
of *Parsifal* were absorbed into it from other well-developed religions
that are quite separate and distinct from Christianity, and that this

120 Kinderman, William and Katherine R. Syer, ed., *A Companion to Wagner's* Parsifal, Rochester, NY, 2005.

turns *Parsifal* into a non-Christian work. The important point is that these were largely taken over into Christianity long ago and so thoroughly absorbed, that they too now add to the Christian flavour of *Parsifal*. Wagner himself was well aware of this absorption process. At the time of *Lohengrin*, he had already made this very point in 'A Communication to my Friends': 'It is a fundamental error of our own superficiality to consider the specific Christian legends as original creations. Not one of the most affecting, not one of the most distinctive Christian myths belongs by right to the Christian spirit; it has inherited them all from the purely human intuition of earlier times and merely moulded them to fit its own peculiar tenets.' The Holy Grail itself had pagan origins; and in the epic of Wolfram von Eschenbach which was one of Wagner's main sources, the Grail was a magical stone. The Grail only gradually evolved through myth and literature into the chalice used by Christ for the institution of Holy Communion, and Derrick Everett has been particularly illuminating in drawing attention to another source for *Parsifal* which Wagner owned and had on the shelves of his Dresden library.[121] This was the story of *Josaphat and Barlaam*, an adaptation by St John of Damascus of the myth brought back from India by Christian missionaries and translated into German in 1325; in it Buddha is transformed into a Christian saint. It rewrites as Christian a central episode in the life of Buddha when Buddha was approaching a state of enlightenment like Parsifal in Act II. In the original Buddhist version, as Derrick Everett explains, Mara, lord of illusion was trying to spoil Buddha's chances of enlightenment, and sent against Buddha an army of demons. Instead of their weapons harming him, they fell round him as flowers. Mara then sent his beautiful daughters, also demons, who attempted but failed to seduce the hero. Finally Mara himself appeared, to launch the final blow with his magic weapon, a discus, but it rose and fell in the air like a dry leaf, and afterwards remained in splendour above Buddha's head. In the version of St John of Damascus, owned by

121 Everett, Derrick, 'Parsifal under the Bodhi Tree', *Wagner*, vol. xxii, no. 2 (2001), Wagner Society of the United Kingdom. p. 67 et seq.

Wagner, the hero becomes Josaphat, a convert to Christianity; Mara becomes a sorcerer, and instead of sending a host of maidens, he sends just one, a beautiful princess. The hero resists her and she promises that she will let herself be saved by him if he will spend a few hours of passion with her. Anyone unaware of the adaptation by St John of Damascus might imagine that this episode was something that Wagner himself had appropriated from Buddhism, and that it was a Buddhist ingredient taken over by Wagner with which he 'watered down the Christianity' in *Parsifal*, but as this account shows it was actually absorbed and metabolised into Christian mythology centuries earlier. It was in the form of a Christian myth that Wagner knew it, and had become so Christian that it reinforces the Christianity of *Parsifal* instead of watering it down.

As mentioned, William Kinderman also suggests that *Parsifal* is less definitely Christian because the name Christus never appears, but one might just as well argue that *Tannhäuser* is the less definitely about Tannhäuser because the name of Tannhäuser never appears. Kinderman's point seems all the more puzzling for two reasons, first that *Parsifal* centres on an idea of Good Friday which is absolutely and uniquely Christian. '*Das ist Charfreitagszauber, Herr!* (That is the spell of Good Friday, Lord!)' is what Gurnemanz tells Parsifal in Act III. Second, Jesus Christ is the only conceivable candidate for Gurnemanz's description, 'He himself on the Cross cannot be perceived by redeemed nature.'[122] Ulrike Kienzle follows the same line as Kinderman when she ends her discussion of whether *Parsifal* is a Christian music drama.[123] She says, 'We need to answer "No" to this

---

122 It is worth remembering that in the nineteenth century there were still conventions that certain names were too sacred to spoken aloud, and that the way round the difficulty of mentioning them was by using some descriptive phrase, and this is a legacy of the Old Testament belief that God was too sacred for human lips to speak. Houston Stewart Chamberlain even argued that Cosima Wagner should belong to this select group of those whose name was too holy to be spoken!

123 in Kinderman and Syer, *op. cit.*

question if we wish to regard Wagner's last work as reinforcing the dogmas of the Church, whether Protestant or Catholic.'

Of course *Parsifal* is not doctrine-reinforcing in any fundamentalist sense. It does not state the Nicene Creed any more than does Milton's *Paradise Lost*, but as far as I know no deconstructionist has ever yet declared that Milton was really a closet atheist. In fact Wagner would have been upset if *Parsifal* had 'reinforced Church dogmas'. He consciously quoted and followed Schiller: 'In the Christian religion I find an intrinsic disposition to all that is highest and noblest, and its various manifestations in life appear to me so vapid and repugnant simply because they fall short of expressing that highest.' He told King Ludwig that true Christianity offered far more than 'a contract where the beneficiary is to obtain eternal never ending bliss on condition of free-willed suffering in this relatively brief and fleeting life'.[124] His objection to churchy, institutionalised Christianity was that it had 'had clutched at the weapons of state jurisdiction, transforming herself into a political power' and entirely perverted Christ's ideals of a universal compassion, by encouraging wars and condoning slavery. However, *Parsifal* is set in the terrain of Christianity even more surely than *Tristan* is set in the terrain of Schopenhauer. *Parsifal* also takes for granted that its Christian beliefs are truths, facts about the world as real as any truths of history and natural science.

What is more, *Parsifal* specifically embodies and promotes the principles of Christianity as taught and lived by Jesus Christ. Wagner confronted the institutionalised distortions of Christianity which he saw all around him and put to himself the question, 'Does this mean that religion itself has ceased?' He answered: 'No, no! It lives, but only at its final source and true dwelling place within the deepest holiest chambers of the individual. For *this* is the essence of true religion; that away from the cheating show of the day-time world, it shines in the night of man's inmost heart.'

124 'On State and Religion' (1865) in *Prose Works*, vol. iv, *Art and Politics*, tr. William Ashton Ellis, London, 1894.

Wagner's disillusioned view of organised religion was not unusual in the nineteenth century and has revealing parallels with Dostoevsky in his story of Christ and the Grand Inquisitor from *The Brothers Karamazov*. It may help with this important point to recall that Dostoevsky's story describes a miraculous reappearance by Christ on earth, this time in Spain during the Inquisition. The earth is straightaway transfigured and the common people are enraptured as he begins to do good and create a world that is both better and happier. Then the Grand Inquisitor appears, the grim representative of organised religion. He frowningly rejects Christ and his principles, his message of love and compassion, because they are a dangerous challenge to the authoritarian church. The Grand Inquisitor asserts that people do not want and cannot manage freedom. They want rules, order, subservience. The Inquisitor arrests Christ as a heretic for threatening to undermine the dogmas which the mass of humanity requires. Wagner's comment that 'True Christianity has not yet begun,' was likewise almost a pre-echo of G.K. Chesterton's gritty observation, that the trouble with Christianity was not that it had been tried and failed, but that it was so difficult that it had never been tried at all.

The question still arises why so many people disapprove and vilify the work, and often so venomously. One reason was Nietzsche (Nietzsche again!) who famously described *Parsifal* as 'an outrage on morals'. People are too ready to believe that because of Nietzsche and his standing, there must be something vaguely but genuinely detestable about *Parsifal*, even if it is not clear what it is. However what Nietzsche detested in *Parsifal* was simply its compassion, not a quality that most people regard as particularly detestable. The advocacy of compassion in *Parsifal* was the reason why Nietzsche pronounced that it was the product of old age, and that his erstwhile hero Wagner now 'sank down suddenly, helpless and broken before the Christian Cross'. It was the compassion in *Parsifal* that proved to Nietzsche that Wagner was now a 'degenerate'. Socrates and Jesus Christ were the other degenerates whom Nietzsche lumped together with Wagner (not bad company!) for being tainted with the same mawkish compassion. It is quite wrong to believe that Nietzsche condemned *Parsifal* for mysterious other reasons, or imagine from Nietzsche that Wagner somehow spent his life mainlining heroin or wallowing in all the perversions, and that *Parsifal* was just as bad.

The context of Nietzsche's views was the climate of Darwinian revolution which had recently swept through Europe and its intellectuals, something already mentioned in connection with Schopenhauer. Against the background of natural selection, Nietzsche spearheaded the idea that compassion for weaker beings was hostile to evolutionary progress; that it resulted in biological and intellectual degeneracy. Compassion gave an undeserved advantage to poor-quality human specimens and to undeserving mentalities which nature and evolution would rightly consign to the bonfire. Most people might feel hesitant about following Nietzsche into this particular brave new world, but unsurprisingly Alfred Rosenberg, the leading Nazi ideologue, adopted it with alacrity. It was he too who (equally unsurprisingly) complained, '*Parsifal* represents a church-influenced enfeeblement in favour of the value of renunciation.' In November 1941, Hitler was thinking on the same lines when he told Goebbels he would 'see to it that religion was banished from *Parsifal*'. Hitler had already held discussions a year earlier with the young Wolfgang Wagner to the effect that after the final victory, *Parsifal* 'was no longer to be done in the Byzantine-sacred style that was common up to then,' and which had been Wagner's own.

Hitler was right to be wary of *Parsifal*. Everything that *Parsifal* represents is at loggerheads with Nazism, whatever compost of ideas had gone into its making. On Good Friday 1865, Wagner wrote to King Ludwig, 'Oh blessed day! Most deeply portentous day in the world! Day of redemption! God's suffering!! Who can grasp the magnitude of it? And yet, this same ineffable mystery – is it not the most familiar of mankind's secrets? God, the creator, must remain totally unintelligible to the world; God, the loving teacher, is dearly beloved, and not understood; but the God who suffers – is inscribed in our hearts in letters of fire; all the obstinacy of existence washed away by our immense pain at seeing God suffering. The teaching which we could not comprehend now touches us: God is within us. The world has been overcome. Who made it? Idle question! Who overcame it? God, whom we comprehend in the deepest anguish of fellow suffering!'[125] Redemption, fellow-feeling, compassion: and yet Hitler could say that he who would understand National Socialism must know Wagner! No wonder that J.R.R. Tolkien would write of his 'private grudge against that ruddy little ignoramus Adolf Hitler for ruining, perverting, misapplying and making forever accursed that noble Northern spirit, a supreme contribution to Europe, which I have ever loved and tried to present in its true light.'[126]

One interesting suggestion offered by *Parsifal* is for a new ordering and structuring of society after feudalism and capitalism have been consigned to history, the very thing which *The Ring* failed to do. In a world of broken communities and societies, *Parsifal* demonstrates a vision and even some definite ideas towards a wholeness of community, as well as ideas towards wholeness for the individual. Although we know nothing of any individual Grail knights except Gurnemanz, their fellowship bears a distant resemblance to the guild of the masters in *Die Meistersinger*. Here in *Parsifal* is another band of dedicated men, guided this time by ethical principles instead of artistic ones, and deploying the will to power to crusade to establish them in the world beyond. As *Parsifal* demonstrates, its members have to believe in a divine power, greater than themselves, which is itself benign and compassionate, and they must willingly and eagerly submit themselves and their own will to power to it and be guided by it. This is a condition of membership and that 'power greater than themselves' is symbolised in the Grail. Its members are nourished by it for their purpose, which is to make a valuable difference to the world; and their guiding star is the compassion which the Grail commands and radiates. The Grail fellowship is thus a mutualist society which is not dominated by the

125 *Selected Letters of Richard Wagner*, ed. Stewart Spencer & Barry Millington, London, 1987; letter of Richard Wagner to King Ludwig, 14 April 1865.
126 Carpenter, Humphrey, *J.R.R. Tolkien: A Biography*, London, 1977, p. 183.

lust for gold or the will to power, but animated by compassion and by a compassionate concern for others. But *Parsifal* is not utopian; far from being removed from harsh reality, it shows a noble community almost broken because headstrong individuals have broken with any submission to divine guidance. Worse, they act without compassion, and whenever things go wrong in *Parsifal* it is because the balance between love as compassion and the will to power has been ructioned. This is exactly the commonest thing that goes wrong with most forms of organised religion and most other human institutions. Even so a human society which accepted compassion for other human beings as an overriding ideal instead of idolising barefaced greed or the will to power might be an interesting and appealing place to live.

Perhaps there is in *Parsifal* submerged somewhere, but yet shining through, the familiar precept: no morality without religion. My personal sense of the religious dimension of *Parsifal* has been coloured by people who did find in it a conduit to the divine and the transcendental. There will be different opinions to the end of time about whether this divinity has an independent existence in whose belief the monk at Ettal so shiningly lived, or is merely an illusion, a man-made fabrication deriving its effect from its power over the imagination. These are deep waters, and to go any deeper is obviously beyond this book. Even so it is not a matter of opinion but a fact that *Parsifal* can be used as a road to the divine, and I owe my awareness of this to Dr Ernst Kirchner, an Austrian country doctor, whom I met at an impressionable stage while in Vienna just after leaving school. Dr Kirchner was not a Wagner expert but a hard-working physician with an altruistic streak, a gentle, civilised man and a liberal intellectual reminiscent of Dr Pusinelli, Wagner's own Dresden doctor. Dr Kirchner was exactly the kind of person that Wagner hoped to address, and it was an eye-opener to spend time with him and hear him explain how *Parsifal* was as religious for him as any service or liturgy in a church. He was a Lutheran, and *Parsifal* was not Lutheran worship, and certainly not like a normal church service where he would reckon to participate actively. However, *Parsifal* still afforded

him a divine connection, a conduit to the Almighty. As it happens
there are denominations of Christianity where the members of the
congregation are silent onlookers, just like the audiences for *Parsifal*,
and yet not the less on that account do they partake in the ritual nor
the encounter with God. The celebrant and sometimes a choir may be
the ones to perform the ritual, but the congregation by its presence
and its active silence participate to the full.

During two performances of Herbert von Karajan's great *Parsifal*
production (Vienna, 1961), I was startled to learn from interval
discussions with several of Dr Kirchner's friends, that his sense of
a religious connection through *Parsifal* was not unique to him or
even unusual. For these people and for others, *Parsifal* inspired
religious experience; it purveyed religious experience; it *was* religious
experience. They felt able to commune through *Parsifal* with a divine
higher power; and when I challenged them brashly about the reality
or otherwise of this communion, one of them explained that it was as
true and authentic as anything that he knew, and that he saw no sense
in doubting it. For them the contact with God mediated by *Parsifal*
was quite as real as talking to me or their relationships with their wives
or husbands, if not more so.

This starts to venture towards those very waters which are beyond
this book, to the questions about the truth value of the beliefs implicit
in *Parsifal*. But whatever the status of these beliefs, it remains true
that *Parsifal* more than anything else by Wagner presses its claims
beyond the footlights, and enjoins ideas that vitally affect us and the
future of the world. Our encounter with Montsalvat comes with a
demand that we accept its standards for actual life. The experience of
Parsifal enjoins kindliness, compassion, loyalty, generosity, integrity,
responsibility, a willingness to get involved and act, and a willingness
to leave well alone – and so much else of value.

There are people who go beyond Dr Kirchner and recognise
Parsifal as evangelism, as preaching Christianity and promoting a
belief in Christianity. It should be clear from the accounts and sources
quoted here that Wagner at times viewed *Parsifal* as evangelism; it was

much the same way as with, say, *The Light of The World* by Holman Hunt.[127] For people affected Wagner could scarcely have invoked and evangelised Christianity more directly if he had brought in Bach's Mass in B minor. It is Bach who has been dubbed the 'fifth evangelist' because of the religious persuasiveness of the *St Matthew Passion* and the Mass in B minor, but there are people who place *Parsifal* in the same category. For them Wagner is almost a sixth evangelist, and even though this idea reduces others to apoplexy, it is likely from what Wagner wrote on the subject that he would have seen this as proper recognition.

Two further points; first, that *Parsifal* can be profoundly constructive as a work of secular spirituality, even for people opposed to its Christianity; but while it can still bring about 'regeneration through identification with Parsifal and through the acquisition of a universal compassion,' the experience is not the same. The difference is like the difference between some theatrical knight declaiming John Donne's sonnets and an ordinary person addressing them to a woman he loves. The professional actor may do a better job artistically, but the young man in love is doing something completely different. The one provides an aesthetic experience, the other makes a personal declaration, and the relative artistic merits of the two are beside the point. The same applies to religion and religious music. Even in the same choir there is all the difference in the world between someone who sings Palestrina simply for the aesthetic experience, and someone who draws on it to worship God.

The second point: some of the reinterpretations that confuse the way to *Parsifal* seem the result of people arranging the work to fit their own convictions, perhaps even their prejudices. Like everything else, *Parsifal* can be twisted to mean almost anything, even its exact opposite, but this is the only way that it can be all things to all men.

127 *The Light of the World* is a picture by Holman Hunt in two versions, one of which now hangs in St Paul's Cathedral in London. After it was painted, this version was shipped round the world making many converts to Christianity, particularly in Australia.

The range of meanings genuinely available in Wagner's works has its limits. It seems inconsistent with all we know of Wagner, to argue that *Parsifal* is really a secret manifesto of racial evil, a cryptic code of satanic principles secretly deployed to infest Teutonic thinking and initiate the Holocaust. Wagner was never secret about anything he believed in; he could not resist broadcasting his every viewpoint from the rooftops, even his racial viewpoints and his paranoid hatred of the Jews – *especially* his racist paranoias, *above all* his hatred of the Jews. It flies in the face of commonsense to maintain that Wagner intended *Parsifal* as surreptitious anti-Jewish propaganda.

Whatever anyone believes, *Parsifal* remains an incomparable refreshment of the spirit. Perhaps the final word can left to Wagner himself. After the first performances in 1883 he asked, 'Who can look, this life-time long, with open eyes and un-pent heart, upon this world of robbery and murder, organised and legalised by lying, deceit and hypocrisy, without being forced to flee from it at times? ... In *Parsifal* you could forget the actual world ... in a dream image of truth, a harbinger of redemption ... You could only seek your quietus in a higher reality. And you found it.'

LIST OF ILLUSTRATIONS

Reproductions are from the author's collection unless stated otherwise. Every reasonable effort has been made to track down copyright holders; any queries should be addressed to the publishers.

VOLUME I

1. **Rosine Wagner**, painted by her husband Ludwig Geyer (1779-1821), oil on canvas, Richard-Wagner-Museum, Bayreuth
2. **Ludwig Geyer**, self-portrait, oil on canvas, Richard-Wagner-Museum, Bayreuth
3. **Adolf Wagner**; German school, early 19th century, oil on canvas, Richard-Wagner-Museum, Bayreuth
4. **Heinrich Laube, writer and leader of the Young Germany movement, in 1836**; lithograph by Friedrich Elias (1813-1845) after Friedrich Randel (1808-1886)
5. **Minna Planer in 1836**, by Alexander von Otterstedt (German, early to mid 19th century), oil on canvas, Richard-Wagner-Museum, Bayreuth
6. **Minna Wagner in 1853 with her dog Peps**, painted by Clementine Stockar-Escher (1816-1886), watercolour, Richard-Wagner-Museum, Bayreuth
7. **Arthur Schopenhauer**, painted in 1859 by Jules Lunteschutz (1822-1893), oil on canvas, Richard-Wagner-Museum, Bayreuth
8. **Franz Liszt in 1865**, oil on canvas, Klassik Stiftung Weimar, Liszt-Haus
9. **Mathilde Wesendonck in 1850**; Karl Ferdinand Sohn (1805-1867), oil on canvas, StadtMuseum Bonn
10. **King Ludwig II of Bavaria as a young man**; colour lithograph, French, after an original photograph c. 1867
11. **Cosima Wagner in 1879**, painted by Franz von Lenbach (1836-1904), oil on canvas, private collection

12.   Richard and Cosima Wagner in Vienna in 1872, photograph by Fritz Luckhardt (1843-1894)

13.   Poster announcing the first *Ring* cycle as a '*Tetralogie*', 1876

14.   Franz Betz, the original Wotan, in 1876

15.   Amalie Materna, the original Brünnhilde, in 1876

16.   Friedrich Schorr, the leading Wotan of the 1920s and 30s

Six Scenes from Wagner's Life; set of six chromolithographed collectible cards advertising Liebig's Fleisch-Extrakt, late 19th century

17.   Wagner plays to his dying stepfather

18.   Wagner as a student

19.   The Asyl (Villa Wesendonck, Zurich)

20.   *Tannhäuser* in Paris

21.   Wagner performs the *Siegfried Idyll* for Cosima at Tribschen

22.   Wagner with Kaiser Wilhelm I at the Opening of the Festspielhaus, Bayreuth

23.   **Richard Wagner at home with Cosima, Franz Liszt and Hans von Wolzogen**; German school, late 19th century, oil on canvas, Richard-Wagner-Museum, Bayreuth

24.   **The Festspielhaus at Bayreuth**, watercolour

Eight photographs of Wieland Wagner productions at the Bayreuth Festival

25.   *Das Rheingold* – **Wotan before Valhalla**, photograph signed by Hans Hotter (1958)

26.   *Das Rheingold* – **The Gods before Valhalla** (1958)

27.   *Die Walküre* – **Brünnhilde's Plea** (Hans Hotter and Astrid Varnay, 1958)

28.   *Die Walküre* – **Wotan's Farewell** (Hans Hotter and Astrid Varnay, 1958)

29.   *Tannhäuser* – **Tannhäuser Prays for his Salvation** (Wolfgang Windgassen, 1960)

30.   *Lohengrin* – **Lohengrin's First Appearance** (Jess Thomas as Lohengrin, 1960)

31.   *Parsifal* – **Grail scene, Act I** (George London as Amfortas, 1962)

32.   *Tristan und Isolde* – **Tristan Drinks the Love Philtre** (Wolfgang Windgassen, Birgit Nilsson, 1962)

VOLUME II

Eight illustrations from *Richard Wagner: 12 Illustrationen von Ferd. Leeke*
Colour lithographs (c. 1900-10) after original oil paintings by Ferdinand
Leeke (1859-1923)

33. *Die Feen*
34. *Der fliegender Holländer* – The Dutchman and Daland
35. *Tannhäuser* – Wolfram Takes his Farewell of Elisabeth
36. *Lohengrin* – Lohengrin Defeats Telramund
37. *Die Walküre* – Brünnhilde and Wotan
38. *Götterdämmerung* – Siegfried and the Rhinemaidens
39. *Die Meistersinger* – Walter's Prize Song
40. *Parsifal* – Parsifal's Journey to the Grail

Tannhäuser
41. John Collier (1850-1934), *Tannhäuser in the Venusberg*, oil on
     canvas, 1901, Atkinson Art Gallery, Southport

Six Scenes from *Tannhäuser*, set of six chromolithographed collectible
cards advertising Liebig's Fleisch-Extrakt, late 19th century
42. Tannhäuser Wanting to Leave the Venusberg, Act I Scene 1
43. Wolfram Recognises Tannhäuser, Act I Scene 4
44. Elisabeth and Tannhäuser, Act II Scene 1
45. Tannhäuser Sings of Venus, Act II Scene 4
46. The Pilgrims' Return from Rome, Act III Scene 1
47. Tannhäuser Dies, Saved, Act III final scene

48. Franz Stuck (1863-1928), *Die Sünde (Sin)*, oil on canvas, 1893,
     Neue Pinakothek, Munich
49. Joseph Tichatschek and Wilhelmine Schröder-Devrient in the
     first performance of *Tannhäuser*, Dresden, 19 October 1845, by F.
     Tischbein (German, mid 19th century); sepia drawing (1845)
50. The Wartburg, scene of Tannhäuser Act II, today

Lohengrin and *Tristan und Isolde*
51. *Lohengrin* Act I
52. *Lohengrin* Act III; René Kollo, Karl Ridderbusch, Anna

Tomowa-Sintow; Salzburg Easter Festival, 1976; set design by
Günther Schneider-Siemssen; Herbert von Karajan, musical and
artistic director. Photographer: Siegfried Lauterwasser

53.   **Tristan and Kurwenal (*Tristan und Isolde*, Act III);** Jon Vickers
and Walter Berry; Salzburg Easter Festival, 1971; artistic and
musical director: Herbert von Karajan

54.   **Henri Fantin-Latour (1836-1904),** *Lohengrin,* oil on canvas,
Musée de la Ville de Paris, Musée du Petit-Palais, Paris

55.   **Ludwig Schnorr von Carolsfeld (1836-1865), self-portrait as
Lohengrin,** 1861

56.   **John William Waterhouse (1849-1917),** *Tristram and Isolde,* oil
on canvas, 1916, private collection

Das Rheingold and *Die Walküre*

57.   **The Rhinemaidens at play;** Arthur Rackham (1867-1939), colour
lithograph, 1910

58.   **The Rhinemaidens enticing Alberich** (Rackham)

59.   **Alberich seizes the gold;** Franz Stassen (1869-1949), colour
lithographs from *Der Ring des Nibelungen,* 4 vols., [1922-32]

60.   **The Rhinemaidens complain to Loge** (Rackham)

61.   **Alberich flogs the Nibelungen** (Rackham)

62.   **Loge: 'Spare me, Dragon!'** (Rackham)

63.   **Erda's Warning** (Rackham)

64.   **Fafner murders Fasolt** (Rackham)

65.   **The Rhinemaidens' lament** (Rackham)

66.   **Sieglinde succours Siegmund** (Rackham)

67.   **Brünnhilde in the joy of youth** (Rackham)

68.   **Fricka rides out in fury** (Rackham)

69.   **Brünnhilde dazed and confused by Wotan's orders** (Rackham)

70.   **Brünnhilde prepares to tell Siegmund he must die** (Rackham)

71.   **The sleep of Brünnhilde** (Rackham)

Siegfried; Arthur Rackham (1867-1939), colour lithographs, 1911

72.   **Sieglinde in the forest**

73.   **Mime at the anvil**

74.   **Siegfried learns what love is like**

75.   **Nothung reforged**

76.   **Wanderer with Mime**

77.   **Siegfried slays Fafner**

78.   Siegfried tastes the dragon's blood
79.   Siegfried overwhelmed by Brünnhilde

Götterdämmerung
80.   Franz Stassen (1869-1949), *The Norns at the World Ash,* colour
       lithograph from *Der Ring des Nibelungen,* 4 vols., [1922-32]

Seven illustrations by Arthur Rackham (1867-1939), colour lithographs,
1911
81.   The Norns fade into nothingness
82   Brünnhilde treasures Siegfried's Ring
83.   Waltraute remonstrates over the Ring
84.   Siegfried with the Rhinemaidens
85.   The Rhinemaidens entreat Siegfried one last time
86.   Brünnhilde rides into the flames
87.   The Rhinemaidens drown Hagen and recover the Ring

88.   Donald McIntyre as Wotan summoning the magic fire, in the
       centenary performance of *The Ring* at Bayreuth, 1976; director
       Patrice Chéreau, musical director Pierre Boulez

A Wagner Miscellany
89.   Seven Valkyries, Covent Garden, 1935
90.   Berta Morena as Brünnhilde, c. 1910
91.   The Ride of the Valkyries; design by Carl Emil Doepler for
       a magic lantern projection used in the original 1876 Bayreuth
       staging.
92.   Hans Sachs the cobbler, *Die Meistersinger* Act II: Liebig's
       Fleisch-Extrakt, late 19th century
93.   Hans Sachs the cobbler, *Die Meistersinger* Act II: Hans Hotter,
       Bayreuth, 1956; production: Wieland Wagner, musical director
       André Cluytens
94.   *The Annunciation,* Marienkapelle, Würzburg, bas-relief, c. 1420
95.   Raphael (1483-1520), *The Sistine Madonna,* oil on canvas, 1513,
       Gemäldegalerie Alte Meister, Dresden
96.   Betsy de la Porte as Waltraute (*Die Walküre,* Covent Garden, 1935)

Parsifal

Six Scenes from *Parsifal*; set of six chromolithographed collectible cards advertising Liebig's Fleisch-Extrakt, late 19th century

97.   **Amfortas tells of the prophecy of the pure fool**, Act I
98.   **Parsifal and Gurnemanz in the Grail Temple**, Act I
99.   **Parsifal and Kundry in Klingsor's castle**, Act II
100.   **Parsifal takes the spear**, Act II
101.   **Parsifal robed by Gurnemanz and Kundry**, Act III
102.   **Parsifal heals Amfortas' wound**, Act III

103.   **Titian (c. 1488-1576),** *Venus of Urbino*, oil on canvas, 1538, Uffizi, Florence.
104.   **Waltraud Meier as Kundry**, Staatsoper Unter den Linden, Berlin, 1990s; production Harry Kupfer, musical director Daniel Barenboim

BIBLIOGRAPHY

Selected Works by Richard Wagner

Das Judenthum in der Musik, (published pseudonymously as by 'K. Freigedenk': Leipzig, 1850,) repr. (as by Wagner,) 1869
My Life, authorized translation from the German, London, 1911, also New York, 1911, (http://catalog.hathitrust.org/Record/001457327)
Prose Works, tr. William Ashton Ellis, 8 vols., London, 1892-9

       'A Communication to my Friends', in *Prose Works*, vol. i
       'Beethoven', in *Prose Works*, vol. v
       'Beethoven's "Heroic Symphony"', in *Prose Works*, vol. iii
       'Ludwig Schnorr of Carolsfeld' in *Prose Works*, vol. iv
       'On State and Religion' in *Prose Works*, vol. iv
       'On the Application of Music to the Drama', in *Prose Works*, vol. vi
       'On the name "Music Drama"', *Prose Works*, vol. v
       'On the Performing of "Tannhäuser"', in *Prose Works*, vol. iii
       Opera and Drama: *Prose Works*, vol. ii
       '"Parsifal" at Bayreuth', in *Prose Works*, vol. vi
       Religion and Art, in *Prose Works*, vol. vi
       The Artwork of the Future, in *Prose Works*, vol. i
       'The Destiny of Opera', in *Prose Works*, vol. v
       'The Nibelungen-Myth Considered as a Sketch for a Drama' (1848), in *Prose Works*, vol. vii

Correspondence of Richard Wagner

Correspondence of Wagner and Liszt, tr. Francis Hueffer, New York, 1889
Richard to Minna Wagner: Letters to his First Wife, tr. William Ashton Ellis, London, 1909
Richard Wagner to Mathilde Wesendonck, tr. William Ashton Ellis, London, 1905

Richard Wagner's Letters to August Röckel, tr. Eleanor C. Sellar, Bristol, [1897]

Richard Wagner's Letters to his Dresden Friends, tr. J.S. Shedlock, London, [1890]

Selected Letters of Richard Wagner, ed. and tr. Stewart Spencer and Barry Millington, London, 1987

The Family Letters of Richard Wagner, tr. William Ashton Ellis, London, 1911

The Letters of Richard Wagner and Anton Pusinelli, tr. Elbert Lenrow, New York, 1932 (repr. 1972)

The Letters of Richard Wagner, The Burrell Collection, tr. Hans Abraham, Henry Lea and Richard Stoehr, ed. John N. Burk, London, 1951

Select General Bibliography

Alcoholics Anonymous, AA World Services Inc., 3rd ed., New York, 1976

Artin, Tom, *The Wagner Complex: Genesis and Meaning in* The Ring, [Sparkill, N.Y.,] 2012

Barth, Herbert, Dietrich Mack and Egon Voss, *Wagner, a Documentary Study*, London, 1975

Beckett, Lucy, *Parsifal*, Cambridge, 1981

Berlin, Isaiah, *Karl Marx*, London, 1939, 3rd ed., Oxford, 1963

Bloom, Paul, *How Pleasure Works*, London, 2011

Bolen, Jean Shinoda, *Ring of Power: The Abandoned Child, the Authoritarian Father, and the Disempowered Feminine*, New York, 1992

Borchmeyer, Dieter, *Richard Wagner: Theory and Theatre*, tr. Stewart Spencer, Oxford, 1991

Brooke, Rupert, *Collected Poems: With a Memoir*, London, 1918

Brown, Callum G., *The Death of Christian Britain: Understanding Secularisation, 1800-2000*, Abingdon, 2001

Browning, Christopher R., *The Origins of the Final Solution*, Lincoln, Nebr. and Jerusalem, 2004

Bülow, Hans von, *Letters of Hans von Bülow*, tr. Scott Goddard, New York, 1972

Carpenter, Humphrey, *J.R.R. Tolkien: A Biography*, London, 1977

Chamberlain, Houston Stewart, *Richard Wagner*, tr. G. Ainslie Height, London, 1900

Cheltenham Festival, *Maestro* Magazine, 4-15 July 2012

Clément, Catherine, *Opera or the Undoing of Women*, tr. Betsy Wing, London, 1989

Cord, William O., 'Assessment of the Secrets of the Power Wagner's Work

Holds over Us', *Leitmotive*, vol. XXI no. 2 (Summer 2007)

Dahlhaus, Carl, *Richard Wagner's Music Dramas*, tr. Mary Whittall, Cambridge, 1979

Deathridge, John, *Wagner beyond Good and Evil*, Berkeley, Cal., 2008

Dickson, Anne, *The Mirror Within: A New Look at Sexuality*, London, 1985

Donington, Robert, *The Ring and its Symbols*, London, 1963

Dreyfus, Laurence, *Wagner and the Erotic Impulse*, Cambridge, Mass., 2010

Ellis, William Ashton, *Life of Richard Wagner*, 6 vols, London, 1900-8

Everett, Derrick, 'Parsifal under the Bodhi Tree', in *Wagner*, vol. xxii, no. 2 (2001)

Exley, Helen, *... And Wisdom Comes Quietly*, Watford, 2000

Freud, Sigmund, *The Interpretation of Dreams*, tr. A.A. Brill, New York, 1913

Fromm, Erich, *The Art of Loving*, New York, 1956

Furtwängler, Wilhelm, *Furtwängler on Music*, tr. Ronald Taylor, Aldershot, 1991

Göllerich, August, and Max Auer, *Anton Bruckner: Ein Lebens- und Schaffens-Bild*, 3 vols., Regensburg, 1932.

Gregor-Dellin, Martin, *Richard Wagner, His Life, his Work and his Century*, tr. J. Maxwell Brownjohn, London, 1983

Greinacher, Norbert, 'How does Tannhäuser find Salvation?', in programme for *Tannhäuser*, Bayreuth, 1986

Hall, Calvin S., *A Primer of Freudian Psychology*, New York, 1954

Harper-Scott, J.P.E. 'Wagner, Sex and Capitalism', in *The Wagner Journal*, vol. v, no. 2 (2011)

Heine, Heinrich, *Memoirs of Herr Schnabelewopski*, in *Complete Works*, tr. Charles Godfrey Leland, vol. i, London, 1891

Heine, Heinrich, *The Rabbi of Bacharach*, in *Complete Works*, tr. Charles Godfrey Leland, vol. i, London, 1891

Hite, Shere, *The Hite Report on Love, Passion and Emotional Violence*, New York, 1987

Hite, Shere, *The Hite Report on Male Sexuality*, New York, 1981

Jung, Carl G., *On the Nature of the Psyche*, tr. R.F.C. Hull, Abingdon, 1969

Jung, Carl G., *Two Essays on Analytical Psychology*, tr. R.F.C. Hull, New York, 1956

Kaplan, Helen Singer, *The New Sex Therapy*, London, 1974

Keller, Hans, *Criticism*, London, 1987

Kinderman, William and Katherine R. Syer, ed., *A Companion to Wagner's Parsifal*, Rochester, NY, 2005

King, Robert, *Henry Purcell*, London, 1994

Kitzinger, Sheila, *Woman's Experience of Sex*, London, 1985

Köhler, Joachim, *Richard Wagner: The Last of the Titans*, tr. Stewart Spencer,
New Haven and London, 2004

Krüger, Johann Gottlob, *Gedanken von der Erziehung der Kinder*, Halle, 1752

Kufferath, Maurice, *Parsifal*, Paris, 1890

Lewis, C.S., *Surprised by Joy, an Autobiography*, London, 1955

Lieberman, D., J. Trooby and L. Cosmides, 'The Architecture of Human Kin
Detection', *Nature*, No. 445 (2007), pp. 727 et seqq.

Lorenz, Alfred, *Der Geheimnis der Form bei Richard Wagner*, Berlin 1924-33

Magee, Bryan, *Aspects of Wagner*, London, 1968

Marek, George R., *Cosima Wagner*, New York, 1981

Marion, Jean-Luc, *The Erotic Phenomenon*, Chicago, 2007

Marx, Karl, *Das Kapital*, tr. (as *Capital*) Eden and Cedar Paul, London, 1930

Matthias, Adolf, *Wie erziehen wir unseren Sohn Benjamin?*, 1902

McPhee, Peter, *A Social History of France, 1780-1880*, London, 1992

Meckel, Christoph, *Suchbild: über meinem Vater*, Düsseldorf, 1979

Menuhin, Yehudi, *Theme and Variations*, New York, 1972

Miller, Alice, *For Your Own Good*, tr. Hildegarde and Hunter Hannum,
London, 1987

Miller, Alice, *The Drama of Being a Child*, tr. Ruth Ward, London, 1987

Nattiez, Jean-Jacques, *Wagner Androgyne*, tr. Stewart Spencer, Princeton, 1993

Neuberger, Julia, *Whatever's Happening to Women?*, London, 1991

Newman, Ernest, *A Study of Wagner*, London, 1899

Newman, Ernest, *The Life of Richard Wagner*, 4 vols., London & New York,
1933–46

Newman, Ernest, *Wagner as Man and Artist*, London, 1914, rev. 1924

Newman, Ernest, *Wagner Nights*, London, 1949

North, Roger, *Wagner's Most Subtle Art*, London, 1996

Norwood, Robin, *Women who Love Too Much*, London, 1986

Osborne, Charles, *The World Theatre of Wagner*, (Preface by Sir Colin Davis,)
London, 1982

Parsons,Tony *On Life, Death and Breakfast*, London, 2010

Peck, M. Scott, *The Road Less Travelled*, New York, 1978

Portillo, Michael, 'Politics in Das Rheingold', in *Der Ring des Nibelungen*,
programme, the Royal Opera House, Covent Garden, 2012

Praeger, Ferdinand, *Wagner as I Knew Him*, London, 1892

Rutschky, Katharina, *Schwarze Pädagogik*, Berlin, 1977

Ryle, Gilbert, *The Concept of Mind*, London, 1951

Sacks, Harvey, *Musicophilia*, New York, 2007

Schonberg, Harold C., *The Lives of the Great Composers*, London, 1971

Scruton, Roger, *Death-Devoted Heart*, Oxford, 1996

Shaw, George Bernard, *The Perfect Wagnerite*, 3rd ed., Leipzig, 1913

Skelton, Geoffrey, *Wagner in Thought and Practice*, London, 1991

Smythers, Ruth, *Instruction and Advice for the Young Bride*, New York, 1894

Snow, C.P. *The Masters*, London, 1951

Spencer, Stewart, 'A Wagnerian Footnote', in *Wagner*, vol. iv, no. 3

Spencer, Stewart, ed., *Wagner Remembered*, London, 2000

Steen, Michael, *Enchantress of Nations: Pauline Viardot, Soprano, Muse and Lover*, Thriplow, 2007

Storr, Anthony, *Music and the Mind*, New York, 1992

Stravinsky, Vera, and Robert Craft, *Stravinsky in Pictures and Documents*, London, 1979

Strohm, Reinhard, '*Zur Werkgeschichte des* Tannhäuser', in programme for *Tannhäuser*, Bayreuth,1983

Sulzer, Johann, *Versuch von der Erziehung und Unterweisung der Kinder*, 1748

Tanner, Michael, *The Faber Pocket Guide to Wagner*, London, 2010

Tanner, Michael, *Wagner*, London, 1996

'The Quest for Reginald Goodall', *Omnibus*, BBC2, 1984

Treadwell, James, *Interpreting Wagner*, New Haven and London, 2003

Trollope, Anthony, *An Autobiography*, Edinburgh and London, 1883

van der Post, Laurens, *Jung and the Story of our Time*, Harmondsworth, 1978

Wagner, Cosima, *Diaries*, ed. Martin Gregor-Dellin and Dietrich Mack, tr. Geoffrey Skelton, 2 vols., London, 1978-80

Walter, Bruno, *Theme and Variations: An Autobiography*, tr. John Galston, London, 1946

Warner, Marina, *Alone of All her Sex: The Myth and Cult of the Virgin Mary*, London, 1976

Wilton, Andrew and Robert Upstone, *The Age of Rossetti, Burne-Jones and Watts: Symbolism in Britain 1860-1910*, London, 1997

Young, Wayland, *Eros Denied*, Brattleboro, Vt., 1964

INDEX

Acton, Lord ii.83, ii.190

Acton, William
  *The Functions and Disorders of
    the Reproductive Organs* ii.83

addiction, addictive personality i.41,
  i.76, i.128, i.176, ii.110

Adler, Alfred i.55

Aeschylus i.28 f., i.33, i.112n., i.133
  Oresteia i.28, i.186, i.195, ii.516

Aesop i.xv

Ahasuerus i.78

Albisbrunn i.9

Alcoholics Anonymous i.247n., ii.213

alienation ii.22 f.

Alt, Pastor i.4

American Centennial March (Wagner)
  i.238, ii.509

anorexia nervosa ii.78 f.

anti-Semitism i.xviii, i.9, i.15, i.32, i.76,
  i.248, i.251 ff., ii.532

Apel, Theodor i.116, i.161

Apollonius Rhodius ii.114
  Argonautica ii.398

archetypes i.xi, i.xvi, i.xxii f., i.53, i.66
  f., i.69, i.122, i.228, ii.29, ii.125, ii.181 f.

Arimathea, Joseph of ii.118n.

Aristotle i.83

Arnim, Achim von ii.73

Art and Revolution (Wagner) i.9, i.28,
  ii.155, ii.157

Artwork of the Future (Wagner) i.9

Ashkenazy, Vladimir i.244

Ashton Ellis, William i.xviii, i.xx, i.133,
  ii.356

Asyl, villa, Zurich i.11, ii.363

atonal music ii.366

atonement i.61, ii.338 f.

attachment theory i.82 f.

Auber, Daniel
  La Muette de Portici ii.84 f.

Auden, W.H. i.133

Augustus the Strong, Elector of Saxony
  and King of Poland ii.494n.

Authorised Version i.64n.

Avenarius, Cäcilie (née Geyer, step-sis-
  ter) i.82, i.118 f., i.122

Avenarius, Ferdinand (brother-in-law)
  i.118 ff.

Bach, Carl Philipp Emanuel i.201

Bach, J.S. i.59 ff., i.117, i.126 f., i.203,
  ii.173, ii.459
  Mass in B minor i.209, ii.382
  'St Anne' Prelude and Fugue i.219
  St Matthew Passion i.59 ff., i.244 f.,
    ii.304, ii.531
  The '48' i.199 and n., i.208
  The Art of Fugue i.207

Bad Lauchstädt i.5, i.159

Bakunin, Mikhail i.9, ii.155 f.

Bandura, Albert i.83

Bartsch, Jürgen i.96 f., ii.213
'base camp' within marriage or
    relationship ii.313 f.
Baudelaire, Charles i.44, i.58, ii.87
Bauer, Bruno i.255
Bayreuth i.16 ff., i.39, i.121, i.140 ff.,
    i.156, i.249, ii.29, ii.109n, ii.443
Bayreuther Blätter ii.423
Beecham, Thomas ii.459
Becker's *Universal History* i.113
Beckett, Lucy i.197, ii.419
Beethoven, Ludwig van i.25n., i.37 f.,
    i.200 f., i.203, ii.66, ii.173, ii.512n.
    Egmont i.125
    Fidelio i.130, ii.9, ii.67
    Symphony No. 3 (*Eroica*) i.38, i.200,
        i.209, i.219
    Symphony No. 7 i.124, i.156
    Symphony No. 9 i.4, i.8, i.16, i.38,
        i.124, ii.12
Berlin i.13, i.18, i.22, i.142, i.164, i.184
    f., i.255, i.266, ii.476
Berlin, Isaiah ii.150
Berlioz, Hector i.11
    Benvenuto Cellini i.265
Bethmann, Heinrich i.5, i.257
Beust, Count von i.174
Biebrich i.13, i.187, i.239
bipolar disorder ii.454 f., ii.464
Bismarck, Otto von ii.423
Bloom, Paul i.45, ii.234
Böhme, Dr i.4, i.82, i.121
Böhme, Kurt ii.460
Borchmeyer, Dieter i.166
Bordeaux i.9
Boulogne i.6
Bowlby, John i.82 f.
'Brahminism' ii.487
Brahms, Johannes i.13, i.15
Brentano, Clemens ii.73

Britten, Benjamin i.208
    Peter Grimes ii.65
Brockhaus, Friedrich i.113
Brooke, Rupert i.245 f.
Brown, Callum G. ii.483
Browning, Christopher R. i.253 f.
Bruckner, Anton i.20, i.44, i.58, i.127,
    i.209, i.227n., ii.175
Brünn (Brno) i.131
'Brünnhilde's Glorification', misla-
    belled i.215
Brussels ii.85n.
Buddhism ii.479, ii.486 f., ii.501, ii.521,
    ii.523 f.
Bülow, Cosima von *see* Wagner
Bülow, Franziska von i.185
Bülow, Hans von i.13 ff., i.137, i.150 f.,
    i.185 ff., i.193, ii.360, ii.362, ii.417,
    ii.478
    Nirwana i.186, ii.368
Burrell, Mary i.127n., i.158 f., i.163,
    i.165
Buxtehude, Diderich ii.459

capitalism ii.153 f., ii.172, ii.182 f.,
    ii.190, ii.210 f., ii.477
Capitulation, A (Wagner) i.15 f.
Cardus, Neville i.47, i.72
Carlyle, Thomas i.xx
Casals, Pablo i.199, i.208
censorship ii.84
Chabrier, Emmanuel
    Gwendoline ii.86
Chamberlain, Houston Stewart i.xviii,
    i.23, ii.499, ii.524n.
Charles, Prince ii.456
chastity ii.499 f.
Chesterton, G.K. ii.526
cholera i.131 f.

Chopin, Frédéric
  Ballade No. 4 i.209
Christ, Jesus i.59 f., i.253, i.260, ii.43,
  ii.80, ii.339, ii.365, ii.383, ii.479,
  ii.483 ff., ii.488 ff., ii.501, ii.507,
  ii.516, ii.518 f., ii.521 ff., ii.525 f.
Christiane F. i.96
Christianity i.42, i.59, i.68, i.106, i.260,
  ii.20, ii.71, ii.79, ii.339, ii.365, ii.415
  f., ii.427, ii.479 ff., ii.490 f., ii.520 f.,
  ii.525, ii.530 f.
Churchill, Winston i.xviii, ii.477
Clément, Catherine ii.179, ii.205
Clinton, Bill i.178n.
closed form i.206 f.
co-dependency i.171, ii.111, ii.143
Colonne, Édouard ii.86
Columbus Overture (Wagner) i.6
commitment to forgiveness ii.145
Como, Lake i.181
compassion i.80, i.84, i.89, i.96, i.128,
  i.130, i.250, ii.80, ii.176, ii.327 f.,
  ii.479, ii.486 ff., ii.511, ii.521, ii.525 ff.
compulsive-obsessive disorder i.75 f.
Constantine, Emperor i.253, ii.71
Cooke, Deryck i.198, i.219, i.240
Cord, William O. i.48, i.69
Cornelius, Peter i.140
Culshaw, John ii.361
cunnilingus see oral sex

d'Agoult, Marie i.181 f., i.185
Dahlhaus, Carl ii.16, ii.28, ii.284,
  ii.480, ii.520
daimon, definition i.118
Dante i.109 f.
Darwin, Charles i.25n., ii.175, ii.409,
  ii.527
David, King ii.425

Davis, Colin i.266 f.
Dawkins, Richard i.26n., ii.157
Debussy, Claude i.216, i.243 f., ii.481,
  ii.503
  Prélude à l'après-midi d'un faune
  i.244
Decca Records
  Ring Cycle i.210 and n., ii.361
  Tristan und Isolde ii.388
dependency see also co-dependency
  and interdependence ii.143
deprivation, psychology of ii.212
Des Knaben Wunderhorn ii.73
Descartes, René ii.403
Devrient, Eduard i.143 f., ii.311
Diana, Princess of Wales i.209
Dietrich i.6, i.257
Donington, Robert ii.178, ii.353
Dorn, Heinrich i.4. i.6, i.126, i.136 f.
Dostoevsky, Fyodor
  The Brothers Karamazov ii.526
drama i.33 f.
dreams i.108
Dresden i.3 f., i.7, i.80 f., i.112, i.114,
  i.121, i.165, i.168, i.172 f., ii.38, ii.43,
  ii.84, ii.90, ii.149, ii.154, ii.169, ii.520
Dresden Amen ii.493 f.
Dresden uprising (1849) i.9, i.129,
  i.170, i.174, i.259, i.263, ii.151,
  ii.156, ii.169, ii.422
Dreyfus, Laurence i.xxi, ii.41, ii.87,
  ii.399
'Drumbeat' Overture (Wagner) i.4,
  i.126
Dryden, John i.34
duelling i.128
Dujardin, Édouard ii.87
E flat, key of i.219
Eagleton, Terry ii.199
ego i.54

Einsiedel, Herr von i.165, ii.246

Eisleben i.3 f., i.80 f., i.107, i.128

Eliot, T.S. i.44
    The Waste Land ii.360, ii.405

elitism i.261

Erlösung see redemption

Eros *see also* romantic passion i.55,
    i.179, ii.37, ii.41, ii.81, ii.114, ii.149,
    ii.399

erotic experience ii.41

erysipelas i.74

Ettal, monastery ii.415, ii.485, ii.529

Evans, Geraint ii.476

Everett, Derrick ii.523 f.

Everyman i.42

Ewig-Weibliche ii.11, ii.328n.

expressionism i.77

factory conditions i.259, ii.155

Fantin-Latour, Henri i.40

Faust Overture (originally Symphony)
    (Wagner) i.6, i.10

Feen, Die (Wagner) i.5, i.159

feminine, femininity i.121 f., ii.234,
    ii.328

Festival March (Wagner) i.156

Fétis, François-Joseph i.141

fetishism i.75 f.

Feuerbach, Ludwig ii.155 f., ii.175 f.,
    ii.235, ii.352 ff., ii.356 f., ii.479

Feustel, Friedrich i.259

fictions, appeal of i.45 ff., i.92

Fisher, Robert S. i.20

Flaubert, Gustave
    Salammbo ii.88

Fliegender Holländer, Der (*The Flying
    Dutchman*) (Wagner) i.6 f., i.17, i.22,
    i.125, i.136, i.169, i.212, i.218, i.233 f.,
    Chapter 10, ii.125, ii.152, ii.414

one-act version ii.29

premiere i.7, ii.40

Flugel, J.C. i.246n.

Förster, Bernhard i.255 f.

Foucault, Michel ii.83

Fourier, Charles ii.150

France, Wagnerism in ii.86 f.

Franco-Prussian War i.15, i.150, ii.92n.,
    ii.422

Frantz, Constantin ii.423

Frazer, J.G. ii.522

free love i.115, i.161, i.178, ii.9

free will ii.36

French Revolution i.114, i.254

Freud, Sigmund i.27, i.30, i.53 f., i.86,
    i.90, i.232n., ii.58, ii.82, ii.400, ii.503

Friedrich August (Frederick Augustus)
    II, King of Saxony i.9, i.137, i.259,
    ii.154, ii.190 f.

Friedrich, Götz i.61n., i.266 f., ii.476

fugue i.203, ii.459

Fürtwängler, Wilhelm i.141 ff., ii.54

gambling i.128, ii.109

Gandhi, Mahatma i.xviii

Gautier, Judith i.17, i.190

generosity i.139 ff.

Geneva i.14

Genghis Khan ii.409

Genoa i.230

German, Beckmesser as a caricatured
    ii.458 f.

Germany, unified ii.422 f.

Geyer, Cäcilie *see* Avenarius

Geyer, Frau (step-grandmother) i.4,
    i.80 f.

Geyer, Karl (step-uncle) i.3, i.80

Geyer, Ludwig (stepfather) i.3, i.79 f.,
    i.101 ff., i.123

ghost stories i.131

Glyndebourne ii.458, ii.476

Gobineau, Count i.25

Goethe, Johann Wolfgang von i.31,
i.73, i.109 f., i.133, i.144, ii.11
Faust i.11

Goodall, Reginald ii.361

Götterdämmerung (Wagner) i.15 ff.,
i.215, i.233, ii.144, ii.288, Chapter 17
premiere ii.359

gratitude, as a cause for romantic passion ii.384

Greek history i.113

Greek War of Independence i.111

Gregor-Dellin, Martin ii.423

Greinacher, Norbert i.255

Gustavus Adolphus, King of Sweden
ii.422

Gutman, Robert i.xviii, i.xix, i.40,
i.256

Haitink, Bernard ii.422

Hall, Calvin ii.108 f.

Hamburg i.7

Hanslick, Eduard i.150, i.160, i.198,
ii.39, ii.66

'Happy birthday to you' i.206, ii.16

'Hapsburg look' i.72n.

Harlow, Harry i.83

Hartleb, Hans ii.476

Haydn, Josef i.203

heart disease i.77, i.175, i.192

Hegel, Georg Wilhelm Friedrich i.xxi,
i.147, ii.126, ii.479, ii.520

Heine, Ferdinand i.160n.

Heine, Heinrich i.257, ii.4 ff., ii.29,
ii.74n., ii.151
Memoirs of Herr von Schnabelewopski
ii.4ff.

Heine, Marie i.160

Henry the Fowler, Duke of Saxony and
King of Germany, historical figure
ii.120 f.

Henry Wood Promenade Concerts
ii.74

Herder, Johann Gottfried i.31

Herheim, Stefan i.266

hero myth i.31, ii.268 ff.

Herwegh, Georg ii.175

Hite, Shere ii.82 f., ii.87, ii.111 f.

Hitler, Adolf i.xviii, i.20, i.96 f., i.248,
i.251, i.253, i.256, ii.212 f., ii.349,
ii.409, ii.424, ii.527 f.

Hoffmann, E.T.A. ii.73

Holy Grail ii.118 and n.

Holy Mary Complex ii.58

Homer i.109
Iliad i.112

honour, obsession with ii.145

Hueffer, Francis i.xx, i.xxi

Hugo, Victor i.185

Hunt, Holman
The Light of the World ii.38, ii.531 and
n.
The Awakening Conscience ii.38

Huxley, Aldous ii.361

id i.54

ideals, value of ii.402

illustrations i.xi

incest i.53, i.122, ii.233 f., ii.237

Industrial Revolution i.254

inequality, in the United States ii.210

infidelity ii.112 ff.

instant gratification i.260

interdependence ii.143

intimacy, mutual ii.144

Irritable Bowel Syndrome i.76 f.

Italy i.15, i.17 f., i.156, i.230

Jameson, Frederick ii.173n.
Jesus of Nazareth (Wagner) i.9
Jewry in Music (Judenthum in der Musik, Das) (Wagner) i.9, i.15, i.120, i.251 f.
Jockey Club i.12, ii.93
Joukovsky, Paul i.135
Judenthum in der Musik see *Jewry*
July Revolution (1830) i.114
Jung, Carl Gustav i.xvi, i.xxii, i.27, i.30, i.54 ff., i.65 f., i.68, i.135, i.179, i.199, i.252, ii.11, ii.23, ii.37, ii.41, ii.47, ii.81, ii.149, ii.397, ii.400, ii.416
Junge Siegfried, Der (Wagner) i.9 f., ii.170

Kant, Immanuel i.xxii, i.6, i.147, ii.224, ii.329n.
Kaplan, Helen ii.82, ii.102 f.
Karajan, Herbert von ii.530
Keller, Hans i.51 f., i.246 f.
Kempis, Thomas à i.184
Keynes, John Maynard i.27
Kienzle, Ulrike ii.524
Kietz, Gustav Adolph i.140, i.168, ii.151
Kinderman, William ii.522, ii.524
King James Bible *see* Authorised Version
Kirchner, Ernst ii.529 f.
Kitzinger, Sheila i.172, ii.83
Klondike ii.184
Köhler, Joachim i.xix, i.78 f., i.100, i.103n., i.256
Kollwitz, Käthe i.250
Kolter, tight-rope walker i.107
Königsberg i.6

Kreuzschule, Dresden i.4, i.82, i.112
Krüger, Johann Gottlob i.86
Kufferath, Maurice i.30

Lacan, Jacques i.24, i.63
Lambeth Conference (1958) ii.115
Lamoureux, Charles ii.86
language i.24, i.62 ff., i.218, ii.466
Laube, Heinrich i.5, i.115, i.127, i.130, i.154, i.159, i.161, i.178, ii.9
Laussot, Jessie i.9, i.89, i.151, i.176 f.
Lawrence, D.H. i.44, ii.360
Leipzig i.4 f., i.76, i.79, i.81 f., i.109, i.113, i.117, i.121, i.159, i.202
University i.4, i.117 f., i.128
Leitfaden i.214
leitmotives i.212 ff., ii.11, ii.32, ii.65, ii.118, ii.368
Lenin, Vladimir Ilyich ii.349
Lenrow, Elbert i.142 and n.
letting go, difficulty of ii.264 ff.
Leubald (Wagner) i.4, i.97, i.117, i.125
Levi, Hermann i.18, ii.519n.
Lewinsky, Monica i.178n.
Lewis, C.S. i.20, i.44, i.58, i.67 ff., i.210, ii.175
Liebesmahl der Apostel (Wagner) i.7
Liebestod ii.368, ii.393
Liebesverbot, Das (Wagner) i.5, i.116, i.159, i.161, i.257n., ii.89
Liebigs Fleisch-Extrakt i.xi, ii.86
Lindau i.9
Liszt, Anna i.182
Liszt, Blandine *see* Ollivier
Liszt, Cosima *see* Wagner
Liszt, Daniel i.181
Liszt, Franz i.9 ff., i.15, i.28, i.95 f., i.137 f., i.173, i.181 ff., i.257, ii.48, ii.100, ii.146, ii.357

The Bells of Strasbourg Cathedral ii.492

The Legend of St Elizabeth ii.71

Logier, Johann Bernhard i.125 and n.

Lohengrin (Wagner) i.8, i.12, i.14, i.17, i.33, i.45, i.49 f., i.97, i.203, i.210, i.230, i.262, Chapter 12, ii.224, ii.304, ii.419, ii.424

premiere i.9, ii.146

London i.6, i.10, i.17, i.144 ff., i.177, ii.409

Longborough i.266

Lorenz, Alfred i.205, i.240, i.264, ii.178

Louis Napoleon *see* Napoleon III

Louis Philippe, King of the French ii.150

Louis XIV, King of France ii.422

Lübeck ii.459

Lucas, C.T.L. ii.73

Lucerne i.12, i.189

Ludwig II, King of Bavaria i.13 ff., i.26n., i.141, i.156, i.188 ff., i.195, i.248 f., ii.151, ii.154, ii.357, ii.365, ii.481

Lueger, Karl i.254, i.256

Luther, Martin i.255, ii.427, ii.461, ii.493

Lüttichau, Baron von i.139, ii.84

Lytton, Lord i.6

McIntyre, Donald ii.454, ii.456

McVicar, David ii.476

Magdeburg i.5, i.159, i.257, ii.150

Magee, Bryan i.52 f.

Magna Carta i.114 and n.

Mahler, Alma i.161

Mahler, Gustav i.208, i.261, ii.73n., ii.92, ii.246

Symphony No. 2 'Resurrection' i.244 f., ii.474

Symphony No. 3 i.198, ii.474

Symphony No. 6 i.208

Symphony No. 8 i.219

Mann, Thomas i.248

Männerlist grosser als Frauenlist (Wagner) i.6

Marek, George R. i.184, i.190

Marie (servant girl) i.250

Marienbad i.8, i.160

Marion, Jean-Luc i.64, f.

marriage ii.313 f.

Marschner, Heinrich

Hans Heiling i.204 f.

Der Vampyr ii.38

Marx, Karl i.26 f., i.101, ii.150 f., ii.154 ff., ii.168, ii.182, ii.190, ii.199, ii.210

Mary Magdalene ii.516

Mary, the Virgin ii.82 f., ii.115, ii.520

maternal love ii.503

Matthias, Adolf i.87

Maxwell, Robert ii.212

Meckel, Christoph i.87, i.94

megalomania i.120 f.

Mein Leben (Wagner) i.22, i.78, i.92 f., i.96, i.101, i.128 ff., i.152, i.158, i.160 f., i.164, i.187, i.237, ii.96 f., ii.99, ii.152, ii.234, ii.420

Meistersinger von Nürnberg, Die (Wagner) i.8, i.12 ff., i.34, i.37, i.84, i.99, i.180, i.196 ff., i.205, i.210, i.237 ff., i.250 f., i.265, ii.168, ii.173 f., ii.287 f., ii.311, ii.406, ii.416, Chapter 19, ii.528

premiere i.15, i.150, ii.478

Mendelssohn, Felix i.233, i.256, ii.494n.

Overture, *The Beautiful Melusine* i.218, i.223, i.232, ii.342

Menuhin, Yehudi i.199

Merlin i.186

mescalin ii.361

Metternich, Princess i.12, ii.91

Meudon i.7

Meyerbeer, Giacomo i.6 f., i.95 f., i.137
  ff., i.256, ii.66
  Les Huguenots ii.38, ii.84, ii.120
  Robert le Diable ii.150

middle ages i.114, i.253, ii.370

Miller, Alice i.85 ff., i.91 f., i.95 f., ii.212

Milton, John i.xviii
  Paradise Lost ii.525

Minne, Frau, goddess of erotic passion
  ii.384, ii.389

Mitterwurzer, Anton ii.115 f., ii.417

Mitzkaserne ii.423

Morgan, Charles ii.113

'Morning Greeting' i.11

Moscow i.13

Mother Fixation ii58

Mozart, Leopold i.102

Mozart, Wolfgang Amadeus
  i.170, i.194, i.200, i.203, ii.66
  Don Giovanni i.5, i.124, i.159
  The Marriage of Figaro ii.39
  Requiem i.124

Müller, Christian Gottlieb i.4, i.126

Munich i.13, i.17, i.20, i.121, i.142, i.189,
  ii.93

music drama ii.65 f.

music, Wagner's i.36 ff., i.47 f., Chapter 8

Musset, Alfred de i.185

myth *see also* hero myth, religion i.xvi,
  i.57, i.65, ii.179, ii.180, ii.284, ii.523
  and fairy tale ii.284

Naples i.140, i.156

Napoleon III i.10, i.12, ii.91, ii.170

narcissism i.134 f.

narrative, as psychotherapeutic method
ii.293 f.

National Theatre, London ii.456

Nattiez, Jean-Jacques i.103n.

Naumann, J.G. ii.494n.

Nazis, Nazism *see also* Hitler i.248,
  i.251, i.258, ii.327, ii.421, ii.527 f.

necrophiles, Valkyries as i.266 f.

Neuberger, Julia ii.112

Newman, Ernest i.xxi f., i.151 ff., i.165,
  i.197, i.264, ii.37, ii.120, ii.304, ii.320,
  ii.363, ii.454, ii.480

Newton, Isaac i.xviii

Nibelungenlied ii.148

'Nibelungen myth considered as a
  sketch for a drama' (Wagner) ii.157 ff.

Nicene Creed ii.483 and n., ii.525

Nicolaischule, Leipzig i.4, i.113, i.117

Nietzsche, Friedrich i.15, i.27, i.40,
  i.55, i.58, i.71, i.133, i.143, i.154, i.247,
  ii.287, ii.319, ii.360, ii.481, ii.526 f.

North, Roger i.xxiii, i.205, i.240

Norwood, Robin i.171

Novalis ii.403

'numbers opera' ii.66

Nuremberg i,20, i.31, i.131, Chapter 19

Old Philharmonic Society, London
  i.10, i.177

Oliveros, Natalie ii.400

Ollivier, Blandine (née Liszt) i.181 ff.,
  i.190 f.

Ollivier, Émile i.184

open fifths, effect of i.123, i.125, ii.4,
  ii.11 f.

open relationships i.163

Opera and Drama (Wagner) i.9, i.23 f.,
  i.28, i.34, ii.172, ii.304 f., ii.365

oral sex *see also* Clinton, Bill ii.112

Orwell, George

Nineteen Eighty-four ii.212

Ostralenka i.129

Otterstedt, Alexander von i.157

Overture in D minor (Wagner) i.5

Pachta sisters i.4

Paetz, (Johanna) Rosine *see* Wagner

Palais Garnier, Paris i.249

Palermo i.18

Palermo i.251

Palestrina, Giovanni Pierluigi da i.203,
    ii.531

parent-offspring relationship ii.264 ff.,
    ii.268 f.

Paris i.6 f.. i.12, i.167, i.180, i.182, i.237,
    i.249, ii.38, ii.86, ii.91, ii.98, ii.149 ff.,
    ii.154, ii.156, ii.169 f.

Parsifal (Wagner) i.17 f., i.42, i.56, i.58,
    i.77, i.97, i.122, i.154, i.190, i.217,
    i.230, i.234 f., i.238, i.260, i.266,
    ii.86, ii.95, ii.154, ii.168, ii.264, ii.287,
    ii.327, ii.365, ii.410, ii.477,
    Chapter 20
    premiere i.18, ii.519n.

Pasdeloup, Jules ii.86

Patersi, Madam i.183 f., i.186

Peabody housing schemes ii.409

Pecht, Friedrich i.160

pedagogy in 18th–19th centuries i.84 ff.

Pedro, Dom, Emperor of Brazil ii.86

Pellet, villa, Starnberger See i.13, i.188

Penzing i.13

Perls, Fritz ii.142

personal integration i.68 ff.

Peston, Robert ii.211

Peter's Denial i.59 f.

Pfistermeister, Herr von i.13

Philip, Timothy ii.458 f.

Piano Fantasy in F sharp minor (Wagner) i.127

Pindar i.133

Pius IX, pope i.255

Planer, Minne *see* Wagner

Planer, Natalie i.159 n., i.165

Plato i.71, ii.126, ii.488

The Symposium ii.398

pleasure principle i.54, i.90

Pol Pot ii.409

Polycrates complex i.246 f.

polyphony i.203

Pontius Pilate i.253

Porter, Andrew i.xxi

Portillo, Michael ii.182

Possendorf i.3, i.80, i.105

Praeger, Ferdinand i.76n., i.144 ff.

Prague i.4, i.81 f.

pregnancy, dangers of i.190 f.

Prince-Bishops ii.80

Pringle, Carrie i.19

Privett, Alan i.266

prodigal son, parable of the ii.489 f.

production styles of Wagner's operas
    i.264 f.

Proudhon, Pierre-Joseph i.144n., ii.150,
    ii.152 ff., ii.156, ii.168

pruritus i.75

Prussia, Prussians i.9, i.114 f., i.174,
    i.185 f., i.250, ii.422 f., ii.477

Puccini, Giacomo i.194

Pueblo Indians i.57 f., ii.416

Purcell, Henry i.34

Hear my Prayer, O Lord i.208

Puschmann, Theodor i.120 f.

Pusinelli, Anton i.7, i.158, i.191 and n.,
    ii.529

Rackham, Arthur i.xi

rape, psychological damage of ii.245 f.

Raphael

Sistine Madonna ii.520

Rattle, Simon i.20
Reagan, Ronald ii.199
reconciliation ii.339
redemption i.58 ff., i.215, ii.20, ii.37,
    ii.65, ii.264, ii.359, ii.488, ii.517 ff.,
    ii.532
regression ii.108 ff., ii.142
reincarnation ii.479, ii.501
Reissiger, Carl Gottlieb i.7
rejection, childhood ii.212
relationship failure ii.142 ff.
Religion and Art (Wagner) i.42, ii.520
Religion and Politics (Wagner) i.26n.
religion *see also* Christianity, Buddhism
    i.57 f., i.65, i.105 f., ii.43, ii.490
    and art ii.520 f.
responsibility, value of shouldering
    ii.516
Revue et Gazette musicale i.7
Revue Germanique i.186
Revue Wagnerienne ii.87
Rheingold, Das (Wagner)
    i.9 f., i.15, i.40, i.70 f., i.122, i.206,
    i.210, i.212, i.214, i.216 f., i.218 ff.,
    i.235 f., i.238 f., Chapter 14, ii.269 f.,
    ii.274, ii.286, ii.424, ii.443
    premiere i.15, ii.220
Rhine, River, Wagner's life likened to
    i.xix
Richter, Hans i.15 ff., i.27, ii.220,
    ii.266, ii.303, ii.359
Rienzi (Wagner) i.6 f., i.136, i.142,
    i.169, i.172 f., ii.38, ii.86, ii.152, ii.478
Riga i.6, i.169, ii.150
Ring des Nibelungen, Der (Wagner)
    i.10, i.16 ff., i.20, i.34, i.55 f., i.97,
    i.112, i.149, i.210, i.212, i.232, i.263,
    i.265 ff., Chapters 13-17, ii.363, ii.419,
    ii.466, ii.476, ii.521, ii.528
    premiere *see also individual operas*

i.17
Ringtheater, Vienna i.96
Ritter, Julie i.9, ii.362
Ritter, Karl i.11, ii.362
Röckel, August i.143, i.263
romantic passion, romantic love *see
    also* Eros ii.29, ii.111, ii.117, ii.366,
    ii.396 ff., ii.401 f., ii.416 f.
    destructive aspects of ii.328
Rosenberg, Alfred ii.527
Rossini, Gioacchino
    The Barber of Seville ii.420
    William Tell Overture i.203
Rowling, J.K. i.45
Royal Albert Hall, London i.17
Royal Opera House, Covent Garden
    i.265, ii.69, ii.182, ii.421 f., ii.476
Rutschky, Katharina i.85
Ryle, Gilbert i.51n., ii.397n.

Sabor, Rudolf i.xxiii
Sachs, Hans, historical figure ii.421
St Apollinaris, church of i.187
St Augustine of Hippo ii.82
Saint-Cher, Hugues de ii.81
St Elisabeth ii.70
St Francis of Assisi ii.70
St John's Gospel i.253
St Paul i.xviii
St John of Damascus
    Josaphat and Barlaam ii.523 f.
Saint-Simon, Henri de ii.150
Samaritans, the ii.294
Samson, Savanna (porn star) *see* Oliveros
Sand, Georges i.185
Sayn-Wittgenstein, Caroline zu i.182
    f., ii.357, ii.363
'scenes opera' ii.39 f., ii.66
Schadenfreude ii.501, ii.508, ii.512 f.

Schiller, Friedrich i.31, i.110, i.144, i.232, ii.84, ii.525

schizoid dissonance i.89

Schlesinger, Maurice i.7

Schnorr von Carolsfeld, Ludwig i.14, ii.93, ii.417

Schoenberg, Arnold ii.366
Gurrelieder i.227n.

Schön, Friedrich von i.259, ii.155

Schonberg, Harold C. i.242 ff., ii.360

Schopenhauer, Arthur i.76n., i.130, i.163, i.197, i.210, i.236 f., i.204, i.263, ii.10, ii.174 ff., ii.328, ii.356 f., ii.362, ii.364, ii.366, ii.370, ii.393, ii.403, ii.409, ii.415 f., ii.419, ii.421, ii.457, ii.461, ii.477, ii.479, ii.486, ii.489, ii.499, ii.502, ii.525, ii.527
The World as Will and Representation i.10, i.39, ii.175, ii.419

Schott, publishers i.13, i.125, i.193

Schreber, Moritz i.85 f.

Schröder-Devrient, Wilhelmine i.5, i.7 f., i.130, ii.9, ii.40, ii.115, ii.175

Schumann, Clara (née Wieck) i.126, ii.385

Schuré, Edouard i.36, i.146 f.

Schütz, Heinrich i.203

Schweitzer, Albert i.207

Scruton, Roger ii.401

Seattle i.266

security needs, incompatible ii.141 f.

Seidel, Anton ii.96

'Sermon on the Mount' ii.485, ii.487

sexuality, Christianity and ii.80 f.

shadow side i.56, i.252, ii.47

Shakespeare, William i.28 f., i.33, i.36, i.109 f.
Hamlet i.112, ii.72 f.
Measure for Measure i.5
Romeo and Juliet ii.398

Shaw, George Bernard   i.xviii, i.199n., i.262, ii.178, ii.233, ii.304, ii.400, ii.418
The Perfect Wagnerite ii.182 ff., ii.370

shingles i.75 and n.

Shinoda Bolen, Jean i.xxiv, ii.178 f., ii.212

Shirley, Hugo i.265

sibling relationships ii.233

Siegfried (Wagner) i.11, i.15 f., i.31, i.45, i.237, i.263, Chapter 16, ii.363 f.
premiere ii.303

Siegfried Idyll (Wagner) i.16

Siegfrieds Tod (Wagner) i.8, i.10, i.219, ii.154, ii.156, ii.168, ii.304, ii.330, ii.352 f.

silks and satins i.75

Sillig, Herr i.112

singleness of mind, shining ii.145 f.

Sipp, Herr i.127

Skelton, Geoffrey ii.97 f.

smoking i.146

Smythers, Ruth ii.83, ii.112

Snow, C.P.
The Masters ii.219

Socrates ii.488, ii.526

Solti, Georg i.210n., ii.388

Somerville and Ross
Experiences of an Irish R.M. ii.86

Sonata Form i.200 f., i.203 ff., i.207

'Song Contest on Wartburg' ii.70

Sophocles
Oedipus at Colonus ii.294
Oedipus Tyrannus i.110

Sozialistengesetze ii.423

Spencer, Stewart i.19, i.215n.

Spezia, 'vision of' i.10, i.230 ff.

Spohr, Louis i.107

Stabreim ii.172 f.

Stalin, Joseph ii.212, ii.409

Stanford, Charles Villiers ii.494n.
Starnberger See i.13, i.188
Steiglitz, Charlotte i.166n.
Stein, Herr von ii.487
Stern, Daniel *see* d'Agoult
    Nélida i.183
Stoeckel, Gustave ii.87 f.
Stokowski, Leopold i.212
Stopes, Marie ii.88
Strassburg, Gottfried von ii.362, ii.399
Strauss, David ii.479
Strauss, Johann i.131 f.
    Die Fledermaus ii.65 f.
Strauss, Richard i.24, i.34n., i.194, i.238
    Die Frau ohne Schatten i.227n.
    Ein Heldenleben i.219, i.227n.
Stravinsky, Igor i.197 f., i.207
    Apollon Musagète i.207
    The Rite of Spring i.228n.
Strecker, Ludwig i.193
Strohm, Reinhard ii.48
Stuck, Franz
    Der Sünde (Sin) ii.82
Stuttgart i.13
suffering, universal ii.409
Sühne see atonement
suicide ii.354
Sulzer, Jakob i.153
super-ego i.55
surgeons, cardiac ii.145 f.
Switzerland i.9, i.74 f., i.141, i.143, i.152,
    i.174, i.186, ii.169, ii.354, ii.486
Syberberg, Hans-Jürgen
    Parsifal i.266
Symphony in C (Wagner) i.5, i.18, i.127
synaesthesia i.109, i.235
syphilis i.120 f., ii.81

taking trouble ii.383 f.

Tanner, Michael ii.370, ii.434
Tannhäuser (Wagner) i.7, i.9, i.12, i.17,
    i.20, i.51n., i.137, i.141, i.180, i.185,
    i.198, i.209, i.213, i.233, i.238, i.263 f.,
    ii.39, Chapter 11, ii.117, ii.287, ii.401,
    ii.419, ii.466 f.
    premiere (Dresden) i.8, ii.43, ii.115 f.
Tapert, Wilhelm ii.85
Tchaikovsky, Pyotr Ilyich ii.263
Teplitz i.7
Tertullian ii.81
Thatcher, Margaret ii.199
Thetis, ship i.169, ii.10 f.
Thirty Years War ii.409
Thomä House, Leipzig i.109 ff.
Thomä, Jeanette i.110 f.
Thomaskirche, Leipzig i.126
Thomasschule, Leipzig i.4, i.117
Tichatschek, Josef i.7 f., i.14, ii.115 f.
Tilly, Charles ii.85
Times, The i.92 f., i.261, ii.113, ii.210
Titian ii.509n.
    The Assumption of the Virgin ii.420
Tolkien, J.R.R. ii.528
transcendental euphoria i.48 ff., i.69
translation of Wagner's German i.xx f.,
    ii.356
trauma, psychology of ii.212
Treadwell, James i.39
treu bis zum Tod (true unto death)
    i.169, ii.11, ii.23, ii.29, ii.36
Tribschen i.14 f., i.143, i.180, i.189,
    i.250, ii.481
'Tristan chord' ii.366
Tristan und Isolde (Wagner) i.10 ff.,
    i.179 f., i.186, i.190, i.196 f., i.201
    ff., i.205, i.207, i.210, i.215, i.218,
    i.228 f., i.238, i.251, i.261, ii.14, ii.37,
    ii.95, ii.173, ii.288, Chapter 18, ii.419,
    ii.477

premiere i.14, i.150, ii.417
Trollope, Anthony i.92
 The Small House at Allington ii.216
Tyszkiewicz, Count i.131 f.

Uhlig, Theodor i.85, i.257
unconscious i.xvi f., i.53 f., i.199, ii.82

van der Post, Laurens i.31, ii.84
Venice i.11 f., i.18 f., i.156, ii.420 f.
Verdi, Giuseppe ii.51, ii.54
Verklärung (transfiguration) ii.368,
 ii.413, ii.420
Versöhnung see reconciliation
Victoria, Queen ii.47, ii.74, ii.191
Vienna i.13, i.17, i.96, i.131, i.139, i.254,
 ii.91 ff., ii.419, ii.421, ii.530
Villiers de l'Isle-Adam, Auguste ii.481
 f., ii.486
Volk i.31 f.
Voltaire, François-Marie (Arouet) de
 ii.215
Vreneli, Frau (housekeeper) i.250

Wadsworth, Stephen i.266
Wagner
 and his sisters i.75 f., i.82, i.121 f.,
  ii.233 f.
 as a philosopher, evaluation of i.xxi f.
 childhood and upbringing i.78 ff.,
  i.101 ff.
 Christianity ii.482, ii.486 ff., ii.520
 health *see also individual conditions
 and* water-cure i.75 ff., i.146, ii.98
 physical and mental characteristics
  i.74 ff.
 prose works i.23 ff.

sensitiveness to sound i.123 f.
Wagner, Adolf (uncle) i.4, i.81, i.109 ff.
Wagner, Albert (brother) i.81
Wagner, (Carl) Friedrich (father) i.3,
 i.79, i.101
Wagner, Clara (sister) *see* Wolfram
Wagner, Cosima (née Liszt, previously
 von Bülow, second wife) i.13 ff., i.120,
 i.139, i.150, i.155 f., i.158, i.164, i.179,
 i.181 ff, i.247, i.249, ii.96, ii.365,
 ii.524n.
 Diaries i.22, i.30, i.108, i.113, i.140,
 i.152, i.189 f., i.215, i.257, ii.487 f.,
 ii.520
Wagner, Eva (daughter) i.14
Wagner, Franziska (niece) i.23
Wagner, Friederike (aunt) i.109 ff.
Wagner, Gottfried i.256
Wagner, Isolde (daughter) i.14, i.189
Wagner, Johanna Jachmann (niece) i.8,
 ii.115 f., ii.266 f., ii.359
Wagner, (Johanna) Rosine (née Paetz,
 mother) i.3, i.8, i.79, i.101, i.104 ff.
Wagner, Julius (brother) i.80
Wagner, Katharina i.265
Wagner, Luise (sister) i.82
Wagner, Minna (née Planer, first wife)
 i.5 ff., i.14, i.76, i.104, i.122 f., i.139,
 i.156, Chapter 7, i.257, ii.9, ii.48,
 ii.97 f., ii.143, ii.175, ii.234, ii.246
Wagner, Ottilie (sister) i.82
Wagner, Rosalie (sister) i.39, i.82, i.122,
 ii.234
Wagner, Siegfried (son) i.15, i.155 ff.
Wagner, Wieland ii.443
Wagner, Wolfgang ii.527
Wagner tuba i.227 and n.
Wahn i.26n., i.99, ii.364, ii.414, ii.457,
 ii.463 f., ii.468 f., ii.475
Wahnfried, villa, Bayreuth i.17, i.156,

i.250

Walküre, Die (Wagner) i.9 f., i.15, i.50,
i.61 f., i.122, i.179, i.202, i.205, i.207,
i.217 f., i.227, i.229, ii.88, Chapter 15,
ii.274, ii.287 f.
premiere i.15, ii.266

Walter, Bruno ii.360 f.

Wandering Jew *see* Ahasuerus

Warner, Keith i.265

Warner, Marina ii.81 f.

water-cure i.9, i.76, i.152 f.

Weber, Carl Maria von i.107, i.123
Der Freischütz i.119 f., i.123 f., ii.38

Weimar i.9, i.31, i.137, i.173, i.265,
ii.100, ii.146, ii.191

Weingartner, Felix von ii.491

Weinlig, Christian Theodor i.4 f., i.126,
i.159, i.202

Weissheimer, Wendelin i.187 f., i.238 ff.

Wellesz, Egon i.198

Wesendonck, Mathilde i.10 ff., i.164,
i.170, i.178 ff., ii.362 f., ii.415, ii.420

Wesendonck, Otto i.10 ff., i.137, i.150,
ii.363, ii.420

western democracies ii.477

Wetzel, Pastor Christian i.3, i.80, i.105

Wieck, Clara *see* Schumann

Wieck, Friedrich i.126

Wilde, Oscar
An Ideal Husband ii.38

will to power i.55, ii.149, ii.178 f.

will, the ii.175 f., ii.364, ii.457
pacification ii.176 f., ii.356, ii.477

Wille, Eliza i.141

Wittgenstein, Ludwig ii.393, ii.397

Wittgenstein, Marie ii.363

Wolfram, Clara (née Wagner, sister)
i.124, i.162

Wolfram, Heinrich (brother-in-law)
i.162

Wolzogen, Hans von i.213, i.215

'woman taken in adultery', parable of
the ii.489

Wordsworth, Dorothy ii.233

Wordsworth, William i.44, i.71, i.120,
ii.233

Würzburg i.5, i.129, i.159, ii.150, ii.520

Young Germany movement i.5, i.115,
i.154, i.161, i.178, ii.9, ii.88 f.

Young, Wayland i.51n.

Zelinsky, Hartmut i.40, i.256

Ziegesar, Baron i.34

Zurich i.9, i.175, ii.90